PROFESSIONAL RESPONSIBILITY STANDARDS, RULES & STATUTES

1999–2000 Abridged Edition

Selected and Edited

By

John S. Dzienkowski
Professor of Law & John S. Redditt Professor in
State and Local Government,
University of Texas

WEST GROUP

ST. PAUL, MINN., 1999

ISBN 0–314–24032–2

PREFACE

In recent years, the ABA, the states, and other entities have been active in the promulgation of standards, rules, and statutes that regulate lawyers' conduct. These sources of the law of professional responsibility have significantly affected the manner in which lawyers analyze problems in this area. Similarly, the existence of different formal sources of professional responsibility have altered the way in which lawyers and law students are taught about ethical problems. This pamphlet of Professional Responsibility Standards, Rules, and Statutes is designed to provide teachers and students with easy access to the important sources of professional responsibility.

Beginning with the 1995 edition of Professional Responsibility Standards Rules and Statutes, this book is now published in a full version and an abridged version. The full version will continue to include various sources of professional responsibility including standards for specialized areas for practice and standards for the organized regulation of the profession. The abridged edition will present the ABA versions of the codes governing lawyers and judges as well as several selected rules of procedure and evidence and selected rules from California and New York. The purpose of the two editions is to allow professors to choose which version best fits the class that they plan to teach. This preface will however cover materials in both versions.

The full version of Professional Responsibility Standards Rules and Statutes is organized into seven different parts: (1) Codes Regulating Lawyers' Conduct; (2) Code of Judicial Conduct; (3) Rules of Evidence and Procedure that Affect the Legal Profession; (4) Statutes that Affect the Legal Profession; (5) Standards for Specialized Areas of Practice; and (6) Standards for the Organized Regulation of Lawyers. The abridged edition includes the first three parts which focus on the ABA's pronouncements as well as the federal rules of evidence and procedure that influence the legal profession.

Both the full and abridged versions continue with two important features contained in past editions of this work: (1) an annotated Model Rules, and (2) selected state versions of the Model Rules. In light of the fact that the American Bar Association has amended the Model Rules of Professional Conduct several times since 1983, it has become necessary to annotate the current version of the Model Rules with indication of the original version of the amended provisions. The annotated version of the Model Rules contained in this pamphlet allows students to compare the current version with the prior version, which appears in a footnote on the same page with the current version. The annotated Model Rules should also facilitate the study of cases and ethics opinions that are based upon prior versions of the Model Rules. Where appropriate, the annotations also contain the text of a prior draft of the Model Rules to illustrate a shift in the final ABA position. In light of the fact that the states have made significant modifications to the ABA's version of the Model Rules, it has become desirable to include a section on selected significant state modifications to the Model Rules. This section allows teachers and students to examine how various states have chosen to modify specific provisions of the Model Rules. Both the full and abridged editions now contain the California and New York state materials.

In 1999, both the full and abridged editions contain the text of the sections in the Restatement of Law Governing Lawyers. This project will occupy a significant role in shaping the law of professional responsibility.

Both the full and abridged versions include the ABA Model Code of Professional Conduct and the 1908 Canons, as well as both the 1972 and the 1990 Codes of Judicial Conduct. The prior standards are included to facilitate study of the evolution of professional standards as well as cases and jurisdictions that rely on the prior rules.

I would like to thank Joanne Pitulla, Assistant Ethics Counsel to the ABA Standing Committee on Ethics and Professional Responsibility, and Associate Dean John S. Jenkins of George Washington University, a member of the ABA House of Delegates, for helping to keep me current with the many changes that the ABA makes during the course of the year. I also sincerely acknowledge the excellent expertise and assistance of David Gunn of the Tarlton Law Library in locating the various state codes of professional responsibility. I would like to thank my administrative assistant, Dottie Lee, for her help in preparing this supplement. I welcome comments and suggestions on the materials contained in this edition. My E mail address is jdzienkowski@mail.law.utexas.edu.

The materials are current through April 1999, and this supplement will be updated periodically to reflect new and amended statutes and rules.

JOHN S. DZIENKOWSKI

Austin, Texas
May 1999

TABLE OF CONTENTS

PART ONE: CODES REGULATING LAWYERS' CONDUCT

PART TWO: CODES OF JUDICIAL CONDUCT

PART THREE: RULES OF EVIDENCE AND PROCEDURE THAT AFFECT THE LEGAL PROFESSION

*

PROFESSIONAL RESPONSIBILITY STANDARDS, RULES & STATUTES

1999–2000 Abridged Edition

*

PART ONE

CODES AND STANDARDS REGULATING LAWYERS' CONDUCT

Table of Contents

Introduction

One of the traditional characteristics of a profession is the attempt to achieve self regulation. Throughout history, professions have enacted codes of conduct to assert control over their members. Various groups within the legal profession have similarly sought to exercise a degree of self regulation by enacting codes of conduct. This part includes several codes and standards which have attempted to regulate the conduct of all lawyers in their practice of law.

The first three codes contained in this section were promulgated by the American Bar Association (ABA), a national voluntary organization of lawyers. The ABA has assumed the primary responsibility for promulgating national ethical standards for the legal profession. In 1908, the ABA enacted 32 Canons of Professional Ethics. In 1969, it replaced the Canons with the Model Code of Professional Responsibility. In 1983, the Model Code was replaced with the Model Rules of Professional Conduct.

Although the ABA's codes of conduct have been influential in shaping the law of professional responsibility, they only have force as a body of rules with its voluntary members. However, the various states and the federal courts have looked to the ABA versions as a basis for regulating lawyers within the jurisdiction. Thus, the ABA's codes have been used as the basis for state and federal codes. With the Model Code, many states adopted the ABA version without many significant changes. However, with the ABA's promulgation of the Model Rules, the states have been less deferential. Many states have made significant modifications to the ABA version. Thus, this part includes a section on significant state modifications to the Model Rules.

In 1997, the ABA commissioned a committee to study and revise the Model Rules. This committee, named "Ethics 2000," has begun to draft a more modern, up-to-date version of the Model Rules. Initially, Ethics 2000 was envisioned as a light revision of the Model Rules. Recent proceedings of the Ethics 2000 committee indicate that, although the new rules will retain the current structure of the Model Rules, the revision of the substantive standards will be more extensive than originally anticipated.

A final series of documents in this part reflect a recent trend on the part of the ABA and the states to focus on lawyer professionalism as a basis for regulating lawyers' conduct. The origin of this movement was a study on professionalism commissioned by the ABA. The results of the study identified several reasons for the decline in lawyer professionalism and offered several suggestions to address this problem. The ABA Creed of Professionalism and the ABA Pledge of Professionalism illustrate attempts to implement the suggestions of the Commission on Professionalism. The Texas Creed on Professionalism provides a similar example of a state effort to address this problem. The ABA's Aspirational Goals on Lawyer Advertising provide a more concrete example of urging standards of professionalism in the communication of advertising to the general public.

AMERICAN BAR ASSOCIATION MODEL RULES OF PROFESSIONAL CONDUCT

Annotated to Reflect Amendments and Prior Text of the Model Rules in Footnotes. Adopted August 1983, as Amended to February 1999.

[Less than a decade after the Model Code of Professional Responsibility was promulgated in 1969, the ABA established a commission to create another code of ethics for the legal profession. Between 1977 to 1983 the Kutak Commission, named after its chairman Robert Kutak, proceeded to write several drafts of a new code of conduct for lawyers. In 1983, the ABA enacted the Model Rules of Professional Conduct based upon the work of the Kutak Commission. The Model Rules were a response to criticisms about the Model Code's focus on litigation and its three tier structure of canons, ethical considerations, and disciplinary rules. The Model Rules follow a UCC or restatement-like approach by placing the rule of professional responsibility in text and including elaborative material in the comments. Since its adoption in 1983, the ABA has amended the Model Rules several times, and thus this version of the Model Rules is annotated to indicate in footnotes the manner in which the ABA has amended the Model Rules since the original adoption in 1983. Although the current ABA version is important, the original version of the Model Rules is more likely to form the basis for the state adoptions of the Model Rules. When studying a case or an ethics opinion in the various states, one should examine whether the decision is based upon the current version of the Model Rules or a prior version. In several instances, the annotations include the text of a prior Kutak draft of the Model Rules to indicate a shift in the ABA position. Additionally, the comments to the Model Rules are numbered sequentially under each Model Rule provision to facilitate citation of a particular comment. Ed.]

CONTENTS

Preamble, Scope, and Terminology

CLIENT–LAWYER RELATIONSHIP

Rules

ABA MODEL RULES

PREAMBLE, SCOPE, AND TERMINOLOGY
Preamble: A Lawyer's Responsibilities

[1]   A lawyer is a representative of clients, an officer of the legal system and a public citizen having special responsibility for the quality of justice.

[2]   As a representative of clients, a lawyer performs various functions. As advisor, a lawyer provides a client with an informed understanding of the client's legal rights and obligations and explains their practical implications. As advocate, a lawyer zealously asserts the client's position under the rules of the adversary system. As negotiator, a lawyer seeks a result advantageous to the client but consistent with requirements of honest dealing with others. As intermediary between clients, a lawyer seeks to reconcile their divergent interests as an advisor and, to a limited extent, as a spokesperson for each client. A lawyer acts as evaluator by examining a client's legal affairs and reporting about them to the client or to others.

[3]   In all professional functions a lawyer should be competent, prompt and diligent. A lawyer should maintain communication with a client concerning the representation. A lawyer should keep in confidence information relating to representation of a client except so far as disclosure is required or permitted by the Rules of Professional Conduct or other law.

[4]   A lawyer's conduct should conform to the requirements of the law, both in professional service to clients and in the lawyer's business and personal affairs. A lawyer should use the law's procedures only for legitimate purposes and not to harass or intimidate others. A lawyer should demonstrate respect for the legal system and for those who serve it, including judges, other lawyers and public officials. While it is a lawyer's duty, when necessary, to challenge the rectitude of official action, it is also a lawyer's duty to uphold legal process.

[5]   As a public citizen, a lawyer should seek improvement of the law, the administration of justice and the quality of service rendered by the legal profession. As a member of a learned profession, a lawyer should cultivate knowledge of the law beyond its use for clients, employ that knowledge in reform of the law and work to strengthen legal education. A lawyer should be mindful of deficiencies in the administration of justice and of the fact that the poor, and sometimes persons who are not poor, cannot afford adequate legal assistance, and should therefore devote professional time and civic influence in their behalf. A lawyer should aid the legal profession in pursuing these objectives and should help the bar regulate itself in the public interest.

[6]   Many of a lawyer's professional responsibilities are prescribed in the Rules of Professional Conduct, as well as substantive and procedural law. However, a lawyer is also guided by personal conscience and the approbation of professional peers. A lawyer should strive to attain the highest level of skill, to improve the law and the legal profession and to exemplify the legal profession's ideals of public service.

[7]   A lawyer's responsibilities as a representative of clients, an officer of the legal system and a public citizen are usually harmonious. Thus, when an opposing party is well represented, a lawyer can be a zealous advocate on behalf of a client and at the same time assume that justice is being done. So also, a lawyer can be sure that preserving client confidences ordinarily serves the public interest because people are more likely to seek legal advice, and thereby heed their legal obligations, when they know their communications will be private.

[8]   In the nature of law practice, however, conflicting responsibilities are encountered. Virtually all difficult ethical problems arise from conflict between a lawyer's responsibilities to clients, to the legal system and to the lawyer's own interest in remaining an upright person while earning a satisfactory living. The Rules of Professional Conduct prescribe terms for resolving such conflicts. Within the framework of these Rules many difficult issues of professional discretion can arise. Such issues must be resolved through the exercise of sensitive professional and moral judgment guided by the basic principles underlying the Rules.

[9]   The legal profession is largely self-governing. Although other professions also have been granted powers of self-government, the legal profession is unique in this respect because of the close relationship between the profession and the processes of government and law en-

forcement. This connection is manifested in the fact that ultimate authority over the legal profession is vested largely in the courts.

[10] To the extent that lawyers meet the obligations of their professional calling, the occasion for government regulation is obviated. Self-regulation also helps maintain the legal profession's independence from government domination. An independent legal profession is an important force in preserving government under law, for abuse of legal authority is more readily challenged by a profession whose members are not dependent on government for the right to practice.

[11] The legal profession's relative autonomy carries with it special responsibilities of self-government. The profession has a responsibility to assure that its regulations are conceived in the public interest and not in furtherance of parochial or self-interested concerns of the bar. Every lawyer is responsible for observance of the Rules of Professional Conduct. A lawyer should also aid in securing their observance by other lawyers. Neglect of these responsibilities compromises the independence of the profession and the public interest which it serves.

[12] Lawyers play a vital role in the preservation of society. The fulfillment of this role requires an understanding by lawyers of their relationship to our legal system. The Rules of Professional Conduct, when properly applied, serve to define that relationship.

Scope

[1] The Rules of Professional Conduct are rules of reason. They should be interpreted with reference to the purposes of legal representation and of the law itself. Some of the Rules are imperatives, cast in the terms "shall" or "shall not." These define proper conduct for purposes of professional discipline. Others, generally cast in the term "may," are permissive and define areas under the Rules in which the lawyer has professional discretion. No disciplinary action should be taken when the lawyer chooses not to act or acts within the bounds of such discretion. Other Rules define the nature of relationships between the lawyer and others. The Rules are thus partly obligatory and disciplinary and partly constitutive and descriptive in that they define a lawyer's professional role. Many of the Comments use the term "should." Comments do not add obligations to the Rules but provide guidance for practicing in compliance with the Rules.

[2] The Rules presuppose a larger legal context shaping the lawyer's role. That context includes court rules and statutes relating to matters of licensure, laws defining specific obligations of lawyers and substantive and procedural law in general. Compliance with the Rules, as with all law in an open society, depends primarily upon understanding and voluntary compliance, secondarily upon reinforcement by peer and public opinion and finally, when necessary, upon enforcement through disciplinary proceedings. The Rules do not, however, exhaust the moral and ethical considerations that should inform a lawyer, for no worth-

while human activity can be completely defined by legal rules. The Rules simply provide a framework for the ethical practice of law.

[3]   Furthermore, for purposes of determining the lawyer's authority and responsibility, principles of substantive law external to these Rules determine whether a client-lawyer relationship exists. Most of the duties flowing from the client-lawyer relationship attach only after the client has requested the lawyer to render legal services and the lawyer has agreed to do so. But there are some duties, such as that of confidentiality under Rule 1.6, that may attach when the lawyer agrees to consider whether a client-lawyer relationship shall be established. Whether a client-lawyer relationship exists for any specific purpose can depend on the circumstances and may be a question of fact.

[4]   Under various legal provisions, including constitutional, statutory and common law, the responsibilities of government lawyers may include authority concerning legal matters that ordinarily reposes in the client in private client-lawyer relationships. For example, a lawyer for a government agency may have authority on behalf of the government to decide upon settlement or whether to appeal from an adverse judgment. Such authority in various respects is generally vested in the attorney general and the state's attorney in state government, and their federal counterparts, and the same may be true of other government law officers. Also, lawyers under the supervision of these officers may be authorized to represent several government agencies in intragovernmental legal controversies in circumstances where a private lawyer could not represent multiple private clients. They also may have authority to represent the "public interest" in circumstances where a private lawyer would not be authorized to do so. These Rules do not abrogate any such authority.

[5]   Failure to comply with an obligation or prohibition imposed by a Rule is a basis for invoking the disciplinary process. The Rules presuppose that disciplinary assessment of a lawyer's conduct will be made on the basis of the facts and circumstances as they existed at the time of the conduct in question and in recognition of the fact that a lawyer often has to act upon uncertain or incomplete evidence of the situation. Moreover, the Rules presuppose that whether or not discipline should be imposed for a violation, and the severity of a sanction, depend on all the circumstances, such as the willfulness and seriousness of the violation, extenuating factors and whether there have been previous violations.

[6]   Violation of a Rule should not give rise to a cause of action nor should it create any presumption that a legal duty has been breached. The Rules are designed to provide guidance to lawyers and to provide a structure for regulating conduct through disciplinary agencies. They are not designed to be a basis for civil liability. Furthermore, the purpose of the Rules can be subverted when they are invoked by opposing parties as procedural weapons. The fact that a Rule is a just basis for a lawyer's self-assessment, or for sanctioning a lawyer under the administration of

a disciplinary authority, does not imply that an antagonist in a collateral proceeding or transaction has standing to seek enforcement of the Rule. Accordingly, nothing in the Rules should be deemed to augment any substantive legal duty of lawyers or the extra-disciplinary consequences of violating such a duty.

[7] Moreover, these Rules are not intended to govern or affect judicial application of either the attorney-client or work product privilege. Those privileges were developed to promote compliance with law and fairness in litigation. In reliance on the attorney-client privilege, clients are entitled to expect that communications within the scope of the privilege will be protected against compelled disclosure. The attorney-client privilege is that of the client and not of the lawyer. The fact that in exceptional situations the lawyer under the Rules has a limited discretion to disclose a client confidence does not vitiate the proposition that, as a general matter, the client has a reasonable expectation that information relating to the client will not be voluntarily disclosed and that disclosure of such information may be judicially compelled only in accordance with recognized exceptions to the attorney-client and work product privileges.

[8] The lawyer's exercise of discretion not to disclose information under Rule 1.6 should not be subject to reexamination. Permitting such reexamination would be incompatible with the general policy of promoting compliance with law through assurances that communications will be protected against disclosure.

[9] The Comment accompanying each Rule explains and illustrates the meaning and purpose of the Rule. The Preamble and this note on Scope provide general orientation. The Comments are intended as guides to interpretation, but the text of each Rule is authoritative. Research notes were prepared to compare counterparts in the ABA Model Code of Professional Responsibility (adopted 1969, as amended) and to provide selected references to other authorities. The notes have not been adopted, do not constitute part of the Model Rules, and are not intended to affect the application or interpretation of the Rules and Comments.

Terminology

[1] "Belief" or "Believes" denotes that the person involved actually supposed the fact in question to be true. A person's belief may be inferred from circumstances.

[2] "Consult" or "Consultation" denotes communication of information reasonably sufficient to permit the client to appreciate the significance of the matter in question.

[3] "Firm" or "Law firm" denotes a lawyer or lawyers in a private firm, lawyers employed in the legal department of a corporation or other organization and lawyers employed in a legal services organization. See Comment, Rule 1.10.

[4] "Fraud" or "Fraudulent" denotes conduct having a purpose to deceive and not merely negligent misrepresentation or failure to apprise another of relevant information.

[5] "Knowingly," "Known," or "Knows" denotes actual knowledge of the fact in question. A person's knowledge may be inferred from circumstances.

[6] "Partner" denotes a member of a partnership and a shareholder in a law firm organized as a professional corporation.

[7] "Reasonable" or "Reasonably" when used in relation to conduct by a lawyer denotes the conduct of a reasonably prudent and competent lawyer.

[8] "Reasonable belief" or "Reasonably believes" when used in reference to a lawyer denotes that the lawyer believes the matter in question and that the circumstances are such that the belief is reasonable.

[9] "Reasonably should know" when used in reference to a lawyer denotes that a lawyer of reasonable prudence and competence would ascertain the matter in question.

[10] "Substantial" when used in reference to degree or extent denotes a material matter of clear and weighty importance.

MODEL RULES OF PROFESSIONAL CONDUCT
CLIENT–LAWYER RELATIONSHIP

RULE 1.1 Competence

A Lawyer shall provide competent representation to a client. Competent representation requires the legal knowledge, skill, thoroughness and preparation reasonably necessary for the representation.

COMMENT:

Legal Knowledge and Skill

[1] In determining whether a lawyer employs the requisite knowledge and skill in a particular matter, relevant factors include the relative complexity and specialized nature of the matter, the lawyer's general experience, the lawyer's training and experience in the field in question, the preparation and study the lawyer is able to give the matter and whether it is feasible to refer the matter to, or associate or consult with, a lawyer of established competence in the field in question. In many instances, the required proficiency is that of a general practitioner. Expertise in a particular field of law may be required in some circumstances.

[2] A lawyer need not necessarily have special training or prior experience to handle legal problems of a type with which the lawyer is unfamiliar. A newly admitted lawyer can be as competent as a practitioner with long experience. Some important legal skills, such as the

analysis of precedent, the evaluation of evidence and legal drafting, are required in all legal problems. Perhaps the most fundamental legal skill consists of determining what kind of legal problems a situation may involve, a skill that necessarily transcends any particular specialized knowledge. A lawyer can provide adequate representation in a wholly novel field through necessary study. Competent representation can also be provided through the association of a lawyer of established competence in the field in question.

[3] In an emergency a lawyer may give advice or assistance in a matter in which the lawyer does not have the skill ordinarily required where referral to or consultation or association with another lawyer would be impractical. Even in an emergency, however, assistance should be limited to that reasonably necessary in the circumstances, for ill considered action under emergency conditions can jeopardize the client's interest.

[4] A lawyer may accept representation where the requisite level of competence can be achieved by reasonable preparation. This applies as well to a lawyer who is appointed as counsel for an unrepresented person. See also Rule 6.2.

Thoroughness and Preparation

[5] Competent handling of a particular matter includes inquiry into and analysis of the factual and legal elements of the problem, and use of methods and procedures meeting the standards of competent practitioners. It also includes adequate preparation. The required attention and preparation are determined in part by what is at stake; major litigation and complex transactions ordinarily require more elaborate treatment than matters of lesser consequence.

Maintaining Competence

[6] To maintain the requisite knowledge and skill, a lawyer should engage in continuing study and education. If a system of peer review has been established, the lawyer should consider making use of it in appropriate circumstances.

MODEL CODE COMPARISON:

DR 6–101(A)(1) provided that a lawyer shall not handle a matter "which he knows or should know that he is not competent to handle, without associating himself with a lawyer who is competent to handle it"; DR 6–101(A)(2) requires "preparation adequate in the circumstances." Rule 1.1 more fully particularizes the elements of competence. Whereas DR 6–101(A)(3) prohibited the "[N]eglect of a legal matter," Rule 1.1 does not contain such a prohibition. Instead, Rule 1.1 affirmatively requires the lawyer to be competent.

11

RULE 1.2   Scope of Representation

(a) A lawyer shall abide by a client's decisions concerning the objectives of representation, subject to paragraphs (c), (d) and (e), and shall consult with the client as to the means by which they are to be pursued. A lawyer shall abide by a client's decision whether to accept an offer of settlement of a matter. In a criminal case, the lawyer shall abide by the client's decision, after consultation with the lawyer, as to a plea to be entered, whether to waive jury trial and whether the client will testify.

(b) A lawyer's representation of a client, including representation by appointment, does not constitute an endorsement of the client's political, economic, social or moral views or activities.

(c) A lawyer may limit the objectives of the representation if the client consents after consultation.

(d) A lawyer shall not counsel a client to engage, or assist a client, in conduct that the lawyer knows is criminal or fraudulent, but a lawyer may discuss the legal consequences of any proposed course of conduct with a client and may counsel or assist a client to make a good faith effort to determine the validity, scope, meaning or application of the law.

(e) When a lawyer knows that a client expects assistance not permitted by the rules of professional conduct or other law, the lawyer shall consult with the client regarding the relevant limitations on the lawyer's conduct.

COMMENT:

Scope of Representation

[1]   Both lawyer and client have authority and responsibility in the objectives and means of representation. The client has ultimate authority to determine the purposes to be served by legal representation, within the limits imposed by law and the lawyer's professional obligations. Within those limits, a client also has a right to consult with the lawyer about the means to be used in pursuing those objectives. At the same time, a lawyer is not required to pursue objectives or employ means simply because a client may wish that the lawyer do so. A clear distinction between objectives and means sometimes cannot be drawn, and in many cases the client-lawyer relationship partakes of a joint undertaking. In questions of means, the lawyer should assume responsibility for technical and legal tactical issues, but should defer to the client regarding such questions as the expense to be incurred and concern for third persons who might be adversely affected. Law defining the lawyer's scope of authority in litigation varies among jurisdictions.

[2]   In a case in which the client appears to be suffering mental disability, the lawyer's duty to abide by the client's decisions is to be guided by reference to Rule 1.14.

Independence from Client's Views or Activities

[3] Legal representation should not be denied to people who are unable to afford legal services, or whose cause is controversial or the subject of popular disapproval. By the same token, representing a client does not constitute approval of the client's views or activities.

Services Limited in Objectives or Means

[4] The objectives or scope of services provided by a lawyer may be limited by agreement with the client or by the terms under which the lawyer's services are made available to the client. For example, a retainer may be for a specifically defined purpose. Representation provided through a legal aid agency may be subject to limitations on the types of cases the agency handles. When a lawyer has been retained by an insurer to represent an insured, the representation may be limited to matters related to the insurance coverage. The terms upon which representation is undertaken may exclude specific objectives or means. Such limitations may exclude objectives or means that the lawyer regards as repugnant or imprudent.

[5] An agreement concerning the scope of representation must accord with the Rules of Professional Conduct and other law. Thus, the client may not be asked to agree to representation so limited in scope as to violate Rule 1.1, or to surrender the right to terminate the lawyer's services or the right to settle litigation that the lawyer might wish to continue.

Criminal, Fraudulent and Prohibited Transactions

[6] A lawyer is required to give an honest opinion about the actual consequences that appear likely to result from a client's conduct. The fact that a client uses advice in a course of action that is criminal or fraudulent does not, of itself, make a lawyer a party to the course of action. However, a lawyer may not knowingly assist a client in criminal or fraudulent conduct. There is a critical distinction between presenting an analysis of legal aspects of questionable conduct and recommending the means by which a crime or fraud might be committed with impunity.

[7] When the client's course of action has already begun and is continuing, the lawyer's responsibility is especially delicate. The lawyer is not permitted to reveal the client's wrongdoing, except where permitted by Rule 1.6. However, the lawyer is required to avoid furthering the purpose, for example, by suggesting how it might be concealed. A lawyer may not continue assisting a client in conduct that the lawyer originally supposes is legally proper but then discovers is criminal or fraudulent. Withdrawal from the representation, therefore, may be required.

[8] Where the client is a fiduciary, the lawyer may be charged with special obligations in dealings with a beneficiary.

[9] Paragraph (d) applies whether or not the defrauded party is a party to the transaction. Hence, a lawyer should not participate in a sham transaction; for example, a transaction to effectuate criminal or fraudulent escape of tax liability. Paragraph (d) does not preclude undertaking a criminal defense incident to a general retainer for legal services to a lawful enterprise. The last clause of paragraph (d) recognizes that determining the validity or interpretation of a statute or regulation may require a course of action involving disobedience of the statute or regulation or of the interpretation placed upon it by governmental authorities.

MODEL CODE COMPARISON:

Paragraph (a) has no counterpart in the Disciplinary Rules of the Model Code. EC 7–7 stated: "In certain areas of legal representation not affecting the merits of the cause or substantially prejudicing the rights of a client, a lawyer is entitled to make decisions on his own. But otherwise the authority to make decisions is exclusively that of the client...." EC 7–8 stated that "[I]n the final analysis, however, the ... decision whether to forego legally available objectives or methods because of nonlegal factors is ultimately for the client.... In the event that the client in a nonadjudicatory matter insists upon a course of conduct that is contrary to the judgment and advice of the lawyer but not prohibited by Disciplinary Rules, the lawyer may withdraw from the employment." DR 7–101(A)(1) provided that a lawyer "shall not intentionally ... fail to seek the lawful objectives of his client through reasonably available means permitted by law.... A lawyer does not violate this Disciplinary Rule, however, by ... avoiding offensive tactics...."

Paragraph (b) has no counterpart in the Model Code.

With regard to paragraph (c), DR 7–101(B)(1) provided that a lawyer may, "where permissible, exercise his professional judgment to waive or fail to assert a right or position of his client."

With regard to paragraph (d), DR 7–102(A)(7) provided that a lawyer shall not "counsel or assist his client in conduct that the lawyer knows to be illegal or fraudulent." DR 7–102(A)(6) provided that a lawyer shall not "participate in the creation or preservation of evidence when he knows or it is obvious that the evidence is false." DR 7–106 provided that a lawyer shall not "advise his client to disregard a standing rule of a tribunal or a ruling of a tribunal ... but he may take appropriate steps in good faith to test the validity of such rule or ruling." EC 7–5 stated that a lawyer "should never encourage or aid his client to commit criminal acts or counsel his client on how to violate the law and avoid punishment therefor."

With regard to Rule 1.2(e), DR 2–110(C)(1)(c) provided that a lawyer may withdraw from representation if a client "insists" that the lawyer engage in "conduct that is illegal or that is prohibited under the Disciplinary Rules." DR 9–101(C) provided that "a lawyer shall not state or imply that he is able to influence improperly ... any tribunal, legislative body or public official.''

RULE 1.3   Diligence

A lawyer shall act with reasonable diligence and promptness in representing a client.

COMMENT:

[1] A lawyer should pursue a matter on behalf of a client despite opposition, obstruction or personal inconvenience to the lawyer, and may take whatever lawful and ethical measures are required to vindicate a client's cause or endeavor. A lawyer should act with commitment and dedication to the interests of the client and with zeal in advocacy upon the client's behalf. However, a lawyer is not bound to press for every advantage that might be realized for a client. A lawyer has professional discretion in determining the means by which a matter should be pursued. See Rule 1.2. A lawyer's workload should be controlled so that each matter can be handled adequately.

[2] Perhaps no professional shortcoming is more widely resented than procrastination. A client's interests often can be adversely affected by the passage of time or the change of conditions; in extreme instances, as when a lawyer overlooks a statute of limitations, the client's legal position may be destroyed. Even when the client's interests are not affected in substance, however, unreasonable delay can cause a client needless anxiety and undermine confidence in the lawyer's trustworthiness.

[3] Unless the relationship is terminated as provided in Rule 1.16, a lawyer should carry through to conclusion all matters undertaken for a client. If a lawyer's employment is limited to a specific matter, the relationship terminates when the matter has been resolved. If a lawyer has served a client over a substantial period in a variety of matters, the client sometimes may assume that the lawyer will continue to serve on a continuing basis unless the lawyer gives notice of withdrawal. Doubt about whether a client-lawyer relationship still exists should be clarified by the lawyer, preferably in writing, so that the client will not mistakenly suppose the lawyer is looking after the client's affairs when the lawyer has ceased to do so. For example, if a lawyer has handled a judicial or administrative proceeding that produced a result adverse to the client but has not been specifically instructed concerning pursuit of an appeal, the lawyer should advise the client of the possibility of appeal before relinquishing responsibility for the matter.

MODEL CODE COMPARISON:

DR 6–101(A)(3) required that a lawyer not ''[n]eglect a legal matter entrusted to him.'' EC 6–4 stated that a lawyer should ''give appropriate attention to his legal work.'' Canon 7 stated that ''a lawyer should represent a client zealously within the bounds of the law.'' DR 7–

101(A)(1) provided that a lawyer "shall not intentionally ... fail to seek the lawful objectives of his client through reasonably available means permitted by law and the Disciplinary Rules...." DR 7–101(A)(3) provided that a lawyer "shall not intentionally ... [p]rejudice or damage his client during the course of the relationship...."

RULE 1.4 Communication

(a) A lawyer shall keep a client reasonably informed about the status of a matter and promptly comply with reasonable requests for information.

(b) A lawyer shall explain a matter to the extent reasonably necessary to permit the client to make informed decisions regarding the representation.

COMMENT:

[1] The client should have sufficient information to participate intelligently in decisions concerning the objectives of the representation and the means by which they are to be pursued, to the extent the client is willing and able to do so. For example, a lawyer negotiating on behalf of a client should provide the client with facts relevant to the matter, inform the client of communications from another party and take other reasonable steps that permit the client to make a decision regarding a serious offer from another party. A lawyer who receives from opposing counsel an offer of settlement in a civil controversy or a proffered plea bargain in a criminal case should promptly inform the client of its substance unless prior discussions with the client have left it clear that the proposal will be unacceptable. See Rule 1.2(a). Even when a client delegates authority to the lawyer, the client should be kept advised of the status of the matter.

[2] Adequacy of communication depends in part on the kind of advice or assistance involved. For example, in negotiations where there is time to explain a proposal the lawyer should review all important provisions with the client before proceeding to an agreement. In litigation a lawyer should explain the general strategy and prospects of success and ordinarily should consult the client on tactics that might injure or coerce others. On the other hand, a lawyer ordinarily cannot be expected to describe trial or negotiation strategy in detail. The guiding principle is that the lawyer should fulfill reasonable client expectations for information consistent with the duty to act in the client's best interests, and the client's overall requirements as to the character of representation.

[3] Ordinarily, the information to be provided is that appropriate for a client who is a comprehending and responsible adult. However, fully informing the client according to this standard may be impracticable, for example, where the client is a child or suffers from mental disability. See Rule 1.14. When the client is an organization or group, it is often impossible or inappropriate to inform every one of its members

about its legal affairs; ordinarily, the lawyer should address communications to the appropriate officials of the organization. See Rule 1.13. Where many routine matters are involved, a system of limited or occasional reporting may be arranged with the client. Practical exigency may also require a lawyer to act for a client without prior consultation.

Withholding Information

[4] In some circumstances, a lawyer may be justified in delaying transmission of information when the client would be likely to react imprudently to an immediate communication. Thus, a lawyer might withhold a psychiatric diagnosis of a client when the examining psychiatrist indicates that disclosure would harm the client. A lawyer may not withhold information to serve the lawyer's own interest or convenience. Rules or court orders governing litigation may provide that information supplied to a lawyer may not be disclosed to the client. Rule 3.4(c) directs compliance with such rules or orders.

MODEL CODE COMPARISON:

Rule 1.4 has no direct counterpart in the Disciplinary Rules of the Model Code. DR 6–101(A)(3) provided that a lawyer shall not "[n]eglect a legal matter entrusted to him." DR 9–102(B)(1) provided that a lawyer shall "[p]romptly notify a client of the receipt of his funds, securities, or other properties." EC 7–8 stated that a lawyer "should exert his best efforts to insure that decisions of his client are made only after the client has been informed of relevant considerations." EC 9–2 stated that "a lawyer should fully and promptly inform his client of material developments in the matters being handled for the client."

RULE 1.5 Fees

(a) A lawyer's fee shall be reasonable. The factors to be considered in determining the reasonableness of a fee include the following:

(1) the time and labor required, the novelty and difficulty of the questions involved, and the skill requisite to perform the legal service properly;

(2) the likelihood, if apparent to the client, that the acceptance of the particular employment will preclude other employment by the lawyer;

(3) the fee customarily charged in the locality for similar legal services;

(4) the amount involved and the results obtained;

(5) the time limitations imposed by the client or by the circumstances;

(6) the nature and length of the professional relationship with the client;

17

(7) the experience, reputation, and ability of the lawyer or lawyers performing the services; and

(8) whether the fee is fixed or contingent.

(b) When the lawyer has not regularly represented the client, the basis or rate of the fee shall be communicated to the client, preferably in writing, before or within a reasonable time after commencing the representation.

(c) A fee may be contingent on the outcome of the matter for which the service is rendered, except in a matter in which a contingent fee is prohibited by paragraph (d) or other law. A contingent fee agreement shall be in writing and shall state the method by which the fee is to be determined, including the percentage or percentages that shall accrue to the lawyer in the event of settlement, trial or appeal, litigation and other expenses to be deducted from the recovery, and whether such expenses are to be deducted before or after the contingent fee is calculated. Upon conclusion of a contingent fee matter, the lawyer shall provide the client with a written statement stating the outcome of the matter and, if there is a recovery, showing the remittance to the client and the method of its determination.

(d) A lawyer shall not enter into an arrangement for, charge, or collect:

(1) any fee in a domestic relations matter, the payment or amount of which is contingent upon the securing of a divorce or upon the amount of alimony or support, or property settlement in lieu thereof; or

(2) a contingent fee for representing a defendant in a criminal case.

(e) A division of fee between lawyers who are not in the same firm may be made only if:

(1) the division is in proportion to the services performed by each lawyer or, by written agreement with the client, each lawyer assumes joint responsibility for the representation;

(2) the client is advised of and does not object to the participation of all the lawyers involved; and

(3) the total fee is reasonable.

COMMENT:

Basis or Rate of Fee

[1] When the lawyer has regularly represented a client, they ordinarily will have evolved an understanding concerning the basis or rate of the fee. In a new client-lawyer relationship, however, an understanding as to the fee should be promptly established. It is not necessary to recite

all the factors that underlie the basis of the fee, but only those that are directly involved in its computation. It is sufficient, for example, to state that the basic rate is an hourly charge or a fixed amount or an estimated amount, or to identify the factors that may be taken into account in finally fixing the fee. When developments occur during the representation that render an earlier estimate substantially inaccurate, a revised estimate should be provided to the client. A written statement concerning the fee reduces the possibility of misunderstanding. Furnishing the client with a simple memorandum or a copy of the lawyer's customary fee schedule is sufficient if the basis or rate of the fee is set forth.

Terms of Payment

[2] A lawyer may require advance payment of a fee, but is obliged to return any unearned portion. See Rule 1.16(d). A lawyer may accept property in payment for services, such as an ownership interest in an enterprise, providing this does not involve acquisition of a proprietary interest in the cause of action or subject matter of the litigation contrary to Rule 1.8(j).* However, a fee paid in property instead of money may be subject to special scrutiny because it involves questions concerning both the value of the services and the lawyer's special knowledge of the value of the property.

[3] An agreement may not be made whose terms might induce the lawyer improperly to curtail services for the client or perform them in a way contrary to the client's interest. For example, a lawyer should not enter into an agreement whereby services are to be provided only up to a stated amount when it is foreseeable that more extensive services probably will be required, unless the situation is adequately explained to the client. Otherwise, the client might have to bargain for further assistance in the midst of a proceeding or transaction. However, it is proper to define the extent of services in light of the client's ability to pay. A lawyer should not exploit a fee arrangement based primarily on hourly charges by using wasteful procedures. When there is doubt whether a contingent fee is consistent with the client's best interest, the lawyer should offer the client alternative bases for the fee and explain their implications. Applicable law may impose limitations on contingent fees, such as a ceiling on the percentage.

Division of Fee

[4] A division of fee is a single billing to a client covering the fee of two or more lawyers who are not in the same firm. A division of fee facilitates association of more than one lawyer in a matter in which neither alone could serve the client as well, and most often is used when

---

* In 1987, the ABA added the following clause to the 1983 version of the Model Rules: "providing this does not involve ac-quisition of a proprietary interest in the cause of action or subject matter of the litigation contrary to Rule 1.8(j)."

the fee is contingent and the division is between a referring lawyer and a trial specialist. Paragraph (e) permits the lawyers to divide a fee on either the basis of the proportion of services they render or by agreement between the participating lawyers if all assume responsibility for the representation as a whole and the client is advised and does not object. It does not require disclosure to the client of the share that each lawyer is to receive. Joint responsibility for the representation entails the obligations stated in Rule 5.1 for purposes of the matter involved.

Disputes Over Fees

[5] If a procedure has been established for resolution of fee disputes, such as an arbitration or mediation procedure established by the bar, the lawyer should conscientiously consider submitting to it. Law may prescribe a procedure for determining a lawyer's fee, for example, in representation of an executor or administrator, a class or a person entitled to a reasonable fee as part of the measure of damages. The lawyer entitled to such a fee and a lawyer representing another party concerned with the fee should comply with the prescribed procedure.

MODEL CODE COMPARISON:

DR 2–106(A) provided that a lawyer "shall not enter into an agreement for, charge, or collect an illegal or clearly excessive fee." DR 2–106(B) provided that a fee is "clearly excessive when, after a review of the facts, a lawyer of ordinary prudence would be left with a definite and firm conviction that the fee is in excess of a reasonable fee." The factors of a reasonable fee in Rule 1.5(a) are substantially identical to those listed in DR 2–106(B). EC 2–17 states that a lawyer "should not charge more than a reasonable fee.... "

There was no counterpart to Rule 1.5(b) in the Disciplinary Rules of the Model Code. EC 2–19 stated that it is "usually beneficial to reduce to writing the understanding of the parties regarding the fee, particularly when it is contingent."

There was no counterpart to paragraph (c) in the Disciplinary Rules of the Model Code. EC 2–20 provided that "[c]ontingent fee arrangements in civil cases have long been commonly accepted in the United States," but that "a lawyer generally should decline to accept employment on a contingent fee basis by one who is able to pay a reasonable fixed fee.... "

With regard to paragraph (d), DR 2–106(C) prohibited "a contingent fee in a criminal case." EC 2–20 provided that "contingent fee arrangements in domestic relation cases are rarely justified."

With regard to paragraph (e), DR 2–107(A) permitted division of fees only if: "(1) The client consents to employment of the other lawyer after a full disclosure that a division of fees will be made. (2) The division is in proportion to the services performed and responsibility assumed by each. (3) The total fee does not exceed clearly reasonable compensation.... " Paragraph (e) permits division without regard to the services rendered by each lawyer if they assume joint responsibility for the representation.

RULE 1.6   Confidentiality of Information*

(a) A lawyer shall not reveal information relating to representation of a client unless the client consents after consultation, except for disclosures that are impliedly authorized in order to carry out the representation, and except as stated in paragraph (b).

(b) A lawyer may reveal such information to the extent the lawyer reasonably believes necessary:

(1) to prevent the client from committing a criminal act that the lawyer believes is likely to result in imminent death or substantial bodily harm; or

(2) to establish a claim or defense on behalf of the lawyer in a controversy between the lawyer and the client, to establish a defense to a criminal charge or civil claim against the lawyer based upon conduct in which the client was involved, or to respond to allegations in any proceeding concerning the lawyer's representation of the client.

COMMENT:

[1]   The lawyer is part of a judicial system charged with upholding the law. One of the lawyer's functions is to advise clients so that they avoid any violation of the law in the proper exercise of their rights.

[2]   The observance of the ethical obligation of a lawyer to hold inviolate confidential information of the client not only facilitates the full development of facts essential to proper representation of the client but also encourages people to seek early legal assistance.

* In 1991, The ABA House of Delegates rejected the ethics committee recommendation that it modify Model Rule 1.6. The rejected language would have inserted the following exception to the general rule of confidentiality under Model Rule 1.6(b): "to rectify the consequences of a client's criminal or fraudulent act in the furtherance of which the lawyer's services had been used." This language is identical to an exception listed in the Kutak Commission's 1982 Final Revised Draft of Model Rule 1.6. The proposed Kutak Rule 1.6(b) would have contained the following exceptions:

(1) to prevent the client from committing a criminal or fraudulent act that the lawyer reasonably believes is likely to result in death or substantial bodily harm, or in substantial injury to the financial interests or property of another;

(2) to rectify the consequences of a client's criminal or fraudulent act in the furtherance of which the lawyer's financial services had been used;

(3) to establish a claim or defense on behalf of the lawyer in a controversy between the lawyer and the client, or to establish a defense to a criminal charge, civil claim or disciplinary complaint against the lawyer based upon conduct in which the client was involved; or

(4) to comply with other law.

Proposed Model Rule 1.6(b) (Revised Final Draft) (June 20, 1982).

[3] Almost without exception, clients come to lawyers in order to determine what their rights are and what is, in the maze of laws and regulations, deemed to be legal and correct. The common law recognizes that the client's confidences must be protected from disclosure. Based upon experience, lawyers know that almost all clients follow the advice given, and the law is upheld.

[4] A fundamental principle in the client-lawyer relationship is that the lawyer maintain confidentiality of information relating to the representation. The client is thereby encouraged to communicate fully and frankly with the lawyer even as to embarrassing or legally damaging subject matter.

[5] The principle of confidentiality is given effect in two related bodies of law, the attorney-client privilege (which includes the work product doctrine) in the law of evidence and the rule of confidentiality established in professional ethics. The attorney-client privilege applies in judicial and other proceedings in which a lawyer may be called as a witness or otherwise required to produce evidence concerning a client. The rule of client-lawyer confidentiality applies in situations other than those where evidence is sought from the lawyer through compulsion of law. The confidentiality rule applies not merely to matters communicated in confidence by the client but also to all information relating to the representation, whatever its source. A lawyer may not disclose such information except as authorized or required by the Rules of Professional Conduct or other law. See also Scope.

[6] The requirement of maintaining confidentiality of information relating to representation applies to government lawyers who may disagree with the policy goals that their representation is designed to advance.

Authorized Disclosure

[7] A lawyer is impliedly authorized to make disclosures about a client when appropriate in carrying out the representation, except to the extent that the client's instructions or special circumstances limit that authority. In litigation, for example, a lawyer may disclose information by admitting a fact that cannot properly be disputed, or in negotiation by making a disclosure that facilitates a satisfactory conclusion.

[8] Lawyers in a firm may, in the course of the firm's practice, disclose to each other information relating to a client of the firm, unless the client has instructed that particular information be confined to specified lawyers.

Disclosure Adverse to Client

[9] The confidentiality rule is subject to limited exceptions. In becoming privy to information about a client, a lawyer may foresee that the client intends serious harm to another person. However, to the extent a lawyer is required or permitted to disclose a client's purposes,

the client will be inhibited from revealing facts which would enable the lawyer to counsel against a wrongful course of action. The public is better protected if full and open communication by the client is encouraged than if it is inhibited.

Several situations must be distinguished.

[10]   First, the lawyer may not counsel or assist a client in conduct that is criminal or fraudulent. See Rule 1.2(d). Similarly, a lawyer has a duty under Rule 3.3(a)(4) not to use false evidence. This duty is essentially a special instance of the duty prescribed in Rule 1.2(d) to avoid assisting a client in criminal or fraudulent conduct.

[11]   Second, the lawyer may have been innocently involved in past conduct by the client that was criminal or fraudulent. In such a situation the lawyer has not violated Rule 1.2(d), because to "counsel or assist" criminal or fraudulent conduct requires knowing that the conduct is of that character.

[12]   Third, the lawyer may learn that a client intends prospective conduct that is criminal and likely to result in imminent death or substantial bodily harm. As stated in paragraph (b)(1), the lawyer has professional discretion to reveal information in order to prevent such consequences. The lawyer may make a disclosure in order to prevent homicide or serious bodily injury which the lawyer reasonable believes is intended by a client. It is very difficult for a lawyer to "know" when such a heinous purpose will actually be carried out, for the client may have a change of mind.

[13]   The lawyer's exercise of discretion requires consideration of such factors as the nature of the lawyer's relationship with the client and with those who might be injured by the client, the lawyer's own involvement in the transaction and factors that may extenuate the conduct in question. Where practical, the lawyer should seek to persuade the client to take suitable action. In any case, a disclosure adverse to the client's interest should be no greater than the lawyer reasonably believes necessary to the purpose. A lawyer's decision not to take preventive action permitted by paragraph (b)(1) does not violate this Rule.

Withdrawal

[14]   If the lawyer's services will be used by the client in materially furthering a course of criminal or fraudulent conduct, the lawyer must withdraw, as stated in Rule 1.16(a)(1).

[15]   After withdrawal the lawyer is required to refrain from making disclosure of the clients' confidences, except as otherwise provided in Rule 1.6. Neither this Rule nor Rule 1.8(b) nor Rule 1.16(d) prevents the lawyer from giving notice of the fact of withdrawal, and the lawyer may also withdraw or disaffirm any opinion, document, affirmation, or the like.

[16]   Where the client is an organization, the lawyer may be in doubt whether contemplated conduct will actually be carried out by the

organization. Where necessary to guide conduct in connection with this Rule, the lawyer may make inquiry within the organization as indicated in Rule 1.13(b).

Dispute Concerning Lawyer's Conduct

[17] Where a legal claim or disciplinary charge alleges complicity of the lawyer in a client's conduct or other misconduct of the lawyer involving representation of the client, the lawyer may respond to the extent the lawyer reasonably believes necessary to establish a defense. The same is true with respect to a claim involving the conduct or representation of a former client. The lawyer's right to respond arises when an assertion of such complicity has been made. Paragraph (b)(2) does not require the lawyer to await the commencement of an action or proceeding that charges such complicity, so that the defense may be established by responding directly to a third party who has made such an assertion. The right to defend, of course, applies where a proceeding has been commenced. Where practicable and not prejudicial to the lawyer's ability to establish the defense, the lawyer should advise the client of the third party's assertion and request that the client respond appropriately. In any event, disclosure should be no greater than the lawyer reasonably believes is necessary to vindicate innocence, the disclosure should be made in a manner which limits access to the information to the tribunal or other persons having a need to know it, and appropriate protective orders or other arrangements should be sought by the lawyer to the fullest extent practicable.

[18] If the lawyer is charged with wrongdoing in which the client's conduct is implicated, the rule of confidentiality should not prevent the lawyer from defending against the charge. Such a charge can arise in a civil, criminal or professional disciplinary proceeding, and can be based on a wrong allegedly committed by the lawyer against the client, or on a wrong alleged by a third person; for example, a person claiming to have been defrauded by the lawyer and client acting together. A lawyer entitled to a fee is permitted by paragraph (b)(2) to prove the services rendered in an action to collect it. This aspect of the rule expresses the principle that the beneficiary of a fiduciary relationship may not exploit it to the detriment of the fiduciary. As stated above, the lawyer must make every effort practicable to avoid unnecessary disclosure of information relating to a representation, to limit disclosure to those having the need to know it, and to obtain protective orders or make other arrangements minimizing the risk of disclosure.

Disclosures Otherwise Required or Authorized

[19] The attorney-client privilege is differently defined in various jurisdictions. If a lawyer is called as a witness to give testimony concerning a client, absent waiver by the client, Rule 1.6(a) requires the lawyer to invoke the privilege when it is applicable. The lawyer must

comply with the final orders of a court or other tribunal of competent jurisdiction requiring the lawyer to give information about the client.

[20] The Rules of Professional Conduct in various circumstances permit or require a lawyer to disclose information relating to the representation. See Rules 2.2, 2.3, 3.3 and 4.1. In addition to these provisions, a lawyer may be obligated or permitted by other provisions of law to give information about a client. Whether another provision of law supersedes Rule 1.6 is a matter of interpretation beyond the scope of these Rules, but a presumption should exist against such a supersession.

Former Client

[21] The duty of confidentiality continues after the client-lawyer relationship has terminated.

MODEL CODE COMPARISON:

Rule 1.6 eliminates the two-pronged duty under the Model Code in favor of a single standard protecting all information about a client "relating to the representation." Under DR 4–101, the requirement applied only to information protected by the attorney-client privilege and to information "gained in" the professional relationship that "the client has requested be held inviolate or the disclosure of which would be embarrassing or would be likely to be detrimental to the client." EC 4–4 added that the duty differed from the evidentiary privilege in that it existed "without regard to the nature or source of information or the fact that others share the knowledge." Rule 1.6 imposes confidentiality on information relating to the representation even if it is acquired before or after the relationship existed. It does not require the client to indicate information that is to be confidential, or permit the lawyer to speculate whether particular information might be embarrassing or detrimental.

Paragraph (a) permits a lawyer to disclose information where impliedly authorized to do so in order to carry out the representation. Under DR 4–101(B) and (C), a lawyer was not permitted to reveal "confidences" unless the client first consented after disclosure.

Paragraph (b) redefines the exceptions to the requirement of confidentiality. Regarding paragraph (b)(1), DR 4–101(C)(3) provided that a lawyer "may reveal ... [t]he intention of his client to commit a crime and the information necessary to prevent the crime." This option existed regardless of the seriousness of the proposed crime.

With regard to paragraph (b)(2), DR 4–101(C)(4) provided that a lawyer may reveal "[c]onfidences or secrets necessary to establish or collect his fee or to defend himself or his employers or associates against an accusation of wrongful conduct." Paragraph (b)(2) enlarges the exception to include disclosure of information relating to claims by the lawyer other than for the lawyer's fee; for example, recovery of property from the client.

RULE 1.7   Conflict of Interest: General Rule

(a) A lawyer shall not represent a client if the representation of that client will be directly adverse to another client, unless:

   (1) the lawyer reasonably believes the representation will not adversely affect the relationship with the other client; and

   (2) each client consents after consultation.

(b) A lawyer shall not represent a client if the representation of that client may be materially limited by the lawyer's responsibilities to another client or to a third person, or by the lawyer's own interests, unless:

   (1) the lawyer reasonably believes the representation will not be adversely affected; and

   (2) the client consents after consultation. When representation of multiple clients in a single matter is undertaken, the consultation shall include explanation of the implications of the common representation and the advantages and risks involved.

COMMENT:

Loyalty to a Client

[1]   Loyalty is an essential element in the lawyer's relationship to a client. An impermissible conflict of interest may exist before representation is undertaken, in which event the representation should be declined. The lawyer should adopt reasonable procedures, appropriate for the size and type of firm and practice, to determine in both litigation and non-litigation matters the parties and issues involved and to determine whether there are actual or potential conflicts of interest.*

[2]   If such a conflict arises after representation has been undertaken, the lawyer should withdraw from the representation. See Rule 1.16. Where more than one client is involved and the lawyer withdraws because a conflict arises after representation, whether the lawyer may continue to represent any of the clients is determined by Rule 1.9. See also Rule 2.2(c). As to whether a client-lawyer relationship exists or, having once been established, is continuing, see Comment to Rule 1.3 and Scope.

[3]   As a general proposition, loyalty to a client prohibits undertaking representation directly adverse to that client without that client's consent. Paragraph (a) expresses that general rule. Thus, a lawyer ordinarily may not act as advocate against a person the lawyer represents in some other matter, even if it is wholly unrelated. On the other

---

* The ABA added this sentence in the comments to the Model Rules in 1987. The remainder of paragraph 1 in the original version of this comment now appears in the current paragraph 2.

hand, simultaneous representation in unrelated matters of clients whose interests are only generally adverse, such as competing economic enterprises, does not require consent of the respective clients. Paragraph (a) applies only when the representation of one client would be directly adverse to the other.

[4] Loyalty to a client is also impaired when a lawyer cannot consider, recommend or carry out an appropriate course of action for the client because of the lawyer's other responsibilities or interests. The conflict in effect forecloses alternatives that would otherwise be available to the client. Paragraph (b) addresses such situations. A possible conflict does not itself preclude the representation. The critical questions are the likelihood that a conflict will eventuate and, if it does, whether it will materially interfere with the lawyer's independent professional judgment in considering alternatives or foreclose courses of action that reasonably should be pursued on behalf of the client. Consideration should be given to whether the client wishes to accommodate the other interest involved.

Consultation and Consent

[5] A client may consent to representation notwithstanding a conflict. However, as indicated in paragraph (a)(1) with respect to representation directly adverse to a client, and paragraph (b)(1) with respect to material limitations on representation of a client, when a disinterested lawyer would conclude that the client should not agree to the representation under the circumstances, the lawyer involved cannot properly ask for such agreement or provide representation on the basis of the client's consent. When more than once client is involved, the question of conflict must be resolved as to each client. Moreover, there may be circumstances where it is impossible to make the disclosure necessary to obtain consent. For example, when the lawyer represents different clients in related matters and one of the clients refuses to consent to the disclosure necessary to permit the other client to make an informed decision, the lawyer cannot properly ask the latter to consent.

Lawyer's Interests

[6] The lawyer's own interests should not be permitted to have adverse effect on representation of a client. For example, a lawyer's need for income should not lead the lawyer to undertake matters that cannot be handled competently and at a reasonable fee. See Rules 1.1 and 1.5. If the probity of a lawyer's own conduct in a transaction is in serious question, it may be difficult or impossible for the lawyer to give a client detached advice. A lawyer may not allow related business interests to affect representation, for example, by referring clients to an enterprise in which the lawyer has an undisclosed interest.

27

Conflicts in Litigation

[7] Paragraph (a) prohibits representation of opposing parties in litigation. Simultaneous representation of parties whose interests in litigation may conflict, such as co-plaintiffs or co-defendants, is governed by paragraph (b). An impermissible conflict may exist by reason of substantial discrepancy in the parties' testimony, incompatibility in positions in relation to an opposing party or the fact that there are substantially different possibilities of settlement of the claims or liabilities in question. Such conflicts can arise in criminal cases as well as civil. The potential for conflict of interest in representing multiple defendants in a criminal case is so grave that ordinarily a lawyer should decline to represent more than one codefendant. On the other hand, common representation of persons having similar interests is proper if the risk of adverse effect is minimal and the requirements of paragraph (b) are met. Compare Rule 2.2 involving intermediation between clients.

[8] Ordinarily, a lawyer may not act as advocate against a client the lawyer represents in some other matter, even if the other matter is wholly unrelated. However, there are circumstances in which a lawyer may act as advocate against a client. For example, a lawyer representing an enterprise with diverse operations may accept employment as an advocate against the enterprise in an unrelated matter if doing so will not adversely affect the lawyer's relationship with the enterprise or conduct of the suit and if both clients consent upon consultation. By the same token, government lawyers in some circumstances may represent government employees in proceedings in which a government agency is the opposing party. The propriety of concurrent representation can depend on the nature of the litigation. For example, a suit charging fraud entails conflict to a degree not involved in a suit for a declaratory judgment concerning statutory interpretation.

[9] A lawyer may represent parties having antagonistic positions on a legal question that has arisen in different cases, unless representation of either client would be adversely affected. Thus, it is ordinarily not improper to assert such positions in cases pending in different trial courts, but it may be improper to do so in cases pending at the same time in an appellate court.

Interest of Person Paying for a Lawyer's Service

[10] A lawyer may be paid from a source other than the client, if the client is informed of that fact and consents and the arrangement does not compromise the lawyer's duty of loyalty to the client. See Rule 1.8(f). For example, when an insurer and its insured have conflicting interests in a matter arising from a liability insurance agreement, and the insurer is required to provide special counsel for the insured, the arrangement should assure the special counsel's professional independence. So also, when a corporation and its directors or employees are involved in a controversy in which they have conflicting interests, the

corporation may provide funds for separate legal representation of the directors or employees, if the clients consent after consultation and the arrangement ensures the lawyer's professional independence.

Other Conflict Situations

[11] Conflicts of interest in contexts other than litigation sometimes may be difficult to assess. Relevant factors in determining whether there is potential for adverse effect include the duration and intimacy of the lawyer's relationship with the client or clients involved, the functions being performed by the lawyer, the likelihood that actual conflict will arise and the likely prejudice to the client from the conflict if it does arise. The question is often one of proximity and degree.

[12] For example, a lawyer may not represent multiple parties to a negotiation whose interests are fundamentally antagonistic to each other, but common representation is permissible where the clients are generally aligned in interest even though there is some difference of interest among them.

[13] Conflict questions may also arise in estate planning and estate administration. A lawyer may be called upon to prepare wills for several family members, such as husband and wife, and, depending upon the circumstances, a conflict of interest may arise. In estate administration the identity of the client may be unclear under the law of a particular jurisdiction. Under one view, the client is the fiduciary; under another view the client is the estate or trust, including its beneficiaries. The lawyer should make clear the relationship to the parties involved.

[14] A lawyer for a corporation or other organization who is also a member of its board of directors should determine whether the responsibilities of the two roles may conflict. The lawyer may be called on to advise the corporation in matters involving actions of the directors. Consideration should be given to the frequency with which such situations may arise, the potential intensity of the conflict, the effect of the lawyer's resignation from the board and the possibility of the corporation's obtaining legal advice from another lawyer in such situations. If there is material risk that the dual role will compromise the lawyer's independence of professional judgment, the lawyer should not serve as a director.

Conflict Charged by an Opposing Party

[15] Resolving questions of conflict of interest is primarily the responsibility of the lawyer undertaking the representation. In litigation, a court may raise the question when there is reason to infer that the lawyer has neglected the responsibility. In a criminal case, inquiry by the court is generally required when a lawyer represents multiple defendants. Where the conflict is such as clearly to call in question the fair or efficient administration of justice, opposing counsel may properly

raise the question. Such an objection should be viewed with caution, however, for it can be misused as a technique of harassment. See Scope.

MODEL CODE COMPARISON:

DR 5–101(A) provided that "[e]xcept with the consent of his client after full disclosure, a lawyer shall not accept employment if the exercise of his professional judgment on behalf of the client will be or reasonably may be affected by his own financial, business, property, or personal interests." DR 5–105(A) provided that a lawyer "shall decline proffered employment if the exercise of his independent professional judgment in behalf of a client will be or is likely to be adversely affected by the acceptance of the proffered employment, or if it would be likely to involve him in representing differing interests, except to the extent permitted under DR 5–105(C)." DR 5–105(C) provided that "a lawyer may represent multiple clients if it is obvious that he can adequately represent the interest of each and if each consents to the representation after full disclosure of the possible effect of such representation on the exercise of his independent professional judgment on behalf of each." DR 5–107(B) provided that a lawyer "shall not permit a person who recommends, employs, or pays him to render legal services for another to direct or regulate his professional judgment in rendering such services."

Rule 1.7 clarifies DR 5–105(A) by requiring that, when the lawyer's other interests are involved, not only must the client consent after consultation but also that, independent of such consent, the representation reasonably appears not to be adversely affected by the lawyer's other interests. This requirement appears to be the intended meaning of the provision in DR 5–105(C) that "it is obvious that he can adequately represent" the client, and was implicit in EC 5–2, which stated that a lawyer "should not accept proffered employment if his personal interests or desires will, or there is a reasonable probability that they will, affect adversely the advice to be given or services to be rendered the prospective client."

RULE 1.8   Conflict of Interest: Prohibited Transactions

(a) A lawyer shall not enter into a business transaction with a client or knowingly acquire an ownership, possessory, security or other pecuniary interest adverse to a client unless:

> **(1) the transaction and terms on which the lawyer acquires the interest are fair and reasonable to the client and are fully disclosed and transmitted in writing to the client in a manner which can be reasonably understood by the client;**

> **(2) the client is given a reasonable opportunity to seek the advice of independent counsel in the transaction; and**

> **(3) the client consents in writing thereto.**

(b) A lawyer shall not use information relating to representation of a client to the disadvantage of the client unless the

client consents after consultation, except as permitted or required by Rule 1.6 or Rule 3.3.

(c) A lawyer shall not prepare an instrument giving the lawyer or a person related to the lawyer as parent, child, sibling, or spouse any substantial gift from a client, including a testamentary gift, except where the client is related to the donee.

(d) Prior to the conclusion of representation of a client, a lawyer shall not make or negotiate an agreement giving the lawyer literary or media rights to a portrayal or account based in substantial part on information relating to the representation.

(e) A lawyer shall not provide financial assistance to a client in connection with pending or contemplated litigation, except that:

(1) a lawyer may advance court costs and expenses of litigation, the repayment of which may be contingent on the outcome of the matter; and

(2) a lawyer representing an indigent client may pay court costs and expenses of litigation on behalf of the client.

(f) A lawyer shall not accept compensation for representing a client from one other than the client unless:

(1) the client consents after consultation;

(2) there is no interference with the lawyer's independence of professional judgment or with the client–lawyer relationship; and

(3) Information relating to representation of a client is protected as required by rule 1.6.

(g) A lawyer who represents two or more clients shall not participate in making an aggregate settlement of the claims of or against the clients, or in a criminal case an aggregated agreement as to guilty or nolo contendere pleas, unless each client consents after consultation, including disclosure of the existence and nature of all the claims or pleas involved and of the participation of each person in the settlement.

(h) A lawyer shall not make an agreement prospectively limiting the lawyer's liability to a client for malpractice unless permitted by law and the client is independently represented in making the agreement, or settle a claim for such liability with an unrepresented client or former client without first advising that person in writing that independent representation is appropriate in connection therewith.

(i) A lawyer related to another lawyer as parent, child, sibling or spouse shall not represent a client in a representation directly adverse to a person who the lawyer knows is represented by the other lawyer except upon consent by the client after consultation regarding the relationship.

(j) A lawyer shall not acquire a proprietary interest in the cause of action or subject matter of litigation the lawyer is conducting for a client, except that the lawyer may:

(1) acquire a lien granted by law to secure the lawyer's fee or expenses; and

(2) contract with a client for a reasonable contingent fee in a civil case.

COMMENT:

Transactions Between Client and Lawyer

[1] As a general principle, all transactions between client and lawyer should be fair and reasonable to the client. In such transactions a review by independent counsel on behalf of the client is often advisable. Furthermore, a lawyer may not exploit information relating to the representation to the client's disadvantage. For example, a lawyer who has learned that the client is investing in specific real estate may not, without the client's consent, seek to acquire nearby property where doing so would adversely affect the client's plan for investment. Paragraph (a) does not, however, apply to standard commercial transactions between the lawyer and the client for products or services that the client generally markets to others, for example, banking or brokerage services, medical services, products manufactured or distributed by the client, and utilities services. In such transactions, the lawyer has no advantage in dealing with the client, and the restrictions in paragraph (a) are unnecessary and impracticable.

[2] A lawyer may accept a gift from a client, if the transaction meets general standards of fairness. For example, a simple gift such as a present given at a holiday or as a token of appreciation is permitted. If effectuation of a substantial gift requires preparing a legal instrument such as a will or conveyance, however, the client should have the detached advice that another lawyer can provide. Paragraph (c) recognizes an exception where the client is a relative of the donee or the gift is not substantial.

Literary Rights

[3] An agreement by which a lawyer acquires literary or media rights concerning the conduct of the representation creates a conflict between the interests of the client and the personal interests of the lawyer. Measures suitable in the representation of the client may detract from the publication value of an account of the representation. Paragraph (d) does not prohibit a lawyer representing a client in a transaction concerning literary property from agreeing that the lawyer's fee shall consist of a share in ownership in the property, if the arrangement conforms to Rule 1.5 and paragraph (j).

Person Paying for Lawyer's Services

[4]   Rule 1.8(f) requires disclosure of the fact that the lawyer's services are being paid for by a third party. Such an arrangement must also conform to the requirements of Rule 1.6 concerning confidentiality and Rule 1.7 concerning conflict of interest. Where the client is a class, consent may be obtained on behalf of the class by court-supervised procedure.

Family Relationships Between Lawyers

[5]   Rule 1.8(i) applies to related lawyers who are in different firms. Related lawyers in the same firm are governed by Rules 1.7, 1.9, and 1.10. The disqualification stated in Rule 1.8(i) is personal and is not imputed to members of firms with whom the lawyers are associated.

Acquisition of Interest in Litigation

[6]   Paragraph (j) states the traditional general rule that lawyers are prohibited from acquiring a proprietary interest in litigation. This general rule, which has its basis in common law champerty and maintenance, is subject to specific exceptions developed in decisional law and continued in these Rules, such as the exception for reasonable contingent fees set forth in Rule 1.5 and the exception for certain advances of the costs of litigation set forth in paragraph (e).

[7]   This Rule is not intended to apply to customary qualification and limitations in legal opinions and memoranda.

MODEL CODE COMPARISON:

With regard to paragraph (a), DR 5–104(A) provided that a lawyer "shall not enter into a business transaction with a client if they have differing interests therein and if the client expects the lawyer to exercise his professional judgment therein for the protection of the client, unless the client has consented after full disclosure." EC 5–3 stated that a lawyer "should not seek to persuade his client to permit him to invest in an undertaking of his client nor make improper use of his professional relationship to influence his client to invest in an enterprise in which the lawyer is interested."

With regard to paragraph (b), DR 4–101(B)(3) provided that a lawyer should not use "a confidence or secret of his client for the advantage of himself, or of a third person, unless the client consents after full disclosure."

There was no counterpart to paragraph (c) in the Disciplinary Rules of the Model Code. EC 5–5 stated that a lawyer "should not suggest to his client that a gift be made to himself or for his benefit. If a lawyer accepts a gift from his client, he is peculiarly susceptible to the charge that he unduly influenced or overreached the client. If a client voluntarily offers to make a gift to his lawyer, the lawyer may accept the gift, but before doing so, he should urge that the client secure disinterested advice from an independent, competent person who is cognizant of all the circumstances. Other than in exceptional circumstances, a lawyer should insist that an instrument in which his client desires to name him beneficially be prepared by another lawyer selected by the client.''

Paragraph (d) is substantially similar to DR 5–104(B), but refers to ''literary or media'' rights, a more generally inclusive term than ''publication'' rights.

Paragraph (e)(1) is similar to DR 5–103(B), but eliminates the requirement that ''the client remains ultimately liable for such expenses.''

Paragraph (e)(2) has no counterpart in the Model Code.

Paragraph (f) is substantially identical to DR 5–107(A)(1).

Paragraph (g) is substantially identical to DR 5–106.

The first clause of paragraph (h) is similar to DR 6–102(A). There was no counterpart in the Model Code to the second clause of paragraph (h).

Paragraph (i) has no counterpart in the Model Code.

Paragraph (j) is substantially identical to DR 5–103(A).

RULE 1.9   Conflict of Interest: Former Client *

(a) A lawyer who has formerly represented a client in a matter shall not thereafter represent another person in the same or a substantially related matter in which that person's interests are materially adverse to the interests of the former client unless the former client consents after consultation.

(b) A lawyer shall not knowingly represent a person in the same or a substantially related matter in which a firm with which the lawyer formerly was associated had previously represented a client,

---

* In 1989, the ABA amended Model Rule 1.9 by moving some of the text in original Model Rule 1.10(b) into current Model Rule 1.9(b). The original Model Rule 1.9(b) was moved to Model Rule 1.9(c). The impetus behind this change was to clarify an overlap between Model Rule 1.9 and 1.10 and to address the question of duties to former clients when a lawyer changes firms and did not represent the former client but may have acquired confidential information about a former client of the old firm. The following represents Model Rule 1.9 as adopted in 1983:

**RULE 1.9   Conflict of Interest: For-
mer Client**

A Lawyer who has formerly represented a client in a matter shall not thereafter:

(a) Represent another person in the same or a substantially related matter in which that person's interests are materially adverse to the interests of the former client unless the former client consents after consultation; or

(b) Use information relating to the representation to the disadvantage of the former client except as Rule 1.6 would permit with respect to a client or when the information has become generally known.

(1) whose interests are materially adverse to that person; and

(2) about whom the lawyer had acquired information protected by Rules 1.6 and 1.9(c) that is material to the matter;

unless the former client consents after consultation.

(c) A lawyer who has formerly represented a client in a matter or whose present or former firm has formerly represented a client in a matter shall not thereafter:

(1) use information relating to the representation to the disadvantage of the former client except as Rule 1.6 or Rule 3.3 would permit or require with respect to a client, or when the information has become generally known; or

(2) reveal information relating to the representation except as Rule 1.6 or Rule 3.3 would permit or require with respect to a client.

COMMENT:

[1]   After termination of a client-lawyer relationship, a lawyer may not represent another client except in conformity with this Rule. The principles in Rule 1.7 determine whether the interests of the present and former client are adverse. Thus, a lawyer could not properly seek to rescind on behalf of a new client a contract drafted on behalf of the former client. So also a lawyer who has prosecuted an accused person could not properly represent the accused in a subsequent civil action against the government concerning the same transaction.

[2]   The scope of a "matter" for purposes of this Rule may depend on the facts of a particular situation or transaction. The lawyer's involvement in a matter can also be a question of degree. When a lawyer has been directly involved in a specific transaction, subsequent representation of other clients with materially adverse interests clearly is prohibited. On the other hand, a lawyer who recurrently handled a type of problem for a former client is not precluded from later representing another client in a wholly distinct problem of that type even though the subsequent representation involves a position adverse to the prior client. Similar considerations can apply to the reassignment of military lawyers between defense and prosecution functions within the same military jurisdiction. The underlying question is whether the lawyer was so involved in the matter that the subsequent representation can be justly regarded as a changing of sides in the matter in question.

Lawyers Moving Between Firms*

[3]   When lawyers have been associated within a firm but then end their association, the question of whether a lawyer should undertake

---

* The comments under this topic originally appeared under Model Rule 1.10. With   the modification of Model Rule 1.9, the ABA

representation is more complicated. There are several competing considerations. First, the client previously represented by the former firm must be reasonably assured that the principle of loyalty to the client is not compromised. Second, the rule should not be so broadly cast as to preclude other persons from having reasonable choice of legal counsel. Third, the rule should not unreasonably hamper lawyers from forming new associations and taking on new clients after having left a previous association. In this connection, it should be recognized that today many lawyers practice in firms, that many lawyers to some degree limit their practice to one field or another, and that many move from one association to another several times in their careers. If the concept of imputation were applied with unqualified rigor, the result would be radical curtailment of the opportunity of lawyers to move from one practice setting to another and of the opportunity of clients to change counsel.

[4] Reconciliation of these competing principles in the past has been attempted under two rubrics. One approach has been to seek per se rules of disqualification. For example, it has been held that a partner in a law firm is conclusively presumed to have access to all confidences concerning all clients of the firm. Under this analysis, if a lawyer has been a partner in one law firm and then becomes a partner in another law firm, there may be a presumption that all confidences known by the partner in the first firm are known to all partners in the second firm. This presumption might properly be applied in some circumstances, especially where the client has been extensively represented, but may be unrealistic where the client was represented only for limited purposes. Furthermore, such a rigid rule exaggerates the difference between a partner and an associate in modern law firms.

[5] The other rubric formerly used for dealing with disqualification is the appearance of impropriety proscribed in Canon 9 of the ABA Model Code of Professional Responsibility. This rubric has a two fold problem. First, the appearance of impropriety can be taken to include any new client-lawyer relationship that might make a former client feel anxious. If that meaning were adopted, disqualification would become little more than a question of subjective judgment by the former client. Second, since "impropriety" is undefined, the term "appearance of impropriety" is question-begging. It therefore has to be recognized that the problem of disqualification cannot be properly resolved either by simple analogy to a lawyer practicing alone or by the very general concept of appearance of impropriety.

*Confidentiality**

[6] Preserving confidentiality is a question of access to information. Access to information, in turn, is essentially a question of fact in

moved these comments under Model Rule 1.9 without significant change.

* The comments under this topic originally appeared under Model Rule 1.10. With the modification of Model Rule 1.9, the ABA

particular circumstances, aided by inferences, deductions or working presumptions that reasonably may be made about the way in which lawyers work together. A lawyer may have general access to files of all clients of a law firm and may regularly participate in discussions of their affairs; it should be inferred that such a lawyer in fact is privy to all information about all the firm's clients. In contrast, another lawyer may have access to the files of only a limited number of clients and participate in discussions of the affairs of no other clients; in the absence of information to the contrary, it should be inferred that such a lawyer in fact is privy to information about the clients actually served but not those of other clients.

[7] Application of paragraph (b) depends on a situation's particular facts. In such an inquiry, the burden of proof should rest upon the firm whose disqualification is sought.

[8] Paragraph (b) operates to disqualify the lawyer only when the lawyer involved has actual knowledge of information protected by Rules 1.6 and 1.9(b). Thus, if a lawyer while with one firm acquired no knowledge or information relating to a particular client of the firm, and that lawyer later joined another firm, neither the lawyer individually nor the second firm is disqualified from representing another client in the same or a related matter even though the interests of the two clients conflict. See Rule 1.10(b) for the restrictions on a firm once a lawyer has terminated association with the firm.

[9] Independent of the question of disqualification of a firm, a lawyer changing professional association has a continuing duty to preserve confidentiality of information about a client formerly represented. See Rules 1.6 and 1.9.

*Adverse Positions**

[10] The second aspect of loyalty to a client is the lawyer's obligation to decline subsequent representations involving positions adverse to a former client arising in substantially related matters. This obligation requires abstention from adverse representation by the individual lawyer involved, but does not properly entail abstention of other lawyers through imputed disqualification. Hence, this aspect of the problem is governed by Rule 1.9(a). Thus, if a lawyer left one firm for another, the new affiliation would not preclude the firms involved from continuing to represent clients with adverse interests in the same or related matters, so long as the conditions of paragraphs (b) and (c) concerning confidentiality have been met.

[11] Information acquired by the lawyer in the course of representing a client may not subsequently be used or revealed by the lawyer to the disadvantage of the client. However, the fact that a lawyer has once served a client does not preclude the lawyer from using generally known information about that client when later representing another client.

moved these comments under Model Rule
1.9 without significant change.

[12] Disqualification from subsequent representation is for the protection of former clients and can be waived by them. A waiver is effective only if there is disclosure of the circumstances, including the lawyer's intended role in behalf of the new client.

[13] With regard to an opposing party's raising a question of conflict of interest, see Comment to Rule 1.7. With regard to disqualification of a firm with which a lawyer is or was formerly associated, see Rule 1.10.

MODEL CODE COMPARISON: **

There was no counterpart to this Rule in the Disciplinary Rules of the Model Code. Representation adverse to a former client was sometimes dealt with under the rubric of Canon 9 of the Model Code, which provided: "A lawyer should avoid even the appearance of impropriety." Also applicable were EC 4–6 which stated that the "obligation of a lawyer to preserve the confidences and secrets of his client continues after the termination of his employment" and Canon 5 which stated that "[a] lawyer should exercise independent professional judgment on behalf of a client."

The provision in paragraph (a) for waiver by the former client is similar to DR 5–105(C).

The exception in the last clause of paragraph (c)(1) permits a lawyer to use information relating to a former client that is in the "public domain," a use that was also not prohibited by the Model Code, which protected only "confidences and secrets." Since the scope of paragraph (a) is much broader than "confidences and secrets," it is necessary to define when a lawyer may make use of information about a client after the client-lawyer relationship has terminated.

RULE 1.10   Imputed Disqualification: General Rule***

(a) While lawyers are associated in a firm, none of them shall knowingly represent a client when any one of them prac-

---

** When ABA modified Model Rule 1.9 in 1989, it did not change the text of the Model Code Comparison. Thus, the current Model Code Comparison only refers to the Model Rule 1.9 as originally enacted. To understand the amended Model Rule 1.9, one must read the following text quoted from the Code Comparison to Model Rule 1.10: "DR 5–105(D) provided that '[i]f a lawyer is required to decline or to withdraw from employment under a Disciplinary Rule, no partner, or associate, or any other lawyer affiliated with him or his firm, may accept or continue such employment.'"

*** In 1989, the ABA amended Model Rule 1.10 to remove original Rule 1.10(b) and move it to Model Rule 1.9(b). The ABA thus renumbered original Model Rule 1.10(c) and 1.10(d) as new Model Rule 1.10(b) and 1.10(c). The impetus behind this change was to clarify an overlap between Model Rule 1.9 and 1.10 and to address the question of duties to former clients when a lawyer changes firms and did not represent the former client but may have acquired confidential information about a former client of the old firm. Also, the ABA added the words "and, not currently represented by the firm" to current Model Rule 1.10(b). This was added to clarify the problem that when a lawyer leaves a firm, Model Rule 1.7's general pro-

ticing alone would be prohibited from doing so by Rules 1.7, 1.8(c), 1.9 or 2.2.

(b) When a lawyer has terminated an association with a firm, the firm is not prohibited from thereafter representing a person with interests materially adverse to those of a client represented by the formerly associated lawyer and not currently represented by the firm, unless:

   (1) the matter is the same or substantially related to that in which the formerly associated lawyer represented the client; and

   (2) any lawyer remaining in the firm has information protected by Rules 1.6 and 1.9(c) that is material to the matter.

(c) A disqualification prescribed by this rule may be waived by the affected client under the conditions stated in Rule 1.7.

COMMENT: *

Definition of "Firm"

[1] For purposes of the Rules of Professional Conduct, the term "firm" includes lawyers in a private firm, and lawyers in the legal

hibition of a directly adverse conflict still applies to the situation. The original version of Model Rule 1.10 is reproduced below:

RULE 1.10 Imputed Disqualification: General Rule

(a) While lawyers are associated in a firm, none of them shall knowingly represent a client when any one of them practicing alone would be prohibited from doing so by Rules 1.7, 1.8(c), 1.9 or 2.2.

(b) When a lawyer becomes associated with a firm, the firm may not knowingly represent a person in the same or a substantially related matter in which that lawyer, or a firm with which the lawyer was associated, had previously represented a client whose interests are materially adverse to that person and about whom the lawyer had acquired information protected by Rules 1.6 and 1.9(b) that is material to the matter.

(c) When a lawyer has terminated an association with a firm, the firm is not prohibited from thereafter representing a person with interests materially adverse to those of a client represented by the formerly associated lawyer unless:

   (1) the matter is the same or substantially related to that in which the formerly associated lawyer represented the client; and

   (2) any lawyer remaining in the firm has information protected by Rules 1.6 and 1.9(b) that is material to the matter.

(d) A disqualification prescribed by this rule may be waived by the affected client under the conditions stated in Rule 1.7.

* When the ABA amended Model Rule 1.10 in 1989, it moved several paragraphs of comments from Model Rule 1.10 to Model Rule 1.9. The paragraphs which appeared in the original version of the Model Rules are reproduced below:

Lawyers Moving Between Firms

When lawyers have been associated in a firm but then end their association, however, the problem is more complicated. The fiction that the law firm is the same as a single lawyer is no longer wholly realistic. There are several competing considerations. First, the client previously represented must be reasonably assured that the principle of loyalty to the client is not compromised. Second, the rule of disqualification should not be so broadly cast as to preclude other persons from having reasonable choice of legal counsel. Third, the rule of disqualification should not unreasonably hamper lawyers from forming new associations and taking on new clients after having left a previous association. In this connection, it should be recognized that today many lawyers practice in firms, that many to some degree limit their practice to one field or another, and that many move from one association to another several times in their careers. If the concept of imputed disqualification were defined with unqualified rigor, the result would be radical curtailment of the opportunity of lawyers to move from one practice setting to another and of the opportunity of clients to change counsel.

Reconciliation of these competing principles in the past has been attempted under two rubrics. One approach has been to seek per se rules of disqualification. For example, it has been held that a partner in a law firm is conclusively presumed to have access to all confidences concerning all clients of the firm. Under this analysis, if a lawyer has been a partner in one law firm and then becomes a partner in another law firm, there is a presumption that all confidences known by a partner in the first firm are known to all partners in the second firm. This presumption might properly be applied in some circumstances, especially where the client has been extensively represented, but may be unrealistic where the client was represented only for limited purposes. Furthermore, such a rigid rule exaggerates the difference between a partner and an associate in modern law firms.

The other rubric formerly used for dealing with vicarious disqualification is the appearance of impropriety proscribed in Canon 9 of the ABA Model Code of Professional Responsibility. This rubric has a twofold problem. First, the appearance of impropriety can be taken to include any new client-lawyer relationship that might make a former client feel anxious. If that meaning were adopted, disqualification would become little more than a question of subjective judgment by the former client. Second, since "impropriety" is undefined, the term "appearance of impropriety" is question-begging. It therefore has to be recognized that the problem of imputed disqualification cannot be properly resolved either by simple analogy to a lawyer practicing alone or by the very general concept of appearance of impropriety.

A rule based on a functional analysis is more appropriate for determining the question of vicarious disqualification. Two functions are involved: preserving confidentiality and avoiding positions adverse to a client.

Confidentiality

Preserving confidentiality is a question of access to information. Access to information, in turn, is essentially a question of fact in particular circumstances, aided by inferences, deductions or working presumptions that reasonably may be made about the way in which lawyers work together. A lawyer may have general access to files of all clients of a law firm and may regularly participate in discussions of their affairs; it should be inferred that such a lawyer in fact is privy to all information about all the firm's clients. In contrast, another lawyer may have access to the files of only a limited number of clients and participate in discussion of the affairs of no other clients; in the absence of information to the contrary, it should be inferred that such a lawyer in fact is privy to information about the clients actually served but not those of other clients.

Application of paragraphs (b) and (c) depends on a situation's particular facts. In any such inquiry, the burden of proof should rest upon the firm whose disqualification is sought.

Paragraphs (b) and (c) operate to disqualify the firm only when the lawyer involved has actual knowledge of information protected by Rules 1.6 and 1.9(b). Thus, if a lawyer while with one firm acquired no knowledge of information relating to a particular client of the firm,

department of a corporation or other organization, or in a legal services organization. Whether two or more lawyers constitute a firm within this definition can depend on the specific facts. For example, two practitioners who share office space and occasionally consult or assist each other ordinarily would not be regarded as constituting a firm. However, if they present themselves to the public in a way suggesting that they are a firm or conduct themselves as a firm, they should be regarded as a firm for the purposes of the Rules. The terms of any formal agreement between associated lawyers are relevant in determining whether they are a firm, as is the fact that they have mutual access to information concerning the clients they serve. Furthermore, it is relevant in doubtful cases to consider the underlying purpose of the Rule that is involved. A group of lawyers could be regarded as a firm for purposes of the rule that the same lawyer should not represent opposing parties in litigation, while it might not be so regarded for purposes of the rule that information acquired by one lawyer is attributed to the other.

[2] With respect to the law department of an organization, there is ordinarily no question that the members of the department constitute a firm within the meaning of the Rules of Professional Conduct. However, there can be uncertainty as to the identity of the client. For example, it may not be clear whether the law department of a corporation represents a subsidiary or an affiliated corporation, as well as the corporation by which the members of the department are directly employed. A similar question can arise concerning an unincorporated association and its local affiliates.

[3] Similar questions can also arise with respect to lawyers in legal aid. Lawyers employed in the same unit of a legal service organization constitute a firm, but not necessarily those employed in separate units. As in the case of independent practitioners, whether the lawyers should be treated as associated with each other can depend on the particular rule that is involved, and on the specific facts of the situation.

and that lawyer later joined another firm, neither the lawyer individually nor the second firm is disqualified from representing another client in the same or a related matter even though the interests of the two clients conflict.

Independent of the question of disqualification of a firm, a lawyer changing professional association has a continuing duty to preserve confidentiality of information about a client formerly represented. See Rules 1.6 and 1.9.

Adverse Positions

The second aspect of loyalty to client is the lawyer's obligation to decline subsequent representations involving positions adverse to a former client arising in substantially related matters. This obligation requires abstention from adverse representation by the individual lawyer involved, but does not properly entail abstention of other lawyers through imputed disqualification. Hence, this aspect of the problem is governed by Rule 1.9(a). Thus, if a lawyer left one firm for another, the new affiliation would not preclude the firms involved from continuing to represent clients with adverse interests in the same or related matters, so long as the conditions of Rule 1.10(b) and (c) concerning confidentiality have been met.

[4] Where a lawyer has joined a private firm after having represented the government, the situation is governed by Rule 1.11(a) and (b); where a lawyer represents the government after having served private clients, the situation is governed by Rule 1.11(c)(1). The individual lawyer involved is bound by the Rules generally, including Rules 1.6, 1.7 and 1.9.

[5] Different provisions are thus made for movement of a lawyer from one private firm to another and for movement of a lawyer between a private firm and the government. The government is entitled to protection of its client confidences and, therefore, to the protections provided in Rules 1.6, 1.9 and 1.11. However, if the more extensive disqualification in Rule 1.10 were applied to former government lawyers, the potential effect on the government would be unduly burdensome. The government deals with all private citizens and organizations and, thus, has a much wider circle of adverse legal interests than does any private law firm. In these circumstances, the government's recruitment of lawyers would be seriously impaired if Rule 1.10 were applied to the government. On balance, therefore, the government is better served in the long run by the protections stated in Rule 1.11.

Principles of Imputed Disqualification

[6] The rule of imputed disqualification stated in paragraph (a) gives effect to the principle of loyalty to the client as it applies to lawyers who practice in a law firm. Such situations can be considered from the premise that a firm of lawyers is essentially one lawyer for purposes of the rules governing loyalty to the client, or from the premise that each lawyer is vicariously bound by the obligation of loyalty owed by each lawyer with whom the lawyer is associated. Paragraph (a) operates only among the lawyers currently associated in a firm. When a lawyer moves from one firm to another, the situation is governed by Rules 1.9(b) and 1.10(b).

[7] * Rule 1.10(b) operates to permit a law firm, under certain circumstances, to represent a person with interests directly adverse to those of a client represented by a lawyer who formerly was associated with the firm. The Rule applies regardless of when the formerly associated lawyer represented the client. However, the law firm may not represent a person with interests adverse to those of a present client of the firm, which would violate Rule 1.7. Moreover, the firm may not represent the person where the matter is the same or substantially related to that in which the formerly associated lawyer represented the client and any other lawyer currently in the firm has material information protected by Rules 1.6 and 1.9(c).

---

* The ABA added this entire paragraph to the comments to Model Rule 1.10 in 1989. Thus, this language does not appear in the original version of the Model Rules.

MODEL CODE COMPARISON:

DR 5–105(D) provided that "[i]f a lawyer is required to decline or to withdraw from employment under a Disciplinary Rule, no partner, or associate, or any other lawyer affiliated with him or his firm, may accept or continue such employment."

RULE 1.11 Successive Government and Private Employment

(a) **Except as law may otherwise expressly permit, a lawyer shall not represent a private client in connection with a matter in which the lawyer participated personally and substantially as a public officer or employee, unless the appropriate government agency consents after consultation. No lawyer in a firm with which that lawyer is associated may knowingly undertake or continue representation in such a matter unless:**

    (1) the disqualified lawyer is screened from any participation in the matter and is apportioned no part of the fee therefrom; and

    (2) written notice is promptly given to the appropriate government agency to enable it to ascertain compliance with the provisions of this rule.

(b) **Except as law may otherwise expressly permit, a lawyer having information that the lawyer knows is confidential government information about a person acquired when the lawyer was a public officer or employee, may not represent a private client whose interests are adverse to that person in a matter in which the information could be used to the material disadvantage of that person. A firm with which that lawyer is associated may undertake or continue representation in the matter only if the disqualified lawyer is screened from any participation in the matter and is apportioned no part of the fee therefrom.**

(c) **Except as law may otherwise expressly permit, a lawyer serving as a public officer or employee shall not:**

    (1) participate in a matter in which the lawyer participated personally and substantially while in private practice or nongovernmental employment, unless under applicable law no one is, or by lawful delegation may be, authorized to act in the lawyer's stead in the matter; or

    (2) negotiate for private employment with any person who is involved as a party or as attorney for a party in a matter in which the lawyer is participating personally and substantially, except that a lawyer serving as a law clerk to a judge, other adjudicative officer or arbitrator may negotiate for private employment as permitted by Rule 1.12(b) and subject to the conditions stated in Rule 1.12(b).

(d) **As used in this rule, the term "matter" includes:**

(1) any judicial or other proceeding, application, request for a ruling or other determination, contract, claim, controversy, investigation, charge, accusation, arrest or other particular matter involving a specific party or parties; and

(2) any other matter covered by the conflict of interest rules of the appropriate government agency.

(e) As used in this rule, the term "confidential government information" means information which has been obtained under governmental authority and which, at the time this rule is applied, the government is prohibited by law from disclosing to the public or has a legal privilege not to disclose, and which is not otherwise available to the public.

COMMENT:

[1] This Rule prevents a lawyer from exploiting public office for the advantage of a private client. It is a counterpart of Rule 1.10(b), which applies to lawyers moving from one firm to another.

[2] A lawyer representing a government agency, whether employed or specially retained by the government, is subject to the Rules of Professional Conduct, including the prohibition against representing adverse interests stated in Rule 1.7 and the protections afforded former clients in Rule 1.9. In addition, such a lawyer is subject to Rule 1.11 and to statutes and government regulations regarding conflict of interest. Such statutes and regulations may circumscribe the extent to which the government agency may give consent under this Rule.

[3] Where the successive clients are a public agency and a private client, the risk exists that power or discretion vested in public authority might be used for the special benefit of a private client. A lawyer should not be in a position where benefit to a private client might affect performance of the lawyer's professional functions on behalf of public authority. Also, unfair advantage could accrue to the private client by reason of access to confidential government information about the client's adversary obtainable only through the lawyer's government service. However, the rules governing lawyers presently or formerly employed by a government agency should not be so restrictive as to inhibit transfer of employment to and from the government. The government has a legitimate need to attract qualified lawyers as well as to maintain high ethical standards. The provisions for screening and waiver are necessary to prevent the disqualification rule from imposing too severe a deterrent against entering public service.

[4] When the client is an agency of one government, that agency should be treated as a private client for purposes of this Rule if the lawyer thereafter represents an agency of another government, as when a lawyer represents a city and subsequently is employed by a federal agency.

[5]   Paragraphs (a)(1) and (b) do not prohibit a lawyer from receiving a salary or partnership share established by prior independent agreement.   They prohibit directly relating the attorney's compensation to the fee in the matter in which the lawyer is disqualified.

[6]   Paragraph (a)(2) does not require that a lawyer give notice to the government agency at a time when premature disclosure would injure the client; a requirement for premature disclosure might preclude engagement of the lawyer.   Such notice is, however, required to be given as soon as practicable in order that the government agency will have a reasonable opportunity to ascertain that the lawyer is complying with Rule 1.11 and to take appropriate action if it believes the lawyer is not complying.

[7]   Paragraph (b) operates only when the lawyer in question has knowledge of the information, which means actual knowledge; it does not operate with respect to information that merely could be imputed to the lawyer.

[8]   Paragraphs (a) and (c) do not prohibit a lawyer from jointly representing a private party and a government agency when doing so is permitted by Rule 1.7 and is not otherwise prohibited by law.

[9]   Paragraph (c) does not disqualify other lawyers in the agency with which the lawyer in question has become associated.

MODEL CODE COMPARISON:

Paragraph (a) is similar to DR 9–101(B), except that the latter used the terms "in which he had substantial responsibility while he was a public employee."

Paragraphs (b), (c), (d) and (e) have no counterparts in the Model Code.

RULE 1.12   Former Judge or Arbitrator

(a) Except as stated in paragraph (d), a lawyer shall not represent anyone in connection with a matter in which the lawyer participated personally and substantially as a judge or other adjudicative officer, arbitrator or law clerk to such a person, unless all parties to the proceeding consent after consultation.

(b) A lawyer shall not negotiate for employment with any person who is involved as a party or as attorney for a party in a matter in which the lawyer is participating personally and substantially as a judge or other adjudicative officer, or arbitrator. A lawyer serving as a law clerk to a judge, other adjudicative officer or arbitrator may negotiate for employment with a party or attorney involved in a matter in which the clerk is participating personally and substantially, but only after the lawyer has notified the judge, other adjudicative officer or arbitrator.

(c) If a lawyer is disqualified by paragraph (a), no lawyer in a firm with which that lawyer is associated may knowingly undertake or continue representation in the matter unless:

(1) the disqualified lawyer is screened from any partic-ipation in the matter and is apportioned no part of the fee therefrom; and

(2) written notice is promptly given to the appropriate tribunal to enable it to ascertain compliance with the provi-sions of this rule.

(d) An arbitrator selected as a partisan of a party in a multi-member arbitration panel is not prohibited from subsequently representing that party.

COMMENT:

This Rule generally parallels Rule 1.11. The term "personally and substantially" signifies that a judge who was a member of a multi-member court, and thereafter left judicial office to practice law, is not prohibited from representing a client in a matter pending in the court, but in which the former judge did not participate. So also the fact that a former judge exercised administrative responsibility in a court does not prevent the former judge from acting as a lawyer in a matter where the judge had previously exercised remote or incidental administrative responsibility that did not affect the merits. Compare the Comment to Rule 1.11. The term "adjudicative officer" includes such officials as judges pro tempore, referees, special masters, hearing officers and other parajudicial officers, and also lawyers who serve as part-time judges. Compliance Canons A(2), B(2) and C of the Model Code of Judicial Conduct provide that a part-time judge, judge pro tempore or retired judge recalled to active service, may not "act as a lawyer in any proceeding in which he served as a judge or in any other proceeding related thereto." Although phrased differently from this Rule, those Rules correspond in meaning.

MODEL CODE COMPARISON:

Paragraph (a) is substantially similar to DR 9–101(A), which provid-ed that a lawyer "shall not accept private employment in a matter upon the merits of which he has acted in a judicial capacity." Paragraph (a) differs, however, in that it is broader in scope and states more specifical-ly the persons to whom it applies. There was no counterpart in the Model Code to paragraphs (b), (c) or (d).

With regard to arbitrators, EC 5–20 stated that "a lawyer [who] has undertaken to act as an impartial arbitrator or mediator, ... should not thereafter represent in the dispute any of the parties involved." DR 9–101(A) did not permit a waiver of the disqualification applied to former judges by consent of the parties. However, DR 5–105(C) was similar in effect and could be construed to permit waiver.

RULE 1.13   Organization as Client *

(a) **A lawyer employed or retained by an organization represents the organization acting through its duly authorized constituents.**

(b) **If a lawyer for an organization knows that an officer, employee or other person associated with the organization is engaged in action, intends to act or refuses to act in a matter related to the representation that is a violation of a legal obligation to the organization, or a violation of law which reasonably might be imputed to the organization, and is likely to result in substantial injury to the organization, the lawyer shall proceed as is reasonably necessary in the best interest of the organization.   In determining how to proceed, the lawyer shall give due consideration to the seriousness of the violation and its consequences, the scope and nature of the lawyer's representation, the responsibility in the organization and the apparent motivation of the person involved, the policies of the organization concerning such matters and any other relevant considerations.   Any measures taken shall be designed to minimize disruption of the organization and the risk of revealing information relating to the representation to persons outside the organization.   Such measures may include among others:**

(1) **asking reconsideration of the matter;**

(2) **advising that a separate legal opinion on the matter be sought for presentation to appropriate authority in the organization; and**

---

* The Kutak Commission's Revised Final Draft contained substantially different language on the lawyer's duty to rectify third party acts which are likely to result in substantial injury to the corporation. Proposed Rule 1.13(a) and (c) are reproduced below. Proposed provision (b) of 1.13 was substantially similar to the final version.

Rule 1.13   Organization as Client

(a) A lawyer employed or retained to represent an organization represents the organization as distinct from its directors, officers, employees, members, shareholders or other constituents.

. . . .

(c) When the organization's highest authority insists upon action, or refuses to take action, that is clearly a violation of a legal obligation to the organization, or a violation of law which reasonably might be imputed to the organization,

and is likely to result in substantial injury to the organization, the lawyer may take further remedial action that the lawyer reasonably believes to be in the best interest of the organization. Such action may include revealing information otherwise protected by Rule 1.6 only if the lawyer reasonably believes that:

(1) the highest authority in the organization has acted to further the personal or financial interests of members of that authority which are in conflict with the interests of the organization; and

(2) revealing the information is necessary in the best interest of the organization.

Proposed Model Rule 1.13(a), (c) (Revised Final Draft) (June 20, 1982).

(3) referring the matter to higher authority in the organization, including, if warranted by the seriousness of the matter, referral to the highest authority that can act in behalf of the organization as determined by applicable law.

(c) If, despite the lawyer's efforts in accordance with paragraph (b), the highest authority that can act on behalf of the organization insists upon action, or a refusal to act, that is clearly a violation of law and is likely to result in substantial injury to the organization, the lawyer may resign in accordance with rule 1.16.

(d) In dealing with an organization's directors, officers, employees, members, shareholders or other constituents, a lawyer shall explain the identity of the client when it is apparent that the organization's interests are adverse to those of the constituents with whom the lawyer is dealing.

(e) A lawyer representing an organization may also represent any of its directors, officers, employees, members, shareholders or other constituents, subject to the provisions of rule 1.7. If the organization's consent to the dual representation is required by rule 1.7, the consent shall be given by an appropriate official of the organization other than the individual who is to be represented, or by the shareholders.

COMMENT:

The Entity as the Client

[1] An organizational client is a legal entity, but it cannot act except through its officers, directors, employees, shareholders and other constituents.

[2] Officers, directors, employees and shareholders are the constituents of the corporate organizational client. The duties defined in this Comment apply equally to unincorporated associations. "Other constituents" as used in this Comment means the positions equivalent to officers, directors, employees and shareholders held by persons acting for organizational clients that are not corporations.

[3] When one of the constituents of an organizational client communicates with the organization's lawyer in that person's organizational capacity, the communication is protected by Rule 1.6. Thus, by way of example, if an organizational client requests its lawyer to investigate allegations of wrongdoing, interviews made in the course of that investigation between the lawyer and the client's employees or other constituents are covered by Rule 1.6. This does not mean, however, that constituents of an organizational client are the clients of the lawyer. The lawyer may not disclose to such constituents information relating to the representation except for disclosures explicitly or impliedly authorized by the organizational client in order to carry out the representation or as otherwise permitted by Rule 1.6.

[4]   When constituents of the organization make decisions for it, the decisions ordinarily must be accepted by the lawyer even if their utility or prudence is doubtful. Decisions concerning policy and operations, including ones entailing serious risk, are not as such in the lawyer's province. However, different considerations arise when the lawyer knows that the organization may be substantially injured by action of [a] constituent that is in violation of law. In such a circumstance, it may be reasonably necessary for the lawyer to ask the constituent to reconsider the matter. If that fails, or if the matter is of sufficient seriousness and importance to the organization, it may be reasonably necessary for the lawyer to take steps to have the matter reviewed by a higher authority in the organization. Clear justification should exist for seeking review over the head of the constituent normally responsible for it. The stated policy of the organization may define circumstances and prescribe channels for such review, and a lawyer should encourage the formulation of such a policy. Even in the absence of organization policy, however, the lawyer may have an obligation to refer a matter to higher authority, depending on the seriousness of the matter and whether the constituent in question has apparent motives to act at variance with the organization's interest. Review by the chief executive officer or by the board of directors may be required when the matter is of importance commensurate with their authority. At some point it may be useful or essential to obtain an independent legal opinion.

[5]   In an extreme case, it may be reasonably necessary for the lawyer to refer the matter to the organization's highest authority. Ordinarily, that is the board of directors or similar governing body. However, applicable law may prescribe that under certain conditions highest authority reposes elsewhere; for example, in the independent directors of a corporation.

Relation to Other Rules

[6]   The authority and responsibility provided in paragraph (b) are concurrent with the authority and responsibility provided in other Rules. In particular, this Rule does not limit or expand the lawyer's responsibility under Rules 1.6, 1.8, and 1.16, 3.3 or 4.1. If the lawyer's services are being used by an organization to further a crime or fraud by the organization, Rule 1.2(d) can be applicable.

Government Agency

[7]   The duty defined in this Rule applies to governmental organizations. However, when the client is a governmental organization, a different balance may be appropriate between maintaining confidentiality and assuring that the wrongful official act is prevented or rectified, for public business is involved. In addition, duties of lawyers employed by the government or lawyers in military service may be defined by statutes

and regulation. Therefore, defining precisely the identity of the client and prescribing the resulting obligations of such lawyers may be more difficult in the government context. Although in some circumstances the client may be a specific agency, it is generally the government as a whole. For example, if the action or failure to act involves the head of a bureau, either the department of which the bureau is a part or the government as a whole may be the client for purpose of this Rule. Moreover, in a matter involving the conduct of government officials, a government lawyer may have authority to question such conduct more extensively than that of a lawyer for a private organization in similar circumstances. This Rule does not limit that authority. See note on Scope.

Clarifying the Lawyer's Role

[8] There are times when the organization's interest may be or become adverse to those of one or more of its constituents. In such circumstances the lawyer should advise any constituent, whose interest the lawyer finds adverse to that of the organization of the conflict or potential conflict of interest, that the lawyer cannot represent such constituent, and that such person may wish to obtain independent representation. Care must be taken to assure that the individual understands that, when there is such adversity of interest, the lawyer for the organization cannot provide legal representation for that constituent individual, and that discussions between the lawyer for the organization and the individual may not be privileged.

[9] Whether such a warning should be given by the lawyer for the organization to any constituent individual may turn on the facts of each case.

Dual Representation

[10] Paragraph (e) recognizes that a lawyer for an organization may also represent a principal officer or major shareholder.

Derivative Actions

[11] Under generally prevailing law, the shareholders or members of a corporation may bring suit to compel the directors to perform their legal obligations in the supervision of the organization. Members of unincorporated associations have essentially the same right. Such an action may be brought nominally by the organization, but usually is, in fact, a legal controversy over management of the organization.

[12] The question can arise whether counsel for the organization may defend such an action. The proposition that the organization is the lawyer's client does not alone resolve the issue. Most derivative actions are a normal incident of an organization's affairs, to be defended by the organization's lawyer like any other suit. However, if the claim involves serious charges of wrongdoing by those in control of the organization, a

conflict may arise between the lawyer's duty to the organization and the lawyer's relationship with the board. In those circumstances, Rule 1.7 governs who should represent the directors and the organization.

MODEL CODE COMPARISON:

There was no counterpart to this Rule in the Disciplinary Rules of the Model Code. EC 5–18 stated that a "lawyer employed or retained by a corporation or similar entity owes his allegiance to the entity and not to a stockholder, director, officer, employee, representative, or other person connected with the entity. In advising the entity, a lawyer should keep paramount its interests and his professional judgment should not be influenced by the personal desires of any person or organization. Occasionally, a lawyer for an entity is requested by a stockholder, director, officer, employee, representative, or other person connected with the entity to represent him in an individual capacity; in such case the lawyer may serve the individual only if the lawyer is convinced that differing interests are not present." EC 5–24 stated that although a lawyer "may be employed by a business corporation with non-lawyers serving as directors or officers, and they necessarily have the right to make decisions of business policy, a lawyer must decline to accept direction of his professional judgment from any layman." DR 5–107(B) provided that a lawyer "shall not permit a person who ... employs ... him to render legal services for another to direct or regulate his professional judgment in rendering such legal services."

RULE 1.14   Client Under a Disability

(a) When a client's ability to make adequately considered decisions in connection with the representation is impaired, whether because of minority, mental disability or for some other reason, the lawyer shall, as far as reasonably possible, maintain a normal client–lawyer relationship with the client.

(b) A lawyer may seek the appointment of a guardian or take other protective action with respect to a client, only when the lawyer reasonably believes that the client cannot adequately act in the client's own interest.

COMMENT:

[1] The normal client-lawyer relationship is based on the assumption that the client, when properly advised and assisted, is capable of making decisions about important matters. When the client is a minor or suffers from a mental disorder or disability, however, maintaining the ordinary client-lawyer relationship may not be possible in all respects. In particular, an incapacitated person may have no power to make legally binding decisions. Nevertheless, a client lacking legal competence often has the ability to understand, deliberate upon, and reach conclusions about matters affecting the client's own well-being. Furthermore, to an increasing extent the law recognizes intermediate de-

grees of competence. For example, children as young as five or six years of age, and certainly those of ten or twelve, are regarded as having opinions that are entitled to weight in legal proceedings concerning their custody. So also, it is recognized that some persons of advanced age can be quite capable of handling routine financial matters while needing special legal protection concerning major transactions.

[2] The fact that a client suffers a disability does not diminish the lawyer's obligation to treat the client with attention and respect. If the person has no guardian or legal representative, the lawyer often must act as de facto guardian. Even if the person does have a legal representative, the lawyer should as far as possible accord the represented person the status of client, particularly in maintaining communication.

[3] If a legal representative has already been appointed for the client, the lawyer should ordinarily look to the representative for decisions on behalf of the client. If a legal representative has not been appointed, the lawyer should see to such an appointment where it would serve the client's best interests. Thus, if a disabled client has substantial property that should be sold for the client's benefit, effective completion of the transaction ordinarily requires appointment of a legal representative. In many circumstances, however, appointment of a legal representative may be expensive or traumatic for the client. Evaluation of these considerations is a matter of professional judgment on the lawyer's part.

[4] If the lawyer represents the guardian as distinct from the ward, and is aware that the guardian is acting adversely to the ward's interest, the lawyer may have an obligation to prevent or rectify the guardian's misconduct. See Rule 1.2(d).

Disclosure of the Client's Condition

[5] Rules of procedure in litigation generally provide that minors or persons suffering mental disability shall be represented by a guardian or next friend if they do not have a general guardian. However, disclosure of the client's disability can adversely affect the client's interests. For example, raising the question of disability could, in some circumstances, lead to proceedings for involuntary commitment. The lawyer's position in such cases is an unavoidably difficult one. The lawyer may seek guidance from an appropriate diagnostician.

Emergency Legal Assistance *

[6] In an emergency where the health, safety or a financial interest of a person under a disability is threatened with imminent and irreparable harm, a lawyer may take legal action on behalf of such a person even though the person is unable to establish a client-lawyer relationship or

---

* In 1997, the ABA House of Delegates added comments 6 and 7 to Model Rule 1.14 in order to clarify a lawyer's role when a disabled person is in need of emergency legal services.

to make or express considered judgments about the matter, when the disabled person or another acting in good faith on that person's behalf has consulted the lawyer. Even in such an emergency, however, the lawyer should not act unless the lawyer reasonably believes that the person has no other lawyer, agent or other representative available. The lawyer should take legal action on behalf of the disabled person only to the extent reasonably necessary to maintain the status quo or otherwise avoid imminent and irreparable harm. A lawyer who undertakes to represent a person in such an exigent situation has the same duties under these Rules as the lawyer would with respect to a client.

[7] A lawyer who acts on behalf of a disabled person in an emergency should keep the confidences of the disabled person as if dealing with a client, disclosing them only to the extent necessary to accomplish the intended protective action. The lawyer should disclose to any tribunal involved and to any other counsel involved the nature of his or her relationship with the disabled person. The lawyer should take steps to regularize the relationship or implement other protective solutions as soon as possible. Normally, a lawyer would not seek compensation for such emergency actions taken on behalf of a disabled person.

MODEL CODE COMPARISON:

There was no counterpart to this Rule in the Disciplinary Rules of the Model Code. EC 7–11 stated that the "responsibilities of a lawyer may vary according to the intelligence, experience, mental condition or age of a client.... Examples include the representation of an illiterate or an incompetent." EC 7–12 stated that "[a]ny mental or physical condition of a client that renders him incapable of making a considered judgment on his own behalf casts additional responsibilities upon his lawyer. Where an incompetent is acting through a guardian or other legal representative, a lawyer must look to such representative for those decisions which are normally the prerogative of the client to make. If a client under disability has no legal representative, his lawyer may be compelled in court proceedings to make decisions on behalf of the client. If the client is capable of understanding the matter in question or of contributing to the advancement of his interests, regardless of whether he is legally disqualified from performing certain acts, the lawyer should obtain from him all possible aid. If the disability of a client and the lack of a legal representative compel the lawyer to make decisions for his client, the lawyer should consider all circumstances then prevailing and act with care to safeguard and advance the interests of his client. But obviously a lawyer cannot perform any act or make any decision which the law requires his client to perform or make, either acting for himself if competent, or by a duly constituted representative if legally incompetent."

RULE 1.15 Safekeeping Property

(a) A lawyer shall hold property of clients or third persons that is in a lawyer's possession in connection with a representa-

tion separate from the lawyer's own property. **Funds shall be kept in a separate account maintained in the state where the lawyer's office is situated, or elsewhere with the consent of the client or third person. Other property shall be identified as such and appropriately safeguarded. Complete records of such account funds and other property shall be kept by the lawyer and shall be preserved for a period of [five years] after termination of the representation.**

(b) Upon receiving funds or other property in which a client or third person has an interest, a lawyer shall promptly notify the client or third person. Except as stated in this rule or otherwise permitted by law or by agreement with the client, a lawyer shall promptly deliver to the client or third person any funds or other property that the client or third person is entitled to receive and, upon request by the client or third person, shall promptly render a full accounting regarding such property.

(c) When in the course of representation a lawyer is in possession of property in which both the lawyer and another person claim interests, the property shall be kept separate by the lawyer until there is an accounting and severance of their interest. If a dispute arises concerning their respective interests, the portion in dispute shall be kept separate by the lawyer until the dispute is resolved.

COMMENT:

[1]   A lawyer should hold property of others with the care required of a professional fiduciary. Securities should be kept in a safe deposit box, except when some other form of safekeeping is warranted by special circumstances. All property which is the property of clients or third persons should be kept separate from the lawyer's business and personal property and, if monies, in one or more trust accounts. Separate trust accounts may be warranted when administering estate monies or acting in similar fiduciary capacities.

[2]   Lawyers often receive funds from third parties from which the lawyer's fee will be paid. If there is risk that the client may divert the funds without paying the fee, the lawyer is not required to remit the portion from which the fee is to be paid. However, a lawyer may not hold funds to coerce a client into accepting the lawyer's contention. The disputed portion of the funds should be kept in trust and the lawyer should suggest means for prompt resolution of the dispute, such as arbitration. The undisputed portion of the funds shall be promptly distributed.

[3]   Third parties, such as a client's creditors, may have just claims against funds or other property in a lawyer's custody. A lawyer may have a duty under applicable law to protect such third-party claims against wrongful interference by the client, and accordingly may refuse to surrender the property to the client. However, a lawyer should not

unilaterally assume to arbitrate a dispute between the client and the third party.

[4] The obligations of a lawyer under this Rule are independent of those arising from activity other than rendering legal services. For example, a lawyer who serves as an escrow agent is governed by the applicable law relating to fiduciaries even though the lawyer does not render legal services in the transaction.

[5] A "client's security fund" provides a means through the collective efforts of the bar to reimburse persons who have lost money or property as a result of dishonest conduct of a lawyer. Where such a fund has been established, a lawyer should participate.

MODEL CODE COMPARISON:

With regard to paragraph (a), DR 9–102(A) provided that "funds of clients" are to be kept in an identifiable bank account in the state in which the lawyer's office is situated. DR 9–102(B)(2) provided that a lawyer shall "identify and label securities and properties of a client . . . and place them in . . . safekeeping. . . ." DR 9–102(B)(3) required that a lawyer "[m]aintain complete records of all funds, securities, and other properties of a client. . . ." Paragraph (a) extends these requirements to property of a third person that is in the lawyer's possession in connection with the representation.

Paragraph (b) is substantially similar to DR 9–102(B)(1), (3) and (4).

Paragraph (c) is similar to DR 9–102(A)(2), except that the requirement regarding disputes applies to property concerning which an interest is claimed by a third person as well as by a client.

RULE 1.16   Declining or Terminating Representation

(a) Except as stated in paragraph (c), a lawyer shall not represent a client or, where representation has commenced, shall withdraw from the representation of a client if:

(1) the representation will result in violation of the rules of professional conduct or other law;

(2) the lawyer's physical or mental condition materially impairs the lawyer's ability to represent the client; or

(3) the lawyer is discharged.

(b) Except as stated in paragraph (c), a lawyer may withdraw from representing a client if withdrawal can be accomplished without material adverse effect on the interests of the client, or if:

(1) the client persists in a course of action involving the lawyer's services that the lawyer reasonably believes is criminal or fraudulent;

(2) the client has used the lawyer's services to perpetrate a crime or fraud;

(3) a client insists upon pursuing an objective that the lawyer considers repugnant or imprudent;

(4) the client fails substantially to fulfill an obligation to the lawyer regarding the lawyer's services and has been given reasonable warning that the lawyer will withdraw unless the obligation is fulfilled;

(5) the representation will result in an unreasonable financial burden on the lawyer or has been rendered unreasonably difficult by the client; or

(6) other good cause for withdrawal exists.

(c) When ordered to do so by a tribunal, a lawyer shall continue representation notwithstanding good cause for terminating the representation.

(d) Upon termination of representation, a lawyer shall take steps to the extent reasonably practicable to protect a client's interests, such as giving reasonable notice to the client, allowing time for employment of other counsel, surrendering papers and property to which the client is entitled and refunding any advance payment of fee that has not been earned. The lawyer may retain papers relating to the client to the extent permitted by other law.

COMMENT:

[1] A lawyer should not accept representation in a matter unless it can be performed competently, promptly, without improper conflict of interest and to completion.

Mandatory Withdrawal

[2] A lawyer ordinarily must decline or withdraw from representation if the client demands that the lawyer engage in conduct that is illegal or violates the Rules of Professional Conduct or other law. The lawyer is not obliged to decline or withdraw simply because the client suggests such a course of conduct; a client may make such a suggestion in the hope that a lawyer will not be constrained by a professional obligation.

[3] When a lawyer has been appointed to represent a client, withdrawal ordinarily requires approval of the appointing authority. See also Rule 6.2. Difficulty may be encountered if withdrawal is based on the client's demand that the lawyer engage in unprofessional conduct. The court may wish an explanation for the withdrawal, while the lawyer may be bound to keep confidential the facts that would constitute such an explanation. The lawyer's statement that professional considerations require termination of the representation ordinarily should be accepted as sufficient.

Discharge

[4]   A client has a right to discharge a lawyer at any time, with or without cause, subject to liability for payment for the lawyer's services. Where future dispute about the withdrawal may be anticipated, it may be advisable to prepare a written statement reciting the circumstances.

[5]   Whether a client can discharge appointed counsel may depend on applicable law. A client seeking to do so should be given a full explanation of the consequences. These consequences may include a decision by the appointing authority that appointment of successor counsel is unjustified, thus requiring the client to represent himself.

[6]   If the client is mentally incompetent, the client may lack the legal capacity to discharge the lawyer, and in any event the discharge may be seriously adverse to the client's interests. The lawyer should make special effort to help the client consider the consequences and, in an extreme case, may initiate proceedings for a conservatorship or similar protection of the client. See Rule 1.14.

Optional Withdrawal

[7]   A lawyer may withdraw from representation in some circumstances. The lawyer has the option to withdraw if it can be accomplished without material adverse effect on the client's interests. Withdrawal is also justified if the client persists in a course of action that the lawyer reasonably believes is criminal or fraudulent, for a lawyer is not required to be associated with such conduct even if the lawyer does not further it. Withdrawal is also permitted if the lawyer's services were misused in the past even if that would materially prejudice the client. The lawyer also may withdraw where the client insists on a repugnant or imprudent objective.

[8]   A lawyer may withdraw if the client refuses to abide by the terms of an agreement relating to the representation, such as an agreement concerning fees or court costs or an agreement limiting the objectives of the representation.

Assisting the Client Upon Withdrawal

[9]   Even if the lawyer has been unfairly discharged by the client, a lawyer must take all reasonable steps to mitigate the consequences to the client. The lawyer may retain papers as security for a fee only to the extent permitted by law.

[10]   Whether or not a lawyer for an organization may under certain unusual circumstances have a legal obligation to the organization after withdrawing or being discharged by the organization's highest authority is beyond the scope of these Rules.

MODEL CODE COMPARISON:

With regard to paragraph (a), DR 2–109(A) provided that a lawyer "shall not accept employment . . . if he knows or it is obvious that [the prospective client] wishes to ... [b]ring a legal action ... or otherwise have steps taken for him, merely for the purpose of harassing or maliciously injuring any person...." Nor may a lawyer accept employment if the lawyer is aware that the prospective client wishes to "[p]resent a claim or defense ... that is not warranted under existing law, unless it can be supported by good faith argument for an extension, modification, or reversal of existing law." DR 2–110(B) provided that a lawyer "shall withdraw from employment ... if:

"(1) He knows or it is obvious that his client is bringing the legal action ... or is otherwise having steps taken for him, merely for the purpose of harassing or maliciously injuring any person.

"(2) He knows or it is obvious that his continued employment will result in violation of a Disciplinary Rule.

"(3) His mental or physical condition renders it unreasonably difficult for him to carry out the employment effectively.

"(4) He is discharged by his client."

With regard to paragraph (b), DR 2–110(C) permitted withdrawal regardless of the effect on the client if:

"(1) His client: (a) Insists upon presenting a claim or defense that is not warranted under existing law and cannot be supported by good faith argument for an extension, modification, or reversal of existing law; (b) Personally seeks to pursue an illegal course of conduct; (c) Insists that the lawyer pursue a course of conduct that is illegal or that is prohibited under the Disciplinary Rules; (d) By other conduct renders it unreasonably difficult for the lawyer to carry out his employment effectively; (e) Insists, in a matter not pending before a tribunal, that the lawyer engage in conduct that is contrary to the judgment and advice of the lawyer but not prohibited under the Disciplinary Rules; (f) Deliberately disregards an agreement or obligation to the lawyer as to expenses and fees.

"(2) His continued employment is likely to result in a violation of a Disciplinary Rule.

"(3) His inability to work with co-counsel indicates that the best interest of the client likely will be served by withdrawal.

"(4) His mental or physical condition renders it difficult for him to carry out the employment effectively.

"(5) His client knowingly and freely assents to termination of his employment.

"(6) He believes in good faith, in a proceeding pending before a tribunal, that the tribunal will find the existence of other good cause for withdrawal."

With regard to paragraph (c), DR 2–110(A)(1) provided: "If permission for withdrawal from employment is required by the rules of a tribunal, the lawyer shall not withdraw ... without its permission."

RULE 1.17 Sale of Law Practice*

A lawyer or a law firm may sell or purchase a law practice, including good will, if the following conditions are satisfied:

(a) The seller ceases to engage in the private practice of law [in the geographic area] [in the jurisdiction] (a jurisdiction may elect either version) in which the practice has been conducted;

(b) The practice is sold as an entirety to another lawyer or law firm;

(c) Actual written notice is given to each of the seller's clients regarding:

(1) the proposed sale;

(2) the terms of any proposed change in the fee arrangement authorized by paragraph (d);

(3) the client's right to retain other counsel or to take possession of the file; and

(4) the fact that the client's consent to the sale will be presumed if the client does not take any action or does not otherwise object within ninety (90) days of receipt of the notice.

If a client cannot be given notice, the representation of that client may be transferred to the purchaser only upon entry of an order so authorizing by a court having jurisdiction. The seller may disclose to the court *in camera* information relating to the representation only to the extent necessary to obtain an order authorizing the transfer of a file.

(d) The fees charged clients shall not be increased by reason of the sale. The purchaser may, however, refuse to undertake the representation unless the client consents to pay the purchaser fees at a rate not exceeding the fees charged by the purchaser for rendering substantially similar services prior to the initiation of the purchase negotiations.

COMMENT:

[1] The practice of law is a profession, not merely a business. Clients are not commodities that can be purchased and sold at will. Pursuant to this Rule, when a lawyer or an entire firm ceases to practice and another lawyer or firm takes over the representation, the selling lawyer or firm may obtain compensation for the reasonable value of the practice as may withdrawing partners of law firms. See Rules 5.4 and 5.6.

---

* Model Rule 1.17 did not appear in the original version of the Model Rules. This provision and its comments were added by the ABA in 1990.

Termination of Practice by the Seller

[2] The requirement that all of the private practice be sold is satisfied if the seller in good faith makes the entire practice available for sale to the purchaser. The fact that a number of the seller's clients decide not to be represented by the purchaser but take their matters elsewhere, therefore, does not result in a violation. Neither does a return to private practice as a result of an unanticipated change in circumstances result in a violation. For example, a lawyer who has sold the practice to accept an appointment to judicial office does not violate the requirement that the sale be attendant to cessation of practice if the lawyer later resumes private practice upon being defeated in a contested or a retention election for the office.

[3] The requirement that the seller cease to engage in the private practice of law does not prohibit employment as a lawyer on the staff of a public agency or a legal services entity which provides legal services to the poor, or as in-house counsel to a business.

[4] The Rule permits a sale attendant upon retirement from the private practice of law within the jurisdiction. Its provisions, therefore, accommodate the lawyer who sells the practice upon the occasion of moving to another state. Some states are so large that a move from one locale therein to another is tantamount to leaving the jurisdiction in which the lawyer has engaged in the practice of law. To also accommodate lawyers so situated, states may permit the sale of the practice when the lawyer leaves the geographic area rather than the jurisdiction. The alternative desired should be indicated by selecting one of the two provided for in Rule 1.17(a).

Single Purchaser

[5] The Rule requires a single purchaser. The prohibition against piecemeal sale of a practice protects those clients whose matters are less lucrative and who might find it difficult to secure other counsel if a sale could be limited to substantial fee-generating matters. The purchaser is required to undertake all client matters in the practice, subject to client consent. If, however, the purchaser is unable to undertake all client matters because of a conflict of interest in a specific matter respecting which the purchaser is not permitted by Rule 1.7 or another rule to represent the client, the requirement that there be a single purchaser is nevertheless satisfied.

Client Confidences, Consent and Notice

[6] Negotiations between seller and prospective purchaser prior to disclosure of information relating to a specific representation of an identifiable client no more violate the confidentiality provisions of Model Rule 1.6 than do preliminary discussions concerning the possible association of another lawyer or mergers between firms, with respect to which client consent is not required. Providing the purchaser access to client-

specific information relating to the representation and to the file, however, requires client consent. The Rule provides that before such information can be disclosed by the seller to the purchaser the client must be given actual written notice of the contemplated sale, including the identity of the purchaser and any proposed change in the terms of future representation, and must be told that the decision to consent or make other arrangements must be made within 90 days. If nothing is heard from the client within that time, consent to the sale is presumed.

[7] A lawyer or law firm ceasing to practice cannot be required to remain in practice because some clients cannot be given actual notice of the proposed purchase. Since these clients cannot themselves consent to the purchase or direct any other disposition of their files, the Rule requires an order from a court having jurisdiction authorizing their transfer or other disposition. The Court can be expected to determine whether reasonable efforts to locate the client have been exhausted, and whether the absent client's legitimate interests will be served by authorizing the transfer of the file so that the purchaser may continue the representation. Preservation of client confidences requires that the petition for a court order be considered *in camera*. (A procedure by which such an order can be obtained needs to be established in jurisdictions in which it presently does not exist.)

[8] All the elements of client autonomy, including the client's absolute right to discharge a lawyer and transfer the representation to another, survive the sale of the practice.

Fee Arrangements Between Client and Purchaser

[9] The sale may not be financed by increases in fees charged the clients of the practice. Existing agreements between the seller and the client as to fees and the scope of the work must be honored by the purchaser, unless the client consents after consultation. The purchaser may, however, advise the client that the purchaser will not undertake the representation unless the client consents to pay the higher fees the purchaser usually charges. To prevent client financing of the sale, the higher fee the purchaser may charge must not exceed the fees charged by the purchaser for substantially similar service rendered prior to the initiation of the purchase negotiations.

[10] The purchaser may not intentionally fragment the practice which is the subject of the sale by charging significantly different fees in substantially similar matters. Doing so would make it possible for the purchaser to avoid the obligation to take over the entire practice by charging arbitrarily higher fees for less lucrative matters, thereby increasing the likelihood that those clients would not consent to the new representation.

Other Applicable Ethical Standards

[11] Lawyers participating in the sale of a law practice are subject to the ethical standards applicable to involving another lawyer in the

representation of a client. These include, for example, the seller's obligation to exercise competence in identifying a purchaser qualified to assume the practice and the purchaser's obligation to undertake the representation competently (see Rule 1.1); the obligation to avoid disqualifying conflicts, and to secure client consent after consultation for those conflicts which can be agreed to (see Rule 1.7); and the obligation to protect information relating to the representation (see Rules 1.6 and 1.9).

[12] If approval of the substitution of the purchasing attorney for the selling attorney is required by the rules of any tribunal in which a matter is pending, such approval must be obtained before the matter can be included in the sale (see Rule 1.16).

Applicability of the Rule

[13] This Rule applies to the sale of a law practice by representatives of a deceased, disabled or disappeared lawyer. Thus, the seller may be represented by a non-lawyer representative not subject to these Rules. Since, however, no lawyer may participate in a sale of a law practice which does not conform to the requirements of this Rule, the representatives of the seller as well as the purchasing lawyer can be expected to see to it that they are met.

[14] Admission to or retirement from a law partnership or professional association, retirement plans and similar arrangements, and a sale of tangible assets of a law practice, do not constitute a sale or purchase governed by this Rule.

[15] This Rule does not apply to the transfers of legal representation between lawyers when such transfers are unrelated to the sale of a practice.

MODEL CODE COMPARISON:

There was no counterpart to this Rule in the Model Code.

COUNSELOR

RULE 2.1 Advisor

In representing a client, a lawyer shall exercise independent professional judgment and render candid advice. In rendering advice, a lawyer may refer not only to law but to other considerations such as moral, economic, social and political factors, that may be relevant to the client's situation.

COMMENT:

Scope of Advice

[1] A client is entitled to straightforward advice expressing the lawyer's honest assessment. Legal advice often involves unpleasant facts and alternatives that a client may be disinclined to confront. In

presenting advice, a lawyer endeavors to sustain the client's morale and may put advice in as acceptable a form as honesty permits. However, a lawyer should not be deterred from giving candid advice by the prospect that the advice will be unpalatable to the client.

[2] Advice couched in narrowly legal terms may be of little value to a client, especially where practical considerations, such as cost or effects on other people, are predominant. Purely technical legal advice, therefore, can sometimes be inadequate. It is proper for a lawyer to refer to relevant moral and ethical considerations in giving advice. Although a lawyer is not a moral advisor as such, moral and ethical considerations impinge upon most legal questions and may decisively influence how the law will be applied.

[3] A client may expressly or impliedly ask the lawyer for purely technical advice. When such a request is made by a client experienced in legal matters, the lawyer may accept it at face value. When such a request is made by a client inexperienced in legal matters, however, the lawyer's responsibility as advisor may include indicating that more may be involved than strictly legal considerations.

[4] Matters that go beyond strictly legal questions may also be in the domain of another profession. Family matters can involve problems within the professional competence of psychiatry, clinical psychology or social work; business matters can involve problems within the competence of the accounting profession or of financial specialists. Where consultation with a professional in another field is itself something a competent lawyer would recommend, the lawyer should make such a recommendation. At the same time, a lawyer's advice at its best often consists of recommending a course of action in the face of conflicting recommendations of experts.

Offering Advice

[5] In general, a lawyer is not expected to give advice until asked by the client. However, when a lawyer knows that a client proposes a course of action that is likely to result in substantial adverse legal consequences to the client, duty to the client under Rule 1.4 may require that the lawyer act if the client's course of action is related to the representation. A lawyer ordinarily has no duty to initiate investigation of a client's affairs or to give advice that the client has indicated is unwanted, but a lawyer may initiate advice to a client when doing so appears to be in the client's interest.

MODEL CODE COMPARISON:

There was no direct counterpart to this Rule in the Disciplinary Rules of the Model Code. DR 5–107(B) provided that a lawyer "shall not permit a person who recommends, employs, or pays him to render legal services for another to direct or regulate his professional judgment in rendering such legal services." EC 7–8 stated that "[a]dvice of a lawyer to his client need not be confined to purely legal considerations. . . . In assisting his client to reach a proper decision, it is often desirable for a lawyer to point out those factors which may lead to a decision that is morally just as well as legally permissible.... In the final analysis, however, ... the decision whether to forego legally available objectives or methods because of nonlegal factors is ultimately for the client...."

RULE 2.2   Intermediary

(a) A lawyer may act as intermediary between clients if:

(1) the lawyer consults with each client concerning the implications of the common representation, including the advantages and risks involved, and the effect on the attorney–client privileges, and obtains each client's consent to the common representation;

(2) the lawyer reasonably believes that the matter can be resolved on terms compatible with the clients' best interests, that each client will be able to make adequately informed decisions in the matter and that there is little risk of material prejudice to the interest of any of the clients if the contemplated resolution is unsuccessful; and

(3) the lawyer reasonably believes that the common representation can be undertaken impartially and without improper effect on other responsibilities the lawyer has to any of the clients.

(b) While acting as intermediary, the lawyer shall consult with each client concerning the decisions to be made and the considerations relevant in making them, so that each client can make adequately informed decisions.

(c) A lawyer shall withdraw as intermediary if any of the clients so request, or if any of the conditions stated in paragraph (a) is no longer satisfied. Upon withdrawal, the lawyer shall not continue to represent any of the clients in the matter that was the subject of the intermediation.

COMMENT:

[1] A lawyer acts as intermediary under this Rule when the lawyer represents two or more parties with potentially conflicting interests. A key factor in defining the relationship is whether the parties share responsibility for the lawyer's fee, but the common representation may be inferred from other circumstances. Because confusion can arise as to the lawyer's role where each party is not separately represented, it is important that the lawyer make clear the relationship.

[2] The Rule does not apply to a lawyer acting as arbitrator or mediator between or among parties who are not clients of the lawyer, even where the lawyer has been appointed with the concurrence of the parties. In performing such a role the lawyer may be subject to applicable codes of ethics, such as the Code of Ethics for Arbitration in

Commercial Disputes prepared by a joint Committee of the American Bar Association and the American Arbitration Association.

[3] A lawyer acts as intermediary in seeking to establish or adjust a relationship between clients on an amicable and mutually advantageous basis; for example, in helping to organize a business in which two or more clients are entrepreneurs, working out the financial reorganization of an enterprise in which two or more clients have an interest, arranging a property distribution in settlement of an estate or mediating a dispute between clients. The lawyer seeks to resolve potentially conflicting interests by developing the parties' mutual interests. The alternative can be that each party may have to obtain separate representation, with the possibility in some situations of incurring additional cost, complication or even litigation. Given these and other relevant factors, all the clients may prefer that the lawyer act as intermediary.

[4] In considering whether to act as intermediary between clients, a lawyer should be mindful that if the intermediation fails the result can be additional cost, embarrassment and recrimination. In some situations the risk of failure is so great that intermediation is plainly impossible. For example, a lawyer cannot undertake common representation of clients between whom contentious litigation is imminent or who contemplate contentious negotiations. More generally, if the relationship between the parties has already assumed definite antagonism, the possibility that the clients' interests can be adjusted by intermediation ordinarily is not very good.

[5] The appropriateness of intermediation can depend on its form. Forms of intermediation range from informal arbitration, where each client's case is presented by the respective client and the lawyer decides the outcome, to mediation, to common representation where the clients' interests are substantially though not entirely compatible. One form may be appropriate in circumstances where another would not. Other relevant factors are whether the lawyer subsequently will represent both parties on a continuing basis and whether the situation involves creating a relationship between the parties or terminating one.

Confidentiality and Privilege

[6] A particularly important factor in determining the appropriateness of intermediation is the effect on client-lawyer confidentiality and the attorney-client privilege. In a common representation, the lawyer is still required both to keep each client adequately informed and to maintain confidentiality of information relating to the representation. See Rules 1.4 and 1.6. Complying with both requirements while acting as intermediary requires a delicate balance. If the balance cannot be maintained, the common representation is improper. With regard to the attorney-client privilege, the prevailing rule is that as between commonly represented clients the privilege does not attach. Hence, it must be assumed that if litigation eventuates between the clients, the privilege

65

will not protect any such communications, and the clients should be so advised.

[7] Since the lawyer is required to be impartial between commonly represented clients, intermediation is improper when that impartiality cannot be maintained. For example, a lawyer who has represented one of the clients for a long period and in a variety of matters might have difficulty being impartial between that client and one to whom the lawyer has only recently been introduced.

Consultation

[8] In acting as intermediary between clients, the lawyer is required to consult with the clients on the implications of doing so, and proceed only upon consent based on such a consultation. The consultation should make clear that the lawyer's role is not that of partisanship normally expected in other circumstances.

[9] Paragraph (b) is an application of the principle expressed in Rule 1.4. Where the lawyer is intermediary, the clients ordinarily must assume greater responsibility for decisions than when each client is independently represented.

Withdrawal

[10] Common representation does not diminish the rights of each client in the client-lawyer relationship. Each has the right to loyal and diligent representation, the right to discharge the lawyer as stated in Rule 1.16, and the protection of Rule 1.9 concerning obligations to a former client.

MODEL CODE COMPARISON:

There was no direct counterpart to this Rule in the Disciplinary Rules of the Model Code. EC 5–20 stated that a "lawyer is often asked to serve as an impartial arbitrator or mediator in matters which involve present or former clients. He may serve in either capacity if he first discloses such present or former relationships." DR 5–105(B) provided that a lawyer "shall not continue multiple employment if the exercise of his independent judgment in behalf of a client will be or is likely to be adversely affected by his representation of another client, or if it would be likely to involve him in representation of differing interests, except to the extent permitted under DR 5–105(C)." DR 5–105(C) provided that "a lawyer may represent multiple clients if it is obvious that he can adequately represent the interests of each and if each consents to the representation after full disclosure of the possible effect of such representation on the exercise of his independent professional judgment on behalf of each."

RULE 2.3 Evaluation for Use by Third Persons

(a) A lawyer may undertake an evaluation of a matter affecting a client for the use of someone other than the client if:

(1) the lawyer reasonably believes that making the evaluation is compatible with other aspects of the lawyer's relationship with the client; and

(2) the client consents after consultation.

(b) Except as disclosure is required in connection with a report of an evaluation, information relating to the evaluation is otherwise protected by rule 1.6.

COMMENT:

Definition

[1] An evaluation may be performed at the client's direction but for the primary purpose of establishing information for the benefit of third parties; for example, an opinion concerning the title of property rendered at the behest of a vendor for the information of a prospective purchaser, or at the behest of a borrower for the information of a prospective lender. In some situations, the evaluation may be required by a government agency; for example, an opinion concerning the legality of the securities registered for sale under the securities laws. In other instances, the evaluation may be required by a third person, such as a purchaser of a business.

[2] Lawyers for the government may be called upon to give a formal opinion on the legality of contemplated government agency action. In making such an evaluation, the government lawyer acts at the behest of the government as the client but for the purpose of establishing the limits of the agency's authorized activity. Such an opinion is to be distinguished from confidential legal advice given agency officials. The critical question is whether the opinion is to be made public.

[3] A legal evaluation should be distinguished from an investigation of a person with whom the lawyer does not have a client-lawyer relationship. For example, a lawyer retained by a purchaser to analyze a vendor's title to property does not have a client-lawyer relationship with the vendor. So also, an investigation into a person's affairs by a government lawyer, or by special counsel employed by the government, is not an evaluation as that term is used in this Rule. The question is whether the lawyer is retained by the person whose affairs are being examined. When the lawyer is retained by that person, the general rules concerning loyalty to client and preservation of confidences apply, which is not the case if the lawyer is retained by someone else. For this reason, it is essential to identify the person by whom the lawyer is retained. This should be made clear not only to the person under examination, but also to others to whom the results are to be made available.

Duty to Third Person

[4] When the evaluation is intended for the information or use of a third person, a legal duty to that person may or may not arise. That

legal question is beyond the scope of this Rule. However, since such an evaluation involves a departure from the normal client-lawyer relationship, careful analysis of the situation is required. The lawyer must be satisfied as a matter of professional judgment that making the evaluation is compatible with other functions undertaken in behalf of the client. For example, if the lawyer is acting as advocate in defending the client against charges of fraud, it would normally be incompatible with that responsibility for the lawyer to perform an evaluation for others concerning the same or a related transaction. Assuming no such impediment is apparent, however, the lawyer should advise the client of the implications of the evaluation, particularly the lawyer's responsibilities to third persons and the duty to disseminate the findings.

Access to and Disclosure of Information

[5] The quality of an evaluation depends on the freedom and extent of the investigation upon which it is based. Ordinarily a lawyer should have whatever latitude of investigation seems necessary as a matter of professional judgment. Under some circumstances, however, the terms of the evaluation may be limited. For example, certain issues or sources may be categorically excluded, or the scope of search may be limited by time constraints or the noncooperation of persons having relevant information. Any such limitations which are material to the evaluation should be described in the report. If after a lawyer has commenced an evaluation, the client refuses to comply with the terms upon which it was understood the evaluation was to have been made, the lawyer's obligations are determined by law, having reference to the terms of the client's agreement and the surrounding circumstances.

Financial Auditors' Requests for Information

[6] When a question concerning the legal situation of a client arises at the instance of the client's financial auditor and the question is referred to the lawyer, the lawyer's response may be made in accordance with procedures recognized in the legal profession. Such a procedure is set forth in the American Bar Association Statement of Policy Regarding Lawyers' Responses to Auditors' Requests for Information, adopted in 1975.

MODEL CODE COMPARISON:

There was no counterpart to this Rule in the Model Code.

ADVOCATE

RULE 3.1 Meritorious Claims and Contentions

A lawyer shall not bring or defend a proceeding, or assert or controvert an issue therein, unless there is a basis for doing so that is not frivolous, which includes a good faith argument for

an extension, modification or reversal of existing law. A lawyer for the defendant in a criminal proceeding, or the respondent in a proceeding that could result in incarceration, may nevertheless so defend the proceeding as to require that every element of the case be established.

COMMENT:

[1] The advocate has a duty to use legal procedure for the fullest benefit of the client's cause, but also a duty not to abuse legal procedure. The law, both procedural and substantive, establishes the limits within which an advocate may proceed. However, the law is not always clear and never is static. Accordingly, in determining the proper scope of advocacy, account must be taken of the law's ambiguities and potential for change.

[2] The filing of an action or defense or similar action taken for a client is not frivolous merely because the facts have not first been fully substantiated or because the lawyer expects to develop vital evidence only by discovery. Such action is not frivolous even though the lawyer believes that the client's position ultimately will not prevail. The action is frivolous, however, if the client desires to have the action taken primarily for the purpose of harassing or maliciously injuring a person or if the lawyer is unable either to make a good faith argument on the merits of the action taken or to support the action taken by a good faith argument for an extension, modification or reversal of existing law.

MODEL CODE COMPARISON:

DR 7–102(A)(1) provided that a lawyer may not "[f]ile a suit, assert a position, conduct a defense, delay a trial, or take other action on behalf of his client when he knows or when it is obvious that such action would serve merely to harass or maliciously injure another." Rule 3.1 is to the same general effect as DR 7–102(A)(1), with three qualifications. First, the test of improper conduct is changed from "merely to harass or maliciously injure another" to the requirement that there be a basis for the litigation measure involved that is "not frivolous." This includes the concept stated in DR 7–102(A)(2) that a lawyer may advance a claim or defense unwarranted by existing law if "it can be supported by good faith argument for an extension, modification, or reversal of existing law." Second, the test in Rule 3.1 is an objective test, whereas DR 7–102(A)(1) applied only if the lawyer "knows or when it is obvious" that the litigation is frivolous. Third, Rule 3.1 has an exception that in a criminal case, or a case in which incarceration of the client may result (for example, certain juvenile proceedings), the lawyer may put the prosecution to its proof even if there is no nonfrivolous basis for defense.

RULE 3.2 Expediting Litigation

A lawyer shall make reasonable efforts to expedite litigation consistent with the interests of the client.

COMMENT:

Dilatory practices bring the administration of justice into disrepute. Delay should not be indulged merely for the convenience of the advocates, or for the purpose of frustrating an opposing party's attempt to obtain rightful redress or repose. It is not a justification that similar conduct is often tolerated by the bench and bar. The question is whether a competent lawyer acting in good faith would regard the course of action as having some substantial purpose other than delay. Realizing financial or other benefit from otherwise improper delay in litigation it not a legitimate interest of the client.

MODEL CODE COMPARISON:

DR 7–101(A)(1) stated that a lawyer does not violate the duty to represent a client zealously "by being punctual in fulfilling all professional commitments." DR 7–102(A)(1) provided that a lawyer "shall not . . . file a suit, assert a position, conduct a defense [or] delay a trial . . . when he knows or when it is obvious that such action would serve merely to harass or maliciously injure another."

RULE 3.3   Candor Toward the Tribunal

(a) **A lawyer shall not knowingly:**

(1) **make a false statement of material fact or law to a tribunal;**

(2) **fail to disclose a material fact to a tribunal when disclosure is necessary to avoid assisting a criminal or fraudulent act by the client;**

(3) **fail to disclose to the tribunal legal authority in the controlling jurisdiction known to the lawyer to be directly adverse to the position of the client and not disclosed by opposing counsel; or**

(4) **offer evidence that the lawyer knows to be false. If a lawyer has offered material evidence and comes to know of its falsity, the lawyer shall take reasonable remedial measures.**

(b) **The duties stated in paragraph (a) continue to the conclusion of the proceeding, and apply even if compliance requires disclosure of information otherwise protected by rule 1.6.**

(c) **A lawyer may refuse to offer evidence that the lawyer reasonably believes is false.**

(d) **In an ex parte proceeding, a lawyer shall inform the tribunal of all material facts known to the lawyer which will enable the tribunal to make an informed decision, whether or not the facts are adverse.**

70

COMMENT:

[1] The advocate's task is to present the client's case with persuasive force. Performance of that duty while maintaining confidences of the client is qualified by the advocate's duty of candor to the tribunal. However, an advocate does not vouch for the evidence submitted in a cause; the tribunal is responsible for assessing its probative value.

Representations by a Lawyer

[2] An advocate is responsible for pleadings and other documents prepared for litigation, but is usually not required to have personal knowledge of matters asserted therein, for litigation documents ordinarily present assertions by the client, or by someone on the client's behalf, and not assertions by the lawyer. Compare Rule 3.1. However, an assertion purporting to be on the lawyer's own knowledge, as in an affidavit by the lawyer or in a statement in open court, may properly be made only when the lawyer knows the assertion is true or believes it to be true on the basis of a reasonably diligent inquiry. There are circumstances where failure to make a disclosure is the equivalent of an affirmative misrepresentation. The obligation prescribed in Rule 1.2(d) not to counsel a client to commit or assist the client in committing a fraud applies in litigation. Regarding compliance with Rule 1.2(d), see the Comment to that Rule. See also the Comment to Rule 8.4(b).

Misleading Legal Argument

[3] Legal argument based on a knowingly false representation of law constitutes dishonesty toward the tribunal. A lawyer is not required to make a disinterested exposition of the law, but must recognize the existence of pertinent legal authorities. Furthermore, as stated in paragraph (a)(3), an advocate has a duty to disclose directly adverse authority in the controlling jurisdiction which has not been disclosed by the opposing party. The underlying concept is that legal argument is a discussion seeking to determine the legal premises properly applicable to the case.

False Evidence

[4] When evidence that a lawyer knows to be false is provided by a person who is not the client, the lawyer must refuse to offer it regardless of the client's wishes.

[5] When false evidence is offered by the client, however, a conflict may arise between the lawyer's duty to keep the client's revelations confidential and the duty of candor to the court. Upon ascertaining that material evidence is false, the lawyer should seek to persuade the client that the evidence should not be offered or, if it has been offered, that its false character should immediately be disclosed. If the persuasion is ineffective, the lawyer must take reasonable remedial measures.

71

[6]   Except in the defense of a criminal accused, the rule generally recognized is that, if necessary to rectify the situation, an advocate must disclose the existence of the client's deception to the court or to the other party.   Such a disclosure can result in grave consequences to the client, including not only a sense of betrayal but also loss of the case and perhaps a prosecution for perjury.   But the alternative is that the lawyer cooperate in deceiving the court, thereby subverting the truth-finding process which the adversary system is designed to implement.   See Rule 1.2(d).   Furthermore, unless it is clearly understood that the lawyer will act upon the duty to disclose the existence of false evidence, the client can simply reject the lawyer's advice to reveal the false evidence and insist that the lawyer keep silent.   Thus the client could in effect coerce the lawyer into being a party to fraud on the court.

Perjury by a Criminal Defendant

[7]   Whether an advocate for a criminally accused has the same duty of disclosure has been intensely debated.   While it is agreed that the lawyer should seek to persuade the client to refrain from perjurious testimony, there has been dispute concerning the lawyer's duty when that persuasion fails.   If the confrontation with the client occurs before trial, the lawyer ordinarily can withdraw.   Withdrawal before trial may not be possible, however, either because trial is imminent, or because the confrontation with the client does not take place until the trial itself, or because no other counsel is available.

[8]   The most difficult situation, therefore, arises in a criminal case where the accused insists on testifying when the lawyer knows that the testimony is perjurious.   The lawyer's effort to rectify the situation can increase the likelihood of the client's being convicted as well as opening the possibility of a prosecution for perjury.   On the other hand, if the lawyer does not exercise control over the proof, the lawyer participates, although in a merely passive way, in deception of the court.

[9]   Three resolutions of this dilemma have been proposed.   One is to permit the accused to testify by a narrative without guidance through the lawyer's questioning.   This compromises both contending principles; it exempts the lawyer from the duty to disclose false evidence but subjects the client to an implicit disclosure of information imparted to counsel.   Another suggested resolution, of relatively recent origin, is that the advocate be entirely excused from the duty to reveal perjury if the perjury is that of the client.   This is a coherent solution but makes the advocate a knowing instrument of perjury.

[10]   The other resolution of the dilemma is that the lawyer must reveal the client's perjury if necessary to rectify the situation.   A criminal accused has a right to the assistance of an advocate, a right to testify and a right of confidential communication with counsel.   However, an accused should not have a right to assistance of counsel in committing perjury.   Furthermore, an advocate has an obligation, not only in professional ethics but under the law as well, to avoid implication

in the commission of perjury or other falsification of evidence. See Rule 1.2(d).

Remedial Measures

[11] If perjured testimony or false evidence has been offered, the advocate's proper course ordinarily is to remonstrate with the client confidentially. If that fails, the advocate should seek to withdraw if that will remedy the situation. If withdrawal will not remedy the situation or is impossible, the advocate should make disclosure to the court. It is for the court then to determine what should be done—making a statement about the matter to the trier of fact, ordering a mistrial or perhaps nothing. If the false testimony was that of the client, the client may controvert the lawyer's version of their communication when the lawyer discloses the situation to the court. If there is an issue whether the client has committed perjury, the lawyer cannot represent the client in resolution of the issue and a mistrial may be unavoidable. An unscrupulous client might in this way attempt to produce a series of mistrials and thus escape prosecution. However, a second such encounter could be construed as a deliberate abuse of the right to counsel and as such a waiver of the right to further representation.

Constitutional Requirements

[12] The general rule—that an advocate must disclose the existence of perjury with respect to a material fact, even that of a client—applies to defense counsel in criminal cases, as well as in other instances. However, the definition of the lawyer's ethical duty in such a situation may be qualified by constitutional provisions for due process and the right to counsel in criminal cases. In some jurisdictions these provisions have been construed to require that counsel present an accused as a witness if the accused wishes to testify, even if counsel knows the testimony will be false. The obligation of the advocate under these Rules is subordinate to such a constitutional requirement.

Duration of Obligation

[13] A practical time limit on the obligation to rectify the presentation of false evidence has to be established. The conclusion of the proceeding is a reasonably definite point for the termination of the obligation.

Refusing to Offer Proof Believed to be False

[14] Generally speaking, a lawyer has authority to refuse to offer testimony or other proof that the lawyer believes is untrustworthy. Offering such proof may reflect adversely on the lawyer's ability to discriminate in the quality of evidence and thus impair the lawyer's effectiveness as an advocate. In criminal cases, however, a lawyer may,

in some jurisdictions, be denied this authority by constitutional requirements governing the right to counsel.

Ex Parte Proceedings

[15] Ordinarily, an advocate has the limited responsibility of presenting one side of the matters that a tribunal should consider in reaching a decision; the conflicting position is expected to be presented by the opposing party. However, in an ex parte proceeding, such as an application for a temporary restraining order, there is no balance of presentation by opposing advocates. The object of an ex parte proceeding is nevertheless to yield a substantially just result. The judge has an affirmative responsibility to accord the absent party just consideration. The lawyer for the represented party has the correlative duty to make disclosures of material facts known to the lawyer and that the lawyer reasonably believes are necessary to an informed decision.

MODEL CODE COMPARISON:

Paragraph (a)(1) is substantially identical to DR 7–102(A)(5), which provided that a lawyer shall not "knowingly make a false statement of law or fact."

Paragraph (a)(2) is implicit in DR 7–102(A)(3), which provided that "a lawyer shall not ... knowingly fail to disclose that which he is required by law to reveal."

Paragraph (a)(3) is substantially identical to DR 7–106(B)(1).

With regard to paragraph (a)(4), the first sentence of this subparagraph is similar to DR 7–102(A)(4), which provided that a lawyer shall not "knowingly use" perjured testimony or false evidence. The second sentence of paragraph (a)(4) resolves an ambiguity in the Model Code concerning the action required of a lawyer who discovers that the lawyer has offered perjured testimony or false evidence. DR 7–102(A)(4), quoted above, did not expressly deal with this situation, but the prohibition against "use" of false evidence can be construed to preclude carrying through with a case based on such evidence when that fact has become known during the trial. DR 7–102(B)(1), also noted in connection with Rule 1.6, provided that a lawyer "who receives information clearly establishing that ... [h]is client has ... perpetrated a fraud upon ... a tribunal shall [if the client does not rectify the situation] ... reveal the fraud to the ... tribunal. ..." Since use of perjured testimony or false evidence is usually regarded as "fraud" upon the court, DR 7–102(B)(1) apparently required disclosure by the lawyer in such circumstances. However, some states have amended DR 7–102(B)(1) in conformity with an ABA-recommended amendment to provide that the duty of disclosure does not apply when the "information is protected as a privileged communication." This qualification may be empty, for the rule of attorney-client privilege has been construed to exclude communications that further a crime, including the crime of perjury. On this interpretation of DR 7–102(B)(1), the lawyer has a duty to disclose the perjury.

74

Paragraph (c) confers discretion on the lawyer to refuse to offer evidence that the lawyer "reasonably believes" is false. This gives the lawyer more latitude than DR 7–102(A)(4), which prohibited the lawyer from offering evidence the lawyer "knows" is false.

There was no counterpart in the Model Code to paragraph (d).

RULE 3.4 Fairness to Opposing Party and Counsel

A lawyer shall not:

(a) unlawfully obstruct another party's access to evidence or unlawfully alter, destroy or conceal a document or other material having potential evidentiary value. A lawyer shall not counsel or assist another person to do any such act;

(b) falsify evidence, counsel or assist a witness to testify falsely, or offer an inducement to a witness that is prohibited by law;

(c) knowingly disobey an obligation under the rules of a tribunal except for an open refusal based on an assertion that no valid obligation exists;

(d) in pretrial procedure, make a frivolous discovery request or fail to make reasonably diligent effort to comply with a legally proper discovery request by an opposing party;

(e) in trial, allude to any matter that the lawyer does not reasonably believe is relevant or that will not be supported by admissible evidence, assert personal knowledge of facts in issue except when testifying as a witness, or state a personal opinion as to the justness of a cause, the credibility of a witness, the culpability of a civil litigant or the guilt or innocence of an accused; or

(f) request a person other than a client to refrain from voluntarily giving relevant information to another party unless:

> **(1) the person is a relative or an employee or other agent of a client; and**

> **(2) the lawyer reasonably believes that the person's interests will not be adversely affected by refraining from giving such information.**

COMMENT:

[1] The procedure of the adversary system contemplates that the evidence in a case is to be marshalled competitively by the contending parties. Fair competition in the adversary system is secured by prohibitions against destruction or concealment of evidence, improperly influencing witnesses, obstructive tactics in discovery procedure, and the like.

[2] Documents and other items of evidence are often essential to establish a claim or defense. Subject to evidentiary privileges, the right of an opposing party, including the government, to obtain evidence through discovery or subpoena is an important procedural right. The

exercise of that right can be frustrated if relevant material is altered, concealed or destroyed. Applicable law in many jurisdictions makes it an offense to destroy material for purpose of impairing its availability in a pending proceeding or one whose commencement can be foreseen. Falsifying evidence is also generally a criminal offense. Paragraph (a) applies to evidentiary material generally, including computerized information.

[3] With regard to paragraph (b), it is not improper to pay a witness's expenses or to compensate an expert witness on terms permitted by law. The common law rule in most jurisdictions is that it is improper to pay an occurrence witness any fee for testifying and that it is improper to pay an expert witness a contingent fee.

[4] Paragraph (f) permits a lawyer to advise employees of a client to refrain from giving information to another party, for the employees may identify their interests with those of the client. See also Rule 4.2.

MODEL CODE COMPARISON:

With regard to paragraph (a), DR 7–109(A) provided that a lawyer "shall not suppress any evidence that he or his client has a legal obligation to reveal." DR 7–109(B) provided that a lawyer "shall not advise or cause a person to secrete himself . . . for the purpose of making him unavailable as a witness. . . ." DR 7–106(C)(7) provided that a lawyer shall not "[i]ntentionally or habitually violate any established rule of procedure or of evidence."

With regard to paragraph (b), DR 7–102(A)(6) provided that a lawyer shall not participate "in the creation or preservation of evidence when he knows or it is obvious that the evidence is false." DR 7–109(C) provided that a lawyer "shall not pay, offer to pay, or acquiesce in the payment of compensation to a witness contingent upon the content of his testimony or the outcome of the case. But a lawyer may advance, guarantee or acquiesce in the payment of: (1) Expenses reasonably incurred by a witness in attending or testifying; (2) Reasonable compensation to a witness for his loss of time in attending or testifying; [or] (3) A reasonable fee for the professional services of an expert witness." EC 7–28 stated that witnesses "should always testify truthfully and should be free from any financial inducements that might tempt them to do otherwise."

Paragraph (c) is substantially similar to DR 7–106(A), which provided that "A lawyer shall not disregard . . . a standing rule of a tribunal or a ruling of a tribunal made in the course of a proceeding, but he may take appropriate steps in good faith to test the validity of such rule or ruling."

Paragraph (d) has no counterpart in the Model Code.

Paragraph (e) substantially incorporates DR 7–106(C)(1), (2), (3) and (4). DR 7–106(C)(2) proscribed asking a question "intended to degrade a witness or other person," a matter dealt with in Rule 4.4. DR 7–106(C)(5), providing that a lawyer shall not "fail to comply with known local customs of courtesy or practice," was too vague to be a rule of conduct enforceable as law.

With regard to paragraph (f), DR 7–104(A)(2) provided that a lawyer shall not "give advice to a person who is not represented . . . other than the advice to secure counsel, if the interests of such person are or have a reasonable possibility of being in conflict with the interests of his client."

RULE 3.5 Impartiality and Decorum of the Tribunal

A lawyer shall not:

(a) seek to influence a judge, juror, prospective juror or other official by means prohibited by law;

(b) communicate ex parte with such a person except as permitted by law; or

(c) engage in conduct intended to disrupt a tribunal.

COMMENT:

[1] Many forms of improper influence upon a tribunal are proscribed by criminal law. Others are specified in the ABA Model Code of Judicial Conduct, with which an advocate should be familiar. A lawyer is required to avoid contributing to a violation of such provisions.

[2] The advocate's function is to present evidence and argument so that the cause may be decided according to law. Refraining from abusive or obstreperous conduct is a corollary of the advocate's right to speak on behalf of litigants. A lawyer may stand firm against abuse by a judge but should avoid reciprocation; the judge's default is no justification for similar dereliction by an advocate. An advocate can present the cause, protect the record for subsequent review and preserve professional integrity by patient firmness no less effectively than by belligerence or theatrics.

MODEL CODE COMPARISON:

With regard to paragraphs (a) and (b), DR 7–108(A) provided that "[b]efore the trial of a case a lawyer . . . shall not communicate with . . . anyone he knows to be a member of the venire. . . ." DR 7–108(B) provided that during the trial of a case a lawyer "shall not communicate with . . . any member of the jury." DR 7–110(B) provided that a lawyer shall not "communicate . . . as to the merits of the cause with a judge or an official before whom the proceeding is pending, except . . . upon adequate notice to opposing counsel," or as "otherwise authorized by law."

With regard to paragraph (c), DR 7–106(C)(6) provided that a lawyer shall not engage in "undignified or discourteous conduct which is degrading to a tribunal."

RULE 3.6   Trial Publicity*

(a) A lawyer who is participating or has participated in the investigation or litigation of a matter shall not make an extraju-

* In August 1994, the ABA House of Delegates amended Model Rule 3.6 to reflect the Supreme Court's decision in Gentile v. Nevada State Bar, 501 U.S. 1030 (1991). The original version of Model Rule 3.6 read as follows:

(a) A lawyer shall not make an extrajudicial statement that a reasonable person would expect to be disseminated by means of public communication if the lawyer knows or reasonably should know that it will have a substantial likelihood of materially prejudicing an adjudicative proceeding.

(b) A statement referred to in paragraph (a) ordinarily is likely to have such an effect when it refers to a civil matter triable to a jury, a criminal matter, or any other proceeding that could result in incarceration, and the statement relates to:

(1) the character, credibility, reputation or criminal record of a party, suspect in a criminal investigation or witness, or the identity of a witness, or the expected testimony of a party or witness;

(2) in a criminal case or proceeding that could result in incarceration, the possibility of a plea of guilty to the offense or the existence or contents of any confession, admission, or statement given by a defendant or suspect or that person's refusal or failure to make a statement;

(3) the performance or results of any examination or test or the refusal or failure of a person to submit to an examination or test, or the identity or nature of physical evidence expected to be presented;

(4) any opinion as to the guilt or innocence of a defendant or suspect in a criminal case or proceeding that could result in incarceration;

(5) information the lawyer knows or reasonably should know is likely to be inadmissible as evidence in a trial and would if disclosed create a substantial risk of prejudicing an impartial trial; or

(6) the fact that a defendant has been charged with a crime, unless there is included therein a statement explaining that the charge is merely an accusation and that the defendant is presumed innocent until and unless proven guilty.

(c) Notwithstanding paragraph (a) and (b)(1–5), a lawyer involved in the investigation or litigation of a matter may state without elaboration:

(1) the general nature of the claim or defense;

(2) the information contained in a public record;

(3) that an investigation of the matter is in progress, including the general scope of the investigation, the offense or claim or defense involved and, except when prohibited by law, the identity of the persons involved;

(4) the scheduling or result of any step in litigation;

(5) a request for assistance in obtaining evidence and information necessary thereto;

(6) a warning of danger concerning the behavior of a person involved, when there is reason to believe that there exists the likelihood of substantial harm to an individual or to the public interest; and

(7) in a criminal case:

(i) the identity, residence, occupation and family status of the accused;

(ii) if the accused has not been apprehended, information necessary to aid in apprehension of that person;

dicial statement that a reasonable person would expect to be disseminated by means of public communication if the lawyer knows or reasonably should know that it will have a substantial likelihood of materially prejudicing an adjudicative proceeding in the matter.

(b) Notwithstanding paragraph (a), a lawyer may state:

(1) the claim, offense or defense involved and, except when prohibited by law, the identity of the persons involved;

(2) information contained in a public record;

(3) that an investigation of a matter is in progress;

(4) the scheduling or result of any step in litigation;

(5) a request for assistance in obtaining evidence and information necessary thereto;

(6) a warning of danger concerning the behavior of a person involved, when there is reason to believe that there exists the likelihood of substantial harm to an individual or to the public interest; and

(7) in a criminal case, in addition to subparagraphs (1) through (6):

(i) the identity, residence, occupation and family status of the accused;

(ii) if the accused has not been apprehended, information necessary to aid in apprehension of that person;

(iii) the fact, time and place of arrest; and

(iv) the identity of investigating and arresting officers or agencies and the length of the investigation.

(c) Notwithstanding paragraph (a), a lawyer may make a statement that a reasonable lawyer would believe is required to protect a client from the substantial undue prejudicial effect of recent publicity not initiated by the lawyer or the lawyer's client. A statement made pursuant to this paragraph shall be limited to such information as is necessary to mitigate the recent adverse publicity.

(d) No lawyer associated in a firm or government agency with a lawyer subject to paragraph (a) shall make a statement prohibited by paragraph (a).

(iii) the fact, time and place of arrest; and

(iv) the identity of investigating and arresting officers or

COMMENT:*

[1]   It is difficult to strike a balance between protecting the right to a fair trial and safeguarding the right of free expression. Preserving the right to a fair trial necessarily entails some curtailment of the information that may be disseminated about a party prior to trial, particularly where trial by jury is involved. If there were no such limits, the result would be the practical nullification of the protective effect of the rules of forensic decorum and the exclusionary rules of evidence. On the other hand, there are vital social interests served by the free dissemination of information about events having legal consequences and about legal proceedings themselves. The public has a right to know about threats to its safety and measures aimed at assuring its security. It also has a legitimate interest in the conduct of judicial proceedings, particularly in matters of general public concern. Furthermore, the subject matter of legal proceedings is often of direct significance in debate and deliberation over questions of public policy.

[2]   Special rules of confidentiality may validly govern proceedings in juvenile, domestic relations and mental disability proceedings, and perhaps other types of litigation. Rule 3.4(c) requires compliance with such Rules.

[3]   The Rule sets forth a basic general prohibition against a lawyer's making statements that the lawyer knows or should know will have a substantial likelihood of materially prejudicing an adjudicative proceeding. Recognizing that the public value of informed commentary is great and the likelihood of prejudice to a proceeding by the commentary of a lawyer who is not involved in the proceeding is small, the rule applies only to lawyers who are, or who have been involved in the investigation or litigation of a case, and their associates.

[4]   Paragraph (b) identifies specific matters about which a lawyer's statements would not ordinarily be considered to present a substantial likelihood of material prejudice, and should not in any event be considered prohibited by the general prohibition of paragraph (a). Paragraph (b) is not intended to be an exhaustive listing of the subjects upon which a lawyer may make a statement, but statements on other matters may be subject to paragraph (a).

[5]   There are, on the other hand, certain subjects which are more likely than not to have a material prejudicial effect on a proceeding, particularly when they refer to a civil matter triable to a jury, a criminal matter, or any other proceeding that could result in incarceration. These subjects relate to:

agencies and the length of the investigation.

* The ABA's amendment of Model Rule 3.6 in August 1994 deleted the original comment 2 and renumbered comment 3 as comment 2 and added comments 3, 4, 5, 6 and 7. The deleted comment 2 read as follows:

[2]   No body of rules can simultaneously satisfy all interests of fair trial and all those of free expression. The formula in this Rule is based upon the ABA Model Code of Professional Responsibility and the ABA Standards Relating to Fair Trial and Free Press, as amended in 1978.

(1) the character, credibility, reputation or criminal record of a party, suspect in a criminal investigation or witness, or the identity of a witness, or the expected testimony of a party or witness;

(2) in a criminal case or proceeding that could result in incarceration, the possibility of a plea of guilty to the offense or the existence or contents of any confession, admission, or statement given by a defendant or suspect or that person's refusal or failure to make a statement;

(3) the performance or results of any examination or test or the refusal or failure of a person to submit to an examination or test, or the identity or nature of physical evidence expected to be presented;

(4) any opinion as to the guilt or innocence of a defendant or suspect in a criminal case or proceeding that could result in incarceration;

(5) information that the lawyer knows or reasonably should know is likely to be inadmissible as evidence in a trial and that would, if disclosed, create a substantial risk of prejudicing an impartial trial; or

(6) the fact that a defendant has been charged with a crime, unless there is included therein a statement explaining that the charge is merely an accusation and that the defendant is presumed innocent until and unless proven guilty.

[6] Another relevant factor in determining prejudice is the nature of the proceeding involved. Criminal jury trials will be most sensitive to extrajudicial speech. Civil trials may be less sensitive. Non-jury hearings and arbitration proceedings may be even less affected. The Rule will still place limitations on prejudicial comments in these cases, but the likelihood of prejudice may be different depending on the type of proceeding.

[7] Finally, extrajudicial statements that might otherwise raise a question under this Rule may be permissible when they are made in response to statements made publicly by another party, another party's lawyer, or third persons, where a reasonable lawyer would believe a public response is required in order to avoid prejudice to the lawyer's client. When prejudicial statements have been publicly made by others, responsive statements may have the salutary effect of lessening any resulting adverse impact on the adjudicative proceeding. Such responsive statements should be limited to contain only such information as is necessary to mitigate undue prejudice created by the statements made by others.

MODEL CODE COMPARISON:

Rule 3.6 is similar to DR 7–107, except as follows: First, Rule 3.6 adopts the general criteria of "substantial likelihood of materially prejudicing an adjudicative proceeding" to describe impermissible conduct.

Second, Rule 3.6 makes clear that only attorneys who are, or have been involved in a proceeding, or their associates, are subject to the Rule. Third, Rule 3.6 omits the particulars in DR 7–107(b), transforming them instead into an illustrative compilation as part of the Rule's commentary that is intended to give fair notice of the kinds of statements that are generally thought to be more likely than other kinds of statements to pose unacceptable dangers to the fair administration of justice. Whether any statement will have a substantial likelihood of materially prejudicing an adjudicatory proceeding will depend upon the facts of each case. The particulars of DR 7–107(c) are retained in Rule 3.6(b), except DR 7–107(C)(7), which provided that a lawyer may reveal "[a]t the time of seizure, a description of the physical evidence seized, other than a confession, admission or statement." Such revelations may be substantially prejudicial and are frequently the subject of pretrial suppression motions whose success would be undermined by disclosure of the suppressed evidence to the press. Finally, Rule 3.6 authorizes a lawyer to protect a client by making a limited reply to adverse publicity substantially prejudicial to the client.

RULE 3.7 Lawyer as Witness

(a) A lawyer shall not act as advocate at a trial in which the lawyer is likely to be a necessary witness except where:

(1) the testimony relates to an uncontested issue;

(2) the testimony relates to the nature and value of legal services rendered in the case; or

(3) disqualification of the lawyer would work substantial hardship on the client.

(b) A lawyer may act as advocate in a trial in which another lawyer in the lawyer's firm is likely to be called as a witness unless precluded from doing so by rule 1.7 or rule 1.9.

COMMENT:

[1]   Combining the roles of advocate and witness can prejudice the opposing party and can involve a conflict of interest between the lawyer and client.

[2]   The opposing party has proper objection where the combination of roles may prejudice that party's rights in the litigation. A witness is required to testify on the basis of personal knowledge, while an advocate is expected to explain and comment on evidence given by others. It may not be clear whether a statement by an advocate-witness should be taken as proof or as an analysis of the proof.

[3]   Paragraph (a)(1) recognizes that if the testimony will be uncontested, the ambiguities in the dual role are purely theoretical. Paragraph (a)(2) recognizes that where the testimony concerns the extent and value of legal services rendered in the action in which the testimony is offered, permitting the lawyers to testify avoids the need for a second

trial with new counsel to resolve that issue. Moreover, in such a situation the judge has first hand knowledge of the matter in issue; hence, there is less dependence on the adversary process to test the credibility of the testimony.

[4] Apart from these two exceptions, paragraph (a)(3) recognizes that a balancing is required between the interests of the client and those of the opposing party. Whether the opposing party is likely to suffer prejudice depends on the nature of the case, the importance and probable tenor of the lawyer's testimony, and the probability that the lawyer's testimony will conflict with that of other witnesses. Even if there is risk of such prejudice, in determining whether the lawyer should be disqualified due regard must be given to the effect of disqualification on the lawyer's client. It is relevant that one or both parties could reasonably foresee that the lawyer would probably be a witness. The principle of imputed disqualification stated in Rule 1.10 has no application to this aspect of the problem.

[5] Whether the combination of roles involves an improper conflict of interest with respect to the client is determined by Rule 1.7 or 1.9. For example, if there is likely to be substantial conflict between the testimony of the client and that of the lawyer or a member of the lawyer's firm, the representation is improper. The problem can arise whether the lawyer is called as a witness on behalf of the client or is called by the opposing party. Determining whether or not such a conflict exists is primarily the responsibility of the lawyer involved. See Comment to Rule 1.7. If a lawyer who is a member of a firm may not act as both advocate and witness by reason of conflict of interest, Rule 1.10 disqualifies the firm also.

MODEL CODE COMPARISON:

DR 5–102(A) prohibited a lawyer, or the lawyer's firm, from serving as advocate if the lawyer "learns or it is obvious that he or a lawyer in his firm ought to be called as a witness on behalf of his client." DR 5–102(B) provided that a lawyer, and the lawyer's firm, may continue representation if the "lawyer learns or it is obvious that he or a lawyer in his firm may be called as a witness other than on behalf of his client ... until it is apparent that his testimony is or may be prejudicial to his client." DR 5–101(B) permitted a lawyer to testify while representing a client: "(1) If the testimony will relate solely to an uncontested matter; (2) If the testimony will relate solely to a matter of formality and there is no reason to believe that substantial evidence will be offered in opposition to the testimony; (3) If the testimony will relate solely to the nature and value of legal services rendered in the case by the lawyer or his firm to the client; (4) As to any matter if refusal would work a substantial hardship on the client because of the distinctive value of the lawyer or his firm as counsel in the particular case."

The exception stated in paragraph (a)(1) consolidates provisions of DR 5–101(B)(1) and (2). Testimony relating to a formality, referred to in DR 5–101(B)(2), in effect defines the phrase "uncontested issue," and is redundant.

RULE 3.8 Special Responsibilities of a Prosecutor*

The prosecutor in a criminal case shall:

(a) refrain from prosecuting a charge that the prosecutor knows is not supported by probable cause;

(b) make reasonable efforts to assure that the accused has been advised of the right to, and the procedure for obtaining, counsel and has been given reasonable opportunity to obtain counsel;

(c) not seek to obtain from an unrepresented accused a waiver of important pretrial rights, such as the right to a preliminary hearing;

(d) make timely disclosure to the defense of all evidence or information known to the prosecutor that tends to negate the guilt of the accused or mitigates the offense, and, in connection with sentencing, disclose to the defense and to the tribunal all unprivileged mitigating information known to the prosecutor, except when the prosecutor is relieved of this responsibility by a protective order of the tribunal; and

(e) exercise reasonable care to prevent investigators, law enforcement personnel, employees or other persons assisting or associated with the prosecutor in a criminal case from making an extrajudicial statement that the prosecutor would be prohibited from making under rule 3.6.

(f) not subpoena a lawyer in a grand jury or other criminal proceeding to present evidence about a past or present client unless:

(i) the prosecutor reasonably believes:

(1) the information sought is not protected from disclosure by any applicable privilege;

---

* In 1990, the ABA House of Delegates added subparagraph (f) to Model Rule 3.8 to address the profession's concerns over the increased use of subpoenas by prosecutors towards attorneys for information about their clients. The original amendment included a statement limiting the situations in which a prosecutor may subpoena a lawyer in a grand jury or criminal proceeding to cases in which "the prosecutor obtains prior judicial approval after an opportunity for an adversarial hearing." This statement was removed by the House of Delegates in August 1995, because several judicial decisions had invalidated this ABA requirement. Thus, under the current rule, a prosecutor must continue to meet the remaining standards in subparagraph (f) to obtain a subpoena against a criminal defense lawyer; however, the prosecutor does not need to obtain prior court approval.

In August 1994, the ABA added the text in subparagraph (g) to the original Model Rule 3.8. This amendment reflects the changes that the ABA made to Model Rule 3.6 as it applies to prosecutors.

(2) the evidence sought is essential to the successful completion of an ongoing investigation or prosecution;

(3) there is no other feasible alternative to obtain the information.

(g) except for statements that are necessary to inform the public of the nature and extent of the prosecutor's action and that serve a legitimate law enforcement purpose, refrain from making extrajudicial comments that have a substantial likelihood of heightening public condemnation of the accused.

COMMENT:

[1] A prosecutor has the responsibility of a minister of justice and not simply that of an advocate. This responsibility carries with it specific obligations to see that the defendant is accorded procedural justice and that guilt is decided upon the basis of sufficient evidence. Precisely how far the prosecutor is required to go in this direction is a matter of debate and varies in different jurisdictions. Many jurisdictions have adopted the ABA Standards of Criminal Justice Relating to Prosecution Function, which in turn are the product of prolonged and careful deliberation by lawyers experienced in both criminal prosecution and defense. See also Rule 3.3(d), governing ex parte proceedings, among which grand jury proceedings are included. Applicable law may require other measures by the prosecutor and knowing disregard of those obligations or a systematic abuse of prosecutorial discretion could constitute a violation of Rule 8.4.

[2] Paragraph (c) does not apply to an accused appearing pro se with the approval of the tribunal. Nor does it forbid the lawful questioning of a suspect who has knowingly waived the rights to counsel and silence.

[3] The exception in paragraph (d) recognizes that a prosecutor may seek an appropriate protective order from the tribunal if disclosure of information to the defense could result in substantial harm to an individual or to the public interest.

[4]* Paragraph (f) is intended to limit the issuance of lawyer subpoenas in grand jury and other criminal proceedings to those situations in which there is a genuine need to intrude into the client-lawyer relationship.

[5] ** Paragraph (g) supplements Rule 3.6, which prohibits extrajudicial statements that have a substantial likelihood of prejudicing an adjudicatory proceeding. In the context of a criminal prosecution, a

---

* The ABA added paragraph [4] in 1990 when it amended Model Rule 3.8 by adding subparagraph (f). The 1995 amendment to subparagraph (f) deleted the following sentence: "The prosecutor is required to obtain court approval for the issuance of the subpoena after an opportunity for an adversarial hearing is afforded in order to assure an independent determination that the applicable standards are met."

** The ABA added paragraph [5] in 1994 when it amended Model Rule 3.8 by adding subparagraph (g).

prosecutor's extrajudicial statement can create the additional problem of increasing public condemnation of the accused. Although the announcement of an indictment, for example, will necessarily have severe consequences for the accused, a prosecutor can, and should, avoid comments which have no legitimate law enforcement purpose and have a substantial likelihood of increasing public opprobrium of the accused. Nothing in this Comment is intended to restrict the statements which a prosecutor may make which comply with Rule 3.6(b) or 3.6(c).

MODEL CODE COMPARISON:

DR 7–103(A) provided that a "public prosecutor ... shall not institute ... criminal charges when he knows or it is obvious that the charges are not supported by probable cause." DR 7–103(B) provided that "[a] public prosecutor ... shall make timely disclosure ... of the existence of evidence, known to the prosecutor ... that tends to negate the guilt of the accused, mitigate the degree of the offense, or reduce the punishment."

RULE 3.9 Advocate in Nonadjudicative Proceedings

A lawyer representing a client before a legislative or administrative tribunal in a nonadjudicative proceeding shall disclose that the appearance is in a representative capacity and shall conform to the provisions of rules 3.3(a) through (c), 3.4(a) through (c), and 3.5.

COMMENT:

[1] In representation before bodies such as legislatures, municipal councils, and executive and administrative agencies acting in a rule-making or policy-making capacity, lawyers present facts, formulate issues and advance argument in the matters under consideration. The decision-making body, like a court, should be able to rely on the integrity of the submissions made to it. A lawyer appearing before such a body should deal with the tribunal honestly and in conformity with applicable rules of procedure.

[2] Lawyers have no exclusive right to appear before nonadjudicative bodies, as they do before a court. The requirements of this Rule therefore may subject lawyers to regulations inapplicable to advocates who are not lawyers. However, legislatures and administrative agencies have a right to expect lawyers to deal with them as they deal with courts.

[3] This Rule does not apply to representation of a client in a negotiation or other bilateral transaction with a governmental agency; representation in such a transaction is governed by Rules 4.1 through 4.4.

MODEL CODE COMPARISON:

EC 7–15 stated that a lawyer "appearing before an administrative agency, regardless of the nature of the proceeding it is conducting, has the continuing duty to advance the cause of his client within the bounds of the law." EC 7–16 stated that "[w]hen a lawyer appears in connection with proposed legislation, he ... should comply with applicable laws and legislative rules." EC 8–5 stated that "[f]raudulent, deceptive, or otherwise illegal conduct by a participant in a proceeding before a ... legislative body ... should never be participated in ... by lawyers." DR 7–106(B)(1) provided that "[i]n presenting a matter to a tribunal, a lawyer shall disclose ... [u]nless privileged or irrelevant, the identity of the clients he represents and of the persons who employed him."

TRANSACTIONS WITH PERSONS OTHER THAN CLIENTS

RULE 4.1 Truthfulness in Statements to Others *

In the course of representing a client a lawyer shall not knowingly:

(a) make a false statement of material fact or law to a third person; or

(b) fail to disclose a material fact to a third person when disclosure is necessary to avoid assisting a criminal or fraudulent act by a client, unless disclosure is prohibited by rule 1.6.

COMMENT:

Misrepresentation

[1] A lawyer is required to be truthful when dealing with others on a client's behalf, but generally has no affirmative duty to inform an opposing party of relevant facts. A misrepresentation can occur if the lawyer incorporates or affirms a statement of another person that the lawyer knows is false. Misrepresentations can also occur by failure to act.

Statements of Fact

[2] This Rule refers to statements of fact. Whether a particular statement should be regarded as one of fact can depend on the circumstances. Under generally accepted conventions in negotiation, certain types of statements ordinarily are not taken as statements of material fact. Estimates of price or value placed on the subject of a transaction and a party's intentions as to an acceptable settlement of a claim are in this category, and so is the existence of an undisclosed principal except where nondisclosure of the principal would constitute fraud.

Fraud by Client

[3] Paragraph (b) recognizes that substantive law may require a lawyer to disclose certain information to avoid being deemed to have

---

* The Kutak Commission's Revised Final Draft contained substantially different language on the interaction of Rules 1.6 and 4.1: "The duties stated in this Rule apply even if compliance requires disclosure of information otherwise protected by Rule 1.6." Proposed Model Rule 4.1(b) (Revised Final Draft) (June 20, 1982).

assisted the client's crime or fraud. The requirement of disclosure created by this paragraph is, however, subject to the obligations created by Rule 1.6.

MODEL CODE COMPARISON:

Paragraph (a) is substantially similar to DR 7–102(A)(5), which stated that "[i]n his representation of a client, a lawyer shall not ... [k]nowingly make a false statement of law or fact."

With regard to paragraph (b), DR 7–102(A)(3) provided that a lawyer shall not "[c]onceal or knowingly fail to disclose that which he is required by law to reveal."

RULE 4.2 Communication With Person Represented by Counsel*

In representing a client, a lawyer shall not communicate about the subject of the representation with a person the lawyer knows to be represented by another lawyer in the matter, unless the lawyer has the consent of the other lawyer or is authorized by law to do so.

COMMENT:†

[1] This Rule does not prohibit communication with a represented person, or an employee or agent of such a person, concerning matters outside the representation. For example, the existence of a controversy between a government agency and a private party, or between two organizations, does not prohibit a lawyer for either from communicating with nonlawyer representatives of the other regarding a separate matter. Also, parties to a matter may communicate directly with each other and a lawyer having independent justification for communicating with the other party is permitted to do so. Communications authorized by law include, for example, the right of a party to a controversy with a government agency to speak with government officials about the matter.

---

* In August 1995, the ABA House of Delegates amended Model Rule 4.2 to substitute the word "person" for the word "party" so as to clarify that the rule applies to situations where a lawyer seeks to contact a represented individual in pre-litigation or pre-custodial settings as well or when a lawyer seeks to contact a non-party such as an informant or undercover agent who is represented by counsel.

† The ABA's amendment of Rule 4.2 in August 1995 included a substantial revision of the comments: (1) to clarify that knowledge of the fact that a person is represented by counsel may be inferred from the circumstances; (2) to elaborate on the situations in which the communication with represented persons is authorized by law; (3) to make clear that the rule applies to persons represented by counsel in all matters (for example, contract or negotiation matters) and not just to parties in formal proceedings; and (4) to cross reference discussions of situations where the person is not represented by counsel to Model Rule 4.3. Comments 2, 5, and 6 are added in this amendment. Comments 1, 3, and 4 are based upon prior comments and rewritten to reflect the clarifications discussed above.

[2]   Communications authorized by law also include constitutionally permissible investigative activities of lawyers representing governmental entities, directly or through investigative agents, prior to the commencement of criminal or civil enforcement proceedings, when there is applicable judicial precedent that either has found the activity permissible under this Rule or has found this Rule inapplicable.   However, the Rule imposes ethical restrictions that go beyond those imposed by constitutional provisions.

[3]   This rule applies to communications with any person, whether or not a party to a formal adjudicative proceeding, contract or negotiation, who is represented by counsel concerning the matter to which the communication relates.

[4]   In the case of an organization, this Rule prohibits communications by a lawyer for another person or entity concerning the matter in representation with persons having a managerial responsibility on behalf of the organization, and with any other person whose act or omission in connection with that matter may be imputed to the organization for purposes of civil or criminal liability or whose statement may constitute an admission on the part of the organization.   If an agent or employee of the organization is represented in the matter by his or her own counsel, the consent by that counsel to a communication will be sufficient for purposes of this Rule.   Compare Rule 3.4(f).

[5]   The prohibition on communications with a represented person only applies, however, in circumstances where the lawyer knows that the person is in fact represented in the matter to be discussed.   This means that the lawyer has actual knowledge of the fact of the representation; but such actual knowledge may be inferred from the circumstances.   See Terminology.   Such an inference may arise in circumstances where there is substantial reason to believe that the person with whom communication is sought is represented in the matter to be discussed.   Thus, a lawyer cannot evade the requirement of obtaining the consent of counsel by closing eyes to the obvious.

[6]   In the event the person with whom the lawyer communicates is not known to be represented by counsel in the matter, the lawyer's communications are subject to Rule 4.3.

MODEL CODE COMPARISON:

This Rule is substantially identical to DR 7–104(A)(1).

RULE 4.3   Dealing With Unrepresented Person

In dealing on behalf of a client with a person who is not represented by counsel, a lawyer shall not state or imply that the lawyer is disinterested.   When the lawyer knows or reasonably should know that the unrepresented person misunderstands the lawyer's role in the matter, the lawyer shall make reasonable efforts to correct the misunderstanding.

COMMENT:

An unrepresented person, particularly one not experienced in dealing with legal matters, might assume that a lawyer is disinterested in loyalties or is a disinterested authority on the law even when the lawyer represents a client. During the course of a lawyer's representation of a client, the lawyer should not give advice to an unrepresented person other than the advice to obtain counsel.

MODEL CODE COMPARISON:

There was no direct counterpart to this Rule in the Model Code. DR 7–104(A)(2) provided that a lawyer shall not "[g]ive advice to a person who is not represented by a lawyer, other than the advice to secure counsel. . . ."

RULE 4.4   Respect for Rights of Third Persons

In representing a client, a lawyer shall not use means that have no substantial purpose other than to embarrass, delay, or burden a third person, or use methods of obtaining evidence that violate the legal rights of such a person.

COMMENT:

Responsibility to a client requires a lawyer to subordinate the interests of others to those of the client, but that responsibility does not imply that a lawyer may disregard the rights of third persons. It is impractical to catalogue all such rights, but they include legal restrictions on methods of obtaining evidence from third persons.

MODEL CODE COMPARISON:

DR 7–106(C)(2) provided that a lawyer shall not "[a]sk any question that he has no reasonable basis to believe is relevant to the case and that is intended to degrade a witness or other person." DR 7–102(A)(1) provided that a lawyer shall not "take . . . action on behalf of his client when he knows or when it is obvious that such action would serve merely to harass or maliciously injure another." DR 7–108(D) provided that "[a]fter discharge of the jury . . . the lawyer shall not ask questions or make comments to a member of that jury that are calculated merely to harass or embarrass the juror. . . ." DR 7–108(E) provided that a lawyer "shall not conduct . . . a vexatious or harassing investigation of either a venireman or a juror."

LAW FIRMS AND ASSOCIATIONS

RULE 5.1   Responsibilities of a Partner or Supervisory Lawyer

(a) A partner in a law firm shall make reasonable efforts to ensure that the firm has in effect measures giving reasonable assurance that all lawyers in the firm conform to the rules of professional conduct.

(b) A lawyer having direct supervisory authority over another lawyer shall make reasonable efforts to ensure that the other lawyer conforms to the rules of professional conduct.

(c) A lawyer shall be responsible for another lawyer's violation of the rules of professional conduct if:

(1) the lawyer orders or, with knowledge of the specific conduct, ratifies the conduct involved; or

(2) the lawyer is a partner in the law firm in which the other lawyer practices, or has direct supervisory authority over the other lawyer, and knows of the conduct at a time when its consequences can be avoided or mitigated but fails to take reasonable remedial action.

COMMENT:

[1] Paragraphs (a) and (b) refer to lawyers who have supervisory authority over the professional work of a firm or legal department of a government agency. This includes members of a partnership and the shareholders in a law firm organized as a professional corporation; lawyers having supervisory authority in the law department of an enterprise or government agency; and lawyers who have intermediate managerial responsibilities in a firm.

[2] The measures required to fulfill the responsibility prescribed in paragraphs (a) and (b) can depend on the firm's structure and the nature of its practice. In a small firm, informal supervision and occasional admonition ordinarily might be sufficient. In a large firm, or in practice situations in which intensely difficult ethical problems frequently arise, more elaborate procedures may be necessary. Some firms, for example, have a procedure whereby junior lawyers can make confidential referral of ethical problems directly to a designated senior partner or special committee. See Rule 5.2. Firms, whether large or small, may also rely on continuing legal education in professional ethics. In any event, the ethical atmosphere of a firm can influence the conduct of all its members and a lawyer having authority over the work of another may not assume that the subordinate lawyer will inevitably conform to the Rules.

[3] Paragraph (c)(1) expresses a general principle of responsibility for acts of another. See also Rule 8.4(a).

[4] Paragraph (c)(2) defines the duty of a lawyer having direct supervisory authority over performance of specific legal work by another lawyer. Whether a lawyer has such supervisory authority in particular circumstances is a question of fact. Partners of a private firm have at least indirect responsibility for all work being done by the firm, while a partner in charge of a particular matter ordinarily has direct authority over other firm lawyers engaged in the matter. Appropriate remedial action by a partner would depend on the immediacy of the partner's involvement and the seriousness of the misconduct. The supervisor is required to intervene to prevent avoidable consequences of misconduct if the supervisor knows that the misconduct occurred. Thus, if a supervis-

ing lawyer knows that a subordinate misrepresented a matter to an opposing party in negotiation, the supervisor as well as the subordinate has a duty to correct the resulting misapprehension.

[5]   Professional misconduct by a lawyer under supervision could reveal a violation of paragraph (b) on the part of the supervisory lawyer even though it does not entail a violation of paragraph (c) because there was no direction, ratification or knowledge or the violation.

[6]   Apart from this Rule and Rule 8.4(a), a lawyer does not have disciplinary liability for the conduct of a partner, associate or subordinate.   Whether a lawyer may be liable civilly or criminally for another lawyer's conduct is a question of law beyond the scope of these Rules.

MODEL CODE COMPARISON:

There was no direct counterpart to this Rule in the Model Code. DR 1–103(A) provided that a lawyer "possessing unprivileged knowledge of a violation of DR 1–102 shall report such knowledge to … authority empowered to investigate or act upon such violation."

RULE 5.2   Responsibilities of a Subordinate Lawyer

(a) A lawyer is bound by the rules of professional conduct notwithstanding that the lawyer acted at the direction of another person.

(b) A subordinate lawyer does not violate the rules of professional conduct if that lawyer acts in accordance with a supervisory lawyer's reasonable resolution of an arguable question of professional duty.

COMMENT:

[1]   Although a lawyer is not relieved of responsibility for a violation by the fact that the lawyer acted at the direction of a supervisor, that fact may be relevant in determining whether a lawyer had the knowledge required to render conduct a violation of the Rules.   For example, if a subordinate filed a frivolous pleading at the direction of a supervisor, the subordinate would not be guilty of a professional violation unless the subordinate knew of the document's frivolous character.

[2]   When lawyers in a supervisor-subordinate relationship encounter a matter involving professional judgment as to ethical duty, the supervisor may assume responsibility for making the judgment.   Otherwise a consistent course of action or position could not be taken.   If the question can reasonably be answered only one way, the duty of both lawyers is clear and they are equally responsible for fulfilling it.   However, if the question is reasonably arguable, someone has to decide upon the course of action.   That authority ordinarily reposes in the supervisor, and a subordinate may be guided accordingly.   For example, if a question arises whether the interests of two clients conflict under Rule 1.7, the supervisor's reasonable resolution of the question should protect

the subordinate professionally if the resolution is subsequently challenged.

MODEL CODE COMPARISON:

There was no counterpart to this Rule in the Model Code.

RULE 5.3 Responsibilities Regarding Nonlawyer Assistants

With respect to a nonlawyer employed or retained by or associated with a lawyer:

(a) a partner in a law firm shall make reasonable efforts to ensure that the firm has in effect measures giving reasonable assurance that the person's conduct is compatible with the professional obligations of the lawyer;

(b) a lawyer having direct supervisory authority over the nonlawyer shall make reasonable efforts to ensure that the person's conduct is compatible with the professional obligations of the lawyer; and

(c) a lawyer shall be responsible for conduct of such a person that would be a violation of the rules of professional conduct if engaged in by a lawyer if:

(1) the lawyer orders or, with the knowledge of the specific conduct, ratifies the conduct involved; or

(2) the lawyer is a partner in the law firm in which the person is employed, or has direct supervisory authority over the person, and knows of the conduct at a time when its consequences can be avoided or mitigated but fails to take reasonable remedial action.

COMMENT:

Lawyers generally employ assistants in their practice, including secretaries, investigators, law student interns, and paraprofessionals. Such assistants, whether employees or independent contractors, act for the lawyer in rendition of the lawyer's professional services. A lawyer should give such assistants appropriate instruction and supervision concerning the ethical aspects of their employment, particularly regarding the obligation not to disclose information relating to representation of the client, and should be responsible for their work product. The measures employed in supervising nonlawyers should take account of the fact that they do not have legal training and are not subject to professional discipline.

MODEL CODE COMPARISON:

There was no direct counterpart to this Rule in the Model Code. DR 4–101(D) provided that a lawyer "shall exercise reasonable care to prevent his employees, associates, and others whose services are utilized by him from disclosing or using confidences or secrets of a client...." DR 7–107(J) provided that "[a] lawyer shall exercise reasonable care to prevent his employees and associates from making an extrajudicial statement that he would be prohibited from making under DR 7–107.''

RULE 5.4   Professional Independence of a Lawyer*

(a) **A lawyer or law firm shall not share legal fees with a nonlawyer, except that:**

(1) **an agreement by a lawyer with the lawyer's firm, partner, or associate may provide for the payment of money, over a reasonable period of time after the lawyer's death, to the lawyer's estate or to one or more specified persons;**

(2) **a lawyer who purchases the practice of a deceased, disabled, or disappeared lawyer may, pursuant to the provisions of Rule 1.17, pay to the estate or other representative of that lawyer the agreed-upon purchase price; and**

(3) **a lawyer or law firm may include nonlawyer employees in a compensation or retirement plan, even though the plan is based in whole or in part on a profit-sharing arrangement.**

(b) **A lawyer shall not form a partnership with a nonlawyer if any of the activities of the partnership consist of the practice of law.**

(c) **A lawyer shall not permit a person who recommends, employs, or pays the lawyer to render legal services for another to direct or regulate the lawyer's professional judgment in rendering such legal services.**

(d) **A lawyer shall not practice with or in the form of a professional corporation or association authorized to practice law for a profit, if:**

(1) **a nonlawyer owns any interest therein, except that a fiduciary representative of the estate of a lawyer may hold the stock or interest of the lawyer for a reasonable time during administration;**

(2) **a nonlawyer is a corporate director or officer thereof; or**

* In 1990, the ABA amended the text of Model Rule 5.4(a)(2) to recognize the addition of Model Rule 1.17 on the sale of a law practice. The original Model Rule 5.4(a)(2) read as follows:

RULE   5.4   Professional   Independence of a Lawyer

(a) A lawyer or law firm shall not share legal fees with a nonlawyer, except that:

* * *

(2) a lawyer who undertakes to complete unfinished legal business of a deceased lawyer may pay to the estate of the deceased lawyer that proportion of the total compensation which fairly represents the services rendered by the deceased lawyer; and

* * *

(3) a nonlawyer has the right to direct or control the professional judgment of a lawyer.

COMMENT:

The provisions of this Rule express traditional limitations on sharing fees. These limitations are to protect the lawyer's professional independence of judgment. Where someone other than the client pays the lawyer's fee or salary, or recommends employment of the lawyer, that arrangement does not modify the lawyer's obligation to the client. As stated in paragraph (c), such arrangements should not interfere with the lawyer's professional judgment.

MODEL CODE COMPARISON:

Paragraph (a) is substantially identical to DR 3–102(A).
Paragraph (b) is substantially identical to DR 3–103(A).
Paragraph (c) is substantially identical to DR 5–107(B).
Paragraph (d) is substantially identical to DR 5–107(C).

RULE 5.5   Unauthorized Practice of Law

A lawyer shall not:

(a) practice law in a jurisdiction where doing so violates the regulation of the legal profession in that jurisdiction; or

(b) assist a person who is not a member of the bar in the performance of activity that constitutes the unauthorized practice of law.

COMMENT:

The definition of the practice of law is established by law and varies from one jurisdiction to another. Whatever the definition, limiting the practice of law to members of the bar protects the public against rendition of legal services by unqualified persons. Paragraph (b) does not prohibit a lawyer from employing the services of paraprofessionals and delegating functions to them, so long as the lawyer supervises the delegated work and retains responsibility for their work. See Rule 5.3. Likewise, it does not prohibit lawyers from providing professional advice and instruction to nonlawyers whose employment requires knowledge of law; for example, claims adjusters, employees of financial or commercial institutions, social workers, accountants and persons employed in government agencies. In addition, a lawyer may counsel nonlawyers who wish to proceed pro se.

MODEL CODE COMPARISON:

With regard to paragraph (a), DR 3–101(B) of the Model Code provided that "[a] lawyer shall not practice law in a jurisdiction where to do so would be in violation of regulations of the profession in that jurisdiction."

With regard to paragraph (b), DR 3–101(A) of the Model Code provided that "[a] lawyer shall not aid a non-lawyer in the unauthorized practice of law."

RULE 5.6   Restrictions on Right to Practice

A lawyer shall not participate in offering or making:

(a) a partnership or employment agreement that restricts the rights of a lawyer to practice after termination of the relationship, except an agreement concerning benefits upon retirement; or

(b) an agreement in which a restriction on the lawyer's right to practice is part of the settlement of a controversy between private parties.

COMMENT:

[1]   An agreement restricting the right of partners or associates to practice after leaving a firm not only limits their professional autonomy but also limits the freedom of clients to choose a lawyer. Paragraph (a) prohibits such agreements except for restrictions incident to provisions concerning retirement benefits for service with the firm.

[2]   Paragraph (b) prohibits a lawyer from agreeing not to represent other persons in connection with settling a claim on behalf of a client.

[3] *   This Rule does not apply to prohibit restrictions that may be included in the terms of the sale of a law practice pursuant to Rule 1.17.

MODEL CODE COMPARISON:

This Rule is substantially similar to DR 2–108.

RULE 5.7   Responsibilities Regarding Law–Related Services†

(a) A lawyer shall be subject to the Rules of Professional Conduct with respect to the provision of law-related services, as defined in paragraph (b), if the law-related services are provided:

(1) by the lawyer in circumstances that are not distinct from the lawyer's provision of legal services to clients; or

(2) by a separate entity controlled by the lawyer individually or with others if the lawyer fails to take reasonable measures to assure that a person obtaining the law-related services knows that the services of the separate entity are not legal services and that the protections of the client-lawyer relationship do not exist.

---

* This paragraph was added by the ABA in 1990 to resolve the potential overlap between this provision and the restrictions placed in Model Rule 1.17 regarding the sale of a law practice.

† See footnote a, page 99 infra, for text and comment to former Rule 5.7, Provision of Ancillary Services (Repealed).

(b) The term "law-related services" denotes services that might reasonably be performed in conjunction with and in substance are related to the provision of legal services, and that are not prohibited as unauthorized practice of law when provided by a nonlawyer.

COMMENT:

[1] When a lawyer performs law-related services or controls an organization that does so, there exists the potential for ethical problems. Principal among these is the possibility that the person for whom the law-related services are performed fails to understand that the services may not carry with them the protections normally afforded as part of the client-lawyer relationship. The recipient of the law-related services may expect, for example, that the protection of client confidences, prohibitions against representation of persons with conflicting interests, and obligations of a lawyer to maintain professional independence apply to the provision of law-related services when that may not be the case. Rule 5.7 applies to the provision of law-related services by a lawyer even when the lawyer does not provide any legal services to the person for whom the law-related services are performed. The Rule identifies the circumstances in which all of the Rules of Professional Conduct apply to the provision of law-related services. Even when those circumstances do not exist, however, the conduct of a lawyer involved in the provision of law-related services is subject to those Rules that apply generally to lawyer conduct, regardless of whether the conduct involves the provision of legal services. See, e.g., Rule 8.4.

[2] When law-related services are provided by a lawyer under circumstances that are not distinct from the lawyer's provision of legal services to clients, the lawyer in providing the law-related services must adhere to the requirements of the Rules of Professional Conduct as provided in Rule 5.7(a)(1).

[3] Law-related services also may be provided through an entity that is distinct from that through which the lawyer provides legal services. If the lawyer individually or with others has control of such an entity's operations, the Rule requires the lawyer to take reasonable measures to assure that each person using the services of the entity knows that the services provided by the entity are not legal services and that the Rules of Professional Conduct that relate to the client-lawyer relationship do not apply. A lawyer's control of an entity extends to the ability to direct its operation. Whether a lawyer has such control will depend upon the circumstances of the particular case.

[4] When a client-lawyer relationship exists with a person who is referred by a lawyer to a separate law-related service entity controlled by the lawyer, individually or with others, the lawyer must comply with Rule 1.8(a).

[5] In taking the reasonable measures referred to in paragraph (a)(2) to assure that a person using law-related services understands the

practical effect or significance of the inapplicability of the Rules of Professional Conduct, the lawyer should communicate to the person receiving the law-related services, in a manner sufficient to assure that the person understands the significance of the fact, that the relationship of the person to the business entity will not be a client-lawyer relationship. The communication should be made before entering into an agreement for provision of or providing law-related services, and preferably should be in writing.

[6] The burden is upon the lawyer to show that the lawyer has taken reasonable measures under the circumstances to communicate the desired understanding. For instance, a sophisticated user of law-related services, such as a publicly held corporation, may require a lesser explanation than someone unaccustomed to making distinctions between legal services and law-related services, such as an individual seeking tax advice from a lawyer-accountant or investigative services in connection with a lawsuit.

[7] Regardless of the sophistication of potential recipients of law-related services, a lawyer should take special care to keep separate the provision of law-related and legal services in order to minimize the risk that the recipient will assume that the law-related services are legal services. The risk of such confusion is especially acute when the lawyer renders both types of services with respect to the same matter. Under some circumstances the legal and law-related services may be so closely entwined that they cannot be distinguished from each other, and the requirement of disclosure and consultation imposed by paragraph (a)(2) of the Rule cannot be met. In such a case a lawyer will be responsible for assuring that both the lawyer's conduct and, to the extent required by Rule 5.3, that of nonlawyer employees in the distinct entity which the lawyer controls complies in all respects with the Rules of Professional Conduct.

[8] A broad range of economic and other interests of clients may be served by lawyers' engaging in the delivery of law-related services. Examples of law-related services include providing title insurance, financial planning, accounting, trust services, real estate counseling, legislative lobbying, economic analysis social work, psychological counseling, tax return preparation, and patient, medical or environmental consulting. When a lawyer is obliged to accord the recipients of such services the protections of those Rules that apply to the client-lawyer relationship, the lawyer must take special care to heed the proscriptions of the Rules addressing conflict of interest (Rules 1.7 through 1.11, especially Rules 1.7(b) and 1.8(a), (b) and (f)), and to scrupulously adhere to the requirements of Rule 1.6 relating to disclosure of confidential information. The promotion of the law-related services must also in all respects comply with Rules 7.1 through 7.3, dealing with advertising and solicitation. In that regard, lawyers should take special care to identify the obligations that may be imposed as a result of a jurisdiction's decisional law.

[9] When the full protections of all of the Rules of Professional Conduct do not apply to the provision of law-related services, principles of law external to the Rules, for example, the law of principal and agent, govern the legal duties owed to those receiving the services. Those other legal principles may establish a different degree of protection for the recipient with respect to confidentiality of information, conflicts of interest and permissible business relationships with clients. See also Rule 8.4 (Misconduct).

a. Model Rule 5.7 did not appear in the original version of the Model Rules. In 1991, the ABA added the provision reproduced in this footnote and its comments in response to the debate created by the adoption of the District of Columbia rule that allows lawyers and non-lawyers to practice together in the same law firm. D.C. Rule 5.4 is contained on pages 200–203. Model Rule 5.7 was passed by a vote of 197 to 186 in the House of Delegates.

In the August 1992 ABA meeting, the House of Delegates voted 190 to 183 to repeal the provision reproduced in this footnote. In February 1994, the ABA passed a new rule dealing with ancillary services. The short-lived Model Rule 5.7 text and comment are reprinted below:

(a) A lawyer shall not practice law in a law firm which owns a controlling interest in, or operates, an entity which provides non-legal services which are ancillary to the practice of law, or otherwise provides such ancillary non-legal services, except as provided in paragraph (b).

(b) A lawyer may practice law in a law firm which provides non-legal services which are ancillary to the practice of law if:

(1) The ancillary services are provided solely to clients of the law firm and are incidental to, in connection with and concurrent to, the provision of legal services by the law firm to such clients;

(2) Such ancillary services are provided solely by employees of the law firm itself and not by a subsidiary or other affiliate of the law firm;

(3) The law firm makes appropriate disclosure in writing to its clients; and

(4) The law firm does not hold itself out as engaging in any non-legal activities except in conjunction with the provision of legal services, as provided in this rule.

(c) One or more lawyers who engage in the practice of law in a law firm shall neither own a controlling interest in, nor operate, an entity which provides non-legal services which are ancillary to the practice of law, nor otherwise provide such ancillary non-legal services, except that their firms may provide such services as provided in paragraph (b).

(d) Two or more lawyers who engage in the practice of law in separate law firms shall neither own a controlling interest in, nor operate, an entity which provides non-legal services which are ancillary to the practice of law, nor otherwise provide such ancillary non-legal services.

COMMENT:

General

[1] For many years, lawyers have provided to their clients non-legal services which are ancillary to the practice of law. Such services included title insurance, trust services and patent consulting. In most instances, these ancillary nonlegal services were provided to law firm clients in connection with, and concurrent to, the provision of legal services by the lawyer or law firm. The provision of such services afforded benefits to clients, including making available a greater range of services from one source and maintaining technical expertise in various fields within a law firm. However, the provision of both legal and ancillary nonlegal

services raises ethical concerns, including conflicts of interest, confusion on the part of clients and possible loss (or inapplicability) of the attorney-client privilege, which may not have been addressed adequately by the other Model Rules of Professional Conduct.

[2] Eventually, law firms began to form affiliates, largely staffed by nonlawyers, to provide ancillary nonlegal services to both clients and customers who were not clients for legal services. In addition to exacerbating the ethical problems of conflicts of interest, confusion and threats to confidentiality, the large-scale movement of law firms into ancillary nonlegal businesses raised serious professionalism concerns, including compromising lawyers' independent judgment, the loss of the bar's right to self-regulation and the provision of legal services by entities controlled by nonlawyers.

[3] Rule 5.7 addresses both the ethical and professionalism concerns implicated by the provision of ancillary nonlegal services by lawyers and law firms. It preserves the ability of lawyers to provide additional services to their clients and maintain within the law firm a broad range of technical expertise. However, Rule 5.7 restricts the ability of law firms to provide ancillary nonlegal services through affiliates to nonclient customers and clients alike, the rendition of which raises serious ethical and professionalism concerns.

Limitations on the Provision of Nonlegal Services Which Are Ancillary to the Practice of Law

[4] Paragraph (a) attempts to forestall the ethical and professional concerns which are raised when law firms own or operate nonlegal businesses which are ancillary to the practice of law or otherwise provide such services. The provision of such ancillary services by law firms has the potential of compromising a lawyer's independent professional judgment and otherwise causing harm to law firm clients (*e.g.*, creating conflicts of interest, jeopardizing clients' expectations of confidentiality and causing confusion on the part of clients). Additionally, serious threats to lawyers' professionalism are

also posed when law firms own or operate ancillary businesses which provide services to persons who are not concurrently seeking legal services from the law firm.

[5] Paragraph (a) prohibits lawyers from practicing in a law firm which owns a controlling interest in, or operates, an entity which provides nonlegal services which are ancillary to the practice of law, or which provides such ancillary services from within the law firm, unless such services are incidental to the law firm's provision of legal services as set forth in Paragraph (b).

[6] The term "nonlegal services which are ancillary to the practice of law" refers to those services which satisfy all or most of the following indicia: (1) are provided to clients of a law firm (or customers of a business owned or controlled by a law firm); (2) clearly do not constitute the practice of law; (3) are readily available from those not licensed to practice law; (4) are functionally connected to the provision of legal services, i.e., services which are often sought or needed in connection with (and in addition to) legal services; (5) involve intellectual ability or learning; and (6) have the potential for creating serious ethical problems in the lawyer-client relationship, such as compromising the independent professional judgment of lawyers; creating conflicts of interest; threatening the clients' (or customers') expectations of confidentiality and/or causing confusion on the part of clients or customers.

[7] Among those activities which are not included in the term "nonlegal services which are ancillary to the practice of law" because they do not pose serious ethical problems in the lawyer-client relationship are:

(1) law firms or lawyers owning, for example, restaurants, shops or taxi services (since these services are not functionally connected to the practice of law);

(2) law firms providing copying services or other clerical services incidental to the practice of law;

(3) law firms owning and managing the buildings in which their offices are

located or other property (since owning and managing property—even through a subsidiary or affiliate—is not functionally connected to the provision of legal services to clients);

(4) a law firm providing services or products intended for use by other lawyers, such as publications, software programs, or legal malpractice insurance (since such services or products are not functionally connected to the provision of legal services to clients);

(5) lawyers serving as fiduciaries of trusts or corporate directors or lawyers serving in quasi-judicial positions such as mediators or arbitrators.

[8] When services provided by a law firm are performed by nonlawyers, there should be an initial presumption that the services do not constitute the practice of law and may be a "nonlegal service which is ancillary to the practice of law." In addition, a presumption that a service is "ancillary to the practice of law" should exist if the service is normally provided by nonlawyers in discrete professions or occupations, e.g., doctors, architects, engineers, real estate brokers, investment bankers or financial consultants.

[9] Note that Paragraph (a) does not prohibit a lawyer from practicing in a law firm which acquires a passive financial interest in an entity which provides nonlegal ancillary services (i.e., purchasing shares of an investment banking firm or a consulting company), provided that the interest is not a controlling one. This rule does not define the concept of control, which is generally a fact-based inquiry dependent on the particular facts and circumstances. However, the existence of an ownership interest by lawyers in other entities (especially clients) may implicate conflict of interest concerns (see Model Rules of Professional Conduct 1.7 and 1.8) and may require disclosure by the lawyers pursuant to these rules.

Connection Between the Provision of Legal and Ancillary Nonlegal Services

[10] Paragraph (b) preserves the ability of law firms to provide nonlegal services which are ancillary to the practice of law, but under conditions designed to ensure that such services are closely re-lated to the firms' provision of legal services and not independent of, and unrelated to, such legal services.

[11] Subsection (1) of Paragraph (b) requires that ancillary nonlegal services be provided solely to law firm clients (as opposed to persons who are not currently seeking legal services from a law firm) and be incidental to, in connection with, and concurrent to, the provision of legal services by the law firm. The requirement that ancillary services be "incidental to" and "in connection with" the firm's provision of legal services seeks to ensure that any nonlegal services be secondary to, strictly related to, and under the supervision of those responsible for, the provision of legal services.

[12] Paragraph (b) permits law firms to employ the services of other professionals if their services are connected to the firm's provision of legal services. For example, an architect on staff at a law firm would be permitted to help clients and lawyers understand the technical issues in a construction contract negotiation, a building accident litigation or the like. However, the requirement in Paragraph (b) that such services be "incidental to" and "in connection with" the provision of legal services would proscribe a law firm from employing architects to design buildings for law firm clients or for nonclient customers who do not use the law firm's legal services. Similarly, an investment banker on staff at a law firm would be permitted to assist lawyers in the negotiation of a transaction or the litigation of valuation issues or the like, as well as to consult with law firm clients when the firm is providing legal services to them, but a law firm would be prohibited from employing investment bankers to seek out acquisitions, sell securities (or otherwise secure financing) or perform other investment banking services unrelated to a pending legal representation. Likewise, a corporation pursuing an acquisition might need the assistance of nonlawyer lobbyists before a state legislature considering anti-takeover legislation. Such lobbying designed to forestall (or attain) a change in the law, if provided by nonlawyers within a law firm, could rea-

sonably be construed to be incidental to the firm's provision of legal services.

[13] Paragraph (b) also requires that the provision of nonlegal services be concurrent with the provision of legal services. In essence, law firm clients (like nonlegal services customers generally) may not obtain ancillary nonlegal services from the law firm (e.g., investment banking services or medical tests), and the firm may not provide them, at a time when the client is not obtaining legal services from the law firm on a related matter.

Provision of Ancillary Nonlegal Services by Employees of Law Firms

[14] Subsection (2) of Paragraph (b), in an effort to vitiate risks of compromise to lawyers' professional judgment, conflicts of interest, client confusion and potential loss of confidentiality, provides that any ancillary services provided by a law firm must be performed within the law firm by employees of the law firm itself (who work together with, and are supervised by, the firm's lawyers), and not through a subsidiary or affiliate of the law firm. This requirement closely unites the provision of legal and nonlegal services under the supervision of lawyers and thereby affords lawyers the opportunity to ensure that their nonlawyer employees are acting responsibly and in accordance with the rules of legal ethics. Such a requirement minimizes the risks of nonlegal employees either providing advice with which the firm's lawyers will disagree and/or engaging in improper behavior for which the firm's lawyers would be responsible. In addition, structuring the provision of nonlegal services in such a way forestalls confusion on the part of clients as to whether the nonlegal services are provided subject to the limitations of the Model Rules (and will prevent lawyers from seeking to provide services outside of the protections afforded to clients by the Model Rules). Finally, if lawyers are present (or otherwise involved) in the provision of nonlegal services ancillary to the practice of law, there is a greater likelihood that client confidences will be protected and a client will be able to maintain evidentiary privileges with respect to communications made by the client to the providers of nonlegal ancillary services. Paragraph (b)(2) is not designed to limit the ability of lawyers to retain outside (i.e., nonaffiliated) consultants such as experts, private investigators or accountants to help them provide legal services to clients.

Disclosure Requirements Relating to the Provision of Ancillary Nonlegal Services

[15] Subsection (3) of Paragraph (b) requires that before providing ancillary services to a client, a law firm must comply with appropriate disclosure requirements (as mandated in Model Rule of Professional Conduct 1.8, relevant case law and other authorities) and fully disclose in writing the firm's interest in the providers of nonlegal services employed by the firm and the potential conflicts of interest inherent in the provision of such services. The law firm should also consider, in appropriate circumstances, recommending that the client seek the advice of independent counsel (or independent providers of nonlegal services) before obtaining nonlegal services from the firm.

Representations Concerning Ancillary and Nonlegal Services

[16] Subsection (4) of Paragraph (b) ensures that when law firms deal with clients (whether prospective or actual) or the public, they do not represent themselves as providing any ancillary nonlegal services independent of the firm's provision of legal services. This proscription attempts to obviate the risks of confusion on the part of clients and the public, actual or apparent overreaching by attorneys and improper solicitation. It ensures that clients and the public are aware that they are dealing with a law firm and can therefore assume that representatives of the firm are bound by the rules of legal ethics; prospective or actual clients do not feel compelled to use the firm's ancillary services; and law firms do not engage in improper solicitation by seeking business for the firm's nonlegal services with an expectation that these nonlegal services will serve as a "feeder" for the firm's legal services. Paragraph (b)(4) also seeks to preserve the unique

and independent status of the legal profession in the public's perception by preventing law firms from representing themselves to clients and the public as multidisciplinary conglomerates or otherwise emphasizing their nonlegal activities.

[17] Paragraph (b)(4) is not intended to preclude law firms from making the existence of their nonlegal business known to clients who have retained the firm for legal services, and who, in the attorney's opinion, might have a need for the firm's ancillary services in addition to legal services (subject to appropriate disclosure requirements). In addition, Paragraph (b)(4) is not intended to prevent individual lawyers from indicating that they are qualified or licensed in other professions, e.g., accounting, where relevant jurisdictions so permit.

Provision of Ancillary Nonlegal Services By One or More Lawyers in a Law Firm

[18] Paragraph (c) prevents one or more lawyers in a single law firm from owning or operating an entity which provides nonlegal services which are ancillary to the practice of law. Paragraph (c) attempts to prevent lawyers or law firms from circumventing the restrictions on law firm ownership and operation of ancillary businesses by vesting ownership not in the entire law firm, but in one or more of the attorneys in a law firm. The ethical and professional concerns inherent in the ownership of ancillary businesses are not vitiated when ownership or operation is vested in several partners in a law firm (as opposed to an entire law firm). However, a law firm itself may provide such ancillary nonlegal services in accordance with Paragraph (b).

Provision of Ancillary Nonlegal Services by Lawyers from Different Law Firms

[19] Paragraph (d) addresses the concerns which may result when lawyers in separate law firms own or operate an entity which provides nonlegal services which are ancillary to the practice of law. The ethical and professional concerns inherent in the ownership and operation of such ancillary businesses by law firms (or one or more lawyers in a firm) are also present (or may be exacerbated) when lawyers in different firms own or operate such businesses.

MODEL CODE COMPARISON

There was no counterpart to this Rule in the Model Code.

PUBLIC SERVICE

RULE 6.1 Voluntary Pro Bono Publico Service *

A lawyer should aspire to render at least (50) hours of pro bono publico legal services per year. In fulfilling this responsibility, the lawyer should:

* In February 1993, the ABA House of Delegates replaced the original version of Model Rule 6.1 with an aspirational plea for 50 hours a year from each lawyer. The amended language also seeks to direct lawyers to provide pro bono services to the economically disadvantaged rather than to charitable and nonprofit organizations. The new rule was adopted by a vote of 228 to 215. The following represents the original text of Model Rule 6.1 and its comments:

RULE 6.1 Pro Bono Publico Service

A lawyer should render public interest legal service. A lawyer may discharge this responsibility by providing professional services at no fee or a reduced fee to persons of limited means or to public service or charitable groups or organizations, by service in activities for improving the law, the legal system or the legal profession, and by financial support

(a) provide a substantial majority of the (50) hours of legal services without fee or expectation of fee to:

(1) persons of limited means or

(2) charitable, religious, civic, community, governmental and educational organizations in matters which are designed primarily to address the needs of persons of limited means; and

(b) provide any additional services through:

(1) delivery of legal services at no fee or substantially reduced fee to individuals, groups or organizations seeking to secure or protect civil rights, civil liberties or public rights, or charitable, religious, civic, community, governmental and educational organizations in matters in furtherance of their organizational purposes, where the payment of standard legal fees would significantly deplete the organization's economic resources or would be otherwise inappropriate;

(2) delivery of legal services at a substantially reduced fee to persons of limited means; or

(3) participation in activities for improving the law, the legal system or the legal profession.

for organizations that provide legal services to persons of limited means.

COMMENT:

[1] The ABA House of Delegates has formally acknowledged "the basic responsibility of each lawyer engaged in the practice of law to provide public interest legal services" without fee, or at a substantially reduced fee, in one or more of the following areas: poverty law, civil rights law, public rights law, charitable organization representation and the administration of justice. This Rule expresses that policy but is not intended to be enforced through disciplinary process.

[2] The rights and responsibilities of individuals and organizations in the United States are increasingly defined in legal terms. As a consequence, legal assistance in coping with the web of statutes, rules and regulations is imperative for persons of modest and limited means, as well as for the relatively well-to-do.

[3] The basic responsibility for providing legal services for those unable to pay ultimately rests upon the individual law-

yer, and personal involvement in the problems of the disadvantaged can be one of the most rewarding experiences in the life of a lawyer. Every lawyer, regardless of professional prominence or professional workload, should find time to participate in or otherwise support the provision of legal services to the disadvantaged. The provision of free legal services to those unable to pay reasonable fees continues to be an obligation of each lawyer as well as the profession generally, but the efforts of individual lawyers are often not enough to meet the need. Thus, it has been necessary for the profession and government to institute additional programs to provide legal services. Accordingly, legal aid offices, lawyer referral services and other related programs have been developed, and others will be developed by the profession and government. Every lawyer should support all proper efforts to meet this need for legal services.

In addition, a lawyer should voluntarily contribute financial support to organizations that provide legal services to persons of limited means.

COMMENT:

[1] Every lawyer, regardless of professional prominence or professional work load, has a responsibility to provide legal services to those unable to pay, and personal involvement in the problems of the disadvantaged can be one of the most rewarding experiences in the life of a lawyer. The American Bar Association urges all lawyers to provide a minimum of 50 hours of pro bono services annually. States, however, may decide to choose a higher or lower number of hours of annual service (which may be expressed as a percentage of a lawyer's professional time) depending upon local needs and local conditions. It is recognized that in some years a lawyer may render greater or fewer hours than the annual standard specified, but during the course of his or her legal career, each lawyer should render on average per year, the number of hours set forth in this Rule. Services can be performed in civil matters or in criminal or quasi-criminal matters for which there is no government obligation to provide funds for legal representation, such as post-conviction death penalty appeal cases.

[2] Paragraphs (a)(1) and (2) recognize the critical need for legal services that exists among persons of limited means by providing that a substantial majority of the legal services rendered annually to the disadvantaged be furnished without fee or expectation of fee. Legal services under these paragraphs consist of a full range of activities, including individual and class representation, the provision of legal advice, legislative lobbying, administrative rule making and the provision of free training or mentoring to those who represent persons of limited means. The variety of these activities should facilitate participation by government attorneys, even when restrictions exist on their engaging in the outside practice of law.

[3] Persons eligible for legal services under paragraphs (a)(1) and (2) are those who qualify for participation in programs funded by the Legal Services Corporation and those whose incomes and financial resources are slightly above the guidelines utilized by such programs but nevertheless, cannot afford counsel. Legal services can be rendered to individuals or to organizations such as homeless shelters, battered women's centers and food pantries that serve those of limited means. The term "governmental organizations" includes, but is not limited to, public protection programs and sections of governmental or public sector agencies.

[4] Because service must be provided without fee or expectation of fee, the intent of the lawyer to render free legal services is essential for the work performed to fall within the meaning of paragraphs (a)(1) and (2). Accordingly, services rendered cannot be considered pro bono if an anticipated fee is uncollected, but the award of statutory attorneys' fees

in a case originally accepted as pro bono would not disqualify such services from inclusion under this section. Lawyers who do receive fees in such cases are encouraged to contribute an appropriate portion of such fees to organizations or projects that benefit persons of limited means.

[5]   While it is possible for a lawyer to fulfill the annual responsibility to perform pro bono services exclusively through activities described in paragraphs (a)(1) and (2), to the extent that any hours of service remained unfulfilled, the remaining commitment can be met in a variety of ways as set forth in paragraph (b). Constitutional, statutory or regulatory restrictions may prohibit or impede government and public sector lawyers and judges from performing the pro bono services outlined in paragraphs (a)(1) and (2). Accordingly, where those restrictions apply, government and public sector lawyers and judges may fulfill their pro bono responsibility by performing services outlined in paragraph (b).

[6]   Paragraph (b)(1) includes the provision of certain types of legal services to those whose incomes and financial resources place them above limited means. It also permits the pro bono attorney to accept a substantially reduced fee for services. Example of the types of issues that may be addressed under this paragraph include First Amendment claims, Title VII claims and environmental protection claims. Additionally, a wide range of organizations may be represented, including social service, medical research, cultural and religious groups.

[7]   Paragraph (b)(2) covers instances in which attorneys agree to and receive a modest fee for furnishing legal services to persons of limited means. Participation in judicare programs and acceptance of court appointments in which the fee is substantially below a lawyer's usual rate are encouraged under this section.

[8]   Paragraph (b)(3) recognizes the value of lawyers engaging in activities that improve the law, the legal system or the legal profession. Serving on bar association committees, serving on boards of pro bono or legal services programs, taking part in Law Day activities, acting as a continuing legal education instructor, a mediator or an arbitrator and engaging in legislative lobbying to improve the law, the legal system or the profession are a few examples of the many activities that fall within this paragraph.

[9]   Because the provision of pro bono services is a professional responsibility, it is the individual ethical commitment of each lawyer. Nevertheless, there may be times when it is not feasible for a lawyer to engage in pro bono services. At such times a lawyer may discharge the pro bono responsibility by providing financial support to organizations providing free legal services to persons of limited means. Such financial support should be reasonably equivalent to the value of the hours of service that would have otherwise been provided. In addition, at times it may be more feasible to satisfy the pro bono responsibility collectively, as by a firm's aggregate pro bono activities.

[10] Because the efforts of individual lawyers are not enough to meet the need for free legal services that exists among persons of limited means, the government and the profession have instituted additional programs to provide those services. Every lawyer should financially support such programs, in addition to either providing direct pro bono services or making financial contributions when pro bono service is not feasible.

[11] The responsibility set forth in this Rule is not intended to be enforced through disciplinary process.

MODEL CODE COMPARISON:

There was no counterpart of this Rule in the Disciplinary Rules of the Model Code. EC 2–25 stated that the "basic responsibility for providing legal services for those unable to pay ultimately rests upon the individual lawyer.... Every lawyer, regardless of professional prominence or professional work load, should find time to participate in serving the disadvantaged." EC 8–9 stated that "[t]he advancement of our legal system is of vital importance in maintaining the rule of law ... [and] lawyers should encourage, and should aid in making, needed changes and improvements." EC 8–3 stated that "[t]hose persons unable to pay for legal services should be provided needed services."

RULE 6.2 Accepting Appointments

A lawyer shall not seek to avoid appointment by a tribunal to represent a person except for good cause, such as:

(a) representing the client is likely to result in violation of the rules of professional conduct or other law;

(b) representing the client is likely to result in an unreasonable financial burden on the lawyer; or

(c) the client or the cause is so repugnant to the lawyer as to be likely to impair the client-lawyer relationship or the lawyer's ability to represent the client.

COMMENT:

[1] A lawyer ordinarily is not obliged to accept a client whose character or cause the lawyer regards as repugnant. The lawyer's freedom to select clients is, however, qualified. All lawyers have a responsibility to assist in providing pro bono publico service. See Rule 6.1. An individual lawyer fulfills this responsibility by accepting a fair share of unpopular matters or indigent or unpopular clients. A lawyer may also be subject to appointment by a court to serve unpopular clients or persons unable to afford legal services.

Appointed Counsel

[2] For good cause a lawyer may seek to decline an appointment to represent a person who cannot afford to retain counsel or whose cause is unpopular. Good cause exists if the lawyer could not handle the matter

competently, see Rule 1.1, or if undertaking the representation would result in an improper conflict of interest, for example, when the client or the cause is so repugnant to the lawyer as to be likely to impair the client-lawyer relationship or the lawyer's ability to represent the client. A lawyer may also seek to decline an appointment if acceptance would be unreasonably burdensome, for example, when it would impose a financial sacrifice so great as to be unjust.

[3]   An appointed lawyer has the same obligations to the client as retained counsel, including the obligations of loyalty and confidentiality, and is subject to the same limitations on the client-lawyer relationship, such as the obligation to refrain from assisting the client in violation of the Rules.

MODEL CODE COMPARISON:

There was no counterpart to this Rule in the Disciplinary Rules of the Model Code.   EC 2–29 stated that when a lawyer is "appointed by a court or requested by a bar association to undertake representation of a person unable to obtain counsel, whether for financial or other reasons, he should not seek to be excused from undertaking the representation except for compelling reasons.   Compelling reasons do not include such factors as the repugnance of the subject matter of the proceeding, the identity or position of a person involved in the case, the belief of the lawyer that the defendant in a criminal proceeding is guilty, or the belief of the lawyer regarding the merits of the civil case."   EC 2–30 stated that "a lawyer should decline employment if the intensity of his personal feelings, as distinguished from a community attitude, may impair his effective representation of a prospective client."

RULE 6.3   Membership in Legal Services Organization

A lawyer may serve as a director, officer or member of a legal services organization, apart from the law firm in which the lawyer practices, notwithstanding that the organization serves persons having interests adverse to a client of the lawyer.   The lawyer shall not knowingly participate in a decision or action of the organization:

(a) if participating in the decision or action would be incompatible with the lawyer's obligations to a client under rule 1.7; or

(b) where the decision or action could have a material adverse effect on the representation of a client of the organization whose interests are adverse to a client of the lawyer.

COMMENT:

[1]   Lawyers should be encouraged to support and participate in legal service organizations.   A lawyer who is an officer or a member of such an organization does not thereby have a client-lawyer relationship with persons served by the organization.   However, there is potential

conflict between the interests of such persons and the interests of the lawyer's clients. If the possibility of such conflict disqualified a lawyer from serving on the board of a legal services organization, the profession's involvement in such organizations would be severely curtailed.

[2] It may be necessary in appropriate cases to reassure a client of the organization that the representation will not be affected by conflicting loyalties of a member of the board. Established, written policies in this respect can enhance the credibility of such assurances.

MODEL CODE COMPARISON:

There was no counterpart to this Rule in the Model Code.

RULE 6.4 Law Reform Activities Affecting Client Interests

A lawyer may serve as a director, officer or member of an organization involved in reform of the law or its administration notwithstanding that the reform may affect the interests of a client of the lawyer. When the lawyer knows that the interests of a client may be materially benefitted by a decision in which the lawyer participates, the lawyer shall disclose that fact but need not identify the client.

COMMENT:

Lawyers involved in organizations seeking law reform generally do not have a client-lawyer relationship with the organization. Otherwise, it might follow that a lawyer could not be involved in a bar association law reform program that might indirectly affect a client. See also Rule 1.2(b). For example, a lawyer specializing in antitrust litigation might be regarded as disqualified from participating in drafting revisions of rules governing that subject. In determining the nature and scope of participation in such activities, a lawyer should be mindful of obligations to clients under other Rules, particularly Rule 1.7. A lawyer is professionally obligated to protect the integrity of the program by making an appropriate disclosure within the organization when the lawyer knows a private client might be materially benefitted.

MODEL CODE COMPARISON:

There was no counterpart to this Rule in the Model Code.

INFORMATION ABOUT LEGAL SERVICES

RULE 7.1 Communications Concerning a Lawyer's Services

A lawyer shall not make a false or misleading communication about the lawyer or the lawyer's services. A communication is false or misleading if it:

(a) contains a material misrepresentation of fact or law, or omits a fact necessary to make the statement considered as a whole not materially misleading;

(b) is likely to create an unjustified expectation about results the lawyer can achieve, or states or implies that the lawyer can achieve results by means that violate the rules of professional conduct or other law; or

(c) compares the lawyer's services with other lawyers' services, unless the comparison can be factually substantiated.

COMMENT:

This Rule governs all communications about a lawyer's services, including advertising permitted by Rule 7.2. Whatever means are used to make known a lawyer's services, statements about them should be truthful. The prohibition in paragraph (b) of statements that may create "unjustified expectations" would ordinarily preclude advertisements about results obtained on behalf of a client, such as the amount of a damage award or the lawyer's record in obtaining favorable verdicts, and advertisements containing client endorsements. Such information may create the unjustified expectation that similar results can be obtained for others without reference to the specific factual and legal circumstances.

MODEL CODE COMPARISON:

DR 2–101 provided that "[a] lawyer shall not ... use ... any form of public communication containing a false, fraudulent, misleading, deceptive, self-laudatory or unfair statement or claim." DR 2–101(B) provided that a lawyer "may publish or broadcast ... the following information ... in the geographic area or areas in which the lawyer resides or maintains offices or in which a significant part of the lawyer's clientele resides, provided that the information ... complies with DR 2–101(A), and is presented in a dignified manner...." DR 2–101(B) then specified twenty-five categories of information that may be disseminated. DR 2–101(C) provided that "[a]ny person desiring to expand the information authorized for disclosure in DR 2–101(B), or to provide for its dissemination through other forums may apply to [the agency having jurisdiction under state law].... The relief granted in response to any such application shall be promulgated as an amendment to DR 2–101(B), universally applicable to all lawyers."

RULE 7.2   Advertising*

(a) Subject to the requirements of rule 7.1 and 7.3, a lawyer may advertise services through public media, such as a tele-

---

* The ABA amended Model Rule 7.2 in 1989 to conform to the holding in Shapero v. Kentucky Bar Ass'n, 486 U.S. 466 (1988) and in 1990 to reflect the addition of Model Rule 1.17 on the sale of a law practice. The original version of Model Rule 7.2 read as follows:

RULE 7.2   Advertising

(a) Subject to the requirements of Rules 7.1, a lawyer may advertise services through public media, such as a telephone directory, legal directory, newspaper or other periodical,

phone directory, legal directory, newspaper or other periodical, outdoor advertising, radio or television, or through written or recorded communication.

(b) A copy or recording of an advertisement or written communication shall be kept for two years after its last dissemination along with a record of when and where it was used.

(c) A lawyer shall not give anything of value to a person for recommending the lawyer's services, except that a lawyer may

(1) pay the reasonable costs of advertisements or communications permitted by this Rule;

(2) pay the usual charges of a not-for-profit lawyer referral service or legal service organization; and

(3) pay for a law practice in accordance with Rule 1.17.

(d) Any communication made pursuant to this rule shall include the name of at least one lawyer responsible for its content.

COMMENT:

[1] To assist the public in obtaining legal services, lawyers should be allowed to make known their services not only through reputation but also through organized information campaigns in the form of advertising. Advertising involves an active quest for clients, contrary to the tradition that a lawyer should not seek clientele. However, the public's need to know about legal services can be fulfilled in part through advertising. This need is particularly acute in the case of persons of moderate means who have not made extensive use of legal services. The interest in expanding public information about legal services ought to prevail over considerations of tradition. Nevertheless, advertising by lawyers entails the risk of practices that are misleading or overreaching.

[2] This Rule permits public dissemination of information concerning a lawyer's name or firm name, address and telephone number; the kinds of services the lawyer will undertake; the basis on which the lawyer's fees are determined, including prices for specific services and payment and credit arrangements; a lawyer's foreign language ability; names of references and, with their consent, names of clients regularly

outdoor, radio or television, or through written communication not involving solicitation as defined in Rule 7.3.

(b) A copy or recording of an advertisement or written communication shall be kept for two years after its last dissemination along with a record of when and where it was used.

(c) A lawyer shall not give anything of value to a person for recommending the lawyer's services, except that a lawyer may pay the reasonable cost of advertising or written communication permitted by this rule and may pay the usual charges of a not-for-profit lawyer referral service or other legal service organization.

(d) Any communication made pursuant to this rule shall include the name of at least one lawyer responsible for its content.

represented; and other information that might invite the attention of those seeking legal assistance.

[3] Questions of effectiveness and taste in advertising are matters of speculation and subjective judgment. Some jurisdictions have had extensive prohibitions against television advertising, against advertising going beyond specified facts about a lawyer, or against "undignified" advertising. Television is now one of the most powerful media for getting information to the public, particularly persons of low and moderate income; prohibiting television advertising, therefore, would impede the flow of information about legal services to many sectors of the public. Limiting the information that may be advertised has a similar effect and assumes that the bar can accurately forecast the kind of information that the public would regard as relevant.

[4] Neither this Rule nor Rule 7.3 prohibits communications authorized by law, such as notice to members of a class in class action litigation.

Record of Advertising

[5] Paragraph (b) requires that a record of the content and use of advertising be kept in order to facilitate enforcement of this Rule. It does not require that advertising be subject to review prior to dissemination. Such a requirement would be burdensome and expensive relative to its possible benefits, and may be of doubtful constitutionality.

Paying Others to Recommend a Lawyer*

[6] A lawyer is allowed to pay for advertising permitted by this Rule and for the purchase of a law practice in accordance with the provisions of Rule 1.17, but otherwise is not permitted to pay another person for channeling professional work. This restriction does not prevent an organization or person other than the lawyer from advertising or recommending the lawyer's services. Thus, a legal aid agency or prepaid legal services plan may pay to advertise legal services provided under its auspices. Likewise, a lawyer may participate in not-for-profit lawyer referral programs and pay the usual fees charged by such programs. Paragraph (c) does not prohibit paying regular compensation to an assistant, such as a secretary, to prepare communications permitted by this Rule.

MODEL CODE COMPARISON:

With regard to paragraph (a), DR 2–101(B) provided that a lawyer "may publish or broadcast, subject to DR 2–103, . . . in print media . . . or television or radio. . . ."

With regard to paragraph (b), DR 2–101(D) provided that if the advertisement is "communicated to the public over television or radio,

---

* In 1990, the ABA added the clause "and for the purchase of a law practice in accordance with the provisions of Rule 1.17" to reflect to addition of this provision to the Model Rules.

... a recording of the actual transmission shall be retained by the lawyer."

With regard to paragraph (c), DR 2–103(B) provided that a lawyer "shall not compensate or give anything of value to a person or organization to recommend or secure his employment ... except that he may pay the usual and reasonable fees or dues charged by any of the organizations listed in DR 2–103(D)." (DR 2–103(D) referred to legal aid and other legal services organizations.) DR 2–101(I) provided that a lawyer "shall not compensate or give anything of value to representatives of the press, radio, television, or other communication medium in anticipation of or in return for professional publicity in a news item."

There was no counterpart to paragraph (d) in the Model Code.

RULE 7.3 Direct Contact With Prospective Clients*

(a) A lawyer shall not by in-person or live telephone contact solicit professional employment from a prospective client with whom the lawyer has no family or prior professional relationship when a significant motive for the lawyer's doing so is the lawyer's pecuniary gain.

(b) A lawyer shall not solicit professional employment from a prospective client by written or recorded communication or by in-person or telephone contact even when not otherwise prohibited by paragraph (a), if:

(1) the prospective client has made known to the lawyer a desire not to be solicited by the lawyer; or

(2) the solicitation involves coercion, duress or harassment.

(c) Every written or recorded communication from a lawyer soliciting professional employment from a prospective client known to be in need of legal services in a particular matter, and

---

* The ABA amended the original version of Model Rule 7.3 in 1989 because in 1988 the Supreme Court had declared a blanket restriction on targeted mailings unconstitutional under the First Amendment. See Shapero v. Kentucky Bar Ass'n, 486 U.S. 466 (1988). The Kentucky rule which was the subject of the Supreme Court decision was identical to the original Model Rule 7.3. This provision read as follows:

RULE 7.3 Direct Contact With Prospective Clients

A lawyer may not solicit professional employment from a prospective client with whom the lawyer has no family or prior professional relationship, by mail, in-person or otherwise, when a significant motive for the lawyer's doing so is the lawyer's pecuniary gain. The term "solicit" includes contact in person, by telephone or telegraph, by letter or other writing or by other communication directed to a specific recipient, but does not include letters addressed or advertising circulars distributed generally to persons not known to need legal services of the kind provided by the lawyer in a particular matter, but who are so situated that they might in general find such services useful.

with whom the lawyer has no family or prior professional relationship, shall include the words "Advertising Material" on the
outside envelope and at the beginning and ending of any recorded communication.

(d) Notwithstanding the prohibitions in paragraph (a), a
lawyer may participate with a prepaid or group legal service
plan operated by an organization not owned or directed by the
lawyer which uses in-person or telephone contact to solicit
memberships or subscriptions for the plan from persons who are
not known to need legal services in a particular matter covered
by the plan.

COMMENT: *

[1]   There is a potential for abuse inherent in direct in-person or
live telephone contact by a lawyer with a prospective client known to
need legal services. These forms of contact between a lawyer and a

---

* The ABA amended the comments to
Model Rule 7.3 in 1989 to reflect changes
made in the text of the Rule brought about
by the *Shapero* decision. The text of the
original comment reads as follows:

COMMENT:

There is a potential for abuse inherent
in direct solicitation by a lawyer of prospective clients known to need legal services. It subjects the lay person to the
private importuning of a trained advocate, in a direct interpersonal encounter.
A prospective client often feels overwhelmed by the situation giving rise to
the need for legal services, and may have
an impaired capacity for reason, judgment and protective self-interest. Furthermore, the lawyer seeking the retainer
is faced with a conflict stemming from
the lawyer's own interest, which may col-
or the advice and representation offered
the vulnerable prospect.

The situation is therefore fraught with
the possibility of undue influence, intimidation, and over-reaching. This potential
for abuse inherent in direct solicitation of
prospective clients justifies its prohibition, particularly since lawyer advertising
permitted under Rule 7.2 offers an alternative means of communicating necessary information to those who may be in
need of legal services.

Advertising makes it possible for a prospective client to be informed about the
need for legal services, and about the

qualifications of available lawyers and
law firms, without subjecting the prospective client to direct personal persuasion
that may overwhelm the client's judgment.

The use of general advertising to
transmit information from lawyer to prospective client, rather than direct private
contact, will help to assure that the information flows cleanly as well as freely.
Advertising is out in public view, thus
subject to scrutiny by those who know
the lawyer. This informal review is itself
likely to help guard against statements
and claims that might constitute false or
misleading communications, in violation
of Rule 7.1. Direct, private communications from a lawyer to a prospective
client are not subject to such third-scru-
tiny and consequently are much more
likely to approach (and occasionally
cross) the dividing line between accurate
representations and those that are false
and misleading.

These dangers attend direct solicitation
whether in-person or by mail. Direct
mail solicitation cannot be effectively regulated by means less drastic than outright prohibition. One proposed safeguard is to require that the designation
"Advertising" be stamped on any envelope containing a solicitation letter. This
would do nothing to assure the accuracy
and reliability of the contents. Another
suggestion is that solicitation letters be

prospective client subject the layperson to the private importuning of the trained advocate in a direct interpersonal encounter. The prospective client, who may already feel overwhelmed by the circumstances giving rise to the need for legal services, may find it difficult fully to evaluate all available alternatives with reasoned judgment and appropriate self-interest in the face of the lawyer's presence and insistence upon being retained immediately. The situation is fraught with the possibility of undue influence, intimidation, and over-reaching.

[2] This potential for abuse inherent in direct in-person or live telephone solicitation of prospective clients justifies its prohibition, particularly since lawyer advertising and written and recorded communication permitted under Rule 7.2 offer alternative means of conveying necessary information to those who may be in need of legal services. Advertising and written and recorded communications which may be mailed or autodialed make it possible for a prospective client to be informed about the need for legal services, and about the qualifications of available lawyers and law firms, without subjecting the prospective client to direct in-person or telephone persuasion that may overwhelm the client's judgment.

[3] The use of general advertising and written and recorded communications to transmit information from lawyer to prospective client,

filed with a state regulatory agency. This would be ineffective as a practical matter. State lawyer discipline agencies struggle for resources to investigate specific complaints, much less for those necessary to screen lawyers' mail solicitation material. Even if they could examine such materials, agency staff members are unlikely to know anything about the lawyer or about the prospective client's underlying problem. Without such knowledge they cannot determine whether the lawyer's representations are misleading. In any event, such review would be after the fact, potentially too late to avert the undesirable consequences of disseminating false and misleading material.

General mailings not speaking to a specific matter do not pose the same danger of abuse as targeted mailings, and therefore are not prohibited by this Rule. The representations made in such mailings are necessarily general rather than tailored, less importuning than informative. They are addressed to recipients unlikely to be specially vulnerable at the time, hence who are likely to be more skeptical about unsubstantiated claims. General mailings not addressed to recipients involved in a specific legal matter or incident, therefore, more closely resemble permissible advertising rather than prohibited solicitation.

Similarly, this Rule would not prohibit a lawyer from contacting representatives of organizations or groups that may be interested in establishing a group or prepaid legal plan for its members, insureds, beneficiaries or other third parties for the purpose of informing such entities of the availability of and details concerning the plan or arrangement which he or his firm is willing to offer. This form of communication is not directed to a specific prospective client known to need legal services related to a particular matter. Rather, it is usually addressed to an individual acting in a fiduciary capacity seeking a supplier of legal services for others who may, if they choose, become prospective clients of the lawyer. Under these circumstances, the activity which the lawyer undertakes in communicating with such representatives and the type of information transmitted to the individual are functionally similar to and serve the same purpose as advertising permitted under Rule 7.2.

115

rather than direct in-person or live telephone contact, will help to assure that the information flows cleanly as well as freely. The contents of advertisements and communications permitted under Rule 7.2 are permanently recorded so that they cannot be disputed and may be shared with others who know the lawyer. This potential for informal review is itself likely to help guard against statements and claims that might constitute false and misleading communications, in violation of Rule 7.1. The contents of direct in-person or live telephone conversations between a lawyer to a prospective client can be disputed and are not subject to third-party scrutiny. Consequently, they are much more likely to approach (and occasionally cross) the dividing line between accurate representations and those that are false and misleading.

[4] There is far less likelihood that a lawyer would engage in abusive practices against an individual with whom the lawyer has a prior personal or professional relationship or where the lawyer is motivated by considerations other than the lawyer's pecuniary gain. Consequently, the general prohibition in Rule 7.3(a) and the requirements of Rule 7.3(c) are not applicable in those situations.

[5] But even permitted forms of solicitation can be abused. Thus, any solicitation which contains information which is false or misleading within the meaning of Rule 7.1, which involves coercion, duress or harassment within the meaning of Rule 7.3(b)(2), or which involves contact with a prospective client who has made known to the lawyer a desire not to be solicited by the lawyer within the meaning of Rule 7.3(b)(1) is prohibited. Moreover, if after sending a letter or other communication to a client as permitted by Rule 7.2 the lawyer receives no response, any further effort to communicate with the prospective client may violate the provisions of Rule 7.3(b).

[6] This Rule is not intended to prohibit a lawyer from contacting representatives of organizations or groups that may be interested in establishing a group or prepaid legal plan for their members, insureds, beneficiaries or other third parties for the purpose of informing such entities of the availability of and details concerning the plan or arrangement which the lawyer or lawyer's firm is willing to offer. This form of communication is not directed to a prospective client. Rather, it is usually addressed to an individual acting in a fiduciary capacity seeking a supplier of legal services for others who may, if they choose, become prospective clients of the lawyer. Under these circumstances, the activity which the lawyer undertakes in communicating with such representatives and the type of information transmitted to the individual are functionally similar to and serve the same purpose as advertising permitted under Rule 7.2.

[7] The requirement in Rule 7.3(c) that certain communications be marked "Advertising Material" does not apply to communications sent in response to requests of potential clients or their spokespersons or sponsors. General announcements by lawyers, including changes in personnel or office location, do not constitute communications soliciting

professional employment from a client known to be in need of legal services within the meaning of this Rule.

[8] Paragraph (d) of this Rule would permit an attorney to participate with an organization which uses personal contact to solicit members for its group or prepaid legal service plan, provided that the personal contact is not undertaken by any lawyer who would be a provider of legal services through the plan. The organization referred to in paragraph (d) must not be owned by or directed (whether as manager or otherwise) by any lawyer or law firm that participates in the plan. For example, paragraph (d) would not permit a lawyer to create an organization controlled directly or indirectly by the lawyer and use the organization for the in-person or telephone solicitation of legal employment of the lawyer through memberships in the plan or otherwise. The communication permitted by these organizations also must not be directed to a person known to need legal services in a particular matter, but is to be designed to inform potential plan members generally of another means of affordable legal services. Lawyers who participate in a legal service plan must reasonably assure that the plan sponsors are in compliance with Rules 7.1, 7.2 and 7.3(a). See 8.4(a).

MODEL CODE COMPARISON:

DR 2–104(A) provided with certain exceptions that "[a] lawyer who has given in-person unsolicited advice to a layperson that he should obtain counsel or take legal action shall not accept employment resulting from that advice...." The exceptions include DR 2–104(A)(1), which provided that a lawyer "may accept employment by a close friend, relative, former client (if the advice is germane to the former employment), or one whom the lawyer reasonably believes to be a client." DR 2–104(A)(2) through DR 2–104(A)(5) provided other exceptions relating, respectively, to employment resulting from public educational programs, recommendation by a legal assistance organization, public speaking or writing and representing members of a class in class action litigation.

RULE 7.4 Communication of Fields of Practice *

A lawyer may communicate the fact that the lawyer does or does not practice in particular fields of law. A lawyer shall not

---

* In August 1992, the ABA House of Delegates modified Model Rule 7.4(c) as a reaction to the Supreme Court's decision in Peel v. Attorney Registration and Disciplinary Commission, 496 U.S. 91 (1990). The 1983 version of 7.4(c) read as follows: "(c) (provisions on designation of specialization of the particular state)." The original intent of the rule was to limit the right of lawyers to state or imply that they are specialists except when a state has an orga-nized plan of specialization or in the two well defined area of law (admiralty and patent) in which a long tradition of specialization exists. In *Peel*, the Supreme Court held that a state could not prohibit a lawyer from stating that he or she is a civil trial specialist certified by the National Board of Trial Advocacy. The revised rule encourages the states to create organizations to certify organizations that seek to qualify lawyers as specialists and requires lawyers

117

state or imply that the lawyer is a specialist in a particular field of law except as follows:

(a) a lawyer admitted to engage in patent practice before the United States Patent and Trademark Office may use the designation "Patent Attorney" or a substantially similar designation;

(b) a lawyer engaged in admiralty practice may use the designation "Admiralty," "Proctor in Admiralty" or a substantially similar designation; and

(c) [for jurisdictions where there is a regulatory authority granting certification or approving organizations that grant certification] a lawyer may communicate the fact that the lawyer has been certified as a specialist in a field of law by a named organization or authority, but only if:

(1) such certification is granted by the appropriate regulatory authority or by an organization which has been approved by the appropriate regulatory authority to grant such certification; or

(2) such certification is granted by an organization that has not yet been approved by, or has been denied the approval available from, the appropriate regulatory authority, and the absence or denial of approval is clearly stated in the communication, and in any advertisement subject to Rule 7.2, such statement appears in the same sentence that communicates the certification.

(c) [for jurisdictions where there is no procedure either for certification of specialties or for approval of organizations granting certification] a lawyer may communicate the fact that the lawyer has been certified as a specialist in a field of law by a named organization, provided that the communication clearly states that there is no procedure in this jurisdiction for approving certifying organizations. If, however, the named organization has been accredited by the American Bar Association to

who wish to advertise specialties by organizations that have either been denied or not approved to disclose such information in the advertisement. In its February 1993 meeting, the ABA adopted "Standards for Accreditation of Specialty Certification Programs for Lawyers." These standards seek to ensure that certification programs ensure that the lawyer has a special proficiency in the specialty and devotes a substantial amount of time to this type of work. They also require that certifying organizations be made up primarily of lawyer members.

In August 1994, the ABA House of Delegates added the last line to alternative paragraph (c): "If, however, the named organization has been accredited by the American Bar Association to certify lawyers as specialists in a particular field of law, the communication need not contain such a statement."

This line reflects the new role of the ABA committee on specialization to accredit organizations.

certify lawyers as specialists in a particular field of law, the communication need not contain such a statement.

COMMENT: *

[1] This Rule permits a lawyer to indicate areas of practice in communications about the lawyer's services. If a lawyer practices only in certain fields, or will not accept matters in a specified field or fields, the lawyer is permitted to so indicate. A lawyer is generally permitted to state that the lawyer is a "specialist," practices a "specialty," or "specializes in" particular fields, but such communications are subject to the "false and misleading" standard applied in Rule 7.1 to communications concerning a lawyer's services.

[2] However, a lawyer may not communicate that the lawyer has been recognized or certified as a specialist in a particular field of law, except as provided by this Rule. Recognition of specialization in patent matters is a matter of long-established policy of the Patent and Trademark Office, as reflected in paragraph (a). Paragraph (b) recognizes that designation of admiralty practice has a long historical tradition associated with maritime commerce and the federal courts.

[3] Paragraph (c) provides for certification as a specialist in a field of law when a state authorizes an appropriate regulatory authority to grant such certification or when the state grants other organizations the right to grant certification. Certification procedures imply that an

---

* In 1989, the ABA amended the comment to Model Rule 7.3 to reflect concerns that the language in the original comment may violate the Supreme Court's legal advertising decisions. The original language read as follows:

COMMENT:

This Rule permits a lawyer to indicate areas of practice in communications about the lawyer's services; for example, in a telephone directory or other advertising. If a lawyer practices only in certain fields, or will not accept matters except in such fields, the lawyer is permitted so to indicate. However, stating that the lawyer is a "specialist" or that the lawyer's practice "is limited to" or "concentrated in" particular fields is not permitted. These terms have acquired a secondary meaning implying formal recognition as a specialist. Hence, use of these terms may be misleading unless the lawyer is certified or recognized in accordance with procedures in the state where the lawyer is licensed to practice.

The 1989 amendment adopted the following language:

COMMENT:

[1] This Rule permits a lawyer to indicate areas of practice in communications about the lawyer's services; for example, in a telephone directory or other advertising. If a lawyer practices only in certain fields, or will not accept matters except in such fields, the lawyer is permitted so to indicate. However, a lawyer is not permitted to state that the lawyer is a "specialist," practices a "specialty," or "specializes in" particular fields. These terms have acquired a secondary meaning implying formal recognition as a specialist and therefore, use of these terms is misleading. [An exception would apply in those states which provide procedures for certification or recognition of specialization and the lawyer has complied with such procedures.]

[2] Recognition of specialization in patent matters is a matter of long-established policy of the Patent and Trademark Office. Designation of admiralty practice has a long historical tradition associated with maritime commerce and the federal courts.

objective entity has recognized a lawyer's higher degree of specialized ability than is suggested by general licensure to practice law. Those objective entities may be expected to apply standards of competence, experience and knowledge to insure that a lawyer's recognition as a specialist is meaningful and reliable. In order to insure that consumers can obtain access to useful information about an organization granting certification, the name of the certifying organization or agency must be included in any communication regarding the certification.

[4] Lawyers may also be certified as specialists by organizations that either have not yet been approved to grant such certification or have been disapproved. In such instances, the consumer may be misled as to the significance of the lawyer's status as a certified specialist. The Rule therefore requires that a lawyer who chooses to communicate recognition by such an organization also clearly state the absence or denial of the organization's authority to grant such certification. Since lawyer advertising through public media and written or recorded communications invites the greatest danger of misleading consumers, the absence or denial of the organization's authority to grant certification must be clearly stated in such advertising in the same sentence that communicates the certification.

[5]* In jurisdictions where no appropriate regulatory authority has a procedure for approving organizations granting certification, the Rule requires that a lawyer clearly state such lack of procedure.

If, however, the named organization has been accredited by the American Bar Association to certify lawyers as specialists in a particular field of law, the communication need not contain such a statement.

MODEL CODE COMPARISON:

DR 2–105(A) provided that a lawyer "shall not hold himself out publicly as a specialist, as practicing in certain areas of law or as limiting his practice . . . except as follows:

"(1) A lawyer admitted to practice before the United States Patent and Trademark Office may use the designation 'Patents,' 'Patent Attorney,' 'Patent Lawyer,' or 'Registered Patent Attorney' or any combination of those terms, on his letterhead and office sign.

"(2) A lawyer who publicly discloses fields of law in which the lawyer . . . practices or states that his practice is limited to one or more fields of law shall do so by using designations and definitions authorized and approved by [the agency having jurisdiction of the subject under state law].

"(3) A lawyer who is certified as a specialist in a particular field of law or law practice by [the authority having jurisdiction under state law over the subject of specialization by lawyers] may hold

---

* The ABA added the last line in this   paragraph (c).
paragraph when it amended alternative

himself out as such, but only in accordance with the rules prescribed by that authority."

EC 2–14 stated that "In the absence of state controls to insure the existence of special competence, a lawyer should not be permitted to hold himself out as a specialist, ... other than in the fields of admiralty, trademark, and patent law where a holding out as a specialist historically has been permitted."

RULE 7.5 Firm Names and Letterheads

(a) A lawyer shall not use a firm name, letterhead or other professional designation that violates rule 7.1. A trade name may be used by a lawyer in private practice if it does not imply a connection with a government agency or with a public or charitable legal services organization and is not otherwise in violation of rule 7.1.

(b) A law firm with offices in more than one jurisdiction may use the same name in each jurisdiction, but identification of the lawyers in an office of the firm shall indicate the jurisdictional limitations on those not licensed to practice in the jurisdiction where the office is located.

(c) The name of a lawyer holding a public office shall not be used in the name of a law firm, or in communications on its behalf, during any substantial period in which the lawyer is not actively and regularly practicing with the firm.

(d) Lawyers may state or imply that they practice in a partnership or other organization only when that is the fact.

COMMENT:

[1] A firm may be designated by the names of all or some of its members, by the names of deceased members where there has been a continuing succession in the firm's identity or by a trade name such as the "ABC Legal Clinic." Although the United States Supreme Court has held that legislation may prohibit the use of trade names in professional practice, use of such names in law practice is acceptable so long as it is not misleading. If a private firm uses a trade name that includes a geographical name such as "Springfield Legal Clinic," an express disclaimer that it is a public legal aid agency may be required to avoid a misleading implication. It may be observed that any firm name including the name of a deceased partner is, strictly speaking, a trade name. The use of such names to designate law firms has proven a useful means of identification. However, it is misleading to use the name of a lawyer not associated with the firm or a predecessor of the firm.

[2] With regard to paragraph (d), lawyers sharing office facilities, but who are not in fact partners, may not denominate themselves as, for example, "Smith and Jones," for that title suggests partnership in the practice of law.

MODEL CODE COMPARISON:

With regard to paragraph (a), DR 2–102(A) provided that "[a] lawyer ... shall not use ... professional announcement cards ... letterheads, or similar professional notices or devices, except ... if they are in dignified form...." DR 2–102(B) provided that "[a] lawyer in private practice shall not practice under a trade name, a name that is misleading as to the identity of the lawyer or lawyers practicing under such name, or a firm name containing names other than those of one or more of the lawyers in the firm, except that ... a firm may use as ... its name the name or names of one or more deceased or retired members of the firm or of a predecessor firm in a continuing line of succession."

With regard to paragraph (b), DR 2–102(D) provided that a partnership "shall not be formed or continued between or among lawyers licensed in different jurisdictions unless all enumerations of the members and associates of the firm on its letterhead and in other permissible listings make clear the jurisdictional limitations on those members and associates of the firm not licensed to practice in all listed jurisdictions; however, the same firm name may be used in each jurisdiction."

With regard to paragraph (c), DR 2–102(B) provided that "[a] lawyer who assumes a judicial, legislative, or public executive or administrative post or office shall not permit his name to remain in the name of a law firm ... during any significant period in which he is not actively and regularly practicing law as a member of the firm...."

Paragraph (d) is substantially identical to DR 2–102(C).

MAINTAINING THE INTEGRITY OF THE PROFESSION

RULE 8.1　Bar Admission and Disciplinary Matters

An applicant for admission to the bar, or a lawyer in connection with a bar admission application or in connection with a disciplinary matter, shall not:

(a) knowingly make a false statement of material fact; or

(b) fail to disclose a fact necessary to correct a misapprehension known by the person to have arisen in the matter, or knowingly fail to respond to a lawful demand for information from an admission or disciplinary authority, except that this rule does not require disclosure of information otherwise protected by rule 1.6.

COMMENT:

[1]　The duty imposed by this Rule extends to persons seeking admission to the bar as well as to lawyers. Hence, if a person makes a material false statement in connection with an application for admission, it may be the basis for subsequent disciplinary action if the person is admitted, and in any event may be relevant in a subsequent admission application. The duty imposed by this Rule applies to a lawyer's own

admission or discipline as well as that of others. Thus, it is a separate professional offense for a lawyer to knowingly make a misrepresentation or omission in connection with a disciplinary investigation of the lawyer's own conduct. This Rule also requires affirmative clarification of any misunderstanding on the part of the admissions or disciplinary authority of which the person involved becomes aware.

[2] This Rule is subject to the provisions of the Fifth Amendment of the United States Constitution and corresponding provisions of state constitutions. A person relying on such a provision in response to a question, however, should do so openly and not use the right of nondisclosure as a justification for failure to comply with this Rule.

[3] A lawyer representing an applicant for admission to the bar, or representing a lawyer who is the subject of a disciplinary inquiry or proceeding, is governed by the rules applicable to the client-lawyer relationship.

MODEL CODE COMPARISON:

DR 1–101(A) provided that a lawyer is "subject to discipline if he has made a materially false statement in, or if he has deliberately failed to disclose a material fact requested in connection with, his application for admission to the bar." DR 1–101(B) provided that a lawyer "shall not further the application for admission to the bar of another person known by him to be unqualified in respect to character, education, or other relevant attribute." With respect to paragraph (b), DR 1–102(A)(5) provided that a lawyer shall not engage in "conduct that is prejudicial to the administration of justice."

RULE 8.2 Judicial and Legal Officials

(a) A lawyer shall not make a statement that the lawyer knows to be false or with reckless disregard as to its truth or falsity concerning the qualifications or integrity of a judge, adjudicatory officer or public legal officer, or of a candidate for election or appointment to judicial or legal office.

(b) A lawyer who is a candidate for judicial office shall comply with the applicable provisions of the code of judicial conduct.

COMMENT:

[1] Assessments by lawyers are relied on in evaluating the professional or personal fitness of persons being considered for election or appointment to judicial office and to public legal offices, such as attorney general, prosecuting attorney and public defender. Expressing honest and candid opinions on such matters contributes to improving the administration of justice. Conversely, false statements by a lawyer can unfairly undermine public confidence in the administration of justice.

[2] When a lawyer seeks judicial office, the lawyer should be bound by applicable limitations on political activity.

[3]   To maintain the fair and independent administration of justice, lawyers are encouraged to continue traditional efforts to defend judges and courts unjustly criticized.

MODEL CODE COMPARISON:

With regard to paragraph (a), DR 8–102(A) provided that a lawyer "shall not knowingly make false statements of fact concerning the qualifications of a candidate for election or appointment to a judicial office." DR 8–102(B) provided that a lawyer "shall not knowingly make false accusations against a judge or other adjudicatory officer."
Paragraph (b) is substantially identical to DR 8–103.

RULE 8.3 Reporting Professional Misconduct*

(a) A lawyer having knowledge that another lawyer has committed a violation of the rules of professional conduct that raises a substantial question as to that lawyer's honesty, trustworthiness or fitness as a lawyer in other respects, shall inform the appropriate professional authority.

(b) A lawyer having knowledge that a judge has committed a violation of applicable rules of judicial conduct that raises a substantial question as to the judge's fitness for office shall inform the appropriate authority.

(c) This rule does not require disclosure of information otherwise protected by Rule 1.6 or information gained by a lawyer or judge while serving as a member of an approved lawyers assistance program to the extent that such information would be confidential if it were communicated subject to the attorney-client privilege.

COMMENT:

[1]   Self-regulation of the legal profession requires that members of the profession initiate disciplinary investigation when they know of a violation of the Rules of Professional Conduct. Lawyers have a similar obligation with respect to judicial misconduct. An apparently isolated violation may indicate a pattern of misconduct that only a disciplinary investigation can uncover. Reporting a violation is especially important where the victim is unlikely to discover the offense.

[2]   A report about misconduct is not required where it would involve violation of Rule 1.6. However, a lawyer should encourage a client to consent to disclosure where prosecution would not substantially prejudice the client's interests.

[3]   If a lawyer were obliged to report every violation of the Rules, the failure to report any violation would itself be a professional offense.

---

* In 1991, the ABA amended Model Rule 8.3(c) to include the reference to the protection of certain information obtained in lawyer assistance programs. The original version of 8.3(c) read as follows: "This rule does not require disclosure of information otherwise protected by Rule 1.6."

Such a requirement existed in many jurisdictions but proved to be unenforceable. This Rule limits the reporting obligation to those offenses that a self-regulating profession must vigorously endeavor to prevent. A measure of judgment is, therefore, required in complying with the provisions of this Rule. The term "substantial" refers to the seriousness of the possible offense and not the quantum of evidence of which the lawyer is aware. A report should be made to the bar disciplinary agency unless some other agency, such as a peer review agency, is more appropriate in the circumstances. Similar considerations apply to the reporting of judicial misconduct.

[4] The duty to report professional misconduct does not apply to a lawyer retained to represent a lawyer whose professional conduct is in question. Such a situation is governed by the rules applicable to the client-lawyer relationship.

[5] Information about a lawyer's or judge's misconduct or fitness may be received by a lawyer in the course of that lawyer's participation in an approved lawyers' or judges' assistance program. In that circumstance, providing for the confidentiality of such information encourages lawyers and judges to seek treatment through such program. Conversely, without such confidentiality, lawyers and judges may hesitate to seek assistance from these programs, which may then result in additional harm to their professional careers and additional injury to the welfare of clients and the public. The Rule therefore exempts the lawyer from the reporting requirements of paragraphs (a) and (b) with respect to information that would be privileged if the relationship between the impaired lawyer or judge and the recipient of the information were that of a client and a lawyer. On the other hand, a lawyer who receives such information would nevertheless be required to comply with the Rule 8.3 reporting provisions to report misconduct if the impaired lawyer or judge indicates an intent to engage in illegal activity, for example, the conversion of client funds to his or her use.

MODEL CODE COMPARISON:

DR 1–103(A) provided that "[a] lawyer possessing unprivileged knowledge of a violation of [a Disciplinary Rule] shall report such knowledge to ... authority empowered to investigate or act upon such violation."

RULE 8.4 Misconduct

It is professional misconduct for a lawyer to:

(a) violate or attempt to violate the rules of professional conduct, knowingly assist or induce another to do so, or do so through the acts of another;

(b) commit a criminal act that reflects adversely on the lawyer's honesty, trustworthiness or fitness as a lawyer in other respects;

   (c) engage in conduct involving dishonesty, fraud, deceit or misrepresentation;

   (d) engage in conduct that is prejudicial to the administration of justice;

   (e) state or imply an ability to influence improperly a government agency or official; or

   (f) knowingly assist a judge or judicial officer in conduct that is a violation of applicable rules of judicial conduct or other law.

COMMENT:

   [1] Many kinds of illegal conduct reflect adversely on fitness to practice law, such as offenses involving fraud and the offense of willful failure to file an income tax return. However, some kinds of offense carry no such implication. Traditionally, the distinction was drawn in terms of offenses involving "moral turpitude." That concept can be construed to include offenses concerning some matters of personal morality, such as adultery and comparable offenses, that have no specific connection to fitness for the practice of law. Although a lawyer is personally answerable to the entire criminal law, a lawyer should be professionally answerable only for offenses that indicate lack of those characteristics relevant to law practice. Offenses involving violence, dishonesty or breach of trust, or serious interference with the administration of justice are in that category. A pattern of repeated offenses, even ones of minor significance when considered separately, can indicate indifference to legal obligation.

   [2] * A lawyer who, in the course of representing a client, knowingly manifests by words or conduct, bias or prejudice based upon race, sex, religion, national origin, disability, age, sexual orientation or socioeconomic status, violates paragraph (d) when such actions are prejudicial to the administration of justice. Legitimate advocacy respecting the foregoing factors does not violate paragraph (d). A trial judge's finding that peremptory challenges were exercised on a discriminatory basis does not alone establish a violation of this rule.

   [3] A lawyer may refuse to comply with an obligation imposed by law upon a good faith belief that no valid obligation exists. The provisions of Rule 1.2(d) concerning a good faith challenge to the validity, scope, meaning or application of the law apply to challenges of legal regulation of the practice of law.

   [4] Lawyers holding public office assume legal responsibilities going beyond those of other citizens. A lawyer's abuse of public office can suggest an inability to fulfill the professional role of attorney. The same is true of abuse of positions of private trust such as trustee, executor,

---

   * The ABA House of Delegates added this comment to Model Rule 8.4 in 1998 after pressure from many groups to amend the text of the rule to prohibit attorney conduct or words based upon bias or prejudice unrelated to the merits of the representation.

administrator, guardian, agent and officer, director or manager of a corporation or other organization.

MODEL CODE COMPARISON:

With regard to paragraphs (a) through (d) DR 1–102(A) provided that a lawyer shall not:

"(1) Violate a Disciplinary Rule.

"(2) Circumvent a Disciplinary Rule through actions of another.

"(3) Engage in illegal conduct involving moral turpitude.

"(4) Engage in conduct involving dishonesty, fraud, deceit, or misrepresentation.

"(5) Engage in conduct that is prejudicial to the administration of justice.

"(6) Engage in any other conduct that adversely reflects on his fitness to practice law."

Paragraph (e) is substantially similar to DR 9–101(C).

There was no direct counterpart to paragraph (f) in the Disciplinary Rules of the Model Code. EC 7–34 stated in part that "[a] lawyer ... is never justified in making a gift or a loan to a [judicial officer] except as permitted by ... the Code of Judicial Conduct." EC 9–1 stated that a lawyer "should promote public confidence in our [legal] system and in the legal profession."

RULE 8.5 Disciplinary Authority; Choice of Law*

(a) Disciplinary Authority. A lawyer admitted to practice in this jurisdiction is subject to the disciplinary authority of this

* In August 1993, the ABA amended Model Rule 8.5 to more clearly address the problem of choice of professional responsibility rules when more than one jurisdiction's rules may potentially apply to the lawyer's conduct. The original Model Rule 8.5 text and comments are reprinted below:

RULE 8.5 Jurisdiction

A lawyer admitted to practice in this jurisdiction is subject to the disciplinary authority of this jurisdiction although engaged in practice elsewhere.

COMMENT:

[1] In modern practice lawyers frequently act outside the territorial limits of the jurisdiction in which they are licensed to practice, either in another state or outside the United States. In doing so, they remain subject to the governing authority of the jurisdiction in which they are licensed to practice. If their activity in another jurisdiction is substantial and continuous, it may constitute practice of law in that jurisdiction. See Rule 5.5.

[2] If the rules of professional conduct in the two jurisdictions differ, principles of conflict of laws may apply. Similar problems can arise when a lawyer is licensed to practice in more than one jurisdiction.

[3] Where the lawyer is licensed to practice law in two jurisdictions which impose conflicting obligations, applicable rules of choice of law may govern the situation. A related problem arises with respect to practice before a federal tribunal, where the general authority of the states to regulate the practice of law must be reconciled with such authority as

jurisdiction, regardless of where the lawyer's conduct occurs. A lawyer may be subject to the disciplinary authority of both this jurisdiction and another jurisdiction where the lawyer is admitted for the same conduct.

(b) Choice of Law. In any exercise of the disciplinary authority of this jurisdiction, the rules of professional conduct to be applied shall be as follows:

(1) for conduct in connection with a proceeding in a court before which a lawyer has been admitted to practice (either generally or for purposes of that proceeding), the rules to be applied shall be the rules of the jurisdiction in which the court sits, unless the rules of the court provide otherwise; and

(2) for any other conduct,

(i) if the lawyer is licensed to practice only in this jurisdiction, the rules to be applied shall be the rules of this jurisdiction, and

(ii) if the lawyer is licensed to practice in this and another jurisdiction, the rules to be applied shall be the rules of the admitting jurisdiction in which the lawyer principally practices; provided, however, that if particular conduct clearly has its predominant effect in another jurisdiction in which the lawyer is licensed to practice, the rules of that jurisdiction shall be applied to that conduct.

COMMENT:

Disciplinary Authority

[1]   Paragraph (a) restates longstanding law.

Choice of Law

[2]   A lawyer may be potentially subject to more than one set of rules of professional conduct which impose different obligations. The lawyer may be licensed to practice in more than one jurisdiction with differing rules, or may be admitted to practice before a particular court with rules that differ from those of the jurisdiction or jurisdictions in which the lawyer is licensed to practice. In the past, decisions have not developed clear or consistent guidance as to which rules apply in such circumstances.

[3]   Paragraph (b) seeks to resolve such potential conflicts. Its premise is that minimizing conflicts between rules, as well as uncertainty about which rules are applicable, is in the best interest of both clients and the profession (as well as the bodies having authority to regulate the profession). Accordingly, it takes the approach of (i) providing that any particular conduct of an attorney shall be subject to only one set of rules

federal tribunals may have to regulate
practice before them.

of professional conduct, and (ii) making the determination of which set of rules applies to particular conduct as straightforward as possible, consistent with recognition of appropriate regulatory interests of relevant jurisdictions.

[4] Paragraph (b) provides that as to a lawyer's conduct relating to a proceeding in a court before which the lawyer is admitted to practice (either generally or pro hac vice), the lawyer shall be subject only to the rules of professional conduct of that court. As to all other conduct, paragraph (b) provides that a lawyer licensed to practice only in this jurisdiction shall be subject to the rules of professional conduct of this jurisdiction, and that a lawyer licensed in multiple jurisdictions shall be subject only to the rules of the jurisdiction where he or she (as an individual, not his or her firm) principally practices, but with one exception: if particular conduct clearly has its predominant effect in another admitting jurisdiction, then only the rules of that jurisdiction shall apply. The intention is for the latter exception to be a narrow one. It would be appropriately applied, for example, to a situation in which a lawyer admitted in, and principally practicing in, State A, but also admitted in State B, handled an acquisition by a company whose headquarters and operations were in State B of another, similar such company. The exception would not appropriately be applied, on the other hand, if the lawyer handled an acquisition by a company whose headquarters and operations were in State A of a company whose headquarters and main operations were in State A, but which also had some operations in State B.

[5] If two admitting jurisdictions were to proceed against a lawyer for the same conduct, they should, applying this rule, identify the same governing ethics rules. They should take all appropriate steps to see that they do apply the same rule to the same conduct, and in all events should avoid proceeding against a lawyer on the basis of two inconsistent rules.

[6] The choice of law provision is not intended to apply to transnational practice. Choice of law in this context should be the subject of agreements between jurisdictions or of appropriate international law.

MODEL CODE COMPARISON:

There was no counterpart to this Rule in the Model Code.

TABLES A AND B: RELATED SECTIONS IN THE ABA MODEL CODE OF PROFESSIONAL RESPONSIBILITY

TABLE A *

ABA Model Rules	ABA Model Code	ABA Model Rules	ABA Model Code
Competence		*Conflict of Interest*	
Rule 1.1	EC 1–1, EC 1–2, EC 6–1, EC 6–2, EC 6–3, EC 6–4, EC 6–5, DR 6–101(A)	Rule 1.7(a)	EC 5–1, EC 5–14, EC 5–15, EC 5–17, EC 5–21, EC 5–22, DR 5–101(A), DR 5–105(A) & (B), DR 5–107(B)
Scope of Representation		Rule 1.7(b) & (b)(1)	EC 2–21, EC 5–1, EC 5–2, EC 5–3, EC 5–9, EC 5–11, EC 5–13, EC 5–14, EC 5–15, EC 5–16, EC 5–17, EC 5–19, EC 5–21, EC 5–22, EC 5–23, DR 5–101(A) & (B), DR 5–102, DR 5–104(A), DR 5–105(A), (B) & (C), DR 5–107(A)
Rule 1.2(a)	EC 5–12, EC 7–7, EC 7–8, DR 7–101(A)(1)		
Rule 1.2(b)	EC 7–17		
Rule 1.2(c)	EC 7–8, EC 7–9, DR 7–101(B)(1)		
Rule 1.2(d)	EC 7–1, EC 7–2, EC 7–5, EC 7–22, DR 7–102(A)(6), (7) & (8), DR 7–106		
Rule 1.2(e)	DR 2–110(C)(1)(c), DR 9–101(C)	Rule 1.7(b)(2)	EC 5–16, EC 5–17, DR 7–106(B)(2)
Diligence		*Prohibited Transactions*	
Rule 1.3	EC 2–31, EC 6–4, EC 7–1, EC 7–38, DR 6–101(A)(3), DR 7–101(A)(1) & (3)	Rule 1.8(a)	EC 5–3, EC 5–5, DR 5–104(A)
		Rule 1.8(b)	EC 4–5, DR 4–101(B)
Communication		Rule 1.8(c)	EC 5–1, EC 5–2, EC 5–5, EC 5–6
Rule 1.4(a)	EC 7–8, EC 9–2, DR 6–101(A)(3), DR 9–102(B)(1)	Rule 1.8(d)	EC 5–1, EC 5–3, EC 5–4, DR 5–104(B)
Rule 1.4(b)	EC 7–8	Rule 1.8(e)	EC 5–1, EC 5–3, EC 5–7, EC 5–8, DR 5–103(B)
Fees			
Rule 1.5(a)	EC 2–16, EC 2–17, EC 2–18, DR 2–106(A) & (B)	Rule 1.8(f)	EC 2–21, EC 5–1, DR 5–107(A) & (B)
Rule 1.5(b)	EC 2–19	Rule 1.8(g)	EC 5–1, DR 5–106(A)
Rule 1.5(c)	EC 2–20, EC 5–7		
Rule 1.5(d)	EC 2–20, DR 2–106(C)	Rule 1.8(h)	EC 6–6, DR 6–102(A)
Rule 1.5(e)	EC 2–22, DR 2–107(A)	Rule 1.8(i)	None
Confidentiality of Information		Rule 1.8(j)	EC 5–1, EC 5–7, DR 5–101(A), DR 5–103(A)
Rule 1.6(a)	EC 4–1, EC 4–2, EC 4–3, EC 4–4, DR 4–101(A), (B) & (C)	*Former Client*	
		Rule 1.9(a)	DR 5–105(C)
Rule 1.6(b)(1)	EC 4–2, DR 4–101(C)(3), DR 7–102(B)	Rule 1.9(b)	EC 4–5, EC 4–6
		Imputed Disqualification	
Rule 1.6(b)(2)	DR 4–101(C)(4)	Rule 1.10(a)	EC 4–5, DR 5–105(D)

* Table A provides cross-references to related provisions, but only in the sense that the provisions consider substantially similar subject matter or reflect similar concerns. A cross-reference does not indicate that a provision of the ABA Model Code of Professional Responsibility has been incorporated by the provision of a Model Rule. The Canons of the Code are not cross-referenced.

TABLES

ABA Model Rules	ABA Model Code	ABA Model Rules	ABA Model Code
Imputed Disqualification		*Declining or Terminating Representation*	
Rule 1.10(b)	EC 4–5, DR 5–105(D)	Rule 1.16(b)(5)	EC 2–32, DR 2–110(C)(1)(d) & (e)
Rule 1.10(c)	DR 5–105(A)	Rule 1.16(b)(6)	EC 2–32, DR 2–110(C)(6)
Rule 1.10(d)	EC 5–16	Rule 1.16(c)	EC 2–32, DR 2–110(A)(1)
Successive Government and Private Employment		Rule 1.16(d)	EC 2–32, DR 2–110(A)(2) & (3)
Rule 1.11(a)	EC 9–3, DR 9–101(B)	*Advisor*	
Rule 1.11(b)	None	Rule 2.1	EC 5–11, EC 7–3, EC 7–8, DR 5–107(B)
Rule 1.11(c)	EC 8–8		
Rule 1.11(d)	None	*Intermediary*	
Rule 1.11(e)	None	Rule 2.2(a)(1)	EC 4–2, EC 5–14, EC 5–15, EC 5–16, EC 5–20, DR 5–105(A) & (C)
Former Judge or Arbitrator			
Rule 1.12(a) & (b)	EC 5–20, EC 9–3, DR 9–101(A) & (B)		
Rule 1.12(c)	DR 5–105(D)	Rule 2.2(a)(2) & (3)	EC 5–14, EC 5–15, DR 5–105(A) & (C)
Rule 1.12(d)	None	Rule 2.2(b)	EC 5–16
Organization as Client		Rule 2.2(c)	EC 5–15, EC 5–19, DR 5–105(B) & (C)
Rule 1.13(a)	EC 5–18, EC 5–24		
Rule 1.13(b)	EC 5–18, EC 5–24, DR 5–107(B)	*Evaluation for Use by Third Persons*	
		Rule 2.3	None
Rule 1.13(c)	EC 5–18, EC 5–24, DR 5–105(D), DR 5–107(B)	*Meritorious Claims and Contentions*	
		Rule 3.1	EC 7–1, EC 7–4, EC 7–5, EC 7–14, EC 7–25, DR 1–102(A)(5), DR 2–109(A)(B)(1), DR 7–102(A)(1) & (2)
Rule 1.13(d)	EC 5–16		
Rule 1.13(e)	EC 4–4, EC 5–16, DR 5–105(B) & (C)		
Disabled Client			
Rule 1.14(a)	EC 7–11, EC 7–12	*Expediting Litigation*	
Rule 1.14(b)	EC 7–12	Rule 3.2	EC 7–20, DR 1–102(A)(5), DR 7–101(A)(1) & (2)
Safekeeping Property			
Rule 1.15	EC 5–7, EC 9–5, EC 9–7, DR 5–103(A)(1), DR 9–102	*Candor Toward the Tribunal*	
		Rule 3.3(a)(1)	EC 7–4, EC 7–32, EC 8–5, DR 1–102(A)(4) & (5), DR 7–102(A)(4) & (5)
Declining or Terminating Representation			
Rule 1.16(a)(1)	EC 2–30, EC 2–31, EC 2–32, DR 2–103(E), DR 2–104(A), DR 2–109(A), DR 2–110(B)(1) & (2)	Rule 3.3(a)(2)	EC 8–5, DR 1–102(A)(4) & (5), DR 7–102(A)(3), DR 7–102(B)(1), DR 7–109(A)
Rule 1.16(a)(2)	EC 1–6, EC 2–30, EC 2–31, EC 2–32, DR 2–110(B)(3), DR 2–110(C)(4)	Rule 3.3(a)(3)	EC 7–23, DR 1–102(A)(5), DR 7–106(B)(1)
		Rule 3.3(a)(4)	EC 7–5, EC 7–26, EC 8–5, DR 1–102(A)(4) & (5), DR 7–102(A)(7), DR 7–102(B)(1)
Rule 1.16(a)(3)	EC 2–31, EC 2–32, DR 2–110(B)(4)		
Rule 1.16(b)(1)	EC 2–31, EC 2–32, DR 2–110(C)(1)(b) & (c), DR 2–110(C)(2)		
		Rule 3.3(b)	EC 8–5, DR 7–102(B)
Rule 1.16(b)(2)	EC 2–31, EC 2–32, DR 2–110(C)(2)	Rule 3.3(c)	EC 7–24, EC 7–25
		Rule 3.3(d)	EC 7–24, EC 7–27
Rule 1.16(b)(3)	EC 2–30, EC 2–31, EC 2–32, DR 2–110(C)(1)(d)	*Fairness to Opposing Party and Counsel*	
		Rule 3.4(a)	EC 7–6, EC 7–27, DR 1–102(A)(4) & (5), DR 7–106(C)(7), DR 7–109(A) & (B)
Rule 1.16(b)(4)	EC 2–31, EC 2–32, DR 2–110(C)(1)(f)(i)(j)		

ABA MODEL RULES

ABA Model Rules	ABA Model Code	ABA Model Rules	ABA Model Code

Fairness to Opposing Party and Counsel

Rule 3.4(b) — EC 7–6, EC 7–28, DR 1–102(A)(4), (5) & (6), DR 7–102(A)(6), DR 7–109(C)

Rule 3.4(c) — EC 7–22, EC 7–25, EC 7–38, DR 1–102(A)(5), DR 7–106(A), DR 7–106(C)(5) & (7)

Rule 3.4(d) — DR 1–102(A)(5), DR 7–106(A), DR 7–106(C)(7)

Rule 3.4(e) — EC 7–24, EC 7–25, DR 1–102(A)(5), DR 7–106(C)(1), (2), (3) & (4)

Rule 3.4(f) — EC 7–27, DR 1–102(A)(5), DR 7–104(A)(2), DR 7–109(B)

Impartiality and Decorum

Rule 3.5(a) — EC 7–20, EC 7–29, EC 7–31, EC 7–32, EC 7–34, DR 7–106, DR 7–108, DR 7–109, DR 7–110, DR 8–101(A)

Rule 3.5(b) — EC 7–35, DR 7–108, DR 7–110(A) & (B)

Rule 3.5(c) — EC 7–20, EC 7–25, EC 7–36, EC 7–37, DR 7–101(A)(1), DR 7–106(C)(6)

Trial Publicity

Rule 3.6 — EC 7–25, EC 7–33, DR 7–107

Lawyer as Witness

Rule 3.7(a) — EC 5–9, EC 5–10, DR 5–101(B)(1) & (2), DR 5–102

Rule 3.7(b) — EC 5–9, DR 5–101(B), DR 5–102

Special Responsibilities of a Prosecutor

Rule 3.8(a) — EC 7–11, EC 7–13, EC 7–14, DR 7–103(A)

Rule 3.8(b) — EC 7–11, EC 7–13

Rule 3.8(c) — EC 7–11, EC 7–13, EC 7–18

Rule 3.8(d) — EC 7–11, EC 7–13, DR 7–103(B)

Rule 3.8(e) — None

Advocate in Nonadjudicative Proceedings

Rule 3.9 — EC 7–11, EC 7–15, EC 7–16, EC 8–4, EC 8–5, DR 7–106(B)(2), DR 9–101(C)

Truthfulness to Others

Rule 4.1 — EC 7–5, DR 7–102(A)(3), (4), (5) & (7), DR 7–102(B)

Communication With Represented Persons

Rule 4.2 — EC 2–30, EC 7–18, DR 7–104(A)(1)

Dealing With Unrepresented Persons

Rule 4.3 — EC 2–3, EC 7–18, DR 7–104(A)(2)

Respect for Rights of Third Persons

Rule 4.4 — EC 7–10, EC 7–14, EC 7–21, EC 7–25, EC 7–29, EC 7–30, EC 7–37, DR 2–110(B)(1), DR 7–101(A)(1), DR 7–102(A)(1), DR 7–106(C)(2), DR 7–107(D), (E) & (F), DR 7–108(D), (E) & (F)

Responsibilities of a Partner or Supervisory Lawyer

Rule 5.1(a) & (b) — EC 4–5, DR 4–101(D), DR 7–107(J)

Rule 5.1(c) — DR 1–102(A)(2), DR 1–103(A), DR 7–108(E)

Responsibilities of a Subordinate Lawyer

Rule 5.2 — None

Responsibilities Regarding Nonlawyer Assistants

Rule 5.3(a) — EC 3–6, EC 4–2, EC 4–5, EC 7–28, DR 4–101(D), DR 7–107(J)

Rule 5.3(b) — DR 1–102(A)(2), DR 7–107(J), DR 7–108(B), DR 7–108(E)

Rule 5.3(c) — None

Professional Independence of Lawyer

Rule 5.4(a) — EC 2–33, EC 3–8, EC 5–24, DR 2–103(D)(4)(d), (e) & (f), DR 3–102(A), DR 5–107(C)(3)

Rule 5.4(b) — EC 2–33, EC 3–8, DR 3–103(A)

Rule 5.4(c) — EC 2–33, EC 5–23, DR 2–103(C), DR 5–107(B)

Rule 5.4(d) — EC 2–33, EC 3–8, DR 5–107(C)

Unauthorized Practice of Law

Rule 5.5 — DR 3–101(A) & (B)

Restrictions on Right to Practice

Rule 5.6 — DR 2–108

Pro Bono Publico Service

Rule 6.1 — EC 1–2, EC 1–4, EC 2–1, EC 2–2, EC 2–16, EC 2–24, EC 2–25, EC 6–2, EC 8–1,

TABLES

ABA Model Code	ABA Model Rules	ABA Model Code	ABA Model Rules

TABLE B*

Canon 1: Integrity of Profession

EC 1–1	Rules 1.1, 8.1(a)		
EC 1–2	Rules 1.1, 6.1, 8.1(a)		
EC 1–3	Rules 8.1(a), 8.3		
EC 1–4	Rule 6.1		
EC 1–5	Rule 8.4(a), (b), (c), (e) & (f)		
EC 1–6	Rules 1.16(a)(2), 8.4(a)		
DR 1–101	Rule 8.1(a)		
DR 1–102(A)(1)	Rule 8.4(a)		
DR 1–102(A)(2)	Rules 5.1(c), 5.3(b), 8.4(a)		
DR 1–102(A)(3)	Rule 8.4(b) & (f)		
DR 1–102(A)(4)	Rules 3.3(a)(1), (2) & (4), 3.4(a) & (b), 8.4(c) & (f)		
DR 1–102(A)(5)	Rules 3.1, 3.2, 3.3(a)(1), (2) & (4), 3.4, 8.4(d) & (f)		
DR 1–102(A)(6)	Rules 3.4(b), 8.4(b) & (f)		
DR 1–103(A)	Rules 5.1(c), 8.3		
DR 1–103(B)	Rule 8.1(b)		

Canon 2: Making Counsel Available

EC 2–1	Rules 6.1, 6.2(a), 7.2(a), 7.4		
EC 2–2	Rules 6.1, 7.2(a)		
EC 2–3	Rules 4.3, 7.3		
EC 2–4	Rule 7.3		
EC 2–5	Rule 7.1(b)		
EC 2–6	Rule 7.2(a)		
EC 2–7	Rules 7.2(a), 7.4		
EC 2–8	Rules 7.1, 7.2(a) & (c), 7.4		
EC 2–9	Rule 7.1		
EC 2–10	Rule 7.1(a) & (c)		
EC 2–11	Rule 7.5		
EC 2–12	Rule 7.5(c)		
EC 2–13	Rule 7.5(a) & (d)		
EC 2–14	Rule 7.4		
EC 2–15	Rule 7.2(a) & (c)		
EC 2–16	Rules 1.5(a), 6.1, 6.2(b)		
EC 2–17	Rule 1.5(a)		
EC 2–18	Rule 1.5(a)		
EC 2–19	Rule 1.5(b)		
EC 2–20	Rule 1.5(c) & (d)		
EC 2–21	Rules 1.7(b), 1.8(f)		
EC 2–22	Rule 1.5(e)		
EC 2–23	None		
EC 2–24	Rule 6.1		
EC 2–25	Rules 6.1, 6.2		

Canon 2: Making Counsel Available

ABA Model Code	ABA Model Rules
EC 2–26	None
EC 2–27	Rule 6.2(a) & (c)
EC 2–28	Rule 6.2(a)
EC 2–29	Rule 6.2
EC 2–30	Rules 1.16(a)(1) & (2), 1.16(b)(3), 4.2, 6.2(b) & (c)
EC 2–31	Rules 1.3, 1.16(a) & (b)
EC 2–32	Rule 1.16(a), (b), (c) & (d)
EC 2–33	Rules 5.4, 6.3, 6.4
DR 2–101(A)	Rule 7.1
DR 2–101(B)	Rules 7.1, 7.2(a)
DR 2–101(C)	Rule 7.1
DR 2–101(D)	Rule 7.2(b)
DR 2–101(E)	Rule 7.1
DR 2–101(F)	Rule 7.1
DR 2–101(G)	Rule 7.1
DR 2–101(H)	Rule 7.2
DR 2–101(I)	Rule 7.2(c)
DR 2–102(A)	Rules 7.2(a), 7.4
DR 2–102(B)	Rules 7.2(a), 7.5(a) & (c)
DR 2–102(C)	Rule 7.5(d)
DR 2–102(D)	Rule 7.5(a) & (b)
DR 2–102(E)	Rules 7.1(a), 7.4, 7.5(a)
DR 2–103(A)	Rule 7.3
DR 2–103(B)	Rule 7.2(a) & (c)
DR 2–103(C)	Rules 5.4(a), 7.2(c), 7.3
DR 2–103(D)	Rules 1.16(a)(1), 5.4(a), 7.2(c), 7.3
DR 2–103(E)	Rules 1.16(a), 7.2(a), 7.3
DR 2–104	Rules 1.16(a), 7.3
DR 2–105	Rule 7.4
DR 2–106(A)	Rule 1.5(a)
DR 2–106(B)	Rule 1.5(a)
DR 2–106(C)	Rule 1.5(d)
DR 2–107(A)	Rule 1.5(e)
DR 2–107(B)	Rule 5.4(a)(1)
DR 2–108(A)	Rule 5.6
DR 2–108(B)	Rule 5.6
DR 2–109(A)	Rules 1.16(a)(1), 3.1
DR 2–110(A)	Rule 1.16(c) & (d)
DR 2–110(B)	Rules 1.16(a), 3.1, 4.4
DR 2–110(C)	Rules 1.2(e), 1.16(a) & (b)

Canon 3: Unauthorized Practice

EC 3–1	None
EC 3–2	None

* Table B provides cross-references to related provisions, but only in the sense that the provisions consider substantially similar subject matter or reflect similar concerns. A cross-reference does not indicate that a provision of the ABA Model Code of Professional Responsibility has been incorporated by the provision of a Model Rule. The Canons of the Code are not cross-referenced.

134

TABLES

ABA Model Code	ABA Model Rules	ABA Model Code	ABA Model Rules
Canon 3: Unauthorized Practice		*Canon 5: Independent Judgment*	
EC 3–3	Rule 8.4(e)	EC 5–22	Rule 1.7
EC 3–4	None	EC 5–23	Rules 1.7(b), 5.4(c)
EC 3–5	None	EC 5–24	Rules 1.13(a), (b) & (c), 5.4(a)
EC 3–6	Rule 5.3(a)		
EC 3–7	None	DR 5–101(A)	Rules 1.7, 1.8(j), 6.3, 6.4
EC 3–8	Rule 5.49(a), (b) & (d)		
		DR 5–101(B)	Rules 1.7(b), 3.7
EC 3–9	Rule 8.4(d)	DR 5–102(A)	Rules 1.7(b), 3.7
DR 3–101(A)	Rule 5.5	DR 5–102(B)	Rules 1.7(b), 3.7
DR 3–101(B)	Rules 5.5, 8.4(d)	DR 5–103(A)	Rules 1.8(j), 1.15
DR 3–102	Rule 5.4(a)	DR 5–103(B)	Rule 1.8(e)
DR 3–103	Rule 5.4(b)	DR 5–104(A)	Rules 1.7(b), 1.8(a)
Canon 4: Confidences and Secrets		DR 5–104(B)	Rule 1.8(d)
EC 4–1	Rule 1.6(a)	DR 5–105(A)	Rules 1.7, 1.10(c), 2.2(a)
EC 4–2	Rules 1.6(a) & (b)(1), 2.2(a)(1), 5.3(a)		
		DR 5–105(B)	Rules 1.7, 1.13(e), 2.2(c)
EC 4–3	Rule 1.6(a)		
EC 4–4	Rules 1.6(a), 1.13(e)	DR 5–105(C)	Rules 1.7(b), 1.13(e), 1.9(a), 2.2
EC 4–5	Rules 1.8(b), 1.9(b), 1.10(a) & (b), 5.1(a) & (c), 5.3(a)		
		DR 5–105(D)	Rules 1.10(a), 1.12(c), 1.13(c)
EC 4–6	Rule 1.9(b)		
DR 4–101(A)	Rule 1.6(a)	DR 5–106	Rule 1.8(g)
DR 4–101(B)	Rules 1.6(a), 1.8(b), 1.9(b)	DR 5–107(A)	Rules 1.7(b), 1.8(f)
		DR 5–107(B)	Rules 1.7(a), 1.8(f), 1.13(b) & (c), 2.1, 5.4(c)
DR 4–101(C)	Rules 1.6(a) & (b)		
DR 4–101(D)	Rules 5.1(a) & (b), 5.3(a) & (b)		
		DR 5–107(C)	Rule 5.4(a) & (d)
Canon 5: Independent Judgment		*Canon 6: Competence*	
EC 5–1	Rules 1.7(a) & (b), 1.8(c), (d), (e), (f), (g) & (j)	EC 6–1	Rule 1.1
		EC 6–2	Rules 1.1, 5.1(a) & (b), 6.1
EC 5–2	Rules 1.7(b), 1.8(c)		
EC 5–3	Rules 1.7(b), 1.8(a), (d) & (e)	EC 6–3	Rule 1.1
		EC 6–4	Rules 1.1, 1.3
EC 5–4	Rule 1.8(d)	EC 6–5	Rule 1.1
EC 5–5	Rule 1.8(a) & (c)	EC 6–6	Rule 1.8(h)
EC 5–6	Rules 1.8(c), 7.3	DR 6–101	Rules 1.1, 1.3, 1.4(a)
EC 5–7	Rules 1.5(c), 1.8(e) & (j), 1.15	DR 6–102	Rule 1.8(h)
		Canon 7: Zeal Within the Law	
EC 5–8	Rule 1.8(e)	EC 7–1	Rules 1.2(d), 1.3, 3.1
EC 5–9	Rules 1.7(b), 3.7	EC 7–2	Rule 1.2(d)
EC 5–10	Rule 3.7(a)	EC 7–3	Rule 2.1
EC 5–11	Rules 1.7(b), 2.1	EC 7–4	Rules 3.1, 3.3(a)(1)
EC 5–12	Rule 1.2(a)	EC 7–5	Rules 1.2(d), 3.1, 3.3(a)(4), 4.1
EC 5–13	Rule 1.7(b)		
EC 5–14	Rules 1.7(a), 2.2(a)	EC 7–6	Rule 3.4(a) & (b)
EC 5–15	Rules 1.7, 2.2(a) & (c)	EC 7–7	Rule 1.2(a)
		EC 7–8	Rules 1.2(a) & (c), 1.4, 2.1
EC 5–16	Rules 1.7(b), 1.10(d), 1.13(d) & (e), 2.2(a)(1) & (b)		
		EC 7–9	Rule 1.2(c)
		EC 7–10	Rule 4.4
EC 5–17	Rule 1.7	EC 7–11	Rules 1.14(a), 3.8(a), (b), (c) & (d), 3.9
EC 5–18	Rule 1.13(a), (b) & (c)		
		EC 7–12	Rule 1.14
EC 5–19	Rules 1.7(b), 2.2(c)	EC 7–13	Rule 3.8
EC 5–20	Rules 1.12(a) & (b), 2.2(a)(1)	EC 7–14	Rules 3.1, 3.8(a), 4.4
		EC 7–15	Rule 3.9
		EC 7–16	Rule 3.9
		EC 7–17	Rule 1.2(b)
		EC 7–18	Rules 3.8(c), 4.2, 4.3
EC 5–21	Rule 1.7	EC 7–19	None

ABA MODEL RULES

ABA Model Code	ABA Model Rules	ABA Model Code	ABA Model Rules
Canon 7: Zeal Within the Law		*Canon 7: Zeal Within the Law*	
EC 7–20	Rules 3.2, 3.5(a) & (c)	DR 7–107(A)–(I)	Rule 3.6
		DR 7–107(D)–(F)	Rule 4.4
EC 7–21	Rule 4.4	DR 7–107(J)	Rules 5.1(a) & (b), 5.3(a) & (b)
EC 7–22	Rules 1.2(d), 3.4(c)		
EC 7–23	Rule 3.3(a)(3)	DR 7–108(A)	Rule 3.5(a) & (b)
EC 7–24	Rules 3.3(c) & (d), 3.4(e)	DR 7–108(B)	Rules 3.5(a), (b), (c), (d) & (f), 5.3(b)
EC 7–25	Rules 3.1, 3.3(c), 3.4(c) & (e), 3.5(c), 3.6, 4.4	DR 7–108(C)	Rule 3.5(a) & (b)
		DR 7–108(D)	Rule 4.4
		DR 7–108(E)	Rules 4.4, 5.1(c), 5.3(b)
EC 7–26	Rule 3.3(a)(4)		
EC 7–27	Rules 3.3(d), 3.4(a) & (f)	DR 7–108(F)	Rule 4.4
		DR 7–108(G)	None
EC 7–28	Rules 3.4(b), 5.3(a)	DR 7–109(A)	Rules 3.3(a)(2), 3.4(a)
EC 7–29	Rules 3.5(a), 4.4		
EC 7–30	Rule 4.4	DR 7–109(B)	Rule 3.4(a) & (f)
EC 7–31	Rule 3.5(a)	DR 7–109(C)	Rule 3.4(b)
EC 7–32	Rules 3.3(a)(1), 3.5(a)	DR 7–110(A)	Rules 3.5(a), 8.4(f)
		DR 7–110(B)	Rule 3.5(a) & (b)
EC 7–33	Rule 3.6	*Canon 8: Improving Legal System*	
EC 7–34	Rules 3.5(a), 8.4(f)	EC 8–1	Rule 6.1
EC 7–35	Rule 3.5(b)	EC 8–2	Rule 6.1
EC 7–36	Rule 3.5(c)	EC 8–3	Rules 6.1, 6.2(a), 8.4(d)
EC 7–37	Rules 3.5(c), 4.4		
EC 7–38	Rules 1.3, 3.4(c)	EC 8–4	Rule 3.9
EC 7–39	None	EC 8–5	Rules 3.3(a)(1), (2) & (4), 3.3(b), 3.9
DR 7–101(A)	Rules 1.2(a), 1.3, 3.2, 3.5(c), 4.4		
		EC 8–6	Rule 8.2(a)
DR 7–101(B)	Rules 1.2, 1.16(b)	EC 8–7	Rule 6.1
DR 7–102(A)(1)	Rules 3.1, 4.4	EC 8–8	Rule 1.11(c)
DR 7–102(A)(2)	Rule 3.1	EC 8–9	Rule 6.1
DR 7–102(A)(3)	Rules 3.3(a)(2), 4.1	DR 8–101	Rules 3.5, 8.4(b), (c) & (f)
DR 7–102(A)(4)	Rules 3.3(a) & (c), 4.1		
		DR 8–102	Rule 8.2(a)
DR 7–102(A)(5)	Rules 3.3(a)(1), 4.1	DR 8–103	Rule 8.2(b)
DR 7–102(A)(6)	Rules 1.2(d), 3.4(b)	*Canon 9: Appearance of Impropriety*	
DR 7–102(A)(7)	Rules 1.2(d), 3.3(a)(4), 4.1	EC 9–1	Rule 8.4(f)
		EC 9–2	Rules 1.4(a), 8.4(e)
DR 7–102(A)(8)	Rules 1.2(d), 8.4(a) & (b)	EC 9–3	Rules 1.11(a), 1.12(a) & (b)
DR 7–102(B)	Rules 1.6(b)(1), 3.3(b), 4.1	EC 9–4	Rules 7.1(b), 8.4(c) & (e)
DR 7–103(A)	Rule 3.8(a)	EC 9–5	Rule 1.15
DR 7–103(B)	Rule 3.8(d)	EC 9–6	Preamble, Rule 8.4(e)
DR 7–104	Rules 3.4(f), 4.2, 4.3		
DR 7–105	None	EC 9–7	Rule 1.15
DR 7–106(A)	Rules 1.2(d), 3.4(c) & (d), 3.5(a)	DR 9–101(A)	Rule 1.12(a) & (b)
		DR 9–101(B)	Rules 1.11(a), 1.12(a) & (b)
DR 7–106(B)	Rules 1.7(b)(2), 3.3(a)(3), 3.9	DR 9–101(C)	Rules 1.2(e), 3.9, 7.1(b), 8.4(e)
DR 7–106(C)	Rules 3.4(a), (c), (d) & (e), 3.5(c), 4.4	DR 9–102	Rules 1.4(a), 1.15

INDEX TO ABA MODEL RULES

A

B

C

137

INDEX

Government lawyer,
> authority established by constitution, statutes and common law, Scope
> conflict of interest, Rule 1.7 (Comment)
> duty of confidentiality, Rule 1.6 (Comment)
> representing multiple clients, Scope
> subject to rules, Rule 1.11 (Comment)

H

Harass,
> law's procedures used to, Preamble

I

Impartiality and decorum of the tribunal, Rule 3.5
Imputed disqualification,
> general rule, Rule 1.10
> government lawyers, Rule 1.11 (Comment)
> witness, when member of firm serves as, Rule 3.7(b)
Incompetent client,
> appointment of guardian for, Rule 1.14(b)
> representation of, Rule 1.14(a)
Independence of the legal profession, Preamble
Independent professional judgment, duty to exercise, Rule 5.4; Rule 2.1
Indigent client, paying court costs and expenses on behalf of, Rule 1.8(e)(2)
Insurance representation, conflict of interest, Rule 1.7 (Comment)
Intermediary,
> between clients, Rule 2.2
> lawyer as, Preamble
> withdrawal as, Rule 2.2(c)
Intimidate,
> law's procedures used to, Preamble

J

Judges,
> duty to show respect for, Preamble
> *ex parte* communication with, Rule 3.5(b)
> former judge, disqualification, Rule 1.12
> improper influence on, Rule 3.5(a)
> misconduct by, Rule 8.3(b)
> statements about, Rule 8.2
Juror,
> improper influence on, Rule 3.5(a)
Jury trial,
> client's right to waive, Rule 1.2(a)

L

Law clerk,
> negotiating for private employment, Rule 1.12(b)
Law firm,
> defined, Terminology
> nonlawyer assistants, responsibility for, Rule 5.3
> responsibility of partner or supervisory lawyer, Rule 5.1
> subordinate lawyer, responsibility of, Rule 5.2
Law reform activities,
> affecting clients' interests, Rule 6.4
Lawyer referral service, Rule 6.1 (Comment)
> costs of, Rule 7.2(c)
Legal education,
> duty to work to strengthen, Preamble
Legislature,
> appearance before on behalf of client, Rule 3.8
Letterheads,
> false or misleading, Rule 7.5(a)
> jurisdictional limitations of members, Rule 7.5(b)
> public officials, Rule 7.5(c)
Liability to client,
> agreements limiting, Rule 1.8(h)
Lien,
> to secure fees and expenses, Rule 1.8(j)(1)
Literary rights,
> acquiring concerning representation, Rule 1.8(d)
Litigation,
> expedite, duty to, Rule 3.2
Loyalty,
> duty of to client, Rule 1.7 (Comment)

M

Malpractice,
> limiting liability to client for, Rule 1.8(h)
Meritorious claims and contentions, Rule 3.1
Military lawyers,
> adverse interests, representation of, Rule 1.9 (Comment)
Misconduct,
> forms of, Rule 8.4
Misleading legal argument, Rule 3.3 (Comment)
Misrepresentation,
> in advertisements, Rule 7.1
> to court, Rule 3.3 (Comment)
Multiple representation, *See under* Conflict of interest; *See also* Intermediary.

N

Negotiation,
conflicting interest, representation of, Rule 1.7 (Comment)
statements made during, Rule 4.1 (Comment)
Negotiator,
lawyer as, Preamble
Nonlawyers,
division of fees with, Rule 5.4(a)
partnership with, Rule 5.4(b)

O

Objectives of the representation,
client's right to determine, Rule 1.2(a)
lawyer's right to limit, Rule 1.2(c)
Opposing party,
communications with represented party, Rule 4.2
duty of fairness to, Rule 3.4
Organization, representation of,
board of directors, lawyer for serving on, Rule 1.7 (Comment)
communication with, Rule 1.4 (Comment)
conflicting interests among officers and employees, Rule 1.7 (Comment)
conflict of interest, Rule 1.7 (Comment)
constituents, representing, Rule 1.13(e)
identity of client, Rule 1.13(a); Rule 1.13(d)
misconduct, client engaged in, Rule 1.13(b)

P

Partner,
defined, Terminology
Patent practice,
advertising, Rule 7.4(a)
Perjury,
criminal defendant, Rule 3.3 (Comment)
disclosure of, Rule 3.3(b)
Personal affairs of lawyer,
duty to conduct in compliance with law, Preamble
Plea bargain,
client's right to accept or reject, Rule 1.2(a)
Pleadings,
verification of, Rule 3.3 (Comment)
Precedent,
failure to disclose to court, Rule 3.3(a)(3)
Prepaid legal services,
advertising for, Rule 7.2 (Comment)
Pro bono publico service, Rule 6.1

Procedural law,
lawyer's professional responsibilities proscribed by, Preamble
Professional corporation,
defined, Terminology
formation of, Rule 5.4(d)
Prompt,
lawyer's duty to be, Preamble
Property of client,
safekeeping, Rule 1.15
Prosecutor,
representing former defendant, Rule 1.9 (Comment)
special responsibilities of, Rule 3.8
Public citizen,
lawyer's duty as, Preamble
Public interest,
government lawyer's authority to represent, Scope
Public interest legal services, *See Pro bono publico* service.
Public office, lawyer holding,
negotiating private employment while, Rule 1.11(c)(2)
Public officials,
lawyer's duty to show respect for, Preamble

R

Recordkeeping,
property of client, Rule 1.15(a)
Referral,
when lawyer not competent to handle matter, Rule 1.1
Regulation of the legal profession,
self-governance, Preamble
Relatives of lawyer,
representing interests adverse to, Rule 1.8(h)
Representation of client,
decisionmaking authority of lawyer and client, Rule 1.2(a)
objectives, lawyer's right to limit, Rule 1.2(c)
termination of, Rule 1.2 (Comment)
Restrictions on right to practice,
partnership or employment agreement imposes, Rule 5.6(a)
settlement imposes, Rule 5.6(b)

S

Sanction,
severity of, Scope
Scope of representation, Rule 1.2
Settlement,
aggregate settlement on behalf of clients, Rule 1.8(g)

SELECTED SIGNIFICANT STATE MODIFICATIONS TO THE ABA MODEL RULES

The ABA Model Rules are designed to serve as a model for the states to consider and adopt. The enactment of the Model Rules caused most of the states to at least reconsider their local codes of ethics. As of the date of this publication, thirty-nine states have replaced codes based upon the Model Code and have enacted codes based upon the structure and content of the Model Rules. Every one of these states has in some way amended the Model Rules provisions. Three states (New York, Oregon, and Virginia) have amended their version of the Model Code to reflect certain Model Rules' provisions. One state, California, did not base its code on the Model Code originally and refused to base a 1989 revision on the Model Rules.

In light of the many state modifications to the Model Rules, it is useful to examine selected significant state amendments. Some of these amendments illustrate substantive disagreements with the position adopted by the ABA in the Model Rules. Other modifications reflect local practices that the states have chosen to memorialize in the local code. Still other changes illustrate the desire to be more elaborative with respect to the language in the text. The selected state variations presented in this section fall within each of these categories.

The selected significant state modifications to the ABA Model Rules are presented under the order of the rules and within this framework by alphabetical order of the states. In the advertising section, however, the Arizona and Texas rules are grouped under each state. This section is intended to be illustrative and not exhaustive of the many state modifications. The comments to the state rule are included only if they are relevant to the difference that is illustrated.

TABLE OF CONTENTS

District of Columbia Rule 1.8.
Illinois Rule 1.8.
Indiana Rule 1.8(k).
Minnesota Rule 1.8(e)(3).
Texas Rule 1.09 (Modification of Model Rule 1.9).
Utah Rule 1.9(a).
District of Columbia Rule 1.11.
New Hampshire Rule 1.11A.
Montana Rule 1.17.

Counsellor

Oregon Rule DR 5–106 (Modification to Model Rule 2.2).

Advocate

Wyoming Rule 3.1.
Kansas Rule 3.5.

Transactions With Persons Other Than Clients

Louisiana Rule 4.2.
New Mexico Rule 16–402 (Modification of Model Rule 4.2).
Texas Rule 4.02 (Modification of Model Rule 4.2).
Minnesota Rule 4.3.
Texas Rule 4.04 (Modification of Model Rule 4.4).

Law Firms and Associations

Texas Rule 5.01 (Modification of Model Rule 5.1).
Texas Rule 5.02 (Modification of Model Rule 5.2).
District of Columbia Rule 5.4.
Pennsylvania Rule 5.7.

Public Service

South Dakota Rule 6.1.

Information About Legal Services

Arizona Rule 7.1.
Arizona Rule 7.2.
Arizona Rule 7.3.
Texas Rule 7.01.
Texas Rule 7.02.
Texas Rule 7.03.
Texas Rule 7.04.
Texas Rule 7.05.
Texas Rule 7.06.
Texas Rule 7.07.

Maintaining the Integrity of the Profession

Kansas Rule 8.3.
Florida Rule 4–8.4(d).
Louisiana Rule 8.4.
Minnesota Rule 8.4.

New Jersey Rule 8.4(g).
District of Columbia Rule 9.1.
Appendix: States That Have Adopted a Version of the Model Rules.

CLIENT–LAWYER RELATIONSHIP

Texas Rule 1.01 *(Modification of Model Rules 1.1 and 1.3)*

[Texas has combined Model Rule 1.1 (competence) and 1.3 (diligence) into one rule.]

RULE 1.01   Competent and Diligent Representation

(a) A lawyer shall not accept or continue employment in a legal matter which the lawyer knows or should know is beyond the lawyer's competence, unless:

(1) another lawyer who is competent to handle the matter is, with the prior informed consent of the client, associated in the matter; or

(2) the advice or assistance of the lawyer is reasonably required in an emergency and the lawyer limits the advice and assistance to that which is reasonably necessary in the circumstances.

(b) In representing a client, a lawyer shall not:

(1) neglect a legal matter entrusted to the lawyer; or

(2) frequently fail to carry out completely the obligations that the lawyer owes to a client or clients.

(c) As used in this Rule, "neglect" signifies inattentiveness involving a conscious disregard for the responsibilities owed to a client or clients.

COMMENT:

Accepting Employment

[1]   A lawyer generally should not accept or continue employment in any area of the law in which the lawyer is not and will not be prepared to render competent legal services. "Competence" is defined in Terminology as possession of the legal knowledge, skill, and training reasonably necessary for the representation. Competent representation contemplates appropriate application by the lawyer of that legal knowledge, skill and training, reasonable thoroughness in the study and analysis of the law and facts, and reasonable attentiveness to the responsibilities owed to the client.

[2]   In determining whether a matter is beyond a lawyer's competence, relevant factors include the relative complexity and specialized nature of the matter, the lawyer's general experience in the field in

question, the preparation and study the lawyer will be able to give the matter, and whether it is feasible either to refer the matter to or associate a lawyer of established competence in the field in question. The required attention and preparation are determined in part by what is at stake; major litigation and complex transactions ordinarily require more elaborate treatment than matters of lesser consequences.

[3] A lawyer may not need to have special training or prior experience to accept employment to handle legal problems of a type with which the lawyer is unfamiliar. Although expertise in a particular field of law may be useful in some circumstances, the appropriate proficiency in many instances is that of a general practitioner. A newly admitted lawyer can be as competent in some matters as a practitioner with long experience. Some important legal skills, such as the analysis of precedent, the evaluation of evidence and legal drafting, are required in all legal problems. Perhaps the most fundamental legal skill consists of determining what kind of legal problems a situation may involve, a skill that necessarily transcends any particular specialized knowledge.

[4] A lawyer possessing the normal skill and training reasonably necessary for the representation of a client in an area of law is not subject to discipline for accepting employment in a matter in which, in order to represent the client properly, the lawyer must become more competent in regard to relevant legal knowledge by additional study and investigation. If the additional study and preparation will result in unusual delay or expense to the client, the lawyer should not accept employment except with the informed consent of the client.

[5] A lawyer offered employment or employed in a matter beyond the lawyer's competence generally must decline or withdraw from the employment or, with the prior informed consent of the client, associate a lawyer who is competent in the matter. Paragraph (a)(2) permits a lawyer, however, to give advice or assistance in an emergency in a matter even though the lawyer does not have the skill ordinarily required if referral to or consultation with another lawyer would be impractical and if the assistance is limited to that which is reasonably necessary in the circumstances.

Competent and Diligent Representation

[6] Having accepted employment, a lawyer should act with competence, commitment and dedication to the interest of the client and with zeal in advocacy upon the client's behalf. A lawyer should feel a moral or professional obligation to pursue a matter on behalf of a client with reasonable diligence and promptness despite opposition, obstruction or personal inconvenience to the lawyer. A lawyer's workload should be controlled so that each matter can be handled with diligence and competence. As provided in paragraph (a), an incompetent lawyer is subject to discipline.

Neglect

[7] Perhaps no professional shortcoming is more widely resented than procrastination. A client's interests often can be adversely affected by the passage of time or the change of conditions; in extreme instances, as when a lawyer overlooks a statute of limitations, the client's legal position may be destroyed. Under paragraph (b), a lawyer is subject to professional discipline for neglecting a particular legal matter as well as for frequent failures to carry out fully the obligations owed to one or more clients. A lawyer who acts in good faith is not subject to discipline, under those provisions for an isolated inadvertent or unskilled act or omission, tactical error, or error of judgment. Because delay can cause a client needless anxiety and undermine confidence in the lawyer's trustworthiness, there is a duty to communicate reasonably with clients; see Rule 1.03.

Maintaining Competence

[8] Because of the vital role of lawyers in the legal process, each lawyer should strive to become and remain proficient and competent in the practice of law. To maintain the requisite knowledge and skill of a competent practitioner, a lawyer should engage in continuing study and education. If a system of peer review has been established, the lawyer should consider making use of it in appropriate circumstances. Isolated instances of faulty conduct or decision should be identified for purposes of additional study or instruction.

Michigan Rule 1.2

[Michigan has amended Model Rule 1.2(a) to read as follows:]

RULE 1.2 Scope of Representation

(a) A lawyer shall seek the lawful objectives of a client through reasonably available means permitted by law and these rules. A lawyer does not violate this rule by acceding to reasonable requests of opposing counsel that do not prejudice the rights of the client, by being punctual in fulfilling all professional commitments, by avoiding offensive tactics. A lawyer shall abide by a client's decision whether to accept an offer of settlement or mediation evaluation of a matter. In a criminal case, the lawyer shall abide by the client's decision, after consultation with the lawyer, as to a plea to be entered, whether to waive jury trial, and whether the client will testify. In representing a client, a lawyer may, where permissible, exercise professional judgment to waive or fail to assert a right or position of the client.

* * *

147

Florida Rule 4–1.5 (Modification of Model Rule 1.5)

[Florida has amended Model Rule 1.5 to read as follows:]

RULE 4–1.5 Fees for Legal Services

(a) Illegal, Prohibited, or Clearly Excessive Fees. An attorney shall not enter into an agreement for, charge, or collect an illegal, prohibited, or clearly excessive fee or a fee generated by employment that was obtained through advertising or solicitation not in compliance with the Rules Regulating The Florida Bar. A fee is clearly excessive when:

(1) after a review of the facts, a lawyer of ordinary prudence would be left with a definite and firm conviction that the fee exceeds a reasonable fee for services provided to such a degree as to constitute clear overreaching or an unconscionable demand by the attorney; or

(2) the fee is sought or secured by the attorney by means of intentional misrepresentation or fraud upon the client, a nonclient party, or any court, as to either entitlement to, or amount of, the fee.

(b) Factors to Be Considered in Determining Reasonable Fee. Factors to be considered as guides in determining a reasonable fee include:

(1) the time and labor required, the novelty, complexity, and difficulty of the questions involved, and the skill requisite to perform the legal service properly;

(2) the likelihood that the acceptance of the particular employment will preclude other employment by the lawyer;

(3) the fee, or rate of fee, customarily charged in the locality for legal services of a comparable or similar nature;

(4) the significance of, or amount involved in, the subject matter of the representation, the responsibility involved in the representation, and the results obtained;

(5) the time limitations imposed by the client or by the circumstances and, as between attorney and client, any additional or special time demands or requests of the attorney by the client;

(6) the nature and length of the professional relationship with the client;

(7) the experience, reputation, diligence, and ability of the lawyer or lawyers performing the service and the skill, expertise, or efficiency of effort reflected in the actual providing of such services; and

(8) whether the fee is fixed or contingent, and, if fixed as to amount or rate, then whether the client's ability to pay rested to any significant degree on the outcome of the representation.

(c) Consideration of All Factors. In determining a reasonable fee, the time devoted to the representation and customary rate of fee need not be the sole or controlling factors. All factors set forth in this rule should be considered, and may be applied, in justification of a fee higher or lower than that which would result from application of only the time and rate factors.

(d) Enforceability of Fee Contracts. Contracts or agreements for attorney's fees between attorney and client will ordinarily be enforceable according to the terms of such contracts or agreements, unless found to be illegal, obtained through advertising or solicitation not in compliance with the Rules Regulating The Florida Bar, prohibited by this rule, or clearly excessive as defined by this rule.

(e) Duty to Communicate Basis or Rate of Fee to Client. When the lawyer has not regularly represented the client, the basis or rate of the fee shall be communicated to the client, preferably in writing, before or within a reasonable time after commencing the representation.

(f) Contingent Fees. As to contingent fees:

(1) A fee may be contingent on the outcome of the matter for which the service is rendered, except in a matter in which a contingent fee is prohibited by paragraph (f)(3) or by law. A contingent fee agreement shall be in writing and shall state the method by which the fee is to be determined, including the percentage or percentages that shall accrue to the lawyer in the event of settlement, trial, or appeal, litigation and other expenses to be deducted from the recovery, and whether such expenses are to be deducted before or after the contingent fee is calculated. Upon conclusion of a contingent fee matter, the lawyer shall provide the client with a written statement stating the outcome of the matter and, if there is a recovery, showing the remittance to the client and the method of its determination.

(2) Every lawyer who accepts a retainer or enters into an agreement, express or implied, for compensation for services rendered or to be rendered in any action, claim, or proceeding whereby the lawyer's compensation is to be dependent or contingent in whole or in part upon the successful prosecution or settlement thereof shall do so only where such fee arrangement is reduced to a written contract, signed by the client, and by a lawyer for the lawyer or for the law firm representing the client. No lawyer or firm may participate in the fee without the consent of the client in writing. Each participating lawyer or law firm shall sign the contract with the client and shall agree to assume joint legal responsibility to the client for the performance of the services in question as if each were partners of the other lawyer or law firm involved. The client shall be furnished with a copy of the signed contract and any subsequent notices or consents. All provisions of this rule shall apply to such fee contracts.

(3) A lawyer shall not enter into an arrangement for, charge, or collect:

(A) any fee in a domestic relations matter, the payment or amount of which is contingent upon the securing of a divorce or upon the amount of alimony or support, or property settlement in lieu thereof; or

(B) a contingent fee for representing a defendant in a criminal case.

(4) A lawyer who enters into an arrangement for, charges, or collects any fee in an action or claim for personal injury or for property damages or for death or loss of services resulting from personal injuries based upon tortious conduct of another, including products liability claims, whereby the compensation is to be dependent or contingent in whole or in part upon the successful prosecution or settlement thereof shall do so only under the following requirements:

(A) The contract shall contain the following provisions:

(i) "The undersigned client has, before signing this contract, received and read the statement of client's rights and understands each of the rights set forth therein. The undersigned client has signed the statement and received a signed copy to refer to while being represented by the undersigned attorney(s)."

(ii) "This contract may be cancelled by written notification to the attorney at any time within 3 business days of the date the contract was signed, as shown below, and if cancelled the client shall not be obligated to pay any fees to the attorney for the work performed during that time. If the attorney has advanced funds to others in representation of the client, the attorney is entitled to be reimbursed for such amounts as the attorney has reasonably advanced on behalf of the client."

(B) The contract for representation of a client in a matter set forth in subdivision (f)(4) may provide for a contingent fee arrangement as agreed upon by the client and the lawyer, except as limited by the following provisions:

(i) without prior court approval as specified below, any contingent fee that exceeds the following standards shall be presumed, unless rebutted, to be clearly excessive:

a. Through the time of filing of an answer or the demand for appointment of arbitrators—33⅓% of any recovery up to $1 million.

b. From the time of filing an answer or the demand for appointment of arbitrators through the entry of judgment:

1. 40% of any recovery up to $1 million; plus

2. 30% of any portion of the recovery between $1 million and $2 million; plus

3. 20% of any portion of the recovery exceeding $2 million,

c. If all defendants admit liability at the time of filing their answers and request a trial only on damages:

1. 33⅓% of any recovery up to $1 million; plus

2. 20% of any portion of the recovery between $1 million and $2 million; plus

3.   15% of any portion of the recovery for any amount exceeding $2 million.

d.   An additional 5% of any recovery after notice of appeal is filed or post-judgment relief or action is required for recovery on the judgment.

(ii) If any client is unable to obtain an attorney of the client's choice because of the limitations set forth in (f)(4)(B)(i), the client may petition the circuit court for approval of any fee contract between the client and an attorney of the client's choosing.   Such authorization shall be given if the court determines the client has a complete understanding of the client's rights and the terms of the proposed contract.   The application for authorization of such a contract can be filed as a separate proceeding before suit or simultaneously with the filing of a complaint.   Proceedings thereon may occur before service on the defendant and this aspect of the file may be sealed.   Authorization of such a contract shall not bar subsequent inquiry as to whether the fee actually claimed or charged is clearly excessive under subdivisions (a) and (b).

(iii) In cases where the client is to receive a recovery that will be paid to the client on a future structured or periodic basis, the contingent fee percentage shall only be calculated on the cost of the structured verdict or settlement or, if the cost is unknown, on the present money value of the structured verdict or settlement, whichever is less.   If the damages and the fee are to be paid out over the long term future schedule, then this limitation does not apply.   No attorney may separately negotiate with the defendant for that attorney's fee in a structured verdict or settlement where such separate negotiations would place the attorney in a position of conflict.

(C) Before a lawyer enters into a contingent fee contract for representation of a client in a matter set forth in this rule, the lawyer shall provide the client with a copy of the statement of client's rights and shall afford the client a full and complete opportunity to understand each of the rights as set forth therein.   A copy of the statement, signed by both the client and the lawyer, shall be given to the client to retain and the lawyer shall keep a copy in the client's file.   The statement shall be retained by the lawyer with the written fee contract and closing statement under the same conditions and requirements as subdivision (f)(5).

(D) As to lawyers not in the same firm, a division of any fee within subdivision (f)(4) shall be on the following basis:

(i) To the lawyer assuming primary responsibility for the legal services on behalf of the client, a minimum of 75% of the total fee.

(ii) To the lawyer assuming secondary responsibility for the legal services on behalf of the client, a maximum of 25% of the total fee. Any fee in excess of 25% shall be presumed to be clearly excessive.

(iii) The 25% limitation shall not apply to those cases in which 2 or more lawyers or firms accept substantially equal active participation in the providing of legal services. In such circumstances counsel shall apply for circuit court authorization of the fee division in excess of 25%, based upon a sworn petition signed by all counsel that shall disclose in detail those services to be performed. The application for authorization of such a contract may be filed as a separate proceeding before suit or simultaneously with the filing of a complaint. Proceedings thereon may occur before service of process on any party and this aspect of the file may be sealed. Authorization of such contract shall not bar subsequent inquiry as to whether the fee actually claimed or charged is clearly excessive. An application under this subdivision shall contain a certificate showing service on the client and The Florida Bar. Counsel may proceed with representation of the client pending court approval.

(iv) The percentages required by this subdivision shall be applicable after deduction of any fee payable to separate counsel retained especially for appellate purposes.

(5) In the event there is a recovery, upon the conclusion of the representation, the lawyer shall prepare a closing statement reflecting an itemization of all costs and expenses, together with the amount of fee received by each participating lawyer or law firm. A copy of the closing statement shall be executed by all participating lawyers, as well as the client, and each shall receive a copy. Each participating lawyer shall retain a copy of the written fee contract and closing statement for 6 years after execution of the closing statement. Any contingent fee contract and closing statement shall be available for inspection at reasonable times by the client, by any other person upon judicial order, or by the appropriate disciplinary agency.

(g) Division of Fees Between Lawyers in Different Firms. Subject to the provisions of subdivision (f)(4)(D), a division of fee between lawyers who are not in the same firm may be made only if the total fee is reasonable and:

(1) the division is in proportion to the services performed by each lawyer; or

(2) by written agreement with the client:

(A) each lawyer assumes joint legal responsibility for the representation and agrees to be available for consultation with the client; and

(B) the agreement fully discloses that a division of fees will be made and the basis upon which the division of fees will be made.

(h) Credit Plans. Charges made by any lawyer or law firm under an approved credit plan shall be only for services actually rendered or cash actually paid on behalf of the client. No higher fee shall be charged and no additional charge shall be imposed by reason of a lawyer's or law firm's participation in an approved credit plan.

STATEMENT OF CLIENT'S RIGHTS
FOR CONTINGENCY FEES

Before you, the prospective client, arrange a contingent fee agreement with a lawyer, you should understand this statement of your rights as a client. This statement is not a part of the actual contract between you and your lawyer, but, as a prospective client, you should be aware of these rights:

1. There is no legal requirement that a lawyer charge a client a set fee or a percentage of money recovered in a case. You, the client, have the right to talk with your lawyer about the proposed fee and to bargain about the rate or percentage as in any other contract. If you do not reach an agreement with one lawyer you may talk with other lawyers.

2. Any contingent fee contract must be in writing and you have 3 business days to reconsider the contract. You may cancel the contract without any reason if you notify your lawyer in writing within 3 business days of signing the contract. If you withdraw from the contract within the first 3 business days, you do not owe the lawyer a fee although you may be responsible for the lawyer's actual costs during that time. If your lawyer begins to represent you, your lawyer may not withdraw from the case without giving you notice, delivering necessary papers to you, and allowing you time to employ another lawyer. Often, your lawyer must obtain court approval before withdrawing from a case. If you discharge your lawyer without good cause after the 3–day period, you may have to pay a fee for work the lawyer has done.

3. Before hiring a lawyer, you, the client, have the right to know about the lawyer's education, training, and experience. If you ask, the lawyer should tell you specifically about the lawyer's actual experience dealing with cases similar to yours. If you ask, the lawyer should provide information about special training or knowledge and give you this information in writing if you request it.

4. Before signing a contingent fee contract with you, a lawyer must advise you whether the lawyer intends to handle your case alone or whether other lawyers will be helping with the case. If your lawyer intends to refer the case to other lawyers, the lawyer should tell you what kind of fee sharing arrangement will be made with the other lawyers. If lawyers from different law firms will represent you, at least 1 lawyer from each law firm must sign the contingent fee contract.

5. If your lawyer intends to refer your case to another lawyer or counsel with other lawyers, your lawyer should tell you about that at the beginning. If your lawyer takes the case and later decides to refer it to another lawyer or to associate with other lawyers, you should sign a new contract that includes the new lawyers. You, the client, also have the right to consult with each lawyer working on your case and each lawyer is legally responsible to represent your interests and is legally responsible for the acts of the other lawyers involved in the case.

6. You, the client, have the right to know in advance how you will need to pay the expenses and the legal fees at the end of the case. If you pay a deposit in advance for costs, you may ask reasonable questions about how the money will be or has been spent and how much of it remains unspent. Your lawyer should give a reasonable estimate about future necessary costs. If your lawyer agrees to lend or advance you money to prepare or research the case, you have the right to know periodically how much money your lawyer has spent on your behalf. You also have the right to decide, after consulting with your lawyer, how much money is to be spent to prepare a case. If you pay the expenses, you have the right to decide how much to spend. Your lawyer should also inform you whether the fee will be based on the gross amount recovered or on the amount recovered minus the costs.

7. You, the client, have the right to be told by your lawyer about possible adverse consequences if you lose the case. Those adverse consequences might include money that you might have to pay to your lawyer for costs and liability you might have for attorney's fees to the other side.

8. You, the client, have the right to receive and approve a closing statement at the end of the case before you pay any money. The statement must list all of the financial details of the entire case, including the amount recovered, all expenses, and a precise statement of your lawyer's fee. Until you approve the closing statement you need not pay any money to anyone, including your lawyer. You also have the right to have every lawyer or law firm working on your case sign this closing statement.

9. You, the client, have the right to ask your lawyer at reasonable intervals how the case is progressing and to have these questions answered to the best of your lawyer's ability.

10. You, the client, have the right to make the final decision regarding settlement of a case. Your lawyer must notify you of all offers of settlement before and after the trial. Offers during the trial must be immediately communicated and you should consult with your lawyer regarding whether to accept a settlement. However, you must make the final decision to accept or reject a settlement.

11. If at any time you, the client, believe that your lawyer has charged an excessive or illegal fee, you have the right to report the matter to The Florida Bar, the agency that oversees the practice and behavior of all lawyers in Florida. For information on how to reach The

Florida Bar, call 904–561–5600, or contact the local bar association. Any disagreement between you and your lawyer about a fee can be taken to court and you may wish to hire another lawyer to help you resolve this disagreement. Usually fee disputes must be handled in a separate lawsuit unless your fee contract provides for arbitration. You can request, but may not require, that a provision for arbitration (under chapter 682, Florida Statutes, or under the fee arbitration rule of the Rules Regulating The Florida Bar) be included in your fee contract.

_____	_____
Client Signature	Attorney Signature
_____	_____
Date	Date

COMMENT:

Basis or rate of fee

When the lawyer has regularly represented a client, they ordinarily will have evolved an understanding concerning the basis or rate of the fee. In a new client-lawyer relationship, however, an understanding as to the fee should be promptly established. It is not necessary to recite all the factors that underlie the basis of the fee but only those that are directly involved in its computation. It is sufficient, for example, to state the basic rate is an hourly charge or a fixed amount or an estimated amount, or to identify the factors that may be taken into account in finally fixing the fee. When developments occur during the representation that render an earlier estimate substantially inaccurate, a revised estimate should be provided to the client. A written statement concerning the fee reduces the possibility of misunderstanding. Furnishing the client with a simple memorandum or a copy of the lawyer's customary fee schedule is sufficient if the basis or rate of the fee is set forth.

Rule 4–1.8(e) should be consulted regarding a lawyer's providing financial assistance to a client in connection with litigation.

Terms of payment

A lawyer may require advance payment of a fee but is obliged to return any unearned portion. See rule 4–1.16(d). A lawyer is not, however, required to return retainers that, pursuant to an agreement with a client, are not refundable. A lawyer may accept property in payment for services, such as an ownership interest in an enterprise, providing this does not involve acquisition of a proprietary interest in the cause of action or subject matter of the litigation contrary to rule 4–1.8(i). However, a fee paid in property instead of money may be subject to special scrutiny because it involves questions concerning both the value of the services and the lawyer's special knowledge of the value of the property.

An agreement may not be made whose terms might induce the lawyer improperly to curtail services for the client or perform them in a way contrary to the client's interest. For example, a lawyer should not enter into an agreement whereby services are to be provided only up to a stated amount when it is foreseeable that more extensive services probably will be required, unless the situation is adequately explained to the client. Otherwise, the client might have to bargain for further assistance in the midst of a proceeding or transaction. However, it is proper to define the extent of services in light of the client's ability to pay. A lawyer should not exploit a fee arrangement based primarily on hourly charges by using wasteful procedures. When there is doubt whether a contingent fee is consistent with the client's best interest, the lawyer should offer the client alternative bases for the fee and explain their implications. Applicable law may impose limitations on contingent fees, such as a ceiling on the percentage.

Rule 4–1.5(f)(3) does not apply to lawyers seeking to obtain or enforce judgments for arrearages.

Contingent fee regulation

Rule 4–1.5(f)(4) should not be construed to apply to actions or claims seeking property or other damages arising in the commercial litigation context.

Rule 4–1.5(f)(4)(B) is intended to apply only to contingent aspects of fee agreements. In the situation where a lawyer and client enter a contract for part noncontingent and part contingent attorney's fees, rule 4–1.5(f)(4)(B) should not be construed to apply to and prohibit or limit the noncontingent portion of the fee agreement. An attorney could properly charge and retain the noncontingent portion of the fee even if the matter was not successfully prosecuted or if the noncontingent portion of the fee exceeded the schedule set forth in rule 4–1.5(f)(4)(B). Rule 4–1.5(f)(4)(B) should, however, be construed to apply to any additional contingent portion of such a contract when considered together with earned noncontingent fees. Thus, under such a contract a lawyer may demand or collect only such additional contingent fees as would not cause the total fees to exceed the schedule set forth in rule 4–1.5(f)(4)(B).

The limitations in rule 4–1.5(f)(4)(B)(i)c are only to be applied in the case where all the defendants admit liability at the time they file their initial answer and the trial is only on the issue of the amount or extent of the loss or the extent of injury suffered by the client. If the trial involves not only the issue of damages but also such questions as proximate cause, affirmative defenses, seat belt defense, or other similar matters, the limitations are not to be applied because of the contingent nature of the case being left for resolution by the trier of fact.

Rule 4–1.5(f)(4)(B)(ii) provides the limitations set forth in subdivision (f)(4)(B)(i) may be waived by the client upon approval by a circuit court judge. This waiver provision may not be used to authorize a lawyer to charge a client a fee that would exceed rule 4–1.5(a) or (b). It is contemplated that this waiver provision will not be necessary except where the client wants to retain a particular lawyer to represent the client or the case involves complex, difficult, or novel questions of law or fact that would justify a contingent fee greater than the schedule but not a contingent fee that would exceed rule 4–1.5(b).

Upon a petition by a client, the trial court reviewing the waiver request must grant that request if the trial court finds the client: (a) understands the right to have the limitations in rule 4–1.5(f)(4)(B) applied in the specific matter; and (b) understands and approves the terms of the proposed contract. The consideration by the trial court of the waiver petition is not to be used as an opportunity for the court to inquire into the merits or details of the particular action or claim that is the subject of the contract.

The proceedings before the trial court and the trial court's decision on a waiver request are to be confidential and not subject to discovery by any of the parties to the action or by any other individual or entity except The Florida Bar. However, terms of the contract approved by the trial court may be subject to discovery if the contract (without court approval) was subject to discovery under applicable case law or rules of evidence.

Rule 4–1.5(f)(4)(B)(iii) prohibits a lawyer from charging the contingent fee percentage on the total, future value of a recovery being paid on a structured or periodic basis. This prohibition does not apply if the lawyer's fee is being paid over the same length of time as the schedule of payments to the client.

Division of fee

A division of fee is a single billing to a client covering the fee of two or more lawyers who are not in the same firm. A division of fee facilitates association of more than one lawyer in a matter in which neither alone could serve the client as well, and most often is used when the fee is contingent and the division is between a referring lawyer and a trial specialist. Subject to the provisions of subdivision (f)(4)(D), subdivision (g) permits the lawyers to divide a fee on either the basis of the proportion of services they render or by agreement between the participating lawyers if all assume responsibility for the representation as a whole and the client is advised and does not object. It does require disclosure to the client of the share that each lawyer is to receive. Joint responsibility for the representation entails the obligations stated in rule 4–5.1 for purposes of the matter involved.

Disputes over fees

Since the fee arbitration rule (Chapter 14) has been established by the bar to provide a procedure for resolution of fee disputes, such as an arbitration or mediation procedure established by the bar, the lawyer should conscientiously consider submitting to it. Where law prescribes a procedure for determining a lawyer's fee, for example, in representation of an executor or administrator, a class, or a person entitled to a reasonable fee as part of the measure of damages, the lawyer entitled to such a fee and a lawyer representing another party concerned with the fee should comply with the prescribed procedure.

Referral fees and practices

A secondary lawyer shall not be entitled to a fee greater than the limitation set forth in rule 4–1.5(f)(4)(D)(ii) merely because the lawyer agrees to do some or all of the following: (a) consults with the client; (b) answers interrogatories; (c) attends depositions; (d) reviews pleadings; (e) attends the trial; or (f) assumes joint legal responsibility to the client. However, the provisions do not contemplate that a secondary lawyer who does more than the above is necessarily entitled to a larger percentage of the fee than that allowed by the limitation.

The provisions of rule 4–1.5(f)(4)(D)(iii) only apply where the participating lawyers have for purposes of the specific case established a co-counsel relationship. The need for court approval of a referral fee arrangement under rule 4–1.5(f)(4)(D)(iii) should only occur in a small percentage of cases arising under rule 4–1.5(f)(4).

In determining if a co-counsel relationship exists, the court should look to see if the lawyers have established a special partnership agreement for the purpose of the specific case or matter. If such an agreement does exist, it must provide for a sharing of services or responsibility and the fee division is based upon a division of the services to be rendered or the responsibility assumed. It is contemplated that a co-counsel situation would exist where a division of responsibility is based upon, but not limited to, the following: (a) based upon geographic considerations, the lawyers agree to divide the legal work, responsibility, and representation in a convenient fashion. Such a situation would occur when different aspects of a case must be handled in different locations; (b) where the lawyers agree to divide the legal work and representation based upon their particular expertise in the substantive areas of law involved in the litigation; or (c) where the lawyers agree to divide the legal work and representation along established lines of division, such as liability and damages, causation and damages, or other similar factors.

The trial court's responsibility when reviewing an application for authorization of a fee division under rule 4–1.5(f)(4)(D)(iii) is to determine if a co-counsel relationship exists in that particular case. If the court determines a co-counsel relationship exists and authorizes the fee division requested, the court does not have any responsibility to review or approve the specific amount of the fee division agreed upon by the lawyers and the client.

Rule 4–1.5(f)(4)(D)(iv) applies to the situation where appellate counsel is retained during the trial of the case to assist with the appeal of the case. The percentages set forth in subdivision (f)(4)(D) are to be applicable after appellate counsel's fee is established. However, the effect should not be to impose an unreasonable fee on the client.

Illinois Rule 1.5

[Illinois has added subsections (g) through (j) to Model Rule 1.5]

RULE 1.5 Fees

* * *

(g) A division of fees shall be made in proportion to the services performed and responsibility assumed by each lawyer, except where the primary service performed by one lawyer is the referral of the client to another lawyer and

(1) the receiving lawyer discloses that the referring lawyer has received or will receive economic benefit from the referral and the extent and basis of such economic benefit, and

(2) the referring lawyer agrees to assume the same legal responsibility for the performance of the services in question as would a partner of the receiving lawyer.

(h) The total fee of the lawyers shall be reasonable.

(i) For purposes of Rule 1.5 "economic benefit" shall include:

(1) the amount of participation in the fee received with regard to the particular matter;

(2) any other form of remuneration passing to the referring lawyer from the receiving lawyer, whether or not with regard to the particular matter; and

(3) an established practice of referrals to and from or from and to the receiving lawyer and the referring lawyer.

(j) Notwithstanding Rule 1.5(f), a payment may be made to a lawyer formerly in the firm, pursuant to a separation or retirement agreement.

Kansas Rule 1.5

[Kansas has substituted the following provisions for Model Rule 1.5(c) through (e):]

RULE 1.5

(c) A lawyer's fee shall be reasonable but a court determination that a fee is not reasonable shall not be presumptive evidence of a violation that requires discipline of the attorney.

(d) A fee may be contingent on the outcome of the matter for which the service is rendered, except in a matter in which a contingent fee is prohibited by paragraph (f) or other law. A contingent fee agreement shall be in writing and shall state the method by which the fee is to be determined, including the percentage or percentages that shall accrue to the lawyer in the event of settlement, trial or appeal, and the litigation and other expenses to be deducted from the recovery. All such expenses shall be deducted before the contingent fee is calculated. Upon conclusion of a contingent fee matter, the lawyer shall provide the client with a written statement stating the outcome of the matter and, if there is a recovery, showing the client's share and amount and the method of its determination. The statement shall advise the client of the right to have the fee reviewed as provided in subsection (e).

(e) Upon application by the client, all fee contracts shall be subject to review and approval by the appropriate court having jurisdiction of the matter and the court shall have the authority to determine whether the contract is reasonable. If the court finds the contract is not reasonable, it shall set and allow a reasonable fee.

Texas Rule 1.04 *(Modification of Model Rule 1.5)*

[Texas has modified several subsections of Model Rule 1.5 (fees) to read as follows:]

RULE 1.04   Fees

(a) A lawyer shall not enter into an arrangement for, charge, or collect an illegal fee or unconscionable fee. A fee is unconscionable if a competent lawyer could not form a reasonable belief that the fee is reasonable.

* * *

(f) A division or agreement for division of a fee between lawyers who are not in the same firm shall not be made unless:

   (1) the division is:

      (i) in proportion to the professional services performed by each lawyer;

      (ii) made with a forwarding lawyer; or

      (iii) made, by written agreement with the client, with a lawyer who assumes joint responsibility for the representation;

   (2) the client is advised of, and does not object to, the participation of all the lawyers involved; and

   (3) the aggregate fee does not violate paragraph (a).

* * *

COMMENT:

1. A lawyer in good conscience should not charge or collect more than a reasonable fee, although he may charge less or no fee at all. The determination of the reasonableness of a fee, or of the range of reasonableness, can be a difficult question, and a standard of "reasonableness" is too vague and uncertain to be an appropriate standard in a disciplinary action. For this reason, paragraph (a) adopts, for disciplinary purposes only, a clearer standard: the lawyer is subject to discipline for an illegal fee or an unconscionable fee. Paragraph (a) defines an unconscionable fee in terms of the reasonableness of the fee but in a way to eliminate factual disputes as to the fee's reasonableness. The Rule's "unconscionable" standard, however, does not preclude use of the "reasonableness" standard of paragraph (b) in other settings.

Basis or Rate of Fee

2. When the lawyer has regularly represented a client, they ordinarily will have evolved an understanding concerning the basis or rate of the fee. If, however, the basis or rate of fee being charged to a regularly represented client differs from the understanding that has evolved, the lawyer should so advise the client. In a new client-lawyer relationship, an understanding as to the fee should be promptly established. It is not necessary to recite all the factors that underlie the basis of the fee, but only those that are directly involved in its computation. It is sufficient, for example, to state that the basic rate is an hourly charge or a fixed amount or an estimated amount, in order to identify the factors that may be taken into account in finally fixing the fee. When developments occur during the representation that render an earlier estimate substantially inaccurate, a revised estimate should be provided to the client. A written statement concerning the fee reduces the possibility of misunderstanding, and when the lawyer has not regularly represented the client it is preferable for the basis or rate of the fee to be communicated to the client in writing. Furnishing the client with a simple memorandum or a copy of the lawyer's customary fee schedule is sufficient if the basis or rate of the fee is set forth. In the case of a contingent fee, a written agreement is mandatory.

　　　* * *

Unconscionable Fees

7. Two principal circumstances combine to make it difficult to determine whether a particular fee is unconscionable within the disciplinary test provided by paragraph (a) of this Rule. The first is the subjectivity of a number of the factors relied on to determine the reasonableness of fees under paragraph (b). Because those factors do not permit more than an approximation of a range of fees that might be found reasonable in any given case, there is a corresponding degree of uncertainty in determining whether a given fee is unconscionable. Sec-

161

ondly, fee arrangements normally are made at the outset of representation, a time when many uncertainties and contingencies exist, while claims of unconscionability are made in hindsight when the contingencies have been resolved. The "unconscionability" standard adopts that difference in perspective and requires that a lawyer be given the benefit of any such uncertainties for disciplinary purposes only. Except in very unusual situations, therefore, the circumstances at the time a fee arrangement is made should control in determining a question of unconscionability.

8. Two factors in otherwise borderline cases might indicate a fee may be unconscionable. The first is overreaching by a lawyer, particularly of a client who was unusually susceptible to such overreaching. The second is a failure of the lawyer to give at the outset a clear and accurate explanation of how a fee was to be calculated. For example, a fee arrangement negotiated at arm's length with an experienced business client would rarely be subject to question. On the other hand, a fee arrangement with an uneducated or unsophisticated individual having no prior experience in such matters should be more carefully scrutinized for overreaching. While the fact that a client was at a marked disadvantage in bargaining with a lawyer over fees will not make a fee unconscionable, application of the disciplinary test may require some consideration of the personal circumstances of the individuals involved.

* * *

Division of Fees

10. A division of fees is a sharing of a single billing to a client between two or more lawyers who are not in the same firm. A division of fees facilitates association of more than one lawyer in a matter in which neither alone could serve the client as well, and most often is used when the fee is contingent and the division is between a referring lawyer and a trial specialist. Because the association of additional counsel normally will result in a further disclosure of client confidences and have a financial impact on a client, advance disclosure of the existence of that proposed association and client consent generally are required. Where those consequences will not arise, however, disclosure is not mandated by this Rule. For example, if a lawyer hires a second lawyer for consultation and advice on a specialized aspect of a matter and that consultation will not necessitate the disclosure of confidential information and the hiring lawyer both absorbs the entire cost of the second lawyer's fees and assumes all responsibility for the advice ultimately given the client, a division of fees within the meaning of this Rule is not involved. See also Comment 3 to Rule 5.04.

11. Paragraph (f) permits lawyers to divide a fee on one of three bases. The first is in proportion to the professional services performed by each. The second continues the Texas practice of permitting a division of fees with a forwarding attorney. The third permits fees to be

divided with a lawyer who, by written agreement with the client, assumes joint responsibility for the representation. The second and the third methods permit the fees to be divided in any mutually agreeable proportion. If the third method is used, a lawyer may satisfy his or her obligations of "joint responsibility" for the representation either by being an attorney of record in the matter or by discharging the responsibilities imposed on a "supervised lawyer" under these rules. See Rule 5.02. Paragraph (f) does not require disclosure to the client of the share that each lawyer is to receive.

Fee Disputes and Determinations

12. If a procedure has been established for resolution of fee disputes, such as an arbitration or mediation procedure established by a bar association, the lawyer should conscientiously consider submitting to it. Law may prescribe a procedure for determining a lawyer's fee, for example, in representation of an executor or administrator, or when a class or a person is entitled to recover a reasonable attorney's fee as part of the measure of damages. All involved lawyers should comply with any prescribed procedures.

Michigan Rule 1.6

[Michigan has modified Model Rule 1.6 to read as follows:]

RULE 1.6 Confidentiality of Information

(a) "Confidence" refers to information protected by the client-lawyer privilege under applicable law, and "secret" refers to other information gained in the professional relationship that the client has requested be held inviolate or the disclosure of which would be embarrassing or would be likely to be detrimental to the client.

(b) Except when permitted under paragraph (c), a lawyer shall not knowingly:

(1) reveal a confidence or secret of a client;

(2) use a confidence or secret of a client to the disadvantage of the client; or

(3) use a confidence or secret of a client for the advantage of the lawyer or of a third person, unless the client consents after full disclosure.

(c) A lawyer may reveal:

(1) confidences or secrets with the consent of the client or clients affected, but only after full disclosure to them;

(2) confidences or secrets when permitted or required by these rules, or when required by law or by court order;

(3) confidences and secrets to the extent reasonably necessary to rectify the consequences of a client's illegal or

fraudulent act in the furtherance of which the lawyer's services have been used;

(4) the intention of a client to commit a crime and the information necessary to prevent the crime; and

(5) confidences or secrets necessary to establish or collect a fee, or to defend the lawyer or the lawyer's employees or associates against an accusation of wrongful conduct.

(d) A lawyer shall exercise reasonable care to prevent employees, associates, and others whose services are utilized by the lawyer from disclosing or using confidences or secrets of a client, except that a lawyer may reveal the information allowed by paragraph (c) through an employee.

COMMENT:

The lawyer is part of a judicial system charged with upholding the law. One of the lawyer's functions is to advise clients so that they avoid any violation of the law in the proper exercise of their rights.

The observance of the ethical obligation of a lawyer to hold inviolate confidential information of the client not only facilitates the full development of facts essential to proper representation of the client, but also encourages people to seek early legal assistance.

Almost without exception, clients come to lawyers in order to determine what their rights are and what is, in the maze of laws and regulations, deemed to be legal and correct. The common law recognizes that the client's confidences must be protected from disclosure. Upon the basis of experience, lawyers know that almost all clients follow the advice given and that the law is upheld.

A fundamental principle in the client-lawyer relationship is that the lawyer maintain confidentiality of information relating to the representation. The client is thereby encouraged to communicate fully and frankly with the lawyer even as to embarrassing or legally damaging subject matter.

The principle of confidentiality is given effect in two related bodies of law, the client-lawyer privilege (which includes the work-product doctrine) in the law of evidence and the rule of confidentiality established in professional ethics. The client-lawyer privilege applies in judicial and other proceedings in which a lawyer may be called as a witness or otherwise required to produce evidence concerning a client. The rule of client-lawyer confidentiality applies in situations other than those where evidence is sought from the lawyer through compulsion of law. The confidentiality rule applies to confidences and secrets as defined in the rule. A lawyer may not disclose such information except as authorized or required by the Rules of Professional Conduct or other law. See also Scope, ante.

The requirement of maintaining confidentiality of information relating to representation applies to government lawyers who may disagree with the policy goals that their representation is designed to advance.

Authorized Disclosure. A lawyer is impliedly authorized to make disclosures about a client when appropriate in carrying out the representation, except to the extent that the client's instructions or special circumstances limit that authority. In litigation, for example, a lawyer may disclose information by admitting a fact that cannot properly be disputed, or, in negotiation, by making a disclosure that facilitates a satisfactory conclusion.

Lawyers in a firm may, in the course of the firm's practice, disclose to each other information relating to a client of the firm, unless the client has instructed that particular information be confined to specified lawyers, or unless the disclosure would breach a screen erected within the firm in accordance with Rules 1.10(b), 1.11(a), or 1.12(c).

Disclosure Adverse to Client. The confidentiality rule is subject to limited exceptions. In becoming privy to information about a client, a lawyer may foresee that the client intends to commit a crime. To the extent a lawyer is prohibited from making disclosure, the interests of the potential victim are sacrificed in favor of preserving the client's confidences even though the client's purpose is wrongful. To the extent a lawyer is required or permitted to disclose a client's purposes, the client may be inhibited from revealing facts which would enable the lawyer to counsel against a wrongful course of action. A rule governing disclosure of threatened harm thus involves balancing the interests of one group of potential victims against those of another. On the assumption that lawyers generally fulfill their duty to advise against the commission of deliberately wrongful acts, the public is better protected if full and open communication by the client is encouraged than if it is inhibited.

Generally speaking, information relating to the representation must be kept confidential as stated in paragraph (b). However, when the client is or will be engaged in criminal conduct or the integrity of the lawyer's own conduct is involved, the principle of confidentiality may appropriately yield, depending on the lawyer's knowledge about and relationship to the conduct in question, and the seriousness of that conduct. Several situations must be distinguished.

First, the lawyer may not counsel or assist a client in conduct that is illegal or fraudulent. See Rule 1.2(c). Similarly, a lawyer has a duty under Rule 3.3(a)(4) not to use false evidence. This duty is essentially a special instance of the duty prescribed in Rule 1.2(c) to avoid assisting a client in illegal or fraudulent conduct. The same is true of compliance with Rule 4.1 concerning truthfulness of a lawyer's own representations.

Second, the lawyer may have been innocently involved in past conduct by the client that was criminal or fraudulent. In such a situation the lawyer has not violated Rule 1.2(c), because to "counsel or assist" criminal or fraudulent conduct requires knowing that the conduct is of that character. Even if the involvement was innocent, however, the fact remains that the lawyer's professional services were made the instrument of the client's crime or fraud. The lawyer, therefore, has a legitimate interest in being able to rectify the consequences of such conduct, and has the professional right, although not a professional duty, to rectify the situation. Exercising that right may require revealing information relating to the representation. Paragraph (c)(3) gives the lawyer professional discretion to reveal such information to the extent necessary to accomplish rectification. However, the constitutional rights of defendants in criminal cases may limit the extent to which counsel for a defendant may correct a misrepresentation that is based on information provided by the client. See comment to Rule 3.3.

Third, the lawyer may learn that a client intends prospective conduct that is criminal. Inaction by the lawyer is not a violation of Rule 1.2(c), except in the limited circumstances where failure to act constitutes assisting the client. See comment to Rule 1.2(c). However, the lawyer's knowledge of the client's purpose may enable the lawyer to prevent commission of the prospective crime. If the prospective crime is likely to result in substantial injury, the lawyer may feel a moral obligation to take preventive action. When the threatened injury is grave, such as homicide or serious bodily injury, a lawyer may have an obligation under tort or criminal law to take reasonable preventive measures. Whether the lawyer's concern is based on moral or legal considerations, the interest in preventing the harm may be more compelling than the interest in preserving confidentiality of information relating to the client. As stated in paragraph (c)(4), the lawyer has professional discretion to reveal information in order to prevent a client's criminal act.

It is arguable that the lawyer should have a professional obligation to make a disclosure in order to prevent homicide or serious bodily injury which the lawyer knows is intended by the client. However, it is very difficult for a lawyer to "know" when such a heinous purpose will actually be carried out, for the client may have a change of mind. To require disclosure when the client intends such an act, at the risk of professional discipline if the assessment of the client's purpose turns out to be wrong, would be to impose a penal risk that might interfere with the lawyer's resolution of an inherently difficult moral dilemma.

The lawyer's exercise of discretion requires consideration of such factors as magnitude, proximity, and likelihood of the contemplated wrong; the nature of the lawyer's relationship with the client and with those who might be injured by the client; the lawyer's own involvement in the transaction; and factors that may extenuate the conduct in question. Where practical, the lawyer should seek to persuade the client to take suitable action. In any case, a disclosure adverse to the client's interest should be no greater than the lawyer reasonably believes necessary to the purpose. A lawyer's decision not to make a disclosure permitted by paragraph (c) does not violate this rule.

Where the client is an organization, the lawyer may be in doubt whether contemplated conduct will actually be carried out by the organization. Where necessary to guide conduct in connection with this rule, the lawyer should make an inquiry within the organization as indicated in Rule 1.13(b).

Paragraph (c)(3) does not apply where a lawyer is employed after a crime or fraud has been committed to represent the client in matters ensuing therefrom.

Withdrawal. If the lawyer's services will be used by the client in materially furthering a course of criminal or fraudulent conduct, the lawyer must withdraw, as stated in Rule 1.16(a)(1).

After withdrawal the lawyer is required to refrain from making disclosure of the client's confidences, except as otherwise provided in Rule 1.6. Neither this rule nor Rule 1.8(b) nor Rule 1.16(d) prevents the lawyer from giving notice of the fact of withdrawal, and the lawyer may also withdraw or disaffirm any opinion, document, affirmation, or the like.

Dispute Concerning Lawyer's Conduct. Where a legal claim or disciplinary charge alleges complicity of the lawyer in a client's conduct or other misconduct of the lawyer involving representation of the client, the lawyer may respond to the extent the lawyer reasonably believes necessary to establish a defense. The same is true with respect to a claim involving the conduct or representation of a former client. The lawyer's right to respond arises when an assertion of complicity or other misconduct has been made. Paragraph (c)(5) does not require the lawyer to await the commencement of an action or proceeding that charges complicity or other misconduct, so that the defense may be established by responding directly to a third party who has made such an assertion. The right to defend, of course, applies where a proceeding has been commenced. Where practicable and not prejudicial to the lawyer's ability to establish the defense, the lawyer should advise the client of the third party's assertion and request that the client respond appropriately. In any event, disclosure should be no greater than the lawyer reasonably believes is necessary to vindicate innocence, the disclosure should be made in a manner which limits access to the information to the tribunal or other persons having a need to know it, and appropriate protective orders or other arrangements should be sought by the lawyer to the fullest extent practicable.

If the lawyer is charged with wrongdoing in which the client's conduct is implicated, the rule of confidentiality should not prevent the lawyer from defending against the charge. Such a charge can arise in a civil, criminal, or professional disciplinary proceeding, and can be based on a wrong allegedly committed by the lawyer against the client, or on a wrong alleged by a third person, for example, a person claiming to have been defrauded by the lawyer and client acting together.

A lawyer entitled to a fee is permitted by paragraph (c)(5) to prove the services rendered in an action to collect it. This aspect of the rule expresses the principle that the beneficiary of a fiduciary relationship may not exploit it to the detriment of the fiduciary. As stated above, the lawyer must make every effort practicable to avoid unnecessary disclosure of information relating to a representation, to limit disclosure to those having the need to know it, and to obtain protective orders or make other arrangements minimizing the risk of disclosure.

Disclosures Otherwise Required or Authorized. The scope of the client-lawyer privilege is a question of law. If a lawyer is called as a witness to give testimony concerning a client, absent waiver by the client, paragraph (b)(1) requires the lawyer to invoke the privilege when it is applicable. The lawyer must comply with the final orders of a court or other tribunal of competent jurisdiction requiring the lawyer to give information about the client.

The Rules of Professional Conduct in various circumstances permit or require a lawyer to disclose information relating to the representation. See Rules 2.2, 2.3, 3.3 and 4.1. In addition to these provisions, a lawyer may be obligated or permitted by other provisions of law to give information about a client. Whether another provision of law supersedes Rule 1.6 is a matter of interpretation beyond the scope of these rules, but a presumption should exist against such a supersession.

Former Client. The duty of confidentiality continues after the client-lawyer relationship has terminated. See Rule 1.9.

Minnesota Rule 1.6

[Minnesota has modified Model Rule 1.6 to read as follows:]

RULE 1.6   Confidentiality of Information

(a) Except when permitted under paragraph (b), a lawyer shall not knowingly:

(1) reveal a confidence or secret of a client;

(2) use a confidence or secret of a client to the disadvantage of the client;

(3) use a confidence or secret of a client for the advantage of the lawyer or a third person, unless the client consents after consultation.

(b) A lawyer may reveal:

(1) confidences or secrets with the consent of the client or clients affected, but only after consultation with them;

(2) confidences or secrets when permitted under the Rules of Professional Conduct or required by law or court order;

(3) the intention of a client to commit a crime and the information necessary to prevent a crime;

(4) confidences and secrets necessary to rectify the consequences of a client's criminal or fraudulent act in the furtherance of which the lawyer's services were used;

(5) confidences or secrets necessary to establish or collect a fee or to defend the lawyer or employees or associates against an accusation of wrongful conduct.

(6) secrets necessary to inform the Office of Lawyers Professional Responsibility of knowledge of another lawyer's violation of the Rules of Professional Conduct that raises a substantial question as to that lawyer's honesty, trustworthiness or fitness as a lawyer in other respects. See Rule 8.3.

(c) A lawyer shall exercise reasonable care to prevent employees, associates and others whose services the lawyer utilizes from disclosing or using confidences or secrets of a client, except that a lawyer may reveal the information allowed by paragraph (b) through an employee.

(d) "Confidence" refers to information protected by the attorney-client privilege under applicable law, and "secret" refers to other information gained in the professional relationship that the client has requested be held inviolate or the disclosure of which would be embarrassing or would be likely to be detrimental to the client.

COMMENT—1991

General

Both the fiduciary relationship existing between lawyer and client and the proper functioning of the legal system require the lawyer to preserve confidences and secrets of one who has employed or sought to employ the lawyer. A client must feel free to discuss whatever the client wishes with the lawyer and a lawyer must be equally free to obtain information beyond what the client volunteers. A lawyer should be fully informed of all the facts of the matter the lawyer is handling in order for the client to obtain the full advantage of our legal system. It is for the lawyer in the exercise of independent professional judgment to separate the relevant and important from the irrelevant and unimportant.

Observance of the lawyer's ethical obligation to hold inviolate the client's confidences and secrets not only facilitates the full development of facts essential to proper representation of the client but also encourages people to seek early legal assistance.

Authorized Disclosure

The obligation to protect confidences and secrets obviously does not preclude a lawyer from revealing information when the client consents after consultation, when necessary to perform professional employment, when permitted by the Rules of Professional Conduct or when required by law.

The confidentiality required under this rule should not allow a client to utilize the lawyer's services in committing a criminal or fraudulent act. A lawyer is permitted to reveal the intention of a client to commit a crime and the information necessary to prevent the crime. In addition, where the lawyer finds out, after the fact, that the lawyer's services were used by the client to commit a criminal or fraudulent act, the lawyer has discretion to reveal information necessary to rectify the consequences of the client's crime or fraud. A lawyer is not permitted, however, to disclose a client's criminal or fraudulent act committed prior to the client's retention of the lawyer's services.

Unless the client otherwise directs, a lawyer may disclose the client's affairs to partners or associates.

It is a matter of common knowledge that the normal operation of a law office exposes confidential professional information to non-lawyer employees of the office, particularly secretaries and those having access to the files; and this obligates a lawyer to exercise care in selecting and training employees so that the sanctity of all confidences and secrets of clients may be preserved.

If the obligation extends to two or more clients as to the same information, a lawyer should obtain the permission of all before revealing the information.

A lawyer must always be sensitive to the client's rights and wishes and act scrupulously in making decisions which may involve disclosure of information obtained in the professional relationship. Thus, in the absence of the client's consent after consultation, a lawyer should not associate another lawyer in handling a matter; nor, in the absence of consent, seek counsel from another lawyer if there is a reasonable possibility that the client's identity or confidences or secrets would be revealed to that lawyer. Both social amenities and professional duty should cause a lawyer to shun indiscreet conversations concerning clients.

Unless the client otherwise directs, it is not improper for a lawyer to give limited information from the lawyer's files to an outside agency necessary for statistical, bookkeeping, accounting, data processing, banking, printing, or other legitimate purposes, provided the lawyer exercises due care in selecting the agency and warns the agency that the information must be kept confidential.

Protecting Confidences

The attorney-client privilege is more limited than the lawyer's ethical obligation to guard the client's confidences and secrets. The ethical obligation, unlike the evidentiary privilege, exists without regard to the nature or source of information or the fact that others share the knowledge.

A lawyer should endeavor to act in a manner which preserves the evidentiary privilege; for example, the lawyer should avoid professional discussions in the presence of persons to whom the privilege does not extend. A lawyer owes an obligation to advise the client of the attorney-client privilege and timely to assert the privilege unless it is waived by the client.

Using Confidences or Secrets

A lawyer should not use information acquired in the course of the representation of a client to the client's disadvantage and a lawyer should not use, except with the client's consent after full disclosure, such information for the lawyer's own purposes.

Likewise, a lawyer should be diligent in efforts to prevent misuse of such information by employees and associates.

A lawyer should exercise care to prevent disclosure of confidences and secrets of one client to another and should accept no employment that might require such disclosure.

Former Client

The lawyer's obligation to preserve the client's confidences and secrets continues after termination of the employment. Thus, a lawyer should not attempt to sell a law practice as a going business because, among other reasons, to do so would involve disclosure of confidences and secrets.

A lawyer should also provide for the protection of the client's confidences and secrets following the termination of the practice of the lawyer, whether termination is due to death, disability or retirement. For example, a lawyer might provide for the client's personal papers to be returned to the client and for the lawyer's papers to be delivered to another lawyer or to be destroyed. In determining the method of disposition, the client's instructions and wishes should be a dominant consideration.

Reporting Obligation

In the course of representation a lawyer may acquire knowledge of another lawyer's violations of the Rules of Professional Conduct. In that instance, a lawyer's obligation to protect client confidences and secrets under Rule 1.6 may appear to conflict with that lawyer's obligations under Rule 8.3 to report professional misconduct by another lawyer. Where "confidences" are involved, the importance of the fiduciary relationship between lawyer and client and the proper functioning of the legal system require that the client retain the veto power over the lawyer's ability to divulge knowledge of another lawyer's violations of the Rules of Professional Conduct.

Until the Rules of Professional Conduct superseded the Code of Professional Responsibility in 1985, Minnesota lawyers were required to report professional misconduct only if their knowledge of the misconduct was "unprivileged." Until 1985, if a lawyer's knowledge of misconduct was a "secret," reporting was required; if the knowledge acquired involved a "confidence," reporting was not allowed, unless some other exception to the confidentiality rule applied. Since September 1, 1985, reporting of misconduct has been forbidden without client consent, if either a confidence or secret is involved.

Under subsection 1.6(b)(6), a lawyer now has the discretion to reveal "secrets," but not client confidences, when necessary to report the lawyer's knowledge of another lawyer's misconduct. This subsection incorporates the language of Rule 8.3 as to the type of reportable misconduct, requiring that the misconduct "raise a substantial question" about the lawyer's honesty, trustworthiness or fitness as a lawyer in other respects.

This discretion to report a lawyer's misconduct balances the policy of confidentiality with the legal profession's obligation to enforce high ethical standards. If the client consents to the lawyer reporting another lawyer's misconduct, no conflict exists between these two policies. Therefore, the lawyer with knowledge of another lawyer's misconduct should seek the client's permission to report the misconduct to the disciplinary authority.

When the client opposes such disclosure, the lawyer then must determine whether knowledge of the misconduct stemmed from a client confidence. If so, the confidentiality rule prevails: disclosure is prohibited. If the knowledge stemmed from a secret, however, the lawyer faces the discretionary decision whether to report the misconduct. Factors pertinent to the discretionary decision include the nature of the lawyer's misconduct, the likelihood that such misconduct will recur if not reported, the possible emotional harm to the client if required to testify in a disciplinary proceeding and/or the likelihood of recovery of embezzled funds.

Other factors that may merit consideration would be the ability to recover funds, such as through frozen assets or a client security fund, in which case, the client's preference might be given less weight.

Texas Rule 1.05 *(Modification of Model Rule 1.6)*

[Texas has modified Model Rule 1.6 (Confidentiality) to read as follows:]

RULE 1.05   Confidentiality of Information

(a) "Confidential information" includes both "privileged information" and "unprivileged client information." "Privileged information" refers to the information of a client protected by the lawyer-client privilege of Rule 503 of the Texas Rules of Evidence or of Rule 503 of the Texas Rules of Criminal Evidence or by the principles of attorney-client privilege governed by Rule 501 of the Federal Rules of Evidence for United States Courts and Magistrates. "Unprivileged client information"

means all information relating to a client or furnished by the client, other than privileged information, acquired by the lawyer during the course of or by reason of the representation of the client.

(b) Except as permitted by paragraphs (c) and (d), or as required by paragraphs (e) and (f), a lawyer shall not knowingly:

(1) Reveal confidential information of a client or a former client to:

> (i) a person that the client has instructed is not to receive the information; or

> (ii) anyone else, other than the client, the client's representatives, or the members, associates, or employees of the lawyer's law firm.

(2) Use confidential information of a client to the disadvantage of the client unless the client consents after consultation.

(3) Use confidential information of a former client to the disadvantage of the former client after the representation is concluded unless the former client consents after consultation or the confidential information has become generally known.

(4) Use privileged information of a client for the advantage of the lawyer or of a third person, unless the client consents after consultation.

(c) A lawyer may reveal confidential information:

(1) When the lawyer has been expressly authorized to do so in order to carry out the representation.

(2) When the client consents after consultation.

(3) To the client, the client's representatives, or the members, associates, and employees of the lawyer's firm, except when otherwise instructed by the client.

(4) When the lawyer has reason to believe it is necessary to do so in order to comply with a court order, a Texas Disciplinary Rule of Professional Conduct, or other law.

(5) To the extent reasonably necessary to enforce a claim or establish a defense on behalf of the lawyer in a controversy between the lawyer and the client.

(6) To establish a defense to a criminal charge, civil claim or disciplinary complaint against the lawyer or the lawyer's associates based upon conduct involving the client or the representation of the client.

(7) When the lawyer has reason to believe it is necessary to do so in order to prevent the client from committing a criminal or fraudulent act.

(8) To the extent revelation reasonably appears necessary to rectify the consequences of a client's criminal or fraudulent act in the commission of which the lawyer's services had been used.

(d) A lawyer also may reveal unprivileged client information:

(1) When impliedly authorized to do so in order to carry out the representation.

(2) When the lawyer has reason to believe it is necessary to do so in order to:

(i) carry out the representation effectively;

(ii) defend the lawyer or the lawyer's employees or associates against a claim of wrongful conduct;

(iii) respond to allegations in any proceeding concerning the lawyer's representation of the client; or

(iv) prove the services rendered to a client, or the reasonable value thereof, or both, in an action against another person or organization responsible for the payment of the fee for services rendered to the client.

(e) When a lawyer has confidential information clearly establishing that a client is likely to commit a criminal or fraudulent act that is likely to result in death or substantial bodily harm to a person, the lawyer shall reveal confidential information to the extent revelation reasonably appears necessary to prevent the client from committing the criminal or fraudulent act.

(f) A lawyer shall reveal confidential information when required to do so by Rule 3.03(a)(2), 3.03(b), or by Rule 4.01(b).

COMMENT:

Confidentiality Generally

1. Both the fiduciary relationship existing between lawyer and client and the proper functioning of the legal system require the preservation by the lawyer of confidential information of one who has employed or sought to employ the lawyer. Free discussion should prevail between lawyer and client in order for the lawyer to be fully informed and for the client to obtain the full benefit of the legal system. The ethical obligation of the lawyer to protect the confidential information of the client not only facilitates the proper representation of the client but also encourages potential clients to seek early legal assistance.

2.   Subject to the mandatory disclosure requirements of paragraphs (e) and (f) the lawyer generally should be required to maintain confidentiality of information acquired by the lawyer during the course of or by reason of the representation of the client. This principle involves an ethical obligation not to use the information to the detriment of the client or for the benefit of the lawyer or a third person. In regard to an evaluation of a matter affecting a client for use by a third person, see Rule 2.02.

3.   The principle of confidentiality is given effect not only in the Texas Rules of Professional Conduct but also in the law of evidence regarding the attorney-client privilege and in the law of agency. The attorney-client privilege, developed through many decades, provides the client a right to prevent certain confidential communications from being revealed by compulsion of law. Several sound exceptions to confidentiality have been developed in the evidence law of privilege. Exceptions exist in evidence law where the services of the lawyer were sought or used by a client in planning or committing a crime or fraud as well as where issues have arisen as to breach of duty by the lawyer or by the client to the other.

4.   Rule 1.05 reinforces the principles of evidence law relating to the attorney-client privilege. Rule 1.05 also furnishes considerable protection to other information falling outside the scope of the privilege. Rule 1.05 extends ethical protection generally to unprivileged information relating to the client or furnished by the client during the course of or by reason of the representation of the client. In this respect Rule 1.05 accords with general fiduciary principles of agency.

5.   The requirement of confidentiality applies to government lawyers who may disagree with the policy goals that their representation is designed to advance.

Disclosure for Benefit of Client

6.   A lawyer may be expressly authorized to make disclosures to carry out the representation and generally is recognized as having implied-in-fact authority to make disclosures about a client when appropriate in carrying out the representation to the extent that the client's instructions do not limit that authority. In litigation, for example, a lawyer may disclose information by admitting a fact that cannot properly be disputed, or in negotiation by making a disclosure that facilitates a satisfactory conclusion. The effect of Rule 1.05 is to require the lawyer to invoke, for the client, the attorney-client privilege when applicable; but if the court improperly denies the privilege, under paragraph (c)(4) the lawyer may testify as ordered by the court or may test the ruling as permitted by Rule 3.04(d).

7.   In the course of a firm's practice, lawyers may disclose to each other and to appropriate employees information relating to a client, unless the client has instructed that particular information be confined to specified lawyers. Subparagraphs (b)(1) and (c)(3) continue these

practices concerning disclosure of confidential information within the firm.

Use of Information

8. Following sound principles of agency law, subparagraphs (b)(2) and (4) subject a lawyer to discipline for using information relating to the representation in a manner disadvantageous to the client or beneficial to the lawyer or a third person, absent the informed consent of the client. The duty not to misuse client information continues after the client-lawyer relationship has terminated. Therefore, the lawyer is forbidden by subparagraph (b)(3) to use, in absence of the client's informed consent, confidential information of the former client to the client's disadvantage, unless the information is generally known.

Discretionary Disclosure Adverse to Client

9. In becoming privy to information about a client, a lawyer may foresee that the client intends serious and perhaps irreparable harm. To the extent a lawyer is prohibited from making disclosure, the interests of the potential victim are sacrificed in favor of preserving the client's information—usually unprivileged information—even though the client's purpose is wrongful. On the other hand, a client who knows or believes that a lawyer is required or permitted to disclose a client's wrongful purposes may be inhibited from revealing facts which would enable the lawyer to counsel effectively against wrongful action. Rule 1.05 thus involves balancing the interests of one group of potential victims against those of another. The criteria provided by the Rule are discussed below.

10. Rule 503(d)(1), Texas Rules of Civil Evidence (Tex.R.Civ.Evid.), and Rule 503(d)(1), Texas Rules of Criminal Evidence (Tex.R.Crim. Evid.), indicate the underlying public policy of furnishing no protection to client information where the client seeks or uses the services of the lawyer to aid in the commission of a crime or fraud. That public policy governs the dictates of Rule 1.05. Where the client is planning or engaging in criminal or fraudulent conduct or where the culpability of the lawyer's conduct is involved, full protection of client information is not justified.

11. Several other situations must be distinguished. First, the lawyer may not counsel or assist a client in conduct that is criminal or fraudulent. See Rule 1.02(c). As noted in the Comment to that Rule, there can be situations where the lawyer may have to reveal information relating to the representation in order to avoid assisting a client's criminal or fraudulent conduct, and sub-paragraph (c)(4) permits doing so. A lawyer's duty under Rule 3.03(a) not to use false or fabricated evidence is a special instance of the duty prescribed in Rule 1.02(c) to avoid assisting a client in criminal or fraudulent conduct, and sub-paragraph (c)(4) permits revealing information necessary to comply with

Rule 3.03(a) or (b). The same is true of compliance with Rule 4.01. See also paragraph (f).

12. Second, the lawyer may have been innocently involved in past conduct by the client that was criminal or fraudulent. In such a situation the lawyer has not violated Rule 1.02(c), because to "counsel or assist" criminal or fraudulent conduct requires knowing that the conduct is of that character. Since the lawyer's services were made an instrument of the client's crime or fraud, the lawyer has a legitimate interest both in rectifying the consequences of such conduct and in avoiding charges that the lawyer's participation was culpable. Subparagraph (c)(6) and (8) give the lawyer professional discretion to reveal both unprivileged and privileged information in order to serve those interests. See paragraph (g). In view of Tex.R.Civ.Evid. Rule 503(d)(1), and Tex.R.Crim.Evid. 503(d)(1), however, rarely will such information be privileged.

13. Third, the lawyer may learn that a client intends prospective conduct that is criminal or fraudulent. The lawyer's knowledge of the client's purpose may enable the lawyer to prevent commission of the prospective crime or fraud. When the threatened injury is grave, the lawyer's interest in preventing the harm may be more compelling than the interest in preserving confidentiality of information. As stated in subparagraph (c)(7), the lawyer has professional discretion, based on reasonable appearances, to reveal both privileged and unprivileged information in order to prevent the client's commission of any criminal or fraudulent act. In some situations of this sort, disclosure is mandatory. See paragraph (e) and Comments 18–20.

14. The lawyer's exercise of discretion under paragraphs (c) and (d) involves consideration of such factors as the magnitude, proximity, and likelihood of the contemplated wrong, the nature of the lawyer's relationship with the client and with those who might be injured by the client, the lawyer's own involvement in the transaction, and factors that may extenuate the client's conduct in question. In any case, a disclosure adverse to the client's interest should be no greater than the lawyer believes necessary to the purpose. Although preventive action is permitted by paragraphs (c) and (d), failure to take preventive action does not violate those paragraphs. But see paragraphs (e) and (f). *Because these rules do not define standards of civil liability of lawyers for professional conduct, paragraphs (c) and (d) do not create a duty on the lawyer to make any disclosure and no civil liability is intended to arise from the failure to make such disclosure.*

15. A lawyer entitled to a fee necessarily must be permitted to prove the services rendered in an action to collect it, and this necessity is recognized by sub-paragraphs (c)(5) and (d)(2)(iv). This aspect of the rule, in regard to privileged information, expresses the principle that the beneficiary of a fiduciary relationship may not exploit the relationship to the detriment of the fiduciary. Any disclosure by the lawyer, however, should be as protective of the client's interests as possible.

16. If the client is an organization, a lawyer also should refer to Rule 1.12 in order to determine the appropriate conduct in connection with this Rule.

Client Under a Disability

17. In some situations, Rule 1.02(g) requires a lawyer representing a client under a disability to seek the appointment of a legal representative for the client or to seek other orders for the protection of the client. The client may or may not, in a particular matter, effectively consent to the lawyer's revealing to the court confidential information and facts reasonably necessary to secure the desired appointment or order. Nevertheless, the lawyer is authorized by paragraph (c)(4) to reveal such information in order to comply with Rule 1.02(g). See also paragraph 5, Comment to Rule 1.03.

Mandatory Disclosure Adverse to Client

18. Rule 1.05(e) and (f) place upon a lawyer professional obligations in certain situations to make disclosure in order to prevent certain serious crimes by a client or to prevent involvement by the lawyer in a client's crimes or frauds. Except when death or serious bodily harm is likely to result, a lawyer's obligation is to dissuade the client from committing the crime or fraud or to persuade the client to take corrective action; see Rule 1.02(d) and (e).

19. Because it is very difficult for a lawyer to know when a client's criminal or fraudulent purpose actually will be carried out, the lawyer is required by paragraph (e) to act only if the lawyer has information "clearly establishing" the likelihood of such acts and consequences. If the information shows clearly that the client's contemplated crime or fraud is likely to result in death or serious injury, the lawyer must seek to avoid those lamentable results by revealing information necessary to prevent the criminal or fraudulent act. When the threatened crime or fraud is likely to have the less serious result of substantial injury to the financial interests or property of another, the lawyer is not required to reveal preventive information but may do so in conformity to paragraph (c)(7). See also paragraph (f); Rule 1.02(d) and (e); and Rule 3.03(b) and (c).

20. Although a violation of paragraph (e) will subject a lawyer to disciplinary action, the lawyer's decisions whether or how to act should not constitute grounds for discipline unless the lawyer's conduct in the light of those decisions was unreasonable under all existing circumstances as they reasonably appeared to the lawyer. This construction necessarily follows from the fact that paragraph (e) bases the lawyer's affirmative duty to act on how the situation "reasonably appears" to the lawyer, while that imposed by paragraph (f) arises only when a lawyer "knows" that the lawyer's services have been misused by the client. See also Rule 3.03(b).

Withdrawal

21.   If the lawyer's services will be used by the client in materially furthering a course of criminal or fraudulent conduct, the lawyer must withdraw, as stated in Rule 1.15(a)(1).   After withdrawal, a lawyer's conduct continues to be governed by Rule 1.05.   However, the lawyer's duties of disclosure under paragraph (e) of the Rule, insofar as such duties are mandatory, do not survive the end of the relationship even though disclosure remains permissible under paragraphs (6), (7), and (8) if the further requirements of such paragraph are met.   Neither this Rule nor Rule 1.15 prevents the lawyer from giving notice of the fact of withdrawal, and no rule forbids the lawyer to withdraw or disaffirm any opinion, document, affirmation, or the like.

Other Rules

22.   Various other Texas Rules of Professional Conduct permit or require a lawyer to disclose information relating to the representation. See Rules 1.07, 1.12, 2.02, 3.03 and 4.01.   In addition to these provisions, a lawyer may be obligated by other provisions of statutes or other law to give information about a client.   Whether another provision of law supersedes Rule 1.05 is a matter of interpretation beyond the scope of these Rules, but sub-paragraph (c)(4) protects the lawyer from discipline who acts on reasonable belief as to the effect of such laws.

Texas Rule 1.06 *(Modification of Model Rule 1.7)*

[Texas has modified Model Rule 1.7 (Conflict of Interest) as follows:]

RULE 1.06   Conflict of Interest: General Rule

(a) A lawyer shall not represent opposing parties to the same litigation.

(b) In other situations and except to the extent permitted by paragraph (c), a lawyer shall not represent a person if the representation of that person:

(1) involves a substantially related matter in which that person's interests are materially and directly adverse to the interests of another client of the lawyer or the lawyer's firm; or

(2) reasonably appears to be or become adversely limited by the lawyer's or law firm's responsibilities to another client or to a third person or by the lawyer's or law firm's own interests.

(c) A lawyer may represent a client in the circumstances described in (b) if:

(1) the lawyer reasonably believes the representation of each client will not be materially affected; and

179

(2) each affected or potentially affected client consents to such representation after full disclosure of the existence, nature, implications, and possible adverse consequences of the common representation and the advantages involved, if any.

(d) A lawyer who has represented multiple parties in a matter shall not thereafter represent any of such parties in a dispute among the parties arising out of the matter, unless prior consent is obtained from all such parties to the dispute.

(e) If a lawyer has accepted representation in violation of this Rule, or if multiple representation properly accepted becomes improper under this Rule, the lawyer shall promptly withdraw from one or more representations to the extent necessary for any remaining representation not to be in violation of these Rules.

(f) If a lawyer would be prohibited by this Rule from engaging in particular conduct, no other lawyer while a member or associated with that lawyer's firm may engage in that conduct.

COMMENT:

Loyalty to a Client

1. Loyalty is an essential element in the lawyer's relationship to a client. An impermissible conflict of interest may exist before representation is undertaken, in which event the representation should be declined. If such a conflict arises after representation has been undertaken, the lawyer must take effective action to eliminate the conflict, including withdrawal if necessary to rectify the situation. See also Rule 1.16. When more than one client is involved and the lawyer withdraws because a conflict arises after representation, whether the lawyer may continue to represent any of the clients is determined by this Rule and Rules 1.05 and 1.09. See also Rule 1.07(c). Under this Rule, any conflict that prevents a particular lawyer from undertaking or continuing a representation of a client also prevents any other lawyer who is or becomes a member of or an associate with that lawyer's firm from doing so. See paragraph (f).

2. A fundamental principle recognized by paragraph (a) is that a lawyer may not represent opposing parties in litigation. The term "opposing parties" as used in this Rule contemplates a situation where a judgment favorable to one of the parties will directly impact unfavorably upon the other party. Moreover, as a general proposition loyalty to a client prohibits undertaking representation directly adverse to the representation of that client in a substantially related matter unless that client's fully informed consent is obtained and unless the lawyer reasonably believes that the lawyer's representation will be reasonably protective of that client's interests. Paragraphs (b) and (c) express that general concept.

Conflicts in Litigation

3. Paragraph (a) prohibits representation of opposing parties in litigation. Simultaneous representation of parties whose interests in litigation are not actually directly adverse but where the potential for conflict exists, such as co-plaintiffs or co-defendants, is governed by paragraph (b). An impermissible conflict may exist or develop by reason of substantial discrepancy in the parties' testimony, incompatibility in positions in relation to an opposing party or the fact that there are substantially different possibilities of settlement of the claims or liabilities in question. Such conflicts can arise in criminal cases as well as civil. The potential for conflict of interest in representing multiple defendants in a criminal case is so grave that ordinarily a lawyer should decline to represent more than one co-defendant. On the other hand, common representation of persons having similar interests is proper if the risk of adverse effect is minimal and the requirements of paragraph (b) are met. Compare Rule 1.07 involving intermediation between clients.

Conflict with Lawyer's Own Interests

4. Loyalty to a client is impaired not only by the representation of opposing parties in situations within paragraphs (a) and (b)(1) but also in any situation when a lawyer may not be able to consider, recommend or carry out an appropriate course of action for one client because of the lawyer's own interests or responsibilities to others. The conflict in effect forecloses alternatives that would otherwise be available to the client. Paragraph (b)(2) addresses such situations. A potential possible conflict does not itself necessarily preclude the representation. The critical questions are the likelihood that a conflict exists or will eventuate and, if it does, whether it will materially and adversely affect the lawyer's independent professional judgment in considering alternatives or foreclose courses of action that reasonably should be pursued on behalf of the client. It is for the client to decide whether the client wishes to accommodate the other interest involved. However, the client's consent to the representation by the lawyer of another whose interests are directly adverse is insufficient unless the lawyer also believes that there will be no materially adverse effect upon the interests of either client. See paragraph (c).

5. The lawyer's own interests should not be permitted to have adverse effect on representation of a client, even where paragraph (b)(2) is not violated. For example, a lawyer's need for income should not lead the lawyer to undertake matters that cannot be handled competently and at a reasonable fee. See Rules 1.01 and 1.04. If the probity of a lawyer's own conduct in a transaction is in question, it may be difficult for the lawyer to give a client detached advice. A lawyer should not allow related business interests to affect representation, for example, by

referring clients to an enterprise in which the lawyer has an undisclosed interest.

Meaning of Directly Adverse

6. Within the meaning of Rule 1.06(b), the representation of one client is "directly adverse" to the representation of another client if the lawyer's independent judgment on behalf of a client or the lawyer's ability or willingness to consider, recommend or carry out a course of action will be or is reasonably likely to be adversely affected by the lawyer's representation of, or responsibilities to, the other client. The dual representation also is directly adverse if the lawyer reasonably appears to be called upon to espouse adverse positions in the same matter or a related matter. On the other hand, simultaneous representation in unrelated matters of clients whose interests are only generally adverse, such as competing economic enterprises, does not constitute the representation of directly adverse interests. Even when neither paragraph (a) nor (b) is applicable, a lawyer should realize that a business rivalry or personal differences between two clients or potential clients may be so important to one or both that one or the other would consider it contrary to its interests to have the same lawyer as its rival even in unrelated matters; and in those situations a wise lawyer would forego the dual representation.

Full Disclosure and Informed Consent

7. A client under some circumstances may consent to representation notwithstanding a conflict or potential conflict. However, as indicated in paragraph (c)(1), when a disinterested lawyer would conclude that the client should not agree to the representation under the circumstances, the lawyer involved should not ask for such agreement or provide representation on the basis of the client's consent. When more than one client is involved, the question of conflict must be resolved as to each client. Moreover, there may be circumstances where it is impossible to make the full disclosure necessary to obtain informed consent. For example, when the lawyer represents different clients in related matters and one of the clients refuses to consent to the disclosure necessary to permit the other client to make an informed decision, the lawyer cannot properly ask the latter to consent.

8. Disclosure and consent are not formalities. Disclosure sufficient for sophisticated clients may not be sufficient to permit less sophisticated clients to provide fully informed consent. While it is not required that the disclosure and consent be in writing, it would be prudent for the lawyer to provide potential dual clients with at least a written summary of the considerations disclosed.

9. In certain situations, such as in the preparation of loan papers or the preparation of a partnership agreement, a lawyer might have properly undertaken multiple representation and be confronted subse-

quently by a dispute among those clients in regard to that matter. Paragraph (d) forbids the representation of any of those parties in regard to that dispute unless informed consent is obtained from all of the parties to the dispute who had been represented by the lawyer in that matter.

10. A lawyer may represent parties having antagonistic positions on a legal question that has arisen in different cases, unless representation of either client would be adversely affected. Thus, it is ordinarily not improper to assert such positions in cases pending in different trial courts, but it may be improper to do so in cases pending at the same time in an appellate court.

11. Ordinarily, it is not advisable for a lawyer to act as advocate against a client the lawyer represents in some other matter, even if the other matter is wholly unrelated and even if paragraphs (a), (b), and (d) are not applicable. However, there are circumstances in which a lawyer may act as advocate against a client, for a lawyer is free to do so unless this Rule or another rule of the Texas Rules of Professional Conduct would be violated. For example, a lawyer representing an enterprise with diverse operations may accept employment as an advocate against the enterprise in a matter unrelated to any matter being handled for the enterprise if the representation of one client is not directly adverse to the representation of the other client. The propriety of concurrent representation can depend on the nature of the litigation. For example, a suit charging fraud entails conflict to a degree not involved in a suit for declaratory judgment concerning statutory interpretation.

Interest of Person Paying for a Lawyer's Service

12. A lawyer may be paid from a source other than the client, if the client is informed of that fact and consents and the arrangement does not compromise the lawyer's duty of loyalty to the client. See Rule 1.08(e). For example, when an insurer and its insured have conflicting interests in a matter arising from a liability insurance agreement, and the insurer is required to provide special counsel for the insured, the arrangement should assure the special counsel's professional independence. So also, when a corporation and its directors or employees are involved in a controversy in which they have conflicting interests, the corporation may provide funds for separate legal representation of the directors or employees, if the clients consent after consultation and the arrangement ensures the lawyer's professional independence.

Non-litigation Conflict Situations

13. Conflicts of interest in contexts other than litigation sometimes may be difficult to assess. Relevant factors in determining whether there is potential for adverse effect include the duration and intimacy of the lawyer's relationship with the client or clients involved, the functions being performed by the lawyer, the likelihood that actual conflict will arise and the likely prejudice to the client from the conflict if it does arise. The question is often one of proximity and degree.

14. For example, a lawyer may not represent multiple parties to a negotiation whose interests are fundamentally antagonistic to each other, but common representation may be permissible where the clients are generally aligned in interest even though there is some difference of interest among them.

15. Conflict questions may also arise in estate planning and estate administration. A lawyer may be called upon to prepare wills for several family members, such as husband and wife, and, depending upon the circumstances, a conflict of interest may arise. In estate administration it may be unclear whether the client is the fiduciary or is the estate or trust, including its beneficiaries. The lawyer should make clear the relationship to the parties involved.

16. A lawyer for a corporation or other organization who is also a member of its board of directors should determine whether the responsibilities of the two roles may conflict. The lawyer may be called on to advise the corporation in matters involving actions of the directors. Consideration should be given to the frequency with which such situations may arise, the potential intensity of the conflict, the effect of the lawyer's resignation from the board and the possibility of the corporation's obtaining legal advice from another lawyer in such situations. If there is material risk that the dual role will compromise the lawyer's independence of professional judgment, the lawyer should not serve as a director.

Conflict Charged by an Opposing Party

17. Raising questions of conflict of interest is primarily the responsibility of the lawyer undertaking the representation. In litigation, a court may raise the question when there is reason to infer that the lawyer has neglected the responsibility. In a criminal case, inquiry by the court is generally required when a lawyer represents multiple defendants. Where the conflict is such as clearly to call in question the fair or efficient administration of justice, opposing counsel may properly raise the question. Such an objection should be viewed with great caution, however, for it can be misused as a technique of harassment. See Preamble: Scope.

18. Except when the absolute prohibition of this rule applies or in litigation when a court passes upon issues of conflicting interests in determining a question of disqualification of counsel, resolving questions of conflict of interests may require decisions by all affected clients as well as by the lawyer.

Utah Rule 1.7(c)

[Utah has added section (c) to Model Rule 1.7]

RULE 1.7 Conflict of Interest: General Rule

(c) A lawyer shall not simultaneously represent the interests of adverse parties in separate matters, unless:

(1) The lawyer reasonably believes the representation of each will not be adversely affected; and

(2) Each client consents after consultation.

District of Columbia Rule 1.8

[The District of Columbia has added subsection (i) to Model Rule 1.8]

RULE 1.8   Conflict of Interest: Prohibited Transactions

* * *

(i) A lawyer may acquire and enforce a lien granted by law to secure the lawyer's fees or expenses, but a lawyer shall not impose a lien upon any part of a client's files, except upon the lawyer's own work product, and then only to the extent that the work product has not been paid for. This work product exception shall not apply when the client has become unable to pay, or when withholding the lawyer's work product would present a significant risk to the client of irreparable harm.

Lawyer's Liens

[8] The substantive law of the District of Columbia has long permitted lawyers to assert and enforce liens against the property of clients. See, e.g., Redevelopment Land Agency v. Dowdey, 618 A.2d 153, 159–60 (D.C.1992), and cases cited therein. Whether a lawyer has a lien on money or property belonging to a client is generally a matter of substantive law as to which the ethics rules take no position. Exceptions to what the common law might otherwise permit are made with respect to contingent fees and retaining liens. See, respectively, Rule 1.5(c) and Rule 1.8(i).

[9] Rule 1.16(d) requires a lawyer to surrender papers and property to which the client is entitled when representation of the client terminates. Paragraph (i) of this Rule states a narrow exception to Rule 1.16(d): a lawyer may retain anything the law permits—including property—except for files. As to files, a lawyer may retain only the lawyer's own work product, and then only if the client has not paid for the work. However, if the client has paid for the work product, the client is entitled to receive it, even if the client has not previously seen or received a copy of the work product. Furthermore, the lawyer may not retain the work product for which the client has not paid, if the client has become unable to pay or if withholding the work product might irreparably harm the client's interest.

[10] Under Rule 1.16(d), for example, a lawyer would be required to return all papers received from a client, such as birth certificates, wills, tax returns, or "green cards." Rule 1.8(i) does not permit retention of such papers to secure payment of any fee due. Only the lawyer's own work product—results of factual investigations, legal research and analysis, and similar materials generated by the lawyer's own effort—

185

could be retained. (The term "work product" as used in paragraph (i) is limited to materials falling within the "work product doctrine," but includes any material generated by the lawyer that would be protected under that doctrine whether or not created in connection with pending or anticipated litigation.) And a lawyer could not withhold all of the work product merely because a portion of the lawyer's fees had not been paid.

[11] There are situations in which withholding the work product would not be permissible because of irreparable harm to the client. The possibility of involuntary incarceration or criminal conviction constitutes one category of irreparable harm. The realistic possibility that a client might irretrievably lose a significant right or become subject to a significant liability because of the withholding of the work product constitutes another category of irreparable harm. On the other hand, the mere fact that the client might have to pay another lawyer to replicate the work product does not, standing alone, constitute irreparable harm. These examples are merely indicative of the meaning of the term "irreparable harm," and are not exhaustive.

Illinois Rule 1.8

[Illinois has added the following provision to Model Rule 1.8]

RULE 1.8   Conflict of Interest: Prohibited Transactions

* * *

(h) A lawyer shall not enter into an agreement with a client or former client limiting or purporting to limit the right of the client or former client to file or pursue any complaint before the Attorney Registration and Disciplinary Commission.

Indiana Rule 1.8(k)

[Indiana has added the following provision to Model Rule 1.8.]

RULE 1.8   Conflict of Interest: Prohibited Transactions

* * *

(k) A part-time prosecutor or deputy prosecutor authorized by statute to otherwise engage in the practice of law shall refrain from representing a private client in any matter wherein exists an issue upon which said prosecutor has statutory prosecutorial authority or responsibilities. This restriction is not intended to prohibit representation in tort cases in which investigation and any prosecution of infractions has terminated, nor to prohibit representation in family law matters involving no issue subject to prosecutorial authority or responsibilities. Upon a prior, express written limitation of responsibility to exclude prosecutorial authority in matters related to family law,

a part-time deputy prosecutor may fully represent private clients in cases involving family law.

Minnesota Rule 1.8(e)(3) & (k)

[Minnesota has added the following provision to Model Rule 1.8:]

RULE 1.8   Conflict of Interest: Prohibited Transactions

    * * *

(e) **A lawyer shall not provide financial assistance to a client in connection with pending or contemplated litigation, except that:**

    * * *

(3) **a lawyer may guarantee a loan reasonably needed to enable the client to withstand delay in litigation that would otherwise put substantial pressure on the client to settle a case because of financial hardship rather than on the merits, provided the client remains ultimately liable for repayment of the loan without regard to the outcome of the litigation and, further provided, that no promise of such financial assistance was made to the client by the lawyer, or by another in the lawyer's behalf, prior to the employment of that lawyer by that client.**

(k) **A lawyer shall not have sexual relations with a current client unless a consensual sexual relationship existed between them when the lawyer-client relationship commenced. For purposes of this paragraph:**

(1) **"Sexual relations" means sexual intercourse or any other intentional touching of the intimate parts of a person or causing the person to touch the intimate parts of the lawyer.**

(2) **If the client is an organization, any individual who oversees the representation and gives instructions to the lawyer on behalf of the organization shall be deemed to be the client. In-house attorneys while representing governmental or corporate entities are governed by Rule 1.7(b) rather than by this rule with respect to sexual relations with other employees of the entity they represent.**

(3) **This paragraph does not prohibit a lawyer from engaging in sexual relations with a client of the lawyer's firm provided that the lawyer has no involvement in the performance of the legal work for the client.**

(4) **If a party other than the client alleges violation of this paragraph, and the complaint is not summarily dismissed, the Director, in determining whether to investigate**

the allegation and whether to charge any violation based on the allegations, shall consider the client's statement regarding whether the client would be unduly burdened by the investigation or charge.

Texas Rule 1.09 (Modification of Model Rule 1.9)

[Texas has modified Rule 1.9 (Former Client Conflicts) as follows:]

RULE 1.09   Conflict of Interest: Former Client

(a) Without prior consent, a lawyer who personally has formerly represented a client in a matter shall not thereafter represent another person in a matter adverse to the former client:

    (1) in which such other person questions the validity of the lawyer's services or work product for the former client; or

    (2) if the representation in reasonable probability will involve a violation of Rule 1.05.

    (3) if it is the same or a substantially related matter;

(b) Except to the extent authorized by Rule 1.10, when lawyers are or have become members of or associated with a firm, none of them shall knowingly represent a client if any one of them practicing alone would be prohibited from doing so by paragraph (a).

(c) When the association of a lawyer with a firm has terminated, the lawyers who were then associated with that lawyer shall not knowingly represent a client if the lawyer whose association with that firm has terminated would be prohibited from doing so by paragraph (a)(1) or if the representation in reasonable probability will involve a violation of Rule 1.05.

COMMENT:

1. Rule 1.09 addresses the circumstances in which a lawyer in private practice, and other lawyers who were, are or become members of or associated with a firm in which that lawyer practiced or practices, may represent a client against a former client of that lawyer or the lawyer's former firm. Whether a lawyer, or that lawyer's present or former firm, is prohibited from representing a client in a matter by reason of the lawyer's successive government and private employment is governed by Rule 1.10 rather than by this Rule.

2. Paragraph (a) concerns the situation where a lawyer once personally represented a client and now wishes to represent a second client against that former client. Whether such a personal attorney-client relationship existed involves questions of both fact and law that are beyond the scope of these Rules. See Preamble: Scope. Among the relevant factors, however, would be how the former representation

actually was conducted within the firm; the nature and scope of the former client's contacts with the firm (including any restrictions the client may have placed on the dissemination of confidential information within the firm); and the size of the firm.

3. Although paragraph (a) does not absolutely prohibit a lawyer from representing a client against a former client, it does provide that the latter representation is improper if any of three circumstances exists, except with prior consent. The first prohibition is against representation adverse to a former client if it is the same or a substantially related matter. The second circumstance is that the lawyer may not represent a client who questions the validity of the lawyer's services or work product for the former client. Thus, for example, a lawyer who drew a will leaving a substantial portion of the testator's property to a designated beneficiary would violate paragraph (a) by representing the testator's heirs at law in an action seeking to overturn the will.

4. Paragraph (a)'s third limitation on undertaking a representation against a former client is that it may not be done if there is a "reasonable probability" that the representation would cause the lawyer to violate the obligations owed the former client under Rule 1.05. Thus, for example, if there were a reasonable probability that the subsequent representation would involve either an unauthorized disclosure of confidential information under Rule 1.05(b)(1) or an improper use of such information to the disadvantage of the former client under Rule 1.05(b)(3), that representation would be improper under paragraph (a). Whether such a reasonable probability exists in any given case will be a question of fact.

5. Paragraph (b) extends paragraph (a)'s limitations on an individual lawyer's freedom to undertake a representation against that lawyer's former client to all other lawyers who are or become members of or associated with the firm in which that lawyer is practicing. Thus, for example, if a client severs the attorney-client relationship with a lawyer who remains in a firm, the entitlement of that individual lawyer to undertake a representation against that former client is governed by paragraph (a); and all other lawyers who are or become members of or associated with that lawyer's firm are treated in the same manner by paragraph (b). Similarly, if a lawyer severs his or her association with a firm and that firm retains as a client a person whom the lawyer personally represented while with the firm, that lawyer's ability thereafter to undertake a representation against that client is governed by paragraph (a); and all other lawyers who are or become members of or associates with that lawyer's new firm are treated in the same manner by paragraph (b).

6. Paragraph (c) addresses the situation of former partners or associates of a lawyer who once had represented a client when the relationship between the former partners or associates and the lawyer has been terminated. In that situation, the former partners or associates are prohibited from questioning the validity of such lawyer's work

product and from undertaking representation which in reasonable probability will involve a violation of Rule 1.05. Such a violation could occur, for example, when the former partners or associates retained materials in their files from the earlier representation of the client that, if disclosed or used in connection with the subsequent representation, would violate Rule 1.05(b)(1) or (b)(3).

7. Thus, the effect of paragraphs (b) and (c) is to extend any inability of a particular lawyer under paragraph (a) to undertake a representation against a former client to all other lawyers who are or become members of or associated with any firm in which that lawyer is practicing. Should those other lawyers cease to be members of the same firm as the lawyer affected by paragraph (a) without themselves coming within its restrictions, they thereafter may undertake the representation against the lawyer's former client unless prevented from doing so by some other of these Rules.

8. Although not required to do so by Rule 1.05 or this Rule, some courts, as a procedural decision, disqualify a lawyer for representing a present client against a former client when the subject matter of the present representation is so closely related to the subject matter of the prior representation that confidences obtained from the former client might be useful in the representation of the present client. See Comment 17 to Rule 1.06. This so-called "substantial relationship" test is defended by asserting that to require a showing that confidences of the first client were in fact used for the benefit of the subsequent client as a condition to procedural disqualification would cause disclosure of the confidences that the court seeks to protect. A lawyer is not subject to discipline under Rule 1.05(b)(1), (3), or (4), however, unless the protected information is actually used. Likewise, a lawyer is not subject to discipline under this Rule unless the new representation by the lawyer in reasonable probability would result in a violation of those provisions.

9. Whether the "substantial relationship" test will continue to be employed as a standard for procedural disqualification is a matter beyond the scope of these Rules. See Preamble: Scope. The possibility that such a disqualification might be sought by the former client or granted by a court, however, is a matter that could be of substantial importance to the present client in deciding whether or not to retain or continue to employ a particular lawyer or law firm as its counsel. Consequently, a lawyer should disclose those possibilities, as well as their potential consequences for the representation, to the present client as soon as the lawyer becomes aware of them; and the client then should be allowed to decide whether or not to obtain new counsel. See Rules 1.03(b) and 1.06(b).

10. This Rule is primarily for the protection of clients and its protections can be waived by them. A waiver is effective only if there is consent after disclosure of the relevant circumstances, including the lawyer's past or intended role on behalf of each client, as appropriate. See Comments 7 and 8 to Rule 1.06.

Utah Rule 1.9(a)

[Utah has modified Model Rule 1.9(a) as follows:]

RULE 1.9 Conflict of Interest: Former Client

A lawyer who has formerly represented a client in a matter shall not thereafter:

(a) Represent another person in the same or a substantially factually related matter in which that person's interests are materially adverse to the interests of the former client unless the former client consents after consultation; or

(b) Use information relating to the representation to the disadvantage of the former client except as Rule 1.6 would permit with respect to a client or when the information has become generally known.

COMMENT:

After termination of a client-lawyer relationship, a lawyer may not represent another client except in conformity with this Rule. The principles in Rule 1.7 determine whether the interests of the present and former client are adverse. Thus, a lawyer could not properly seek to rescind on behalf of a new client a contract drafted on behalf of the former client. So also a lawyer who has prosecuted an accused person could not properly represent the accused in a subsequent civil action against the government concerning the same transaction.

The scope of a "matter" for purposes of Rule 1.9(a) may depend on the facts of a particular situation or transaction. The lawyer's involvement in a matter can also be a question of degree. When a lawyer has been directly involved in a specific transaction, subsequent representation of other clients with materially adverse interests clearly is prohibited. On the other hand, a lawyer who recurrently handled a type of problem for a former client is not precluded from later representing another client in a wholly distinct problem of that type even though the subsequent representation involves a position adverse to the prior client. Similar considerations can apply to the reassignment of military lawyers between defense and prosecution functions within the same military jurisdiction. The underlying question is whether the lawyer was so involved in the matter that the subsequent representation can be justly regarded as a changing of sides in the matter in question.

Information acquired by the lawyer in the course of representing a client may not subsequently be used by the lawyer to the disadvantage of the client. However, the fact that a lawyer has once served a client does not preclude the lawyer from using generally known information about the client when later representing another client.

Disqualification from subsequent representation is for the protection of clients and can be waived by them. A waiver is effective only if there is disclosure of the circumstances, including the lawyer's intended role in behalf of the new client.

With regard to an opposing party's raising a question of conflict of interest, see Comment to Rule 1.7. With regard to disqualification of a firm with which a lawyer is associated, see Rule 1.10.

District of Columbia Rule 1.11

[The District of Columbia has added the following provisions to Model Rule 1.11]

RULE 1.11   Successive Government and Private Employment

* * *

(d) Except as provided in paragraph (e), when any of counsel, lawyer, partner, or associate of a lawyer personally disqualified under paragraph (a) accepts employment in connection with a matter giving rise to the personal disqualification, the following notifications shall be required:

(1) The personally disqualified lawyer shall submit to the public department or agency by which the lawyer was formerly employed and serve on each other party to any pertinent proceeding a signed document attesting that during the period of disqualification the personally disqualified lawyer will not participate in any manner in the matter or the representation, will not discuss the matter or the representation with any partner, associate, or of counsel lawyer, and will not share in any fees for the matter or the representation.

(2) At least one affiliated lawyer shall submit to the same department or agency and serve on the same parties a signed document attesting that all affiliated lawyers are aware of the requirement that the personally disqualified lawyer be screened from participating in or discussing the matter or the representation and describing the procedures being taken to screen the personally disqualified lawyer.

(e) If a client requests in writing that the fact and subject matter of a representation subject to paragraph (d) not be disclosed by submitting the signed statements referred to in paragraph (d), such statements shall be prepared concurrently with undertaking the representation and filed with bar counsel under seal. If at any time thereafter the fact and subject matter of the representation are disclosed to the public or become a part of the public record, the signed statements previously prepared shall be promptly submitted as required by paragraph (d).

(f) Signed documents filed pursuant to paragraph (d) shall be available to the public, except to the extent that a lawyer submitting a signed document demonstrates to the satisfaction of the public department or agency upon which such documents

are served that public disclosure is inconsistent with Rule 1.6 or provisions of law.

(g) This Rule applies to any matter involving a specific party or parties.

(h) A lawyer who participates in a program of temporary service to the office of corporation counsel of the kind described in Rule 1.10(e) shall be treated as having served as a public officer or employee for purposes of paragraph (a), and the provisions of paragraphs (b)–(e) shall apply to the lawyer and to lawyers affiliated with the lawyer.

New Hampshire Rule 1.11A

[New Hampshire has added the following provision to address the conduct of lawyer officials:]

RULE 1.11A   Conduct of Lawyer–Officials

(a) **Definitions.** As used in this rule:

(1) lawyer-official means a lawyer actively engaged in the practice of law, who is a member of the governmental body;

(2) government body means any state or local governmental agency, board, body, council or commission; and

(3) interest means a direct, personal and pecuniary interest, individually or on a client's behalf, in a matter which is under consideration by the governmental body of which the lawyer-official is a member.

(b) No lawyer-official shall:

(1) participate in any hearing, debate, discussion or vote, or in any manner otherwise attempt to influence the outcome of a matter in which he or she has an interest;

(2) utilize information obtained in such capacity for his or her own personal benefit or that of his or her clients or the clients of the firm with which the lawyer-official is associated;

(3) appear on behalf of a client before any governmental body of which the lawyer-official is a member or whose members have been appointed by the governmental body of which the lawyer-official is a member;

(4) accept anything of value from any person or organization when the lawyer-official knows or reasonably should know that the offer is for the purpose of influencing the lawyer-official's actions or decisions;

(5) use his or her official position to influence or to attempt to influence any governmental body to act in favor of the lawyer-official or the lawyer-official's clients or

clients of the firm with which the lawyer-official is associated.

(c) Other lawyers in the firm with which the lawyer-official is associated may not appear on behalf of clients before the governmental body of which the lawyer-official is a member, or any governmental body whose members have been appointed by the body of which the lawyer-official is a member, unless the lawyer-official publicly disqualifies himself or herself and refrains from participation in the matter in accordance with paragraph (b)(1) of this Rule, and otherwise conducts himself or herself with respect to the matter in accordance with paragraph (b) of this Rule.

Montana Rule 1.17

[Montana has added Rule 1.17 which has no counterpart in the Model Rules]

RULE 1.17 Government Employment

An attorney employed by a department of the State of Montana or municipality on a part-time or fee basis shall not accept other employment during the course of which it would be possible to use or otherwise rely on information obtained by reason of government employment that is injurious, confidential or privileged and not otherwise discoverable.

COUNSELLOR

Oregon Rule DR 5–106 (Modification to Model Rule 2.2)

[Oregon has modified Model Rule 2.2 to read as follows:]

DR 5–106. Mediation

(A) A lawyer may act as a mediator for multiple parties in any matter if:

(1) The lawyer clearly informs the parties of the lawyer's role and they consent to this arrangement; and

(2) The lawyer gives advice to a party only in the presence of all parties in the matter.

(B) A lawyer serving as a mediator may draft a settlement agreement but must advise and encourage the parties to seek independent legal advice before executing it.

(C) A lawyer serving as a mediator may not act on behalf of any party in court nor represent one party against the other in any related legal proceeding.

(D) A lawyer shall withdraw as mediator if any of the parties so request, or if any of the conditions stated in DR 5–106(A) are no longer satisfied. Upon withdrawal, the lawyer shall not continue to act on behalf of any of the parties in the matter that was the subject of the mediation.

ADVOCATE

Wyoming Rule 3.1

[Wyoming has modified Model Rule 3.1 to read as follows:]

RULE 3.1   Meritorious Claims and Contentions

A lawyer shall not bring or defend a proceeding, or assert or controvert an issue therein, unless there is a basis for doing so that is not frivolous, which includes a good faith argument for an extension, modification or reversal of existing law. A lawyer for the defendant in a criminal proceeding, or the respondent in a proceeding that could result in incarceration, may nevertheless so defend the proceeding as to require that every element of the case be established. The signature of an attorney constitutes a certificate by him that he has read the pleading, motion, or other court document; that to the best of his knowledge, information, and belief, formed after reasonable inquiry, it is well grounded in fact and is warranted by existing law or a good faith argument for the extension, modification, or reversal of existing law; and that it is not interposed for any improper purpose such as to harass or to cause unnecessary delay or needless increase in the cost of litigation.

COMMENT:

[1] The advocate has a duty to use legal procedure for the fullest benefit of the client's cause, but also a duty not to abuse legal procedure. The law, both procedural and substantive, establishes the limits within which an advocate may proceed. However, the law is not always clear and never is static. Accordingly, in determining the proper scope of advocacy, account must be taken of the law's ambiguities and potential for change.

[2] The filing of an action, defense or other document in court is not frivolous merely because the facts have not first been fully substantiated or because the lawyer expects to develop vital evidence by discovery. Such action is not frivolous even though the lawyer believes that the client's position ultimately will not prevail. The action is frivolous, however, if the client or attorney desires to have the action taken primarily for the purpose of harassing, delaying or causing unnecessary expense or if the lawyer is unable either to make a good faith argument on the merits of the action taken or to support the action taken by a good faith argument for an extension, modification or reversal of existing law. The last sentence of Rule 3.1 is based on Rule 11 of the Federal Rules of Civil Procedure. It imposes an affirmative duty on an advocate to make reasonable inquiry, both as to the facts and law, before filing a

pleading or other court document. A violation subjects the lawyer to discipline.

Kansas Rule 3.5

[Kansas has modified Model Rule 3.5 to read as follows:]

RULE 3.5   Impartiality and Decorum of the Tribunal

A lawyer shall not:

(a) give or lend anything of value to a judge, official, or employee of a tribunal except as permitted by Section C(4) of Canon 5 of the Code of Judicial Conduct as it may, from time to time be adopted in Kansas, nor may a lawyer attempt to improperly influence a judge, official or employee of a tribunal, but a lawyer may make a contribution to the campaign fund of a candidate for judicial office in conformity with Section B(2) under Canon 7 of the Code of Judicial Conduct;

(b) communicate or cause another to communicate with a member of a jury or the venire from which the jury will be selected about the matters under consideration other than in the course of official proceedings until after the discharge of the jury from further consideration of the case;

(c) communicate or cause another to communicate as to the merits of a cause with a judge or official before whom an adversary proceeding is pending except:

(1) in the course of official proceedings in the cause;

(2) in writing, if the lawyer promptly delivers a copy of the writing to opposing counsel or to the adverse party if unrepresented;

(3) orally upon adequate notice to opposing counsel or the adverse party if unrepresented;

(4) as otherwise authorized by law or court rule;

(d) engage in undignified or discourteous conduct degrading to a tribunal.

KANSAS COMMENT:

Rule 3.5 in the proposed Model Rules as adopted by the ABA has been substantially modified to include more specific guidelines and prohibitions such as were included in the Model Code. The reason for this is that the Kansas committee felt that existing disciplinary rules, 7.106(C)(6), 7.108, 7.109, 7.110 were more specific and preferable in many respects to the proposed model rule. Model Rule 3.5 prohibits a lawyer from seeking to influence a judge, juror, prospective juror or other official by means prohibited by law. The Kansas committee felt that this is too narrow a prohibition and would permit some things that should not be permitted. The committee has reimposed the absolute prohibition of DR 7–110(A) upon a lawyer giving or lending anything of value to a judge or official; except as permitted by the Canons of Judicial Ethics. In other words, a lawyer may ethically give what a judge may ethically receive. It was felt that such a *per se* rule is preferable to one that would require proof that the gift or loan was prompted by an attempt to influence the official.

Similarly, it was felt by the Kansas committee that the more specific provisions found in DR 7–108 regarding communication with jurors was preferable in that they give more guidance to the lawyer as to what communications are permitted and what communications are not permitted and further would give more guidance to the disciplinary authority as to when a violation had been committed.

Section (c) of the Model Rule prohibited conduct intended to disrupt a tribunal and, therefore, impliedly would authorize undignified or discourteous conduct degrading to a tribunal, prohibited under DR 7–106(C)(6), unless the intent to disrupt is established. The Kansas committee is of the opinion that standards of lawyer conduct in the courtroom should not be lowered as the model rule would appear to do.

TRANSACTIONS WITH PERSONS OTHER THAN CLIENTS

Louisiana Rule 4.2
[Louisiana has modified Model Rule 4.2 to read as follows:]

RULE 4.2 Communication With Person Represented by Counsel

In representing a client, a lawyer shall not communicate about the subject of the representation with a party the lawyer knows to be represented by another lawyer in the matter, unless the lawyer has the consent of the other lawyer or is authorized by law to do so. A lawyer shall not effect the prohibited communication through a third person, including the lawyer's client.

New Mexico Rule 16–402 (Modification of Model Rule 4.2)
[New Mexico has modified Model Rule 4.2 to read as follows:]

RULE 16–402. Communication With Person Represented by Counsel

In representing a client, a lawyer shall not communicate about the subject of the representation with a party the lawyer knows to be represented by another lawyer in the matter, unless the lawyer has the consent of the other lawyer or is authorized by law to do so. Except for persons having a managerial responsibility on behalf of the organization, an attorney is not prohibited from communicating directly with employees of a corporation, partnership or other entity about the subject matter of the representation even though the corporation, partnership or entity itself is represented by counsel.

Texas Rule 4.02 (Modification of Model Rule 4.2)
[Texas has modified Model Rule 4.2 as follows:]

RULE 4.02.   Communication With One Represented by Counsel

(a) In representing a client, a lawyer shall not communicate or cause or encourage another to communicate about the subject of the representation with a person, organization or entity of government the lawyer knows to be represented by another lawyer regarding that subject, unless the lawyer has the consent of the other lawyer or is authorized by law to do so.

(b) In representing a client a lawyer shall not communicate or cause another to communicate about the subject of representation with a person or organization a lawyer knows to be employed or retained for the purpose of conferring with or advising another lawyer about the subject of the representation, unless the lawyer has the consent of the other lawyer or is authorized by law to do so.

(c) For the purpose of this rule, "organization or entity of government" includes: (1) those persons presently having a managerial responsibility with an organization or entity of government that relates to the subject of the representation, or (2) those persons presently employed by such organization or entity and whose act or omission in connection with the subject of representation may make the organization or entity of government vicariously liable for such act or omission.

(d) When a person, organization, or entity of government that is represented by a lawyer in a matter seeks advice regarding that matter from another lawyer, the second lawyer is not prohibited by paragraph (a) from giving such advice without notifying or seeking consent of the first lawyer.

COMMENT:

1.   Paragraph (a) of this Rule is directed at efforts to circumvent the lawyer-client relationship existing between other persons, organizations or entities of government and their respective counsel. It prohibits communications that in form are between a lawyer's client and another person, organization or entity of government represented by counsel where, because of the lawyer's involvement in devising and controlling their content, such communications in substance are between the lawyer and the represented person, organization or entity of government.

2.   Paragraph (a) does not, however, prohibit communication between a lawyer's client and persons, organizations, or entities of government represented by counsel, as long as the lawyer does not cause or encourage the communication without the consent of the lawyer for the other party. Consent may be implied as well as expressed, as, for example, where the communication occurs in the form of a private

placement memorandum or similar document that obviously is intended for multiple recipients and that normally is furnished directly to persons, even if known to be represented by counsel. Similarly, that paragraph does not impose a duty on a lawyer to affirmatively discourage communication between the lawyer's client and other represented persons, organizations or entities of government. Furthermore, it does not prohibit client communications concerning matters outside the subject of the representation with any such person, organization, or entity of government. Finally, it does not prohibit a lawyer from furnishing a "second opinion" in a matter to one requesting such opinion, nor from discussing employment in the matter if requested to do so. But see Rule 7.02.

3. Paragraph (b) of this Rule provides that unless authorized by law, experts employed or retained by a lawyer for a particular matter should not be contacted by opposing counsel regarding that matter without the consent of the lawyer who retained them. However, certain governmental agents or employees such as police may be contacted due to their obligations to the public at large.

4. In the case of an organization or entity of government, this Rule prohibits communications by a lawyer for one party concerning the subject of the representation with persons having a managerial responsibility on behalf of the organization that relates to the subject of the representation and with those persons presently employed by such organization or entity whose act or omission may make the organization or entity vicariously liable for the matter at issue, without the consent of the lawyer for the organization or entity of government involved. This Rule is based on the presumption that such persons are so closely identified with the interests of the organization or entity of government that its lawyers will represent them as well. If, however, such an agent or employee is represented in the matter by his or her own counsel that presumption is inapplicable. In such cases, the consent by that counsel to communicate will be sufficient for purposes of this Rule. Compare Rule 3.04(f). Moreover, this Rule does not prohibit a lawyer from contacting a former employee of a represented organization or entity of a government, nor from contacting a person presently employed by such an organization or entity whose conduct is not a matter at issue but who might possess knowledge concerning the matter at issue.

Minnesota Rule 4.3

[Minnesota has modified Model Rule 4.3 to read as follows:]

RULE 4.3 Dealing With Unrepresented Person

(a) In dealing on behalf of a client with a person who is not represented by counsel, a lawyer shall clearly disclose whether the client's interests are adverse to the interests of such person and shall not state or imply that the lawyer is disinterested.

(b) When the lawyer knows or reasonably should know that the unrepresented person misunderstands the lawyer's role in

the matter, the lawyer shall make reasonable efforts to correct the misunderstanding.

(c) During the course of representation of a client a lawyer shall not give advice to a person who is not represented by a lawyer, other than the advice to secure counsel, on those issues as to which the interests of each person are or have a reasonable possibility of being in conflict with the interests of the client.

COMMENT—1985:

An unrepresented person, particularly one not experienced in dealing with legal matters, might assume that a lawyer is disinterested in loyalties or is a disinterested authority on the law even when the lawyer represents a client.

Texas Rule 4.04 (Modification of Model Rule 4.4)

[Texas has modified Model Rule 4.4 as follows:]

RULE 4.04   Respect for Rights of Third Persons

* * *

(b) A lawyer shall not present, participate in presenting, or threaten to present:

(1) criminal or disciplinary charges solely to gain an advantage in a civil matter; or

(2) civil, criminal or disciplinary charges against a complainant, a witness, or a potential witness in a bar disciplinary proceeding solely to prevent participation by the complainant, witness or potential witness therein.

LAW FIRMS AND ASSOCIATIONS

Texas Rule 5.01 (Modification of Model Rule 5.1)

[Texas has modified Model Rule 5.1 as follows:]

RULE 5.01   Responsibilities of a Partner or Supervisory Lawyer

A lawyer shall be subject to discipline because of another lawyer's violation of these rules of professional conduct if:

(a) The lawyer is a partner or supervising lawyer and orders, encourages, or knowingly permits the conduct involved; or

(b) The lawyer is a partner in the law firm in which the other lawyer practices, is the general counsel of a government agency's legal department in which the other lawyer is employed, or has direct supervisory authority over the other lawyer, and with knowledge of the other lawyer's violation of these rules knowingly fails to take reasonable remedial action to avoid or mitigate the consequences of the other lawyer's violation.

COMMENT:

1. Rule 5.01 conforms to the general principle that a lawyer is not vicariously subjected to discipline for the misconduct of another person, under Rule 8.04, a lawyer is subject to discipline if the lawyer knowingly assists or induces another to violate these rules. Rule 5.01(a) additionally provides that a partner or supervising lawyer is subject to discipline for ordering or encouraging another lawyer's violation of these rules. Moreover, a partner or supervising lawyer is in a position of authority over the work of other lawyers and the partner or supervising lawyer may be disciplined for permitting another lawyer to violate these rules.

2. Rule 5.01(b) likewise is concerned with the lawyer who is in a position of authority over another lawyer and who knows that the other lawyer has committed a violation of a rule of professional conduct. A partner in a law firm, the general counsel of a government agency's legal department, or a lawyer having direct supervisory authority over specific legal work by another lawyer, occupies the position of authority contemplated by Rule 5.01(b).

3. Whether a lawyer has "direct supervisory authority over the other lawyer" in particular circumstances is a question of fact. In some instances, a senior associate may be a supervising attorney.

4. The duty imposed upon the partner or other authoritative lawyer by Rule 5.01(b) is to take reasonable remedial action to avoid or mitigate the consequences of the other lawyer's known violation. Appropriate remedial action by a partner or other supervisory lawyer would depend on may factors, such as the immediacy of the partner's or supervisory lawyer's knowledge and involvement, the nature of the action that can reasonably be expected to avoid or mitigate injurious consequences, and the seriousness of the anticipated consequences. In some circumstances, it may be sufficient for a junior partner to refer the ethical problem directly to a designated senior partner or a management committee. A lawyer supervising a specific legal matter may be required to intervene more directly. For example if a supervising lawyer knows that a supervised lawyer misrepresented a matter to an opposing party in negotiation, the supervisor as well as the other lawyer may be required by Rule 5.01(b) to correct the resulting misapprehension.

5. Thus, neither Rule 5.01(a) nor Rule 5.01(b) visits vicarious disciplinary liability upon the lawyer in a position of authority. Rather, the lawyer in such authoritative position is exposed to discipline only for his or her own knowing actions or failures to act. Whether a lawyer may be liable civilly or criminally for another lawyer's conduct is a question of law beyond the scope of these rules.

6. Wholly aside from the dictates of these rules for discipline, a lawyer in a position of authority in a firm or government agency or over another lawyer should feel a moral compunction to make reasonable efforts to ensure that the office, firm, or agency has in effect appropriate procedural measures giving reasonable assurance that all lawyers in the

office conform to these rules. This moral obligation, although not required by these rules, should fall also upon lawyers who have intermediate managerial responsibilities in the law department of an organization or government agency.

7. The measures that should be undertaken to give such reasonable assurance may depend on the structure of the firm or organization and upon the nature of the legal work performed. In a small firm, informal supervision and an occasional admonition ordinarily will suffice. In a large firm, or in practice situations where intensely difficult ethical problems frequently arise, more elaborate procedures may be called for in order to give such assurance. Obviously, the ethical atmosphere of a firm influences the conduct of all of its lawyers. Lawyers may rely also on continuing legal education in professional ethics to guard against unintentional misconduct by members of their firm or organization.

Texas Rule 5.02 (Modification of Model Rule 5.2)

[Texas has modified Model Rule 5.2 as follows:]

RULE 5.02   Responsibilities of a Supervised Lawyer

A lawyer is bound by these rules notwithstanding that the lawyer acted under the supervision of another person, except that a supervised lawyer does not violate these rules if that lawyer acts in accordance with a supervisory lawyer's reasonable resolution of an arguable question of professional conduct.

COMMENT:

1. Rule 5.02 embodies the fundamental concept that every lawyer is a trained, mature, licensed professional who has sworn to uphold ethical standards and who is responsible for the lawyer's own conduct. Accordingly, a lawyer is not relieved from compliance with these rules because the lawyer acted under the supervision of an employer or other person. In some situations, the fact that a lawyer acted at the direction or order of another person may be relevant in determining whether the lawyer had the knowledge required to render the conduct a violation of these rules. The fact of supervision may also, of course, be a circumstance to be considered by a grievance committee or court in mitigation of the penalty to be imposed for violation of a rule.

2. In many law firms and organizations, the relatively inexperienced lawyer works as an assistant to a more experienced lawyer or is directed, supervised or given guidance by an experienced lawyer in the firm. In the normal course of practice the senior lawyer has the responsibility for making the decisions involving professional judgment as to procedures to be taken, the status of the law, and the propriety of actions to be taken by the lawyers. Otherwise a consistent course of action could not be taken on behalf of clients. The junior lawyer

reasonably can be expected to acquiesce in the decisions made by the senior lawyer unless the decision is clearly wrong.

3. Rule 5.02 take a realistic attitude toward those prevailing modes of practice by lawyers not engaged in solo practice. Accordingly, Rule 5.02 provides the supervised lawyer with a special defense in a disciplinary proceeding in which the lawyer is charged with having violated a rule of professional conduct. The supervised lawyer is entitled to this defense only if it appears that an arguable question of professional conduct was resolved by a supervising lawyer and that a resolution made by the supervising lawyer was a reasonable resolution. The resolution is a reasonable one, even if it is ultimately found to be officially unacceptable, provided it would have appeared reasonable to a disinterested, competent lawyer based on the information reasonably available to the supervising lawyer at the time the resolution was made. "Supervisory lawyer" as used in Rule 5.02 should be construed in conformity with prevailing modes of practice in firms and other groups and, therefore, should include a senior lawyer who undertakes to resolve the question of professional propriety as well as a lawyer who more directly supervises the supervised lawyer.

4. By providing such a defense to the supervised lawyer, Rule 5.02 recognizes that the inexperienced lawyer working under the direction or supervision of an employer or senior attorney is not in a favorable position to disagree with reasonable decisions made by the experienced lawyer. Often, the only choices available to the supervised lawyer would be to accept the decision made by the senior lawyer or to resign or otherwise lose the employment. This provision of Rule 5.02 also recognizes that it is not necessarily improper for the inexperienced lawyer to rely, reasonably and in good faith, upon decisions made in unclear matters by senior lawyers in the organization.

5. The defense provided by this Rule is available without regard to whether the conduct in question was originally proposed by the supervised lawyer or another person. Nevertheless, the supervised lawyer is not permitted to accept an unreasonable decision as to the propriety of professional conduct. The Rule obviously provides no defense to the supervised lawyer who participates in clearly wrongful conduct. Reliance can be placed only upon a reasonable resolution made by the supervisory lawyer.

6. The protection afforded by Rule 5.02 to a supervised lawyer relates only to professional disciplinary proceedings. Whether a similar defense may exist in actions in tort or for breach of contract is a question beyond the scope of the Texas Rules of Professional Conduct.

District of Columbia Rule 5.4

RULE 5.4 **Professional Independence of a Lawyer**

(a) A lawyer or law firm shall not share legal fees with a nonlawyer, except that:

(1) an agreement by a lawyer with the lawyer's firm, partner, or associate may provide for the payment of money, over a reasonable period of time after the lawyer's death, to the lawyer's estate or to one or more specified persons;

(2) a lawyer who undertakes to complete unfinished legal business of a deceased lawyer may pay to the estate of the deceased lawyer that proportion of the total compensation which fairly represents the services rendered by the deceased lawyer;

(3) a lawyer or law firm may include nonlawyer employees in a compensation or retirement plan, even though the plan is based in whole or in part on a profit-sharing arrangement; and

(4) sharing of fees is permitted in a partnership or other form of organization which meets the requirements of paragraph (b).

(b) A lawyer may practice law in a partnership or other form of organization in which a financial interest is held or managerial authority is exercised by an individual nonlawyer who performs professional services which assist the organization in providing legal services to clients, but only if:

(1) the partnership or organization has as its sole purpose providing legal services to clients;

(2) all persons having such managerial authority or holding a financial interest undertake to abide by these rules of professional conduct;

(3) the lawyers who have a financial interest or managerial authority in the partnership or organization undertake to be responsible for the nonlawyer participants to the same extent as if nonlawyer participants were lawyers under rule 5.1;

(4) the foregoing conditions are set forth in writing.

(c) A lawyer shall not permit a person who recommends, employs, or pays the lawyer to render legal services for another to direct or regulate the lawyer's professional judgment in rendering such legal services.

COMMENT:

[1] The provisions of this Rule express traditional limitations on sharing fees with nonlawyers. (On sharing fees among lawyers not in the same firm, see Rule 1.5(e).) These limitations are to protect the lawyer's professional independence of judgment. Where someone other than the client pays the lawyer's fee or salary, or recommends employment of the lawyer, that arrangement does not modify the lawyer's

obligation to the client. As stated in paragraph (c), such arrangements should not interfere with the lawyer's professional judgment.

[2] Traditionally, the canons of legal ethics and disciplinary rules prohibited lawyers from practicing law in a partnership that includes nonlawyers or in any other organization where a nonlawyer is a shareholder, director, or officer. Notwithstanding these strictures, the profession implicitly recognized exceptions for lawyers who work for corporate law departments, insurance companies, and legal service organizations.

[3] As the demand increased for a broad range of professional services from a single source, lawyers employed professionals from other disciplines to work for them. So long as the nonlawyers remained employees of the lawyers, these relationships did not violate the disciplinary rules. However, when lawyers and nonlawyers considered forming partnerships and professional corporations to provide a combination of legal and other services to the public, they faced serious obstacles under the former rules.

[4] This Rule rejects an absolute prohibition against lawyers and nonlawyers joining together to provide collaborative services, but continues to impose traditional ethical requirements with respect to the organization thus created. Thus, a lawyer may practice law in an organization where nonlawyers hold a financial interest or exercise managerial authority, but only if the conditions set forth in subparagraphs (b)(1), (b)(2), and (b)(3) are satisfied, and, pursuant to subparagraph (b)(4), satisfaction of these conditions is set forth in a written instrument. The requirement of a writing helps ensure that these important conditions are not overlooked in establishing the organizational structure of entities in which nonlawyers enjoy an ownership or managerial role equivalent to that of a partner in a traditional law firm.

[5] Nonlawyer participants under Rule 5.4 ought not be confused with nonlawyer assistants under Rule 5.3. Nonlawyer participants are persons having managerial authority or financial interests in organizations which provide legal services. Within such organizations, lawyers with financial interests or managerial authority are held responsible for ethical misconduct by nonlawyer participants about which the lawyers know or reasonably should know. This is the same standard of liability contemplated by Rule 5.1, regarding the responsibilities of lawyers with direct supervisory authority over other lawyers.

[6] Nonlawyer assistants under Rule 5.3 do not have managerial authority or financial interests in the organization. Lawyers having direct supervisory authority over nonlawyer assistants are held responsible only for ethical misconduct by assistants about which the lawyers actually know.

[7] As the introductory portion of Subparagraph (b) makes clear, the purpose of liberalizing the rules regarding the possession of a financial interest or the exercise of management authority by a nonlawyer is to permit nonlawyer professionals to work with lawyers in the delivery of legal services without being relegated to the role of an

employee. For example, the Rule permits economists to work in a firm
with antitrust or public utility practitioners, psychologists or psychiatric
social workers to work with family law practitioners to assist in counseling clients, nonlawyer lobbyists to work with lawyers who perform
legislative services, certified public accountants to work in conjunction
with tax lawyers or others who use accountants' services in performing
legal services, and professional managers to serve as office managers,
executive directors, or in similar positions. In all of these situations, the
professionals may be given financial interests or managerial responsibility, so long as all of the requirements of subparagraph (c) are met.

[8] Subparagraph (b) does not permit an individual or entity to
acquire all or any part of the ownership of a law partnership or other
form of law practice organization for investment or other purposes. It
thus does not permit a corporation, an investment banking firm, an
investor, or any other person or entity to entitle itself to all or any
portion of the income or profits of a law firm or other similar organization. Since such an investor would not be an individual performing
professional services within the law firm or other organization, the
requirements of subparagraph (b) would not be met.

[9] The term "individual" in subparagraph (b) is not intended to
preclude the participation in a law firm or other organization by an
individual professional corporation in the same manner as lawyers who
have incorporated as a professional corporation currently participate in
partnerships which include professional corporations.

[10] Some sharing of fees is likely to occur in the kinds of organizations permitted by paragraph (b). Subparagraph (a)(4) makes it clear
that such fee-sharing is not prohibited.

* * *

Pennsylvania Rule 5.7

*[Pennsylvania has enacted its own Rule 5.7 to govern lawyer involvement
    in nonlegal services.]*

Rule 5.7. Responsibilities Regarding Nonlegal Services

(a) A lawyer who provides nonlegal services to a recipient
that are not distinct from legal services provided to that recipient is subject to the Rules of Professional Conduct with respect
to the provision of both legal and nonlegal services.

(b) A lawyer who provides nonlegal services to a recipient
that are distinct from any legal services provided to the recipient is subject to the Rules of Professional Conduct with respect
to the nonlegal services if the lawyer knows or reasonably
should know that the recipient might believe that the recipient
is receiving the protection of a client-lawyer relationship.

(c) A lawyer who is an owner, controlling party, employee,
agent, or is otherwise affiliated with an entity providing nonle-

gal services to a recipient is subject to the Rules of Professional Conduct with respect to the nonlegal services if the lawyer knows or reasonably should know that the recipient might believe that the recipient is receiving the protection of a client-lawyer relationship.

(d) Paragraph (b) or (c) does not apply if the lawyer makes reasonable efforts to avoid any misunderstanding by the recipient receiving nonlegal services. Those efforts must include advising the recipient that the services are not legal services and that the protection of a client-lawyer relationship does not exist with respect to the provision of nonlegal services to the recipient.

COMMENT

For many years, lawyers have provided to their clients nonlegal services that are ancillary to the practice of law. Nonlegal services are those that are not prohibited as unauthorized practice of law when provided by a nonlawyer. Examples of nonlegal services include providing title insurance, financial planning, accounting, trust services, real estate counseling, legislative lobbying, economic analysis, social work, psychological counseling, tax return preparation, and patent, medical or environmental consulting. A broad range of economic and other interests of clients may be served by lawyers participating in the delivery of these services. In recent years, however, there has been significant debate about the role the Rules of Professional Conduct should play in regulating the degree and manner in which a lawyer participates in the delivery of nonlegal services. The ABA, for example, adopted, repealed and then adopted a different version of Rule 5.7. In the course of this debate, several ABA sections offered competing versions of Rule 5.7.

One approach to the issue of nonlegal services is to try to substantively limit the type of nonlegal services a lawyer may provide to a recipient or the manner in which the services are provided. A competing approach does not try to substantively limit the lawyer's provision of nonlegal services, but instead attempts to clarify the conduct to which the Rules of Professional Conduct apply and to avoid misunderstanding on the part of the recipient of the nonlegal services. This Rule adopts the latter approach.

The Potential for Misunderstanding

Whenever a lawyer directly provides nonlegal services, there exists the potential for ethical problems. Principal among these is the possibility that the person for whom the nonlegal services are performed may fail to understand that the services may not carry with them the protection normally afforded by the client-lawyer relationship. The recipient of the nonlegal services may expect, for example, that the protection of client confidences, prohibitions against representation of persons with conflicting interests, and obligations of a lawyer to maintain professional independence apply to the provision of nonlegal services when that may not be the case. The risk of such confusion is especially acute when the lawyer renders both types of services with respect to the same matter.

Providing Nonlegal Services That Are Not Distinct From Legal Services

Under some circumstances, the legal and nonlegal services may be so closely entwined that they cannot be distinguished from each other. In this situation, confusion by the recipient as to when the protection of the client-lawyer relationship applies are likely to be unavoidable. Therefore, Rule 5.7(a) requires that the lawyer providing the nonlegal services adhere to all of the requirements of the Rules of Professional Conduct.

In such a case, a lawyer will be responsible for assuring that both the lawyer's conduct and, to the extent required by Rule 5.3, that of nonlawyer employees comply in all respects with the Rules of Professional Conduct. When a lawyer is obliged to accord the recipients of such nonlegal services the protection of those Rules that apply to the client-lawyer relationship, the lawyer must take special care to heed the proscriptions of the Rules addressing conflict of interest (Rules 1.7 through 1.11, especially Rules 1.7(b) and 1.8(a), (b) and (f)), and to scrupulously adhere to the requirements of Rule 1.6 relating to disclosure of confidential information. The promotion of the nonlegal services must also in all respects comply with Rules 7.1 through 7.3, dealing with advertising and solicitation.

Rule 5.7(a) applies to the provision of nonlegal services by a lawyer even when the lawyer does not personally provide any legal services to the person for whom the nonlegal services are performed if the person is also receiving legal services from another lawyer that are not distinct from the nonlegal services.

Avoiding Misunderstanding When A Lawyer Directly Provides Nonlegal Services That Are Distinct From Legal Services

Even when the lawyer believes that his or her provision of nonlegal services is distinct from any legal services provided to the recipient, there is still a risk that the recipient of the nonlegal services will misunderstand the implications of receiving nonlegal services from a lawyer; the recipient might believe that the recipient is receiving the protection of a client-lawyer relationship. Where there is such a risk of misunderstanding, Rule 5.7(b) requires that the lawyer providing the nonlegal services adhere to all the Rules of Professional Conduct, unless exempted by Rule 5.7(d).

Avoiding Misunderstanding When a Lawyer is Indirectly Involved in the Provision of Nonlegal Services

Nonlegal services also may be provided through an entity with which a lawyer is somehow affiliated, for example, as owner, employee, controlling party or agent. In this situation, there is still a risk that the recipient of the nonlegal services might believe that the recipient is receiving the protection of a client-lawyer relationship. Where there is such a risk of misunderstanding, Rule 5.7(c) requires that the lawyer involved with the entity providing nonlegal services adhere to all the Rules of Professional Conduct, unless exempted by Rule 5.7(d).

Avoiding the Application of Paragraphs (b) and (c)

Paragraphs (b) and (c) specify that the Rules of Professional Conduct apply to a lawyer who directly provides or is otherwise involved in the provision of nonlegal services if there is a risk that the recipient might believe that the recipient is receiving the protection of a client-lawyer relationship. Neither the Rules of Professional Conduct nor paragraphs (b) or (c) will apply, however, if pursuant to paragraph (d), the lawyer takes reasonable efforts to avoid any misunderstanding by the recipient. In this respect, Rule 5.7 is analogous to Rule 4.3(c).

In taking the reasonable measures referred to in paragraph (d), the lawyer must communicate to the person receiving the nonlegal services that the relationship will not be a client-lawyer relationship. The communication should be made before entering into an agreement for the provision of nonlegal services, in a manner sufficient to assure that the person understands the significance of the communication, and preferably should be in writing.

The burden is upon the lawyer to show that the lawyer has taken reasonable measures under the circumstances to communicate the desired understanding. For instance, a sophisticated user of nonlegal services, such as a publicly-held corporation, may require a lesser explanation than someone unaccustomed to making distinctions between legal services and nonlegal services, such as an individual seeking tax advice from a lawyer-accountant or investigative services in connection with a lawsuit.

The Relationship Between Rule 5.7 and Other Rules of Professional Conduct

Even before Rule 5.7 was adopted, a lawyer involved in the provision of nonlegal services was subject to those Rules of Professional Conduct that apply generally. For example, Rule 8.4(c) makes a lawyer responsible for fraud committed with respect to the provision of nonlegal services. Such a lawyer must also comply with Rule 1.8(a). Nothing in this rule is intended to suspend the effect of any otherwise applicable Rule of Professional Conduct such as Rule 1.7(b), Rule 1.8(a) and Rule 8.4(c).

In addition to the Rules of Professional Conduct, principles of law external to the Rules, for example, the law of principal and agent, may govern the legal duties owed by a lawyer to those receiving the nonlegal services.

PUBLIC SERVICE

South Dakota Rule 6.1

[South Dakota has modified Model Rule 6.1 to read as follows:]

RULE 6.1 Pro Bono Publico Service

A lawyer should render public interest legal service.

A lawyer may discharge this responsibility by:

(a) providing professional services at no fee or a reduced fee to persons of limited means or to public service or charitable groups or organizations; or

(b) by service without compensation in public interest activities that improve the law, the legal system or the legal profession; or

(c) by financial support for organizations that provide legal services to persons of limited means.

COMMENT:

Each lawyer engaged in the practice of law has a responsibility to provide public interest legal services without fee, or at a substantially reduced fee, in one or more of the following areas: poverty law, civil rights law, public rights law, charitable organization representation and the administration of justice. This Rule expresses that policy but is not intended to be enforced through disciplinary process.

The rights and responsibilities of individuals and organizations in the United States are increasingly defined in legal terms. As a consequence, legal assistance in coping with the web of statutes, rules and regulations is imperative for all persons.

The basic responsibility for providing legal services for those unable to pay ultimately rests upon the individual lawyer, and personal involvement in the problems of the disadvantaged can be one of the most rewarding experiences in the life of a lawyer. Every lawyer, regardless of professional prominence or professional workload, should find time to participate in or otherwise support the provision of legal services to the disadvantaged. The provision of free legal services to those unable to pay reasonable fees continues to be an obligation of each lawyer as well as the profession generally, but the efforts of individual lawyers are often not enough to meet the need. Thus, it has been necessary for the profession and government to institute additional programs to provide legal services. Accordingly, legal aid offices, lawyer referral services and other related programs have been developed, and others will be developed by the profession and government. Every lawyer should support all proper efforts to meet this need for legal services.

The Rule has been restructured to make it clear that the "pro bono publico" obligation can also be discharged by uncompensated service in public interest activities and by financial support for legal service organizations.

INFORMATION ABOUT LEGAL SERVICES

Arizona Rule 7.1

[Arizona has modified Model Rule 7.1 to read as follows:]

ER 7.1 Communications and Advertising Concerning a Lawyer's Services

(a) A lawyer shall not make a false or misleading communication about the lawyer or the lawyer's services. A communication is false or misleading if it:

(1) contains a material misrepresentation of fact or law or omits a fact necessary to make the statement considered as a whole not materially misleading;

(2) is likely to create an unjustified expectation about results the lawyer can achieve or states or implies that the lawyer can achieve results by means that violate the rules of professional conduct or other law;

(3) compares the lawyer's services with any other lawyers' services, unless the comparison can be factually substantiated;

(4) is a factual statement which cannot be factually substantiated.

(b) All communications and advertising concerning a lawyer's services shall be predominantly informational. As used in this rule, "predominantly informational" shall mean that, in both quantity and quality, the communication of factual information rationally related to the need for and selection of an attorney predominates.

(c) Subject to all the requirements set forth in these rules, a lawyer may advertise services through public media, such as a telephone directory, legal directory, newspaper or other periodical, billboards and other signs, radio, television and recorded messages the public may access by dialing a telephone number, or through written communication. These rules shall not apply to any advertisement broadcast or disseminated in another jurisdiction in which the advertising lawyer is admitted if such advertisement complies with the rules governing lawyer advertising in that jurisdiction and is not intended for broadcast or dissemination within the State of Arizona.

(d) The following information in advertisements and written communications, if truthful, shall be presumed not to violate the provisions of ER 7.1:

(1) the name of the lawyer or law firm, a listing of lawyers associated with the firm, office addresses and tele-

phone numbers, office and telephone service hours, and a designation such as "attorney" or "law firm";

(2) date of admission to the State Bar of Arizona and any other bar associations and a listing of federal courts and jurisdictions other than Arizona where the lawyer is licensed to practice;

(3) technical and professional licenses granted by the state or other recognized licensing authorities;

(4) language ability in addition to English;

(5) fields of law in which the lawyer is certified subject to the requirements of ER 7.4;

(6) prepaid or group legal service plans or programs in which the lawyer participates;

(7) acceptance of credit cards;

(8) information concerning fees and costs, or the availability of such information on request, subject to the requirements of these rules;

(9) a listing of a lawyer or law firm as a sponsor of charitable, civic or community program or event or public service announcement. Such listing shall not exceed the traditional description of sponsors of or contributors to the charitable, civic or community program or event or public service announcement, and such listing must comply with the provisions of these rules;

(10) schools attended, with dates of graduation, degrees and other scholastic distinctions;

(11) public or quasi-public offices;

(12) military service;

(13) legal authorships;

(14) legal teaching positions;

(15) memberships, offices and committee assignments in bar associations;

(16) memberships and offices in legal fraternities and legal societies;

(17) memberships in scientific, technical and professional associations and societies;

(18) names and addresses of bank references;

(19) with their written consent, names of clients regularly represented;

(20) office and telephone answering service hours;

(21) availability upon request of written schedule of fees and/or an estimate of the fee to be charged for specific services.

(e) Every advertisement (including advertisement by written solicitation) that contains information about the lawyer's fees shall be subject to the following requirements:

(1) Advertisements and written communications indicating that the charging of a fee is contingent on outcome or that the fee will be a percentage of the recovery shall disclose (A) that the client will be liable for expenses regardless of outcome and (B) whether the percentage fee will be computed before expenses are deducted from the recovery.

(2) Range of fees or hourly rates for services may be communicated provided that the client is informed in writing at the commencement of any attorney-client relationship that the total fee within the range which will be charged or the total hours to be devoted will vary depending upon that particular matter to be handled for each client and the client is entitled without obligation to an estimate of the fee within the range likely to be charged.

(3) Fixed fees for specific routine legal services, the description of which would not be misunderstood or be deceptive, may be communicated provided that the client is informed in writing at the commencement of any attorney-client relationship that the quoted fee will be available only to clients whose matters fall within the services described and that the client is entitled without obligation to a specific estimate of the fee likely to be charged.

(4) A lawyer who advertises a specific fee, range of fees or hourly rate for a particular service shall honor the advertised fee, or range of fees, for at least ninety (90) days unless the advertisement specifies a shorter period; provided, for advertisements in the yellow pages of telephone directories or other media not published more frequently than annually, the advertised fee or range of fees shall be honored for no less than one year following publication.

(f) A lawyer shall not advertise services or communicate in writing under a name that violates the provisions of these rules.

(g) All advertisements and written communications provided for under these rules shall disclose the cities, towns or counties in which the lawyer or lawyers who will actually perform the services advertised maintain an office or principally practice law.

(h) No lawyer shall, directly or indirectly, pay all or a part of the cost of an advertisement by a lawyer not in the same firm unless the advertisement discloses the name and address of the non-advertising lawyer, the relationship between the advertising lawyer and the non-advertising lawyer, and whether the advertising lawyer may refer any case received through the advertisement to the non-advertising lawyer.

(i) Nothing in this rule prohibits a lawyer or law firm from permitting the inclusion in reputable law lists and law directories intended primarily for the use of the legal profession of such information as has traditionally been included in these publications, subject to the requirements of these rules.

(j) A lawyer shall not give anything of value to a person for recommending the lawyer's services, except that a lawyer may pay the reasonable cost of advertising or written or recorded communications permitted by these rules and may pay the usual charges of a lawyer referral service or other legal service organization.

(k) This rule does not apply to identification of a lawyer as a lawyer as well as by name:

(1) in political advertisements when the professional status is germane to the political campaign or to a political issue;

(2) in public notices when the name and profession of a lawyer are required or authorized by law or are reasonably pertinent for a purpose other than the attraction of potential clients;

(3) in routine reports and announcements of a bona fide business, civic, professional, or political organization in which the lawyer serves as a director or officer;

(4) in and on legal documents prepared by the lawyer;

(5) in and on legal textbooks, treatises, and other legal publications, and in dignified advertisements thereof;

(6) in communications by a qualified legal assistance organization, along with the biographical information permitted in these rules, directed to a member or beneficiary of such organization;

(7) in a brief announcement in any of the public media that identifies a lawyer or law firm as a contributor to a specified charity or as a sponsor of a specified charitable, community or public interest program, activity or event;

(8) in a newsletter mailed only to existing clients or other lawyers;

(9) in professional announcement cards stating new or changed associations, new offices, and similar changes relating to a lawyer or law firm, and which are mailed only to

other lawyers, relatives, close personal friends and existing clients.

(*l*) A lawyer shall not, on behalf of himself, his partner or associate, or any other lawyer affiliated with him or his firm, use or participate in the use of any form of public communication which:

   (1) is intended or is likely to result in a legal action or a legal position being asserted merely to harass or maliciously injure another;

   (2) contains a prediction of future success; or

   (3) contains an opinion, representation or implication regarding the quality of legal services which is not susceptible of reasonable verification by the public.

(m) A lawyer shall not accept employment when he knows or should know that the person who seeks his services does so as a result of conduct prohibited under this rule.

(n) All advertisements and written communications pursuant to these rules shall include the name of at least one lawyer or the lawyer referral service responsible for its content.

(*o*) A copy or recording of an advertisement or written or recorded communication shall be kept for three years after its last dissemination along with a record of when and where it was used.

(p) No communication, advertisement or other professional designation shall state or imply a relationship between any member in private practice and a government agency or instrumentality, or a public or non-public legal services organization; or that a member has a relationship to any other member or a law firm as a partner or associate, or officer or shareholder unless such relationship in fact exists or that a member or a law firm is "of counsel" to another member or law firm unless the former has a relationship with the latter which is close, personal, continuous and regular.

(q) Advertisements on the electronic media, such as television and radio, may contain the same information as permitted in advertisements in the print media, subject to the following requirements:

   (1) Impersonations, dramatizations and recreations shall comply with all the requirements set forth in these rules, and shall be designed to further the informational purposes of legal advertisement.

   (2) If a law firm advertises on television and a person appears on screen purporting to be a lawyer, such person shall in fact be a lawyer employed full-time at the advertising law firm. If a law firm advertises a particular legal

service on television, and a lawyer appears on screen as the person purporting to render the service, the lawyer appearing on screen shall be the lawyer who will actually perform the service advertised unless the advertisement discloses that the service may be performed by other lawyers in the firm.

(r) A lawyer or his partner or associate or any other lawyer affiliated with him or his firm may be recommended, employed or paid by, or may cooperate with, one of the following offices or organizations that promote the use of his services or those of his partner or associate or any other lawyer affiliated with him or his firm if there is no interference with the exercise of independent professional judgment in behalf of his client:

(1) a legal aid office or public defender office which is operated or sponsored by a duly accredited law school, by a bona fide non-profit community organization, or by a governmental agency; or which is operated, sponsored, or approved by a bar association;

(2) a military legal assistance office;

(3) a lawyer referral service operated, sponsored, or approved by a bar association. A lawyer shall not accept referrals from a lawyer referral service unless the service:

(A) engages in no communication with the public and in no direct contact with prospective clients in a manner that would violate the rules of professional conduct if the communication or contact were made by the lawyer;

(B) receives no fee or charge that constitutes a division or sharing of fees;

(C) refers clients only to lawyers lawfully permitted to practice law in Arizona when the services to be rendered constitute the practice of law in Arizona;

(D) furnishes the state bar on a quarterly basis with the names of all lawyers participating in the service; and

(E) neither represents nor implies to the public that this service is operated, endorsed, sponsored or approved by the state bar, unless the service is operated, endorsed, sponsored or expressly approved by the state bar.

(4) any bona fide organization that recommends, furnishes or pays for legal services to its members or beneficiaries, provided the following conditions are satisfied:

(A) such organization, including any affiliate, is so organized and operated that no profit is derived by it from the rendition of legal services by lawyers, and that, if the organization is organized for profit, the legal services are not rendered by lawyers employed, directed, supervised or selected by it, except in connection with matters where such organization bears ultimate liability of its members or beneficiary;

(B) neither the lawyer, nor his partner or associate, nor any other lawyer affiliated with him or his firm, nor any non-lawyer, shall have initiated or promoted such organization for the primary purpose of providing financial or other benefit to such lawyer, partner, associate or affiliated lawyer;

(C) such organization is not operated for the purpose of procuring legal work or financial benefit for any lawyer as a private practitioner outside of the legal services program of the organization;

(D) the member or beneficiary to whom the legal services are furnished, and not such organization, is recognized as the client of the lawyer in the matter;

(E) any member or beneficiary who is entitled to have legal services furnished or paid for by the organization may, if such member or beneficiary so desires, select counsel other than that furnished, selected or approved by the organization for the particular matter involved; and the legal service plan of such organization provides appropriate relief for any member or beneficiary who asserts a claim that representation by counsel furnished, selected or approved would be unethical, improper or inadequate under the circumstances of the matter involved and the plan provides an appropriate procedure for seeking such relief;

(F) the lawyer does not know or have cause to know that such organization is in violation of applicable laws, rules of court and other legal requirements that govern its legal service operations; and

(G) such organization has filed with the appropriate disciplinary authority at least annually a report with respect to its legal service plan, if any, showing its terms, schedule of benefits, subscription charges, agreements with counsel, and financial results of its legal service activities, or if it has failed to do so, the lawyer does not know or have cause to know of such failure.

(5) A public interest law firm, which is defined as: A nonprofit firm which provides, without cost or at a substantially reduced fee, legal services which would not be provided by a governmental agency or by any other means, and has been recognized and approved as such by the Board of Governors of the State Bar of Arizona, and which falls exclusively into one or more of the following areas:

(A) Poverty Law: Legal services in civil and criminal matters of importance to a client who does not have the financial resources to compensate counsel.

(B) Individual Civil Rights Laws: Legal representation of an important right of an individual which society has a special interest in protecting, but which the client would not otherwise seek to vindicate.

(C) Public Rights Law: Legal representation of an important right belonging to the public at large, where those asserting the right would not otherwise seek its vindication.

(D) Charitable Organization Representation: Legal service to charitable, religious, civic and educational institutions in matters in furtherance of their organizational purpose where the payment of customary legal fees would significantly deplete the organization's economic resources.

Arizona Rule 7.2

[Arizona has modified Model Rule 7.2 to read as follows:]

ER 7.2   Legal Service Information

(a) Each lawyer or law firm that advertises (including by written solicitation) his, her or its availability to provide legal services shall have a factual statement detailing the background, training and experience of each lawyer or law firm available for delivery upon request to any potential client in a form to be prescribed by the state bar and approved by the court.

(b) If the lawyer or law firm claims expertise beyond that possessed by competent and experienced lawyers in general practice in the representation of clients in particular matters or publicly designated or limits the lawyer's or law firm's practice to particular types of cases or clients, the written information shall comply with ER 7.4.

(c) Whenever a potential client requests information regarding a lawyer or law firm for the purpose of making a decision regarding employment of the lawyer or law firm:

(1) the lawyer or law firm shall promptly furnish (by mail if requested) the written information described in paragraphs (a) and (b).

(2) the lawyer or law firm may furnish such additional factual information regarding the lawyer or law firm deemed valuable to assist the client.

(d) A copy of all information furnished to clients by reason of this rule shall be retained by the lawyer or law firm for a period of three (3) years after last regular use of the information.

(e) Upon reasonable request by the state bar, a lawyer shall promptly provide proof that any statement or claim made in any advertisement or written communication, as well as the information furnished to a prospective client as authorized by these rules, is in compliance with paragraphs (a) and (b) above.
Amended July 27, 1989, effective Aug. 1, 1989; July 16, 1992, effective Dec. 1, 1992.

STATE BAR OF ARIZONA
LAW FIRM INFORMATION STATEMENT
(eff. Dec. 1, 1994)

1. Firm name _____
2. Firm address(es) _____
3. Telephone number(s) _____
4. Number of Lawyers in firm _____
5. Areas of law firm practice _____
6. Courts to which members of the law firm are admitted to practice
   _____
7. Areas in which lawyers are certified by the Arizona Board of Legal Specialization or Equivalent Certification, and number of lawyers certified by each organization in each area of specialization _____
   _____
8. Year in which firm originally was established _____
9. List attorneys in firm having experience in each advertised area of practice. (For a description of the experience, see each attorney's Lawyer Information Statement.) _____

STATE BAR OF ARIZONA
LAWYER INFORMATION STATEMENT

1. Lawyer's name _____
2. Office address(es) _____
3. Telephone number(s) _____
4. Date of admission to State Bar of Arizona _____
5. Courts to which lawyer is admitted and dates of admission to each
   _____
6. Technical and professional licenses granted by state or other licensing authorities _____

7. Areas of law in which lawyer practices _____
8. Areas of law in which lawyer is certified by the Arizona Board of Legal Specialization or equivalent certification _____
9. For each advertised area of law in which the lawyer practices, please give the following information:
    —Number of years of experience in the area of law _____
    —Percentage of practice devoted to the area of law, and for how long _____
    —Approximate total number of cases or matters in the area which have been handled by the lawyer _____
    —Pertinent publications, if any _____
    —Special training in the area _____
    —Pertinent awards and recognition _____
    If the advertised area of law is litigation or personal injury law, please specify the following information for cases in which you have served either as sole or lead counsel or associate counsel:

    Arizona Superior Court or U.S. District Court
    Number of civil jury trials completed
     sole or lead counsel _____
     associate counsel _____
    Number of civil bench trials completed
     sole or lead counsel _____
     associate counsel _____
    Number of criminal jury trials completed
     sole or lead counsel _____
     associate counsel _____
    Number of criminal bench trials completed
     sole or lead counsel _____
     associate counsel _____

    Municipal or Justice Courts
    Number of civil jury trials completed
     sole or lead counsel _____
     associate counsel _____
    Number of civil bench trials completed
     sole or lead counsel _____
     associate counsel _____
    Number of criminal jury trials completed
     sole or lead counsel _____
     associate counsel _____
    Number of criminal bench trials completed
     sole or lead counsel _____
     associate counsel _____

    Contested Arbitration Proceedings
    Number of completed arbitration hearings
     sole or lead counsel _____
     associate counsel _____

    Other Evidentiary Hearings
    Number of other evidentiary hearings that have exceeded three hours of in-court appearance (e.g., judicial administrative hearings, temporary restraining orders, preliminary injunc-

tions, provisional remedy hearings, criminal motions to suppress, temporary orders in marital dissolutions, etc.).
sole or lead counsel _____
associate counsel _____
10.   Membership in professional organizations _____
11.   School(s) attended, dates of graduation, degrees received, honors or
distinctions _____
12.   Public or quasi-public offices held _____
13.   Military service _____
14.   Legal authorships _____
15.   Legal teaching positions _____
16.   Memberships, offices and committee assignments in bar associations _____
17.   Language ability in addition to English _____

Arizona Rule 7.3

[Arizona has modified Model Rule 7.3 to read as follows:]

ER 7.3   Direct Contact With Prospective Clients

(a) A lawyer may not solicit professional employment from a prospective client with whom the lawyer has no family or prior professional relationship in person or by telephone, when a motive for the lawyer's doing so is the lawyer's pecuniary gain.

(b) Subject to all of the requirements of these rules concerning communications and advertising and the specific additional requirements of this section, a lawyer may initiate written communication, not involving personal or telephone contact, with persons known to need legal services of the kind provided by the lawyer in a particular matter, for the purpose of obtaining professional employment. Such written communication shall be clearly marked on the envelope and on the first page of the communication contained in the envelope, as follows:

ADVERTISING MATERIAL:

THIS IS A COMMERCIAL SOLICITATION

Said notification shall be printed in red ink, in all capital letters, in type size at least double the largest type size used in the body of the communication. No other statement shall be placed on the envelope which makes reference to the contents of the solicitation. If the solicitation advertises representation on a contingent or "no recovery, no fee" basis, it shall also state that the client may be liable for costs and expenses.

(c) At the time of dissemination of such written communication, a copy shall be forwarded to the Clerk of the Arizona Supreme Court and the State Bar of Arizona at its Phoenix office. If a written communication identical in content is sent to two or more prospective clients, the lawyer may comply with

this requirement by forwarding a single copy together with a list of the names and addresses of persons to whom the written communication was sent.

(d) A lawyer shall not send, or knowingly permit to be sent, on behalf of himself, his firm, his partner, an associate, or any other lawyer affiliated with him or his firm a written communication to a prospective client for the purpose of obtaining professional employment if:

(1) it has been made known to the lawyer that the person does not want to receive such communications from the lawyer;

(2) the communication involves coercion, duress, fraud, overreaching, harassment, intimidation, or undue influence;

(3) the communication contains a false, fraudulent, misleading, deceptive or unfair statement or claim or is otherwise improper under these rules;

(4) the lawyer knows or reasonably should know that the physical, emotional, or mental state of the person makes it unlikely that the person would exercise reasonable judgment in employing a lawyer.

(e) Written communications mailed to prospective clients shall be sent only by regular U.S. mail, not by registered mail or other forms of restricted delivery.

(f) No reference shall be made in the communication to the communication having received any kind of approval from the state bar.

(g) If a contract for representation is mailed with the written communication, the contract shall be marked "sample" in red ink and shall contain the words "do not sign" on the client signature line.

(h) Written communications shall be on letter-sized paper rather than legal-sized paper and shall not be made to resemble legal pleadings or other legal documents. This provision does not preclude the mailing of brochures and pamphlets.

(i) If a lawyer other than the lawyer whose name or signature appears on the communication will actually handle the case or matter or if the case or matter will be referred to another lawyer or law firm, any written communication concerning a specific matter shall include a statement so advising the client.

(j) Any written communication prompted by a specific occurrence involving or affecting the intended recipient of the communication or a family member shall disclose how the lawyer obtained the information prompting the communication. If the information prompting the communication is a public document obtained from a commercial service or subscription, the disclosure shall identify the fact and role of the commercial service or subscription.

(k) A written communication seeking employment by a specific prospective client in a specific matter shall not reveal on the envelope, or on the outside of a self-mailing brochure or pamphlet, the nature of the client's legal problem.

(*l*) All statements required by this rule shall be displayed conspicuously in type size at least equal to the largest type used in the communication.

(m) The lawyer initiating the communication shall bear the burden of proof regarding the truthfulness of all facts contained in the communication, and shall, upon request of the State Bar or the recipient of the communication, disclose:

(1) how the identity and specific legal need of the potential recipient were discovered; and

(2) how the identity and knowledge of the specific need of the potential recipient were verified by the soliciting lawyer.

Texas Disciplinary Rules 7.01–7.07

[In 1995, Texas substantially revised its advertising rules. In 1998, the State Bar of Texas proposed new revisions of the advertising rules. The members of the bar have passed these rules; however, they await adoption by the Texas Supreme Court.]

RULE 7.01   Firm Names and Letterhead

(a) A lawyer in private practice shall not practice under a trade name, a name that is misleading as to the identity of the lawyer or lawyers practicing under such name, or a firm name containing names other than those of one or more of the lawyers in the firm, except that the names of a professional corporation, professional association, limited liability partnership, or professional limited liability company may contain "P.C.," "P.A.," "L.L.P.," "P.L.L.C.," or similar symbols indicating the nature of the organization, and if otherwise lawful a firm may use as, or continue to include in, its name the name or names of one or more deceased or retired members of the firm or of a predecessor firm in a continuing line of succession. Nothing herein shall prohibit a married woman from practicing under her maiden name.

(b) A firm with offices in more than one jurisdiction may use the same name in each jurisdiction, but identification of the lawyers in an office of the firm shall indicate the jurisdictional limitations on those not licensed to practice in the jurisdiction where the office is located.

(c) The name of a lawyer occupying a judicial, legislative, or public executive or administrative position shall not be used in the name of a firm, or in communications on its behalf, during any substantial period in which the lawyer is not actively and regularly practicing with the firm.

(d) A lawyer shall not hold himself or herself out as being a partner, shareholder, or associate with one or more other lawyers unless they are in fact partners, shareholders, or associates.

(e) A lawyer shall not advertise in the public media or seek professional employment by ~~written~~ any communication under a trade or fictitious name, except that a lawyer who practices under a ~~trade~~ firm name as authorized by paragraph (a) of this Rule may use that name in such advertisement or ~~such written~~ communication but only if that name is the firm name that appears on the lawyer's letterhead, business cards, office sign, fee contracts, and with the lawyer's signature on pleadings and other legal documents.

(f) A lawyer shall not use a firm name, letterhead, or other professional designation that violates Rule 7.02(a).

(Former Rule 7.04 adopted eff. Jan. 1, 1990; redesignated and amended to be eff. April 1, 1995; on March 31, 1995, the Texas Supreme Court extended the effective date 120 days after the date of judgment of the U.S. District Court in Texans Against Censorship, Inc. v. State Bar of Texas, 888 F.Supp. 1328 (E.D.Tex. 1995).)

COMMENT

1. A lawyer or law firm may not practice law using a name that is misleading as to the identity of the lawyers practicing under such name, but the continued use of the name of a deceased or retired member of the firm or of a predecessor firm is not considered to be misleading. Trade names are generally considered inherently misleading. Other types of firm names can be misleading as well, such as a firm name that creates the appearance that lawyers are partners or employees of a single law firm when in fact they are merely associated for the purpose of sharing expenses. In such cases, the lawyers involved may not denominate themselves in any manner suggesting such an ongoing professional relationship as, for example, "Smith and Jones" or "Smith and Jones Associates" or "Smith and Associates." Such titles create the false impression that the lawyers named have assumed a joint professional responsibility for clients' legal affairs. See paragraph (d).

2. The practice of law firms having offices in more than one state is commonplace. Although it is not necessary that the name of an interstate firm include Texas lawyers, a letterhead including the name of any lawyer not licensed in Texas must indicate the lawyer is not licensed in Texas.

3. Paragraph (c) is designed to prevent the exploitation of a lawyer's public position for the benefit of the lawyer's firm. Likewise, because it may be misleading under paragraph (a), a lawyer who occupies a judicial, legislative, or public executive or administrative position should not indicate that fact on a letterhead which identifies that person as an attorney in the private practice of law. However, a firm name may

include the name of a public official who is actively and regularly practicing law with the firm. But see Rule 7.02(a)(4).

4. With certain limited exceptions, paragraph (a) forbids a lawyer from using a trade name or fictitious name. Paragraph (e) sets out this same prohibition with respect to advertising in public media or written communications seeking professional employment and contains additional restrictions on the use of trade names or fictitious names in those contexts. In a largely overlapping measure, paragraph (f) forbids the use of any such name or designation if it would amount to a "false or misleading communication" under Rule 7.02(a).

(Comment amended by State Bar Board of Directors Jan. 20, 1995.)

RULE 7.02 Communications Concerning a Lawyer's Services

(a) **A lawyer shall not make a false or misleading communication about the qualifications or the services of any lawyer or firm. A communication is false or misleading if it:**

(1) **contains a material misrepresentation of fact or law, or omits a fact necessary to make the statement considered as a whole not materially misleading;**

(2) **is likely to create an unjustified expectation about results the lawyer can achieve, or states or implies that the lawyer can achieve results by means that violate these rules or other law;**

(3) **compares the lawyer's services with other lawyers' services, unless the comparison can be substantiated by reference to verifiable, objective data;**

(4) **states or implies that the lawyer is able to influence improperly or upon irrelevant grounds any tribunal, legislative body, or public official; or**

(5) **designates one or more specific areas of practice in an advertisement in the public media or in a ~~written~~ solicitation communication unless the advertising or soliciting lawyer is competent to handle legal matters in each such area of practice.**

(b) **Rule 7.02(a)(5) does not require that a lawyer be certified by the Texas Board of Legal Specialization at the time of advertising in a specific area of practice, but such certification shall conclusively establish that such lawyer satisfies the requirements of Rule 7.02(a)(5) with respect to the area(s) of practice in which such lawyer is certified.**

(c) **A lawyer shall not advertise in the public media or state in a solicitation communication that the lawyer is a specialist, except as permitted under Rule 7.04.**

(d) **Any statement or disclaimer required by these rules shall be made in each language used in the advertisement or ~~writing~~ solicitation communication with respect to which such**

required statement or disclaimer relates; provided however, the mere statement that a particular language is spoken or understood shall not alone result in the need for a statement or disclaimer in that language.

(Former Rule 7.01 adopted eff. Jan. 1, 1990; redesignated and amended to be eff. April 1, 1995; on March 31, 1995, the Texas Supreme Court extended the effective date 120 days after the date of judgment of the U.S. District Court in Texans Against Censorship, Inc. v. State Bar of Texas, 888 F.Supp. 1328 (E.D.Tex. 1995).)

COMMENT

1. The Rules within Part VII are intended to regulate communications made for the purpose of obtaining professional employment. They are not intended to affect other forms of speech by lawyers, such as political advertisements or political commentary, except insofar as a lawyer's effort to obtain employment is linked to a matter of current public debate.

2. Whatever means are used to make known a lawyer's services, statements about them should be truthful and nondeceptive. Sub-paragraph (a)(1) recognizes that statements can be misleading both by what they contain and what they leave out. Statements that are false or misleading for either reason are prohibited. The prohibitions in sub-paragraph (a)(2) of statements that may create an "unjustified expectation" and in sub-paragraph (a)(3) of comparisons of lawyers' services unless those comparisons "can be substantiated by reference to verifiable objective data" are each designated to prevent lawyers from misleading members of the public as they seek legal services. Those provisions would ordinarily preclude advertisements in the public media and written solicitation communications that discuss the results obtained on behalf of a client, such as the amount of a damage award, the lawyer's record in obtaining favorable settlements or verdicts, as well as those that contain client endorsements. Unless accompanied by appropriate, prominent qualifications and disclaimers, that information can readily mislead prospective clients into believing that similar results can be obtained for them without reference to their specific factual and legal circumstances. Similarly, statements comparing a lawyer's services with those of another where the comparisons are not susceptible of precise measurement or verification, such as "we are the toughest lawyers in town", "we will get money for you when other lawyers can't", or "we are the best law firm in Texas if you want a large recovery" can deceive or mislead prospective clients. On the other hand, a simple statement of a lawyer's own qualifications devoid of comparisons to other lawyers does not pose the same risk of being misleading and does not fall within this Rule. See Rule 7.04. A lawyer making a referral to another lawyer may, of course, express a good faith subjective opinion regarding that lawyer.

3. This Rule does not prohibit communication of information concerning a lawyer's name or firm name, address and telephone numbers;

the basis on which the lawyer's fees are determined, including prices for specific services and payment and credit arrangements; names of references and, with their consent, names of clients regularly represented; and other truthful information that might invite the attention of those seeking legal assistance. When a communication permitted by Rule 7.02 is made in the public media, the lawyer should consult Rule 7.04 for further guidance and restrictions. When a communication permitted by Rule 7.02 is made by a lawyer through a written solicitation, the lawyer should consult Rule 7.05 for further guidance and restrictions.

Communication of Fields of Practice

4. Paragraphs (a)(5), (b) and (c) of Rule 7.02 regulate communications concerning a lawyer's fields of practice and should be construed together with Rule 7.04 or 7.05, as applicable. If a lawyer in a public media advertisement or in a written solicitation designates one or more specific areas of practice, that designation is at least an implicit representation that the lawyer is qualified in the areas designated. Accordingly, Rule 7.02(a)(5) prohibits the designation of a field of practice unless the communicating lawyer is in fact competent in the area.

5. Typically, one would expect competency to be measured by special education, training, or experience in the particular area of law designated. Because certification by the Texas Board of Legal Specialization involves special education, training, and experience, certification by the Texas Board of Legal Specialization conclusively establishes that a lawyer meets the requirements of Rule 7.02(a)(5) in any area in which the Board has certified the lawyer. However, competency may be established by means other than certification by the Texas Board of Legal Specialization. See Rule 7.04(b).

6. Lawyers who wish to advertise in the public media that they specialize should refer to Rule 7.04(a), (b) and (c). Lawyers who wish to assert a specialty in a written solicitation should refer to Rule 7.05(a)(4) and (b)(1).

Communication in a Second Language

7. The ability of lawyers to communicate in a second language can facilitate the delivery and receipt of legal services. Accordingly, it is in the best interest of the public that potential clients be made aware of a lawyer's language ability. A lawyer may state an ability to communicate in a second language without any further elaboration. However, if a lawyer chooses to communicate with potential clients in a second language, all statements or disclaimers required by the Texas Disciplinary Rules of Professional Conduct must also be made in that language. See paragraph (d). Communicating some information in one language while communicating the rest in another is potentially misleading if the recipient understands only one of the languages.

(Comment amended by State Bar Board of Directors Jan. 20, 1995.)

RULE 7.03   **Prohibited Solicitations and Payments**

(a) A lawyer shall not by in-person, ~~or telephone,~~ or regulated telephone or other electronic contact as defined in paragraph (f) seek professional employment concerning a matter arising out of a particular occurrence or event, or series of occurrences or events, from a prospective client or nonclient who has not sought the lawyer's advice regarding employment or with whom the lawyer has no family or past or present attorney-client relationship when a significant motive for the lawyer's doing so is the lawyer's pecuniary gain. Notwithstanding the provisions of this paragraph, a lawyer for a qualified nonprofit organization may communicate with the organization's members for the purpose of educating the members to understand the law, to recognize legal problems, to make intelligent selection of counsel, or to use legal services. In those situations where in-person, ~~or~~ telephone, or other electronic contact is permitted by this paragraph, a lawyer shall not have such a contact with a prospective client if:

(1) the communication involves coercion, duress, fraud, overreaching, intimidation, undue influence, or harassment;

(2) the communication contains information prohibited by Rule 7.02(a); or

(3) the communication contains a false, fraudulent, misleading, deceptive, or unfair statement or claim.

(b) A lawyer shall not pay, give, or offer to pay or give anything of value to a person not licensed to practice law for soliciting prospective clients for, or referring clients or prospective clients to, any lawyer or firm, except that a lawyer may pay reasonable fees for advertising and public relations services rendered in accordance with this Rule and may pay the usual charges of a lawyer referral service that meets the requirements of Article 320d, Revised Statutes.

(c) A lawyer, in order to solicit professional employment, shall not pay, give, advance, or offer to pay, give, or advance anything of value, other than actual litigation expenses and other financial assistance as permitted by Rule 1.08(d), to a prospective client or any other person; provided however, this provision does not prohibit the payment of legitimate referral fees as permitted by Rule 1.04(f) or by paragraph (b) of this Rule.

(d) A lawyer shall not enter into an agreement for, charge for, or collect a fee for professional employment obtained in violation of Rule 7.03(a), (b), or (c).

(e) A lawyer shall not participate with or accept referrals from a lawyer referral service unless the lawyer knows or reasonably believes that the lawyer referral service meets the requirements of Article 320d, Revised Statutes.

(f) As used in paragraph (a), "regulated telephone or other electronic contact" means any electronic communication initiated by a lawyer or by any person acting on behalf of a lawyer or law firm that will result in the person contacted communicating in a live, interactive manner with any other person by telephone or other electronic means. For purposes of this Rule a website for a lawyer or law firm is not considered a communication initiated by or on behalf of that lawyer or firm.

(Former Rule 7.02 adopted eff. Jan. 1, 1990; redesignated and amended to be eff. April 1, 1995; on March 31, 1995, the Texas Supreme Court extended the effective date 120 days after the date of judgment of the U.S. District Court in Texans Against Censorship, Inc. v. State Bar of Texas, 888 F.Supp. 1328 (E.D.Tex. 1995).)

COMMENT

1. In many situations, in-person or telephone solicitations by lawyers involve well-known opportunities for abuse of prospective clients. Nonetheless, paragraph (a) unconditionally prohibits those activities only when profit for the lawyer is a significant motive and the solicitation concerns matters arising out of a particular occurrence, event, or series of occurrences or events. The reason for this limited outright ban is that there are circumstances where the dangers of such contacts can be reduced. As long as the conditions of subparagraphs (a)(1) through (a)(3) are not violated by a given contact, a lawyer may engage in telephone or in-person solicitations when the solicitation is unrelated to a specific occurrence, event, or series of occurrences or events. Similarly, subject to the same restrictions, in-person or telephone solicitations are permitted where the prospective client either has a family or past or present attorney-client relationship with the lawyer or where the potential client had previously contacted the lawyer about possible employment in the matter.

2. In addition, Rule 7.03(a) does not prohibit a lawyer for a qualified non-profit organization from in-person or telephone solicitation of prospective clients for purposes related to that organization. Historically and by law, nonprofit legal aid agencies, unions, and other qualified nonprofit organizations and their lawyers have been permitted to solicit clients in-person or by telephone, and Rule 7.03(a) is not in derogation of their constitutional rights to do so. Attorneys for such nonprofit organizations, however, remain subject to this Rule's general prohibitions against undue influence, intimidation, overreaching, and the like.

Paying for Solicitation

3. Rule 7.03(b) does not prohibit a lawyer from paying standard commercial fees for advertising or public relations services rendered in accordance with these Rules. In addition, a lawyer may pay the fees required by a lawyer referral service that meets the requirements of Article 320(d), Revised Statutes. However, paying, giving, or offering to

pay or give anything of value to persons not licensed to practice law who solicit prospective clients for lawyers has always been considered to be against the best interest of both the public and the legal profession. Such actions circumvent these Rules by having a nonlawyer do what a lawyer is ethically proscribed from doing. Accordingly, the practice is forbidden by Rule 7.03(b). As to payments or gifts of value to licensed lawyers for soliciting prospective clients, see Rule 1.04(f).

4. Rule 7.03(c) prohibits a lawyer from paying or giving value directly to a prospective client or any other person as consideration for employment by that client except as permitted by Rule 1.08(d).

5. Paragraph (d) prohibits a lawyer from agreeing to or charging for professional employment obtained in violation of Rule 7.03. Paragraph (e) further requires a lawyer to decline business generated by a lawyer referral service unless the lawyer knows or reasonably believes that service is operated in conformity with statutory requirements.

6. References to "a lawyer" in this and other Rules include lawyers who practice in law firms. A lawyer associated with a firm cannot circumvent these Rules by soliciting or advertising in the name of that firm in a way that violates these Rules. See Rule 7.04(e).

(Comment amended by State Bar Board of Directors Jan. 20, 1995.)

RULE 7.04 Advertisements in the Public Media

(a) A lawyer shall not advertise in the public media by stating or implying that the lawyer is a specialist, except as permitted under Rule 7.04(b) or as follows:

(1) A lawyer admitted to practice before the United States Patent Office may use the designation "Patents," "Patent Attorney," or "Patent Lawyer," or any combination of those terms. A lawyer engaged in the trademark practice may use the designation "Trademark," "Trademark Attorney," or "Trademark Lawyer," or any combination of those terms. A lawyer engaged in patent and trademark practice may hold himself or herself out as specializing in "Intellectual Property Law," "Patent, Trademark, Copyright Law and Unfair Competition," or any of those terms.

(2) A lawyer may permit his or her name to be listed in lawyer referral service offices that meet the requirements of Article 320d, Revised Statutes, according to the areas of law in which the lawyer will accept referrals.

(3) A lawyer available to practice in a particular area of law or legal service may distribute to other lawyers and publish in legal directories and legal newspapers (whether written or electronic) a listing or an announcement of such availability. The listing shall not contain a false or misleading representation of special competence or experience, but

may contain the kind of information that traditionally has been included in such publications.

(b) A lawyer who advertises in the public media:

(1) shall publish or broadcast the name of at least one lawyer who is responsible for the content of such advertisement.

(2) shall not include a statement that the lawyer has been certified or designated by an organization as possessing special competence or a statement that the lawyer is a member of an organization the name of which implies that its members possess special competence, except that:

(i) a lawyer who has been awarded a Certificate of Special Competence by the Texas Board of Legal Specialization in the area so advertised, may state with respect to each such area, "Board Certified, [area of specialization]—Texas Board of Legal Specialization;" and

(ii) a lawyer who is a member of an organization the name of which implies that its members possess special competence, or who has been certified or designated by an organization as possessing special competence, may include a factually accurate statement of such membership or may include a factually accurate statement, "Certified [area of specialization] [name of certifying organization]," but such statements may be made only if that organization has been accredited by the Texas Board of Legal Specialization as a bona fide organization that admits to membership or grants certification only on the basis of objective, exacting, publicly available standards (including high standards of individual character, conduct, and reputation) that are reasonably relevant to the special training or special competence that is implied and that are in excess of the level of training and competence generally required for admission to the Bar.~~; and~~

~~(3) shall state with respect to each area advertised in which the lawyer has not been awarded a Certificate of Special Competence by the Texas Board of Legal Specialization, "Not Certified by the Texas Board of Legal Specialization," however, if an area of law so advertised has not been designated as an area in which a lawyer may be awarded a Certificate of Special Competence by the Texas Board of Legal Specialization, the lawyer may also state, "No designation has been made by the Texas Board of Legal Specialization for a Certificate of Special Competence in this area."~~

(4) shall, in the case of an infomercial or comparable presentation, state that the presentation is an advertisement:

(i) both verbally and in writing at its outset, after any commercial interruption, and at its conclusion; and

(ii) in writing during any portion of the presentation that explains how to contact a lawyer or law firm.

(c) Separate and apart from any other statements, the statements referred to in paragraph (b) shall be displayed conspicuously and, in the case of subparagraph (b)(2), do so with no abbreviations, changes, or additions in the quoted language set forth, in paragraph (b) so as to be easily seen or understood by an ordinary consumer.

(d) Subject to the requirements of Rules 7.02 and 7.03 and of paragraphs (a), (b), and (c) of this Rule, a lawyer may, either directly or through a public relations or advertising representative, advertise services in the public media, such as (but not limited to) a telephone directory, legal directory, newspaper or other periodical, outdoor display, radio, or television, the Internet, or other electronic media.

(e) All advertisements in the public media for a lawyer or firm must be reviewed and approved in writing by the lawyer or a lawyer in the firm.

(f) A copy or recording of each advertisement in the public media and relevant approval referred to in paragraph (e), and a record of when and where the advertisement was used, shall be kept by the lawyer or firm for four years after its last dissemination.

(g) In advertisements utilizing video or comparable visual images, any person who portrays a lawyer whose services or whose firm's services are being advertised, or who narrates an advertisement as if he or she were such a lawyer, shall be one or more of the lawyers whose services are being advertised. In advertisements utilizing audio recordings, any person who narrates an advertisement as if he or she were a lawyer whose services or whose firm's services are being advertised, shall be one or more of the lawyers whose services are being advertised.

(h) If an advertisement in the public media by a lawyer or firm discloses the willingness or potential willingness of the lawyer or firm to render services on a contingent fee basis, the advertisement must state whether the client will be obligated to pay all or any portion of the court costs and, if a client may be liable for other expenses, this fact must be disclosed. If specific percentage fees or fee ranges of contingent fee work are disclosed in such advertisement, it must also disclose whether the percentage is computed before or after expenses are deducted from the recovery.

(i) A lawyer who advertises in the public media a specific fee or range of fees for a particular service shall conform to the advertised fee or range of fees for the period during which the advertisement is reasonably expected to be in circulation or otherwise expected to be effective in attracting clients, unless the advertisement specifies a shorter period; but in no instance is the lawyer bound to conform to the advertised fee or range of fees for a period of more than one year after the date of publication.

* (j) A lawyer or firm who advertises in the public media must disclose the geographic location, by city or town, of the lawyer's or firm's principal office. A lawyer or firm shall not advertise the existence of any office other than the principal office unless:

(1) that other office is staffed by a lawyer at least three days a week; or

(2) the advertisement states:

(i) the days and times during which a lawyer will be present at that office, or

(ii) that meetings with lawyers will be by appointment only.

* **Publisher's Note**: In Texans Against Censorship, Inc. v. State Bar of Texas, 888 F.Supp. 1328 (E.D.Tex. 1995), the U.S. District Court for the Eastern District of Texas held Rule 7.04(j) unconstitutional as applied to one of the plaintiffs. Affirmed, Texans v. State Bar of Texas, 100 F.3d 953 (5th Cir. 1996).

(k) A lawyer may not, directly or indirectly, pay all or a part of the cost of an advertisement in the public media for a lawyer not in the same firm unless such advertisement discloses the name and address of the financing lawyer, the relationship between the advertising lawyer and the financing lawyer, and whether the advertising lawyer is likely to refer cases received through the advertisement to the financing lawyer.

(*l*) If an advertising lawyer knows or should know at the time of an advertisement in the public media that a case or matter will likely be referred to another lawyer or firm, a statement of such fact shall be conspicuously included in such advertisement.

(m) No motto, slogan, or jingle that is false or misleading may be used in any advertisement in the public media.

(n) A lawyer shall not include in any advertisement in the public media the lawyer's association with a lawyer referral service unless the lawyer knows or reasonably believes that the lawyer referral service meets the requirements of Article 320d, Revised Statutes.

(*o*) A lawyer may not advertise in the public media as part of an advertising cooperative or venture of two or more lawyers not in the same firm unless each such advertisement:

(1) states that the advertisement is paid for by the cooperating lawyers;

(2) names each of the cooperating lawyers;

(3) sets forth conspicuously the special competency requirements required by Rule 7.04(b) of lawyers who advertise in the public media;

(4) does not state or imply that the lawyers participating in the advertising cooperative or venture possess professional superiority, are able to perform services in a superior manner, or possess special competence in any area of law advertised, except that the advertisement may contain the information permitted by Rule 7.04(b)(2); and

(5) does not otherwise violate the Texas Disciplinary Rules of Professional Conduct.

(p) Each lawyer who advertises in the public media as part of an advertising cooperative or venture shall be individually responsible for:

(1) ensuring that each advertisement does not violate this Rule; and

(2) complying with the filing requirements of Rule 7.07.

(Adopted to be eff. April 1, 1995; on March 31, 1995, the Texas Supreme Court extended the effective date 120 days after the date of judgment of the U.S. District Court in Texans Against Censorship, Inc. v. State Bar of Texas, 888 F.Supp. 1328 (E.D.Tex. 1995).)

COMMENT

1. Neither Rule 7.04 nor Rule 7.05 prohibits communications authorized by law, such as notice to members of a class in class action litigation.

Advertising Areas of Practice and Special Competence

2. Paragraphs (a) and (b) permit a lawyer, under the restrictions set forth, to indicate areas of practice in advertisements about the lawyer's services. See also paragraph (d). The restrictions are designed primarily to require that accurate information be conveyed. These restrictions recognize that a lawyer has a right protected by the United States Constitution to advertise publicly, but that the right may be regulated by reasonable restrictions designed to protect the public from false or misleading information. The restrictions contained in Rule 7.04 are based on the experience of the legal profession in the State of Texas and are designed to curtail what experience has shown to be misleading and deceptive advertising. To ensure accountability, sub-paragraph (b)(1) requires identification of at least one lawyer responsible for the content of the advertisement.

3. Because of long-standing tradition a lawyer admitted to practice before the United States Patent Office may use the designation "patents," "patent attorney" or "patent lawyer" or any combination of those terms. As recognized by paragraph (a)(1), a lawyer engaged in patent and trademark practice may hold himself or herself out as concentrating

in "intellectual property law," "patents, or trademarks and related matters," or "patent, trademark, copyright law and unfair competition" or any of those terms.

4. Paragraph (a)(2) recognizes the propriety of listing a lawyer's name in legal directories according to the areas of law in which the lawyer will accept new matters. The same right is given with respect to lawyer referral service offices, but only if those services comply with statutory guidelines. The restriction in paragraph (a)(2) does not prevent a legal aid agency or prepaid legal services plan from advertising legal services provided under its auspices.

5. Paragraph (a)(3) permits advertisements by lawyers to other lawyers in legal directories and legal newspapers, subject to the same requirements of truthfulness that apply to all other forms of lawyer advertising. Such advertisements traditionally contain information about the name, location, telephone numbers, and general availability of a lawyer to work on particular legal matters. Other information may be included so long as it is not false or misleading. Because advertisements in these publications are not available to the general public, lawyers who list various areas of practice are not required to comply with paragraph (b).

6. Some advertisements, sometimes known as tombstone advertisements, mention only such matters as the name of the lawyer or law firm, a listing of lawyers associated with the firm, office addresses and telephone numbers, office and telephone service hours, dates of admission to bars, the acceptance of credit cards, and fees. The content of such advertisements is not the kind of information intended to be regulated by Rule 7.04(b). However, if the advertisement in the public media mentions any area of the law in which the lawyer practices, then, because of the likelihood of misleading material, the lawyer must comply with paragraph (b).

7. Sometimes lawyers choose to advertise in the public media the fact that they have been certified or designated by a particular organization or that they are members of a particular organization. Such statements naturally lead the public to believe that the lawyer possesses special competence in the area of law mentioned. Consequently, in order to ensure that the public will not be misled by such statements, sub-paragraph (b)(2) and paragraph (c) place limited but necessary restrictions upon a lawyer's basic right to advertise those affiliations.

8. Rule 7.04(b)(2) gives lawyers who possess certificates of specialization from the Texas Board of Legal Specialization or other meritorious credentials from organizations approved by the Board the option of stating that fact. If a lawyer mentions in an advertisement in the public media an area of the law in which the lawyer practices and that lawyer has not been awarded a Certificate in the area advertised, then the lawyer must disclaim or, where applicable, state that no certification is available. See sub-paragraph (b)(3). Sub-paragraphs (b)(2) and (b)(3)

require that the restrictions set forth be complied with as to each area of law advertised.

9. Paragraph (c) is intended to ensure against misleading or material variations from the statements required by paragraph (b).

10. Paragraphs (e) and (f) provide the advertising lawyer, the Bar, and the public with requisite records should questions arise regarding the propriety of a public media advertisement. Paragraph (e), like paragraph (b)(1), ensures that a particular attorney accepts responsibility for the advertisement. It is in the public interest and in the interest of the legal profession that the records of those advertisements and approvals be maintained.

Examples of Prohibited Advertising

11. Paragraphs (g) through (o) regulate conduct that has been found to mislead or be likely to mislead the public. Each paragraph is designed to protect the public and to guard the legal profession against these documented misleading practices while at the same time respecting the constitutional rights of any lawyer to advertise.

12. Paragraph (g) is a limited regulation of video and audio forms of advertising. It prohibits lawyers from misleading the public into believing a nonlawyer portrayor or narrator in the advertisement is one of the lawyers prepared to perform services for the public. It does not prohibit the narration of an advertisement in the third person by an actor, as long as it is clear to those hearing or seeing the advertisement that the actor is not a lawyer prepared to perform services for the public.

13. Contingent fee contracts present unusual opportunities for deception by lawyers or for misunderstanding by the public. By requiring certain disclosures, paragraph (h) safeguards the public from misleading or potentially misleading advertisements that involve representation on a contingent fee basis. The affirmative requirements of paragraph (h) are not triggered solely by the expression of "contingent fee" or "percentage fee" in the advertisement. To the contrary, they encompass advertisements in the public media where the lawyer or firm expresses a mere willingness or potential willingness to render services for a contingent fee. Therefore, statements in an advertisement such as "no fee if no recovery" or "fees in the event of recovery only" are clearly included as a form of advertisement subject to the disclosure requirements of paragraph (h).

14. Paragraphs (i), (j), (k) and (l) jointly address the problem of advertising that experience has shown misleads the public concerning the fees that will be charged, the location where services will be provided, or the attorney who will be performing these services. Together they prohibit the same sort of "bait and switch" advertising tactics by lawyers that are universally condemned.

15. Paragraph (i) requires a lawyer who advertises a specific fee or range of fees in the public media to honor those commitments for the period during which the advertisement is reasonably expected to be in

circulation or otherwise expected to be effective in attracting clients, unless the advertisement itself specifies a shorter period. In no event, however, is a lawyer required to honor an advertised fee or range of fees for more than one year after publication.

16. Paragraph (j) prohibits advertising the availability of a satellite office that is not staffed by a lawyer at least on a part-time basis. Paragraph (j) does not require, however, that a lawyer or firm identify the particular office as its principal one. Experience has shown that, in the absence of such regulation, members of the public have been misled into employing a lawyer in a distant city who advertises that there is a nearby satellite office, only to learn later that the lawyer is rarely available to the client because the nearby office is seldom open or is staffed only by lay personnel. Paragraph (k) is not intended to restrict the ability of legal services programs to advertise satellite offices in remote parts of the program's service area even if those satellite offices are staffed irregularly by attorneys. Otherwise low-income individuals in and near such communities might be denied access to the only legal services truly available to them.

17. When a lawyer or firm advertises, the public has a right to expect that lawyer or firm will perform the legal services. Experience has shown that attorneys not in the same firm may create a relationship wherein one will finance advertising for the other in return for referrals. Nondisclosure of such a referral relationship is misleading to the public. Accordingly, paragraph (k) prohibits such a relationship between an advertising lawyer and a lawyer who finances the advertising unless the advertisement discloses the nature of the financial relationship between the two lawyers. Paragraph (*l*) addresses the same problem from a different perspective, requiring a lawyer who advertises the availability of legal services and who knows or should know at the time that the advertisement is placed in the media that business will likely be referred to another lawyer or firm, to include a conspicuous statement of that fact in any such advertising. This requirement applies whether or not the lawyer to whom the business is referred is financing the advertisements of the referring lawyer. It does not, however, require disclosure of all possible scenarios under which a referral could occur, such as an unforeseen need to associate with a specialist in accordance with Rule 1.01(a) or the possibility of a referral if a prospective client turns out to have a conflict of interest precluding representation by the advertising lawyer.

18. Paragraph (m) protects the public by forbidding mottos, slogans, and jingles that are false or misleading. There are, however, mottos, slogans, and jingles that are informative rather than false or misleading. Accordingly, paragraph (m) recognizes an advertising lawyer's constitutional right to include appropriate mottos, slogans, and jingles in advertising.

19. Some lawyers choose to band together in a cooperative or joint venture to advertise. Although those arrangements are lawful, the fact

that several independent lawyers have joined together in a single advertisement increases the risk of misrepresentation or other forms of inappropriate expression. Special care must be taken to ensure that cooperative advertisements identify each cooperating lawyer, state that each cooperating lawyer is paying for the advertisement, and accurately describe the professional qualifications of each cooperating lawyer. See paragraph (*o*). Furthermore, each cooperating lawyer must comply with the filing requirements of Rule 7.07. See paragraph (p).

(Comment adopted by State Bar Board of Directors Jan. 20, 1995.)

RULE 7.05   Prohibited Written, Recorded, Or Other Electronic Solicitations

(a) **A lawyer shall not send, ~~or~~ deliver, transmit ~~on the lawyer's behalf~~, or cause another to send, deliver, or transmit, a written, audio, audio-visual, CD-ROM, recorded telephone message, or other electronic communication to a prospective client for the purpose of obtaining professional employment on behalf of any lawyer or law firm if:**

    (1) the communication involves coercion, duress, fraud, overreaching, intimidation, undue influence, or harassment;

    (2) the communication contains information prohibited by Rule 7.02 or fails to satisfy each of the requirements of Rule 7.04(a) through (c), and (h) through (*o*) that would be applicable to the communication if it were an advertisement in the public media; or

    (3) the communication contains a false, fraudulent, misleading, deceptive, or unfair statement or claim.

(b) **Except as provided in paragraph ~~(e)~~(f) of this Rule, a written solicitation communication to prospective clients for the purpose of obtaining professional employment:**

    (1) ~~shall conform to the provisions of Rule 7.04(a) through (c);~~

    ~~(2)~~ shall, in the case of a non-electronically transmitted written communication, be plainly marked "ADVERTISEMENT" on ~~the~~ its first page ~~of the written communication~~, and on the face of the envelope or other packaging used to transmit the communication. ~~also shall be plainly marked "ADVERTISEMENT."~~ If the written communication is in the form of a self-mailing brochure or pamphlet, the word "ADVERTISEMENT" shall be:

        (i) in a color that contrasts sharply with the background color; and

        (ii) in a size of at least 3/8″ vertically or three times the vertical height of the letters used in the body of such communication, whichever is larger~~.~~;

238

(2) shall, in the case of an electronic mail message, be plainly marked "ADVERTISEMENT" in the "subject" portion of the standard electronic mail format and at the beginning of the message's text;

(3) shall not be made to resemble legal pleadings or other legal documents;

(4) [Deleted by the Supreme Court of Texas July 1, 1998.]

(5) [Deleted by the Supreme Court of Texas July 1, 1998.]

(4)(6) shall not reveal on the envelope or other packaging or electronic mail subject line used for to transmit the communication, or on the outside of a self-mailing brochure or pamphlet, the nature of the legal problem of the prospective client or nonclient; and

(5)(7) shall disclose how the lawyer obtained the information prompting such written the communication to solicit professional employment if such contact was prompted by a specific occurrence involving the recipient of the communication or a family member of such person(s).

(c) Except as provided in paragraph (f) of this Rule, an audio, audio-visual, CD-ROM, recorded telephone message, or other electronic communication sent to prospective clients for the purpose of obtaining professional employment:

(1) shall, in the case of any such communication delivered to the recipient by non-electronic means, plainly and conspicuously state in writing on the outside of any envelope or other packaging used to transmit the communication, that it is an "ADVERTISEMENT."

(2) shall not reveal on any such envelope or other packaging the nature of the legal problem of the prospective client or non-client;

(3) shall disclose, either in the communication itself or in accompanying transmittal message, how the lawyer obtained the information prompting such audio, audio-visual, CD-ROM, recorded telephone message, or other electronic communication to solicit professional employment, if such contact was prompted by a specific occurrence involving the recipient of the communication or a family member of such person(s);

(4) shall, in the case of a recorded audio presentation or a recorded telephone message, plainly state that it is an advertisement prior to any other words being spoken and again at the presentation's or message's conclusion;

(5) shall, in the case of an audio-visual or CD-ROM presentation, plainly state that the presentation is an advertisement;

(i) both verbally and in writing at the outset of the presentation and again at its conclusion; and

(ii) in writing during any portion of the presentation that explains how to contact a lawyer or law firm.

~~(c)~~(d) All written, audio, audio-visual, CD-ROM, recorded telephone message, or other electronic communications made to a prospective client for the purpose of obtaining professional employment of a lawyer or law firm must be reviewed and either signed by or approved in writing by the lawyer or a lawyer in the firm.

~~(d)~~(e) A copy of each written, audio, audio-visual, CD-ROM, recorded telephone message, or other electronic solicitation communication, the relevant approval thereof, and a record of the date of each such communication; the name, ~~and~~ address, telephone number, or electronic address to which each such communication was sent; and the means by which each such communication was sent shall be kept by the lawyer or firm for four years after its dissemination.

~~(e)~~(f) The provisions of paragraphs (b) and (c) of this Rule do not apply to a written, audio, audio-visual, CD-ROM, recorded telephone message, or other form of electronic solicitation communication:

(1) directed to a family member or a person with whom the lawyer had or has an attorney-client relationship;

(2) that is not motivated by or concerned with a particular past occurrence or event or a particular series of past occurrences or events, and also is not motivated by or concerned with the prospective client's specific existing legal problem of which the lawyer is aware;

(3) if the lawyer's use of the communication to secure professional employment was not significantly motivated by a desire for, or by the possibility of obtaining, pecuniary gain; or

(4) that is requested by the prospective client.

(Adopted to be eff. April 1, 1995; on March 31, 1995, the Texas Supreme Court extended the effective date 120 days after the date of judgment of the U.S. District Court in Texans Against Censorship, Inc. v. State Bar of Texas, 888 F.Supp. 1328 (E.D.Tex. 1995).)

COMMENT

1. Rule 7.03 deals with in-person or telephone contact between a lawyer and a prospective client wherein the lawyer seeks professional employment. Rule 7.04 deals with advertisements in the public media

by a lawyer seeking professional employment. This Rule deals with written solicitations between a lawyer and a prospective client. Typical examples are letters or other forms of correspondence addressed to a prospective client.

2. Written solicitations raise more concerns than do comparable written advertisements. Being private, they are more difficult to monitor, and for that reason paragraph (d) requires retention for four years of certain information regarding written solicitations. See also Rule 7.07(a). Paragraph (a) addresses such concerns as well as problems stemming from exceptionally outrageous communications such as written solicitations involving fraud, intimidation, or deceptive and misleading claims. Because receipt of multiple solicitations appears to be most pronounced and vexatious in situations involving accident victims, paragraph (b)(7) requires disclosure of the source of information if the solicitation was prompted by a specific occurrence.

3. Because experience has shown that many written solicitations have been intrusive or misleading by reason of being personalized or being disguised as some form of official communication special prohibitions against such practices are necessary. The requirements of paragraph (b) greatly lessen those dangers of deception and harassment.

4. Newsletters or other works published by a lawyer that are not circulated for the purpose of obtaining professional employment are not within the ambit of paragraph (b).

5. In addition to addressing these special problems posed by written solicitations, Rule 7.05 regulates the content of those communications. It does so by incorporating the standards of Rule 7.02 and those of Rule 7.04 that would apply to the written solicitation were it instead a written advertisement in the public media. See paragraphs (a)(2), (3), and (b)(1). In brief, this approach means that, a lawyer may not include or omit anything from a written solicitation unless the lawyer could do so were the communication a written advertisement in the public media, except for those statements or disclaimers required by Rule 7.04(a)–(c). See sub-paragraph (b)(1).

6. Paragraph (e) provides that none of the restrictions in paragraph (b) apply in certain situations because the dangers of deception, harassment, vexation and overreaching are quite low. For example, a written solicitation may be directed to a family member or a present or a former client, or in response to a request by a prospective client. Similarly, a written solicitation may be used in seeking general employment in commercial matters from a bank or other corporation, when there is neither concern with specific existing legal problems nor concern with a particular past event or series of events. All such communications, however, remain subject to Rule 7.02 and paragraphs (h) through (o) of Rule 7.04. See sub-paragraph (a)(2).

7. In addition, paragraph (e) allows such communications in situations not involving the lawyer's pecuniary gain. For purposes of these rules, it is presumed that communications made on behalf of a nonprofit

legal aid agency, union, or other qualified nonprofit organization are not motivated by a desire for, or by the possibility of obtaining, pecuniary gain, but that presumption may be rebutted.

(Comment adopted by State Bar Board of Directors Jan. 20, 1995.)

RULE 7.06 Prohibited Employment

(a) A lawyer shall not accept or continue employment in a matter when ~~the lawyer knows or reasonably should know~~ that employment was procured by conduct prohibited by any of Rules 7.01 through 7.05, 8.04(a)(2), or 8.04(a)(9), engaged in by that lawyer personally or by any other person whom the lawyer ordered, encouraged, or knowingly permitted to engage in such conduct.

(b) A lawyer shall not accept or continue employment in a matter when the lawyer knows or reasonably should know that employment was procured by conduct prohibited by any of Rules 7.01 through 7.05, 8.04(a)(2), or 8.04(a)(9), engaged in by any other person or entity that is a shareholder, partner, or member of, an associate in, or of counsel to that lawyer's firm; or by any other person whom any of the foregoing persons or entities ordered, encouraged, or knowingly permitted to engage in such conduct.

(c) A lawyer who has not violated paragraph (a) or (b) in accepting employment in a matter shall not continue employment in that matter once the lawyer knows or reasonably should know that the person procuring the lawyer's employment in the matter engaged in, or ordered, encouraged, or knowingly permitted another to engage in, conduct prohibited by any of Rules 7.01 through 7.05, 8.04(a)(2), or 8.04(a)(9) in connection with the matter unless nothing of value is given thereafter in return for that employment. ~~the person who seeks the lawyer's services does so as a result of conduct prohibited by these Rules.~~

(Former Rule 7.03 adopted eff. Jan. 1, 1990; redesignated and amended to be eff. April 1, 1995; on March 31, 1995, the Texas Supreme Court extended the effective date 120 days after the date of judgment of the U.S. District Court in Texans Against Censorship, Inc. v. State Bar of Texas, 888 F.Supp. 1328 (E.D.Tex. 1995).)

COMMENT

Selection of a lawyer by a client often is a result of the advice and recommendation of third parties—relatives, friends, acquaintances, business associates and other lawyers. Although that method of referral is perfectly legitimate, the client is best served if the recommendation is disinterested and informed. All lawyers must guard against creating situations where referral from others is the consequence of some form of prohibited compensation or from some form of false or misleading communication, or by virtue of some other violation of these rules. This prohibition on accepting or continuing employment applies even if the lawyer whose services are involved had no direct or indirect involvement with the underlying violation of these Rules, provided that lawyer knows of the violation. See also Rule 7.03(d), forbidding a lawyer to charge or collect a fee where the misconduct involves violations of Rule 7.03(a), (b), or (c).

(Comment amended by State Bar Board of Directors Jan. 20, 1995.)

RULE 7.07   Filing Requirements for Public Advertisements and Written, Recorded, or Other Electronic Solicitations

(a) Except as provided in paragraphs ~~(d)~~ (c) and (e) of this Rule, a lawyer shall file with the ~~Lawyer Advertisement and Solicitation~~ Advertising Review Committee of the State Bar of Texas, ~~either before or concurrently with~~ no later than the mailing or sending by any means, including electronic, of a written, audio, audio-visual, or other electronic solicitation communication:

(1) a copy of the ~~written~~ solicitation communication being sent or to be sent to one or more prospective clients for the purpose of obtaining professional employment, together with a representative sample of the envelopes or other packaging in which the communications are enclosed; ~~and~~

(2) a completed lawyer advertising and solicitation communication application form; and

(3) a check or money order payable to the State Bar of Texas for the fee set by the Board of Directors. Such fee shall be for the sole purpose of defraying the expense of enforcing the rules related to such solicitations.

(b) Except as provided in paragraph ~~(d)~~(e) of this Rule, a lawyer shall file with the ~~Lawyer Advertisement and Solicitation~~ Advertising Review Committee of the State Bar of Texas, ~~either before or concurrently with~~ no later than the first dissemination of an advertisement in the public media, a copy of that advertisement. The filing shall include:

(1) a copy of the advertisement in the form in which it appears ~~or is~~ or will appear upon dissemination ~~be disseminated,~~ such as a videotape, an audiotape, a print copy, or a photograph of outdoor advertising;

(2) a production script of the advertisement setting forth all words used and describing in detail the actions, events, scenes, and background sounds used in such advertisement together with a listing of the names and addresses of persons portrayed or heard to speak, if the advertisement is in or will be in a form in which the advertised message is not fully revealed by a print copy or photograph;

(3) a statement of when and where the advertisement has been, is, or will be used; ~~and~~

(4) a completed lawyer advertising and solicitation communication application form; and

(5) a check or money order payable to the State Bar of Texas for the fee set by the Board of Directors. Such fee shall be for the sole purpose of defraying the expense of enforcing the rules related to such advertisements.

(c) Except as provided in paragraph (e) of this Rule, a lawyer shall file with the Advertising Review Committee of the State Bar of Texas no later than its first posting on the Internet or other comparable network of computers information concerning the lawyer's or lawyer's firm's website. As used in this Rule, a "website" is a publication on the Internet or other network of computers, consisting of a file, a part of a file, or a collection of files, that is accessible to the general public. The filing shall include:

(1) each unit of the website up to a maximum of ten (10) of those units that, standing alone, would not be exempt from filing under paragraph (e). As used in this subparagraph (1), a "unit" of a website is the equivalent of one 8½ × 11″ printed page of text or one minute of audio or audiovisual production script;

(2) a completed lawyer advertising and solicitation communication application form; and

(3) a check or money order payable to the State Bar of Texas for the fee set by the Board of Directors. Such fee shall be set for the sole purpose of defraying the expense of enforcing the rules related to such websites. In addition, the fee set shall permit the filing party to submit any modifications made to the units of its website filed pursuant to subparagraph (c)(1) within one year of their initial approval or pre-approval, for review by the Advertising Review Committee at no additional charge.

~~(e)~~(d) A lawyer who desires to secure an advance advisory opinion, referred to as a request for pre-approval, concerning compliance of a contemplated ~~written~~ solicitation communication or advertisement (including all or portions of a website) may submit to the ~~Lawyer Advertisement and Solicitation~~ Advertising Review Committee, not less than thirty (30) days prior to the date of first dissemination, the material specified in paragraph (a) or (b), or all or any filed portion of a website submitted pursuant to paragraph (c) ~~of this Rule~~, including the application form and required fee; provided however, it shall not be necessary to submit a videotape if the videotape has not then been prepared and the production script submitted reflects in detail and accurately the actions, events, scenes, and background sounds that will be depicted or contained on such videotapes, when prepared, as well as the narrative transcript of the verbal and printed portions of such advertisement. A lawyer who wishes to request a pre-approval of an advertisement in a telephone directory or similar publication for which the date of dissemination is preceded by a period of time during which the advertisement cannot be changed must submit to the Advertising Review Committee, not less than thirty (30) days prior to the change deadline of the publication, the material specified in paragraph (b) of this Rule. If a lawyer submits an advertisement or written solicitation communication for pre-approval. ~~An advisory opinion of the Lawyer Advertisement and Solicitation Review Committee~~ a finding of noncompliance by the Advertising Review Committee is not binding in a disciplinary proceeding or disciplinary action but a finding of compliance is binding in favor of the submitting lawyer as to all materials actually submitted for pre-approval if the representations, statements, materials, facts and written assurances received in connection therewith are true and are not misleading. The finding of compliance constitutes admissible evidence if offered by a party.

~~(d)~~(e) The filing requirements of paragraphs (a)~~,~~ ~~and~~ (b), and (c) do not extend to any of the following materials, provided those materials comply with Rule 7.02(a) through (c) and, where applicable, Rule 7.04(a) through (c):

(1) an advertisement in the public media (including a website) that contains only part or all of the following information~~, provided the information is not false or misleading~~:

(i) the name of a lawyer or firm and lawyers associated with the firm, with office addresses, electronic addresses, telephone numbers, office and telephone service hours, telecopier numbers, and a designation of the profession such as "attorney," "lawyer," "law office," or "firm";

(ii) the ~~fields~~ particular areas of law in which the lawyer or firm specializes or possesses special competence ~~advertises specialization and the statements required by Rule 7.04(a) through (c)~~;

(iii) the particular areas of law in which the lawyer or firm practices or concentrates or to which it limits its practice

~~(iii)~~(iv) the date of admission of the lawyer or lawyers to the State Bar of Texas, to particular federal courts, and to the bars of other jurisdictions;

(iv)(v) technical and professional licenses granted by this state and other recognized licensing authorities;

(v)(vi) foreign language ability;

~~(vi) fields of law in which one or more lawyers are certified or designated, provided the statement of this information is in compliance with Rule 7.02(a) through (c);~~

(vii) identification of prepaid or group legal service plans in which the lawyer participates;

(viii) the acceptance or nonacceptance of credit cards;

(ix) any fee for initial consultation and fee schedule;

(x) in the case of a website, other publicly available information concerning legal issues, not prepared or paid for by the firm or any of its lawyers, such as news articles, legal articles, editorial opinions, or other legal developments or events, such as proposed or enacted rules, regulations, or legislation;

(xi) in the case of a website, links to other websites;

(xii) that the lawyer or firm is a sponsor of a charitable, civic, or community program or event, or is a sponsor of a public service announcement;

(xiii) any disclosure or statement required by these rules; and

(xivi) any other information specified from time to time in orders promulgated by the Supreme Court of Texas:

(2) an advertisement in the public media (including a website) that:

(i) identifies one or more lawyers or a firm as a contributor to a specified charity or as a sponsor of a specified charitable, community, or public interest program, activity, or event; and

(ii) contains no information about the lawyers or firm other than name* of the lawyers or firm or both, location of the law offices, and the fact of the sponsorship or contribution;

* So in February 23, 1995 Order.

(3) a listing or entry in a regularly published law list, whether written or electronic;

(4) an announcement card stating new or changed associations, new offices, or similar changes relating to a lawyer or firm, or a tombstone professional card;

(5) in the case of communications sent, delivered, or transmitted to, rather than accessed by, intended recipients, a newsletter, whether written or electronic, provided that it is sent, delivered, or transmitted ~~mailed~~ only to:

> **(i)** existing or former clients;
>
> **(ii)** other lawyers or professionals; ~~and~~ or
>
> **(iii)** members of a nonprofit organization that meets the following conditions: the primary purposes of the organization do not include the rendition of legal services; the recommending, furnishing, paying for, or educating persons regarding legal services is incidental and reasonably related to the primary purposes of the organization; the organization does not derive a financial benefit from the rendition of legal services by a lawyer; and the person for whom the legal services are rendered, and not the organization, is recognized as the client of the lawyer who is recommended, furnished, or paid by the organization;

(6) a ~~written~~ solicitation communication that is not motivated by or concerned with a particular past occurrence or event or a particular series of past occurrences or events, and also is not motivated by or concerned with the prospective client's specific existing legal problem of which the lawyer is aware;

(7) a ~~written~~ solicitation communication if the lawyer's use of the communication to secure professional employment was not significantly motivated by a desire for, or by the possibility of obtaining, pecuniary gain; or

(8) a ~~written~~ solicitation communication that is requested by the prospective client.

~~(e)~~(f) If requested by the ~~Lawyer Advertisement and Solicitation~~ Advertising Review Committee, a lawyer shall promptly submit information to substantiate statements or representations made or implied in any advertisement in the public media (including a website) ~~and/~~or ~~written~~ solicitation communication.

(Adopted to be eff. April 1, 1995; on March 31, 1995, the Texas Supreme Court extended the effective date 120 days after the date of judgment of the U.S. District Court in Texans Against Censorship, Inc. v. State Bar of Texas, 888 F.Supp. 1328 (E.D.Tex. 1995).)

COMMENT

1. Rule 7.07 covers the filing requirements for public media advertisements (see Rule 7.04) and written solicitations (see Rule 7.05). Rule

7.07(a) deals with those written solicitations sent by a lawyer to one or more specified prospective clients. Rule 7.07(b) deals with advertisements in the public media. Each provision allows the Bar to charge a fee for reviewing submitted materials, but requires that fee be set solely to defray the expenses of enforcing those provisions.

2. Copies of non-exempt written solicitations or advertisements in the public media must be provided to the Advertising Review Committee of the State Bar of Texas either in advance or concurrently with dissemination, together with the fee required by the State Bar of Texas Board of Directors. Presumably, the Advertising Review Committee will report to the appropriate grievance committee any lawyer whom it finds from the reviewed products has disseminated an advertisement in the public media or written solicitation that violates Rules 7.02, 7.03, 7.04, or 7.05, or, at a minimum, any lawyer whose violation raises a substantial question as to that lawyer's honesty, trustworthiness, or fitness as a lawyer in other respects. See Rule 8.03(a).

3. Paragraphs (a) and (b) do not require that a lawyer submit a copy of each and every written solicitation letter a lawyer sends. If the same form letter is sent to several people, only a representative sample of each form letter, along with a representative sample of the envelopes used to mail the letters, need be filed.

4. A lawyer wishing to do so may secure an advisory opinion from the Advertising Review Committee concerning any proposed advertisement in the public media or any written solicitation in advance of its first use or mailing by complying with Rule 7.07(c). This procedure is intended as a service to those lawyers who want to resolve any possible doubts about their proposed advertisements' or written solicitations' compliance with these Rules before utilizing them. Its use is purely optional. No lawyer is required to obtain advance clearance of any advertisement or written solicitation communication from the State Bar. Although a finding of noncompliance by the Advertising Review Committee is not binding in a disciplinary proceeding, a finding of compliance is binding in favor of the submitting lawyer, as long as the lawyer's presentation to the Advertising Review Committee in connection with that advisory opinion is true and not misleading.

5. Under its Internal Rules and Operating Procedures, the Advertising Review Committee is to complete its evaluations no later than 25 days after the date of receipt of a filing. The only way that the Committee can extend that review period is to: (1) determine that there is reasonable doubt whether the advertisement or written solicitation communication complies with these Rules; (2) conclude that further examination is warranted but cannot be completed within the 25-day period; and (3) advise the lawyer of those determinations in writing within that 25-day period. The Committee's Internal Rules and Operating Procedures also provide that a failure to send such a communication to the lawyer within the 25-day period constitutes approval of the advertisement or written solicitation communication. Consequently, if

an attorney submits an advertisement in the public media or written solicitation communication to the Committee for advance approval not less than 30 days prior to the date of first dissemination as required by these Rules, the attorney will receive an assessment of that advertisement or communication before the date of its first intended use.

6. Consistent with the effort to protect the first amendment rights of lawyers while ensuring the right of the public to be free from misleading advertising and the right of the Texas legal profession to maintain its integrity, paragraph (d) exempts certain types of advertisements and written solicitations prepared for the purpose of seeking paid professional employment from the filing requirements of paragraphs (a) and (b). Those types of communications need not be filed at all if they were not prepared to secure paid professional employment.

7. For the most part, the types of exempted advertising listed in subparagraphs (d)(1)–(5) are objective and less likely to result in false, misleading or fraudulent content. Similarly the types of exempted written solicitations listed in subparagraphs (d)(6)–(8) are those found least likely to result in harm to the public. See Rule 7.05(e), and comment 5 to Rule 7.05. The fact that a particular advertisement or written solicitation made by a lawyer is exempted from the filing requirements of this Rule does not exempt a lawyer from the other applicable obligations of these Rules. See generally Rules 7.01 through 7.06.

8. Paragraph (e) does not empower the Advertising Review Committee to seek information from a lawyer to substantiate statements or representations made or implied in advertisements or written communications that do not seek to obtain paid professional employment for that lawyer.

(Comment adopted by State Bar Board of Directors Jan. 20, 1995.)

MAINTAINING THE INTEGRITY OF THE PROFESSION

Kansas Rule 8.3

[Kansas amended Model Rule 8.3 as follows:]

RULE 8.3 Reporting Professional Misconduct

(a) A lawyer having knowledge that another lawyer has committed a violation of the Rules of Professional Conduct that raises a substantial question as to that lawyer's honesty, trustworthiness or fitness as a lawyer in other respects, shall inform the appropriate professional authority.

(b) A lawyer having knowledge that a judge has committed a violation of applicable rules of judicial conduct that raises a substantial question as to the judge's fitness for office shall inform the appropriate authority.

(c) This rule does not require disclosure of information otherwise protected by Rule 1.6. In addition, a lawyer is not

required to disclose information concerning any such violation which is discovered through participation in a Substance Abuse Committee, Service to the Bar Committee or similar committee sponsored by a state or local bar association, or by participation in a self-help organization such as Alcoholics Anonymous, through which aid is rendered to another lawyer who may be impaired in the practice of law.

* * *

KANSAS COMMENT:

Substance Abuse Committees have earned an important position in the organization of bar association activities and render a valuable and important service to the profession and the public. As such, these committees and other recognized self-help organizations, and the lawyers who serve on them should be allowed to function without fear of the requirement to report every violation which might be uncovered during the course of their service. To provide otherwise might inhibit free and open communication by the incapacitated lawyer and result in neglected matters remaining so. In this instance, the Kansas Committee feels that the public is better served by providing a measure of confidentiality to the incapacitated lawyer's communications with those who would help the lawyer in serving clients.

Florida Rule 8.4(d)

[Florida has modified Model Rule 8.4 to read as follows:]

RULE 4–8.4 Misconduct

A lawyer shall not:

* * *

(d) engage in conduct in connection with the practice of law that is prejudicial to the administration of justice, including to knowingly, or through callous indifference, disparage, humiliate, or discriminate against litigants, jurors, witnesses, court personnel, or other lawyers on any basis, including, but not limited to, on account of race, ethnicity, gender, religion, national origin, disability, marital status, sexual orientation, age, socioeconomic status, employment, or physical characteristic;

* * *

COMMENT:

Many kinds of illegal conduct reflect adversely on fitness to practice law, such as offenses involving fraud and the offense of willful failure to file.

Louisiana Rule 8.4

[Louisiana has amended Model Rule 8.4 to add the following:]

RULE 8.4 Misconduct

It is professional misconduct for a lawyer to:

* * *

(g) Except upon the expressed assertion of a constitutional privilege, to fail to cooperate with the Committee on Professional Responsibility in its investigation of alleged misconduct.

(h) Present, participate in presenting, or threaten to present criminal charges solely to obtain an advantage in a civil matter.

Minnesota Rule 8.4

[Minnesota, one of the first states to include a prohibition against discriminatory conduct by lawyers, has amended Model Rule 8.4 to add the following:]

RULE 8.4 Misconduct

It is professional misconduct for a lawyer to:

* * *

(g) harass a person on the basis of sex, race, age, creed, religion, color, national origin, disability, sexual preference or marital status in connection with a lawyer's professional activities;

(h) commit a discriminatory act, prohibited by federal, state or local statute or ordinance, that reflects adversely on the lawyer's fitness as a lawyer. Whether a discriminatory act reflects adversely on a lawyer's fitness as a lawyer shall be determined after consideration of all the circumstances, including (1) the seriousness of the act, (2) whether the lawyer knew that it was prohibited by statute or ordinance, (3) whether it was part of a pattern of prohibited conduct, and (4) whether it was committed in connection with the lawyer's professional activities.

COMMENT–1991

* * *

Paragraph (g) specifies a particularly egregious type of discriminatory act—harassment on the basis of sex, race, age, creed, religion, color, national origin, disability, sexual preference, or marital status. What constitutes harassment in this context may be determined with reference to antidiscrimination legislation and case law thereunder. This harass-

251

ment ordinarily involves the active burdening of another, rather than mere passive failure to act properly.

Harassment on the basis of sex, race, age, creed, religion, color, national origin, disability, sexual preference, or marital status may violate either paragraph (g) or paragraph (h). The harassment violates paragraph (g) if the lawyer committed it in connection with the lawyer's professional activities. Harassment, even if not committed in connection with the lawyer's professional activities, violates paragraph (h) if the harassment (1) is prohibited by antidiscrimination legislation and (2) reflects adversely on the lawyer's fitness as a lawyer, determined as specified in paragraph (h).

Paragraph (h) reflects the premise that the concept of human equality lies at the very heart of our legal system. A lawyer whose behavior demonstrates hostility toward or indifference to the policy of equal justice under the law may thereby manifest a lack of character required of members of the legal profession. Therefore, a lawyer's discriminatory act prohibited by statute or ordinance may reflect adversely on his or her fitness as a lawyer even if the unlawful discriminatory act was not committed in connection with the lawyer's professional activities.

Whether an unlawful discriminatory act reflects adversely on fitness as a lawyer is determined after consideration of all relevant circumstances, including the four factors listed in paragraph (h). It is not required that the listed factors be considered equally, nor is the list intended to be exclusive. For example, it would also be relevant that the lawyer reasonably believed that his or her conduct was protected under the state or federal constitution or that the lawyer was acting in a capacity for which the law provides an exemption from civil liability. See, e.g., Minn.Stat. Section 317A.257 (unpaid director or officer of nonprofit organization acting in good faith and not willfully or recklessly).

A lawyer may refuse to comply with an obligation imposed by law upon a good faith belief that no valid obligation exists. The provisions of Rule 1.2(c)(d) concerning a good faith challenge to the validity, scope, meaning or application of the law apply to challenges of legal regulation of the practice of law.

New Jersey Rule 8.4(g)

[New Jersey has modified Model Rule 8.4 to read as follows:]

RULE 8.4 Misconduct

It is professional misconduct for a lawyer to:

   * * *

(g) engage, in a professional capacity, in conduct involving discrimination (except employment discrimination unless resulting in a final agency or judicial determination) because of race,

color, religion, age, sex, sexual orientation, national origin, marital status, socioeconomic status, or handicap, where the conduct is intended or likely to cause harm.

COMMENT BY SUPREME COURT:

This rule amendment (the addition of paragraph g) is intended to make discriminatory conduct unethical when engaged in by lawyers in their professional capacity. It would, for example, cover activities in the court house, such as a lawyer's treatment of court support staff, as well as conduct more directly related to litigation; activities related to practice outside of the court house, whether or not related to litigation, such as treatment of other attorneys and their staff; bar association and similar activities; and activities in the lawyer's office and firm. Except to the extent that they are closely related to the foregoing, purely private activities are not intended to be covered by this rule amendment, although they may possibly constitute a violation of some other ethical rule. Nor is employment discrimination in hiring, firing, promotion, or partnership status intended to be covered unless it has resulted in either an agency or judicial determination of discriminatory conduct. The Supreme Court believes that existing agencies and courts are better able to deal with such matters, that the disciplinary resources required to investigate and prosecute discrimination in the employment area would be disproportionate to the benefits to the system given remedies available elsewhere, and that limiting ethics proceedings in this area to cases where there has been an adjudication represents a practical resolution of conflicting needs.

"Discrimination" is intended to be construed broadly. It includes sexual harassment, derogatory or demeaning language, and, generally, any conduct towards the named groups that is both harmful and discriminatory.

Case law has already suggested both the area covered by this amendment and the possible direction of future cases. *In re Vincenti*, 114 N.J. 275 (554 A.2d 470) (1989). The Court believes the administration of justice would be better served, however, by the adoption of this general rule than by a case by case development of the scope of the professional obligation.

While the origin of this rule was a recommendation of the Supreme Court's Task Force on Women in the Courts, the Court concluded that the protection, limited to women and minorities in that recommendation, should be expanded. The groups covered in the initial proposed amendment to the rule are the same as those named in Canon 3A(4) of the Code of Judicial Conduct.

Following the initial publication of this proposed subsection (g) and receipt of various comments and suggestions, the Court revised the proposed amendment by making explicit its intent to limit the rule to conduct by attorneys in a professional capacity, to exclude employment discrimination unless adjudicated, to restrict the scope to conduct intended or likely to cause harm, and to include discrimination because of sexual orientation or socioeconomic status, these categories having been proposed by the ABA's Standing Committee on Ethics and Professional Responsibility as additions to the groups now covered in Canon 3A(4) of the New Jersey Code of Judicial Conduct. That Committee has also proposed that judges require attorneys, in proceedings before a judge, refrain from manifesting by words or conduct any bias or prejudice based on any of these categories. See proposed Canon 3A(6). This revision to the RPC further reflects the Court's intent to cover all discrimination where the attorney intends to cause harm such as inflicting emotional distress or obtaining a tactical advantage and not to cover instances when no harm is intended unless its occurrence is likely regardless of intent, e.g., where discriminatory comments or behavior is repetitive. While obviously the language of the rule cannot explicitly cover every instance of possible discriminatory conduct, the Court believes that, along with existing case law, it sufficiently narrows the breadth of the rule to avoid any suggestion that it is overly broad. See, e.g., *In re Vincenti,* 114 N.J. 275 (554 A.2d 470) (1989).

District of Columbia Rule 9.1

[The District of Columbia has added the following provision which has no counterpart in the Model Rules]

NONDISCRIMINATION BY MEMBERS OF THE BAR

RULE 9.1   Discrimination in Employment

A lawyer shall not discriminate against any individual in conditions of employment because of the individual's race, color, religion, national origin, sex, age, marital status, sexual orientation, family responsibility, or physical handicap.

COMMENT:

[1]   This provision is modeled after the D.C. Human Rights Act, D.C. Code § 1–2512 (1981), though in some respects more limited in scope. There are also provisions of federal law that contain certain prohibitions on discrimination in employment. The rule is not intended to create ethical obligations that exceed those imposed on a lawyer by applicable law.

    * * *

[3]   The investigation and adjudication of discrimination claims may involve particular expertise of the kind found within the D.C. Office of Human Rights and the federal Equal Employment Opportunity Commission. Such experience may involve, among other things, methods of analysis of statistical data regarding discrimination claims. These agencies also have, in appropriate circumstances, the power to award reme-

dies to the victims of discrimination, such as reinstatement or back pay, which extend beyond the remedies that are available through the disciplinary process. Remedies available through the disciplinary process include such sanctions as disbarment, suspension, censure, and admonition, but do not extend to monetary awards or other remedies that could alter the employment status to take into account the impact of prior acts of discrimination.

[4] If proceedings are pending before other organizations, such as the D.C. Office of Human Rights or the Equal Employment Opportunity Commission, the processing of complaints by Bar Counsel may be deferred or abated where there is substantial similarity between the complaint filed with Bar Counsel and material allegations involved in such other proceedings. See § 19(d) of Rule XI of the Rules Governing the Bar of the District of Columbia.

Appendix:
States That Have Adopted a Version of the Model Rules *

Alabama

Alaska

Arizona

Arkansas

Colorado

Connecticut

Delaware

District of Columbia

Florida

Hawaii

Idaho

Illinois

Indiana

Kansas

Kentucky

Louisiana

Maryland

Massachusetts

Michigan

Minnesota

Mississippi

Missouri

Montana

Nevada

New Hampshire

New Jersey

New Mexico

North Carolina (structure of Rules and Comment but organized under
the Canons of the Model Code)

North Dakota

Oklahoma

* Source: ABA/BNA Manual on Professional Conduct 01:3 (1998) (State Ethics
Rules).

STATE MODIFICATIONS

Pennsylvania
Rhode Island
South Carolina
South Dakota
Texas
Utah
Washington
West Virginia
Wisconsin
Wyoming

*

OTHER SELECTED STATE STANDARDS, RULES, AND STATUTES

Table of Contents

Introduction

This section presents a more in depth perspective on how two states have chosen to regulate lawyers. The California Rules of Professional Conduct for governing lawyers' conduct differ substantially from the ABA codes of ethics. The California approach to regulating lawyer must also consider the legislature's control over lawyers. This form of regulation is contained in the California Business and Professions Code. Selected sections are reproduced below. We include the Disciplinary Rules of the New York Code of Professional Responsibility as an example of a state that continues to retain a code based upon the ABA Model Code of Professional Responsibility. As of the date of publication of this supplement, New York was in the process of revising their Code of Professional Responsibility.

CALIFORNIA RULES OF PROFESSIONAL CONDUCT

Approved by Supreme Court August 13, 1992
Effective September 14, 1992

CHAPTER 1. PROFESSIONAL INTEGRITY IN GENERAL

CHAPTER 2. RELATIONSHIP AMONG MEMBERS

CHAPTER 3. PROFESSIONAL RELATIONSHIP WITH CLIENTS

CHAPTER 4. FINANCIAL RELATIONSHIP WITH CLIENTS

CHAPTER 1. PROFESSIONAL INTEGRITY IN GENERAL

Rule 1–100. Rules of Professional Conduct, in General

(A) Purpose and Function.

The following rules are intended to regulate professional conduct of members of the State Bar through discipline. They have been adopted by the Board of Governors of the State Bar of California and approved by the Supreme Court of California pursuant to Business and Professions Code sections 6076 and 6077 to protect the public and to promote respect and confidence in the legal profession. These rules together with any standards adopted by the Board of Governors pursuant to these rules shall be binding upon all members of the State Bar.

For a willful breach of any of these rules, the Board of Governors has the power to discipline members as provided by law.

The prohibition of certain conduct in these rules is not exclusive. Members are also bound by applicable law including the State Bar Act (Bus. & Prof. Code, § 6000 et seq.) and opinions of California courts. Although not binding, opinions of ethics committees in California should be consulted by members for guidance on proper professional conduct. Ethics opinions and rules and standards promulgated by other jurisdictions and bar associations may also be considered.

These rules are not intended to create new civil causes of action. Nothing in these rules shall be deemed to create, augment, diminish, or eliminate any substantive legal duty of lawyers or the non-disciplinary consequences of violating such a duty.

(B) Definitions.

(1) "Law Firm" means:

    (a) two or more lawyers whose activities constitute the practice of law, and who share its profits, expenses, and liabilities; or

    (b) a law corporation which employs more than one lawyer; or

    (c) a division, department, office, or group within a business entity, which includes more than one lawyer who performs legal services for the business entity; or

    (d) a publicly funded entity which employs more than one lawyer to perform legal services.

(2) "Member" means a member of the State Bar of California.

(3) "Lawyer" means a member of the State Bar of California or a person who is admitted in good standing of and eligible to practice before the bar of any United States court or the highest court of the District of Columbia or any state, territory, or insular possession of the United States or is licensed to practice law is, or is admitted in good standing and is eligible to practice before the bar of the highest court of a foreign country or any political subdivision thereof.

(4) "Associate" means an employee or fellow employee who is employed as a lawyer.

(5) "Shareholder" means a shareholder in a professional corporation pursuant to Business and Professions Code section 6160 et seq.

(C) Purpose of Discussions.

Because it is a practical impossibility to convey in black letter form all of the nuances of these disciplinary rules, the comments contained in the Discussions of the rules, while they do not add independent basis for imposing discipline, are intended to provide guidance for interpreting the rules and practicing in compliance with them.

(D) Geographic Scope of Rules.

    (1) As to members:

        These rules shall govern the activities of members in and outside this state, except as members lawfully practicing outside this state may be specifically required by a jurisdiction in which they are practicing to follow rules of professional conduct different from these rules.

    (2) As to lawyers from other jurisdictions who are not members:

        These rules shall also govern the activities of lawyers while engaged in the performance of lawyer functions in this state; but nothing contained in these rules shall be deemed to authorize the performance of such functions by such persons in this state except as otherwise permitted by law.

(E) These rules may be cited and referred to as "Rules of Professional Conduct of the State Bar of California."

Discussion:

The Rules of Professional Conduct are intended to establish the standards for members for purposes of discipline. (See *Ames v. State Bar* (1973) 8 Cal.3d 910 [106 Cal.Rptr. 489].) The fact that a member has engaged in conduct that may be contrary to these rules does not automatically give rise to a civil cause of action. (See *Noble v. Sears, Roebuck & Co.* (1973) 33 Cal.App.3d 654 [109 Cal.Rptr. 269]; *Wilhelm v. Pray, Price, Williams & Russell* (1986) 186 Cal.App.3d 1324 [231 Cal. Rptr. 355].) These rules are not intended to supercede existing law relating to members in non-disciplinary contexts. (See, e.g., *Klemm v. Superior Court* (1977) 75 Cal.App.3d 893 [142 Cal.Rptr. 509] (motion for disqualification of counsel due to a conflict of interest); *Academy of California Optometrists, Inc. v. Superior Court* (1975) 51 Cal.App.3d 999 [124 Cal.Rptr. 668] (duty to return client files); *Chronometrics, Inc. v. Sysgen, Inc.* (1980) 110 Cal.App.3d 597 [168 Cal.Rptr. 196] (disqualification of member appropriate remedy for improper communication with adverse party).

Law firm, as defined by subparagraph (B)(1), is not intended to include an association of lawyers who do not share profits, expenses, and liabilities. The subparagraph is not intended to imply that a law firm may include a person who is not a member in violation of the law governing the unauthorized practice of law.

Rule 1-110. Disciplinary Authority of the State Bar

A member shall comply with conditions attached to public or private reprovals or other discipline administered by the State Bar pursuant to Business and Professions Code sections 6077 and 6078 and rule 956, California Rules of Court.

Rule 1-120. Assisting, Soliciting, or Inducing Violations

A member shall not knowingly assist in, solicit, or induce any violation of these rules or the State Bar Act.

Rule 1-200. False Statement Regarding Admission to the State Bar

(A) A member shall not knowingly make a false statement regarding a material fact or knowingly fail to disclose a material fact in connection with an application for admission to the State Bar.

(B) A member shall not further an application for admission to the State Bar of a person whom the member knows to be unqualified in respect to character, education, or other relevant attributes.

(C) This rule shall not prevent a member from serving as counsel of record for an applicant for admission to practice in proceedings related to such admission.

Discussion:

For purposes of rule 1–200 "admission" includes readmission.

Rule 1–300.   Unauthorized Practice of Law

(A) A member shall not aid any person or entity in the unauthorized practice of law.

(B) A member shall not practice law in a jurisdiction where to do so would be in violation of regulations of the profession in that jurisdiction.

Rule 1–310.   Forming a Partnership With a Non-lawyer

A member shall not form a partnership with a person who is not a lawyer if any of the activities of that partnership consist of the practice of law.

Discussion:

Rule 1–310 is not intended to govern members' activities which cannot be considered to constitute the practice of law. It is intended solely to preclude a member from being involved in the practice of law with a person who is not lawyer.

Rule 1–311.   Employment of Disbarred, Suspended, Resigned, or Involuntarily Inactive Member

(A) For purposes of this rule:

   (1) "Employ" means to engage the services of another, including employees, agents, independent contractors and consultants, regardless of whether any compensation is paid;
   (2) "Involuntarily inactive member" means a member who is ineligible to practice law as a result of action taken pursuant to Business and Professions Code sections 6007, 6203(c), or California Rule of Court 958(d); and
   (3) "Resigned member" means a member who has resigned from the State Bar while disciplinary charges are pending.

(B) A member shall not employ, associate professionally with, or aid a person the member knows or reasonably should know is a disbarred, suspended, resigned, or involuntarily inactive member to perform the following on behalf of the member's client:

   (1) Render legal consultation or advice to the client;
   (2) Appear on behalf of a client in any hearing or proceeding or before any judicial officer, arbitrator, mediator, court, public agency, referee, magistrate, commissioner, or hearing officer;
   (3) Appear as a representative of the client at a deposition or other discovery matter;
   (4) Negotiate or transact any matter for or on behalf of the client with third parties;

(5) Receive, disburse or otherwise handle the client's funds; or

(6) Engage in activities which constitute the practice of law.

(C) A member may employ, associate professionally with, or aid a disbarred, suspended, resigned, or involuntarily inactive member to perform research, drafting or clerical activities, including but not limited to:

(1) Legal work of a preparatory nature, such as legal research, the assemblage of data and other necessary information, drafting of pleadings, briefs, and other similar documents;

(2) Direct communication with the client or third parties regarding matters such as scheduling, billing, updates, confirmation of receipt or sending of correspondence and messages; or

(3) Accompanying an active member in attending a deposition or other discovery matter for the limited purpose of providing clerical assistance to the active member who will appear as the representative of the client.

(D) Prior to or at the time of employing a person the member knows or reasonably should know is a disbarred, suspended, resigned, or involuntarily inactive member, the member shall serve upon the State Bar written notice of the employment, including a full description of such person's current bar status. The written notice shall also list the activities prohibited in paragraph (B) and state that the disbarred, suspended, resigned, or involuntarily inactive member will not perform such activities. The member shall serve similar written notice upon each client on whose specific matter such person will work, prior to or at the time of employing such person to work on the client's specific matter. The member shall obtain proof of service of the client's written notice and shall retain such proof and a true and correct copy of the client's written notice for two years following termination of the member's employment with the client.

(E) A member may, without client or State Bar notification, employ a disbarred, suspended, resigned or involuntarily inactive member whose sole function is to perform office physical plant or equipment maintenance, courier or delivery services, catering, reception, typing or transcription, or other similar support activities.

(F) Upon termination of the disbarred, suspended, resigned, or involuntarily inactive member, the member shall promptly serve upon the State Bar written notice of the termination.

Discussion

For discussion of the activities that constitute the practice of law, see *Farnham v. State Bar* (1976) 17 Cal.3d 605 [131 Cal.Rptr. 611]; *Bluestein v. State Bar* (1974) 13 Cal.3d 162 [118 Cal.Rptr. 175]; *Baron v. City of Los Angeles* (1970) 2 Cal.3d 535 [86 Cal.Rptr. 673]; *Crawford v.*

State Bar (1960) 54 Cal.2d 659 [7 Cal.Rptr. 746]; *People v. Merchants Protective Corporation* (1922) 189 Cal. 531, 535 [209 P. 363]; *People v. Landlords Professional Services* (1989) 215 Cal.App.3d 1599 [264 Cal. Rptr. 548]; and *People v. Sipper* (1943) 61 Cal.App.2d Supp. 844 [142 P.2d 960].)

Paragraph (D) is not intended to prevent or discourage a member from fully discussing with the client the activities that will be performed by the disbarred, suspended, resigned, or involuntarily inactive member on the client's matter. If a member's client is an organization, then the written notice required by paragraph (D) shall be served upon the highest authorized officer, employee, or constituent overseeing the particular engagement. (See rule 3–600.)

Nothing in rule 1–311 shall be deemed to limit or preclude any activity engaged in pursuant to rules 983, 983.1, 983.2, and 988 of the California Rules of Court, or any local rule of a federal district court concerning admission pro hac vice.

Rule 1–320. Financial Arrangements With Non-lawyers

(A) Neither a member nor a law firm shall directly or indirectly share legal fees with a person who is not a lawyer, except that:

   (1) An agreement between a member and a law firm, partner, or associate may provide for the payment of money after the member's death to the member's estate or to one or more specified persons over a reasonable period of time; or

   (2) A member or law firm undertaking to complete unfinished legal business of a deceased member may pay to the estate of the deceased member or other person legally entitled thereto that proportion of the total compensation which fairly represents the services rendered by the deceased member;

   (3) A member or law firm may include non-member employees in a compensation, profit-sharing, or retirement plan even though the plan is based in whole or in part on a profit-sharing arrangement, if such plan does not circumvent these rules or Business and Professions Code section 6000 et seq.; or

   (4) A member may pay a prescribed registration, referral, or participation fee to a lawyer referral service established, sponsored, and operated in accordance with the State Bar of California's Minimum Standards for a Lawyer Referral Service in California.

(B) A member shall not compensate, give, or promise anything of value to any person or entity for the purpose of recommending or securing employment of the member or the member's law firm by a client, or as a reward for having made a recommendation resulting in employment of the member or the member's law firm by a client. A member's offering of or giving a gift or gratuity to any person or entity having made a recommendation resulting in the employment of the member or the member's law firm shall not of itself violate this rule, provided that the gift or gratuity was not offered or given in consideration of any promise, agreement, or understanding that such a gift or gratuity would be forthcoming or that referrals would be made or encouraged in the future.

(C) A member shall not compensate, give, or promise anything of value to any representative of the press, radio, television, or other communication medium in anticipation of or in return for publicity of the member, the law firm, or any other member as such in a news item, but the incidental provision of food or beverage shall not of itself violate this rule.

Discussion:

Rule 1-320(C) is not intended to preclude compensation to the communications media in exchange for advertising the member's or law firm's availability for professional employment.

Rule 1-400. Advertising and Solicitation

(A) For purposes of this rule, "communication" means any message or offer made by or on behalf of a member concerning the availability for professional employment of a member or a law firm directed to any former, present, or prospective client, including but not limited to the following:

    (1) Any use of firm name, trade name, fictitious name, or other professional designation of such member or law firm; or

    (2) Any stationery, letterhead, business card, sign, brochure, or other comparable written material describing such member, law firm, or lawyers; or

    (3) Any advertisement (regardless of medium) of such member or law firm directed to the general public or any substantial portion thereof; or

    (4) Any unsolicited correspondence from a member or law firm directed to any person or entity.

(B) For purposes of this rule, a "solicitation" means any communication:

    (1) Concerning the availability for professional employment of a member or a law firm in which a significant motive is pecuniary gain; and

    (2) Which is;

        (a) delivered in person or by telephone, or

        (b) directed by any means to a person known to the sender to be represented by counsel in a matter which is a subject of the communication.

(C) A solicitation shall not be made by or on behalf of a member or law firm to a prospective client with whom the member or law firm has no family or prior professional relationship, unless the solicitation is protected from abridgment by the Constitution of the United States or by the Constitution of the State of California. A solicitation to a former or present client in the discharge of a member's or law firm's professional duties is not prohibited.

(D) A communication or a solicitation (as defined herein) shall not:

(1) Contain any untrue statement; or

(2) Contain any matter, or present or arrange any matter in a manner or format which is false, deceptive, or which tends to confuse, deceive, or mislead the public; or

(3) Omit to state any fact necessary to make the statements made, in the light of circumstances under which they are made, not misleading to the public; or

(4) Fail to indicate clearly, expressly, or by context, that it is a communication or solicitation, as the case may be; or

(5) Be transmitted in any manner which involves intrusion, coercion, duress, compulsion, intimidation, threats, or vexatious or harassing conduct.

(6) State that a member is a "certified specialist" unless the member holds a current certificate as a specialist issued by the Board of Legal Specialization, or any other entity accredited by the State Bar to designate specialists pursuant to standards adopted by the Board of Governors, and states the complete name of the entity which granted certification.

(E) The Board of Governors of the State Bar shall formulate and adopt standards as to communications which will be presumed to violate this rule 1–400. The standards shall only be used as presumptions affecting the burden of proof in disciplinary proceedings involving alleged violations of these rules. "Presumption affecting the burden of proof" means that presumption defined in Evidence Code sections 605 and 606. Such standards formulated and adopted by the Board, as from time to time amended, shall be effective and binding on all members.

(F) A member shall retain for two years a true and correct copy or recording of any communication made by written or electronic media. Upon written request, the member shall make any such copy or recording available to the State Bar, and, if requested, shall provide to the State Bar evidence to support any factual or objective claim contained in the communication.

Standards:

Pursuant to Rule 1–400(E) the Board of Governors of the State Bar has adopted the following standards effective May 27, 1989 as forms of "communication" defined in rule 1–400(A) which are presumed to be in violation of Rule 1–400:

(1) A "communication" which contains guarantees, warranties, or predictions regarding the result of the representation.

(2) A "communication" which contains testimonials about or endorsements of a member unless such communication also contains an express disclaimer such as "this testimonial or endorse-

ment does not constitute a guarantee, warranty, or prediction regarding the outcome of your legal matter."

(3) A "communication" which is delivered to a potential client whom the member knows or should reasonably know is in such a physical, emotional, or mental state that he or she would not be expected to exercise reasonable judgment as to the retention of counsel.

(4) A "communication" which is transmitted at the scene of an accident or at or en route to a hospital, emergency care center, or other health care facility.

(5) A "communication," except professional announcements, seeking professional employment for pecuniary gain, which is transmitted by mail or equivalent means which does not bear the word "Advertisement," "Newsletter" or words of similar import in 12 point print on the first page. If such communication, including firm brochures, newsletters, recent legal development advisories, and similar materials, is transmitted in an envelope, the envelope shall bear the word "Advertisement," "Newsletter" or words of similar import on the outside thereof.*

(6) A "communication" in the form of a firm name, trade name, fictitious name, or other professional designation which states or implies a relationship between any member in private practice and a government agency or instrumentality or a public or non-profit legal services organization.

(7) A "communication" in the form of a firm name, trade name, fictitious name, or other professional designation which states or implies that a member has a relationship to any other lawyer or a law firm as a partner or associate, or officer or shareholder pursuant to Business and Professions Code sections 6160–6172 unless such relationship in fact exists.

(8) A "communication" which states or implies that a member or law firm is "of counsel" to another lawyer or a law firm unless the former has a relationship with the latter (other than as a partner or associate, or officer or shareholder pursuant to Business and Professions Code sections 6160–6172) which is close, personal, continuous, and regular.

(9) A "communication" in the form of a firm name, trade name, fictitious name, or other professional designation used by a member or law firm in private practice which differs materially from any other such designation used by such member or law firm at the same time in the same community.

(10) A "communication" which implies that the member or law firm is participating in a lawyer referral service which has been certified by the State Bar of California or as having satisfied the Minimum Standards for Lawyer Referral Services in California, when that is not the case.

* Amended, effective May 11, 1994.

(11) [Repealed eff. June 1, 1997.] A "communication" which states or implies that a member is a "certified specialist" unless such communication also states the complete name of the entity which granted the certification as a specialist.

(12) A "communication," except professional announcements, in the form of an advertisement primarily directed to seeking professional employment primarily for pecuniary gain transmitted to the general public or any substantial portion thereof by mail or equivalent means or by means of television, radio, newspaper, magazine or other form of commercial mass media which does not state the name of the member responsible for the communication. When the communication is made on behalf of a law firm, the communication shall state the name of at least one member responsible for it.**

(13) A "communication" which contains a dramatization unless such communication contains a disclaimer which states "this is a dramatization" or words of similar import.*

(14) A "communication" which states or implies "no fee without recovery" unless such communication also expressly discloses whether or not the client will be liable for costs.*

(15) A "communication" which states or implies that a member is able to provide legal services in a language other than English unless the member can actually provide legal services in such language or the communication also states in the language of the communication (a) the employment title of the person who speaks such language and (b) that the person is not a member of the State Bar of California, if that is the case.*

(16) An unsolicited "communication" transmitted to the general public or any substantial portion thereof primarily directed to seeking professional employment primarily for pecuniary gain which sets forth a specific fee or range of fees for a particular service where, in fact, the member charges a greater fee than advertised in such communication within a period of 90 days following dissemination of such communication, unless such communication expressly specifies a shorter period of time regarding the advertised fee. Where the communication is published in the classified or "yellow pages" section of telephone, business or legal directories or in other media not published more frequently than once a year, the member shall conform to the advertised fee for a period of one year from initial publication, unless such communication expressly specifies a shorter period of time regarding the advertised fee.*

Rule 1-500. Agreements Restricting a Member's Practice

(A) A member shall not be a party to or participate in offering or making an agreement, whether in connection with the settlement of a lawsuit or otherwise, if the agreement restricts the right of a

** Added, effective May 11, 1994.

member to practice law, except that this rule shall not prohibit such an agreement which:

(1) Is a part of an employment, shareholders' or partnership agreement among members provided the restrictive agreement does not survive the termination of the employment, shareholder, or partnership relationship; or

(2) Requires payments to a member upon the member's retirement from the practice of law.

(3) Is authorized by Business and Professions Code Sections 6092.5, subdivision (i) on 6093.

(B) A member shall not be a party to or participate in offering or making an agreement which precludes the reporting of a violation of these rules.

Discussion:

Paragraph (A) makes it clear that the practice, in connection with settlement agreements, of proposing that a member refrain from representing other clients in similar litigation, is prohibited. Neither counsel may demand or suggest such provisions nor may opposing counsel accede or agree to such provisions.

Paragraph (A) permits a restrictive covenant in a law corporation, partnership, or employment agreement. The law corporation shareholder, partner, or associate may agree not to have a separate practice during the existence of the relationship; however, upon termination of the relationship (whether voluntary or involuntary), the member is free to practice law without any contractual restriction except in the case of retirement from the active practice of law.

Rule 1-600. Legal Service Programs

(A) A member shall not participate in a nongovernmental program activity, or organization furnishing, recommending, or paying for legal services, which allows any third person or organization to interfere with the member's independence of professional judgment, or with the client-lawyer relationship, or allows unlicensed persons to practice law, or allows any third person or organization to receive directly or indirectly any part of the consideration paid to the member except as permitted by these rules, or otherwise violates the State Bar Act or these rules.

(B) The Board of Governors of the State Bar shall formulate and adopt Minimum Standards for Lawyer Referral Services, which, as from time to time amended, shall be binding on members.

Discussion:

The participation of a member in a lawyer referral service established, sponsored, supervised, and operated in conformity with the

Minimum Standards for a Lawyer Referral Service in California is encouraged and is not, of itself, a violation of these rules.

Rule 1–600 is not intended to override any contractual agreement or relationship between insurers and insureds regarding the provision of legal services.

Rule 1–600 is not intended to apply to the activities of a public agency responsible for providing legal services to a government or to the public.

For purposes of paragraph (A), "a nongovernmental program, activity, or organization" includes, but is not limited to group, prepaid, and voluntary legal service programs, activities, or organizations.

Rule 1–700.   Member as Candidate for Judicial Office

(A) A member who is a candidate for judicial office in California shall comply with Canon 5 of the Code of Judicial Ethics.

(B) For purposes of this rule, "candidate for judicial office" means a member seeking judicial office by election. The determination of when a member is a candidate for judicial office is defined in the terminology section of the California Code of Judicial Ethics. A member's duty to comply with paragraph (A) shall end when the member announces withdrawal of the member's candidacy or when the results of the election are final, whichever occurs first.

Discussion

Nothing in rule 1–700 shall be deemed to limit the applicability of any rule or law.

(Approved by order of the Supreme Court, effective November 21, 1967.)

CHAPTER 2.   RELATIONSHIP AMONG MEMBERS

Rule 2–100.   Communication With a Represented Party

(A) While representing a client, a member shall not communicate directly or indirectly about the subject of the representation with a party the member knows to be represented by another lawyer in the matter, unless the member has the consent of the other lawyer.

(B) For purposes of this rule, a "party" includes:

   (1) An officer, director, or managing agent of a corporation or association, and a partner or managing agent of a partnership; or

   (2) An association member or an employee of an association, corporation, or partnership, if the subject of the communication is any act or omission of such person in connection with the matter which may be binding upon or imputed to the organization for purposes of civil or criminal liability or whose statement may constitute an admission on the part of the organization.

(C) This rule shall not prohibit:

(1) Communications with a public officer, board, committee, or body;

(2) Communications initiated by a party seeking advice or representation from an independent lawyer of the party's choice; or

(3) Communications otherwise authorized by law.

Discussion:

Rule 2–100 is intended to control communications between a member and persons the member knows to be represented by counsel unless a statutory scheme or case law will override the rule. There are a number of express statutory schemes which authorize communications between a member and person who would otherwise be subject to this rule. These statutes protect a variety of other rights such as the right of employees to organize and to engage in collective bargaining, employee health and safety, or equal employment opportunity. Other applicable law also includes the authority of government prosecutors and investigators to conduct criminal investigations, as limited by the relevant decisional law.

Rule 2–100 is not intended to prevent the parties themselves from communicating with respect to the subject matter of the representation, and nothing in the rule prevents a member from advising the client that such communication can be made. Moreover, the rule does not prohibit a member who is also a party to a legal matter from directly or indirectly communicating on his or her own behalf with a represented party. Such a member has independent rights as a party which should not be abrogated because of his or her professional status. To prevent any possible abuse in such situations, the counsel for the opposing party may advise that party (1) about the risks and benefits of communications with a lawyer-party, and (2) not to accept or engage in communications with the lawyer-party.

Rule 2–100 also addresses the situation in which member A is contacted by an opposing party who is represented and, because of dissatisfaction with that party's counsel, seeks A's independent advice. Since A is employed by the opposition, the member cannot give independent advice.

As used in paragraph (A), "the subject of the representation," "matter," and "party" are not limited to a litigation context.

Paragraph (B) is intended to apply only to persons employed at the time of the communication. See *Triple A Machine Shop, Inc. v. State of California* (1989) 213 Cal.App.3d 131 [261 Cal.Rptr. 493].

Subparagraph (C)(2) is intended to permit a member to communicate with a party seeking to hire new counsel or to obtain a second opinion. A member contacted by such a party continues to be bound by other Rules of Professional Conduct. (See, e.g., rules 1–400 and 3–310.)

273

Rule 2–200.   Financial Arrangements Among Lawyers

(A) A member shall not divide a fee for legal services with a lawyer who is not a partner of, associate of, or shareholder with the member unless:

    (1) The client has consented in writing thereto after a full disclosure has been made in writing that a division of fees will be made and the terms of such division; and

    (2) The total fee charged by all lawyers is not increased solely by reason of the provision for division of fees and is not unconscionable as that term is defined in rule 4–200.

(B) Except as permitted in paragraph (A) of this rule or rule 2–300, a member shall not compensate, give, or promise anything of value to any lawyer for the purpose of recommending or securing employment of the member or the member's law firm by a client, or as a reward for having made a recommendation resulting in employment of the member or the member's law firm by a client. A member's offering of or giving a gift or gratuity to any lawyer who has made a recommendation resulting in the employment of the member or the member's law firm shall not of itself violate this rule, provided that the gift or gratuity was not offered in consideration of any promise, agreement, or understanding that such a gift or gratuity would be forthcoming or that referrals would be made or encouraged in the future.

Rule 2–300.   Sale or Purchase of a Law Practice of a Member, Living or Deceased

All or substantially all of the law practice of a member, living or deceased, including goodwill, may be sold to another member or law firm subject to all the following conditions:

(A) Fees charged to clients shall not be increased solely by reason of such sale.

(B) If the sale contemplates the transfer of responsibility for work not yet completed or responsibility for client files or information protected by Business and Professions Code section 6068, subdivision (e), then;

    (1) if the seller is deceased, has a conservator or other person acting in a representative capacity, and no member has been appointed to act for the seller pursuant to Business and Professions Code section 6180.5, then prior to the transfer;

        (a) the purchaser shall cause a written notice to be given to the client stating that the interest in the law practice is being transferred to the purchaser; that the client has the right to retain other counsel; that the client may take possession of any client papers and property, as required by rule 3–700(D); and that if no response is received to the notification within 90 days of the sending of such notice, or in the event the client's rights would be prejudiced by a failure to act during that time, the purchaser may act on behalf of the client until otherwise notified by the client. Such notice shall comply with the requirements as set forth in rule 1–400(D) and any provisions relating to attorney-client fee arrangements, and

(b) the purchaser shall obtain the written consent of the client provided that such consent shall be presumed until otherwise notified by the client if no response is received to the notification specified in subparagraph (a) within 90 days of the date of the sending of such notification to the client's last address as shown on the records of the seller, or the client's rights would be prejudiced by a failure to act during during such 90-day period.

(2) in all other circumstances, not less than 90 days prior to the transfer;

(a) the seller, or the member appointed to act for the seller pursuant to Business and Professions Code section 6180.5 shall cause a written notice to be given to the client stating that the interest in the law practice is being transferred to the purchaser; that the client has the right to retain other counsel; that the client may take possession of any client papers and property, as required by rule 3–700(D); and that if no response is received to the notification within 90 days of the sending of such notice, the purchaser may act on behalf of the client until otherwise notified by the client. Such notice shall comply with the requirements as set forth in rule 1–400(D) and any provisions relating to attorney-client fee arrangements, and

(b) the seller, or the member appointed to act for the seller pursuant to Business and Professions Code section 6180.5 shall obtain the written consent of the client prior to the transfer provided that such consent shall be presumed until otherwise notified by the client if no response is received to the notification specified in subparagraph (a) within 90 days of the date of the sending of such notification to the client's last address as shown on the records of the seller.

(C) If substitution is required by the rules of a tribunal in which a matter is pending, all steps necessary to substitute a member shall be taken.

(D) All activity of a purchaser or potential purchaser under this rule shall be subject to compliance with rules 3–300 and 3–310 where applicable.

(E) Confidential information shall not be disclosed to a nonmember in connection with a sale under this rule.

(F) Admission to or retirement from a law partnership or law corporation, retirement plans and similar arrangements, or sale of tangible assets of a law practice shall not be deemed a sale or purchase under this rule.

Discussion:

Paragraph (A) is intended to prohibit the purchaser from charging the former clients of the seller a higher fee than the purchaser is charging his or her existing clients.

"All or substantially all of the law practice of a member" means, for purposes of rule 2–300, that, for example, a member may retain one or two clients who have such a longstanding personal and professional relationship with the member that transfer of those clients' files is not feasible. Conversely, rule 2–300 is not intended to authorize the sale of a law practice in a piecemeal fashion except as may be required by subparagraph (B)(1)(a) or paragraph (D).

Transfer of individual client matters, where permitted, is governed by rule 2–200. Payment of a fee to a non-lawyer broker for arranging the sale or purchase of a law practice is governed by rule 1–320.

Rule 2–400. Prohibited Discriminatory Conduct in a Law Practice

(A) For purposes of this rule:

    (1) "law practice" includes sole practices, law partnerships, law corporations, corporate and governmental legal departments, and other entities which employ members to practice law;

    (2) "knowingly permit" means a failure to advocate corrective action where the member knows of a discriminatory policy or practice which results in the unlawful discrimination prohibited in paragraph (B); and

    (3) "unlawfully" and "unlawful" shall be determined by reference to applicable state or federal statutes or decisions making unlawful discrimination in employment and in offering goods and services to the public.

(B) In the management or operation of a law practice, a member shall not unlawfully discriminate or knowingly permit unlawful discrimination on the basis of race, national origin, sex, sexual orientation, religion, age or disability in:

    (1) hiring, promoting, discharging or otherwise determining the conditions of employment of any person; or

    (2) accepting or terminating representation of any client.

(C) No disciplinary investigation or proceeding may be initiated by the State Bar against a member under this rule unless and until a tribunal of competent jurisdiction, other than a disciplinary tribunal, shall have first adjudicated a complaint of alleged discrimination and found that unlawful conduct occurred. Upon such adjudication, the tribunal finding or verdict shall then be admissible evidence of the occurrence or non-occurrence of the alleged discrimination in any disciplinary proceeding initiated under this rule. In order for discipline to be imposed under this rule, however, the finding of unlawfulness must be upheld and final after appeal, the time for filing an appeal must have expired, or the appeal must have been dismissed.

Discussion:

In order for discriminatory conduct to be actionable under this rule, it must first be found to be unlawful by an appropriate civil administrative or judicial tribunal under applicable state or federal law. Until there is a finding of civil unlawfulness, there is no basis for disciplinary action under this rule.

A complaint of misconduct based on this rule may be filed with the State Bar following a finding of unlawfulness in the first instance even though that finding is thereafter appealed.

A disciplinary investigation or proceeding for conduct coming within this rule may be initiated and maintained, however, if such conduct warrants discipline under California Business and Professions Code sections 6106 and 6068, the California Supreme Court's inherent authority to impose discipline, or other disciplinary standard.

Adopted, eff. March 1, 1994.

CHAPTER 3. PROFESSIONAL RELATIONSHIP WITH CLIENTS

Rule 3–110. Failing to Act Competently

(A) A member shall not intentionally, recklessly, or repeatedly fail to perform legal services with competence.

(B) For purposes of this rule, "competence" in any legal service shall mean to apply the 1) diligence, 2) learning and skill, and 3) mental, emotional, and physical ability reasonably necessary for the performance of such service.

(C) If a member does not have sufficient learning and skill when the legal service is undertaken, the member may nonetheless perform such services competently by 1) associating with or, where appropriate, professionally consulting another lawyer reasonably believed to be competent, or 2) by acquiring sufficient learning and skill before performance is required.

Discussion:

The duties set forth in rule 3–110 include the duty to supervise the work of subordinate attorney and non-attorney employees or agents. (See, e.g., *Waysman v. State Bar* (1986) 41 Cal.3d 452; *Trousil v. State Bar* (1985) 38 Cal.3d 337, 342 [211 Cal.Rptr. 525]; *Palomo v. State Bar* (1984) 36 Cal.3d 785 [205 Cal.Rptr. 834]; *Crane v. State Bar* (1981) 30

Cal.3d 117, 122; *Black v. State Bar* (1972) 7 Cal.3d 676, 692 [103 Cal.Rptr. 288; 499 P.2d 968]; *Vaughn v. State Bar* (1972) 6 Cal.3d 847, 857–858 [100 Cal.Rptr. 713; 494 P.2d 1257]; *Moore v. State Bar* (1964) 62 Cal.2d 74, 81 [41 Cal.Rptr. 161; 396 P.2d 577].)

In an emergency a lawyer may give advice or assistance in a matter in which the lawyer does not have the skill ordinarily required where referral to or consultation with another lawyer would be impractical. Even in an emergency, however, assistance should be limited to that reasonably necessary in the circumstances.

Rule 3–120. Sexual Relations With Client

(A) For purposes of this rule, "sexual relations" means sexual intercourse or the touching of an intimate part of another person for the purpose of sexual arousal, gratification, or abuse.

(B) A member shall not:

   (1) Require or demand sexual relations with a client incident to or as a condition of any professional representation; or

   (2) Employ coercion, intimidation, or undue influence in entering into sexual relations with a client; or

   (3) Continue representation of a client with whom the member has sexual relations if such sexual relations cause the member to perform legal services incompetently in violation of rule 3–110.

(C) Paragraph (B) shall not apply to sexual relations between members and their spouses or to ongoing consensual sexual relationships which predate the initiation of the lawyer-client relationship.

(D) Where a lawyer in a firm has sexual relations with a client but does not participate in the representation of that client, the lawyers in the firm shall not be subject to discipline under this rule solely because of the occurrence of such sexual relations.

Discussion:

Rule 3–120 is intended to prohibit sexual exploitation by a lawyer in the course of a professional representation. Often, based upon the nature of the underlying representation, a client exhibits great emotional vulnerability and dependence upon the advice and guidance of counsel. Attorneys owe the utmost duty of good faith and fidelity to clients. (See, e.g., Greenbaum v. State Bar (1976) 15 Cal.3d 893, 903 [126 Cal.Rptr. 785]; Alkow v. State Bar (1971) 3 Cal.3d 924, 935 [92 Cal.Rptr. 279]; Cutler v. State Bar (1969) 71 Cal.2d 241, 251 [78 Cal.Rptr. 172]; Clancy v. State Bar (1969) 71 Cal.2d 140, 146 [77 Cal.Rptr. 657].) The relationship between an attorney and client is a fiduciary relationship of the very highest character and all dealings between an attorney and client that are beneficial to the attorney will be closely scrutinized with the utmost strictness for unfairness. (See, e.g., Giovanazzi v. State Bar (1980) 28 Cal.3d 465, 472 [169 Cal.Rptr. 581]; Benson v. State Bar

(1975) 13 Cal.3d 581, 586 [119 Cal.Rptr. 297]; Lee v. State Bar (1970) 2 Cal.3d 927, 939 [88 Cal.Rptr. 361]; Clancy v. State Bar (1969) 71 Cal.2d 140, 146 [77 Cal.Rptr. 657].) Where attorneys exercise undue influence over clients or take unfair advantage of clients, discipline is appropriate. (See, e.g., Magee v. State Bar (1962) 58 Cal.2d 423 [24 Cal.Rptr. 839]; Lantz v. State Bar (1931) 212 Cal. 213 [298 P. 497].) In all client matters, a member is advised to keep clients' interests paramount in the course of the member's representation.

For purposes of this rule, if the client is an organization, any individual overseeing the representation shall be deemed to be the client. (See rule 3–600.)

Although paragraph (C) excludes representation of certain clients from the scope of rule 3–120, such exclusion is not intended to preclude the applicability of other Rules of Professional Conduct, including rule 3–110.

Rule 3–200. Prohibited Objectives of Employment

A member shall not seek, accept, or continue employment if the member knows or should know that the objective of such employment is:

(A) To bring an action, conduct a defense, assert a position in litigation, or take an appeal, without probable cause and for the purpose of harassing or maliciously injuring any person; or

(B) To present a claim or defense in litigation that is not warranted under existing law, unless it can be supported by a good faith argument for an extension, modification, or reversal of such existing law.

Rule 3–210. Advising the Violation of Law

A member shall not advise the violation of any law, rule, or ruling of a tribunal unless the member believes in good faith that such law, rule, or ruling is invalid. A member may take appropriate steps in good faith to test the validity of any law, rule, or ruling of a tribunal.

Discussion:

Rule 3–210 is intended to apply not only to the prospective conduct of a client but also to the interaction between the member and client and to the specific legal service sought by the client from the member. An example of the former is the handling of physical evidence of a crime in the possession of the client and offered to the member. (See *People v. Meredith* (1981) 29 Cal.3d 682 [175 Cal.Rptr. 612].) An example of the latter is a request that the member negotiate the return of stolen property in exchange for the owner's agreement not to report the theft to the police or prosecutorial authorities. (See *People v. Pic'l* (1982) 31 Cal.3d 731 [183 Cal.Rptr. 685].)

Rule 3–300. Avoiding Interests Adverse to a Client

A member shall not enter into a business transaction with a client; or knowingly acquire an ownership, possessory, security, or other pecuniary interest adverse to a client, unless each of the following requirements has been satisfied:

(A) The transaction or acquisition and its terms are fair and reasonable to the client and are fully disclosed and transmitted in writing to the client in a manner which should reasonably have been understood by the client; and

(B) The client is advised in writing that the client may seek the advice of an independent lawyer of the client's choice and is given a reasonable opportunity to seek that advice; and

(C) The client thereafter consents in writing to the terms of the transaction or the terms of the acquisition.

Discussion:

Rule 3–300 is not intended to apply to the agreement by which the member is retained by the client, unless the agreement confers on the member an ownership, possessory, security, or other pecuniary interest adverse to the client. Such an agreement is governed, in part, by rule 4–200.

Rule 3–300 is not intended to apply where the member and client each make an investment on terms offered to the general public or a significant portion thereof. For example, rule 3–300 is not intended to apply where A, a member, invests in a limited partnership syndicated by a third party. B, A's client, makes the same investment. Although A and B are each investing in the same business, A did not enter into the transaction "with" B for the purposes of the rule.

Rule 3–300 is intended to apply where the member wishes to obtain an interest in client's property in order to secure the amount of the member's past due or future fees.

Rule 3–310. Avoiding the Representation of Adverse Interests

(A) For purposes of this rule:

    (1) "Disclosure" means informing the client or former client of the relevant circumstances and of the actual and reasonably foreseeable adverse consequences to the client or former client;

    (2) "Informed written consent" means the client's or former client's written agreement to the representation following written disclosure;

    (3) "Written" means any writing as defined in Evidence Code section 250.

(B) A member shall not accept or continue representation of a client without providing written disclosure to the client where:

    (1) The member has a legal, business, financial, professional, or personal relationship with a party or witness in the same matter; or

(2) The member knows or reasonably should know that:

    (a) the member previously had a legal, business, financial, professional, or personal relationship with a party or witness in the same matter; and

    (b) the previous relationship would substantially affect the member's representation; or

(3) The member has or had a legal, business, financial, professional, or personal relationship with another person or entity the member knows or reasonably should know would be affected substantially by resolution of the matter; or

(4) The member has or had a legal, business, financial, or professional interest in the subject matter of the representation.

(C) A member shall not, without the informed written consent of each client:

    (1) Accept representation of more than one client in a matter in which the interests of the clients potentially conflict; or

    (2) Accept or continue, representation of more than one client in a matter in which the interests of the clients actually conflict; or

    (3) Represent a client in a matter and at the same time in a separate matter accept as a client a person or entity whose interest in the first matter is adverse to the client in the first matter.

(D) A member who represents two or more clients shall not enter into an aggregate settlement of the claims of or against the clients without the informed written consent of each client.

(E) A member shall not, without the informed written consent of the client or former client, accept employment adverse to the client or former client where, by reason of the representation of the client or former client, the member has obtained confidential information material to the employment.

(F) A member shall not accept compensation for representing a client from one other than the client unless:

    (1) There is no interference with the member's independence of professional judgment or with the client-lawyer relationship; and

    (2) Information relating to representation of the client is protected as required by Business and Professions Code section 6068, subdivision (e); and

    (3) The member obtains the client's informed written consent, provided that no disclosure or consent is required if:

        (a) such nondisclosure is otherwise authorized by law; or

        (b) the member is rendering legal services on behalf of any public agency which provides legal services to other public agencies or the public.

Discussion:

    Rule 3–310 is not intended to prohibit a member from representing parties having antagonistic positions on the same legal question that has arisen in different cases, unless representation of either client would be adversely affected.

Other rules and laws may preclude making adequate disclosure under this rule. If such disclosure is precluded, informed written consent is likewise precluded. (See, e.g., Business and Professions Code section 6068, subsection (e).)

Paragraph (B) is not intended to apply to the relationship of a member to another party's lawyer. Such relationships are governed by rule 3–320.

Paragraph (B) is not intended to require either the disclosure of the new engagement to a former client or the consent of the former client to the new engagement. However, such disclosure or consent is required if paragraph (E) applies.

While paragraph (B) deals with the issues of adequate disclosure to the present client or clients of the member's present or past relationships to other parties or witnesses or present interest in the subject matter of the representation, paragraph (E) is intended to protect the confidences of another present or former client. These two paragraphs are to apply as complementary provisions.

Paragraph (B) is intended to apply only to a member's own relationships or interests, unless the member knows that a partner or associate in the same firm as the member has or had a relationship with another party or witness or has or had an interest in the subject matter of the representation.

Subparagraphs (C)(1) and (C)(2) are intended to apply to all types of legal employment, including the concurrent representation of multiple parties in litigation or in a single transaction or in some other common enterprise or legal relationship. Examples of the latter include the formation of a partnership for several partners or a corporation for several shareholders, the preparation of an ante-nuptial agreement, or joint or reciprocal wills for a husband and wife, or the resolution of an "uncontested" marital dissolution. In such situations, for the sake of convenience or economy, the parties may well prefer to employ a single counsel, but a member must disclose the potential adverse aspects of such multiple representation (e.g., Evid.Code, § 962) and must obtain the informed written consent of the clients thereto pursuant to subparagraph (C)(1). Moreover, if the potential adversity should become actual, the member must obtain the further informed written consent of the clients pursuant to subparagraph (C)(2).

Subparagraph (C)(3) is intended to apply to representations of clients in both litigation and transactional matters.

There are some matters in which the conflicts are such that written consent may not suffice for non-disciplinary purposes. (See Woods v. Superior Court (1983) 149 Cal.App.3d 931 [197 Cal.Rptr. 185]; Klemm v. Superior Court (1977) 75 Cal.App.3d 893 [142 Cal.Rptr. 509]; Ishmael v. Millington (1966) 241 Cal.App.2d 520 [50 Cal.Rptr. 592].)

Paragraph (D) is not intended to apply to class action settlements subject to court approval.

Paragraph (F) is not intended to abrogate existing relationships between insurers and insureds whereby the insurer has the contractual right to unilaterally select counsel for the insured, where there is no conflict of interest. (See San Diego Navy Federal Credit Union v. Cumis Insurance Society (1984) 162 Cal.App.3d 358 [208 Cal.Rptr. 494].)

Rule 3–320. Relationship With Other Party's Lawyer

A member shall not represent a client in a matter in which another party's lawyer is a spouse, parent, child, or sibling of the member, lives with the member, is a client of the member, or has an intimate personal relationship with the member, unless the member informs the client in writing of the relationship.

Discussion:

Rule 3–320 is not intended to apply to circumstances in which a member fails to advise the client of a relationship with another lawyer who is merely a partner or associate in the same law firm as the adverse party's counsel, and who has no direct involvement in the matter.

Rule 3–400. Limiting Liability to Client

A member shall not:
(A) Contract with a client prospectively limiting the member's liability to the client for the member's professional malpractice; or
(B) Settle a claim or potential claim for the member's liability to the client for the member's professional malpractice unless the client is informed in writing that the client may seek the advice of an independent lawyer of the client's choice regarding the settlement and is given a reasonable opportunity to seek that advice.

Discussion:

Rule 3–400 is not intended to apply to customary qualifications and limitations in legal opinions and memoranda, nor is it intended to prevent a member from reasonably limiting the scope of the member's employment or representation.

Rule 3–500. Communication

A member shall keep a client reasonably informed about significant developments relating to the employment or representation, including promptly complying with reasonable requests for information and copies of significant documents when necessary to keep the client so informed.

Discussion:

Rule 3–500 is not intended to change a member's duties to his or her clients. It is intended to make clear that, while a client must be informed of significant developments in the matter, a member will not be disciplined for failing to communicate insignificant or irrelevant information. (See Bus. & Prof.Code, § 6068, subd. (m).)

A member may contract with the client in their employment agreement that the client assumes responsibility for the cost of copying significant documents. This rule is not intended to prohibit a claim for the recovery of the member's expense in any subsequent legal proceeding.

Rule 3-500 is not intended to create. augment, diminish, or eliminate any application of the work product rule. The obligation of the member to provide work product to the client shall be governed by relevant statutory and decisional law. Additionally, this rule is not intended to apply any document or correspondence that is subject to a protective order or non-disclosure agreement, or to override applicable statutory or decisional law requiring that certain information not be provided to criminal defendants who are clients of the member.
(Amended by order of the Supreme Court, operative June 5, 1997.)

Rule 3-510. Communication of Settlement Offer

(A) A member shall promptly communicate to the member's client:

    (1) All terms and conditions of any offer made to the client in a criminal matter; and

    (2) All amounts, terms, and conditions of any written offer of settlement made to the client in all other matters.

(B) As used in this rule, "client" includes a person who possesses the authority to accept an offer of settlement or plea, or, in a class action, all the named representatives of the class.

Discussion:

Rule 3-510 is intended to require that counsel in a criminal matter convey all offers, whether written or oral, to the client, as give and take negotiations are less common in criminal matters, and, even were they to occur, such negotiations should require the participation of the accused.

Any oral offers of settlement made to the client in a civil matter should also be communicated if they are "significant" for the purposes of rule 3-500.

Rule 3-600. Organization as Client

(A) In representing an organization, a member shall conform his or her representation to the concept that the client is the organization itself, acting through its highest authorized officer, employee, body, or constituent overseeing the particular engagement.

(B) If a member acting on behalf of an organization knows that an actual or apparent agent of the organization acts or intends or refuses to act in a manner that is or may be a violation of law reasonably imputable to the organization, or in a manner which is likely to result in substantial injury to the organization, the member shall not violate his or her duty of protecting all confidential information as provided in Business and Professions Code section 6068, subdivision (e). Subject to Business and Professions Code section 6068, subdivision (e), the member may take such actions as appear to the member to be in the best lawful interest of the organization. Such actions may include among others:

(1) Urging reconsideration of the matter while explaining its likely consequences to the organization; or

(2) Referring the matter to the next higher authority in the organization, including, if warranted by the seriousness of the matter, referral to the highest internal authority that can act on behalf of the organization.

(C) If, despite the member's actions in accordance with paragraph (B), the highest authority that can act on behalf of the organization insists upon action or a refusal to act that is a violation of law and is likely to result in substantial injury to the organization, the member's response is limited to the member's right, and, where appropriate, duty to resign in accordance with rule 3–700.

(D) In dealing with an organization's directors, officers, employees, members, shareholders, or other constituents, a member shall explain the identity of the client for whom the member acts, whenever it is or becomes apparent that the organization's interests are or may become adverse to those of the constituent(s) with whom the member is dealing. The member shall not mislead such a constituent into believing that the constituent may communicate confidential information to the member in a way that will not be used in the organization's interest if that is or becomes adverse to the constituent.

(E) A member representing an organization may also represent any of its directors, officers, employees, members, shareholders, or other constituents, subject to the provisions of rule 3–310. If the organization's consent to the dual representation is required by rule 3–310, the consent shall be given by an appropriate constituent of the organization other than the individual or constituent who is to be represented, or by the shareholder(s) or organization members.

Discussion:

Rule 3–600 is not intended to enmesh members in the intricacies of the entity and aggregate theories of partnership.

Rule 3–600 is not intended to prohibit members from representing both an organization and other parties connected with it, as for instance (as simply one example) in establishing employee benefit packages for closely held corporations or professional partnerships.

Rule 3–600 is not intended to create or to validate artificial distinctions between entities and their officers, employees, or members, nor is it the purpose of the rule to deny the existence or importance of such formal distinctions. In dealing with a close corporation or small association, members commonly perform professional engagements for both the organization and its major constituents. When a change in control occurs or is threatened, members are faced with complex decisions involving personal and institutional relationships and loyalties and have frequently had difficulty in perceiving their correct duty. (See *People ex rel. Deukmejian v. Brown* (1981) 29 Cal.3d 150 [172 Cal.Rptr. 478]; *Goldstein v. Lees* (1975) 46 Cal.App.3d 614 [120 Cal.Rptr. 253]; *Woods v. Superior Court* (1983) 149 Cal.App.3d 931 [197 Cal.Rptr. 185]; *In re Banks* (1978) 283 Ore. 459 [584 P.2d 284]; 1 A.L.R.4th 1105.) In resolving such multiple relationships, members must rely on case law.

Rule 3–700. Termination of Employment

(A) In General.
  (1) If permission for termination of employment is required by the rules of a tribunal, a member shall not withdraw from employment in a proceeding before that tribunal without its permission.
  (2) A member shall not withdraw from employment until the member has taken reasonable steps to avoid reasonably foreseeable prejudice to the rights of the client, including giving due notice to the client, allowing time for employment of other counsel, complying with rule 3–700(D), and complying with applicable laws and rules.
(B) Mandatory Withdrawal.

A member representing a client before a tribunal shall withdraw from employment with the permission of the tribunal, if required by its rules, and a member representing a client in other matters shall withdraw from employment, if:

  (1) The member knows or should know that the client is bringing an action, conducting a defense, asserting a position in litigation, or taking an appeal, without probable cause and for the purpose of harassing or maliciously injuring any person; or
  (2) The member knows or should know that continued employment will result in violation of these rules or of the State Bar Act; or
  (3) The member's mental or physical condition renders it unreasonably difficult to carry out the employment effectively.
(C) Permissive Withdrawal.

If rule 3–700(B) is not applicable, a member may not request permission to withdraw in matters pending before a tribunal, and may not withdraw in other matters, unless such request or such withdrawal is because:

(1) The client
    (a) insists upon presenting a claim or defense that is not warranted under existing law and cannot be supported by good faith argument for an extension, modification, or reversal of existing law, or

(b) seeks to pursue an illegal course of conduct, or

(c) insists that the member pursue a course of conduct that is illegal or that is prohibited under these rules or the State Bar Act, or

(d) by other conduct renders it unreasonably difficult for the member to carry out the employment effectively, or

(e) insists, in a matter not pending before a tribunal, that the member engage in conduct that is contrary to the judgment and advice of the member but not prohibited under these rules or the State Bar Act, or

(f) breaches an agreement or obligation to the member as to expenses or fees.

(2) The continued employment is likely to result in a violation of these rules or of the State Bar Act; or

(3) The inability to work with co-counsel indicates that the best interests of the client likely will be served by withdrawal; or

(4) The member's mental or physical condition renders it difficult for the member to carry out the employment effectively; or

(5) The client knowingly and freely assents to termination of the employment; or

(6) The member believes in good faith, in a proceeding pending before a tribunal, that the tribunal will find the existence of other good cause for withdrawal.

(D) Papers, Property and Fees.

A member whose employment has terminated shall:

(1) Subject to any protective order or non-disclosure agreement, promptly release to the client, at the request of the client, all the client papers and property. "Client papers and property" includes correspondence, pleadings, deposition transcripts, exhibits, physical evidence, expert's reports, and other items reasonably necessary to the client's representation, whether the client has paid for them or not; and

(2) Promptly refund any part of a fee paid in advance that has not been earned. This provision is not applicable to a true retainer fee which is paid solely for the purpose of ensuring the availability of the member for the matter.

Discussion:

Subparagraph (A)(2) provides that "a member shall not withdraw from employment until the member has taken reasonable steps to avoid reasonably foreseeable prejudice to the rights of the clients." What such steps would include, of course, will vary according to the circumstances. Absent special circumstances, "reasonable steps" do not include providing additional services to the client once the successor counsel has been employed and rule 3–700(D) has been satisfied.

Paragraph (D) makes clear the member's duties in the recurring situation in which new counsel seeks to obtain client files from a member discharged by the client. It codifies existing case law. (See *Academy of California Optometrists v. Superior Court* (1975) 51 Cal. App.3d 999 [124 Cal.Rptr. 668]; *Weiss v. Marcus* (1975) 51 Cal.App.3d 590 [124 Cal.Rptr. 297].) Paragraph (D) also requires that the member "promptly" return unearned fees paid in advance. If a client disputes the amount to be returned, the member shall comply with rule 4–100(A)(2).

Paragraph (D) is not intended to prohibit a member from making, at the member's own expense, and retaining copies of papers released to the client, nor to prohibit a claim for the recovery of the member's expense in any subsequent legal proceeding.

CHAPTER 4. FINANCIAL RELATIONSHIP WITH CLIENTS

Rule 4–100. Preserving Identity of Funds and Property of a Client

(A) All funds received or held for the benefit of clients by a member or law firm, including advances for costs and expenses, shall be deposited in one or more identifiable bank accounts labelled "Trust Account," "Client's Funds Account" or words of similar import, maintained in the State of California, or, with written consent of the client, in any other jurisdiction where there is a substantial relationship between the client or the client's business and the other jurisdiction. No funds belonging to the member or the law firm shall be deposited therein or otherwise commingled therewith except as follows:

(1) Funds reasonably sufficient to pay bank charges.

(2) In the case of funds belonging in part to a client and in part presently or potentially to the member or the law firm, the portion belonging to the member or law firm must be withdrawn at the earliest reasonable time after the member's interest in that portion becomes fixed. However, when the right of the member or law firm to receive a portion of trust funds is disputed by the client, the disputed portion shall not be withdrawn until the dispute is finally resolved.

(B) A member shall:

(1) Promptly notify a client of the receipt of the client's funds, securities, or other properties.

(2) Identify and label securities and properties of a client promptly upon receipt and place them in a safe deposit box or other place of safekeeping as soon as practicable.

(3) Maintain complete records of all funds, securities, and other properties of a client coming into the possession of the member or law firm and render appropriate accounts to the client regarding them; preserve such records for a period of no less than five years after final appropriate distribution of such funds or proper-

ties; and comply with any order for an audit of such records issued pursuant to the Rules of Procedure of the State Bar.

(4) Promptly pay or deliver, as requested by the client, any funds, securities, or other properties in the possession of the member which the client is entitled to receive.

(C) The Board of Governors of the State Bar shall have the authority to formulate and adopt standards as to what "records" shall be maintained by members and law firms in accordance with subparagraph (B)(3). The standards formulated and adopted by the Board, as from time to time amended, shall be effective and binding on all members.

Standards:

Pursuant to rule 4–100(C) the Board of Governors of the State Bar adopted the following standards as to what "records" shall be maintained by members and law firms in accordance with subparagraph (B)(3).

(1) A member shall, from the date of receipt of client funds through the period ending five years from the date of appropriate disbursement of such funds, maintain:

(a) a written ledger for each client on whose behalf funds are held that sets forth:

(i) the name of such client,

(ii) the date, amount and source of all funds received on behalf of such client,

(iii) the date, amount, payee and purpose of each disbursement made on behalf of such client, and

(iv) the current balance for such client;

(b) a written journal for each bank account that sets forth:

(i) the name of such account,

(ii) the date, amount and client affected by each debit and credit, and

(iii) the current balance in such account;

(c) all bank statements and cancelled checks for each bank account; and

(d) each monthly reconciliation (balancing) of (a), (b), and (c).

(2) A member shall, from the date of receipt of all securities and other properties held for the benefit of client through the period ending five years from the date of appropriate disbursement of such securities and other properties, maintain a written journal that specifies:

(a) each item of security and property held;

(b) the person on whose behalf the security or property is held;

(c) the date of receipt of the security or property;

(d) the date of distribution of the security or property; and

(e) person to whom the security or property was distributed.

(Trust Account Record Keeping Standards as Adopted by the Board of Governors on July 11, 1992 Effective on January 1, 1993)

Rule 4–200. Fees for Legal Services

(A) A member shall not enter into an agreement for, charge, or collect an illegal or unconscionable fee.

(B) Unconscionability of a fee shall be determined on the basis of all the facts and circumstances existing at the time the agreement is entered into except where the parties contemplate that the fee will be affected by later events. Among the factors to be considered, where appropriate, in determining the conscionability of a fee are the following:

(1) The amount of the fee in proportion to the value of the services performed.

(2) The relative sophistication of the member and the client.

(3) The novelty and difficulty of the questions involved and the skill requisite to perform the legal service properly.

(4) The likelihood, if apparent to the client, that the acceptance of the particular employment will preclude other employment by the member.

(5) The amount involved and the results obtained.

(6) The time limitations imposed by the client or by the circumstances.

(7) The nature and length of the professional relationship with the client.

(8) The experience, reputation, and ability of the member or members performing the services.

(9) Whether the fee is fixed or contingent.

(10) The time and labor required.

(11) The informed consent of the client to the fee.

Rule 4–210. Payment of Personal or Business Expenses Incurred by or for a Client

(A) A member shall not directly or indirectly pay or agree to pay, guarantee, represent, or sanction a representation that the member or member's law firm will pay the personal or business expenses of a prospective or existing client, except that this rule shall not prohibit a member:

(1) With the consent of the client, from paying or agreeing to pay such expenses to third persons from funds collected or to be collected for the client as a result of the representation; or

(2) After employment, from lending money to the client upon the client's promise in writing to repay such loan; or

(3) From advancing the costs of prosecuting or defending a claim or action or otherwise protecting or promoting the client's interests, the repayment of which may be contingent on the outcome of the matter. Such costs within the meaning of this subparagraph (3) shall be limited to all reasonable expenses of litigation or reasonable expenses in preparation for litigation or in providing any legal services to the client.

(B) Nothing in rule 4–210 shall be deemed to limit rules 3–300, 3–310, and 4–300.

Rule 4–300. Purchasing Property at a Foreclosure or a Sale Subject to Judicial Review

(A) A member shall not directly or indirectly purchase property at a probate, foreclosure, receiver's, trustee's or judicial sale in an action or proceeding in which such member or any lawyer affiliated by reason of personal, business, or professional relationship with that member or with that member's law firm is acting as a lawyer for a party or as executor, receiver, trustee, administrator, guardian, or conservator.

(B) A member shall not represent the seller at a probate, foreclosure, receiver, trustee, or judicial sale in an action or proceeding in which the purchaser is a spouse or relative of the member or of another lawyer in the member's law firm or is an employee of the member or the member's law firm.

Rule 4–400. Gifts From Client

A member shall not induce a client to make a substantial gift, including a testamentary gift, to the member or to the member's parent, child, sibling, or spouse, except where the client is related to the member.

Discussion:

A member may accept a gift from a member's client, subject to general standards of fairness and absence of undue influence. The member who participates in the preparation of an instrument memorializing a gift which is otherwise permissible ought not to be subject to professional discipline. On the other hand, where impermissible influence occurred, discipline is appropriate. (See *Magee v. State Bar* (1962) 58 Cal.2d 423 [24 Cal.Rptr. 839].)

CHAPTER 5.   ADVOCACY AND REPRESENTATION

Rule 5–100.   Threatening Criminal, Administrative, or Disciplinary Charges

(A) A member shall not threaten to present criminal, administrative, or disciplinary charges to obtain an advantage in a civil dispute.

(B) As used in paragraph (A) of this rule, the term "administrative charges" means the filing or lodging of a complaint with a federal, state, or local governmental entity which may order or recommend the loss or suspension of a license, or may impose or recommend the imposition of a fine, pecuniary sanction, or other sanction of a quasi-criminal nature but does not include filing charges with an administrative entity required by law as a condition precedent to maintaining a civil action.

(C) As used in paragraph (A) of this rule, the term "civil dispute" means a controversy or potential controversy over the rights and duties of two or more parties under civil law, whether or not an action has been commenced, and includes an administrative proceeding of a quasi-civil nature pending before a federal, state, or local governmental entity.

Discussion:

Rule 5–100 is not intended to apply to a member's threatening to initiate contempt proceedings against a party for a failure to comply with a court order.

Paragraph (B) is intended to exempt the threat of filing an administrative charge which is a prerequisite to filing a civil complaint on the same transaction or occurrence.

For purposes of paragraph (C), the definition of "civil dispute" makes clear that the rule is applicable prior to the formal filing of a civil action.

Rule 5–110.   Performing the Duty of Member in Government Service

A member in government service shall not institute or cause to be instituted criminal charges when the member knows or should know that the charges are not supported by probable cause. If, after the institution of criminal charges, the member in government service having responsibility for prosecuting the charges becomes aware that those charges are not supported by probable cause, the member shall promptly so advise the court in which the criminal matter is pending.

Rule 5–120. Trial Publicity

(A) A member who is participating or has participated in the investigation or litigation of a matter shall not make an extrajudicial statement that a reasonable person would expect to be disseminated by means of public communication if the member knows or reasonably should know that it will have a substantial likelihood of materially prejudicing an adjudicative proceeding in the matter.

(B) Notwithstanding paragraph (A), a member may state:
  (1) the claim, offense or defense involved and, except when prohibited by law, the identity of the persons involved;
  (2) the information contained in a public record;
  (3) that an investigation of the matter is in progress;
  (4) the scheduling or result of any step in litigation;
  (5) a request for assistance in obtaining evidence and information necessary thereto;
  (6) a warning of danger concerning the behavior of a person involved, when there is reason to believe that there exists the likelihood of substantial harm to an individual or the public interest; and
  (7) in a criminal case, in addition to subparagraphs (1) through (6):
    (a) the identity, residence, occupation, and family status of the accused;
    (b) if the accused has not been apprehended, information necessary to aid in apprehension of that person;
    (c) the fact, time, and place of arrest; and
    (d) the identity of investigating and arresting officers or agencies and the length of the investigation.

(C) Notwithstanding paragraph (A), a member may make a statement that a reasonable member would believe is required to protect a client from the substantial undue prejudicial effect of recent publicity not initiated by the member or the member's client. A statement made pursuant to this paragraph shall be limited to such information as is necessary to mitigate the recent adverse publicity.

Discussion

Rule 5–120 is intended to apply equally to prosecutors and criminal defense counsel. Whether an extrajudicial statement violates rule 5–120 depends on many factors, including:

(1) whether the extrajudicial statement presents information clearly inadmissible as evidence in the matter for the purpose of proving or disproving a material fact in issue;

(2) whether the extrajudicial statement presents information the member knows is false, deceptive, or the use of which would violate Business and Professions Code section 6068(d);

(3) whether the extrajudicial statement violates a lawful "gag" order, or protective order, statute, rule of court, or special rule of confidentiality (for example, in juvenile, domestic, mental disability, and certain criminal proceedings); and

(4) the timing of the statement.

Paragraph (A) is intended to apply to statements made by or on behalf of the member. Subparagraph (B)(6) is not intended to create, augment, diminish, or eliminate any application of the lawyer-client privilege or of Business and Professions Code section 6068(e) regarding the member's duty to maintain client confidence and secrets.

Rule 5–200.   Trial Conduct

In presenting a matter to a tribunal, a member:

(A) Shall employ, for the purpose of maintaining the causes confided to the member such means only as are consistent with truth;

(B) Shall not seek to mislead the judge, judicial officer, or jury by an artifice or false statement of fact or law;

(C) Shall not intentionally misquote to a tribunal the language of a book, statute, or decision;

(D) Shall not, knowing its invalidity, cite as authority a decision that has been overruled or a statute that has been repealed or declared unconstitutional; and

(E) Shall not assert personal knowledge of the facts at issue, except when testifying as a witness.

Rule 5–210.   Member as Witness

A member shall not act as an advocate before a jury which will hear testimony from the member unless:

(A) The testimony relates to an uncontested matter; or

(B) The testimony relates to the nature and value of legal services rendered in the case; or

(C) The member has the informed, written consent of the client. If the member represents the People or a governmental entity, the consent shall be obtained from the head of the office or a designee of the head of the office by which the member is employed and shall be consistent with principles of recusal.

Discussion:

Rule 5–210 is intended to apply to situations in which the member knows or should know that he or she ought to be called as a witness in litigation in which there is a jury. This rule is not intended to encompass situations in which the member is representing the client in an adversarial proceeding and is testifying before a judge. In non-adversarial proceedings, as where the lawyer testifies on behalf of the client, in a hearing before a legislative body, rule 5–210 is not applicable.

Rule 5–210 is not intended to apply to circumstances in which a lawyer in an advocate's firm will be a witness.

Rule 5–220. Suppression of Evidence

A member shall not suppress any evidence that the member or the member's client has a legal obligation to reveal or to produce.

Rule 5–300. Contact With Officials

(A) A member shall not directly or indirectly give or lend anything of value to a judge, official, or employee of a tribunal unless the personal or family relationship between the member and the judge, official, or employee is such that gifts are customarily given and exchanged. Nothing contained in this rule shall prohibit a member from contributing to the campaign fund of a judge running for election or confirmation pursuant to applicable law pertaining to such contributions.

(B) A member shall not directly or indirectly communicate with or argue to a judge or judicial officer upon the merits of a contested matter pending before such judge or judicial officer, except:

    (1) In open court; or

    (2) With the consent of all other counsel in such matter; or

    (3) In the presence of all other counsel in such matter; or

    (4) In writing with a copy thereof furnished to such other counsel; or

    (5) In ex parte matters.

(C) As used in this rule, "judge" and "judicial officer" shall include law clerks, research attorneys, or other court personnel who participate in the decision-making process.

Rule 5–310. Prohibited Contact With Witnesses

A member shall not:

(A) Advise or directly or indirectly cause a person to secrete himself or herself or to leave the jurisdiction of a tribunal for the purpose of making that person unavailable as a witness therein.

(B) Directly or indirectly pay, offer to pay, or acquiesce in the payment of compensation to a witness contingent upon the content of the witness's testimony or the outcome of the case. Except where prohibited by law, a member may advance, guarantee, or acquiesce in the payment of:

    (1) Expenses reasonably incurred by a witness in attending or testifying.

    (2) Reasonable compensation to a witness for loss of time in attending or testifying.

    (3) A reasonable fee for the professional services of an expert witness.

Rule 5–320. Contact With Jurors

(A) A member connected with a case shall not communicate directly or indirectly with anyone the member knows to be a member of the venire from which the jury will be selected for trial of that case.

(B) During trial a member connected with the case shall not communicate directly or indirectly with any juror.

(C) During trial a member who is not connected with the case shall not communicate directly or indirectly concerning the case with anyone the member knows is a juror in the case.

(D) After discharge of the jury from further consideration of a case a member shall not ask questions of or make comments to a member of that jury that are intended to harass or embarrass the juror or to influence the juror's actions in future jury service.

(E) A member shall not directly or indirectly conduct an out of court investigation of a person who is either a member of the venire or a juror in a manner likely to influence the state of mind of such person in connection with present or future jury service.

(F) All restrictions imposed by this rule also apply to communications with or investigations of members of the family of a person who is either a member of the venire or a juror.

(G) A member shall reveal promptly to the court improper conduct by a person who is either a member of a venire or a juror, or by another toward a person who is either a member of a venire or a juror or a member of his or her family, of which the member has knowledge.

(H) This Rule does not prohibit a member from communicating with persons who are members of a venire or jurors as a part of the official proceedings.

(I) For purposes of this Rule, "juror" means any empaneled, discharged, or excused juror.

CALIFORNIA BUSINESS AND PROFESSIONS CODE

(Selected Sections)

Table of Contents

CHAPTER 4. ATTORNEYS

ARTICLE 4. ADMISSION TO THE PRACTICE OF LAW

ARTICLE 6. DISCIPLINARY AUTHORITY OF THE COURTS

ARTICLE 4. ADMISSION TO THE PRACTICE OF LAW

§ 6067. Oath

Every person on his admission shall take an oath to support the Constitution of the United States and the Constitution of the State of California, and faithfully to discharge the duties of any attorney at law to the best of his knowledge and ability. A certificate of the oath shall be indorsed upon his license.

§ 6068. Duties of attorney

It is the duty of an attorney:

(a) To support the Constitution and laws of the United States and of this State.

(b) To maintain the respect due to the courts of justice and judicial officers.

(c) To counsel or maintain such actions, proceedings or defenses only as appear to him legal or just, except the defense of a person charged with a public offense.

(d) To employ, for the purpose of maintaining the causes confided to him such means only as are consistent with truth, and never to seek to mislead the judge or any judicial officer by an artifice or false statement of fact or law.

(e) To maintain inviolate the confidence, and at every peril to himself to preserve the secrets, of his client.

(f) To abstain from all offensive personality, and to advance no fact prejudicial to the honor or reputation of a party or witness, unless required by the justice of the cause with which he is charged.

(g) Not to encourage either the commencement or the continuance of an action or proceeding from any corrupt motive of passion or interest.

(h) Never to reject, for any consideration personal to himself, the cause of the defenseless or the oppressed.

(i) To cooperate and participate in any disciplinary investigation or other regulatory or disciplinary proceeding pending against the attorney. However, this subdivision shall not be construed to deprive an attorney of any privilege guaranteed by the Fifth Amendment to the Constitution of the United States or any other constitutional or statutory privileges.

(j) To comply with the requirements of Section 6002.1.

(k) To comply with all conditions attached to any disciplinary probation, including a probation imposed with the concurrence of the attorney.

(l) To keep all agreements made in lieu of disciplinary prosecution with the agency charged with attorney discipline.

(m) To respond promptly to reasonable status inquiries of clients and to keep clients reasonably informed of significant developments in matters with regard to which the attorney has agreed to provide legal services.

(n) To provide copies to the client of certain documents under time limits and as prescribed in a rule of professional conduct which the board shall adopt.

(o) To report to the agency charged with attorney discipline, in writing, within 30 days of the time the attorney has knowledge of any of the following:

(1) The filing of three or more lawsuits in a 12-month period against the attorney for malpractice or other wrongful conduct committed in a professional capacity.

(2) The entry of judgment against the attorney in any civil action for fraud, misrepresentation, breach of fiduciary duty, or gross negligence committed in a professional capacity.

(3) The imposition of any judicial sanctions against the attorney, except for sanctions for failure to make discovery or monetary sanctions of less than one thousand dollars ($1,000).

(4) The bringing of an indictment or information charging a felony against the attorney.

(5) The conviction of the attorney, including any verdict of guilty, or plea of guilty or no contest, of any felony, or any misdemeanor committed in the course of the practice of law, or in any manner such that a client of the attorney was the victim, or a necessary element of which, as determined by the statutory or common law definition of the misdemeanor, involves improper conduct of an attorney, including dishonesty or other moral turpitude, or an attempt or a conspiracy or solicitation of another to commit a felony or any such misdemeanor.

(6) The imposition of discipline against the attorney by any professional or occupational disciplinary agency or licensing board, whether in California or elsewhere.

(7) Reversal of judgment in a proceeding based in whole or in part upon misconduct, grossly incompetent representation, or wilful misrepresentation by an attorney.

(8) As used in this subdivision, "against the attorney" includes claims and proceedings against any firm of attorneys for the practice of law in which the attorney was a partner at the time of the conduct complained of and any law corporation in which the attorney was a shareholder at the time of the conduct complained of unless the matter has to the attorney's knowledge already been reported by the law firm or corporation.

(9) The State Bar may develop a prescribed form for the making of reports required by this section, usage of which it may require by rule or regulation.

(10) This subdivision is only intended to provide that the failure to report as required herein may serve as a basis of discipline.

§ 6090.5 Settlements; prohibited agreements

(a) It is cause for suspension, disbarment, or other discipline for any member, whether as a party or as an attorney for a party, to agree or seek agreement, that:

(1) The professional misconduct or the terms of a settlement of a claim for professional misconduct shall not be reported to the disciplinary agency.

(2) The plaintiff shall withdraw a disciplinary complaint or shall not cooperate with the investigation or prosecution conducted by the disciplinary agency.

(3) The record of any civil action for professional misconduct shall be sealed from review by the disciplinary agency.

(b) The section applies to all settlements, whether made before or after the commencement of a civil action.
(Amended by Stats.1996, c. 1104 (A.B.2787), § 4.)

ARTICLE 6. DISCIPLINARY AUTHORITY OF THE COURTS

§ 6100. Disbarment or suspension

For any of the causes provided in this article, arising after an attorney's admission to practice, he or she may be disbarred or suspended by the Supreme Court. Nothing in this article limits the inherent power of the Supreme Court to discipline, including to summarily disbar, any attorney.

§ 6101. Conviction of crime; notice of pendency of action; record of conviction; proceedings

(a) Conviction of a felony or misdemeanor, involving moral turpitude, constitutes a cause for disbarment or suspension.

In any proceeding, whether under this article or otherwise, to disbar or suspend an attorney on account of that conviction, the record of conviction shall be conclusive evidence of guilt of the crime of which he or she has been convicted.

(b) The district attorney, city attorney, or other prosecuting agency shall notify the Office of the State Bar of the State of California of the pendency of an action against an attorney charging a felony or misdemeanor immediately upon obtaining information that the defendant is an attorney. The notice shall identify the attorney and describe the crimes charged and the alleged facts. The prosecuting agency shall also notify the clerk of the court in which the action is pending that the defendant is an attorney, and the clerk shall record prominently in the file that the defendant is an attorney.

(c) The clerk of the court in which an attorney is convicted of a crime shall, within 48 hours after the conviction, transmit a certified copy of the record of conviction to the Office of the State Bar. Within five days of receipt, the Office of the State Bar shall transmit the record of any conviction which involves or may involve moral turpitude to the Supreme Court with such other records and information as may be appropriate to establish the Supreme Court's jurisdiction. The State Bar of California may procure and transmit the record of conviction to the Supreme Court when the clerk has not done so or when the conviction was had in a court other than a court of this state.

(d) The proceedings to disbar or suspend an attorney on account of such a conviction shall be undertaken by the Supreme Court pursuant to the procedure provided in this section and Section 6102, upon the receipt of the certified copy of the record of conviction.

(e) A plea or verdict of guilty, an acceptance of a nolo contendere plea, or a conviction after a plea of nolo contendere is deemed to be a conviction within the meaning of those sections.

§ 6102. Immediate suspension and subsequent disbarment upon conviction of crime; crimes involving moral turpitude or felonies; procedure

(a) Upon the receipt of the certified copy of the record of conviction, if it appears therefrom that the crime of which the attorney was convicted involved or that there is probable cause to believe that it involved moral turpitude or is a felony under the laws of California, the United States, or any state or territory thereof, the Supreme Court shall suspend the attorney until the time for appeal has elapsed, if no appeal has been taken, or until the judgment of conviction has been affirmed on appeal, or has otherwise become final, and until the further order of the court. Upon its own motion or upon good cause shown the court may decline to impose, or may set aside, the suspension when it appears to be in the interest of justice to do so, with due regard being given to maintaining the integrity of and confidence in the profession.

(b) For the purposes of this section, a crime is a felony under the law of California if it is declared to be so specifically or by subdivision (a) of Section 17 of the Penal Code, unless it is charged as a misdemeanor pursuant to paragraph (4) or (5) of subdivision (b) of Section 17 of the Penal Code, irrespective of whether in a particular case the crime may be considered a misdemeanor as a result of postconviction proceedings, including proceedings resulting in punishment or probation set forth in paragraph (1) or (3) of subdivision (b) of Section 17 of the Penal Code.

(c) After the judgment of conviction of an offense specified in subdivision (a) has become final or, irrespective of any subsequent order under Section 1203.4 of the Penal Code or similar statutory provision, an order granting probation has been made suspending the imposition of sentence, the Supreme Court shall summarily disbar the attorney if the offense is a felony under the laws of California, the United States, or any state or territory thereof, and an element of the offense is the specific intent to deceive, defraud, steal, or make or suborn a false statement or involved moral turpitude.

(d) For purposes of this section, a conviction under the laws of another state or territory of the United States shall be deemed a felony if:

    (1) The judgment or conviction was entered as a felony irrespective of any subsequent order suspending sentence or granting probation and irrespective of whether the crime may be considered a misdemeanor as a result of postconviction proceedings.

    (2) The elements of the offense for which the member was convicted would constitute a felony under the laws of the State of California at the time the offense was committed.

(e) Except as provided in subdivision (c), if after adequate notice and opportunity to be heard (which hearing shall not be had until the judgment of conviction has become final or, irrespective of any subsequent order under Section 1203.4 of the Penal Code, an order granting probation has been made suspending the imposition of sentence), the court finds that the crime of which the attorney was convicted, or the circumstances of its commission, involved moral turpitude, it shall enter an order disbarring the attorney or suspending him or her from practice for a limited time, according to the gravity of the crime and the circumstances of the case; otherwise it shall dismiss the proceedings. In determining the extent of the discipline to be imposed in a proceeding pursuant to this article any prior discipline imposed upon the attorney may be considered.

(f) The court may refer the proceedings or any part thereof or issue therein, including the nature or extent of discipline, to the State Bar for hearing, report, and recommendation.

(g) The record of the proceedings resulting in the conviction, including a transcript of the testimony therein, may be received in evidence.

(h) The Supreme Court shall prescribe rules for the practice and procedure in proceedings had pursuant to this section and Section 6101.

(i) The other provisions of this article providing a procedure for the disbarment or suspension of an attorney do not apply to proceedings pursuant to this section and Section 6101, unless expressly made applicable.

§ 6103. Disobedience of court order; violation of oath or attorney's duties

A wilful disobedience or violation of an order of the court requiring him to do or forbear an act connected with or in the course of his profession, which he ought in good faith to do or forbear, and any violation of the oath taken by him, or of his duties as such attorney, constitute causes for disbarment or suspension.

§ 6103.5 Written offers of settlement; required communication to client; discovery

(a) A member of the State Bar shall promptly communicate to the member's client all amounts, terms, and conditions of any written offer of settlement made by or on behalf of an opposing party. As used in this section, "client" includes any person employing the member of the State Bar who possesses the authority to accept an offer of settlement, or in a class action, who is a representative of the class.

(b) Any written offer of settlement or any required communication of a settlement offer, as described in subdivision (a), shall be discoverable by either party in any action in which the existence or communication of the offer of settlement is an issue before the trier of fact.

§ 6104. Unauthorized appearance

Corruptly or wilfully and without authority appearing as attorney for a party to an action or proceeding constitutes a cause for disbarment or suspension.

§ 6105. Permitting misuse of name

Lending his name to be used as attorney by another person who is not an attorney constitutes a cause for disbarment or suspension.

§ 6106. Moral turpitude, dishonesty or corruption irrespective of criminal conviction

The commission of any act involving moral turpitude, dishonesty or corruption, whether the act is committed in the course of his relations as an attorney or otherwise, and whether the act is a felony or misdemeanor or not, constitutes a cause for disbarment or suspension.

If the act constitutes a felony or misdemeanor, conviction thereof in a criminal proceeding is not a condition precedent to disbarment or suspension from practice therefor.

§ 6106.1 Advocacy of overthrow of government

Advocating the overthrow of the Government of the United States or of this State by force, violence, or other unconstitutional means, constitutes a cause for disbarment or suspension.

§ 6106.5 Insurance claims; fraud

It shall constitute cause for disbarment or suspension for an attorney to engage in any conduct prohibited under Section 1871.1 or 1871.4 of the Insurance Code.

§ 6106.7 Miller–Ayala Athlete Agents Act; violation of requirements

It shall constitute cause for the imposition of discipline of an attorney within the meaning of this chapter for an attorney to violate any provision of the Miller–Ayala Athlete Agents Act (Chapter 2.5 (commencing with Section 18895) of Division 8), or to violate any provision of Chapter 1 (commencing with Section 1500) of Part 6 of Division 2 of the Labor Code, prior to January 1, 1997, or to violate any provision of the law of any other state regulating athlete agents.

§ 6106.8 Sexual involvement between lawyers and clients; rule of professional conduct

(a) The Legislature hereby finds and declares that there is no rule that governs propriety of sexual relationships between lawyers and clients. The Legislature further finds and declares that it is difficult to separate sound judgment from emotion or bias which may result from sexual involvement between a lawyer and his or her client during the period that an attorney-client relationship exists, and that emotional detachment is essential to the lawyer's ability to render competent legal services. Therefore, in order to ensure that a lawyer acts in the best interest of his or her client, a rule of professional conduct governing sexual relations between attorneys and their clients shall be adopted.

(b) With the approval of the Supreme Court, the State Bar shall adopt a rule of professional conduct governing sexual relations between attorneys and their clients in cases involving, but not limited to, probate matters and domestic relations, including dissolution proceedings, child custody cases, and settlement proceedings.

(c) The State Bar shall submit the proposed rule to the Supreme Court for approval no later than January 1, 1991.

(d) Intentional violation of this rule shall constitute a cause for suspension or disbarment.

§ 6106.9 Sexual relations between attorney and client; cause for discipline; complaints to state bar

(a) It shall constitute cause for the imposition of discipline of an attorney within the meaning of this chapter for an attorney to do any of the following:

(1) Expressly or impliedly condition the performance of legal services for a current or prospective client upon the client's willingness to engage in sexual relations with the attorney.

(2) Employ coercion, intimidation, or undue influence in entering into sexual relations with a client.

(3) Continue representation of a client with whom the attorney has sexual relations if the sexual relations cause the attorney to perform legal services incompetently in violation of Rule 3–110 of

the Rules of Professional Conduct of the State Bar of California, or if the sexual relations would, or would be likely to, damage or prejudice the client's case.

(b) Subdivision (a) shall not apply to sexual relations between attorneys and their spouses or persons in an equivalent domestic relationship or to ongoing consensual sexual relationships that predate the initiation of the attorney-client relationship.

(c) Where an attorney in a firm has sexual relations with a client but does not participate in the representation of that client, the attorneys in the firm shall not be subject to discipline under this section solely because of the occurrence of those sexual relations.

(d) For the purposes of this section, "sexual relations" means sexual intercourse or the touching of an intimate part of another person for the purpose of sexual arousal, gratification, or abuse.

(e) Any complaint made to the State Bar alleging a violation of subdivision (a) shall be verified under oath by the person making the complaint.

§ 6107. Proceedings upon court's own knowledge or upon information

The proceedings to disbar or suspend an attorney, on grounds other than the conviction of a felony or misdemeanor, involving moral turpitude, may be taken by the court for the matters within its knowledge, or may be taken upon the information of another.

§ 6108. Accusation

If the proceedings are upon the information of another, the accusation shall be in writing and shall state the matters charged, and be verified by the oath of some person, to the effect that the charges therein contained are true.

The verification may be made upon information and belief when the accusation is presented by an organized bar association.

§ 6109. Order to appear and answer; service

Upon receiving the accusation, the court shall make an order requiring the accused to appear and answer it at a specified time, and shall cause a copy of the order and of the accusation to be served upon the accused at least five days before the day appointed in the order.

§ 6110. Citation

The court or judge may direct the service of a citation to the accused, requiring him to appear and answer the accusation, to be made by publication for thirty days in a newspaper of general circulation published in the county in which the proceeding is pending, if it appears by affidavit to the satisfaction of the court or judge that the accused either:

    (a) Resides out of the State.

    (b) Has departed from the State.

    (c) Can not, after due diligence, be found within the State.

    (d) Conceals himself to avoid the service of the order to show cause.

The citation shall be:

    (a) Directed to the accused.

    (b) Recite the date of the filing of the accusation, the name of the accuser, and the general nature of the charges against him.

    (c) Require him to appear and answer the accusation at a specified time.

On proof of the publication of the citation as herein required, the court has jurisdiction to proceed to hear the accusation and render judgment with like effect as if an order to show cause and a copy of the accusation had been personally served on the accused.

§ 6111. Appearance; determination upon default

The accused shall appear at the time appointed in the order, and answer the accusation, unless, for sufficient cause, the court assigns another day for that purpose. If he does not appear, the court may proceed and determine the accusation in his absence.

§ 6112. Answer

The accused may answer to the accusation either by objecting to its sufficiency or by denying it.

If he objects to the sufficiency of the accusation, the objection shall be in writing, but need not be in any specific form. It is sufficient if it presents intelligibly the grounds of the objection.

If he denies the accusation, the denial may be oral and without oath, and shall be entered upon the minutes.

§ 6113. Time for answer after objection

If an objection to the sufficiency of the accusation is not sustained, the accused shall answer within the time designated by the court.

§ 6114. Judgment upon plea of guilty or failure to answer; trial upon denial of charges

If the accused pleads guilty, or refuses to answer the accusation, the court shall proceed to judgment of disbarment or suspension.

If he denies the matters charged, the court shall, at such time as it may appoint, proceed to try the accusation.

§ 6115. Reference to take depositions

The court may, in its discretion, order a reference to a committee to take depositions in the matter.

§ 6116. Judgment

When an attorney has been found guilty of the charges made in proceedings not based upon a record of conviction, judgment shall be rendered disbarring the attorney or suspending him from practice for a limited time, according to the gravity of the offense charged.

§ 6117. Effect of disbarment or suspension

During such disbarment or suspension, the attorney shall be precluded from practicing law.

When disbarred, his name shall be stricken from the roll of attorneys.

ARTICLE 7.   UNLAWFUL PRACTICE OF LAW

§ 6125. Necessity of active membership in state bar

No person shall practice law in California unless the person is an active member of the State Bar.

§ 6126. Unauthorized practice, advertising or holding out; penalties

(a) Any person advertising or holding himself or herself out as practicing or entitled to practice law or otherwise practicing law who is not an active member of the State Bar, is guilty of a misdemeanor.

(b) Any person who has been involuntarily enrolled as an inactive member of the State Bar, or has been suspended from membership from the State Bar, or has been disbarred, or has resigned from the State Bar with charges pending, and thereafter advertises or holds himself or herself out as practicing or otherwise entitled to practice law, is guilty of a crime punishable by imprisonment in the state prison or county jail. However, any person who has been involuntarily enrolled as an inactive member of the State Bar pursuant to paragraph (1) of subdivision (e) of Section 6007 and who knowingly thereafter advertises or holds himself or herself out as practicing or otherwise entitled to practice law, is guilty of a crime punishable by imprisonment in the state prison or county jail.

(c) The willful failure of a member of the State Bar, or one who has resigned or been disbarred, to comply with an order of the Supreme Court to comply with Rule 955, constitutes a crime punishable by imprisonment in the state prison or county jail.

§ 6127. Contempt of court

The following acts or omissions in respect to the practice of law are contempts of the authority of the courts:

(a) Assuming to be an officer or attorney of a court and acting as such, without authority.

(b) Advertising or holding oneself out as practicing or as entitled to practice law or otherwise practicing law in any court, without being an active member of the State Bar.

Proceedings to adjudge a person in contempt of court under this section are to be taken in accordance with the provisions of Title V of Part III of the Code of Civil Procedure.

§ 6127.5 Law corporation under professional corporation act

Nothing in Sections 6125, 6126 and 6127 shall be deemed to apply to the acts and practices of a law corporation duly certificated pursuant to the Professional Corporation Act, as contained in Part 4 (commencing with Section 13400) of Division 3 of Title 1 of the Corporations Code, and pursuant to Article 10 (commencing with Section 6160) of Chapter 4 of Division 3 of this code, when the law corporation is in compliance with the requirements of (a) the Professional Corporation Act; (b) Article 10 (commencing with Section 6160) of Chapter 4 of Division 3 of this code; and (c) all other statutes and all rules and regulations now or hereafter enacted or adopted pertaining to such corporation and the conduct of its affairs.

§ 6128. Deceit, collusion, delay of suit and improper receipt of money as misdemeanors

Every attorney is guilty of a misdemeanor who either:

(a) Is guilty of any deceit or collusion, or consents to any deceit or collusion, with intent to deceive the court or any party.

(b) Wilfully delays his client's suit with a view to his own gain.

(c) Wilfully receives any money or allowance for or on account of any money which he has not laid out or become answerable for.

Any violation of the provisions of this section is punishable by imprisonment in the county jail not exceeding six months, or by a fine not exceeding two thousand five hundred dollars ($2,500), or by both.

§ 6129. Buying claim as misdemeanor

Every attorney who, either directly or indirectly, buys or is interested in buying any evidence of debt or thing in action, with intent to bring suit thereon, is guilty of a misdemeanor.

Any violation of the provisions of this section is punished by imprisonment in the county jail not exceeding six months, or by a fine not exceeding two thousand five hundred dollars ($2,500), or by both.

§ 6130. Disbarred or suspended attorney suing as assignee

No person, who has been an attorney, shall while a judgment of disbarment or suspension is in force appear on his own behalf as plaintiff in the prosecution of any action where the subject of the action has been assigned to him subsequent to the entry of the judgment of disbarment or suspension and solely for purpose of collection.

§ 6131. Aiding defense where partner or self has acted as public prosecutor; misdemeanor and disbarment

Every attorney is guilty of a misdemeanor and, in addition to the punishment prescribed therefor, shall be disbarred:

(a) Who directly or indirectly advises in relation to, or aids, or promotes the defense of any action or proceeding in any court the prosecution of which is carried on, aided or promoted by any person as district attorney or other public prosecutor with whom such person is directly or indirectly connected as a partner.

(b) Who, having himself prosecuted or in any manner aided or promoted any action or proceeding in any court as district attorney or other public prosecutor, afterwards, directly or indirectly, advises in relation to or takes any part in the defense thereof, as attorney or otherwise, or who takes or receives any valuable consideration from or on behalf of any defendant in any such action upon any understanding or agreement whatever having relation to the defense thereof.

This section does not prohibit an attorney from defending himself in person, as attorney or counsel, when prosecuted, either civilly or criminally.

ARTICLE 8.5   FEE AGREEMENTS

§ 6146. Limitations; periodic payments

(a) An attorney shall not contract for or collect a contingency fee for representing any person seeking damages in connection with an action for injury or damage against a health care provider based upon such person's alleged professional negligence in excess of the following limits:

(1) Forty percent of the first fifty thousand dollars ($50,000) recovered.

(2) Thirty-three and one-third percent of the next fifty thousand dollars ($50,000) recovered.

(3) Twenty-five percent of the next five hundred thousand dollars ($500,000) recovered.

(4) Fifteen percent of any amount on which the recovery exceeds six hundred thousand dollars ($600,000).

The limitations shall apply regardless of whether the recovery is by settlement, arbitration, or judgment, or whether the person for whom the recovery is made is a responsible adult, an infant, or a person of unsound mind.

(b) If periodic payments are awarded to the plaintiff pursuant to Section 667.7 of the Code of Civil Procedure, the court shall place a total value on these payments based upon the projected life expectancy of the plaintiff and include this amount in computing the total award from which attorney's fees are calculated under this section.

(c) For purposes of this section:

(1) "Recovered" means the net sum recovered after deducting any disbursements or costs incurred in connection with prosecution or settlement of the claim. Costs of medical care incurred by the plaintiff and the attorney's office-overhead costs or charges are not deductible disbursements or costs for such purpose.

(2) "Health care provider" means any person licensed or certified pursuant to Division 2 (commencing with Section 500), or licensed pursuant to the Osteopathic Initiative Act, or the Chiropractic Initiative Act, or licensed pursuant to Chapter 2.5 (commencing with Section 1440) of Division 2 of the Health and Safety Code; and any clinic, health dispensary, or health facility, licensed pursuant to Division 2 (commencing with Section 1200) of the Health and Safety Code. "Health care provider" includes the legal representatives of a health care provider.

(3) "Professional negligence" is a negligent act or omission to act by a health care provider in the rendering of professional services, which act or omission is the proximate cause of a personal injury or wrongful death, provided that the services are within the scope of services for which the provider is licensed and which are not within any restriction imposed by the licensing agency or licensed hospital.

§ 6147. Contingency fee contract; duplicate copy; contents; effect of noncompliance; recovery of workers' compensation benefits

Text of section operative until Jan. 1, 2000.

(a) An attorney who contracts to represent a client on a contingency fee basis shall, at the time the contract is entered into, provide a duplicate copy of the contract, signed by both the attorney and the client, or that client's guardian or representative, to the client, or to the client's guardian or representative. The contract shall be in writing and shall include, but is not limited to, all of the following:

(1) A statement of the contingency fee rate that the client and attorney have agreed upon.

(2) A statement as to how disbursements and costs incurred in connection with the prosecution or settlement of the claim will affect the contingency fee and the client's recovery.

(3) A statement as to what extent, if any, the client could be required to pay any compensation to the attorney for related matters that arise out of their relationship not covered by their contingency fee contract. This may include any amounts collected for the plaintiff by the attorney.

(4) Unless the claim is subject to the provisions of Section 6146, a statement that the fee is not set by law but is negotiable between attorney and client.

(5) If the claim is subject to the provisions of Section 6146, a statement that the rates set forth in that section are the maximum limits for the contingency fee agreement, and that the attorney and client may negotiate a lower rate.

(6) If the attorney does not meet any of the following criteria, a statement disclosing that fact:

(A) Maintains errors and omissions insurance coverage.

(B) Has filed with the State Bar an executed copy of a written agreement guaranteeing payment of all claims established against the attorney by his or her clients for errors or omissions arising out of the practice of law by the attorney in the amount specified in paragraph (c) of subsection (1) of Section B of Rule IV of the Law Corporation Rules of the State Bar. The State Bar may charge a filing fee not to exceed five dollars ($5).

(C) If a law corporation, has filed with the State Bar an executed copy of the written agreement required pursuant to paragraph (a), (b), or (c) of subsection (1) of Section B of Rule IV of the Law Corporation Rules of the State Bar.

(b) Failure to comply with any provision of this section renders the agreement voidable at the option of the client, and the attorney shall thereupon be entitled to collect a reasonable fee.

(c) This section shall not apply to contingency fee contracts for the recovery of workers' compensation benefits.

(d) This section shall remain in effect only until January 1, 2000, and of that date is repealed, unless a later enacted statute, which is enacted before January 1, 2000, deletes or extends that date.

§ 6147. Contingency fee contracts; duplicate copy; contents; effect of noncompliance; recovery of workers' compensation benefits

Text of section operative Jan. 1, 2000.

(a) An attorney who contracts to represent a client on a contingency fee basis shall, at the time the contract is entered into, provide a duplicate copy of the contract, signed by both the attorney and the client, or the client's guardian or representative, to the client, or to the client's guardian or representative. The contract shall be in writing and shall include, but is not limited to, all of the following:

(1) A statement of the contingency fee rate that the client and attorney have agreed upon.

(2) A statement as to how disbursements and costs incurred in connection with the prosecution or settlement of the claim will affect the contingency fee and the client's recovery.

(3) A statement as to what extent, if any, the client could be required to pay any compensation to the attorney for related matters that arise out of their relationship not covered by their contingency fee contract. This may include any amounts collected for the plaintiff by the attorney.

(4) Unless the claim is subject to the provisions of Section 6146, a statement that the fee is not set by law but is negotiable between attorney and client.

(5) If the claim is subject to the provisions of Section 6146, a statement that the rates set forth in that section are the maximum limits for the contingency fee agreement, and that the attorney and client may negotiate a lower rate.

(b) Failure to comply with any provision of this section renders the agreement voidable at the option of the plaintiff, and the attorney shall thereupon be entitled to collect a reasonable fee.

(c) This section shall not apply to contingency fee contracts for the recovery of workers' compensation benefits.

(d) This section shall become operative on January 1, 2000.

§ 6147.5 Contingency fee contracts; recovery of claims between merchants

(a) Sections 6147 and 6148 shall not apply to contingency fee contracts for the recovery of claims between merchants as defined in Section 2104 of the Commercial Code, arising from the sale or lease of goods or services rendered, or money loaned for use, in the conduct of a business or profession if the merchant contracting for legal services employs 10 or more individuals.

(b)(1) In the instances in which no written contract for legal services exists as permitted by subdivision (a), an attorney shall not contract for or collect a contingency fee in excess of the following limits:

(A) Twenty percent of the first three hundred dollars ($300) collected.

(B) Eighteen percent of the next one thousand seven hundred dollars ($1,700) collected.

(C) Thirteen percent of sums collected in excess of two thousand dollars ($2,000).

(2) However, the following minimum charges may be charged and collected:

(A) Twenty-five dollars ($25) in collections of seventy-five dollars ($75) to one hundred twenty-five dollars ($125).

(B) Thirty-three and one-third percent of collections less than seventy-five dollars ($75).

§ 6148. Contracts for services in cases not coming within § 6147; bills rendered by attorney; contents; failure to comply

Text of section operative until Jan. 1, 2000.

(a) In any case not coming within Section 6147 in which it is reasonably foreseeable that total expense to a client, including attorney fees will exceed one thousand dollars ($1,000), the contract for services in the case shall be in writing. At the time the contract is entered into, the attorney shall provide a duplicate copy of the contract signed by both the attorney and the client, or the client's guardian or representative, to the client or the client's guardian or representative. The written contract shall contain all of the following:

(1) Any basis of compensation including, but not limited to, hourly rates, statutory fees or flat fees, and other standard rates, fees, and charges applicable to the case.

(2) The general nature of the legal services to be provided to the client.

(3) The respective responsibilities of the attorney and the client as to the performance of the contract.

(4) If the attorney does not meet any of the following criteria, a statement disclosing that fact:

(A) Maintains errors and omissions insurance coverage.

(B) Has filed with the State Bar an executed copy of a written agreement guaranteeing payment of all claims established against the attorney by his or her clients for errors or omissions arising out of the practice of law by the attorney in the amount specified in paragraph (c) of subdivision (1) of Section B of Rule IV of the Law Corporation Rules of the State Bar. The State Bar may charge a filing a fee not to exceed five dollars ($5).

(C) If a law corporation, has filed with the State Bar an executed copy of the written agreement required pursuant to paragraph (a), (b), or (c) of subsection (1) of Section B of Rule IV of the Law Corporation Rules of the State Bar.

(b) All bills rendered by an attorney to a client shall clearly state the basis thereof. Bills for the fee portion of the bill shall include the amount, rate, basis for calculation, or other method of determination of the attorney's fees and costs. Bills for the cost and expense portion of the bill shall clearly identify the costs and expenses incurred and the amount of the costs and expenses. Upon request by the client, the attorney shall provide a bill to the client no later than 10 days following the request unless the attorney has provided a bill to the client within 31 days prior to the request, in which case the attorney may provide a bill to the client no later than 31 days following the date the most recent bill was provided. The client is entitled to make similar requests at intervals of no less than 30 days following the initial request. In providing responses to client requests for billing information, the attorney may use billing data that is currently effective on the date of the request, or, if any fees or costs to that date cannot be accurately determined, they shall be described and estimated.

(c) Failure to comply with any provision of this section renders the agreement voidable at the option of the client, and the attorney shall, upon the agreement being voided, be entitled to collect a reasonable fee.

(d) This section shall not apply to any of the following:

(1) Services rendered in an emergency to avoid foreseeable prejudice to the rights or interests of the client or where a writing is otherwise impractical.

(2) An arrangement as to the fee implied by the fact that the attorney's services are of the same general kind as previously rendered to and paid for by the client.

(3) If the client knowingly states in writing, after full disclosure of this section, that a writing concerning fees is not required.

(4) If the client is a corporation.

(e) This section applies prospectively only to fee agreements following its operative date.

(f) This section shall remain in effect only until January 1, 2000, and as of that date is repealed, unless a later enacted statute, which is enacted before January 1, 2000, deletes or extends that date.

§ 6148. Contracts for services in cases not coming within § 6147; bills rendered by attorney; contents; failure to comply

Text of section operative Jan. 1, 2000.

(a) In any case not coming within Section 6147 in which it is reasonably foreseeable that total expense to a client, including attorney fees will exceed one thousand dollars ($1,000), the contract for services in the case shall be in writing. At the time the contract is entered into, the attorney shall provide a duplicate copy of the contract signed by both the attorney and the client, or the client's guardian or representative, to the client or the client's guardian or representative. The written contract shall contain all of the following:

(1) Any basis of compensation including, but not limited to, hourly rates, statutory fees or flat fees, and other standard rates, fees, and charges applicable to the case.

(2) The general nature of the legal services to be provided to the client.

(3) The respective responsibilities of the attorney and the client as to the performance of the contract.

(b) All bills rendered by an attorney to a client shall clearly state the basis thereof. Bills for the fee portion of the bill shall include the amount, rate, basis for calculation, or other method of determination of the attorney's fees and costs. Bills for the cost and expense portion of the bill shall clearly identify the costs and expenses incurred and the amount of the costs and expenses. Upon request by the client, the attorney shall provide a bill to the client no later than 10 days following the request unless the attorney has provided a bill to the client within 31 days prior to the request, in which case the attorney may provide a bill to the client no later than 31 days following the date the most recent bill was provided. The client is entitled to make similar requests at intervals of no less than 30 days following the initial request. In providing responses to client requests for billing information, the attorney may use billing data that is currently effective on the date of the request, or, if any fees or costs to that date cannot be accurately determined, they shall be described and estimated.

(c) Failure to comply with any provision of this section renders the agreement voidable at the option of the client, and the attorney shall, upon the agreement being voided, be entitled to collect a reasonable fee.

(d) This section shall not apply to any of the following:

(1) Services rendered in an emergency to avoid foreseeable prejudice to the rights or interests of the client or where a writing is otherwise impractical.

(2) An arrangement as to the fee implied by the fact that the attorney's services are of the same general kind as previously rendered to and paid for by the client.

(3) If the client knowingly states in writing, after full disclosure of this section, that a writing concerning fees is not required.

(4) If the client is a corporation.

(e) This section applies prospectively only to fee agreements following its operative date.

(f) This section shall become operative on January 1, 2000.

§ 6149. Written fee contract as confidential communication

A written fee contract shall be deemed to be a confidential communication within the meaning of subdivision (e) of Section 6068 and of Section 952 of the Evidence Code.

§ 6149.5 Third-party liability claim; settlement by insurer; notice to claimant; effect on action or defense

(a) Upon the payment of one hundred dollars ($100) or more in settlement of any third-party liability claim the insurer shall provide written notice to the claimant if both of the following apply:

(1) The claimant is a natural person.

(2) The payment is delivered to the claimant's lawyer or other representative by draft, check, or otherwise.

(b) For purposes of this section, "written notice" includes providing to the claimant a copy of the cover letter sent to the claimant's attorney or other representative that accompanied the settlement payment.

(c) This section shall not create any cause of action for any person against the insurer based upon the insurer's failure to provide the notice to a claimant required by this section. This section shall not create a defense for any party to any cause of action based upon the insurer's failure to provide this notice.

ARTICLE 9.   UNLAWFUL SOLICITATION

§ 6150. Relation of article to chapter

This article is a part of Chapter 4 of this division of the Business and Professions Code, but the phrase "this chapter" as used in Chapter 4 does not apply to the provisions of this article unless expressly made applicable.

§ 6151. Definitions

As used in this article:

(a) A runner or capper is any person, firm, association or corporation acting for consideration in any manner or in any capacity as an agent for an attorney at law or law firm, whether the attorney or any member of the law firm is admitted in California or any other jurisdiction, in the solicitation or procurement of business for the attorney at law or law firm as provided in this article.

(b) An agent is one who represents another in dealings with one or more third persons.

§ 6152. Prohibition of solicitation

(a) It is unlawful for:

(1) Any person, in an individual capacity or in a capacity as a public or private employee, or for any firm, corporation, partnership or association to act as a runner or capper for any attorneys or to solicit any business for any attorneys in and about the state prisons, county jails, city jails, city prisons, or other places of detention of persons, city receiving hospitals, city and county receiving hospitals, county hospitals, municipal courts, superior courts, or in any public institution or in any public place or upon any public street or highway or in and about private hospitals, sanitariums or in and about any private institution or upon private property of any character whatsoever.

(2) Any person to solicit another person to commit or join in the commission of a violation of subdivision (a).

(b) A general release from a liability claim obtained from any person during the period of the first physical confinement, whether as an inpatient or outpatient, in a clinic or health facility, as defined in Sections 1203 and 1250 of the Health and Safety Code, as a result of the injury alleged to have given rise to the claim and primarily of treatment of the injury, is presumed fraudulent if such release is executed within 15 days after the commencement of confinement or prior to release from confinement, which ever occurs first.

(c) Nothing in this section shall be construed to prevent the recommendation of professional employment where that recommendation is not prohibited by the Rules of Professional Conduct of the State Bar of California.

(d) Nothing in this section shall be construed to mean that a public defender or assigned counsel may not make known his or her services as a criminal defense attorney to persons unable to afford legal counsel whether those persons are in custody or otherwise.

§ 6153. Violation; penalty

Any person, firm, partnership, association, or corporation violating subdivision (a) of Section 6152 is punishable, upon a first conviction by imprisonment in a county jail for not more than one year. Upon a second or subsequent conviction, a person, firm, partnership, association, or corporation is punishable by imprisonment in a county jail for not more than one year, or by imprisonment in the state prison for 16 months or 2 or 3 years, or by a fine up to ten thousand dollars ($10,000), or by both that imprisonment and fine.

Any person employed either as an officer, director, trustee, clerk, servant or agent of this State or of any county or other municipal corporation or subdivision thereof, who is found guilty of violating any of the provisions of this article, shall forfeit the right to his office and employment in addition to any other penalty provided in this article.

§ 6154. Runner or capper used to procure business's void contract; divesting of fees and other compensation; fees recovered from workers' compensation actions

(a) Any contract for professional services secured by any attorney at law or law firm in this state through the services of a runner or capper is void. In any action against any attorney or law firm under the Unfair Practices Act, Chapter 4 (commencing with Section 17000) of Division 7, or Chapter 5 (commencing with Section 17200) of Division 7, any judgment shall include an order divesting the attorney or law firm of any fees and other compensation received pursuant to any such void contract. Those fees and compensation shall be recoverable as additional civil penalties under Chapter 4 (commencing with Section 17000) or Chapter 5 (commencing with Section 17200) of Division 7.

(b) Notwithstanding Section 17206 or any other provision of law, any fees recovered pursuant to subdivision (a) in an action involving professional services related to the provision of workers' compensation shall be allocated as follows: if the action is brought by the Attorney General, one-half of the penalty collected shall be paid to the State General Fund, and one-half of the penalty collected shall be paid to the Workers' Compensation Fraud Account in the Insurance Fund; if the action is brought by a district attorney, one-half of the penalty collected shall be paid to the treasurer of the county in which the judgment was entered, and one-half of the penalty collected shall be paid to the Workers' Compensation Fraud Account in the Insurance Fund; if the action is brought by a city attorney or city prosecutor, one-half of the penalty collected shall be paid to the Workers' Compensation Fraud Account in the Insurance Fund. Moneys deposited into the Workers' Compensation Fraud Account pursuant to this subdivision shall be used in the investigation and prosecution of workers' compensation fraud, as appropriated by the Legislature.

§ 6155. Referral services; conflicts of interest; enforcement; rules and regulations; duration of section

(a) An individual, partnership, corporation, association, or any other entity shall not operate for the direct or indirect purpose, in whole or in part, of referring potential clients to attorneys, and no attorney shall accept a referral of such potential clients, unless all of the following requirements are met:

(1) The service is registered with the State Bar of California and (a) on July 1, 1988, is operated in conformity with minimum standards for a lawyer referral service established by the State Bar, or (b) upon approval by the Supreme Court of minimum standards for a lawyer referral service, is operated in conformity with those standards.

(2) The combined charges to the potential client by the referral service and the attorney to whom the potential client is referred do

not exceed the total cost that the client would normally pay if no referral service were involved.

(b) A referral service shall not be owned or operated, in whole or in part, directly or indirectly, by those lawyers to whom, individually or collectively, more than 20 percent of referrals are made. For purposes of this subdivision, a referral service that is owned or operated by a bar association, as defined in the minimum standards, shall be deemed to be owned or operated by its governing committee so long as the governing committee is constituted and functions in the manner prescribed by the minimum standards.

(c) None of the following is a lawyer referral service:

(1) A plan of legal insurance as defined in Section 119.6 of the Insurance Code.

(2) A group or prepaid legal plan, whether operated by a union, trust, mutual benefit or aid association, public or private corporation, or other entity or person, which meets both of the following conditions:

(A) It recommends, furnishes, or pays for legal services to its members or beneficiaries.

(B) It provides telephone advice or personal consultation.

(3) A program having as its purpose the referral of clients to attorneys for representation on a pro bono basis.

(d) The following are in the public interest and do not constitute an unlawful restraint of trade or commerce:

(1) An agreement between a referral service and a participating attorney to eliminate or restrict the attorney's fee for an initial office consultation for each potential client or to provide free or reduced fee services.

(2) Requirements by a referral service that attorneys meet reasonable participation requirements, including experience, education, and training requirements.

(3) Provisions of the minimum standards as approved by the Supreme Court.

(4) Requirements that the application and renewal fees for certification as a lawyer referral service be determined, in whole or in part, by a consideration of any combination of the following factors: a referral service's gross annual revenues, number of panels, number of panel members, amount of fees charged to panel members, or for-profit or nonprofit status; provided that the application and renewal fees do not exceed ten thousand dollars ($10,000) or 1 percent of the gross annual revenues, whichever is less.

(5) Requirements that, to increase access to the justice system for all Californians, lawyer referral services establish separate ongoing activities or arrangements that serve persons of limited means.

(e) A violation or threatened violation of this section may be enjoined by any person.

(f) With the approval of the Supreme Court, the State Bar shall formulate and enforce rules and regulations for carrying out this section, including rules and regulations which do the following:

(1) Establish minimum standards for lawyer referral services. The minimum standards shall include provisions ensuring that panel membership shall be open to all attorneys practicing in the geographical area served who are qualified by virtue of suitable experience, and limiting attorney registration and membership fees to reasonable sums which do not discourage widespread attorney membership.

(2) Require that an entity seeking to qualify as a lawyer referral service register with the State Bar and obtain from the State Bar a certificate of compliance with the minimum standards for lawyer referral services.

(3) Require that the certificate may be obtained, maintained, suspended, or revoked pursuant to procedures set forth in the rules and regulations.

(4) Require the lawyer referral service to pay an application and renewal fee for the certificate in such reasonable amounts as may be determined by the State Bar. The State Bar shall adopt rules authorizing the waiver or reduction of the fees upon a demonstration of financial necessity. The State Bar may require that the application and renewal fees for certification as a lawyer referral service be determined, in whole or in part, by a consideration of any combination of the following factors: a referral service's gross annual revenues, number of panels, number of panel members, amount of fees charged to panel members, or for-profit or nonprofit status; provided that the application and renewal fees do not exceed ten thousand dollars ($10,000) or 1 percent of the gross annual revenues, whichever is less.

(5) Require that, to increase access to the justice system for all Californians, lawyer referral services establish separate ongoing activities or arrangements that serve persons of limited means.

(6) Require each lawyer who is a member of a certified lawyer referral service to comply with all applicable professional standards, rules, and regulations, and to possess a policy of errors and omissions insurance in an amount not less than one hundred thousand dollars ($100,000) for each occurrence and three hundred thousand dollars ($300,000) aggregate, per year. By rule, the State Bar may

provide for alternative proof of financial responsibility to meet this requirement.

(g) Provide that cause for denial of certification or recertification or revocation of certification of a lawyer referral service shall include, but not be limited to:

(1) Noncompliance with the statutes or minimum standards governing lawyer referral services as adopted and from time to time amended.

(2) Sharing common or cross ownership, interests, or operations with any entity which engages in referrals to licensed or unlicensed health care providers.

(3) Direct or indirect consideration regarding referrals between an owner, operator, or member of a lawyer referral service and any licensed or unlicensed health care provider.

(4) Advertising on behalf of attorneys in violation of the Rules of Professional Conduct or the Business and Professions Code.

(h) This section shall not be construed to prohibit attorneys from jointly advertising their services.

(1) Permissible joint advertising, among other things, identifies by name the advertising attorneys or law firms whom the consumer of legal services may select and initiate contact with.

(2) Certifiable referral activity involves, among other things, some person or entity other than the consumer and advertising attorney or law firms which, in person, electronically, or otherwise, refers the consumer to an attorney or law firm not identified in the advertising.

(i) A lawyer referral service certified under this section and operating in full compliance with this section, and in full compliance with the minimum standards and the rules and regulations of the State Bar governing lawyer referral services, shall not be deemed to be in violation of Section 3215 of the Labor Code or Section 750 of the Insurance Code.

(j) The payment by an attorney or law firm member of a certified referral service of the normal fees of that service shall not be deemed to be in violation of Section 3215 of the Labor Code or Section 750 of the Insurance Code, provided that the attorney or law firm member is in full compliance with the minimum standards and the rules and regulations of the State Bar governing lawyer referral services.

(k) Certifications of lawyer referral services issued by the State Bar shall not be transferable.

[Ed. Note: The California Bar has prepared two documents relating to referral services: (1) Minimum Standards for a Lawyer Referral Service in California, and (2) Certification and Renewal Fees for Lawyer Referral Services. These documents are omitted from this publication.]

ARTICLE 9.5   LEGAL ADVERTISING

§ 6157. Definitions

As used in this article, the following definitions apply:

(a) "Member" means a member in good standing of the State Bar and includes the terms "lawyer" and "attorney" and includes any agent of the member and any law firm or law corporation doing business in the State of California.

(b) "Lawyer" means a member of the State Bar or a person who is admitted in good standing and eligible to practice before the bar of any United States court or the highest court of the District of Columbia or any state, territory, or insular possession of the United States, or is licensed to practice law in, or is admitted in good standing and eligible to practice before the bar of the highest court of, a foreign country or any political subdivision thereof, and includes any agent of the lawyer or law firm or law corporation doing business in the this state.

(c) "Advertise" or "advertisement" means any communication, disseminated by television or radio, by any print medium including, but not limited to, newspapers and billboards, or by means of a mailing directed generally to members of the public and not to a specific person, that solicits employment of legal services provided by a member, and is directed to the general public and is paid for by, or on the behalf of, an attorney.

(d) "Electronic medium" means television, radio, or computer networks.

§ 6157.1 False, misleading or deceptive statements; prohibition

No advertisement shall contain any false, misleading, or deceptive statement or omit to state any fact necessary to make the statements made, in light of circumstances under which they are made, not false, misleading, or deceptive.

§ 6157.2 Prohibited statements regarding outcome; dramatizations; contingent fee basis representations

No advertisement shall contain or refer to any of the following:

(a) Any guarantee or warranty regarding the outcome of a legal matter as a result of representation by the member.

(b) Statements or symbols stating that the member featured in the advertisement can generally obtain immediate cash or quick settlements.

(c)(1) An impersonation of the name, voice, photograph, or electronic image of any person other than the lawyer, directly or implicitly purporting to be that of a lawyer.

(2) An impersonation of the name, voice, photograph, or electronic image of any person directly or implicitly purporting to be a

client of the member featured in the advertisement, or a dramatization of events, unless disclosure of the impersonation or dramatization is made in the advertisement.

(3) A spokesperson, including a celebrity spokesperson, unless there is a disclosure of the spokesperson's title.

(d) A statement that a member offers representation on a contingent basis unless the statement also advises whether a client will be held responsible for any costs advanced by the member when no recovery is obtained on behalf of the client. If the client will not be held responsible for costs, no disclosure is required.

§ 6157.3 Advertisements made on behalf of member; required representations

Any advertisement made on behalf of a member, which is not paid for by the member, shall disclose any business relationship, past or present, between the member and the person paying for the advertisement.

§ 6157.4 Lawyer referral service advertising

Any advertisement that is created or disseminated by a lawyer referral service shall disclose whether the attorneys on the organization's referral list, panel, or system, paid any consideration, other than a proportional share of actual cost, to be included on that list, panel, or system.

§ 6158. Electronic media advertising; false, misleading or deceptive message; factual substantiation

In advertising by electronic media, to comply with Sections 6157.1 and 6157.2, the message as a whole may not be false, misleading, or deceptive, and the message as a whole must be factually substantiated. The message means the effect in combination of the spoken word, sound, background, action, symbols, visual image, or any other technique employed to create the message. Factually substantiated means capable of verification by a credible source.

§ 6158.1. False, misleading or deceptive messages; rebuttable presumption

There shall be a rebuttable presumption affecting the burden of producing evidence that the following messages are false, misleading, or deceptive within the meaning of Section 6158:

(a) A message as to the ultimate result of a specific case or cases presented out of context without adequately providing information as to the facts or law giving rise to the result.

(b) The depiction of an event through methods such as the use of displays of injuries, accident scenes, or portrayals of other injurious events which may or may not be accompanied by sound effects and which may give rise to a claim for compensation.

(c) A message referring to or implying money received by or for a client in a particular case or cases, or to potential monetary recovery for a prospective client. A reference to money or monetary recovery includes, but is not limited to, a specific dollar amount, characterization of a sum of money, monetary symbols, or the implication of wealth.

§ 6158.2.   Information presumed to be in compliance with article

The following information shall be presumed to be in compliance with this article for purposes of advertising by electronic media, provided the message as a whole is not false, misleading, or deceptive:

(a) Name, including name of law firm, names of professional associates, addresses, telephone numbers, and the designation "lawyer," "attorney," "law firm," or the like.

(b) Fields of practice, limitation of practice, or specialization.

(c) Fees for routine legal services, subject to the requirements of subdivision (d) of Section 6157.2 and the Rules of Professional Conduct.

(d) Date and place of birth.

(e) Date and place of admission to the bar of state and federal courts.

(f) Schools attended, with dates of graduation, degrees, and other scholastic distinctions.

(g) Public or quasi-public offices.

(h) Military service.

(i) Legal authorship.

(j) Legal teaching positions.

(k) Memberships, offices, and committee assignments in bar associations.

(l) Memberships and offices in legal fraternities and legal societies.

(m) Technical and professional licenses.

(n) Memberships in scientific, technical, and professional associations and societies.

(o) Foreign language ability of the advertising lawyer or a member of lawyer's firm.

§ 6158.3.   Electronic media advertising; required disclosures

In addition to any disclosure required by Section 6157.2, Section 6157.3, and the Rules of Professional Conduct, the following disclosure shall appear in advertising by electronic media. Use of the following disclosure alone may not rebut any presumption created in Section 6158.1. If an advertisement in the electronic media conveys a message portraying a result in a particular case or cases, the advertisement must state, in either an oral or printed communication, either of the following disclosures: The advertisement must adequately disclose the factual and legal circumstances that justify the result portrayed in the message, including the basis for liability and the nature of injury or damage sustained, or the advertisement must state that the result portrayed in the advertisement was dependent on the facts of that case, and that the results will differ if based on different facts.

§ 6158.4.   Violation; complaint; contents; procedure

(a) Any person claiming a violation of Section 6158, 6158.1, or 6158.3 may file a complaint with the State Bar that states the name of the advertiser, a description of the advertisement claimed to violate these sections, and that specifically identifies the alleged violation. A copy of the complaint shall be served simultaneously upon the advertiser. The advertiser shall have nine days from the date of service of the complaint to voluntarily withdraw from broadcast the advertisement that is the subject of the complaint. If the advertiser elects to withdraw the advertisement, the advertiser shall notify the State Bar of that fact, and no further action may be taken by the complainant. The advertiser shall provide a copy of the complained of advertisement to the State Bar for review within seven days of service of the complaint. Within 21 days of the delivery of the complained of advertisement, the State Bar shall determine whether substantial evidence of a violation of these sections exists. The review shall be conducted by a State Bar attorney who has expertise in the area of lawyer advertising.

(b)(1) Upon a State Bar determination that substantial evidence of a violation exists, if the member or certified lawyer referral service withdraws that advertisement from broadcast within 72 hours, no further action may be taken by the complainant.

(2) Upon a State Bar determination that substantial evidence of a violation exists, if the member or certified lawyer referral service fails to withdraw the advertisement within 72 hours, a civil enforcement action brought pursuant to subdivision (e) may be commenced within one year of the State Bar decision. If the member or certified lawyer referral service withdraws an advertisement upon a State Bar determination that substantial evidence of a violation exists and subsequently rebroadcasts the same advertisement without a finding by the trier of fact in an action brought pursuant to subdivision (c) or (e) that the advertisement does not violate Section 6158, 6158.1, or 6158.3, a civil enforcement action may be commenced within one year of the rebroadcast.

(3) Upon a determination that substantial evidence of a violation does not exist, the complainant is barred from bringing a civil enforcement action pursuant to subdivision (e), but may bring an action for declaratory relief pursuant to subdivision (c).

(c) Any member or certified lawyer referral service who was the subject of a complaint and any complainant affected by the decision of the State Bar may bring an action for declaratory relief in the superior court to obtain a judicial declaration of whether Section 6158, 6158.1, or

6158.3 has been violated, and, if applicable, may also request injunctive relief. Any defense otherwise available at law may be raised for the first time in the declaratory relief action, including any constitutional challenge. Any civil enforcement action filed pursuant to subdivision (e) shall be stayed pending the resolution of the declaratory relief action. The action shall be defended by the real party in interest. The State Bar shall not be considered a party to the action unless it elects to intervene in the action.

(1) Upon a State Bar determination that substantial evidence of a violation exists, if the complainant or the member or certified lawyer referral service brings an action for declaratory relief to obtain a judicial declaration of whether the advertisement violates Section 6158, 6158.1, or 6158.3, and the court declares that the advertisement violates one or more of the sections, a civil enforcement action pursuant to subdivision (e) may be filed or maintained if the member or certified lawyer referral service failed to withdraw the advertisement within 72 hours of the State Bar determination. The decision of the court that an advertisement violates Section 6158, 6158.1, or 6158.3 shall be binding on the issue of whether the advertisement is unlawful in any pending or prospective civil enforcement action brought pursuant to subdivision (e) if that binding effect is supported by the doctrine of collateral estoppel or res judicata.

If, in that declaratory relief action, the court declares that the advertisement does not violate Section 6158, 6158.1, or 6158.3, the member or lawyer referral service may broadcast the advertisement. The decision of the court that an advertisement does not violate Section 6158, 6158.1, or 6158.3 shall bar any pending or prospective civil enforcement action brought pursuant to subdivision (e) if that prohibitive effect is supported by the doctrine of collateral estoppel or res judicata.

(2) If, following a State Bar determination that does not find substantial evidence that an advertisement violates Section 6158, 6158.1, or 6158.3, the complainant or the member or certified lawyer referral service brings an action for declaratory relief to obtain a judicial declaration of whether the advertisement violates Section 6158, 6158.1, or 6158.3, and the court declares that the advertisement violates one or more of the sections, a civil enforcement action pursuant to subdivision (e) may be filed or maintained if the member or certified lawyer referral service broadcasts the same advertisement following the decision in the declaratory relief action. The decision of the court that an advertisement violates Section 6158, 6158.1, or 6158.3 shall be binding on the issue of whether the advertisement is unlawful in any pending or prospective civil enforcement action brought pursuant to subdivision (e) if that binding effect is supported by the doctrine of collateral estoppel or res judicata.

If, in that declaratory relief action, the court declares that the advertisement does not violate Section 6158, 6158.1, or 6158.3, the member or lawyer referral service may continue broadcast of the advertisement. The decision of the court that an advertisement does not violate Section 6158, 6158.1, or 6158.3 shall bar any pending or prospective civil enforcement action brought pursuant to subdivision (e) if that prohibitive effect is supported by the doctrine of collateral estoppel or res judicata.

(d) The State Bar review procedure shall apply only to members and certified referral services. A direct civil enforcement action for a violation of Section 6158, 6158.1, or 6158.3 may be maintained against any other advertiser after first giving 14 days' notice to the advertiser of the alleged violation. If the advertiser does not withdraw from broadcast the advertisement that is the subject of the notice within 14 days of service of the notice, a civil enforcement action pursuant to subdivision (e) may be commenced. The civil enforcement action shall be commenced within one year of the date of the last publication or broadcast of the advertisement that is the subject of the action.

(e) Subject to Section 6158.5, a violation of Section 6158, 6158.1, or 6158.3 shall be cause for a civil enforcement action brought by any person residing within the State of California for an amount up to five thousand dollars ($5,000) for each individual broadcast that violates Section 6158, 6158.1, or 6158.3. Venue shall be in a county where the advertisement was broadcast.

(f) In any civil action brought pursuant to this section, the matter shall be determined according to the law and procedure relating to the trial of civil actions, including trial by jury, if demanded.

(g) The decision of the State Bar pursuant to subdivision (a) shall be admissible in the civil enforcement action brought pursuant to subdivision (e). However, the State Bar shall not be a party or a witness in either a declaratory relief proceeding brought pursuant to subdivision (c) or the civil enforcement action brought pursuant to subdivision (e). Additionally, no direct action may be filed against the State Bar challenging the State Bar's decision pursuant to subdivision (a).

(h) Amounts recovered pursuant to this section shall be paid into the Client Security Fund maintained by the State Bar.

(i) In any civil action brought pursuant to this section, the court shall award attorney's fees pursuant to Section 1021.5 of the Code of Civil Procedure if the court finds that the action has resulted in the enforcement of an important public interest or that a significant benefit has been conferred on the public.

(j) The State Bar shall maintain records of all complainants and complaints filed pursuant to subdivision (a) for a period of seven years. If a complainant files five or more unfounded complaints within seven years, the complainant shall be considered a vexatious litigant for purposes of this section. The State Bar shall require any person deemed a vexatious litigant to post security in the minimum amount of twenty-five thousand dollars ($25,000) prior to considering any complaint filed by that person and shall refrain from taking any action until the security is posted. In any civil action arising from this section brought by a person deemed a vexatious litigant, the defendant may advise the court and trier of fact that the plaintiff is deemed to be a vexatious litigant under the provisions of this section and disclose the basis for this determination.

(k) Nothing in this section shall restrict any other right available under existing law or otherwise available to a citizen seeking redress for false, misleading, or deceptive advertisements.

§ 6158.5.   Application of article

This article applies to all lawyers, members, law partnerships, law corporations, entities subject to regulation under Section 6155, advertising collectives, cooperatives, or other individuals, including nonlawyers, or groups advertising the availability of legal services. Subdivisions (a) to (k), inclusive, of Section 6158.4 do not apply to qualified legal services projects as defined in Article 14 (commencing with Section 6210) and nonprofit lawyer referral services certified under Section 6155. Sections 6157 to 6158.5, inclusive, do not apply to the media in which the advertising is displayed or to an advertising agency that prepares the contents of an advertisement and is not directly involved in the formation or operation of lawyer advertising collectives or cooperatives, referral services, or other groups existing primarily for the purpose of advertising the availability of legal services or making referrals to attorneys.

§ 6158.7.   Violation as cause for discipline by state bar

A violation of Section 6158, 6158.1, or 6158.3 by a member shall be cause for discipline by the State Bar. In addition to the existing grounds for initiating a disciplinary proceeding set forth in a statute or in the Rules of Professional Conduct, the State Bar may commence an investigation based upon a complaint filed by a person pursuant to Section 6158.4. The State Bar's decision pursuant to subdivision (a) of Section 6158.4 shall be admissible, but shall not be determinative, in any disciplinary proceeding brought as a result of that complaint.

§ 6159.   Report by court of article violators

The court shall report the name, address, and professional license number of any person found in violation of this article to the appropriate professional licensing agency for review and possible disciplinary action.

§ 6159.1   Retention of advertising copy by payor

A true and correct copy of any advertisement made by a person or member shall be retained for one year by the person or member who pays for an advertisement soliciting employment of legal services.

§ 6159.2 Rights and duties under other laws

(a) Nothing in this article shall be deemed to limit or preclude enforcement of any other provision of law, or of any court rule, or of the State Bar Rules of Professional Conduct.

(b) Nothing in this article shall limit the right of advertising protected under the Constitution of the State of California or of the United States. If any provision of this article is found to violate either Constitution, that provision is severable and the remaining provisions shall be enforceable without the severed provision.

ARTICLE 13. ARBITRATION OF ATTORNEYS' FEES

§ 6200. Establishment of system and procedure; applicability of article; voluntary or mandatory nature; rules; immunity of arbitrator; powers of arbitrator; confidentiality of mediation

(a) The board of governors shall, by rule, establish, maintain, and administer a system and procedure for the arbitration, and may establish, maintain, and administer a system and procedure for mediation of disputes concerning fees, costs, or both, charged for professional services by members of the State Bar or by members of the bar of other jurisdictions. The rules may include provision for a filing fee in such amount as the board may, from time to time, determine.

(b) This article shall not apply to any of the following:

(1) Disputes where a member of the State Bar of California is also admitted to practice in another jurisdiction or where an attorney is only admitted to practice in another jurisdiction, and he or she maintains no office in the State of California, and no material portion of the services were rendered in the State of California.

(2) Claims for affirmative relief against the attorney for damages or otherwise based upon alleged malpractice or professional misconduct, except as provided in subdivision (a) of Section 6203.

(3) Disputes where the fee or cost to be paid by the client or on his or her behalf has been determined pursuant to statute or court order.

(c) Unless the client has agreed in writing to arbitration under this article of all disputes concerning fees, costs, or both, arbitration under this article shall be voluntary for a client and shall be mandatory for an attorney if commenced by a client. Mediation under this article shall be voluntary for an attorney and a client.

(d) The board of governors shall adopt rules to allow arbitration and mediation of attorney fee and cost disputes under this article to proceed under arbitration and mediation systems sponsored by local bar associations in this state. Rules of procedure promulgated by local bar associations are subject to review by the board to insure that they provide for a fair, impartial, and speedy hearing and award.

(e) In adopting or reviewing rules of arbitration under this section the board shall provide that the panel shall include one attorney member whose area of practice is either, at the option of the client, civil law, if the attorney's representation involved civil law, or criminal law, if the attorney's representation involved criminal law, as follows:

   (1) If the panel is composed of three members the panel shall include one attorney member whose area of practice is either, at the option of the client, civil or criminal law, and shall include one lay member.

   (2) If the panel is composed of one member, that member shall be an attorney whose area of practice is either, at the option of the client, civil or criminal law.

(f) In any arbitration or mediation conducted pursuant to this article by the State Bar or by a local bar association, pursuant to rules of procedure approved by the board of governors, an arbitrator or mediator, as well as the arbitrating association and its directors, officers, and employees, shall have the same immunity which attaches in judicial proceedings.

(g) In the conduct of arbitrations under this article the arbitrator or arbitrators may do all of the following:

   (1) Take and hear evidence pertaining to the proceeding.

   (2) Administer oaths and affirmations.

   (3) Compel, by subpoena, the attendance of witnesses and the production of books, papers, and documents pertaining to the proceeding.

(h) Participation in mediation is a voluntary consensual process, based on direct negotiations between the attorney and his or her client, and is an extension of the negotiated settlement process. All discussions and offers of settlement are confidential and may not be disclosed in any subsequent arbitration or other proceedings.

§ 6201. Notice to client and state bar; stay of action; right to arbitration; waiver by client

(a) The rules adopted by the board of governors shall provide that an attorney shall forward a written notice to the client prior to or at the time of service of summons or claim in an action against the client or prior to or at the commencement of any other proceeding against client under a contract between attorney and client which provides for an alternative to arbitration under this article, for recovery of fees, costs, or both. The written notice shall be in the form that the board of governors prescribes, and shall include a statement of the client's right to arbitration under this article. Failure to give this notice shall be a ground for the dismissal of the action or other proceeding. The notice shall not be required, however, prior to initiating mediation of the dispute.

The rules adopted by the board of governors shall provide that the client's failure to request arbitration within 30 days after receipt of notice from the attorney shall be deemed a waiver of the client's right to arbitration under the provisions of this article.

(b) If an attorney, or the attorney's assignee, commences an action in any court or any other proceeding and the client is entitled to maintain arbitration under this article, and the dispute is not one to which subdivision (b) of Section 6200 applies, the client may stay the action or other proceeding by serving and filing a request for arbitration in accordance with the rules established by the board of governors pursuant to subdivision (a) of Section 6200. The request for arbitration shall be served and filed prior to the filing of an answer in the action or equivalent response in the other proceeding; failure to so request arbitration prior to the filing of an answer or equivalent response shall be deemed a waiver of the client's right to arbitration under the provisions of this article if notice of the client's right to arbitration was given pursuant to subdivision (a).

(c) Upon filing and service of the request for arbitration, the action or other proceeding shall be automatically stayed until the award of the arbitrators is issued or the arbitration is otherwise terminated. The stay may be vacated in whole or in part, after a hearing duly noticed by any party or the court, if and to the extent the court finds that the matter is not appropriate for arbitration under the provisions of this article. The action or other proceeding may thereafter proceed subject to the provisions of Section 6204.

(d) A client's right to request or maintain arbitration under the provisions of this article is waived by the client commencing an action or filing any pleading seeking either of the following: (1) Judicial resolution of a fee dispute to which this article applies. (2) Affirmative relief against the attorney for damages or otherwise based upon alleged malpractice or professional misconduct.

(e) If the client waives the right to arbitration under this article, the parties may stipulate to set aside the waiver and to proceed with arbitration.

§ 6203. Award; contents; damages and offset; fees and costs; finality of award; appellate fees and costs; attorney inactive status and penalties

(a) The award shall be in writing and signed by the arbitrators concurring therein. It shall include a determination of all the questions submitted to the arbitrators, the decision of which is necessary in order to determine the controversy. The award shall not include any award to either party for costs or attorney's fees incurred in preparation for or in the course of the fee arbitration proceeding, notwithstanding any contract between the parties providing for such an award or attorney's fees. However, the filing fee paid may be allocated between the parties by the arbitrators. This section shall not preclude an award of costs or attorney's fees to either party by a court pursuant to subdivision (c) of this section or of subdivision (d) of Section 6204. The State Bar, or the local bar association delegated by the State Bar to conduct the arbitration, shall deliver to each of the parties with the award, an original declaration of service of the award.

Evidence relating to claims of malpractice and professional misconduct, shall be admissible only to the extent that those claims bear upon the fees, costs, or both, to which the attorney is entitled. The arbitrators shall not award affirmative relief, in the form of damages or offset or otherwise, for injuries underlying any such claim. Nothing in this section shall be construed to prevent the arbitrators from awarding a refund of unearned prepaid fees.

(b) Even if the parties to the arbitration have not agreed in writing to be bound, the arbitration award shall become binding upon the passage of 30 days after mailing of notice of the award, unless a party has, within the 30 days, sought a trial after arbitration pursuant to Section 6204. If an action has previously been filed in any court, any petition to confirm, correct, or vacate the award shall be to the court in which the action is pending, and may be served by mail on any party who has appeared, as provided in Chapter 4 (commencing with Section 1003) of Title 14 of Part 2 of the Code of Civil Procedure; otherwise it shall be in the same manner as provided in Chapter 4 (commencing with Section 1285) of Title 9 of Part 3 of the Code of Civil Procedure. If no action is pending in any court, the award may be confirmed, corrected, or vacated by petition to the court having jurisdiction over the amount of the arbitration award, but otherwise in the same manner as provided in Chapter 4 (commencing with Section 1285) of Title 9 of Part 3 of the Code of Civil Procedure.

(c) Neither party to the arbitration may recover costs or attorney's fees incurred in preparation for or in the course of the fee arbitration proceeding with the exception of the filing fee paid pursuant to subdivision (a) of this section. However, a court confirming, correcting, or vacating an award under this section may award to the prevailing party reasonable fees and costs including, if applicable, fees or costs on appeal, incurred in obtaining confirmation, correction, or vacation of the award. The party obtaining judgment confirming, correcting, or vacating the award shall be the prevailing party except that, without regard to consideration of who the prevailing party may be, if a party did not appear at the arbitration hearing in the manner provided by the rules adopted by the board of governors, that party shall not be entitled to attorney's fees or costs upon confirmation, correction, or vacation of the award.

(d)(1) In any matter arbitrated under this article in which the award is binding or has become binding by operation of law or has become a judgment either after confirmation under subdivision (c) or after a trial after arbitration under Section 6204, or in any matter mediated under this article, if: (A) the award, judgment, or agreement reached after mediation includes a refund of fees or costs, or both, to the client and (B) the attorney has not complied with that award, judgment, or agreement the State Bar shall enforce the award, judgment, or agreement by placing the attorney on involuntary inactive status until the refund has been paid.

(2) The State Bar shall provide for an administrative procedure to determine whether an award, judgment, or agreement should be enforced pursuant to this subdivision. An award, judgment, or agreement shall be so enforced if either of the following applies:

> (A) The State Bar shows that the attorney has failed to comply with a binding fee arbitration award, judgment, or agreement rendered pursuant to this article.

> (B) The attorney has not proposed a payment plan acceptable to the client or the State Bar.

However, the award, judgment, or agreement shall not be so enforced if the attorney has demonstrated that he or she (i) is not personally responsible for making or ensuring payment of the refund, or (ii) is unable to pay the refund.

(3) An attorney who has failed to comply with a binding award, judgment, or agreement shall pay administrative penalties or reasonable costs, or both, as directed by the State Bar. Penalties imposed shall not exceed 20 percent of the amount to be refunded to the client or one thousand dollars ($1,000), whichever is greater. Any penalties or costs, or both, that are not paid shall be added to the membership fee of the attorney for the next calendar year.

(4) The board shall terminate the inactive enrollment upon proof that the attorney has complied with the award, judgment, or agreement and upon payment of any costs or penalties, or both, assessed as a result of the attorney's failure to comply.

(5) A request for enforcement under this subdivision shall be made within four years from the date (A) the arbitration award was mailed, (B) the judgment was entered, or (C) the date the agreement was signed. In an arbitrated matter, however, in no event shall a request be made prior to 100 days from the date of the service of a signed copy of the award. In cases where the award is appealed, a request shall not be made prior to 100 days from the date the award has become final as set forth in this section.

ARTICLE 14. FUNDS FOR THE PROVISION OF LEGAL SERVICES TO INDIGENT PERSONS

§ 6210. Legislative findings; purpose

The Legislature finds that, due to insufficient funding, existing programs providing free legal services in civil matters to indigent persons, especially underserved client groups, such as the elderly, the disabled, juveniles, and non-English-speaking persons, do not adequately meet the needs of these persons. It is the purpose of this article to expand the availability and improve the quality of existing free legal services in civil matters to indigent persons, and to initiate new programs that will provide services to them. The Legislature finds that the use of funds collected by the State Bar pursuant to this article for these purposes is in the public interest, is a proper use of the funds, and is consistent with essential public and governmental purposes in the judicial branch of government. The Legislature further finds that the expansion, improvement, and initiation of legal services to indigent persons will aid in the advancement of the science of jurisprudence and the improvement of the administration of justice.

§ 6211. Establishment by attorney of demand trust account; interest earned to be paid to state bar; other accounts not prohibited; rules of professional conduct, authority of supreme court or state bar not affected

(a) An attorney or law firm, which in the course of the practice of law receives or disburses trust funds, shall establish and maintain an interest bearing demand trust account and shall deposit therein all client deposits that are nominal in amount or are on deposit for a short period of time. All such client funds may be deposited in a single unsegregated account. The interest earned on all such accounts shall be paid to the State Bar of California to be used for the purposes set forth in this article.

(b) Nothing in this article shall be construed to prohibit an attorney or law firm from establishing one or more interest bearing bank accounts or other trust investments as may be permitted by the Supreme Court, with the interest or dividends earned on the accounts payable to clients for trust funds not deposited in accordance with subdivision (a).

(c) With the approval of the Supreme Court, the State Bar may formulate and enforce rules of professional conduct pertaining to the use by attorneys or law firms of interest bearing trust accounts for unsegregated client funds pursuant to this article.

(d) Nothing in this article shall be construed as affecting or impairing the disciplinary powers and authority of the Supreme Court or of the State Bar or as modifying the statutes and rules governing the conduct of members of the State Bar.

§ 6212. Establishment by attorney of demand trust account; amount of interest; remittance to state bar; statements and reports

An attorney who, or a law firm which, establishes an interest bearing demand trust account pursuant to subdivision (a) of Section 6211 shall comply with all of the following provisions:

(a) The interest bearing trust account shall be established with a bank or such other financial institution as are authorized by the Supreme Court.

(b) The rate of interest payable on any interest bearing demand trust account shall not be less than the rate paid by the depository institution to regular, nonattorney depositors. Higher rates offered by the institution to customers whose deposits exceed certain time or quantity qualifications, such as those offered in the form of certificates of deposit, may be obtained by an attorney or law firm so long as there is no impairment of the right to withdraw or transfer principal immediately (except as accounts generally may be subject to statutory notification requirements), even though interest may be sacrificed thereby.

(c) The depository institution shall be directed to do all of the following:

(1) To remit interest on the average daily balance in the account, less reasonable service charges, to the State Bar, at least quarterly.

(2) To transmit to the State Bar with each remittance a statement showing the name of the attorney or law firm for whom the remittance is sent, the rate of interest applied, and the amount of service charges deducted, if any.

(3) To transmit to the depositing attorney or law firm at the same time a report showing the amount paid to the State Bar for that period, the rate of interest applied, the amount of service charges deducted, if any, and the average daily account balance for each month of the period for which the report is made.

§ 6213. Definitions

As used in this article:

(a) "Qualified legal services project" means either of the following:

(1) A nonprofit project incorporated and operated exclusively in California which provides as its primary purpose and function legal services without charge to indigent persons and which has quality control procedures approved by the State Bar of California.

(2) A program operated exclusively in California by a nonprofit law school accredited by the State Bar of California which meets the requirements of subparagraphs (A) and (B).

(A) The program shall have operated for at least two years at a cost of at least twenty thousand dollars ($20,000) per year as an identifiable law school unit with a primary purpose and function of providing legal services without charge to indigent persons.

(B) The program shall have quality control procedures approved by the State Bar of California.

(b) "Qualified support center" means an incorporated nonprofit legal services center, which has as its primary purpose and function the provision of legal training, legal technical assistance, or advocacy support without charge and which actually provides through an office in California a significant level of legal training, legal technical assistance, or advocacy support without charge to qualified legal services projects on a statewide basis in California.

(c) "Recipient" means a qualified legal services project or support center receiving financial assistance under this article.

(d) "Indigent person" means a person whose income is (1) 125 percent or less of the current poverty threshold established by the United States Office of Management and Budget, or (2) who is eligible for Supplemental Security Income or free services under the Older Americans Act or Developmentally Disabled Assistance Act. With regard to a project which provides free services of attorneys in private practice without compensation, "indigent person" also means a person whose income is 75 percent or less of the maximum levels of income for lower income households as defined in Section 50079.5 of the Health and Safety Code. For the purpose of this subdivision, the income of a person who is disabled shall be determined after deducting the costs of medical and other disability-related special expenses.

(e) "Fee generating case" means any case or matter which, if undertaken on behalf of an indigent person by an attorney in private practice, reasonably may be expected to result in payment of a fee for legal services from an award to a client, from public funds, or from the opposing party. A case shall not be considered fee generating if adequate representation is unavailable and any of the following circumstances exist:

(1) The recipient has determined that free referral is not possible because of any of the following reasons:

(A) The case has been rejected by the local lawyer referral service, or if there is no such service, by two attorneys in private practice who have experience in the subject matter of the case.

(B) Neither the referral service nor any attorney will consider the case without payment of a consultation fee.

(C) The case if of the type that attorneys in private practice in the area ordinarily do not accept, or do not accept without prepayment of a fee.

(D) Emergency circumstances compel immediate action before referral can be made, but the client is advised that, if appropriate and consistent with professional responsibility, referral will be attempted at a later time.

(2) Recovery of damages is not the principal object of the case and a request for damages is merely ancillary to an action for equitable or other nonpecuniary relief, or inclusion of a counterclaim requesting damages is necessary for effective defense or because of applicable rules governing joinder of counterclaims.

(3) A court has appointed a recipient or an employee of a recipient pursuant to a statute or a court rule or practice of equal applicability to all attorneys in the jurisdiction.

(4) The case involves the rights of a claimant under a publicly supported benefit program for which entitlement to benefit is based on need.

(f) "Legal Services Corporation" means the Legal Services Corporation established under the Legal Services Corporation Act of 1974, (Public Law 93–355; 42 U.S.C. Sec. 2996 et seq.).

(g) "Older Americans Act" means the Older Americans Act of 1965, as amended (Public Law 89–73; 42 U.S.C. Sec. 3001 et seq.).

(h) "Developmentally Disabled Assistance Act" means the Developmentally Disabled Assistance and Bill of Rights Act of 1975, as amended (Public Law 94–103; 42 U.S.C. Sec. 6001 et seq.).

(i) "Supplemental security income recipient" means an individual receiving or eligible to receive payments under Title XVI of the federal Social Security Act, or payments under Chapter 3 (commencing with Section 12000) of Part 3 of Division 9 of the Welfare and Institutions Code.

§ 6214. Qualified legal service projects

(a) Projects meeting the requirements of subdivision (a) of Section 6213 which are funded either in whole or part by the Legal Services Corporation or with Older American Act funds shall be presumed qualified legal services projects for the purpose of this article.

(b) Projects meeting the requirements of subdivision (a) of Section 6213 but not qualifying under the presumption specified in subdivision (a) shall qualify for funds under this article if they meet all of the following additional criteria:

(1) They receive cash funds from other sources in the amount of at least twenty thousand dollars ($20,000) per year to support free legal representation to indigent persons.

(2) They have demonstrated community support for the operation of a viable ongoing program.

(3) They provide one or both of the following special services:

(A) The coordination of the recruitment of substantial numbers of attorneys in private practice to provide free legal representation to indigent persons or to qualified legal services projects in California.

(B) The provision of legal representation, training, or technical assistance on matters concerning special client groups, including the elderly, the disabled, juveniles, and non-English-speaking groups, or on matters of specialized substantive law important to the special client groups.

§ 6214.5 Qualified legal services projects; eligibility for distributions of funds

A law school program that meets the definition of a "qualified legal services project" as defined in paragraph (2) of subdivision (a) of Section 6213, and that applied to the State Bar for funding under this article not later than February 17, 1984, shall be deemed eligible for all distributions of funds made under Section 6216.

§ 6215. Qualified support centers

(a) Support centers satisfying the qualifications specified in subdivision (b) of Section 6213 which were operating an office and providing services in California on December 31, 1980, shall be presumed to be qualified support centers for the purposes of this article.

(b) Support centers not qualifying under the presumption specified in subdivision (a) may qualify as a support center by meeting both of the following additional criteria:

(1) Meeting quality control standards established by the State Bar.

(2) Being deemed to be of special need by a majority of the qualified legal services projects.

§ 6216. Distribution of funds

The State Bar shall distribute all moneys received under the program established by this article for the provision of civil legal services to indigent persons. The funds first shall be distributed 18 months from the effective date of this article, or upon such a date, as shall be determined by the State Bar, that adequate funds are available to initiate the program. Thereafter, the funds shall be distributed on an annual basis. All distributions of funds shall be made in the following order and in the following manner:

(a) To pay the actual administrative costs of the program, including any costs incurred after the adoption of this article and a reasonable reserve therefor.

(b) Eighty-five percent of the funds remaining after payment of administrative costs allocated pursuant to this article shall be distributed to qualified legal services projects. Distribution shall be by a pro rata county-by-county formula based upon the number of persons whose income is 125 percent or less of the current poverty threshold per county. For the purposes of this section, the source of data identifying the number of persons per county shall be the latest available figures from the United States Department of Commerce, Bureau of the Census. Projects from more than one county may pool their funds to operate a joint, multicounty legal services project serving each of their respective counties.

(1)(A) In any county which is served by more than one qualified legal services project, the State Bar shall distribute funds for the county to those projects which apply on a pro rata basis, based upon the amount of their total budget expended in the prior year for legal services in that county as compared to the total expended in the prior year for legal services by all qualified legal services projects applying therefor in the county. In determining the amount of funds to be allocated to a qualified legal services project specified in paragraph (2) of subdivision (a) of Section 6213, the State Bar shall recognize only expenditures attributable to the representation of indigent persons as constituting the budget of the program.

(B) The State Bar shall reserve 10 percent of the funds allocated to the county for distribution to programs meeting the standards of subparagraph (A) of paragraph (3) and paragraphs (1) and (2) of subdivision (b) of Section 6214 and which perform the services described in subparagraph (A) of paragraph (3) of Section 6214 as their principal means of delivering legal services. The State Bar shall distribute the funds for that county to those programs which apply on a pro rata basis, based upon the amount of their total budget expended for free legal services in that county as compared to the total expended for free legal services by all programs meeting the standards of subparagraph (A) of paragraph (3) and paragraphs (1) and (2) of subdivision (b) of Section 6214 in that county. The State Bar shall distribute any funds for which no program has qualified pursuant hereto, in accordance with the provisions of subparagraph (A) of paragraph (1) of this subdivision.

(2) In any county in which there is no qualified legal services projects providing services, the State Bar shall reserve for the remainder of the fiscal year for distribution the pro rata share of funds as provided for by this article. Upon application of a qualified legal services project proposing to provide legal services to the indigent of the county, the State Bar shall distribute the funds to the project. Any funds not so distributed shall be added to the funds to be distributed the following year.

(c) Fifteen percent of the funds remaining after payment of administrative costs allocated for the purposes of this article shall be distributed equally by the State Bar to qualified support centers which apply for the funds. The funds provided to support centers shall be used only for the provision of legal services within California. Qualified support centers that receive funds to provide services to qualified legal services projects from sources other than this article, shall submit and shall have approved by the State Bar a plan assuring that the services funded under this article are in addition to those already funded for qualified legal services projects by other sources.

§ 6217. Maintenance of quality services, professional standards, attorney-client privilege; funds to be expended in accordance with article; interference with attorney prohibited

With respect to the provision of legal assistance under this article, each recipient shall ensure all of the following:

(a) The maintenance of quality service and professional standards.

(b) The expenditure of funds received in accordance with the provisions of this article.

(c) The preservation of the attorney-client privilege in any case, and the protection of the integrity of the adversary process from any impairment in furnishing legal assistance to indigent persons.

(d) That no one shall interfere with any attorney funded in whole or in part by this article in carrying out his or her professional responsibility to his or her client as established by the rules of professional responsibility and this chapter.

§ 6218. Eligibility for services; establishment of guidelines; funds to be expended in accordance with article

All legal services projects and support centers receiving funds pursuant to this article shall adopt financial eligibility guidelines for indigent persons.

(a) Qualified legal services programs shall ensure that funds appropriated pursuant to this article shall be used solely to defray the costs of providing legal services to indigent persons or for such other purposes as set forth in this article.

(b) Funds received pursuant to this article by support centers shall only be used to provide services to qualified legal services projects as defined in subdivision (a) of Section 6213 which are used pursuant to a plan as required by subdivision (c) of Section 6216, or as permitted by Section 6219.

§6219. Provision of work opportunities and scholarships for disadvantaged law students

Qualified legal services projects and support centers may use funds provided under this article to provide work opportunities with pay, and where feasible, scholarships for disadvantaged law students to help defray their law school expenses.

§6220. Private attorneys providing legal services without charge; support center services

Attorneys in private practice who are providing legal services without charge to indigent persons shall not be disqualified from receiving the services of the qualified support centers.

§6221. Services for indigent members of disadvantaged and underserved groups

Qualified legal services projects shall make significant efforts to utilize 20 percent of the funds allocated under this article for increasing the availability of services to the elderly, the disabled, juveniles, or other indigent persons who are members of disadvantaged and underserved groups within their service area.

§6222. Financial statements; submission to state bar; state bar report

A recipient of funds allocated pursuant to this article annually shall submit a financial statement to the State Bar, including an audit of the funds by a certified public accountant or a fiscal review approved by the State Bar, a report demonstrating the programs on which they were expended, a report on the recipient's compliance with the requirements of Section 6217, and progress in meeting the service expansion requirements of Section 6221.

The Board of Governors of the State Bar shall include a report of receipts of funds under this article, expenditures for administrative costs, and disbursements of the funds, on a county-by-county basis, in the annual report of State Bar receipts and expenditures required pursuant to Section 6145.

§6223. Expenditure of funds; prohibitions

No funds allocated by the State Bar pursuant to this article shall be used for any of the following purposes:

(a) The provision of legal assistance with respect to any fee generating case, except in accordance with guidelines which shall be promulgated by the State Bar.

(b) The provision of legal assistance with respect to any criminal proceeding.

(c) The provision of legal assistance, except to indigent persons or except to provide support services to qualified legal services projects as defined by this article.

§ 6224. State bar; powers; determination of qualifications to receive funds; denial of funds; termination; procedures

The State Bar shall have the power to determine that an applicant for funding is not qualified to receive funding, to deny future funding, or to terminate existing funding because the recipient is not operating in compliance with the requirements or restrictions of this article.

A denial of an application for funding or for future funding or an action by the State Bar to terminate an existing grant of funds under this article shall not become final until the applicant or recipient has been afforded reasonable notice and an opportunity for a timely and fair hearing. Pending final determination of any hearing held with reference to termination of funding, financial assistance shall be continued at its existing level on a month-to-month basis. Hearings for denial shall be conducted by an impartial hearing officer whose decision shall be final. The hearing officer shall render a decision no later than 30 days after the conclusion of the hearing. Specific procedures governing the conduct of the hearings of this section shall be determined by the State Bar pursuant to Section 6225.

§ 6225. Implementation of article; adoption of rules and regulations; procedures

The Board of Governors of the State Bar shall adopt the regulations and procedures necessary to implement this article and to ensure that the funds allocated herein are utilized to provide civil legal services to indigent persons, especially underserved client groups such as but not limited to the elderly, the disabled, juveniles, and non-English-speaking persons.

In adopting the regulations the Board of Governors shall comply with the following procedures:

(a) The board shall publish a preliminary draft of the regulations and procedures, which shall be distributed, together with notice of the hearings required by subdivision (b), to commercial banking institutions, to members of the State Bar, and to potential recipients of funds.

(b) The board shall hold at least two public hearings, one in southern California and one in northern California where affected and interested parties shall be afforded an opportunity to present oral and written testimony regarding the proposed regulations and procedures.

§ 6226. Implementation of article; resolution

The program authorized by this article shall become operative only upon the adoption of a resolution by the Board of Governors of the State Bar stating that regulations have been adopted pursuant to Section 6225 which conform the program to all applicable tax and banking statutes, regulations, and rulings.

§ 6227. Credit of state not pledged

Nothing in this article shall create an obligation or pledge of the credit of the State of California or of the State Bar of California. Claims arising by reason of acts done pursuant to this article shall be limited to the moneys generated hereunder.

§ 6228. Severability

If any provision of this article or the application thereof to any group or circumstances is held invalid, such invalidity shall not affect the other provisions or applications of this article which can be given effect without the invalid provision or application, and to this end the provisions of this article are severable.

NEW YORK CODE OF PROFESSIONAL RESPONSIBILITY: CANONS AND DISCIPLINARY RULES

[In 1990, the Appellate Divisions of the Supreme Court promulgated the following Code of Professional Responsibility. The New York Code continues to retain the Canons and the Ethical Considerations; however, the ethical considerations are not reprinted below. Ed.]

Table of Contents

PREAMBLE AND PRELIMINARY STATEMENT

Preamble

The continued existence of a free and democratic society depends upon recognition of the concept that justice is based upon the rule of law grounded in respect for the dignity of the individual and his capacity through reason for enlightened self-government. Law so grounded makes justice possible, for only through such law does the dignity of the individual attain respect and protection. Without it, individual rights

347

become subject to unrestrained power, respect for law is destroyed, and rational self-government is impossible.

Lawyers, as guardians of the law, play a vital role in the preservation of society. The fulfillment of this role requires an understanding by lawyers of their relationship with and function in our legal system. A consequent obligation of lawyers is to maintain the highest standards of ethical conduct.

In fulfilling his professional responsibilities, a lawyer necessarily assumes various roles that require the performance of many difficult tasks. Not every situation which he may encounter can be foreseen, but fundamental ethical principles are always present to guide him. Within the framework of these principles, a lawyer must with courage and foresight be able and ready to shape the body of the law to the ever-changing relationships of society.

The Code of Professional Responsibility points the way to the aspiring and provides standards by which to judge the transgressor. Each lawyer must find within his own conscience the touchstone against which to test the extent to which his actions should rise above minimum standards. But in the last analysis it is the desire for the respect and confidence of the members of his profession and of the society which he serves that should provide to a lawyer the incentive for the highest possible degree of ethical conduct. The possible loss of that respect and confidence is the ultimate sanction. So long as its practitioners are guided by these principles, the law will continue to be a noble profession. This is its greatness and its strength, which permit of no compromise.

Preliminary Statement

In furtherance of the principles stated in the Preamble, the American Bar Association has promulgated this Code of Professional Responsibility, consisting of three separate but interrelated parts: Canons, Ethical Considerations, and Disciplinary Rules. The Code is designed to be adopted by appropriate agencies both as an inspirational guide to the members of the profession and as a basis for disciplinary action when the conduct of a lawyer falls below the required minimum standards stated in the Disciplinary Rules.

Obviously the Canons, Ethical Considerations, and Disciplinary Rules cannot apply to non-lawyers; however, they do define the type of ethical conduct that the public has a right to expect not only of lawyers but also of their non-professional employees and associates in all matters pertaining to professional employment. A lawyer should ultimately be responsible for the conduct of his employees and associates in the course of the professional representation of the client.

The Canons are statements of axiomatic norms, expressing in general terms the standards of professional conduct expected of lawyers in their relationships with the public, with the legal system, and with the legal profession. They embody the general concepts from which the Ethical Considerations and the Disciplinary Rules are derived.

The Ethical Considerations are aspirational in character and represent the objectives toward which every member of the profession should strive. They constitute a body of principles upon which the lawyer can rely for guidance in many specific situations.

The Disciplinary Rules, unlike the Ethical Considerations, are mandatory in character. The Disciplinary Rules state the minimum level of conduct below which no lawyer can fall without being subject to disciplinary action. Within the framework of fair trial, the Disciplinary Rules should be uniformly applied to all lawyers, regardless of the nature of their professional activities. The Code makes no attempt to prescribe either disciplinary procedures or penalties for violation of a Disciplinary Rule, nor does it undertake to define standards for civil liability of lawyers for professional conduct. The severity of judgment against one found guilty of violating a Disciplinary Rule should be determined by the character of the offense and the attendant circumstances. An enforcing agency, in applying the Disciplinary Rules, may find interpretive guidance in the basic principles embodied in the Canons and in the objectives reflected in the Ethical Considerations.

DEFINITIONS

As used in the Disciplinary Rules of the Code of Professional Responsibility[1]:

1. "Differing interests" include every interest that will adversely affect either the judgment or the loyalty of a lawyer to a client, whether it be a conflicting, inconsistent, diverse, or other interest.

2. "Law firm" includes, but is not limited to, a professional legal corporation, the legal department of a corporation or other organization and a legal services organization.

3. "Person" includes a corporation, an association, a trust, a partnership, and any other organization or legal entity.

4. "Professional legal corporation" means a corporation, or an association treated as a corporation, authorized by law to practice law for profit.

5. "State" includes the District of Columbia, Puerto Rico, and other federal territories and possessions.

6. "Tribunal" includes all courts and all other adjudicatory bodies. A tribunal shall be deemed "available" when it would have jurisdiction to hear a complaint, if timely brought.

7. "Bar association" includes a bar association of specialists as referred to in DR 2–105(B).

8. "Qualified legal assistance organization" means an office or organization of one of the four types listed in DR 2–103(D)(1) through (4), inclusive, that meets all the requirements thereof.

9. "Fraud" does not include conduct, although characterized as fraudulent by statute or administrative rule, which lacks an element of

---

1. "Confidence" and "Secret" are defined in DR 4–101(A).

scienter deceit, intent to mislead, or knowing failure to correct misrepresentations which can be reasonably expected to induce detrimental reliance by another.

CANON 1

A Lawyer Should Assist in Maintaining the Integrity and Competence of the Legal Profession

DISCIPLINARY RULES

DR 1-101. Maintaining Integrity and Competence of the Legal Profession

A. A lawyer is subject to discipline if the lawyer has made a materially false statement in, or has deliberately failed to disclose a material fact requested in connection with, the lawyer's application for admission to the bar.

B. A lawyer shall not further the application for admission to the bar of another person that the lawyer knows to be unqualified in respect to character, education, or other relevant attribute.

DR 1-102. Misconduct

A.[1] A lawyer shall not:

1. Violate a Disciplinary Rule.

2. Circumvent a Disciplinary Rule through actions of another.

3. Engage in illegal conduct involving moral turpitude.

4. Engage in conduct involving dishonesty, fraud, deceit, or misrepresentation.

5. Engage in conduct that is prejudicial to the administration of justice.

6. Unlawfully discriminate in the practice of law, including in hiring, promoting or otherwise determining conditions of employment, on the basis of age, race, creed, color, national origin, sex, disability, marital status, or sexual orientation.

Where there is available a tribunal of competent jurisdiction, other than a Departmental Disciplinary Committee, a complaint of professional misconduct based on unlawful discrimination shall be brought before such tribunal in the first instance. A certified copy of a determination by such a tribunal, which has become final and enforceable, and as to which the right to judicial or appellate review has been exhausted, finding that the lawyer has engaged in an unlawful discriminatory practice shall constitute *prima facie* evidence of professional misconduct in a disciplinary proceeding.

7. Begin a sexual relationship with a client during the course of the lawyer's representation of the client.

---

1. So in original. No par. B has been enacted.

8. Engage in any other conduct that adversely reflects on the lawyer's fitness to practice law.

DR 1–103. Disclosure of Information to Authorities

A. A lawyer possessing knowledge, (1) not protected as a confidence or secret, of a violation, or (2), not gained in the lawyer's capacity as a member of a bona fide lawyer assistance or similar program or committee, of DR 1–102 that raises a substantial question as to another lawyer's honesty, trustworthiness or fitness in other respects as a lawyer shall report such knowledge to a tribunal or other authority empowered to investigate or act upon such violation.

B. A lawyer possessing knowledge or evidence, not protected as a confidence or secret, concerning another lawyer or a judge shall reveal fully such knowledge or evidence upon proper request of a tribunal or other authority empowered to investigate or act upon the conduct of lawyers or judges.

DR 1–104. Responsibilities of a Partner or Supervisory Lawyer

(a) A law firm shall make reasonable efforts to ensure that all lawyers in the firm conform to the disciplinary rules.

(b) A lawyer with management responsibility in the law firm or direct supervisory authority over another lawyer shall make reasonable efforts to ensure that the other lawyer conforms to the disciplinary rules.

(c) A law firm shall adequately supervise, as appropriate, the work of partners, associates and nonlawyers who work at the firm. The degree of supervision required is that which is reasonable under the circumstances, taking into account factors such as the experience of the person whose work is being supervised, the amount of work involved in a particular matter, and the likelihood that ethical problems might arise in the course of working on the matter.

(d) A lawyer shall be responsible for a violation of the disciplinary rules by another lawyer or for conduct of a nonlawyer employed or retained by or associated with the lawyer that would be a violation of the disciplinary rules if engaged in by a lawyer if:

(1) The lawyer orders, or directs the specific conduct, or, with knowledge of the specific conduct, ratifies it; or

(2) The lawyer is a partner in the law firm in which the other lawyer practices or the nonlawyer is employed, or has supervisory authority over the other lawyer or the nonlawyer, and knows of such conduct, or in the exercise or reasonable management or supervisory authority should have known of the conduct so that reasonable remedial action could be or could have been taken at a time when its consequences could be or could have been avoided or mitigated.

CANON 2

A Lawyer Should Assist the Legal Profession in Fulfilling Its Duty to Make Legal Counsel Available

DR 2–101. Publicity and Advertising

A. A lawyer on behalf of himself or herself or partners or associates, shall not use or disseminate or participate in the preparation or dissemination of any public communication containing statements or claims that are false, deceptive, misleading or cast reflection on the legal profession as a whole.

B. Advertising or other publicity by lawyers, including participation in public functions, shall not contain puffery, self-laudation, claims regarding the quality of the lawyers' legal services, or claims that cannot be measured or verified.

C. It is proper to include information, provided its dissemination does not violate the provisions of subdivisions (A) and (B) of this section, as to:

1. education, degrees and other scholastic distinctions, dates of admission to any bar; areas of the law in which the lawyer or law firm practices, as authorized by the Code of Professional Responsibility; public offices and teaching positions held; memberships in bar associations or other professional societies or organizations, including offices and committee assignments therein; foreign language fluency;

2. names of clients regularly represented, provided that the client has given prior written consent;

3. bank references; credit arrangements accepted; prepaid or group legal services programs in which the attorney or firm participates; and

4. legal fees for initial consultation; contingent fee rates in civil matters when accompanied by a statement disclosing the information required by subdivision (1) of this section; range of fees for services, provided that there be available to the public free of charge a written statement clearly describing the scope of each advertised service; hourly rates; and fixed fees for specified legal services.

D. Advertising and publicity shall be designed to educate the public to an awareness of legal needs and to provide information relevant to the selection of the most appropriate counsel. Information other than that specifically authorized in subdivision (C) of this section that is consistent with these purposes may be disseminated providing that it does not violate any other provisions of this Rule.

E. A lawyer or law firm advertising any fixed fee for specified legal services shall, at the time of fee publication, have available to the public a written statement clearly describing the scope of each advertised service, which statement shall be delivered to the client at the time of retainer for any such service. Such legal services shall include all those services which are recognized as reasonable and necessary under local custom in the area of practice in the community where the services are performed.

F. If the advertisement is broadcast, it shall be prerecorded or taped and approved for broadcast by the lawyer, and a recording or videotape of the actual transmission shall be retained by the lawyer for a period of not less than one year following such transmission. All advertisements of legal services that are mailed, or are distributed other than by radio, television, directory, newspaper, magazine or other periodical, by a lawyer or law firm with an office for the practice of law in this state, shall also be subject to the following provisions:

1. A copy of each advertisement shall at the time of its initial mailing or distribution be filed with the Departmental Disciplinary Committee of the appropriate judicial department.

2. Such advertisement shall contain no reference to the fact of filing.

3. If such advertisement is directed to a predetermined addressee, a list, containing the names and addresses of all persons to whom the advertisement is being or will thereafter be mailed or distributed, shall be retained by the lawyer or law firm for a period of not less than one year following the last date of mailing or distribution.

4. The advertisements filed pursuant to this subdivision shall be open to public inspection.

5. The requirements of this subdivision shall not apply to such professional cards or other announcements the distribution of which is authorized by DR 2–102(A).

G. If a lawyer or law firm advertises a range of fees or an hourly rate for services, the lawyer or law firm may not charge more than the fee advertised for such services. If a lawyer or law firm advertises a fixed fee for specified legal services, or performs services described in a fee schedule, the lawyer or law firm may not charge more than the fixed fee for such stated legal service as set forth in the advertisement or fee schedule, unless the client agrees in writing that the services performed or to be performed were not legal services referred to or implied in the advertisement or in the fee schedule and, further, that a different fee arrangement shall apply to the transaction.

H. Unless otherwise specified in the advertisement, if a lawyer publishes any fee information authorized under this Disciplinary Rule in a publication which is published more frequently than once per month, the lawyer shall be bound by any representation made therein for a period of not less than 30 days after such publication. If a lawyer publishes any fee information authorized under this Rule in a publication which is published once per month or less frequently, the lawyer shall be bound by any representation made therein until the publication of the succeeding issue. If a lawyer publishes any fee information authorized under this Rule in a publication which has no fixed date for publication of a succeeding issue, the lawyer shall be bound by any representation made therein for a reasonable period of time after publication, but in no event less than 90 days.

I. Unless otherwise specified, if a lawyer broadcasts any fee information authorized under this Rule, the lawyer shall be bound by any representation made therein for a period of not less than 30 days after such broadcast.

J. A lawyer shall not compensate or give any thing of value to representatives of the press, radio, television or other communication medium in anticipation of or in return for professional publicity in a news item.

K. All advertisements of legal services shall include the name, office address and telephone number of the attorney or law firm whose services are being offered.

(L) A lawyer or law firm advertising any contingent fee rates shall, at the time of the fee publication, disclose;

    1. Whether percentages are computed before or after deduction of costs, disbursements and other expenses of litigation;

    2. That, in the event there is no recovery, the client shall remain liable for the expenses of litigation, including court costs and disbursements.

DR 2-102. Professional Notices, Letterheads, and Signs

A. A lawyer or law firm may use professional cards, professional announcement cards, office signs, letterheads or similar professional notices or devices, provided the same do not violate any statute or court rule, and are in accordance with DR 2-101, including the following:

    1. A professional card of a lawyer identifying the lawyer by name and as a lawyer, and giving addresses, telephone numbers, the name of the law firm, and any information permitted under DR 2-105. A professional card of a law firm may also give the names of members and associates.

    2. A professional announcement card stating new or changed associations or addresses, change of firm name, or similar matters pertaining to the professional offices of a lawyer or law firm. It may state biographical data, the names of members of the firm and associates and the names and dates of predecessor firms in a continuing line of succession. It shall not state the nature of the practice except as permitted under DR 2-105.

3. A sign in or near the office and in the building directory identifying the law office. The sign shall not state the nature of the practice, except as permitted under DR 2–105.

4. A letterhead identifying the lawyer by name and as a lawyer, and giving addresses, telephone numbers, the name of the law firm, associates and any information permitted under DR 2–105. A letterhead of a law firm may also give the names of members and associates, and names and dates relating to deceased and retired members. A lawyer may be designated "Of Counsel" on a letterhead if there is a continuing relationship with a lawyer or law firm, other than as a partner or associate. A lawyer or law firm may be designated as "General Counsel" or by similar professional reference on stationery of a client if the lawyer or the firm devotes a substantial amount of professional time in the representation of that client. The letterhead of a law firm may give the names and dates of predecessor firms in a continuing line of succession.

B. A lawyer in private practice shall not practice under a trade name, a name that is misleading as to the identity of the lawyer or lawyers practicing under such name, or a firm name containing names other than those of one or more of the lawyers in the firm, except that the name of a professional corporation may contain "P.C." or such symbols permitted by law, and, if otherwise lawful, a firm may use as, or continue to include in its name the name or names of one or more deceased or retired members of the firm or of a predecessor firm in a continuing line of succession. Such terms as "legal clinic", "legal aid", "legal service office", "legal assistance office", "defender office" and the like, may be used only by qualified legal assistance organizations described in DR 2–103(D), except that the term "legal clinic" may be used by any lawyer or law firm provided the name of a participating lawyer or firm is incorporated therein. A lawyer who assumes a judicial, legislative or public executive or administrative post or office shall not permit his or her name to remain in the name of the law firm or be used in professional notices of the firm during any significant period in which the lawyer is not actively and regularly practicing law as a member of the firm and, during such period, other members of the firm shall not use the lawyer's name in the firm name or in professional notices of the firm.

C. A lawyer shall not hold himself or herself out as having a partnership with one or more other lawyers unless they are in fact partners.

D. A partnership shall not be formed or continued between or among lawyers licensed in different jurisdictions unless all enumerations of the members and associates of the firm on its letterhead and in other permissible listings make clear the jurisdictional limitations on those members and associates of the firm not licensed to practice in all listed jurisdictions; however, the same firm name may be used in each jurisdiction.

DR 2-103.   Solicitation and Recommendation of Professional Employment

A.   A lawyer shall not, directly or indirectly, seek professional employment for the lawyer or a partner or associate of the lawyer from a person who has not sought advice regarding employment of the lawyer in violation of any statute or existing court rule in the judicial department in which the lawyer practices.

B.   A lawyer shall not compensate or give anything of value to a person or organization to recommend or obtain employment by a client, or as a reward for having made a recommendation resulting in employment by a client, except by any of the organizations listed in DR 2-103(D).

C.   A lawyer shall not request a person or organization to recommend or promote the use of the lawyer's services or those of the lawyer's partner or associate, or any other affiliated lawyer as a private practitioner, other than by advertising or publicity not proscribed by DR 2-101, except that:

1.   The lawyer may request referrals from a lawyer referral service operated, sponsored or approved by a bar association and may pay its fees incident thereto.

2.   The lawyer may cooperate with the legal service activities of any of the offices or organizations enumerated in DR 2-103(D)(1) through (4) and may perform legal services for those to whom the lawyer was recommended by such an office or organization to do such work if:

a.   The person to whom the recommendation is made is a member or beneficiary of such office or organization; and

b.   The lawyer remains free to exercise independent professional judgment on behalf of the client.

3.   The lawyer may request such a recommendation from another lawyer or an organization performing legal services.

D.   A lawyer or the lawyer's partner or associate or any other affiliated lawyer may be recommended, employed or paid by, or may cooperate with one of the following offices or organizations which promote the use of the lawyer's services or those of a partner or associate or any other affiliated lawyer if there is no interference with the exercise of independent professional judgment on behalf of the client:

1.   A legal aid office or public defender office:

a.   Operated or sponsored by a duly accredited law school;

b.   Operated or sponsored by a bona fide, non-profit community organization;

c. Operated or sponsored by a governmental agency; or

d. Operated, sponsored, or approved by a bar association;

2. A military legal assistance office;

3. A lawyer referral service operated, sponsored or approved by a bar association;

4. Any bona fide organization which recommends, furnishes or pays for legal services to its members or beneficiaries provided the following conditions are satisfied:

a. Neither the lawyer, nor the lawyer's partner, nor associate, nor any other affiliated lawyer nor any non-lawyer, shall have initiated or promoted such organization for the primary purpose of providing financial or other benefit to such lawyer, partner, associate or affiliated lawyer.

b. Such organization is not operated for the purpose of procuring legal work or financial benefit for any lawyer as a private practitioner outside of the legal services program of the organization.

c. The member or beneficiary to whom the legal services are furnished, and not such organization, is recognized as the client of the lawyer in the matter.

d. Any member or beneficiary who is entitled to have legal services furnished or paid for by the organization may, if such member or beneficiary so desires, select counsel other than that furnished, selected or approved by the organization for the particular matter involved; and the legal service plan of such organization provides appropriate relief for any member or beneficiary who asserts a claim that representation by counsel furnished, selected or approved would be unethical, improper or inadequate under the circumstances of the matter involved; and the plan provides an appropriate procedure for seeking such relief.

e. The lawyer does not know or have cause to know that such organization is in violation of applicable laws, rules of court or other legal requirements that govern its legal service operations.

f. Such organization has filed with the appropriate disciplinary authority, to the extent required by such authority, at least annually a report with respect to its legal service plan, if any, showing its terms, its schedule of benefits, its subscription charges, agreements with counsel and financial results of its legal service activities or, if it has failed to do so, the lawyer does not know or have cause to know of such failure.

E.   A lawyer shall not accept employment when the lawyer knows or it is obvious that the person who seeks services does so as a result of conduct prohibited under this Disciplinary Rule.

F.   Advertising not proscribed under DR 2–101 shall not be deemed in violation of any provision of this Disciplinary Rule.

DR 2-104.   Suggestion of Need of Legal Services

A.   A lawyer who has given unsolicited advice to an individual to obtain counsel or take legal action shall not accept employment resulting from that advice, in violation of any statute or court rule.

B.   A lawyer may accept employment by a close friend, relative, former client (if the advice is germane to the former employment) or one whom the lawyer reasonably believes to be a client.

C.   A lawyer may accept employment which results from participation in activities designed to educate the public to recognize legal problems, to make intelligent selection of counsel or to utilize available legal services.

D.   A lawyer who is recommended, furnished or paid by a qualified legal assistance organization enumerated in DR 2–103(D)(1) through (4) may represent a member or beneficiary thereof, to the extent and under the conditions prescribed therein.

E.   Without affecting the right to accept employment, a lawyer may speak publicly or write for publication on legal topics so long as the lawyer does not undertake to give individual advice.

F.   Subject to compliance with the provisions of DR 2–103(A), if success in asserting rights or defenses of a client in litigation in the nature of a class action is dependent upon the joinder of others, a lawyer may accept employment from those contacted for the purpose of obtaining their joinder.

DR 2-105.   Identification of Practice and Specialty

A.   A lawyer or law firm may publicly identify one or more areas of law in which the lawyer or the law firm practices, or may state that the practice of the lawyer or law firm is limited to one or more areas of law.

B.   A lawyer who is certified as a specialist in a particular area of law or law practice by the authority having jurisdiction under the laws of this state over the subject of specialization by lawyers may hold himself or herself out as a specialist, but only in accordance with the rules prescribed by that authority.

In domestic relations matters to which Part 1400 of the joint rules of the Appellate Divisions is applicable, a lawyer shall provide a prospective client with a statement of client's rights and responsibilities at the initial conference and prior to the signing of a written retainer statement.

DR 2-106. Fee for Legal Services

A. A lawyer shall not enter into an agreement for, charge or collect an illegal or excessive fee.

B. A fee is excessive when, after a review of the facts, a lawyer of ordinary prudence would be left with a definite and firm conviction that the fee is in excess of a reasonable fee. Factors to be considered as guides in determining the reasonableness of a fee include the following:

1. The time and labor required, the novelty and difficulty of the questions involved and the skill requisite to perform the legal service properly.

2. The likelihood, if apparent or made known to the client, that the acceptance of the particular employment will preclude other employment by the lawyer.

3. The fee customarily charged in the locality for similar legal services.

4. The amount involved and the results obtained.

5. The time limitations imposed by the client or by circumstances.

6. The nature and length of the professional relationship with the client.

7. The experience, reputation and ability of the lawyer or lawyers performing the services.

8. Whether the fee is fixed or contingent.

C. A lawyer shall not enter into an arrangement for, charge or collect:

1. A contingent fee for representing a defendant in a criminal case; or

2. any fee in a domestic relations matter to which Part 1400 of the joint rules of the Appellate Divisions is applicable:

i. the payment or amount of which is contingent upon the securing of a divorce or upon the amount of maintenance, support, equitable distribution, or property settlement; or

ii. unless a written retainer agreement is signed by the lawyer and client setting forth in plain language the nature of the relationship and the details of the fee arrangement. A lawyer shall not include in the written retainer agreement a nonrefundable fee clause; or

iii. based upon a security interest, confession of judgment or other lien, without prior notice to the client in a signed retainer agreement and approval from the court after notice to the adversary. A lawyer shall not foreclose on a mortgage placed on the marital residence while the spouse who consents to the mortgage remains the titleholder and the residence remains the spouse's primary residence; and

3. A fee proscribed by law or rule of court.

D. Promptly after a lawyer has been employed in a contingent fee matter, the lawyer shall provide the client with a writing stating the method by which the fee is to be determined, including the percentage or percentages that shall accrue to the lawyer in the event of settlement, trial or appeal, litigation and other expenses to be deducted from the recovery and whether such expenses are to be deducted before or after the contingent fee is calculated. Upon conclusion of a contingent fee matter, the lawyer shall provide the client with a written statement stating the outcome of the matter, and if there is a recovery, showing the remittance to the client and the method of its determination.

E. In domestic relations matters to which Part 1400 of the joint rules of the Appellate Divisions is applicable, a lawyer shall resolve fee disputes by arbitration at the election of the client.

DR 2-107. Division of Fees Among Lawyers

A. A lawyer shall not divide a fee for legal services with another lawyer who is not a partner in or associate of the lawyer's law firm or law office, unless:

1. The client consents to employment of the other lawyer after a full disclosure that a division of fees will be made.

2. The division is in proportion to the services performed by each lawyer or, by a writing given to the client, each lawyer assumes joint responsibility for the representation.

3. The total fee of the lawyers does not exceed reasonable compensation for all legal services they rendered the client.

B. This Disciplinary Rule does not prohibit payment to a former partner or associate pursuant to a separation or retirement agreement.

DR 2-108. Agreements Restricting the Practice of a Lawyer

A. A lawyer shall not be a party to or participate in a partnership or employment agreement with another lawyer that restricts the right of a lawyer to practice law after the termination of a relationship created by the agreement, except as a condition to payment of retirement benefits.

B. In connection with the settlement of a controversy or suit, a lawyer shall not enter into an agreement that restricts the right of a lawyer to practice law.

DR 2–109. Acceptance of Employment

A.[1] A lawyer shall not accept employment on behalf of a person if the lawyer knows or it is obvious that such person wishes to:

1. Bring a legal action, conduct a defense, or assert a position in litigation, or otherwise have steps taken for such person merely for the purpose of harassing or maliciously injuring any person.

2. Present a claim or defense in litigation that is not warranted under existing law, unless it can be supported by good faith argument for an extension, modification, or reversal of existing law.

DR 2–110. Withdrawal From Employment

A. In general. 1. If permission for withdrawal from employment is required by the rules of a tribunal, a lawyer shall not withdraw from employment in a proceeding before that tribunal without its permission.

2. Even when withdrawal is otherwise permitted or required under DR 2–110(A)(1), (B) or (C), a lawyer shall not withdraw from employment until the lawyer has taken steps to the extent reasonably practicable to avoid foreseeable prejudice to the rights of the client, including giving due notice to the client, allowing time for employment of other counsel, delivering to the client all papers and property to which the client is entitled and complying with applicable laws and rules.

3. A lawyer who withdraws from employment shall refund promptly any part of a fee paid in advance that has not been earned.

4. In domestic relations matters, a lawyer shall forward the case file to the client within thirty days after withdrawal.

B. Mandatory withdrawal. A lawyer representing a client before a tribunal, with its permission if required by its rules, shall withdraw from employment, and a lawyer representing a client in other matters shall withdraw from employment, if:

1. The lawyer knows or it is obvious that the client is bringing the legal action, conducting the defense, or asserting a position in the litigation, or is otherwise having steps taken, merely for the purpose of harassing or maliciously injuring any person.

2. The lawyer knows or it is obvious that continued employment will result in violation of a Disciplinary Rule.

3. The lawyer's mental or physical condition renders it unreasonably difficult to carry out the employment effectively.

4. The lawyer is discharged by his or her client.

C. Permissive withdrawal. Except as stated in DR 2–110(A), a lawyer may withdraw from representing a client if withdrawal can be

---

1. So in original. No par. B has been enacted.

accomplished without material adverse effect on the interests of the client, or if:

  1.   The client:

    a.   Insists upon presenting a claim or defense that is not warranted under existing law and cannot be supported by good faith argument for an extension, modification, or reversal of existing law.

    b.   Persists in a course of action involving the lawyer's services that the lawyer reasonably believes is criminal or fraudulent.

    c.   Insists that the lawyer pursue a course of conduct which is illegal or prohibited under the Disciplinary Rules.

    d.   By other conduct renders it unreasonably difficult for the lawyer to carry out employment effectively.

    e.   Insists, in a matter not pending before a tribunal, that the lawyer engage in conduct which is contrary to the judgment and advice of the lawyer but not prohibited under the Disciplinary Rules.

    f.   Deliberately disregards an agreement or obligation to the lawyer as to expenses or fees.

    g.   Has used the lawyer's services to perpetrate a crime or fraud.

  2.   The lawyer's continued employment is likely to result in a violation of a Disciplinary Rule.

  3.   The lawyer's inability to work with co-counsel indicates that the best interests of the client likely will be served by withdrawal.

  4.   The lawyer's mental or physical condition renders it difficult for the lawyer to carry out the employment effectively.

  5.   The lawyer's client knowingly and freely assents to termination of the employment.

  6.   The lawyer believes in good faith, in a proceeding pending before a tribunal, that the tribunal will find the existence of other good cause for withdrawal.

DR 2–111.   Sale of Law Practice

  A.   A lawyer retiring from a private practice of law, a law firm one or more members of which are retiring from the private practice of law with the firm, or the personal representative of a deceased, disabled or missing lawyer, may sell a law practice, including good will, to one or more lawyers or law firms, who may purchase the practice. The seller and the buyer may agree on reasonable restrictions on the seller's private practice of law, notwithstanding any other provision of this Code.

Retirement shall include the cessation of the private practice of law in the geographic area, that is, the county and city and any county or city contiguous thereto, in which the practice to be sold has been conducted.

B. Confidences and Secrets.

1. With respect to each matter subject to the contemplated sale, the seller may provide prospective buyers with any information not protected as a confidence or secret under DR 4–101.

2. Notwithstanding DR 4–101, the seller may provide the prospective buyer with information as to individual clients:

(i) concerning the identity of the client, except as provided in DR 2–111(B)(6);

(ii) concerning the status and general nature of the matter;

(iii) available in public court files; and,

(iv) concerning the financial terms of the attorney-client relationship and the payment status of the client's account.

3. Prior to making any disclosure of confidences or secrets that may be permitted under DR 2–111(B)(2), the seller shall provide the prospective buyer with information regarding the matters involved in the proposed sale sufficient to enable the prospective buyer to determine whether any conflicts of interest exist. Where sufficient information cannot be disclosed without revealing client confidences or secrets, the seller may make the disclosures necessary for the prospective buyer to determine whether any conflict of interest exists, subject to DR 2–111(B)(6). If the prospective buyer determines that conflicts of interest exist prior to reviewing the information, or determines during the course of review that a conflict of interest exists, the prospective buyer shall not review or continue to review the information unless seller shall have obtained the consent of the client in accordance with DR 4–101(C)(1).

4. Prospective buyers shall maintain the confidentiality of and shall not use any client information received in connection with the proposed sale in the same manner and not to the same extent as if the prospective buyers represented the client.

5. Absent the consent of the client after full disclosure, a seller shall not provide a prospective buyer with information if doing so would cause a violation of the attorney-client privilege.

6. If the seller has reason to believe that the identity of the client or the fact of the representation itself constitutes a confidence or secret in the circumstances, the seller may not provide such information to a prospective buyer without first advising the client of the identity of the prospective buyer and obtaining the client's consent to the proposed disclosure.

C. Written notice of the sale shall be given jointly by the seller and the buyer to each of the seller's clients and shall include information regarding:

1. The client's right to retain other counsel or to take possession of the file;

2. That fact that the client's consent to the transfer of the client's file or matter to the buyer will be presumed if the client does not take any action or otherwise object within 90 days of the sending of the notice, subject to any court rule or statute requiring express approval by the client or a court;

3. The fact that agreements between the seller and the seller's clients as to fees will be honored by the buyer;

4. Proposed fee increases, if any, permitted under DR 2–111(E); and

5. The identity and background of the buyer or buyers, including principal office address, bar admissions, number of years in practice in the state, whether the buyer has ever been disciplined for professional misconduct or convicted of a crime, and whether the buyer currently intends to re-sell the practice.

D. When the buyer's representation of a client of the seller would give rise to a waivable conflict of interest, the buyer shall not undertake such representation unless the necessary waiver or waivers have been obtained in writing.

E. The fee charged a client by the buyer shall not be increased by reason of the sale, unless permitted by a retainer agreement with the client or otherwise specifically agreed to by the client.

CANON 3

A Lawyer Should Assist in Preventing the Unauthorized Practice of Law

DR 3–101. Aiding Unauthorized Practice of Law

A. A lawyer shall not aid a non-lawyer in the unauthorized practice of law.

B. A lawyer shall not practice law in a jurisdiction where to do so would be in violation of regulations of the profession in that jurisdiction.

DR 3–102. Dividing Legal Fees With a Non–lawyer

A.[1] A lawyer or law firm shall not share legal fees with a non-lawyer, except that:

1. An agreement by a lawyer with his or her firm, partner, or associate may provide for the payment of money, over a reasonable period of time after the lawyer's death, to the lawyer's estate or to one or more specified persons.

2. A lawyer who undertakes to complete unfinished legal business of a deceased lawyer may pay to the estate of the deceased

---

1. So in original. No par. B has been enacted.

lawyer that proportion of the total compensation which fairly represents the services rendered by the deceased lawyer.

3. A lawyer or law firm may include non-lawyer employees in a retirement plan, even though the plan is based in whole or in part on a profit-sharing arrangement.

DR 3–103. Forming a Partnership With a Non–lawyer

A.1 A lawyer shall not form a partnership with a non-lawyer if any of the activities of the partnership consist of the practice law.

CANON 4

A Lawyer Should Preserve the Confidences and Secrets of a Client

DR 4–101. Preservation of Confidences and Secrets of a Client

A. "Confidence" refers to information protected by the attorney-client privilege under applicable law, and "secret" refers to other information gained in the professional relationship that the client has requested be held inviolate or the disclosure of which would be embarrassing or would be likely to be detrimental to the client.

B. Except when permitted under DR 4–101(C), a lawyer shall not knowingly:

1. Reveal a confidence or secret of a client.

2. Use a confidence or secret of a client to the disadvantage of the client.

3. Use a confidence or secret of a client for the advantage of the lawyer or of a third person, unless the client consents after full disclosure.

C. A lawyer may reveal:

1. Confidences or secrets with the consent of the client or clients affected, but only after a full disclosure to them.

2. Confidences or secrets when permitted under Disciplinary Rules or required by law or court order.

3. The intention of a client to commit a crime and the information necessary to prevent the crime.

4. Confidences or secrets necessary to establish or collect the lawyer's fee or to defend the lawyer or his or her employees or associates against an accusation of wrongful conduct.

5. Confidences or secrets to the extent implicit in withdrawing a written or oral opinion or representation previously given by the lawyer and believed by the lawyer still to be relied upon by a third person where the lawyer has discovered that the opinion or repre-

sentation was based on materially inaccurate information or is being used to further a crime or fraud.

D. A lawyer shall exercise reasonable care to prevent his or her employees, associates, and others whose services are utilized by the lawyer from disclosing or using confidences or secrets of a client, except that a lawyer may reveal the information allowed by DR 4–101(C) through an employee.

CANON 5

A Lawyer Should Exercise Independent Professional Judgment on Behalf of a Client

DR 5–101. Refusing Employment When the Interest of the Lawyer May Impair Independent Professional Judgment

A. Except with the consent of the client after full disclosure, a lawyer shall not accept employment if the exercise of professional judgment on behalf of the client will be or reasonably may be affected by the lawyer's own financial, business, property, or personal interests.

B. A lawyer shall not act, or accept employment that contemplates the lawyer's acting, as an advocate before any tribunal if the lawyer knows or it is obvious that the lawyer ought to be called as a witness on behalf of the client, except that the lawyer may act as an advocate and also testify:

1. If the testimony will relate solely to an uncontested issue.

2. If the testimony will relate solely to a matter of formality and there is no reason to believe that substantial evidence will be offered in opposition to the testimony.

3. If the testimony will relate solely to the nature and value of legal services rendered in the case by the lawyer or the lawyer's firm to the client.

4. As to any matter, if disqualification as an advocate would work a substantial hardship on the client because of the distinctive value of the lawyer as counsel in the particular case.

C. Neither a lawyer nor the lawyer's firm shall accept employment in contemplated or pending litigation if the lawyer knows or it is obvious that the lawyer or another lawyer in the lawyer's firm may be called as a witness other than on behalf of the client, and it is apparent that the testimony would or might be prejudicial to the client.

DR 5–102. Withdrawal as Counsel When the Lawyer Becomes a Witness

A. If, after undertaking employment in contemplated or pending litigation, a lawyer learns or it is obvious that the lawyer ought to be called as a witness on behalf of the client, the lawyer shall withdraw as an advocate before the tribunal, except that the lawyer may continue as an advocate and may testify in the circumstances enumerated in DR 5–101(B)(1) through (4).

B. If, after undertaking employment in contemplated or pending litigation, a lawyer learns or it is obvious that the lawyer or a lawyer in his or her firm may be called as a witness other than on behalf of the client, the lawyer may continue the representation until it is apparent that the testimony is or may be prejudicial to the client at which point the lawyer and the firm must withdraw from acting as an advocate before the tribunal.

DR 5–103. Avoiding Acquisition of Interest in Litigation

A. A lawyer shall not acquire a proprietary interest in the cause of action or subject matter of litigation he or she is conducting for a client, except that the lawyer may:

    1. Acquire a lien granted by law to secure the lawyer's fee or expenses.

    2. Except as provided in DR 2–106(C)(2) or (3), contract with a client for a reasonable contingent fee in a civil case.

B. While representing a client in connection with contemplated or pending litigation, a lawyer shall not advance or guarantee financial assistance to the client, except that:

    1. A lawyer may advance or guarantee the expenses of litigation, including court costs, expenses of investigation, expenses of medical examination, and costs of obtaining and presenting evidence, provided the client remains ultimately liable for such expenses.

    2. Unless prohibited by law or rule of court, a lawyer representing an indigent client on a pro bono basis may pay court costs and reasonable expenses of litigation on behalf of the client.

DR 5–104. Limiting Business Relations With a Client

A. A lawyer shall not enter into a business transaction with a client if they have differing interests therein and if the client expects the lawyer to exercise professional judgment therein for the protection of the client, unless the client has consented after full disclosure.

B. Prior to conclusion of all aspects of the matter giving rise to employment, a lawyer shall not enter into any arrangement or understanding with a client or a prospective client by which the lawyer acquires an interest in literary or media rights with respect to the subject matter of the employment or proposed employment.

DR 5–105. Refusing to Accept or Continue Employment if the Interests of Another Client May Impair the Independent Professional Judgment of the Lawyer

A. A lawyer shall decline proffered employment if the exercise of independent professional judgment in behalf of a client will be or is likely to be adversely affected by the acceptance of the proffered employment, or if it would be likely to involve the lawyer in representing differing interests, except to the extent permitted under DR 5–105(C).

B. A lawyer shall not continue multiple employment if the exercise of independent professional judgment in behalf of a client will be or is likely to be adversely affected by the lawyer's representation of another client, or if it would be likely to involve the lawyer in representing differing interests, except to the extent permitted under DR 5–105(C).

C. In the situations covered by DR 5–105(A) and (B), a lawyer may represent multiple clients if it is obvious that the lawyer can adequately represent the interest of each and if each consents to the representation after full disclosure of the possible effect of such representation on the exercise of the lawyer's independent professional judgment on behalf of each.

D. While lawyers are associated in a law firm, none of them shall knowingly accept or continue employment when any one of them practicing alone would be prohibited from doing so under DR 5–101(A), DR 5–105(A), (B) or (C), DR 5–108, or DR 9–101(B) except as otherwise provided therein.

E. A law firm shall keep records of prior engagements, which records shall be made at or near the time of such engagements and shall have a policy implementing a system by which proposed engagements are checked against current and previous engagements, so as to render effective assistance to lawyers within the firm in complying with subdivision (d) of this disciplinary rule. Failure to keep records or to have a policy which complies with this subdivision, whether or not a violation of subdivision (d) of this disciplinary rule occurs, shall be a violation by the firm. In cases where a violation of this subdivision by the firm is a substantial factor in causing a violation of subdivision (d) by a lawyer, the firm, as well as the individual lawyer, shall also be responsible for the violation of subdivision (d).

DR 5–106. Settling Similar Claims of Clients

A.[1] A lawyer who represents two or more clients shall not make or participate in the making of an aggregate settlement of the claims of or against the clients, unless each client has consented to the settlement after being advised of the existence and nature of all the claims involved in the proposed settlement, of the total amount of the settlement, and of the participation of each person in the settlement.

---

1. So in original. No par. B has been enacted.

DR 5–107. Avoiding Influence by Others Than the Client

A. Except with the consent of the client after full disclosure a lawyer shall not:

1. Accept compensation for legal services from one other than the client.

2. Accept from one other than the client any thing of value related to his or her representation of or employment by the client.

B. A lawyer shall not permit a person who recommends, employs, or pays the lawyer to render legal service for another to direct or regulate his or her professional judgment in rendering such legal services.

C. A lawyer shall not practice with or in the form of a professional corporation or association authorized to practice law for a profit, if:

1. A non-lawyer owns any interest therein, except that a fiduciary representative of the estate of a lawyer may hold the stock or interest of the lawyer for a reasonable time during administration;

2. A non-lawyer is a corporate director or officer thereof; or

3. A non-lawyer has the right to direct or control the professional judgment of a lawyer.

DR 5–108. Conflict of Interest—Former Client

A.[1] Except with the consent of a former client after full disclosure a lawyer who has represented the former client in a matter shall not:

1. Thereafter represent another person in the same or a substantially related matter in which that person's interests are materially adverse to the interests of the former client.

2. Use any confidences or secrets of the former client except as permitted by DR 4–101(C) or when the confidence or secret has become generally known.

DR 5–109. Conflict of Interest—Organization as Client

A.[1] When a lawyer employed or retained by an organization is dealing with the organization's directors, officers, employees, members, shareholders or other constituents, and it appears that the organization's interests may differ from those of the constituents with whom the lawyer is dealing, the lawyer shall explain that the lawyer is the lawyer for the organization and not for any of the constituents.

DR 5–110. Membership in Legal Services Organization

A.[1] A lawyer may serve as a director, officer or member of a not-for-profit legal services organization, apart from the law firm in which the lawyer practices, notwithstanding that the organization serves persons having interests that differ from those of a client of the lawyer or

369

the lawyer's firm, provided that the lawyer shall not knowingly participate in a decision or action of the organization.

1.   If participating in the decision or action would be incompatible with the lawyer's duty of loyalty to a client under Canon 5; or

2.   Where the decision or action could have a material adverse effect on the representation of a client of the organization whose interests differ from those of a client of the lawyer or the lawyer's firm.

CANON 6

A Lawyer Should Represent a Client Competently

DR 6–101.   Failing to Act Competently

A.[1]   A lawyer shall not:

1.   Handle a legal matter which the lawyer knows or should know that he or she is not competent to handle, without associating with a lawyer who is competent to handle it.

2.   Handle a legal matter without preparation adequate in the circumstances.

3.   Neglect a legal matter entrusted to the lawyer.

DR 6–102.   Limiting Liability to Client

A.[1]   A lawyer shall not seek, by contract or other means, to limit prospectively the lawyer's individual liability to a client for malpractice, or, without first advising that person that independent representation is appropriate in connection therewith, to settle a claim for such liability with an unrepresented client or former client.

CANON 7

A Lawyer Should Represent a Client Zealously
Within the Bounds of the Law

DR 7–101.   Representing a Client Zealously

A.   A lawyer shall not intentionally:

1.   Fail to seek the lawful objectives of the client through reasonably available means permitted by law and the Disciplinary Rules, except as provided by DR 7–101(B).   A lawyer does not violate this Disciplinary Rule, however, by acceding to reasonable requests of opposing counsel which do not prejudice the rights of the client, by being punctual in fulfilling all professional commitments, by avoiding offensive tactics, or by treating with courtesy and consideration all persons involved in the legal process.

---

1. So in original.   No par. B has been enacted.

2.   Fail to carry out a contract of employment entered into with a client for professional services, but the lawyer may withdraw as permitted under DR 2–110, DR 5–102, and DR 5–105.

3.   Prejudice or damage the client during the course of the professional relationship, except as required under DR 7–102(B).

B.   In the representation of a client, a lawyer may:

1.   Where permissible, exercise professional judgment to waive or fail to assert a right or position of the client.

2.   Refuse to aid or participate in conduct that the lawyer believes to be unlawful, even though there is some support for an argument that the conduct is legal.

DR 7–102.   Representing a Client Within the Bounds of the Law

A.   In the representation of a client, a lawyer shall not:

1.   File a suit, assert a position, conduct a defense, delay a trial, or take other action on behalf of the client when the lawyer knows or when it is obvious that such action would serve merely to harass or maliciously injure another.

2.   Knowingly advance a claim or defense that is unwarranted under existing law, except that the lawyer may advance such claim or defense if it can be supported by good faith argument for an extension, modification, or reversal of existing law.

3.   Conceal or knowingly fail to disclose that which the lawyer is required by law to reveal.

4.   Knowingly use perjured testimony or false evidence.

5.   Knowingly make a false statement of law or fact.

6.   Participate in the creation or preservation of evidence when the lawyer knows or it is obvious that the evidence is false.

7.   Counsel or assist the client in conduct that the lawyer knows to be illegal or fraudulent.

8.   Knowingly engage in other illegal conduct or conduct contrary to a Disciplinary Rule.

B.   A lawyer who receives information clearly establishing that:

1.   The client has, in the course of the representation, perpetrated a fraud upon a person or tribunal shall promptly call upon the client to rectify the same, and if the client refuses or is unable to do so, the lawyer shall reveal the fraud to the affected person or tribunal, except when the information is protected as a confidence or secret.

2.   A person other than the client has perpetrated a fraud upon a tribunal shall promptly reveal the fraud to the tribunal.

DR 7–103. Performing the Duty of Public Prosecutor or Other Government Lawyer

A. A public prosecutor or other government lawyer shall not institute or cause to be instituted criminal charges when he or she knows or it is obvious that the charges are not supported by probable cause.

B. A public prosecutor or other government lawyer in criminal litigation shall make timely disclosure to counsel for the defendant, or to a defendant who has no counsel, of the existence of evidence, known to the prosecutor or other government lawyer, that tends to negate the guilt of the accused, mitigate the degree of the offense or reduce the punishment.

DR 7–104. Communicating With One of Adverse Interest

A.[1] During the course of the representation of a client a lawyer shall not:

    1. Communicate or cause another to communicate on the subject of the representation with a party the lawyer knows to be represented by a lawyer in that matter unless the lawyer has the prior consent of the lawyer representing such other party or is authorized by law to do so.

    2. Give advice to a person who is not represented by a lawyer, other than the advice to secure counsel, if the interests of such person are or have a reasonable possibility of being in conflict with the interests of the lawyer's client.

DR 7–105. Threatening Criminal Prosecution

A.[1] A lawyer shall not present, participate in presenting, or threaten to present criminal charges solely to obtain an advantage in a civil matter.

DR 7–106. Trial Conduct

A. A lawyer shall not disregard or advise the client to disregard a standing rule of a tribunal or a ruling of a tribunal made in the course of a proceeding, but the lawyer may take appropriate steps in good faith to test the validity of such rule or ruling.

B. In presenting a matter to a tribunal, a lawyer shall disclose:

    1. Controlling legal authority known to the lawyer to be directly adverse to the position of the client and which is not disclosed by opposing counsel.

    2. Unless privileged or irrelevant, the identities of the clients the lawyer represents and of the persons who employed the lawyer.

C. In appearing as a lawyer before a tribunal, a lawyer shall not:

---

1. So in original. No par. B has been enacted.

1. State or allude to any matter that he or she has no reasonable basis to believe is relevant to the case or that will not be supported by admissible evidence.

2. Ask any question that he or she has no reasonable basis to believe is relevant to the case and that is intended to degrade a witness or other person.

3. Assert personal knowledge of the facts in issue, except when testifying as a witness.

4. Assert a personal opinion as to the justness of a cause, as to the credibility of a witness, as to the culpability of a civil litigant, or as to the guilt or innocence of an accused; but the lawyer may argue, upon analysis of the evidence, for any position or conclusion with respect to the matters stated herein.

5. Fail to comply with known local customs of courtesy or practice of the bar or a particular tribunal without giving to opposing counsel timely notice of the intent not to comply.

6. Engage in undignified or discourteous conduct which is degrading to a tribunal.

7. Intentionally or habitually violate any established rule of procedure or of evidence.

DR 7–107. Trial Publicity

A. A lawyer participating in or associated with a criminal or civil matter shall not make an extrajudicial statement that a reasonable person would expect to be disseminated by means of public communication if the lawyer knows or reasonably should know that it will have a substantial likelihood of materially prejudicing an adjudicative proceeding.

B. A statement ordinarily is likely to prejudice materially an adjudicative proceeding when it refers to a civil matter triable to a jury, a criminal matter, or any other proceeding that could result in incarceration, and the statement relates to:

1. The character, credibility, reputation or criminal record of a party, suspect in a criminal investigation or witness, or the identity of a witness, or the expected testimony of a party or witness.

2. In a criminal case or proceeding that could result in incarceration, the possibility of a plea of guilty to the offense or the existence or contents of any confession, admission, or statement given by a defendant or suspect or that person's refusal or failure to make a statement.

3. The performance or results of any examination or test or the refusal or failure of a person to submit to an examination or test, or the identity or nature of physical evidence expected to be presented.

4. Any opinion as to the guilt or innocence of a defendant or suspect in a criminal case or proceeding that could result in incarceration.

5. Information the lawyer knows or reasonably should know is likely to be inadmissible as evidence in a trial and would if disclosed create a substantial risk of prejudicing an impartial trial.

6. The fact that a defendant has been charged with a crime, unless there is included therein a statement explaining that the charge is merely an accusation and that the defendant is presumed innocent until and unless proven guilty.

C. Provided that the statement complies with DR 7–107(A), a lawyer involved with the investigation or litigation of a matter may state the following without elaboration:

1. The general nature of the claim or defense.

2. The information contained in a public record.

3. That an investigation of the matter is in progress.

4. The scheduling or result of any step in litigation.

5. A request for assistance in obtaining evidence and information necessary thereto.

6. A warning of danger concerning the behavior of a person involved, when there is reason to believe that there exists the likelihood of substantial harm to an individual or to the public interest.

7. In a criminal case:

a. The identity, age, residence, occupation and family status of the accused.

b. If the accused has not been apprehended, information necessary to aid in apprehension of that person.

c. The fact, time and place of arrest, resistance, pursuit, use of weapons, and a description of physical evidence seized, other than as contained only in a confession, admission, or statement.

d. The identity of investigating and arresting officers or agencies and the length of the investigation.

DR 7–108. Communication With or Investigation of Jurors

A. Before the trial of a case a lawyer connected therewith shall not communicate with or cause another to communicate with anyone the lawyer knows to be a member of the venire from which the jury will be selected for the trial of the case.

B. During the trial of a case:

1. A lawyer connected therewith shall not communicate with or cause another to communicate with any member of the jury.

2. A lawyer who is not connected therewith shall not communicate with or cause another to communicate with a juror concerning the case.

C. DR 7–108(A) and (B) do not prohibit a lawyer from communicating with members of the venire or jurors in the course of official proceedings.

D. After discharge of the jury from further consideration of a case with which the lawyer was connected, the lawyer shall not ask questions of or make comments to a member of that jury that are calculated merely to harass or embarrass the juror or to influence the juror's actions in future jury service.

E. A lawyer shall not conduct or cause, by financial support or otherwise, another to conduct a vexatious or harassing investigation of either a member of the venire or a juror.

F. All restrictions imposed by DR 7–108 upon a lawyer also apply to communications with or investigations of members of a family of a member of the venire or a juror.

G. A lawyer shall reveal promptly to the court improper conduct by a member of the venire or a juror, or by another toward a member of the venire or a juror or a member of his or her family of which the lawyer has knowledge.

DR 7–109. Contact With Witnesses

A. A lawyer shall not suppress any evidence that the lawyer or the client has a legal obligation to reveal or produce.

B. A lawyer shall not advise or cause a person to hide or to leave the jurisdiction of a tribunal for the purpose of making the person unavailable as a witness therein.

C. A lawyer shall not pay, offer to pay, or acquiesce in the payment of compensation to a witness contingent upon the content of his or her testimony or the outcome of the case. But a lawyer may advance, guarantee, or acquiesce in the payment of:

1. Expenses reasonably incurred by a witness in attending or testifying.

2. Reasonable compensation to a witness for the loss of time in attending or testifying.

3. A reasonable fee for the professional services of an expert witness.

DR 7–110. Contact With Officials

A. A lawyer shall not give or lend anything of value to a judge, official, or employee of a tribunal except as permitted by Section C(4) of Canon 5 of the Code of Judicial Conduct, but a lawyer may make a contribution to the campaign fund of a candidate for judicial office in conformity with Section B(2) under Canon 7 of the Code of Judicial Conduct.

B. In an adversary proceeding, a lawyer shall not communicate, or cause another to communicate, as to the merits of the cause with a judge or an official before whom the proceeding is pending, except:

1. In the course of official proceedings in the cause.

2. In writing if the lawyer promptly delivers a copy of the writing to opposing counsel or to an adverse party who is not represented by a lawyer.

3. Orally upon adequate notice to opposing counsel or to an adverse party who is not represented by a lawyer.

4. As otherwise authorized by law, or by Section A(4) under Canon 3 of the Code of Judicial Conduct.

CANON 8

A Lawyer Should Assist in Improving the Legal System

DR 8–101. Action as a Public Official

A.[1] A lawyer who holds public office shall not:

1. Use the public position to obtain, or attempt to obtain, a special advantage in legislative matters for the lawyer or for a client under circumstances where the lawyer knows or it is obvious that such action is not in the public interest.

2. Use the public position to influence, or attempt to influence, a tribunal to act in favor of the lawyer or of a client.

3. Accept any thing of value from any person when the lawyer knows or it is obvious that the offer is for the purpose of influencing the lawyer's action as a public official.

DR 8–102. Statements Concerning Judges and Other Adjudicatory Officers

A. A lawyer shall not knowingly make false statements of fact concerning the qualifications of a candidate for election or appointment to a judicial office.

B. A lawyer shall not knowingly make false accusations against a judge or other adjudicatory officer.

DR 8–103. Lawyer Candidate for Judicial Office

A.[1] A lawyer who is a candidate for judicial office shall comply with the applicable provisions of Canon 7 of the Code of Judicial Conduct.

---

1. So in original. No par. B has been enacted.

1. So in original. No par. B has been enacted.

CANON 9

A Lawyer Should Avoid Even the Appearance of Professional Impropriety

DR 9-101. Avoiding Even the Appearance of Impropriety

A. A lawyer shall not accept private employment in a matter upon the merits of which the lawyer has acted in a judicial capacity.

B. Except as law may otherwise expressly permit:

1. A lawyer shall not represent a private client in connection with a matter in which the lawyer participated personally and substantially as a public officer or employee, and no lawyer in a firm with which that lawyer is associated may knowingly undertake or continue representation in such a matter unless:

a. The disqualified lawyer is effectively screened from any participation, direct or indirect, including discussion, in the matter and is apportioned no part of the fee therefrom; and

b. There are no other circumstances in the particular representation that create an appearance of impropriety.

2. A lawyer having information that the lawyer knows is confidential government information about a person, acquired when the lawyer was a public officer or employee, may not represent a private client whose interests are adverse to that person in a matter in which the information could be used to the material disadvantage of that person. A firm with which that lawyer is associated may knowingly undertake or continue representation in the matter only if the disqualified lawyer is effectively screened from any participation, direct or indirect, including discussion, in the matter and is apportioned no part of the fee therefrom.

3. A lawyer serving as a public officer or employee shall not:

a. Participate in a matter in which the lawyer participated personally and substantially while in private practice or nongovernmental employment, unless under applicable law no one is, or by lawful delegation may be, authorized to act in the lawyer's stead in the matter; or

b. Negotiate for private employment with any person who is involved as a party or as attorney for a party in a matter in which the lawyer is participating personally and substantially.

C. A lawyer shall not state or imply that the lawyer is able to influence improperly or upon irrelevant grounds any tribunal, legislative body, or public official.

D. A lawyer related to another lawyer as parent, child, sibling or spouse shall not represent in any matter a client whose interests differ from those of another party to the matter who the lawyer knows is represented by the other lawyer unless the client consents to the representation after full disclosure and the lawyer concludes that the lawyer can adequately represent the interests of the client.

DR 9-102. Preserving Identity of Funds and Property of Others; Fiduciary Responsibility; Maintenance of Bank Accounts; Recordkeeping; Examination of Records

A. Prohibition Against Commingling. A lawyer in possession of any funds or other property belonging to another person, where such possession is incident to his or her practice of law, is a fiduciary, and must not commingle such property with his or her own.

B. Separate Accounts. 1. A lawyer who is in possession of funds belonging to another person incident to the lawyer's practice of law, shall maintain such funds in a banking institution within the State of New York which agrees to provide dishonored check reports in accordance with the provisions of Part 1300 of these rules (22 NYCRR Part 1300). "Banking institution" means a state or national bank, trust company, savings bank, savings and loan association or credit union. Such funds shall be maintained, in the lawyer's own name, or in the name of a firm of lawyers of which he or she is a member, or in the name of the lawyer or firm of lawyers by whom he or she is employed, in a special account or accounts, separate from any business or personal accounts of the lawyer or lawyer's firm, and separate from any accounts which the lawyer may maintain as executor, guardian, trustee or receiver, or in any other fiduciary capacity, into which special account or accounts all funds held in escrow or otherwise entrusted to the lawyer or firm shall be deposited; provided, however, that such funds may be maintained in a banking institution located outside the State of New York if such banking institution complies with such Part 1300, and the lawyer has obtained the prior written approval of the person to whom such funds belong which specifies the name and address of the office or branch of the banking institution where such funds are to be maintained.

2. A lawyer or the lawyer's firm shall identify the special bank account or accounts required by subdivision (b)(1) of this section as an "Attorney Special Account", or "Attorney Trust Account", or "Attorney Escrow Account", and shall obtain checks and deposit slips that bear such title. Such title may be accompanied by such other descriptive language as the lawyer may deem appropriate, provided that such additional language distinguishes such special account or accounts from other bank accounts that are maintained by the lawyer or the lawyer's firm.

3. Funds reasonably sufficient to maintain the account or to pay account charges may be deposited therein.

4. Funds belonging in part to a client or third person and in part presently or potentially to the lawyer or law firm shall be kept in such special account or accounts, but the portion belonging to the lawyer or law firm may be withdrawn when due unless the right of the lawyer or law firm to receive it is disputed by the client or third person, in which event the disputed portion shall not be withdrawn until the dispute is finally resolved.

Appellate Division Rule Regarding Dishonored Check Reporting

Effective September 1, 1992, all four Appellate Divisions adopted 22 NYCRR Part 1300 to be read in conjunction with DR 9–102. Part 1300 is set out in its entirety below.

§ 1300.1 [Dishonored Check Reporting Rules for Attorney Special, Trust and Escrow Accounts]

(a) Special bank accounts required by Disciplinary Rule 9–102 shall be maintained only in banking institutions which have agreed to provide dishonored check reports in accordance with the provisions of this section.

(b) An agreement to provide dishonored check reports shall be filed with the Lawyers' Fund for Client Protection, which shall maintain a central registry of all banking institutions which have been approved in accordance with this section, and the current status of each such agreement. The agreement shall apply to all branches of each banking institution that provides special bank accounts for attorneys engaged in the practice of law in this state, and shall not be cancelled by a banking institution except on thirty days prior written notice to the Lawyers' Fund for Client Protection.

(c) A dishonored check report by a banking institution shall be required whenever a properly payable instrument is presented against an attorney special, trust or escrow account which contains insufficient available funds, and the banking institution dishonors the instrument for that reason. A "properly payable instrument" means an instrument which, if presented in the normal course of business, is in a form requiring payment under the laws of the State of New York.

(d) A dishonored check report shall be substantially in the form of the notice of dishonor which the banking institution customarily forwards to its customer, and may include a photocopy or a computer generated duplicate of such notice.

(e) Dishonored check reports shall be mailed to the Lawyers' Fund for Client Protection, 55 Elk Street, Albany, New York 12210, within five banking days after the date of presentment against insufficient available funds.

(f) The Lawyers' Fund for Client Protection shall hold each dishonored check report for ten business days to enable the banking institution to withdraw a report provided by inadvertence or mistake; except that the curing of an insufficiency of available funds by a lawyer or law firm by the deposit of additional funds shall not constitute reason for withdrawing a dishonored check report.

(g) After holding the dishonored check report for ten business days, the Lawyers' Fund for Client Protection shall forward it to the attorney disciplinary committee for the judicial department or district having jurisdiction over the account holder, as indicated by the law office or other address on the report, for such inquiry and action that attorney disciplinary committee deems appropriate.

(h) Every lawyer admitted to the Bar of the State of New York shall be deemed to have consented to the dishonored check reporting requirements of this section. Lawyers and law firms shall promptly notify their banking institutions of existing or new attorney special, trust, or escrow accounts for the purpose of facilitating the implementation and administration of the provisions of this section.

C. Notification of Receipt of Property; Safekeeping; Rendering Accounts; Payment or Delivery of Property. A lawyer shall:

1. Promptly notify a client or third person of the receipt of funds, securities, or other properties in which the client or third person has an interest.

2. Identify and label securities and properties of a client or third person promptly upon receipt and place them in a safe deposit box or other place of safekeeping as soon as practicable.

3. Maintain complete records of all funds, securities, and other properties of a client or third person coming into the possession of the lawyer and render appropriate accounts to the client or third person regarding them.

4. Promptly pay or deliver to the client or third person as requested by the client or third person the funds, securities, or other properties in the possession of the lawyer which the client or third person is entitled to receive.

D. Required Bookkeeping Records. A lawyer shall maintain for seven years after the events which they record:

1. The records of all deposits in and withdrawals from special accounts specified in DR 9-102(B) and of any other bank account which records the operations of the lawyer's practice of law. These records shall specifically identify the date, source and description of each item deposited, as well as the date, payee and purpose of each withdrawal or disbursement.

2. A record for special accounts, showing the source of all funds deposited in such accounts, the names of all persons for whom the funds are or were held, the amount of such funds, the descrip-

tion and amounts, and the names of all persons to whom such funds were disbursed.

3. Copies of all retainer and compensation agreements with clients.

4. Copies of all statements to clients or other persons showing the disbursement of funds to them or on their behalf.

5. Copies of all bills rendered to clients.

6. Copies of all records showing payments to lawyers, investigators or other persons, not in the lawyer's regular employ, for services rendered or performed.

7. Copies of all retainer and closing statements filed with the Office of Court Administration.

8. All checkbooks and checkstubs, bank statements, prenumbered cancelled checks and duplicate deposit slips with respect to the special accounts specified in DR 9-102(B) and any other bank account which records the operations of the lawyer's practice of law.

Lawyers shall make accurate entries of all financial transactions in their records of receipts and disbursements, in their special accounts, in their ledger books or similar records, and in any other books of account kept by them in the regular course of their practice, which entries shall be made at or near the time of the act, condition or event recorded.

E. Authorized Signatories. All special account withdrawals shall be made only to a named payee and not to cash. Such withdrawals shall be made by check or, with the prior written approval of the party entitled to the proceeds, by bank transfer. Only an attorney admitted to practice law in New York State shall be an authorized signatory of a special account.

F-1. Missing Clients. Whenever any sum of money is payable to a client and the lawyer is unable to locate the client, the lawyer shall apply to the court in which the action was brought if in the unified court system, or, if no action was commenced in the unified court system, to the Supreme Court in the county in which the lawyer maintains an office for the practice of law, for an order directing payment to the lawyer of any fees and disbursements that are owed by the client and the balance, if any, to the Lawyers' Fund for Client Protection for safeguarding and disbursement to persons who are entitled thereto.

F-2. Designation of Successor Signatories. (1) Upon the death of a lawyer who was the sole signatory on an attorney trust, escrow or special account, an application may be made to the Supreme court for an order designating a successor signatory for such trust, escrow or special account who shall be a member of the bar in good standing and admitted to the practice of law in New York State.

(2) An application to designate a successor signatory shall be made to the Supreme Court in the judicial district in which the deceased lawyer maintained an office for the practice of law. The application may be made by the legal representative of the deceased lawyer's estate; a lawyer who was affiliated with the deceased lawyer in the practice of law; any person who has a beneficial interest in such trust, escrow or special account; an officer of a city or county bar association; or counsel for an attorney disciplinary committee. No lawyer may charge a legal fee for assisting with an application to designate a successor signatory pursuant to this rule.

(3) The Supreme Court may designate a successor signatory and may direct the safeguarding of funds from such trust, escrow or special account, and the disbursement of such funds to persons who are entitled thereto, and may order that funds in such account be deposited with the Lawyers' Fund for Client Protection for safeguarding and disbursement to persons who are entitled thereto.

G. Dissolution of a Firm. Upon the dissolution of any firm of lawyers, the former partners or members shall make appropriate arrangements for the maintenance by one of them or by a successor firm of the records specified in DR 9–102(D). In the absence of agreement on such arrangements, any partner or former partner or member of a firm in dissolution may apply to the Appellate Division in which the principal office of the law firm is located or its designee for direction and such direction shall be binding upon all partners, former partners or members.

H. Availability of Bookkeeping Records; Records Subject to Production in Disciplinary Investigations and Proceedings. The financial records required by this Disciplinary Rule shall be located, or made available, at the principal New York State office of the lawyers subject hereto and any such records shall be produced in response to a notice or subpoena duces tecum issued in connection with a complaint before or any investigation by the appropriate grievance or departmental disciplinary committee, or shall be produced at the direction of the appropriate Appellate Division before any person designated by it. All books and records produced pursuant to this subdivision shall be kept confidential, except for the purpose of the particular proceeding, and their contents shall not be disclosed by anyone in violation of the lawyer-client privilege.

I. Disciplinary Action. A lawyer who does not maintain and keep the accounts and records as specified and required by this Disciplinary Rule, or who does not produce any such records pursuant to this Rule, shall be deemed in violation of these Rules and shall be subject to disciplinary proceedings.

AMERICAN BAR ASSOCIATION MODEL CODE OF PROFESSIONAL RESPONSIBILITY

As Amended and in Effect as of 1983.

[The Model Code of Professional Responsibility was the product of the Wright Committee's efforts to replace the Canons of Professional Ethics, which had grown from 32 canons in 1908 to 47 canons in 1964. The Model Code was enacted by the ABA in 1969, and subsequently, most states adopted codes of professional responsibility based upon the Model Code. The distinctive feature of the Model Code is its organization into canons, ethical considerations, and disciplinary rules. The canons provided the Model Code with a theoretical structure. Each canon was a general directive to lawyers about the law of professional responsibility. The ethical considerations were more detailed in that they discussed actual fact situations that arose under each canon. Each ethical consideration, however, was only aspirational in nature. Lawyers were supposed to strive to follow the ethical considerations, but they were not considered binding. The disciplinary rules were the provisions that lawyers needed to follow to avoid disciplinary liability. These rules established minimum standards that lawyers were required to follow and standards that were enforced by the disciplinary committees. The ABA replaced the Model Code with the Model Rules of Professional Conduct in 1983. Ed.]

TABLE OF CONTENTS *

* Prepared by Editor.

PREAMBLE AND PRELIMINARY STATEMENT

Preamble [1]

The continued existence of a free and democratic society depends upon recognition of the concept that justice is based upon the rule of law grounded in respect for the dignity of the individual and his capacity through reason for enlightened self-government.[2]   Law so grounded makes justice possible, for only through such law does the dignity of the individual attain respect and protection.   Without it, individual rights become subject to unrestrained power, respect for law is destroyed, and rational self-government is impossible.

Lawyers as guardians of the law, play a vital role in the preservation of society.   The fulfillment of this role requires an understanding by lawyers of their relationship with and function in our legal system.[3]   A consequent obligation of lawyers is to maintain the highest standards of ethical conduct.

In fulfilling his professional responsibilities, a lawyer necessarily assumes various roles that require the performance of many difficult tasks.   Not every situation which he may encounter can be foreseen,[4] but fundamental ethical principles are always present to guide him.   Within the framework of these principles, a lawyer must with courage

1.   The footnotes are intended merely to enable the reader to relate the provisions of this Code to the ABA Canons of Professional Ethics adopted in 1908, as amended, the Opinions of the ABA Committee on Professional Ethics, and a limited number of other sources; they are not intended to be an annotation of the views taken by the ABA Special Committee on Evaluation of Ethical Standards.   Footnotes citing ABA Canons refer to the ABA Canons of Professional Ethics, adopted in 1908, as amended.

2.   Cf. ABA Canons, Preamble.

3.   "[T]he lawyer stands today in special need of a clear understanding of his obligations and of the vital connection between these obligations and the role his profession plays in society."   *Professional Responsibility: Report of the Joint Conference,* 44 A.B.A.J. 1159, 1160 (1958).

4.   "No general statement of the responsibilities of the legal profession can encompass all the situations in which the lawyer may be placed.   Each position held by him makes its own peculiar demands.   These demands the lawyer must clarify for himself in the light of the particular role in which he serves."   *Professional Responsibility: Report of the Joint Conference,* 44 A.B.A.J. 1159, 1218 (1958).

and foresight be able and ready to shape the body of the law to the ever-changing relationships of society.[5]

The Code of Professional Responsibility points the way to the aspiring and provides standards by which to judge the transgressor. Each lawyer must find within his own conscience the touchstone against which to test the extent to which his actions should rise above minimum standards. But in the last analysis it is the desire for the respect and confidence of the members of his profession and of the society which he serves that should provide to a lawyer the incentive for the highest possible degree of ethical conduct. The possible loss of that respect and confidence is the ultimate sanction. So long as its practitioners are guided by these principles, the law will continue to be a noble profession. This is its greatness and its strength, which permit of no compromise.

Preliminary Statement

In furtherance of the principles stated in the Preamble, the American Bar Association has promulgated this Code of Professional Responsibility, consisting of three separate but interrelated parts: Canons, Ethical Considerations, and Disciplinary Rules.[6] The Code is designed to be adopted by appropriate agencies both as an inspirational guide to the members of the profession and as a basis for disciplinary action when the conduct of a lawyer falls below the required minimum standards stated in the Disciplinary Rules.

Obviously the Canons, Ethical Considerations, and Disciplinary Rules cannot apply to non-lawyers; however, they do define the type of ethical conduct that the public has a right to expect not only of lawyers but also of their non-professional employees and associates in all matters pertaining to professional employment. A lawyer should ultimately be responsible for the conduct of his employees and associates in the course of the professional representation of the client.

---

5. "The law and its institutions change as social conditions change. They must change if they are to preserve, much less advance, the political and social values from which they derive their purposes and their life. This is true of the most important of legal institutions, the profession of law. The profession, too, must change when conditions change in order to preserve and advance the social values that are its reasons for being." Cheatham, *Availability of Legal Services: The Responsibility of the Individual Lawyer and the Organized Bar,* 12 U.C.L.A.L.Rev. 438, 440 (1965).

6. The Supreme Court of Wisconsin adopted a Code of Judicial Ethics in 1967. "The code is divided into standards and rules, the standards being statements of what the general desirable level of conduct should be, the rules being particular canons, the violation of which shall subject an individual judge to sanctions." In re Promulgation of a Code of Judicial Ethics, 36 Wis.2d 252, 255, 153 N.W.2d 873, 874 (1967).

The portion of the Wisconsin Code of Judicial Ethics entitled "Standards" states that "[t]he following standards set forth the significant qualities of the ideal judge...." Id., 36 Wis.2d at 256, 153 N.W.2d at 875. The portion entitled "Rules" states that "[t]he court promulgates the following rules because the requirements of judicial conduct embodied therein are of sufficient gravity to warrant sanctions if they are not obeyed...." Id., 36 Wis.2d at 259, 153 N.W.2d at 876.

PROFESSIONAL RESPONSIBILITY

The Canons are statements of axiomatic norms, expressing in general terms the standards of professional conduct expected of lawyers in their relationships with the public, with the legal system, and with the legal profession. They embody the general concepts from which the Ethical Considerations and the Disciplinary Rules are derived.

The Ethical Considerations are aspirational in character and represent the objectives toward which every member of the profession should strive. They constitute a body of principles upon which the lawyer can rely for guidance in many specific situations.[7]

The Disciplinary Rules, unlike the Ethical Considerations, are mandatory in character. The Disciplinary Rules state the minimum level of conduct below which no lawyer can fall without being subject to disciplinary action. Within the framework of fair trial,[8] the Disciplinary Rules should be uniformly applied to all lawyers,[9] regardless of the

---

7. "Under the conditions of modern practice is it peculiarly necessary that the lawyer should understand, not merely the established standards of professional conduct, but the reasons underlying these standards. Today the lawyer plays a changing and increasingly varied role. In many developing fields the precise contribution of the legal profession is as yet undefined." *Professional Responsibility: Report of the Joint Conference,* 44 A.B.A.J. 1159 (1958).

"A true sense of professional responsibility must derive from an understanding of the reasons that lie back of specific restraints, such as those embodied in the Canons. The grounds for the lawyer's peculiar obligations are to be found in the nature of his calling. The lawyer who seeks a clear understanding of his duties will be led to reflect on the special services his profession renders to society and the services it might render if its full capacities were realized. When the lawyer fully understands the nature of his office, he will then discern what restraints are necessary to keep that office wholesome and effective." *Id.*

8. "Disbarment, designed to protect the public, is a punishment or penalty imposed on the lawyer. * * * He is accordingly entitled to procedural due process, which includes fair notice of the charge." In re Ruffalo, 390 U.S. 544, 550, 20 L.Ed.2d 117, 122, 88 S.Ct. 1222, 1226 (1968), rehearing denied, 391 U.S. 961, 20 L.Ed.2d 874, 88 S.Ct. 1833 (1968).

"A State cannot exclude a person from the practice of law or from any other occupation in a manner or for reasons that contravene the Due Process or Equal Protection Clause of the Fourteenth Amendment.... A State can require high standards of qualification ... but any qualification must have a rational connection with the applicant's fitness or capacity to practice law." Schware v. Bd. of Bar Examiners, 353 U.S. 232, 239, 1 L.Ed.2d 796, 801–02, 77 S.Ct. 752, 756 (1957).

"[A]n accused lawyer may expect that he will not be condemned out of a capricious self-righteousness or denied the essentials of a fair hearing." Kingsland v. Dorsey, 338 U.S. 318, 320, 94 L.Ed. 123, 126, 70 S.Ct. 123, 124–25 (1949).

"The attorney and counsellor being, by the solemn judicial act of the court, clothed with his office, does not hold it as a matter of grace and favor. The right which it confers upon him to appear for suitors, and to argue causes is something more than a mere indulgence, revocable at the pleasure of the court, or at the command of the legislature. It is a right of which he can only be deprived by the judgment of the court, for moral or professional delinquency." Ex parte Garland, 71 U.S. (4 Wall.) 333, 378–79, 18 L.Ed. 366, 370 (1866).

See generally Comment, *Procedural Due Process and Character Hearings for Bar Applicants,* 15 Stan.L.Rev. 500 (1963).

9. "The canons of professional ethics must be enforced by the Courts and must

387

nature of their professional activities.[10] The Code makes no attempt to prescribe either disciplinary procedures or penalties [11] for violation of a Disciplinary Rule,[12] nor does it undertake to define standards for civil liability of lawyers for professional conduct. The severity of judgment against one found guilty of violating a Disciplinary Rule should be determined by the character of the offense and the attendant circumstances.[13] An enforcing agency, in applying the Disciplinary Rules, may find interpretive guidance in the basic principles embodied in the Canons and in the objectives reflected in the Ethical Considerations.

CANON 1

A Lawyer Should Assist in Maintaining the Integrity and Competence of the Legal Profession

ETHICAL CONSIDERATIONS

EC 1–1 A basic tenet of the professional responsibility of lawyers is that every person in our society should have ready access to the independent professional services of a lawyer of integrity and competence.

be respected by members of the Bar if we are to maintain public confidence in the integrity and impartiality of the administration of justice." In re Meeker, 76 N.M. 354, 357, 414 P.2d 862, 864 (1966), appeal dismissed, 385 U.S. 449 (1967).

10. See ABA Canon 45.

"The Canons of this Association govern all its members, irrespective of the nature of their practice, and the application of the Canons is not affected by statutes or regulations governing certain activities of lawyers which may prescribe less stringent standards." ABA Comm. on Professional Ethics, Opinions, No. 203 (1940) [hereinafter each Opinion is cited as "ABA Opinion"].

Cf. *ABA Opinion* 152 (1936).

11. "There is generally no prescribed discipline for any particular type of improper conduct. The disciplinary measures taken are discretionary with the courts, which may disbar, suspend, or merely censure the attorney as the nature of the offense and past indicia of character may warrant." Note, 43 Cornell L.Q. 489, 495 (1958).

12. The Code seeks only to specify conduct for which a lawyer should be disciplined. Recommendations as to the procedures to be used in disciplinary actions and the gravity of disciplinary measures appro-

priate for violations of the Code are within the jurisdiction of the American Bar Association Special Committee on Evaluation of Disciplinary Enforcement.

13. "The severity of the judgment of this court should be in proportion to the gravity of the offenses, the moral turpitude involved, and the extent that the defendant's acts and conduct affect his professional qualifications to practice law." Louisiana State Bar Ass'n v. Steiner, 204 La. 1073, 1092–93, 16 So.2d 843, 850 (1944) (Higgins, J., concurring in decree).

"Certainly an erring lawyer who has been disciplined and who having paid the penalty has given satisfactory evidence of repentance and has been rehabilitated and restored to his place at the bar by the court which knows him best ought not to have what amounts to an order of permanent disbarment entered against him by a federal court solely on the basis of an earlier criminal record and without regard to his subsequent rehabilitation and present good character. . . . We think, therefore, that the district court should reconsider the appellant's application for admission and grant it unless the court finds it to be a fact that the appellant is not presently of good moral or professional character." In re Dreier, 258 F.2d 68, 69–70 (3d Cir.1958).

Maintaining the integrity and improving the competence of the bar to meet the highest standards is the ethical responsibility of every lawyer.

EC 1–2 The public should be protected from those who are not qualified to be lawyers by reason of a deficiency in education [1] or moral standards [2] or of other relevant factors [3] but who nevertheless seek to practice law. To assure the maintenance of high moral and educational standards of the legal profession, lawyers should affirmatively assist courts and other appropriate bodies in promulgating, enforcing, and improving requirements for admission to the bar. [4] In like manner, the

1. "[W]e cannot conclude that all educational restrictions [on bar admission] are unlawful. We assume that few would deny that a grammar school education requirement, before taking the bar examination, was reasonable. Or that an applicant had to be able to read or write. Once we conclude that *some* restriction is proper, then it becomes a matter of degree—the problem of drawing the line.

. . .

"We conclude the fundamental question here is whether Rule IV, Section 6 of the Rules Pertaining to Admission of Applicants to the State Bar of Arizona is 'arbitrary, capricious and unreasonable.' We conclude an educational requirement of graduation from an accredited law school is not." Hackin v. Lockwood, 361 F.2d 499, 503–04 (9th Cir.1966), cert. denied, 385 U.S. 960, 17 L.Ed.2d 305, 87 S.Ct. 396 (1966).

2. "Every state in the United States, as a prerequisite for admission to the practice of law, requires that applicants possess 'good moral character.' Although the requirement is of judicial origin, it is now embodied in legislation in most states." Comment, *Procedural Due Process and Character Hearings for Bar Applicants*, 15 Stan.L.Rev. 500 (1963).

"Good character in the members of the bar is essential to the preservation of the integrity of the courts. The duty and power of the court to guard its portals against intrusion by men and women who are mentally and morally dishonest, unfit because of bad character, evidenced by their course of conduct, to participate in the administrative law, would seem to be unquestioned in the matter of preservation of judicial dignity and integrity." In re Monaghan, 126 Vt. 53, 222 A.2d 665, 670 (1966).

"Fundamentally, the question involved in both situations [i.e. admission and disciplinary proceedings] is the same—is the applicant for admission or the attorney sought to be disciplined a fit and proper person to be permitted to practice law, and that usually turns upon whether he has committed or is likely to continue to commit acts of moral turpitude. At the time of oral argument the attorney for respondent frankly conceded that the test for admission and for discipline is and should be the same. We agree with this concession." Hallinan v. Comm. of Bar Examiners, 65 Cal.2d 447, 453, 421 P.2d 76, 81, 55 Cal.Rptr. 228, 233 (1966).

3. "Proceedings to gain admission to the bar are for the purpose of protecting the public and the courts from the ministrations of persons unfit to practice the profession. Attorneys are officers of the court appointed to assist the court in the administration of justice. Into their hands are committed the property, the liberty and sometimes the lives of their clients. This commitment demands a high degree of intelligence, knowledge of the law, respect for its function in society, sound and faithful judgment and, above all else, integrity of character in private and professional conduct." In re Monaghan, 126 Vt. 53, 222 A.2d 665, 676 (1966) (Holden, C.J., dissenting).

4. "A bar composed of lawyers of good moral character is a worthy objective but it is unnecessary to sacrifice vital freedoms in order to obtain that goal. It is also important both to society and the bar itself that lawyers be unintimidated—free to think, speak, and act as members of an Independent Bar." Konigsberg v. State Bar, 353 U.S. 252, 273, 1 L.Ed.2d 810, 825, 77 S.Ct. 722, 733 (1957).

bar has a positive obligation to aid in the continued improvement of all phases of pre-admission and post-admission legal education.

EC 1-3 Before recommending an applicant for admission, a lawyer should satisfy himself that the applicant is of good moral character. Although a lawyer should not become a self-appointed investigator or judge of applicants for admission, he should report to proper officials all unfavorable information he possesses relating to the character or other qualifications of an applicant.[5]

EC 1-4 The integrity of the profession can be maintained only if conduct of lawyers in violation of the Disciplinary Rules is brought to the attention of the proper officials. A lawyer should reveal voluntarily to those officials all unprivileged knowledge of conduct of lawyers which he believes clearly to be in violation of the Disciplinary Rules.[6] A lawyer should, upon request, serve on and assist committees and boards having responsibility for the administration of the Disciplinary Rules.[7]

EC 1-5 A lawyer should maintain high standards of professional conduct and should encourage fellow lawyers to do likewise. He should be temperate and dignified, and he should refrain from all illegal and morally reprehensible conduct.[8] Because of his position in society, even minor violations of law by a lawyer may tend to lessen public confidence in the legal profession. Obedience to law exemplifies respect for law. To lawyers especially, respect for the law should be more than a platitude.

EC 1-6 An applicant for admission to the bar or a lawyer may be unqualified, temporarily or permanently, for other than moral and educational reasons, such as mental or emotional instability. Lawyers should be diligent in taking steps to see that during a period of disqualification such person is not granted a license or, if licensed, is not permitted to practice.[9] In like manner, when the disqualification has

---

5. *See* ABA Canon 29.

6. ABA Canon 28 designates certain conduct as unprofessional and then states that: "A duty to the public and to the profession devolves upon every member of the Bar having knowledge of such practices upon the part of any practitioner immediately to inform thereof, to the end that the offender may be disbarred." ABA Canon 29 states a broader admonition: "Lawyers should expose without fear or favor before the proper tribunals corrupt or dishonest conduct in the profession."

7. "It is the obligation of the organized Bar and the individual lawyer to give unstinted cooperation and assistance to the highest court of the state in discharging its function and duty with respect to discipline

and in purging the profession of the unworthy." *Report of the Special Committee on Disciplinary Procedures,* 80 A.B.A.Rep. 463, 470 (1955).

8. Cf. ABA Canon 32.

9. "We decline, on the present record, to disbar Mr. Sherman or to reprimand him—not because we condone his actions, but because, as heretofore indicated, we are concerned with whether he is mentally responsible for what he has done.

"The logic of the situation would seem to dictate the conclusion that, if he was mentally responsible for the conduct we have outlined, he should be disbarred; and, if he was not mentally responsible, he should not be permitted to practice law.

terminated, members of the bar should assist such person in being licensed, or, if licensed, in being restored to his full right to practice.

DISCIPLINARY RULES

DR 1–101   Maintaining Integrity and Competence of the Legal Profession.

(A) A lawyer is subject to discipline if he has made a materially false statement in, or if he has deliberately failed to disclose a material fact requested in connection with, his application for admission to the bar.[10]

(B) A lawyer shall not further the application for admission to the bar of another person known by him to be unqualified in respect to character, education, or other relevant attribute.[11]

DR 1–102   Misconduct.

(A) A lawyer shall not:
    (1) Violate a Disciplinary Rule.
    (2) Circumvent a Disciplinary Rule through actions of another.[12]

"However, the flaw in the logic is that he may have been mentally irresponsible [at the time of his offensive conduct] . . ., and, yet, have sufficiently improved in the almost two and one-half years intervening to be able to capably and competently represent his clients. . . .

. . .

"We would make clear that we are satisfied that a case has been made against Mr. Sherman, warranting a refusal to permit him to further practice law in this state unless he can establish his mental irresponsibility at the time of the offenses charged. The burden of proof is upon him.

"If he establishes such mental irresponsibility, the burden is then upon him to establish his present capability to practice law." In re Sherman, 58 Wash.2d 1, 6–7, 354 P.2d 888, 890 (1960), cert. denied, 371 U.S. 951, 9 L.Ed.2d 499, 83 S.Ct. 506 (1963).

10. "This Court has the inherent power to revoke a license to practice law in this State, where such license was issued by this Court, and its issuance was procured by the fraudulent concealment, or by the false and fraudulent representation by the applicant of a fact which was manifestly material to the issuance of the license." North Carolina ex rel. Attorney General v. Gorson, 209 N.C. 320, 326, 183 S.E. 392, 395 (1936), cert. denied, 298 U.S. 662, 80 L.Ed. 1387, 56 S.Ct. 752 (1936).

See also Application of Patterson, 318 P.2d 907, 913 (Or.1957), cert. denied, 356 U.S. 947, 2 L.Ed.2d 822, 78 S.Ct. 795 (1958).

11. See ABA Canon 29.

12. In *ABA Opinion 95* (1933), which held that a municipal attorney could not permit police officers to interview persons with claims against the municipality when the attorney knew the claimants to be represented by counsel, the Committee on Professional Ethics said:

"The law officer is, of course, responsible for the acts of those in his department who are under his supervision and control." *Opinion 85.* In re Robinson, 136 N.Y.S. 548 (affirmed 209 N.Y. 354–1912) held that it was a matter of disbarment for an attorney to adopt a general course of approving the unethical conduct of employees of his client, even though he did not actively participate therein.

(3) Engage in illegal conduct involving moral turpitude.[13]

(4) Engage in conduct involving dishonesty, fraud, deceit, or misrepresentation.

(5) Engage in conduct that is prejudicial to the administration of justice.

(6) Engage in any other conduct that adversely reflects on his fitness to practice law.[14]

" '... The attorney should not advise or sanction acts by his client which he himself should not do.' *Opinion 75.*"

13. "The most obvious non-professional ground for disbarment is conviction for a felony. Most states make conviction for a felony grounds for automatic disbarment. Some of these states, including New York, make disbarment mandatory upon conviction for *any* felony, while others require disbarment only for those felonies which involve moral turpitude. There are strong arguments that some felonies, such as involuntary manslaughter, reflect neither on an attorney's fitness, trustworthiness, nor competence and, therefore, should not be grounds for disbarment, but most states tend to disregard these arguments and, following the common law rule, make disbarment mandatory on conviction for any felony." Note, 43 Cornell L.Q. 489, 490 (1958).

"Some states treat conviction for misdemeanors as grounds for automatic disbarment.... However, the vast majority, accepting the common law rule, require that the misdemeanor involve moral turpitude. While the definition of moral turpitude may prove difficult, it seems only proper that those minor offenses which do not affect the attorney's fitness to continue in the profession should not be grounds for disbarment. A good example is an assault and battery conviction which would not involve moral turpitude unless done with malice and deliberation." Id. at 491.

"The term 'moral turpitude' has been used in the law for centuries. It has been the subject of many decisions by the courts but has never been clearly defined because of the nature of the term. Perhaps the best general definition of the term 'moral turpitude' is that it imports an act of baseness, vileness or depravity in the duties which one person owes to another or to society in general, which is contrary to the usual, accepted and customary rule of right and

duty which a person should follow. 58 C.J.S. at page 1201. Although offenses against revenue laws have been held to be crimes of moral turpitude, it has also been held that the attempt to evade the payment of taxes due to the government or any subdivision thereof, while wrong and unlawful, does not involve moral turpitude. 58 C.J.S. at page 1205." Comm. on Legal Ethics v. Scheer, 149 W.Va. 721, 726–27, 143 S.E.2d 141, 145 (1965).

"The right and power to discipline an attorney, as one of its officers, is inherent in the court.... This power is not limited to those instances of misconduct wherein he has been employed, or has acted, in a professional capacity; but, on the contrary, this power may be exercised where his misconduct outside the scope of his professional relations shows him to be an unfit person to practice law." In re Wilson, 391 S.W.2d 914, 917–18 (Mo.1965).

14. "It is a fair characterization of the lawyer's responsibility in our society that he stands 'as a shield,' to quote Devlin, J., in defense of right and to ward off wrong. From a profession charged with these responsibilities there must be exacted those qualities of truth-speaking, of a high sense of honor, of granite discretion, of the strictest observance of fiduciary responsibility, that have, throughout the centuries, been compendiously described as 'moral character.' " Schware v. Bd. of Bar Examiners, 353 U.S. 232, 247 L.Ed.2d 796, 806, 77 S.Ct. 752, 761 (1957) (Frankfurter, J., concurring).

"Particularly applicable here is Rule 4.47 providing that 'A lawyer should always maintain his integrity; and shall not willfully commit any act against the interest of the public; nor shall he violate his duty to the courts or his clients; *nor shall he, by any misconduct, commit any offense against the laws of Missouri or the United States of*

DR 1–103   Disclosure of Information to Authorities.

(A) A lawyer possessing unprivileged knowledge of a violation of DR 1–102 shall report such knowledge to a tribunal or other authority empowered to investigate or act upon such violation.[15]

(B) A lawyer possessing unprivileged knowledge or evidence concerning another lawyer or a judge shall reveal fully such knowledge or evidence upon proper request of a tribunal or other authority empowered to investigate or act upon the conduct of lawyers or judges.[16]

CANON 2

A Lawyer Should Assist the Legal Profession in Fulfilling Its Duty to Make Legal Counsel Available

ETHICAL CONSIDERATIONS

EC 2–1   The need of members of the public for legal services[1] is met only if they recognize their legal problems, appreciate the importance of seeking assistance,[2] and are able to obtain the services of acceptable legal counsel.[3]   Hence, important functions of the legal profession are to educate laymen to recognize their problems, to facilitate the process of

America, which amounts to a crime involving acts done by him contrary to justice, honesty, modesty or good morals; nor shall he be guilty of any other misconduct whereby, for the protection of the public and those charged with the administration of justice, he should no longer be entrusted with the duties and responsibilities belonging to the office of an attorney.' " In re Wilson, 391 S.W.2d 914, 917 (Mo.1965).

15.   See ABA Canon 29; cf. ABA Canon 28.

16.   Cf. ABA Canons 28 and 29.

1.   "Men have need for more than a system of law; they have need for a system of law which functions, and that means they have need for lawyers." Cheatham, *The Lawyer's Role and Surroundings*, 25 Rocky Mt.L.Rev. 405 (1953).

2.   "Law is not self-applying; men must apply and utilize it in concrete cases. But the ordinary man is incapable. He cannot know the principles of law or the rules guiding the machinery of law administration; he does not know how to formulate his desires with precision and to put them into writing; he is ineffective in the presen-

tation of his claims." Cheatham, *The Lawyer's Role and Surroundings*, 25 Rocky Mt. L.Rev. 405 (1953).

3.   "This need [to provide legal services] was recognized by . . . Mr. [Lewis F.] Powell [Jr., President, American Bar Association, 1963–64], who said: 'Looking at contemporary America realistically, we must admit that despite all our efforts to date (and these have not been insignificant), far too many persons are not able to obtain equal justice under law. This usually results because their poverty or their ignorance has prevented them from obtaining legal counsel.' "   Address by E. Clinton Bamberger, Association of American Law Schools 1965 Annual Meeting, Dec. 28, 1965, in Proceedings, Part II, 1965, 61, 63–64 (1965).

"A wide gap separates the need for legal services and its satisfaction, as numerous studies reveal.   Looked at from the side of the layman, one reason for the gap is poverty and the consequent inability to pay legal fees.   Another set of reasons is ignorance of the need for and the value of legal services, and ignorance of where to find a dependable lawyer.   There is fear of the mysterious

intelligent selection of lawyers, and to assist in making legal services fully available.[4]

Recognition of Legal Problems

EC 2–2 The legal profession should assist lay-persons to recognize legal problems because such problems may not be self-revealing and often are not timely noticed. Therefore, lawyers should encourage and participate in educational and public relations programs concerning our legal system with particular reference to legal problems that frequently arise. Preparation of advertisements and professional articles for lay publications [5] and participation in seminars, lectures, and civic programs should be motivated by a desire to educate the public to an awareness of legal needs and to provide information relevant to the selection of the most appropriate counsel rather than to obtain publicity for particular lawyers. The problems of advertising on television require special consideration, due to the style, cost, and transitory nature of such media. If the interests of laypersons in receiving relevant lawyer advertising are not adequately served by print media and radio advertising, and if adequate safeguards to protect the public can reasonably be formulated, television advertising may serve a public interest.

As amended in 1977.

EC 2–3 Whether a lawyer acts properly in volunteering in-person advice to a layperson to seek legal services depends upon the circumstances.[6] The giving of advice that one should take legal action could well be in fulfillment of the duty of the legal profession to assist laypersons in recognizing legal problems.[7] The advice is proper only if

---

processes and delays of the law, and there is fear of overreaching and overcharging by lawyers, a fear stimulated by the occasional exposure of shysters." Cheatham, *Availability of Legal Services: The Responsibility of the Individual Lawyer and of the Organized Bar*, 12 U.C.L.A.L.Rev. 438 (1965).

4. "It is not only the right but the duty of the profession as a whole to utilize such methods as may be developed to bring the services of its members to those who need them, so long as this can be done ethically and with dignity." *ABA Opinion* 320 (1968).

"[T]here is a responsibility on the bar to make legal services available to those who need them. The maxim, 'privilege brings responsibilities,' can be expanded to read, exclusive privilege to render public service brings responsibility to assure that the service is available to those in need of it." Cheatham, *Availability of Legal Services: The Responsibility of the Individual Lawyer*

and of the Organized Bar, 12 U.C.L.A.L.Rev. 438, 443 (1965).

"The obligation to provide legal services for those actually caught up in litigation carries with it the obligation to make preventive legal advice accessible to all. It is among those unaccustomed to business affairs and fearful of the ways of the law that such advice is often most needed. If it is not received in time, the most valiant and skillful representation in court may come too late." *Professional Responsibility: Report of the Joint Conference*, 44 A.B.A.J. 1159, 1216 (1958).

5. "A lawyer may with propriety write articles for publications in which he gives information upon the law...." A.B.A. Canon 40.

6. See ABA Canon 28.

7. This question can assume constitutional dimensions: "We meet at the outset the contention that 'solicitation' is wholly motivated by a desire to protect one who does not recognize that he may have legal problems or who is ignorant of his legal rights or obligations. It is improper if motivated by a desire to obtain personal benefit, secure personal publicity, or cause legal action to be taken merely to harass or injure another. A lawyer should not initiate an in-person contact with a non-client, personally or through a representative, for the purpose of being retained to represent him for compensation.

As amended in 1977.

EC 2–4 Since motivation is subjective and often difficult to judge, the motives of a lawyer who volunteers in-person advice likely to produce legal controversy may well be suspect if he receives professional employment or other benefits as a result.[8] A lawyer who volunteers in-person advice that one should obtain the services of a lawyer generally should not himself accept employment, compensation, or other benefit in connection with that matter. However, it is not improper for a lawyer to volunteer such advice and render resulting legal services to close friends, relatives, former clients (in regard to matters germane to former employment), and regular clients.[9]

As amended in 1977.

EC 2–5 A lawyer who writes or speaks for the purpose of educating members of the public to recognize their legal problems should carefully refrain from giving or appearing to give a general solution applicable to

outside the area of freedoms protected by the First Amendment. To this contention there are two answers. The first is that a State cannot foreclose the exercise of constitutional rights by mere labels. The second is that abstract discussion is not the only species of communication which the Constitution protects; the First Amendment also protects vigorous advocacy, certainly of lawful ends, against governmental intrusion. . . .

. . .

"However valid may be Virginia's interest in regulating the traditionally illegal practice of barratry, maintenance and champerty, that interest does not justify the prohibition of the NAACP activities disclosed by this record. Malicious intent was of the essence of the common-law offenses of fomenting or stirring up litigation. And whatever may be or may have been true of suits against governments in other countries, the exercise in our own, as in this case of First Amendment rights to enforce Constitutional rights through litigation, as a matter of law, cannot be deemed malicious." NAACP v. Button, 371 U.S. 415, 429, 439–40, 9 L.Ed.2d 405, 415–16, 422, 83 S.Ct. 328, 336, 341 (1963).

8. "It is disreputable for an attorney to breed litigation by seeking out those who have claims for personal injuries or other grounds of action in order to secure them as clients, or to employ agents or runners, or to reward those who bring or influence the bringing of business to his office. . . . Moreover, it tends quite easily to the institution of baseless litigation and the manufacture of perjured testimony. From early times, this danger has been recognized in the law by the condemnation of the crime of common barratry, or the stirring up of suits or quarrels between individuals at law or otherwise." In re Ades, 6 F.Supp. 467, 474–75 (D.Mary.1934).

9. "*Rule 2.*

"§ a. . . .

"[A] member of the State Bar shall not solicit professional employment by

"(1) Volunteering counsel or advice except where ties of blood relationship or trust make it appropriate." Cal.Business and Professions Code § 6076 (West 1962).

all apparently similar individual problems,[10] since slight changes in fact situations may require a material variance in the applicable advice; otherwise, the public may be mislead and misadvised. Talks and writings by lawyers for laypersons should caution them not to attempt to solve individual problems upon the basis of the information contained therein.[11]

As amended in 1977.

Selection of a Lawyer

EC 2–6 Formerly a potential client usually knew the reputations of local lawyers for competency and integrity and therefore could select a practitioner in whom he had confidence. This traditional selection process worked well because it was initiated by the client and the choice was an informed one.

EC 2–7 Changed conditions, however, have seriously restricted the effectiveness of the traditional selection process. Often the reputations of lawyers are not sufficiently known to enable laypersons to make intelligent choices.[12] The law has become increasingly complex and specialized. Few lawyers are willing and competent to deal with every kind of legal matter, and many laypersons have difficulty in determining the competence of lawyers to render different types of legal services. The selection of legal counsel is particularly difficult for transients, persons moving into new areas, persons of limited education or means, and others who have little or no contact with lawyers.[13] Lack of information about the availability of lawyers, the qualifications of particular lawyers, and the expense of legal representation leads laypersons to avoid seeking legal advice.

As amended in 1977.

10. *"Rule 18* ... A member of the State Bar shall not advise inquirers or render opinions to them through or in connection with a newspaper, radio or other publicity medium of any kind in respect to their specific legal problems, whether or not such attorney shall be compensated for his services." Cal.Business and Professions Code § 6076 (West 1962).

11. "In any case where a member might well apply the advice given in the opinion to his individual affairs, the lawyer rendering the opinion [concerning problems common to members of an association and distributed to the members through a periodic bulletin] should specifically state that this opinion should not be relied on by any member as a basis for handling his individual affairs, but that in every case he should con-

sult his counsel. In the publication of the opinion the association should make a similar statement." *ABA Opinion* 273 (1946).

12. "A group of recent interrelated changes bears directly on the availability of legal services.... [One] change is the constantly accelerating urbanization of the country and the decline of personal and neighborhood knowledge of whom to retain as a professional man." Cheatham, *Availability of Legal Services: The Responsibility of the Individual Lawyer and of the Organized Bar,* 12 U.C.L.A.L.Rev. 438, 440 (1965).

13. Cf. Cheatham, *A Lawyer When Needed: Legal Services for the Middle Classes,* 63 Colum.L.Rev. 973, 974 (1963).

EC 2-8 Selection of a lawyer by a layperson should be made on an informed basis. Advice and recommendation of third parties—relatives, friends, acquaintances, business associates, or other lawyers—and disclosure of relevant information about the lawyer and his practice may be helpful. A layperson is best served if the recommendation is disinterested and informed. In order that the recommendation be disinterested, a lawyer should not seek to influence another to recommend his employment. A lawyer should not compensate another person for recommending him, for influencing a prospective client to employ him, or to encourage future recommendations.[14] Advertisements and public communications, whether in law lists, telephone directories, newspapers, other forms of print media, television or radio, should be formulated to convey only information that is necessary to make an appropriate selection. Such information includes: (1) office information, such as, name, including name of law firm and names of professional associates; addresses; telephone numbers; credit card acceptability; fluency in foreign languages; and office hours; (2) relevant biographical information; (3) description of the practice, but only by using designations and definitions authorized by [the agency having jurisdiction of the subject under state law], for example, one or more fields of law in which the lawyer or law firm practices; a statement that practice is limited to one or more fields of law; and/or a statement that the lawyer or law firm specializes in a particular field of law practice, but only by using designations, definitions and standards authorized by [the agency having jurisdiction of the subject under state law]; and (4) permitted fee information. Self-laudation should be avoided.

As amended in 1978.

Selection of a Lawyer: Lawyer Advertising

EC 2-9 The lack of sophistication on the part of many members of the public concerning legal services, the importance of the interests affected by the choice of a lawyer and prior experience with unrestricted lawyer advertising, require that special care be taken by lawyers to avoid misleading the public and to assure that the information set forth in any advertising is relevant to the selection of a lawyer. The lawyer must be mindful that the benefits of lawyer advertising depend upon its reliability and accuracy. Examples of information in lawyer advertising that would be deceptive include misstatements of fact, suggestions that the ingenuity or prior record of a lawyer rather than the justice of the claim are the principal factors likely to determine the result, inclusion of information irrelevant to selecting a lawyer, and representations concerning the quality of service, which cannot be measured or verified. Since lawyer advertising is calculated and not spontaneous, reasonable regulation of lawyer advertising designed to foster compliance with

14. See ABA Canon 28.

appropriate standards serves the public interest without impeding the flow of useful, meaningful, and relevant information to the public.

As amended in 1977.

EC 2-10 A lawyer should ensure that the information contained in any advertising which the lawyer publishes, broadcasts or causes to be published or broadcast is relevant, is disseminated in an objective and understandable fashion, and would facilitate the prospective client's ability to compare the qualifications of the lawyers available to represent him. A lawyer should strive to communicate such information without undue emphasis upon style and advertising stratagems which serve to hinder rather than to facilitate intelligent selection of counsel. Because technological change is a recurrent feature of communications forms, and because perceptions of what is relevant in lawyer selection may change, lawyer advertising regulations should not be cast in rigid, unchangeable terms. Machinery is therefore available to advertisers and consumers for prompt consideration of proposals to change the rules governing lawyer advertising. The determination of any request for such change should depend upon whether the proposal is necessary in light of existing Code provisions, whether the proposal accords with standards of accuracy, reliability and truthfulness, and whether the proposal would facilitate informed selection of lawyers by potential consumers of legal services. Representatives of lawyers and consumers should be heard in addition to the applicant concerning any proposed change. Any change which is approved should be promulgated in the form of an amendment to the Code so that all lawyers practicing in the jurisdiction may avail themselves of its provisions.

As amended in 1977.

EC 2-11 The name under which a lawyer conducts his practice may be a factor in the selection process.[15] The use of a trade name or an assumed name could mislead laypersons concerning the identity, responsibility, and status of those practicing thereunder.[16] Accordingly, a lawyer in private practice should practice only under a designation containing his own name, the name of a lawyer employing him, the name of one or more of the lawyers practicing in a partnership, or, if permitted by law, the name of a professional legal corporation, which should be clearly designated as such. For many years some law firms have used a firm name retaining one or more names of deceased or retired partners and such practice is not improper if the firm is a bona fide successor of a firm in which the deceased or retired person was a member, if the use of the name is authorized by law or by contract, and if the public is not misled thereby.[17] However, the name of a partner who withdraws from

---

15. *Cf. ABA Opinion* 303 (1961).

16. *See* ABA Canon 33.

17. Id.

"The continued use of a firm name by one or more surviving partners after the death of a member of the firm whose name is in the firm title is expressly permitted by the Canons of Ethics. The reason for this

a firm but continues to practice law should be omitted from the firm name in order to avoid misleading the public.

As amended in 1977.

EC 2–12 A lawyer occupying a judicial, legislative, or public executive or administrative position who has the right to practice law concurrently may allow his name to remain in the name of the firm if he actively continues to practice law as a member thereof. Otherwise, his name should be removed from the firm name,[18] and he should not be identified as a past or present member of the firm; and he should not hold himself out as being a practicing lawyer.

EC 2–13 In order to avoid the possibility of misleading persons with whom he deals, a lawyer should be scrupulous in the representation of his professional status.[19] He should not hold himself out as being a partner or associate of a law firm if he is not one in fact,[20] and thus should not hold himself out as partner or associate if he only shares offices with another lawyer.[21]

EC 2–14 In some instances a lawyer confines his practice to a particular field of law.[22] In the absence of state controls to insure the existence

---

is that all of the partners have by their joint and several efforts over a period of years contributed to the good will attached to the firm name. In the case of a firm having widespread connections, this good will is disturbed by a change in firm name every time a name partner dies, and that reflects a loss in some degree of the good will to the building up of which the surviving partners have contributed their time, skill and labor through a period of years. To avoid this loss the firm name is continued, and to meet the requirements of the Canon the individuals constituting the firm from time to time are listed." *ABA Opinion* 267 (1945).

"Accepted local custom in New York recognizes that the name of a law firm does not necessarily identify the individual members of the firm, and hence the continued use of a firm name after the death of one or more partners is not a deception and is permissible.... The continued use of a deceased partner's name in the firm title is not affected by the fact that another partner withdraws from the firm and his name is dropped, or the name of the new partner is added to the firm name." *Opinion* No. 45, Committee on Professional Ethics, New York State Bar Ass'n, 39 N.Y.St.B.J. 455 (1967).

18. Cf. ABA Canon 33 and *ABA Opinion* 315 (1965).

19. Cf. *ABA Opinions* 283 (1950) and 81 (1932).

20. See *ABA Opinion* 316 (1967).

21. "The word 'associates' has a variety of meanings. Principally through custom the word when used on the letterheads of law firms has come to be regarded as describing those who are employees of the firm. Because the word has acquired this special significance in connection with the practice of the law the use of the word to describe lawyer relationships other than employer-employee is likely to be misleading." In re Sussman and Tanner, 241 Ore. 246, 248, 405 P.2d 355, 356 (1965).

According to *ABA Opinion* 310 (1963), use of the term "associates" would be misleading in two situations: (1) where two lawyers are partners and they share both responsibility and liability for the partnership; and (2) where two lawyers practice separately, sharing no responsibility or liability, and only share a suite of offices and some costs.

22. "For a long time, many lawyers have, of necessity, limited their practice to certain branches of law. The increasing complexity of the law and the demand of

of special competence, a lawyer should not be permitted to hold himself out as a specialist or as having official recognition as a specialist, other than in the fields of admiralty, trademark, and patent law where a holding out as a specialist historically has been permitted. A lawyer may, however, indicate in permitted advertising, if it is factual, a limitation of his practice or one or more particular areas or fields of law in which he practices using designations and definitions authorized for that purpose by [the state agency having jurisdiction]. A lawyer practicing in a jurisdiction which certifies specialists must also be careful not to confuse laypersons as to his status. If a lawyer discloses areas of law in which he practices or to which he limits his practice, but is not certified in [the jurisdiction], he, and the designation authorized in [the jurisdiction], should avoid any implication that he is in fact certified.

As amended in 1977.

EC 2–15 The legal profession has developed lawyer referral systems designed to aid individuals who are able to pay fees but need assistance in locating lawyers competent to handle their particular problems. Use of a lawyer referral system enables a layman to avoid an uninformed selection of a lawyer because such a system makes possible the employment of competent lawyers who have indicated an interest in the subject matter involved. Lawyers should support the principle of lawyer referral systems and should encourage the evolution of other ethical plans which aid in the selection of qualified counsel.

Financial Ability to Employ Counsel: Generally

EC 2–16 The legal profession cannot remain a viable force in fulfilling its role in our society unless its members receive adequate compensation for services rendered, and reasonable fees [23] should be charged in appropriate cases to clients able to pay them. Nevertheless, persons unable to pay all or a portion of a reasonable fee should be able to obtain necessary legal services,[24] and lawyers should support and participate in ethical activities designed to achieve that objective.[25]

Financial Ability to Employ Counsel: Persons Able to Pay Reasonable Fees

EC 2–17 The determination of a proper fee requires consideration of

the public for more expertness on the part of the lawyer has, in the past few years—particularly in the last ten years—brought about specialization on an increasing scale." *Report of the Special Committee on Specialization and Specialized Legal Services,* 79 A.B.A.Rep. 582, 584 (1954).

23. See ABA Canon 12.

24. Cf. ABA Canon 12.

25. "If there is any fundamental proposition of government on which all would agree, it is that one of the highest goals of society must be to achieve and maintain equality before the law. Yet this ideal remains an empty form of words unless the legal profession is ready to provide adequate representation for those unable to pay the usual fees." *Professional Representation: Report of the Joint Conference,* 44 A.B.A.J. 1159, 1216 (1958).

the interests of both client and lawyer.[26] A lawyer should not charge more than a reasonable fee,[27] for excessive cost of legal service would deter laymen from utilizing the legal system in protection of their rights. Furthermore, an excessive charge abuses the professional relationship between lawyer and client. On the other hand, adequate compensation is necessary in order to enable the lawyer to serve his client effectively and to preserve the integrity and independence of the profession.[28]

EC 2–18 The determination of the reasonableness of a fee requires consideration of all relevant circumstances,[29] including those stated in the Disciplinary Rules. The fees of a lawyer will vary according to many factors, including the time required, his experience, ability, and reputation, the nature of the employment, the responsibility involved, and the results obtained. It is a commendable and long-standing tradition of the bar that special consideration is given in the fixing of any fee for services rendered a brother lawyer or a member of his immediate family.

As amended in 1974.

EC 2–19 As soon as feasible after a lawyer has been employed, it is desirable that he reach a clear agreement with his client as to the basis of the fee charges to be made. Such a course will not only prevent later misunderstanding but will also work for good relations between the lawyer and the client. It is usually beneficial to reduce to writing the understanding of the parties regarding the fee, particularly when it is contingent. A lawyer should be mindful that many persons who desire to employ him may have had little or no experience with fee charges of lawyers, and for this reason he should explain fully to such persons the reasons for the particular fee arrangement he proposes.

EC 2–20 Contingent fee arrangements [30] in civil cases have long been commonly accepted in the United States in proceedings to enforce claims. The historical bases of their acceptance are that (1) they often, and in a variety of circumstances, provide the only practical means by which one having a claim against another can economically afford, finance, and obtain the services of a competent lawyer to prosecute his claim, and (2) a successful prosecution of the claim produces a *res* out of

---

26. See ABA Canon 12.

27. Cf. ABA Canon 12.

28. "When members of the Bar are induced to render legal services for inadequate compensation as a consequence the quality of the service rendered may be lowered, the welfare of the profession injured and the administration of justice made less efficient." *ABA Opinion* 302 (1961).

Cf. *ABA Opinion* 307 (1962).

29. See ABA Canon 12.

30. See ABA Canon 13; see also MacKinnon, Contingent Fees for Legal Services

(1964) (A report of the American Bar Foundation).

"A contract for a reasonable contingent fee where sanctioned by law is permitted by *Canon 13*, but the client must remain responsible to the lawyer for expenses advanced by the latter. 'There is to be no barter of the privilege of prosecuting a cause for gain in exchange for the promise of the attorney to prosecute at his own expense.' (Cardozo, C.J. In Matter of Gilman, 251 N.Y. 265, 270–271.)" *ABA Opinion* 246 (1942).

which the fee can be paid.[31] Although a lawyer generally should decline to accept employment on a contingent fee basis by one who is able to pay a reasonable fixed fee, it is not necessarily improper for a lawyer, where justified by the particular circumstances of a case, to enter into a contingent fee contract in a civil case with any client who, after being fully informed of all relevant factors, desires that arrangement. Because of the human relationships involved and the unique character of the proceedings, contingent fee arrangements in domestic relation cases are rarely justified. In administrative agency proceedings contingent fee contracts should be governed by the same consideration as in other civil cases. Public policy properly condemns contingent fee arrangements in criminal cases, largely on the ground that legal services in criminal cases do not produce a *res* with which to pay the fee.

EC 2–21 A lawyer should not accept compensation or any thing of value incident to his employment or services from one other than his client without the knowledge and consent of his client after full disclosure.[32]

EC 2–22 Without the consent of his client, a lawyer should not associate in a particular matter another lawyer outside his firm. A fee may properly be divided between lawyers [33] properly associated if the division is in proportion to the services performed and the responsibility assumed by each lawyer [34] and if the total fee is reasonable.

EC 2–23 A lawyer should be zealous in his efforts to avoid controversies over fees with clients [35] and should attempt to resolve amicably any differences on the subject.[36] He should not sue a client for a fee unless

---

31. See Comment, *Providing Legal Services for the Middle Class in Civil Matters: The Problem, the Duty and a Solution,* 26 U.Pitt.L.Rev. 811, 829 (1965).

32. See ABA Canon 38.

"Of course, as . . . [Informal Opinion 679] points out, there must be full disclosure of the arrangement [that an entity other than the client pays the attorney's fee] by the attorney to the client...." *ABA Opinion* 320 (1968).

33. "Only lawyers may share in . . . a division of fees, but . . . it is not necessary that both lawyers be admitted to practice in the same state, so long as the division was based on the division of services or responsibility." *ABA Opinion* 316 (1967).

34. See ABA Canon 34.

"We adhere to our previous rulings that where a lawyer merely brings about the employment of another lawyer *but renders no service and assumes no responsibility in the matter,* a division of the latter's fee is improper. *(Opinions 18 and 153).*

"It is assumed that the bar, generally, understands what acts or conduct of a lawyer may constitute 'services' to a client within the intendment of *Canon 12.* Such acts or conduct invariably, if not always involve 'responsibility' on the part of the lawyer, whether the word 'responsibility' be construed to denote the possible resultant legal or moral liability on the part of the lawyer to the client or to others, or the onus of deciding what should or should not be done in behalf of the client. The word 'services' in *Canon 12* must be construed in this broad sense and may apply to the selection and retainer of associate counsel as well as to others acts or conduct in the client's behalf." *ABA Opinion* 204 (1940).

35. See ABA Canon 14.

36. Cf. *ABA Opinion* 320 (1968).

necessary to prevent fraud or gross imposition by the client.[37]

Financial Ability to Employ Counsel: Persons Unable to Pay Reasonable Fees

EC 2–24 A layman whose financial ability is not sufficient to permit payment of any fee cannot obtain legal services, other than in cases where a contingent fee is appropriate, unless the services are provided for him. Even a person of moderate means may be unable to pay a reasonable fee which is large because of the complexity, novelty, or difficulty of the problem or similar factors.[38]

EC 2–25 Historically, the need for legal services of those unable to pay reasonable fees has been met in part by lawyers who donated their services or accepted court appointments on behalf of such individuals. The basic responsibility for providing legal services for those unable to pay ultimately rests upon the individual lawyer, and personal involvement in the problems of the disadvantaged can be one of the most rewarding experiences in the life of a lawyer. Every lawyer, regardless of professional prominence or professional workload, should find time to participate in serving the disadvantaged. The rendition of free legal services to those unable to pay reasonable fees continues to be an obligation of each lawyer, but the efforts of individual lawyers are often not enough to meet the need.[39] Thus it has been necessary for the

37. See ABA Canon 14.

"Ours is a learned profession, not a mere money-getting trade.... Suits to collect fees should be avoided. Only where the circumstances imperatively require, should resort be had to a suit to compel payment. And where a lawyer does resort to a suit to enforce payment of fees which involves a disclosure, he should carefully avoid any disclosure not clearly necessary to obtaining or defending his rights." *ABA Opinion* 250 (1943).

But cf. *ABA Opinion* 320 (1968).

38. "As a society increases in size, sophistication and technology, the body of laws which is required to control that society also increases in size, scope and complexity. With this growth, the law directly affects more and more facets of individual behavior, creating an expanding need for legal services on the part of the individual members of the society.... As legal guidance in social and commercial behavior increasingly becomes necessary, there will come a concurrent demand from the layman that such guidance be made available to him. This demand will not come from those who are able to employ the best legal talent, nor from those who can obtain legal assistance at little or no cost. It will come from the large 'forgotten middle income class,' who can neither afford to pay proportionately large fees nor qualify for ultra-low-cost services. The legal profession must recognize this inevitable demand and consider methods whereby it can be satisfied. If the profession fails to provide such methods, the laity will." Comment, *Providing Legal Services for the Middle Class in Civil Matters: The Problem, the Duty and a Solution,* 26 U.Pitt.L.Rev. 811, 811–12 (1965).

"The issue is not whether we shall do something or do nothing. The demand for ordinary everyday legal justice is so great and the moral nature of the demand is so strong that the issue has become whether we devise, maintain, and support suitable agencies able to satisfy the demand, or by our own default, force the government to take over the job, supplant us, and ultimately dominate us." Smith, *Legal Service Offices for Persons of Moderate Means,* 1949 Wis.L.Rev. 416, 418 (1949).

39. "Lawyers have peculiar responsibilities for the just administration of the law, and these responsibilities include providing

profession to institute additional programs to provide legal services.[40] Accordingly, legal aid offices,[41] lawyer referral services, and other related programs have been developed, and others will be developed, by the profession.[42] Every lawyer should support all proper efforts to meet this need for legal services.[43]

Acceptance and Retention of Employment

EC 2–26 A lawyer is under no obligation to act as advisor or advocate for every person who may wish to become his client; but in furtherance of the objective of the bar to make legal services fully available, a lawyer should not lightly decline proffered employment. The fulfillment of this objective requires acceptance by a lawyer of his share of tendered employment which may be unattractive both to him and the bar generally.[44]

advice and representation for needy persons. To a degree not always appreciated by the public at large, the bar has performed these obligations with zeal and devotion. The Committee is persuaded, however, that a system of justice that attempts, in mid-twentieth century America, to meet the needs of the financially incapacitated accused through primary or exclusive reliance on the uncompensated services of counsel will prove unsuccessful and inadequate.... A system of adequate representation, therefore, should be structured and financed in a manner reflecting its public importance.... We believe that fees for private appointed counsel should be set by the court within maximum limits established by the statute." Report of the Att'y Gen's Comm. on Poverty and the Administration of Criminal Justice 41–43 (1963).

40. "At present this representation [of those unable to pay usual fees] is being supplied in some measure through the spontaneous generosity of individual lawyers, through legal aid societies, and—increasingly—through the organized efforts of the Bar. If those who stand in need of this service know of its availability and their need is in fact adequately met, the precise mechanism by which this service is provided becomes of secondary importance. It is of great importance, however, that both the impulse to render this service and the plan for making that impulse effective, should arise within the legal profession itself." *Professional Responsibility: Report of the*

Joint Conference, 44 A.B.A.J. 1159, 1216 (1958).

41. "Free legal clinics carried on by the organized bar are not ethically objectionable. On the contrary, they serve a very worthwhile purpose and should be encouraged." *ABA Opinion* 191 (1939).

42. "Whereas the American Bar Association believes that it is a fundamental duty of the bar to see to it that all persons requiring legal advice be able to attain it, irrespective of their economic status....

"Resolved, that the Association approves and sponsors the setting up by state and local bar associations of lawyer referral plans and low-cost legal service methods for the purpose of dealing with cases of persons who might not otherwise have the benefit of legal advice...." *Proceedings of the House of Delegates of the American Bar Association,* Oct. 30, 1946, 71 A.B.A.Rep. 103, 109–10 (1946).

43. "The defense of indigent citizens, without compensation, is carried on throughout the country by lawyers representing legal aid societies, not only with the approval, but with the commendation of those acquainted with the work. Not infrequently services are rendered out of sympathy or for other philanthropic reasons, by individual lawyers who do not represent legal aid societies. There is nothing whatever in the Canons to prevent a lawyer from performing such an act, nor should there be." *ABA Opinion* 148 (1935).

44. But cf. ABA Canon 31.

EC 2–27 History is replete with instances of distinguished and sacrificial services by lawyers who have represented unpopular clients and causes. Regardless of his personal feelings, a lawyer should not decline representation because a client or a cause is unpopular or community reaction is adverse.[45]

EC 2–28 The personal preference of a lawyer to avoid adversary alignment against judges, other lawyers,[46] public officials, or influential members of the community does not justify his rejection of tendered employment.

EC 2–29 When a lawyer is appointed by a court or requested by a bar association to undertake representation of a person unable to obtain counsel, whether for financial or other reasons, he should not seek to be excused from undertaking the representation except for compelling reasons.[47] Compelling reasons do not include such factors as the repugnance of the subject matter of the proceeding, the identity[48] or position of a person involved in the case, the belief of the lawyer that the defendant in a criminal proceeding is guilty,[49] or the belief of the lawyer regarding the merits of the civil case.[50]

45. "One of the highest services the lawyer can render to society is to appear in court on behalf of clients whose causes are in disfavor with the general public." *Professional Responsibility: Report of the Joint Conference,* 44 A.B.A.J. 1159, 1216 (1958).

One author proposes the following proposition to be included in "A Proper Oath for Advocates": "I recognize that it is sometimes difficult for clients with unpopular causes to obtain proper legal representation. I will do all that I can to assure that the client with the unpopular cause is properly represented, and that the lawyer representing such a client receives credit from and support of the bar for handling such a matter." Thode, *The Ethical Standard for the Advocate,* 39 Texas L.Rev. 575, 592 (1961).

"§ 6068. ... It is the duty of an attorney.

. . .

"(h) Never to reject, for any consideration personal to himself, the cause of the defenseless or the oppressed." Cal.Business and Professions Code § 6068 (West 1962). Virtually the same language is found in the Oregon statutes at Ore.Rev. Stats. Ch. 9, § 9.460(8).

See Rostow, *The Lawyer and His Client,* 48 A.B.A.J. 25 and 146 (1962).

46. See ABA Canons 7 and 29.

"We are of the opinion that it is not professionally improper for a lawyer to accept employment to compel another lawyer to honor the just claim of a layman. On the contrary, it is highly proper that he do so. Unfortunately, there appears to be a widespread feeling among laymen that it is difficult, if not impossible, to obtain justice when they have claims against members of the Bar because other lawyers will not accept employment to proceed against them. The honor of the profession, whose members proudly style themselves officers of the court, must surely be sullied if its members bind themselves by custom to refrain from enforcing just claims of laymen against lawyers." *ABA Opinion* 144 (1935).

47. ABA Canon 4 uses a slightly different test, saying, "A lawyer assigned as counsel for an indigent prisoner ought not to ask to be excused for any trivial reason...."

48. Cf. ABA Canon 7.

49. See ABA Canon 5.

50. Dr. Johnson's reply to Boswell upon being asked what he thought of "supporting a cause which you know to be bad" was: "Sir, you do not know it to be good or bad till the Judge determines it. I have said

EC 2-30 Employment should not be accepted by a lawyer when he is unable to render competent service [51] or when he knows or it is obvious that the person seeking to employ him desires to institute or maintain an action merely for the purpose of harassing or maliciously injuring another.[52] Likewise, a lawyer should decline employment if the intensity of his personal feeling, as distinguished from a community attitude, may impair his effective representation of a prospective client. If a lawyer knows a client has previously obtained counsel, he should not accept employment in the matter unless the other counsel approves [53] or withdraws, or the client terminates the prior employment.[54]

EC 2-31 Full availability of legal counsel requires both that persons be able to obtain counsel and that lawyers who undertake representation complete the work involved. Trial counsel for a convicted defendant should continue to represent his client by advising whether to take an appeal and, if the appeal is prosecuted, by representing him through the appeal unless new counsel is substituted or withdrawal is permitted by the appropriate court.

EC 2-32 A decision by a lawyer to withdraw should be made only on the basis of compelling circumstances,[55] and in a matter pending before a tribunal he must comply with the rules of the tribunal regarding withdrawal. A lawyer should not withdraw without considering carefully and endeavoring to minimize the possible adverse effect on the rights of his client and the possibility of prejudice to his client [56] as a result of

that you are to state facts fairly; so that your thinking, or what you call knowing, a cause to be bad, must be from reasoning, must be from supposing your arguments to be weak and inconclusive. But, Sir, that is not enough. An argument which does not convince yourself, may convince the Judge to whom you urge it; and if it does convince him, why, then, Sir, you are wrong, and he is right." 2 Boswell, The Life of Johnson 47–48 (Hill ed. 1887).

51. "The lawyer deciding whether to undertake a case must be able to judge objectively whether he is capable of handling it and whether he can assume its burdens without prejudice to previous commitments...." *Professional Responsibility: Report of the Joint Conference,* 44 A.B.A.J. 1158, 1218 (1958).

52. "The lawyer must decline to conduct a civil cause or to make a defense when convinced that it is intended merely to harass or to injure the opposite party or to work oppression or wrong." ABA Canon 30.

53. See ABA Canon 7.

54. Id.

"From the facts stated we assume that the client has discharged the first attorney and given notice of the discharge. Such being the case, the second attorney may properly accept employment. *Canon 7; Opinions 10, 130, 149.*" ABA Opinion 209 (1941).

55. See ABA Canon 44.

"I will carefully consider, before taking a case, whether it appears that I can fully represent the client within the framework of law. If the decision is in the affirmative, then it will take extreme circumstances to cause me to decide later that I cannot so represent him." Thode, *The Ethical Standard for the Advocate,* 39 Texas L.Rev. 575, 592 (1961) (from "A Proper Oath for Advocates").

56. *ABA Opinion* 314 (1965) held that a lawyer should not disassociate himself from a cause when "it is obvious that the very act of disassociation would have the effect of violating *Canon 37.*"

his withdrawal. Even when he justifiably withdraws, a lawyer should protect the welfare of his client by giving due notice of his withdrawal,[57] suggesting employment of other counsel, delivering to the client all papers and property to which the client is entitled, cooperating with counsel subsequently employed, and otherwise endeavoring to minimize the possibility of harm. Further, he should refund to the client any compensation not earned during the employment.[58]

EC 2-33 As a part of the legal profession's commitment to the principle that high quality legal services should be available to all, attorneys are encouraged to cooperate with qualified legal assistance organizations providing prepaid legal services. Such participation should at all times be in accordance with the basic tenets of the profession: independence, integrity, competence and devotion to the interests of individual clients. An attorney so participating should make certain that his relationship with a qualified legal assistance organization in no way interferes with his independent, professional representation of the interests of the individual client. An attorney should avoid situations in which officials of the organization who are not lawyers attempt to direct attorneys concerning the manner in which legal services are performed for individual members, and should also avoid situations in which considerations of economy are given undue weight in determining the attorneys employed by an organization or the legal services to be performed for the member or beneficiary rather than competence and quality of service. An attorney interested in maintaining the historic traditions of the profession and preserving the function of a lawyer as a trusted and independent advisor to individual members of society should carefully assess such factors when accepting employment by, or otherwise participating in, a particular qualified legal assistance organization, and while so participating should adhere to the highest professional standards of effort and competence.

Added in 1974; amended in 1975.

DISCIPLINARY RULES

DR 2-101   Publicity.

(A) A lawyer shall not, on behalf of himself, his partner, associate or any other lawyer affiliated with him or his firm, use or participate in the use of any form of public communication containing a false, fraudulent, misleading, deceptive, self-laudatory or unfair statement or claim.

57. ABA Canon 44 enumerates instances in which "... the lawyer may be warranted in withdrawing on due notice to the client, allowing him time to employ another lawyer."

58. *See* ABA Canon 44.

(B) In order to facilitate the process of informed selection of a lawyer by potential consumers of legal services, a lawyer may publish or broadcast, subject to DR 2-103, the following information in print media distributed or over television or radio broadcast in the geographic area or areas in which the lawyer resides or maintains offices or in which a significant part of the lawyer's clientele resides, provided that the information disclosed by the lawyer in such publication or broadcast complies with DR 2-101(A), and is presented in a dignified manner:

(1) Name, including name of law firm and names of professional associates; addresses and telephone numbers;

(2) One or more fields of law in which the lawyer or law firm practices, a statement that practice is limited to one or more fields of law, or a statement that the lawyer or law firm specializes in a particular field of law practice, to the extent authorized under DR 2-105;

(3) Date and place of birth;

(4) Date and place of admission to the bar of state and federal courts;

(5) Schools attended, with dates of graduation, degrees and other scholastic distinctions;

(6) Public or quasi-public offices;

(7) Military service;

(8) Legal authorships;

(9) Legal teaching positions;

(10) Memberships, offices, and committee assignments, in bar associations;

(11) Membership and offices in legal fraternities and legal societies;

(12) Technical and professional licenses;

(13) Memberships in scientific, technical and professional associations and societies;

(14) Foreign language ability;

(15) Names and addresses of bank references;

(16) With their written consent, names of clients regularly represented;

(17) Prepaid or group legal services programs in which the lawyer participates;

(18) Whether credit cards or other credit arrangements are accepted;

(19) Office and telephone answering service hours;

(20) Fee for an initial consultation;

(21) Availability upon request of a written schedule of fees and/or an estimate of the fee to be charged for specific services;

(22) Contingent fee rates subject to DR 2-106(C), provided that the statement discloses whether percentages are computed before or after deduction of costs;

(23) Range of fees for services, provided that the statement discloses that the specific fee within the range which will be charged will vary depending upon the particular matter to be handled for each client and the client is entitled without obligation to an estimate of the fee within the range likely to be charged. In print size equivalent to the largest print used in setting forth the fee information;

(24) Hourly rate, provided that the statement discloses that the total fee charged will depend upon the number of hours which must be devoted to the particular matter to be handled for each client and the client is entitled to without obligation an estimate of the fee likely to be charged, in print size at least equivalent to the largest print used in setting forth the fee information;

(25) Fixed fees for specific legal services,* the description of which would not be misunderstood or be deceptive, provided that the statement discloses that the quoted fee will be available only to clients whose matters fall into the services described and that the client is entitled without obligation to a specific estimate of the fee likely to be charged in print size at least equivalent to the largest print used in setting forth the fee information.

(C) Any person desiring to expand the information authorized for disclosure in DR 2-101(B), or to provide for its dissemination through other forums may apply to [the agency having jurisdiction under state law]. Any such application shall be served upon [the agencies having jurisdiction under state law over the regulation of the legal profession and consumer matters] who shall be heard, together with the applicant, on the issue of whether the proposal is necessary in light of the existing provisions of the Code, accords with standards of accuracy, reliability and truthfulness, and would facilitate the process of informed selection of lawyers by potential consumers of legal services. The relief granted in response to any such application shall be promulgated as an amendment to DR 2-101(B), universally applicable to all lawyers.*

(D) If the advertisement is communicated to the public over television or radio, it shall be prerecorded, approved for broadcast by the lawyer, and a recording of the actual transmission shall be retained by the lawyer.

---

* The agency having jurisdiction under state law may desire to issue appropriate guidelines defining "specific legal services."

* The agency having jurisdiction under state law should establish orderly and expeditious procedures for ruling on such applications.

(E) If a lawyer advertises a fee for a service, the lawyer must render that service for no more than the fee advertised.

(F) Unless otherwise specified in the advertisement if a lawyer publishes any fee information authorized under DR 2-101(B) in a publication that is published more frequently than one time per month, the lawyer shall be bound by any representation made therein for a period of not less than 30 days after such publication. If a lawyer publishes any fee information authorized under DR 2-101(B) in a publication that is published once a month or less frequently, he shall be bound by any representation made therein until the publication of the succeeding issue. If a lawyer publishes any fee information authorized under DR 2-101(B) in a publication which has no fixed date for publication of a succeeding issue, the lawyer shall be bound by any representation made therein for a reasonable period of time after publication but in no event less than one year.

(G) Unless otherwise specified, if a lawyer broadcasts any fee information authorized under DR 2-101(B), the lawyer shall be bound by any representation made therein for a period of not less than 30 days after such broadcast.

(H) This rule does not prohibit limited and dignified identification of a lawyer as a lawyer as well as by name:

   (1) In political advertisements when his professional status is germane to the political campaign or to a political issue.

   (2) In public notices when the name and profession of a lawyer are required or authorized by law or are reasonably pertinent for a purpose other than the attraction of potential clients.

   (3) In routine reports and announcements of a bona fide business, civic, professional, or political organization in which he serves as a director or officer.

   (4) In and on legal documents prepared by him.

   (5) In and on legal textbooks, treatises, and other legal publications, and in dignified advertisements thereof.

(I) A lawyer shall not compensate or give any thing of value to representatives of the press, radio, television, or other communication medium in anticipation of or in return for professional publicity in a news item.

As amended in 1974, 1975, 1977 and 1978.

DR 2-102 Professional Notices, Letterheads and Offices.

(A) A lawyer or law firm shall not use or participate in the use of professional cards, professional announcement cards, office signs, letterheads, or similar professional notices or devices, except that the following may be used if they are in dignified form:

(1) A professional card of a lawyer identifying him by name and as a lawyer, and giving his addresses, telephone numbers, the name of his law firm, and any information permitted under DR 2-105. A professional card of a law firm may also give the names of members and associates. Such cards may be used for identification.

(2) A brief professional announcement card stating new or changed associations or addresses, change of firm name, or similar matters pertaining to the professional offices of a lawyer or law firm, which may be mailed to lawyers, clients, former clients, personal friends, and relatives.[59] It shall not state biographical data except to the extent reasonably necessary to identify the lawyer or to explain the change in his association, but it may state the immediate past position of the lawyer.[60] It may give the names and dates of predecessor firms in a continuing line of succession. It shall not state the nature of the practice except as permitted under DR 2-105.[61]

(3) A sign on or near the door of the office and in the building directory identifying the law office. The sign shall not state the nature of the practice, except as permitted under DR 2-105.

(4) A letter head of a lawyer identifying him by name and as a lawyer, and giving his addresses, telephone numbers, the name of his law firm, associates and any information permitted under DR 2-105. A letterhead of a law firm may also give the names of members and associates,[62] and names and dates relating to deceased and retired members.[63] A lawyer may be designated "Of Counsel" on a letterhead if he has a continuing relationship with a lawyer or law firm, other than as a partner or associate. A lawyer or law firm may be designated as "General Counsel" or by similar professional reference on stationary of a client if he or the firm devotes a substantial amount of professional time in the representation of that client.[64] The letterhead of a law firm may give the names and dates of predecessor firms in a continuing line of succession.

(B) A lawyer in private practice shall not practice under a trade name, a name that is misleading as to the identity of the

---

59. See *ABA Opinion* 301 (1961).

60. "[I]t has become commonplace for many lawyers to participate in government service; to deny them the right, upon their return to private practice, to refer to their prior employment in a brief and dignified manner, would place an undue limitation upon a large element of our profession. It is entirely proper for a member of the profession to explain his absence from private practice, where such is the primary purpose of the announcement, by a brief and dignified reference to the prior employment.

". . . [A]ny such announcement should be limited to the immediate past connection of the lawyer with the government, made upon his leaving that position to enter private practice." *ABA Opinion* 301 (1961).

61. See *ABA Opinion* 251 (1943).

62. "Those lawyers who are working for an individual lawyer or a law firm may be designated on the letterhead and in other appropriate places as 'associates'." *ABA Opinion* 310 (1963).

63. See ABA Canon 33.

64. But see *ABA Opinion* 285 (1951).

lawyer or lawyers practicing under such name, or a firm name containing names other than those of one or more of the lawyers in the firm, except that the name of a professional corporation or professional association may contain "P.C." or "P.A." or similar symbols indicating the nature of the organization, and if otherwise lawful a firm may use as, or continue to include in, its name the name or names of one or more deceased or retired members of the firm or of a predecessor firm in a continuing line of succession.[65]   A lawyer who assumes a judicial, legislative, or public executive or administrative post or office shall not permit his name to remain in the name of a law firm or to be used in professional notices of the firm during any significant period in which he is not actively and regularly practicing law as a member of the firm,[66] and during such period other members of the firm shall not use his name in the firm name or in professional notices of the firm.[67]

(C) A lawyer shall not hold himself out as having a partnership with one or more other lawyers or professional corporations unless they are in fact partners.[68]

(D) A partnership shall not be formed or continued between or among lawyers licensed in different jurisdictions unless all enumerations of the members and associates of the firm on its letterhead and in other permissible listings make clear the jurisdictional limitations on those members and associates of the firm not licensed to practice in all listed jurisdictions;[69] however, the same firm name may be used in each jurisdiction.

65. See ABA Canon 33; cf. *ABA Opinions* 318 (1967), 267 (1945), 219 (1941), 208 (1940), 192 (1939), 97 (1933), and 6 (1925).

66. *ABA Opinion* 318 (1967) held, anything to the contrary in Formal Opinion 315 or in the other opinions cited notwithstanding that: Where a partner whose name appears in the name of a law firm is elected or appointed to high local, state or federal office, which office he intends to occupy only temporarily, at the end of which time he intends to return to his position with the firm, and provided that he is not precluded by holding such office from engaging in the practice of law and does not in fact sever his relationship with the firm but only takes a leave of absence, and provided that there is no local law, statute or custom to the contrary, his name may be retained in the firm name during his term or terms of office, but only if proper precautions are taken not to mislead the public as to his degree of participation in the firm's affairs.

Cf. *ABA Opinion* 143 (1935). New York County Opinion 67, and New York City Opinions 36 and 798; but cf. *ABA Opinion* 192 (1939) and Michigan Opinion 164.

67. Cf. ABA Canon 33.

68. See *ABA Opinion* 277 (1948); cf. ABA Canon 33 and *ABA Opinions* 318 (1967), 126 (1935), 115 (1934), and 106 (1934).

69. See *ABA Opinions* 318 (1967) and 316 (1967); cf. ABA Canon 33.

(E) Nothing contained herein shall prohibit a lawyer from using or permitting the use of, in connection with his name, an earned degree or title derived therefrom indicating his training in the law.

As amended in 1976, 1977, 1979 and 1980.

DR 2-103 Recommendation of Professional Employment.[70]

(A) A lawyer shall not, except as authorized in DR 2-101(B), recommend employment as a private practitioner,[71] of himself, his partner, or associate to a layperson who has not sought his advice regarding employment of a lawyer.[72]

(B) A lawyer shall not compensate or give anything of value to a person or organization to recommend or secure his employment [73] by a client, or as a reward for having made a recommendation resulting in his employment [74] by a client, except that he may pay the usual and reasonable fees or dues charged by any of the organizations listed in DR 2-103(D).

(C) A lawyer shall not request a person or organization to recommend or promote the use of his services or those of his partner or associate, or any other lawyer affiliated with him or his firm, as a private practitioner,[75] except as authorized in DR 2-101, and except that

(1) He may request referrals from a lawyer referral service operated, sponsored, or approved by a bar association and may pay its fees incident thereto.[76]

70. Cf. ABA Canon 28.

71. "We think it clear that a lawyer's seeking employment in an ordinary law office, or appointment to a civil service position, is not prohibited by ... [Canon 27]." *ABA Opinion* 197 (1939).

72. "[A] lawyer may not seek from persons not his clients the opportunity to perform ... a [legal] checkup." *ABA Opinion* 307 (1962).

73. Cf. *ABA Opinion* 78 (1932).

74. " 'No financial connection of any kind between the Brotherhood and any lawyer is permissible. No lawyer can properly pay any amount whatsoever to the Brotherhood or any of its departments, officers or members as compensation, reimbursement of expenses or gratuity in connection with the procurement of a case.' " In re Brotherhood of R.R. Trainmen, 13 Ill.2d 391, 398, 150 N.E.2d 163, 167 (1958), quoted in In re Ratner, 194 Kan. 362, 372, 399 P.2d 865, 873 (1956).

See *ABA Opinion* 147 (1935).

75. "This Court has condemned the practice of ambulance chasing through the media of runners and touters. In similar fashion we have with equal emphasis condemned the practice of direct solicitation by a lawyer. We have classified both offenses as serious breaches of the Canons of Ethics demanding severe treatment of the offending lawyer." State v. Dawson, 111 So.2d 427, 431 (Fla.1959).

76. "Registrants [of a lawyer referral plan] may be required to contribute to the expense of operating it by a reasonable registration charge or by a reasonable percentage of fees collected by them." *ABA Opinion* 291 (1956).

Cf. *ABA Opinion* 227 (1941).

(2) He may cooperate with the legal service activities of any of the offices or organizations enumerated in DR 2-103(D)(1) through (4) and may perform legal services for those to whom he was recommended by it to do such work if:

    (a) The person to whom the recommendation is made is a member or beneficiary of such office or organization; and

    (b) The lawyer remains free to exercise his independent professional judgment on behalf of his client.

(D) A lawyer or his partner or associate or any other lawyer affiliated with him or his firm may be recommended, employed or paid by, or may cooperate with, one of the following offices or organizations that promote the use of his services or those of his partner or associate or any other lawyer affiliated with him or his firm if there is no interference with the exercise of independent professional judgment in behalf of his client:

(1) A legal aid office or public defender office:

    (a) Operated or sponsored by a duly accredited law school.

    (b) Operated or sponsored by a bona fide nonprofit community organization.

    (c) Operated or sponsored by a governmental agency.

    (d) Operated, sponsored, or approved by a bar association.[77]

(2) A military legal assistance office.

(3) A lawyer referral service operated, sponsored, or approved by a bar association.

(4) Any bona fide organization that recommends, furnishes or pays for legal services to its members or beneficiaries [78] provided the following conditions are satisfied:

    (a) Such organization, including any affiliate, is so organized and operated that no profit is derived by it from the rendition of legal services by lawyers, and that, if the organization is organized for profit, the legal services are not rendered by lawyers employed, directed, supervised or selected by it except in connection with matters where such organization bears ultimate liability of its member or beneficiary.

---

77. Cf. *ABA Opinion* 148 (1935).

78. United Mine Workers v. Ill. State Bar Ass'n., 389 U.S. 217, 19 L.Ed.2d 426, 88 S.Ct. 353 (1967); Brotherhood of R.R. Trainmen v. Virginia, 371 U.S. 1, 12 L.Ed.2d 89, 84 S.Ct. 1113 (1964); NAACP v. Button, 371 U.S. 415, 9 L.Ed.2d 405, 83 S.Ct. 328 (1963).

(b) Neither the lawyer, nor his partner, nor associate, nor any other lawyer affiliated with him or his firm, nor any non-lawyer, shall have initiated or promoted such organization for the primary purpose of providing financial or other benefit to such lawyer, partner, associate or affiliated lawyer.

(c) Such organization is not operated for the purpose of procuring legal work or financial benefit for any lawyer as a private practitioner outside of the legal services program of the organization.

(d) The member or beneficiary to whom the legal services are furnished, and not such organization, is recognized as the client of the lawyer in the matter.

(e) Any member or beneficiary who is entitled to have legal services furnished or paid for by the organization may, if such member or beneficiary so desires, select counsel other than that furnished, selected or approved by the organization for the particular matter involved; and the legal service plan of such organization provides appropriate relief for any member or beneficiary who asserts a claim that representation by counsel furnished, selected or approved would be unethical, improper or inadequate under the circumstances of the matter involved and the plan provides an appropriate procedure for seeking such relief.

(f) The lawyer does not know or have cause to know that such organization is in violation of applicable laws, rules of court and other legal requirements that govern its legal service operations.

(g) Such organization has filed with the appropriate disciplinary authority at least annually a report with respect to its legal service plan, if any, showing its terms, its schedule of benefits, its subscription charges, agreements with counsel, and financial results of its legal service activities or, if it has failed to do so, the lawyer does not know or have cause to know of such failure.

(E) A lawyer shall not accept employment when he knows or it is obvious that the person who seeks his services does so as a result of conduct prohibited under this Disciplinary Rule.

As amended in 1974, 1975 and 1977.

DR 2-104 Suggestion of Need of Legal Services.[79, 80]

79. "If a bar association has embarked on a program of institutional advertising for an annual legal check-up and provides brochures and reprints, it is not improper to have these available in the lawyer's office for persons to read and take." *ABA Opinion* 307 (1962).

Cf. *ABA Opinion* 121 (1934).

80. ABA Canon 28.

(A) **A lawyer who has given in-person unsolicited advice to a layperson that he should obtain counsel or take legal action shall not accept employment resulting from that advice,**[81] **except that:**

   (1) **A lawyer may accept employment by a close friend, relative, former client (if the advice is germane to the former employment), or one whom the lawyer reasonably believes to be a client.**[82]

   (2) **A lawyer may accept employment that results from his participation in activities designed to educate laypersons to recognize legal problems, to make intelligent selection of counsel, or to utilize available legal services if such activities are conducted or sponsored by a qualified legal assistance organization.**

   (3) **A lawyer who is recommended, furnished or paid by a qualified legal assistance organization enumerated in DR 2–103(D)(1) through (4) may represent a member or beneficiary thereof, to the extent and under the conditions prescribed therein.**

   (4) **Without affecting his right to accept employment, a lawyer may speak publicly or write for publication on legal topics**[83] **so long as he does not emphasize his own professional experience or reputation and does not undertake to give individual advice.**

   (5) **If success in asserting rights or defenses of his client in litigation in the nature of a class action is dependent upon the joinder of others, a lawyer may accept, but shall not seek, employment from those contacted for the purpose of obtaining their joinder.**[84]

As amended in 1974, 1975 and 1977.

81. Cf. *ABA Opinions* 229 (1941) and 173 (1937).

82. "It certainly is not improper for a lawyer to advise his regular clients of new statutes, court decisions, and administrative rulings, which may affect the client's interests, provided the communication is strictly limited to such information. . . .

"When such communications go to concerns or individuals other than regular clients of the lawyer, they are thinly disguised advertisements for professional employment, and are obviously improper." *ABA Opinion* 213 (1941).

"It is our opinion that where the lawyer has no reason to believe that he has been supplanted by another lawyer, it is not only his right, but it might even be his duty to advise his client of any change of fact or law which might defeat the client's testamentary purpose as expressed in the will.

"Periodic notices might be sent to the client for whom a lawyer has drawn a will, suggesting that it might be wise for the client to reexamine his will to determine whether or not there has been any change in his situation requiring a modification of his will." *ABA Opinion* 210 (1941).

Cf. ABA Canon 28.

83. Cf. *ABA Opinion* 168 (1937).

84. But cf. *ABA Opinion* 111 (1934).

DR 2-105 Limitation of Practice.[85]

(A) A lawyer shall not hold himself out publicly as a specialist, as practicing in certain areas of law or as limiting his practice permitted under DR 2-101(B), except as follows:

(1) A lawyer admitted to practice before the United States Patent and Trademark Office may use the designation "Patents," "Patent Attorney," "Patent Lawyer," or "Registered Patent Attorney" or any combination of those terms, on his letterhead and office sign.

(2) A lawyer who publicly discloses fields of law in which the lawyer or the law firm practices or states that his practice is limited to one or more fields of law shall do so by using designations and definitions authorized and approved by [the agency having jurisdiction of the subject under state law].

(3) A lawyer who is certified as a specialist in a particular field of law or law practice by [the authority having jurisdiction under state law over the subject of specialization by lawyers] may hold himself out as such, but only in accordance with the rules prescribed by that authority.[86]

As amended in 1977.

DR 2-106 Fees for Legal Services.[87]

(A) A lawyer shall not enter into an agreement for, charge, or collect an illegal or clearly excessive fee.[88]

(B) A fee is clearly excessive when, after a review of the facts, a lawyer of ordinary prudence would be left with a definite and firm conviction that the fee is in excess of a reasonable fee. Factors to be considered as guides in determining the reasonableness of a fee include the following:

(1) The time and labor required, the novelty and difficulty of the questions involved, and the skill requisite to perform the legal service properly.

85. See ABA Canon 45; cf. ABA Canons 43, and 46.

86. This provision is included to conform to action taken by the ABA House of Delegates at the Mid-Winter Meeting, January, 1969.

87. See ABA Canon 12.

88. The charging of a "clearly excessive fee" is a ground for discipline. State ex rel. Nebraska State Bar Ass'n. v. Richards, 165 Neb. 80, 90, 84 N.W.2d 136, 143 (1957).

"An attorney has the right to contract for any fee he chooses so long as it is not excessive (see Opinion 190), and this Committee is not concerned with the amount of such fees unless so excessive as to constitute a misappropriation of the client's funds (see Opinion 27)." *ABA Opinion* 320 (1968).

Cf. *ABA Opinions* 209 (1940), 190 (1939), and 27 (1930) and State ex rel. Lee v. Buchanan, 191 So.2d 33 (Fla.1966).

(2) **The likelihood, if apparent to the client, that the acceptance of the particular employment will preclude other employment by the lawyer.**

(3) **The fee customarily charged in the locality for similar legal services.**

(4) **The amount involved and the results obtained.**

(5) **The time limitations imposed by the client or by the circumstances.**

(6) **The nature and length of the professional relationship with the client.**

(7) **The experience, reputation, and ability of the lawyer or lawyers performing the services.**

(8) **Whether the fee is fixed or contingent.[89]**

(C) **A lawyer shall not enter into an arrangement for, charge, or collect a contingent fee for representing a defendant in a criminal case.[90]**

DR 2-107   Division of Fees Among Lawyers.

(A) **A lawyer shall not divide a fee for legal services with another lawyer who is not a partner in or associate of his law firm or law office, unless:**

(1) **The client consents to employment of the other lawyer after a full disclosure that a division of fees will be made.**

(2) **The division is made in proportion to the services performed and responsibility assumed by each.[91]**

(3) **The total fee of the lawyers does not clearly exceed reasonable compensation for all legal services they rendered the client.[92]**

---

89. Cf. ABA Canon 13; see generally MacKinnon, Contingent Fees for Legal Services (1964) (A Report of the American Bar Foundation).

90. "Contingent fees, whether in civil or criminal cases, are a special concern of the law....

"In criminal cases, the rule is stricter because of the danger of corrupting justice. The second part of Section 542 of the Restatement [of Contracts] reads: 'A bargain to conduct a criminal case ... in consideration of a promise of a fee contingent on success is illegal....'" Peyton v. Margiotti, 398 Pa. 86, 156 A.2d 865, 967 (1959).

"The third area of practice in which the use of the contingent fee is generally considered to be prohibited is the prosecution and defense of criminal cases. However,

there are so few cases, and these are predominantly old, that it is doubtful that there can be said to be any current law on the subject.... In the absence of cases on the validity of contingent fees for defense attorneys, it is necessary to rely on the consensus among commentators that such a fee is void as against public policy. The nature of criminal practice itself makes unlikely the use of contingent fee contracts." MacKinnon, Contingent Fees for Legal Services 52 (1964) (A Report of the American Bar Foundation).

91. See ABA Canon 34 and *ABA Opinions* 316 (1967) and 294 (1958); see generally *ABA Opinions* 265 (1945), 204 (1940), 190 (1939), 171 (1937), 153 (1936), 97 (1933), 63 (1932), 28 (1930), 27 (1930), and 18 (1930).

92. "*Canon 12* contemplates that a lawyer's fee should not exceed *the value of the*

(B) This Disciplinary Rule does not prohibit payment to a former partner or associate pursuant to a separation or retirement agreement.

DR 2–108 Agreements Restricting the Practice of a Lawyer.

(A) A lawyer shall not be a party to or participate in a partnership or employment agreement with another lawyer that restricts the right of a lawyer to practice law after the termination of a relationship created by the agreement, except as a condition to payment of retirement benefits.[93]

(B) In connection with the settlement of a controversy or suit, a lawyer shall not enter into an agreement that restricts his right to practice law.

DR 2–109 Acceptance of Employment.

(A) A lawyer shall not accept employment on behalf of a person if he knows or it is obvious that such person wishes to:

(1) Bring a legal action, conduct a defense, or assert a position in litigation, or otherwise have steps taken for him, merely for the purpose of harassing or maliciously injuring any person.[94]

(2) Present a claim or defense in litigation that is not warranted under existing law, unless it can be supported by good faith argument for an extension, modification, or reversal of existing law.

DR 2–110 Withdrawal From Employment.[95]

(A) In general.

(1) If permission for withdrawal from employment is required by the rules of a tribunal, a lawyer shall not withdraw from employment in a proceeding before that tribunal without its permission.

---

services rendered. . . .

"*Canon 12* applies, whether joint or separate fees are charged [by associate attorneys]. . . ." *ABA Opinion* 204 (1940).

93. "[A] general covenant restricting an employed lawyer, after leaving the employment, from practicing in the community for a stated period, appears to this Committee to be an unwarranted restriction on the right of a lawyer to choose where he will practice and inconsistent with our professional status. Accordingly, the Committee

is of the opinion it would be improper for the employing lawyer to require the covenant and likewise for the employed lawyer to agree to it." *ABA Opinion* 300 (1961).

94. See ABA Canon 30.

"*Rule 13.* . . . A member of the State Bar shall not accept employment to prosecute or defend a case solely out of spite, or solely for the purpose of harassing or delaying another. . . ." Cal.Business and Professions Code § 6067 (West 1962).

95. Cf. ABA Canon 44.

(2) In any event, a lawyer shall not withdraw from employment until he has taken reasonable steps to avoid foreseeable prejudice to the rights of his client, including giving due notice to his client, allowing time for employment of other counsel, delivering to the client all papers and property to which the client is entitled, and complying with applicable laws and rules.

(3) A lawyer who withdraws from employment shall refund promptly any part of a fee paid in advance that has not been earned.

(B) Mandatory withdrawal.

A lawyer representing a client before a tribunal, with its permission if required by its rules, shall withdraw from employment, and a lawyer representing a client in other matters shall withdraw from employment, if:

(1) He knows or it is obvious that his client is bringing the legal action, conducting the defense, or asserting a position in the litigation, or is otherwise having steps taken for him, merely for the purpose of harassing or maliciously injuring any person.

(2) He knows or it is obvious that his continued employment will result in violation of a Disciplinary Rule.[96]

(3) His mental or physical condition renders it unreasonably difficult for him to carry out the employment effectively.

(4) He is discharged by his client.

(C) Permissive withdrawal.[97]

If DR 2-110(B) is not applicable, a lawyer may not request permission to withdraw in matters pending before a tribunal, and may not withdraw in other matters, unless such request or such withdrawal is because:

(1) His client:

(a) Insists upon presenting a claim or defense that is not warranted under existing law and cannot be supported by good faith argument for an extension, modification, or reversal of existing law.[98]

(b) Personally seeks to pursue an illegal course of conduct.

(c) Insists that the lawyer pursue a course of conduct that is illegal or that is prohibited under the Disciplinary Rules.

96. See also Code of Professional Responsibility, DR 5-102 and DR 5-105.

97. Cf. ABA Canon 4.

98. Cf. Anders v. California, 386 U.S. 738, 18 L.Ed.2d 493, 87 S.Ct. 1396 (1967), rehearing denied, 388 U.S. 924, 18 L.Ed.2d 1377, 87 S.Ct. 2094 (1967).

(d) By other conduct renders it unreasonably difficult for the lawyer to carry out his employment effectively.

(e) Insists, in a matter not pending before a tribunal, that the lawyer engage in conduct that is contrary to the judgment and advice of the lawyer but not prohibited under the Disciplinary Rules.

(f) Deliberately disregards an agreement or obligation to the lawyer as to expenses or fees.

(2) His continued employment is likely to result in a violation of a Disciplinary Rule.

(3) His inability to work with co-counsel indicates that the best interests of the client likely will be served by withdrawal.

(4) His mental or physical condition renders it difficult for him to carry out the employment effectively.

(5) His client knowingly and freely assents to termination of his employment.

(6) He believes in good faith, in a proceeding pending before a tribunal, that the tribunal will find the existence of other good cause for withdrawal.

CANON 3

A Lawyer Should Assist in Preventing the Unauthorized Practice of Law

ETHICAL CONSIDERATIONS

EC 3–1 The prohibition against the practice of law by a layman is grounded in the need of the public for integrity and competence of those who undertake to render legal services. Because of the fiduciary and personal character of the lawyer-client relationship and the inherently complex nature of our legal system, the public can better be assured of the requisite responsibility and competence if the practice of law is confined to those who are subject to the requirements and regulations imposed upon members of the legal profession.

EC 3–2 The sensitive variations in the considerations that bear on legal determinations often make it difficult even for a lawyer to exercise appropriate professional judgment, and it is therefore essential that the personal nature of the relationship of client and lawyer be preserved. Competent professional judgment is the product of a trained familiarity with law and legal processes, a disciplined, analytical approach to legal problems, and a firm ethical commitment.

EC 3–3 A non-lawyer who undertakes to handle legal matters is not governed as to integrity or legal competence by the same rules that govern the conduct of a lawyer. A lawyer is not only subject to that regulation but also is committed to high standards of ethical conduct.

The public interest is best served in legal matters by a regulated profession committed to such standards.[1] The Disciplinary Rules protect the public in that they prohibit a lawyer from seeking employment by improper overtures, from acting in cases of divided loyalties, and from submitting to the control of others in the exercise of his judgment. Moreover, a person who entrusts legal matters to a lawyer is protected by the attorney-client privilege and by the duty of the lawyer to hold inviolate the confidences and secrets of his client.

EC 3-4 A layman who seeks legal services often is not in a position to judge whether he will receive proper professional attention. The entrustment of a legal matter may well involve the confidences, the reputation, the property, the freedom, or even the life of the client. Proper protection of members of the public demands that no person be permitted to act in the confidential and demanding capacity of a lawyer unless he is subject to the regulations of the legal profession.

EC 3-5 It is neither necessary nor desirable to attempt the formulation of a single, specific definition of what constitutes the practice of law.[2] Functionally, the practice of law relates to the rendition of services for others that call for the professional judgment of a lawyer. The essence of the professional judgment of the lawyer is his educated ability to relate the general body and philosophy of law to a specific legal problem of a client; and thus, the public interest will be better served if only lawyers are permitted to act in matters involving professional judgment. Where this professional judgment is not involved, non-lawyers, such as court clerks, police officers, abstracters, and many governmental employees, may engage in occupations that require a special knowledge of law in certain areas. But the services of a lawyer are essential in the public interest whenever the exercise of professional legal judgment is required.

EC 3-6 A lawyer often delegates tasks to clerks, secretaries, and other lay persons. Such delegation is proper if the lawyer maintains a direct relationship with his client, supervises the delegated work, and has complete professional responsibility for the work product.[3] This delega-

---

1. "The condemnation of the unauthorized practice of law is designed to protect the public from legal services by persons unskilled in the law. The prohibition of lay intermediaries is intended to insure the loyalty of the lawyer to the client unimpaired by intervening and possibly conflicting interests." Cheatham, *Availability of Legal Services: The Responsibility of the Individual Lawyer and of the Organized Bar*, 12 U.C.L.A.L.Rev. 438, 439 (1965).

2. "What constitutes unauthorized practice of the law in a particular jurisdiction is a matter for determination by the courts of that jurisdiction." *ABA Opinion* 198 (1939).

"In the light of the historical development of the lawyer's functions, it is impossible to lay down an exhaustive definition of 'the practice of law' by attempting to enumerate every conceivable act performed by lawyers in the normal course of their work." State Bar of Arizona v. Arizona Land Title & Trust Co., 90 Ariz. 76, 87, 366 P.2d 1, 8-9 (1961), modified, 91 Ariz. 293, 371 P.2d 1020 (1962).

3. "A lawyer can employ lay secretaries, lay investigators, lay detectives, lay re-

tion enables a lawyer to render legal service more economically and efficiently.

EC 3–7 The prohibition against a non-lawyer practicing law does not prevent a layman from representing himself, for then he is ordinarily exposing only himself to possible injury. The purpose of the legal profession is to make educated legal representation available to the public; but anyone who does not wish to avail himself of such representation is not required to do so. Even so, the legal profession should help members of the public to recognize legal problems and to understand why it may be unwise for them to act for themselves in matters having legal consequences.

EC 3–8 Since a lawyer should not aid or encourage a layman to practice law, he should not practice law in association with a layman or otherwise share legal fees with a layman.[4] This does not mean, however, that the pecuniary value of the interest of a deceased lawyer in his firm or practice may not be paid to his estate or specified persons such as his widow or heirs.[5] In like manner, profit-sharing retirement plans of a

searchers, accountants, lay scriveners, nonlawyer draftsmen or nonlawyer researchers. In fact he may employ nonlawyers to do any task for him except counsel clients about law matters, engage directly in the practice of law, appear in court or appear in formal proceedings a part of the judicial process, so long as it is he who takes the work and vouches for it to the client and becomes responsible to the client." *ABA Opinion* 316 (1967).

ABA Opinion 316 (1967) also stated that if a lawyer practices law as part of a law firm which includes lawyers from several states, he may delegate tasks to firm members in other states so long as he "is the person who, on behalf of the firm, vouched for the work of all of the others and, with the client and in the courts, did the legal acts defined by that state as the practice of law."

"A lawyer cannot delegate his professional responsibility to a law student employed in his office. He may avail himself of the assistance of the student in many of the fields of the lawyer's work, such as examination of case law, finding and interviewing witnesses, making collections of claims, examining court records, delivering papers, conveying important messages, and other similar matters. But the student is not permitted, until he is admitted to the Bar, to perform the professional functions of a lawyer, such as conducting court trials, giv-

ing professional advice to clients or drawing legal documents for them. The student in all his work must act as agent for the lawyer employing him, who must supervise his work and be responsible for his good conduct." *ABA Opinion* 85 (1932).

4. "No division of fees for legal services is proper, except with another lawyer...." ABA Canon 34. Otherwise, according to *ABA Opinion* 316 (1967), "[t]he Canons of Ethics do not examine into the method by which such persons are remunerated by the lawyer.... They may be paid a salary, a per diem charge, a flat fee, a contract price, etc."

See ABA Canons 33 and 47.

5. "Many partnership agreements provide that the active partners, on the death of any one of them, are to make payments to the estate or to the nominee of a deceased partner on a pre-determined formula. It is only where the effect of such an arrangement is to make the estate or nominee a member of the partnership along with the surviving partners that it is prohibited by *Canon 34*. Where the payments are made in accordance with a pre-existing agreement entered into by the deceased partner during his lifetime and providing for a fixed method for determining their amount based upon the value of services rendered during the partner's lifetime and

lawyer or law firm which include non-lawyer office employees are not improper.[6] These limited exceptions to the rule against sharing legal fees with laymen are permissible since they do not aid or encourage laymen to practice law.

EC 3–9 Regulation of the practice of law is accomplished principally by the respective states.[7] Authority to engage in the practice of law conferred in any jurisdiction is not per se a grant of the right to practice elsewhere, and it is improper for a lawyer to engage in practice where he is not permitted by law or by court order to do so. However, the demands of business and the mobility of our society pose distinct problems in the regulation of the practice of law by the states.[8] In furtherance of the public interest, the legal profession should discourage regulation that unreasonably imposes territorial limitations upon the right of a lawyer to handle the legal affairs of his client or upon the opportunity of a client to obtain the services of a lawyer of his choice in all matters including the presentation of a contested matter in a tribunal before which the lawyer is not permanently admitted to practice.[9]

DISCIPLINARY RULES

providing for a fixed period over which the payments are to be made, this is not the case. Under these circumstances, whether the payments are considered to be delayed payment of compensation earned but withheld during the partner's lifetime, or whether they are considered to be an approximation of his interest in matters pending at the time of his death, is immaterial. In either event, as Henry S. Drinker says in his book, Legal Ethics, at page 189: 'It would seem, however, that a reasonable agreement to pay the estate a proportion of the receipts for a reasonable period is a proper practical settlement for the lawyer's services to his retirement or death.' " *ABA Opinion* 308 (1963).

6. Cf. ABA Opinion 311 (1964).

7. "That the States have broad power to regulate the practice of law is, of course, beyond question." United Mine Workers v. Ill. State Bar Ass'n, 389 U.S. 217, 222 (1967).

"It is a matter of law, not of ethics, as to where an individual may practice law. Each state has its own rules." *ABA Opinion* 316 (1967).

8. "Much of clients' business crosses state lines. People are mobile, moving from state to state. Many metropolitan areas cross state lines. It is common today to have a single economic and social community involving more than one state. The business of a single client may involve legal problems in several states." *ABA Opinion* 316 (1967).

9. "[W]e reaffirmed the general principle that legal services to New Jersey residents with respect to New Jersey matters may ordinarily be furnished only by New Jersey counsel; but we pointed out that there may be multistate transactions where strict adherence to this thesis would not be in the public interest and that, under the circumstances, it would have been not only more costly to the client but also 'grossly impractical and inefficient' to have had the settlement negotiations conducted by separate lawyers from different states." In re Estate of Waring, 47 N.J. 367, 376, 221 A.2d 193, 197 (1966).

Cf. ABA Opinion 316 (1967).

DR 3–101   Aiding Unauthorized Practice of Law.[10]

(A) A lawyer shall not aid a non-lawyer in the unauthorized practice of law.[11]

(B) A lawyer shall not practice law in a jurisdiction where to do so would be in violation of regulations of the profession in that jurisdiction.[12]

DR 3–102   Dividing Legal Fees With a Non-lawyer.

(A) A lawyer or law firm shall not share legal fees with a non-lawyer,[13] **except that:**

    (1) An agreement by a lawyer with his firm, partner, or associate may provide for the payment of money, over a reasonable period of time after his death, to his estate or to one or more specified persons.[14]

    (2) A lawyer who undertakes to complete unfinished legal business of a deceased lawyer may pay to the estate of the deceased lawyer that proportion of the total compensation which fairly represents the services rendered by the deceased lawyer.

    (3) A lawyer or law firm may include non-lawyer employees in a compensation or retirement plan, even though the plan is based in whole or in part on a profit-sharing arrangement[15] **providing such plan does not circumvent another disciplinary rule.**[16]

As amended in 1980.

DR 3–103   Forming a Partnership With a Non-lawyer.

(A) A lawyer shall not form a partnership with a non-lawyer if any of the activities of the partnership consist of the prac-

---

10. Conduct permitted by the Disciplinary Rules of Canons 2 and 5 does not violate DR 3–101.

11. See ABA Canon 47.

12. It should be noted, however, that a lawyer may engage in conduct, otherwise prohibited by this Disciplinary Rule, where such conduct is authorized by preemptive federal legislation. See Sperry v. Florida, 373 U.S. 379, 10 L.Ed.2d 428, 83 S.Ct. 1322 (1963).

13. See ABA Canon 34 and *ABA Opinions* 316 (1967), 180 (1938), and 48 (1931).

"The receiving attorney shall not under any guise or form share his fee for legal services with a lay agency, personal or corporate, without prejudice, however, to the right of the lay forwarder to charge and collect from the creditor proper compensation for non-legal services rendered by the law [*sic*] forwarder which are separate and apart from the services performed by the receiving attorney." *ABA Opinion* 294 (1958).

14. See *ABA Opinion* 266 (1945).

15. Cf. *ABA Opinion* 311 (1964).

16. See ABA Informal Opinion 1440 (1979).

tice of law.[17]

CANON 4

A Lawyer Should Preserve the Confidences and Secrets of a Client

ETHICAL CONSIDERATIONS

EC 4–1 Both the fiduciary relationship existing between lawyer and client and the proper functioning of the legal system require the preservation by the lawyer of confidences and secrets of one who has employed or sought to employ him.[1] A client must feel free to discuss whatever he wishes with his lawyer and a lawyer must be equally free to obtain information beyond that volunteered by his client.[2] A lawyer should be fully informed of all the facts of the matter he is handling in order for his client to obtain the full advantage of our legal system. It is for the

---

17. See ABA Canon 33; cf. *ABA Opinions* 239 (1942) and 201 (1940).

ABA Opinion 316 (1967) states that lawyers licensed in different jurisdictions may, under certain conditions, enter "into an arrangement for the practice of law" and that a lawyer licensed in State A is not, for such purpose a layman in State B.

1. See ABA Canons 6 and 37 and *ABA Opinions* 287 (1953). "The reason underlying the rule with respect to confidential communications between attorney and client is well stated in Mechem on Agency, 2d Ed., Vol. 2, § 2297, as follows: 'The purposes and necessities of the relation between a client and his attorney require, in many cases on the part of the client, the fullest and freest disclosures to the attorney of the client's objects, motives and acts. This disclosure is made in the strictest confidence, relying upon the attorney's honor and fidelity. To permit the attorney to reveal to others what is so disclosed, would be not only a gross violation of a sacred trust upon his part, but it would utterly destroy and prevent the usefulness and benefits to be derived from professional assistance. Based upon considerations of public policy, therefore, the law wisely declares that all confidential communications and disclosures, made by a client to his legal adviser for the purpose of obtaining his professional aid or advice, shall be strictly privileged:—that the attorney shall not be permitted, without the consent of his

client,—and much less will he be compelled—to reveal or disclose communications made to him under such circumstances.' " *ABA Opinion* 250 (1943).

"While it is true that complete revelation of relevant facts should be encouraged for trial purposes, nevertheless an attorney's dealings with his client, if both are sincere, and if the dealings involve more than mere technical matters, should be immune to discovery proceedings. There must be freedom from fear of revealment of matters disclosed to an attorney because of the peculiarly intimate relationship existing." Ellis-Foster Co. v. Union Carbide & Carbon Corp., 159 F.Supp. 917, 919 (D.N.J.1958).

Cf. *ABA Opinions* 314 (1965), 274 (1946) and 268 (1945).

2. "While it is the great purpose of law to ascertain the truth, there is the countervailing necessity of insuring the right of every person to freely and fully confer and confide in one having knowledge of the law, and skilled in its practice, in order that the former may have adequate advice and a proper defense. This assistance can be made safely and readily available only when the client is free from the consequences of apprehension of disclosure by reason of the subsequent statements of the skilled lawyer." Baird v. Koerner, 279 F.2d 623, 629–30 (9th Cir.1960).

Cf. *ABA Opinion* 150 (1936).

lawyer in the exercise of his independent professional judgment to separate the relevant and important from the irrelevant and unimportant. The observance of the ethical obligation of a lawyer to hold inviolate the confidences and secrets of his client not only facilitates the full development of facts essential to proper representation of the client but also encourages laymen to seek early legal assistance.

EC 4–2 The obligation to protect confidences and secrets obviously does not preclude a lawyer from revealing information when his client consents after full disclosure,[3] when necessary to perform his professional employment, when permitted by a Disciplinary Rule, or when required by law. Unless the client otherwise directs, a lawyer may disclose the affairs of his client to partners or associates of his firm. It is a matter of common knowledge that the normal operation of a law office exposes confidential professional information to non-lawyer employees of the office, particularly secretaries and those having access to the files; and this obligates a lawyer to exercise care in selecting and training his employees so that the sanctity of all confidences and secrets of his clients may be preserved. If the obligation extends to two or more clients as to the same information, a lawyer should obtain the permission of all before revealing the information. A lawyer must always be sensitive to the rights and wishes of his client and act scrupulously in the making of decisions which may involve the disclosure of information obtained in his professional relationship.[4] Thus, in the absence of consent of his client after full disclosure, a lawyer should not associate another lawyer in the handling of a matter; nor should he, in the absence of consent, seek counsel from another lawyer if there is a reasonable possibility that the identity of the client or his confidences or secrets would be revealed to such lawyer. Both social amenities and professional duty should cause a lawyer to shun indiscreet conversations concerning his clients.

EC 4–3 Unless the client otherwise directs, it is not improper for a lawyer to give limited information from his files to an outside agency necessary for statistical, bookkeeping, accounting, data processing, banking, printing, or other legitimate purposes, provided he exercises due care in the selection of the agency and warns the agency that the information must be kept confidential.

3. "Where ... [a client] knowingly and after full disclosure participates in a [legal fee] financing plan which requires the furnishing of certain information to the bank, clearly by his conduct he has waived any privilege as to that information." *ABA Opinion* 320 (1968).

4. "The lawyer must decide when he takes a case whether it is a suitable one for him to undertake and after this decision is made, he is not justified in turning against his client by exposing injurious evidence entrusted to him.... [D]oing something intrinsically regrettable, because the only alternative involves worse consequences, is a necessity in every profession." Williston, Life and Law 271 (1940).

Cf. *ABA Opinions* 177 (1938) and 83 (1932).

EC 4–4 The attorney-client privilege is more limited than the ethical obligation of a lawyer to guard the confidence and secrets of his client. This ethical precept, unlike the evidentiary privilege, exists without regard to the nature or source of information or the fact that others share the knowledge. A lawyer should endeavor to act in a manner which preserves the evidentiary privilege; for example, he should avoid professional discussions in the presence of persons to whom the privilege does not extend. A lawyer owes an obligation to advise the client of the attorney-client privilege and timely to assert the privilege unless it is waived by the client.

EC 4–5 A lawyer should not use information acquired in the course of the representation of a client to the disadvantage of the client and a lawyer should not use, except with the consent of his client after full disclosure, such information for his own purposes.[5] Likewise, a lawyer should be diligent in his efforts to prevent the misuse of such information by his employees and associates.[6] Care should be exercised by a lawyer to prevent the disclosure of the confidences and secrets of one client to another,[7] and no employment should be accepted that might require such disclosure.

EC 4–6 The obligation of a lawyer to preserve the confidences and secrets of his client continues after the termination of his employment.[8] Thus a lawyer should not attempt to sell a law practice as a going business because, among other reasons, to do so would involve the disclosure of confidences and secrets.[9] A lawyer should also provide for the protection of the confidences and secrets of his client following the termination of the practice of the lawyer, whether termination is due to death, disability, or retirement. For example, a lawyer might provide for the personal papers of the client to be returned to him and for the papers of the lawyer to be delivered to another lawyer or to be destroyed. In determining the method of disposition, the instructions and wishes of the client should be a dominant consideration.

DISCIPLINARY RULES

DR 4–101 Preservation of Confidences and Secrets of a

5. See ABA Canon 11.

6. See ABA Canon 37.

7. See ABA Canons 6 and 37.

"[A]n attorney must not accept professional employment against a client or a former client which will, or even *may* require him to use confidential information obtained by the attorney in the course of his professional relations with such client regarding the subject matter of the employment...." *ABA Opinion* 165 (1936).

8. See ABA Canon 37.

"Confidential communications between an attorney and his client, made because of the relationship and concerning the subject-matter of the attorney's employment, are generally privileged from disclosure without the consent of the client, and this privilege outlasts the attorney's employment. *Canon 37.*" *ABA Opinion* 154 (1936).

9. Cf. *ABA Opinion* 266 (1945).

Client.[10]

(A) "Confidence" refers to information protected by the attorney-client privilege under applicable law, and "secret" refers to other information gained in the professional relationship that the client has requested be held inviolate or the disclosure of which would be embarrassing or would be likely to be detrimental to the client.

(B) Except when permitted under DR 4–101(C), a lawyer shall not knowingly:

(1) Reveal a confidence or secret of his client.[11]

(2) Use a confidence or secret of his client to the disadvantage of the client.

(3) Use a confidence or secret of his client for the advantage of himself [12] or of a third person,[13] unless the client consents after full disclosure.

(C) A lawyer may reveal:

(1) Confidences or secrets with the consent of the client or clients affected, but only after a full disclosure to them.[14]

(2) Confidences or secrets when permitted under Disciplinary Rules or required by law or court order.[15]

---

10. See ABA Canon 37; cf. ABA Canon 6.

11. "§ 6068 ... It is the duty of an attorney: ....

"(e) To maintain inviolate the confidence, and at every peril to himself to preserve the secrets, of his client." Cal. Business and Professions Code § 6068 (West 1962). Virtually the same provision is found in the Oregon statutes. Ore.Rev. Stat. ch. 9, § 9.460(5).

"Communications between lawyer and client are privileged (Wigmore on Evidence, 3d Ed., Vol. 8, §§ 2290–2329). The modern theory underlying the privilege is subjective and is to give the client freedom of apprehension in consulting his legal advisor (ibid., § 2290, p. 548). The privilege applies to communications made in seeking legal advice for any purpose (ibid., § 2294, p. 563). The mere circumstance that the advice is given without charge therefore does not nullify the privilege (ibid., § 2303)." *ABA Opinion* 216 (1941).

"It is the duty of an attorney to maintain the confidence and preserve inviolate the secrets of his client...." *ABA Opinion* 155 (1936).

12. See ABA Canon 11.

"The provision respecting employment is in accord with the general rule announced in the adjudicated cases that a lawyer may not make use of knowledge or information acquired by him through his professional relations with his client, or in the conduct of his client's business, to his own advantage or profit (7 C.J.S., § 125, p. 958; Healy v. Gray, 184 Iowa 111, 168 N.W. 222; Baumgardner v. Hudson, D.C.App., 277 F. 552; Goodrum v. Clement, D.C.App., 277 F. 586)." *ABA Opinion* 250 (1943).

13. See *ABA Opinion* 177 (1938).

14. "[A lawyer] may not divulge confidential communications, information, and secrets imparted to him by the client or acquired during their professional relations, unless he is authorized to do so by the client (People v. Gerold, 265 Ill. 448, 107 N.E. 165, 178; Murphy v. Riggs, 238 Mich. 151, 213 N.W. 110, 112; Opinion of this Committee, No. 91)." *ABA Opinion* 202 (1940).

Cf. *ABA Opinion* 91 (1933).

15. "A defendant in a criminal case when admitted to bail is not only regarded as in the custody of his bail, but he is also in the custody of the law, and admission to bail does not deprive the court of its inher-

(3) The intention of his client to commit a crime [16] and the information necessary to prevent the crime.[17]

(4) Confidences or secrets necessary to establish or collect his fee [18] or to defend himself or his employees or associates against an accusation of wrongful conduct.[19]

ent power to deal with the person of the prisoner. Being in lawful custody, the defendant is guilty of an escape when he gains his liberty before he is delivered in due process of law, and is guilty of a separate offense for which he may be punished. In failing to disclose his client's whereabouts as a fugitive under these circumstances the attorney would not only be aiding his client to escape trial on the charge for which he was indicted, but would likewise be aiding him in evading prosecution for the additional offense of escape.

"It is the opinion of the committee that under such circumstances the attorney's knowledge of his client's whereabouts is not privileged, and that he may be disciplined for failing to disclose that information to the proper authorities...." *ABA Opinion* 155 (1936).

"We held in *Opinion* 155 that a communication by a client to his attorney in respect to the future commission of an unlawful act or to a continuing wrong is not privileged from disclosure. Public policy forbids that the relation of attorney and client should be used to conceal wrongdoing on the part of the client.

. . .

"When an attorney representing a defendant in a criminal case applies on his behalf for probation or suspension of sentence, he represents to the court, by implication at least, that his client will abide by the terms and conditions of the court's order. When that attorney is later advised of a violation of that order, it is his duty to advise his client of the consequences of his act, and endeavor to prevent a continuance of the wrongdoing. If his client thereafter persists in violating the terms and conditions of his probation, it is the duty of the attorney as an officer of the court to advise the proper authorities concerning his client's conduct. Such information, even though coming to the attorney from the client in the course of his professional relations with

respect to other matters in which he represents the defendant, is not privileged from disclosure...." *ABA Opinion* 156 (1936).

See *ABA Opinion* 155 (1936).

16. *ABA Opinion* 314 (1965) indicates that a lawyer must disclose even the confidences of his clients if "the facts in the attorney's possession indicate beyond reasonable doubt that a crime will be committed."

See *ABA Opinion* 155 (1936).

17. See ABA Canon 37 and *ABA Opinion* 202 (1940).

18. Cf. *ABA Opinion* 250 (1943).

19. See ABA Canon 37 and *ABA Opinions* 202 (1940) and 19 (1930).

"[T]he adjudicated cases recognize an exception to the rule [that a lawyer shall not reveal the confidences of his client], where disclosure is necessary to protect the attorney's interests arising out of the relation of attorney and client in which disclosure was made.

"The exception is stated in Mechem on Agency, 2d Ed., Vol. 2, § 2313, as follows: 'But the attorney may disclose information received from the client when it becomes necessary for his own protection, as if the client should bring an action against the attorney for negligence or misconduct, and it became necessary for the attorney to show what his instructions were, or what was the nature of the duty which the client expected him to perform. So if it became necessary for the attorney to bring an action against the client, the client's privilege could not prevent the attorney from disclosing what was essential as a means of obtaining or defending his own rights.'

"Mr. Jones, in his Commentaries on Evidence, 2d Ed., Vol. 5, § 2165, states the exception thus: 'It has frequently been held that the rule as to privileged communications does not apply when litigation arises

(D) A lawyer shall exercise reasonable care to prevent his employees, associates, and others whose services are utilized by him from disclosing or using confidences or secrets of a client, except that a lawyer may reveal the information allowed by DR 4–101(C) through an employee.

CANON 5

A Lawyer Should Exercise Independent Professional Judgment on Behalf of a Client

ETHICAL CONSIDERATIONS

EC 5–1 The professional judgment of a lawyer should be exercised, within the bounds of the law, solely for the benefit of his client and free of compromising influences and loyalties.[1] Neither his personal interests, the interests of other clients, nor the desires of third persons should be permitted to dilute his loyalty to his client.

between attorney and client to the extent that their communications are relevant to the issue. In such cases, if the disclosure of privileged communications becomes necessary to protect the attorney's rights, he is released from those obligations of secrecy which the law places upon him. He should not, however, disclose more than is necessary for his own protection. It would be a manifest injustice to allow the client to take advantage of the rule of exclusion as to professional confidence to the prejudice of his attorney, or that it should be carried to the extent of depriving the attorney of the means of obtaining or defending his own rights. In such cases the attorney is exempted from the obligations of secrecy.' " *ABA Opinion* 250 (1943).

  1. Cf. ABA Canon 35.

"[A lawyer's] fiduciary duty is of the highest order and he must not represent interests adverse to those of the client. It is true that because of his professional responsibility and the confidence and trust which his client may legitimately repose in him, he must adhere to a high standard of honesty, integrity and good faith in dealing with his client. He is not permitted to take advantage of his position or superior knowledge to impose upon the client; nor to conceal facts or law, nor in any way deceive him without being held responsible therefor." Smoot v. Lund, 13 Utah 2d 168, 172, 369 P.2d 933, 936 (1962).

"When a client engages the services of a lawyer in a given piece of business he is entitled to feel that, until that business is finally disposed of in some manner, he has the undivided loyalty of the one upon whom he looks as his advocate and champion. If, as in this case, he is sued and his home attached by his own attorney, who is representing him in another matter, all feeling of loyalty is necessarily destroyed, and the profession is exposed to the charge that it is interested only in money." Grievance Comm. v. Rattner, 152 Conn. 59, 65, 203 A.2d 82, 84 (1964).

"One of the cardinal principles confronting every attorney in the representation of a client is the requirement of complete loyalty and service in good faith to the best of his ability. In a criminal case the client is entitled to a fair trial, but not a perfect one. These are fundamental requirements of due process under the Fourteenth Amendment.... The same principles are applicable in Sixth Amendment cases (not pertinent herein) and suggest that an attorney should have no conflict of interest and that he must devote his full and faithful efforts toward the defense of his client." Johns v. Smyth, 176 F.Supp. 949, 952 (E.D.Va.1959), modified, United States ex rel. Wilkins v. Banmiller, 205 F.Supp. 123, 128 n. 5 (E.D.Pa.1962), aff'd 325 F.2d 514 (3d Cir. 1963), cert. denied, 379 U.S. 847, 13 L.Ed.2d 51, 85 S.Ct. 87 (1964).

Interests of a Lawyer That May Affect His Judgment

EC 5-2 A lawyer should not accept proffered employment if his personal interests or desires will, or there is a reasonable probability that they will, affect adversely the advice to be given or services to be rendered the prospective client.[2] After accepting employment, a lawyer carefully should refrain from acquiring a property right or assuming a position that would tend to make his judgment less protective of the interests of his client.

EC 5-3 The self-interest of a lawyer resulting from his ownership of property in which his client also has an interest or which may affect property of his client may interfere with the exercise of free judgment on behalf of his client. If such interference would occur with respect to a prospective client, a lawyer should decline employment proffered by him. After accepting employment, a lawyer should not acquire property rights that would adversely affect his professional judgment in the representation of his client. Even if the property interests of a lawyer do not presently interfere with the exercise of his independent judgment, but the likelihood of interference can reasonably be foreseen by him, a lawyer should explain the situation to his client and should decline employment or withdraw unless the client consents to the continuance of the relationship after full disclosure. A lawyer should not seek to persuade his client to permit him to invest in an undertaking of his client nor make improper use of his professional relationship to influence his client to invest in an enterprise in which the lawyer is interested.

EC 5-4 If, in the course of his representation of a client, a lawyer is permitted to receive from his client a beneficial ownership in publication rights relating to the subject matter of the employment, he may be tempted to subordinate the interests of his client to his own anticipated pecuniary gain. For example, a lawyer in a criminal case who obtains from his client television, radio, motion picture, newspaper, magazine, book, or other publication rights with respect to the case may be influenced, consciously or unconsciously, to a course of conduct that will enhance the value of his publication rights to the prejudice of his client.

---

2. "Attorneys must not allow their private interests to conflict with those of their clients.... They owe their entire devotion to the interests of their clients." United States v. Anonymous, 215 F.Supp. 111, 113 (E.D.Tenn.1963).

"[T]he court [below] concluded that a firm may not accept any action against a person whom they are presently representing even though there is no relationship between the two cases. In arriving at this conclusion, the court cites an opinion of the Committee on Professional Ethics of the New York County Lawyers' Association which stated in part: 'While under the circumstances ... there may be no actual conflict of interest ... "maintenance of public confidence in the Bar requires an attorney who has accepted representation of a client to decline, while representing such client, any employment from an adverse party in any matter even though wholly unrelated to the original retainer." See Question and Answer No. 350, N.Y. County L. Ass'n, Questions and Answer No. 450 (June 21, 1956).'" Grievance Comm. v. Rattner, 152 Conn. 59, 65, 203 A.2d 82, 84 (1964).

To prevent these potentially differing interests, such arrangements should be scrupulously avoided prior to the termination of all aspects of the matter giving rise to the employment, even though his employment has previously ended.

EC 5–5 A lawyer should not suggest to his client that a gift be made to himself or for his benefit. If a lawyer accepts a gift from his client, he is peculiarly susceptible to the charge that he unduly influenced or over-reached the client. If a client voluntarily offers to make a gift to his lawyer, the lawyer may accept the gift, but before doing so, he should urge that his client secure disinterested advice from an independent, competent person who is cognizant of all the circumstances.[3] Other than in exceptional circumstances, a lawyer should insist that an instrument in which his client desires to name him beneficially be prepared by another lawyer selected by the client.[4]

EC 5–6 A lawyer should not consciously influence a client to name him as executor, trustee, or lawyer in an instrument. In those cases where a client wishes to name his lawyer as such, care should be taken by the lawyer to avoid even the appearance of impropriety.[5]

EC 5–7 The possibility of an adverse effect upon the exercise of free judgment by a lawyer on behalf of his client during litigation generally makes it undesirable for the lawyer to acquire a proprietary interest in the cause of his client or otherwise to become financially interested in the outcome of the litigation.[6] However, it is not improper for a lawyer to protect his right to collect a fee for his services by the assertion of legally permissible liens, even though by doing so he may acquire an interest in the outcome of litigation. Although a contingent fee arrangement[7] gives a lawyer a financial interest in the outcome of litigation, a

3. "Courts of equity will scrutinize with jealous vigilance transactions between parties occupying fiduciary relations toward each other.... A deed will not be held invalid, however, if made by the grantor with full knowledge of its nature and effect, and because of the deliberate, voluntary and intelligent desire of the grantor.... Where a fiduciary relation exists, the burden of proof is on the grantee or beneficiary of an instrument executed during the existence of such relationship to show the fairness of the transaction, that it was equitable and just and that it did not proceed from undue influence.... The same rule has application where an attorney engages in a transaction with a client during the existence of the relation and is benefited thereby.... Conversely, an attorney is not prohibited from dealing with his client or buying his property, and such contracts, if open, fair and honest, when deliberately made, are as valid as contracts between other parties.... [I]mportant factors in determining whether a transaction is fair include a showing by the fiduciary (1) that he made a full and frank disclosure of all the relevant information that he had: (2) that the consideration was adequate; and (3) that the principal had independent advice before completing the transaction." McFail v. Braden, 19 Ill.2d 108, 117–18, 166 N.E.2d 46, 52 (1960).

4. See State ex rel. Nebraska State Bar Ass'n v. Richards, 165 Neb. 80, 94–95, 84 N.W.2d 136, 146 (1957).

5. See ABA Canon 9.

6. See ABA Canon 10.

7. See Code of Professional Responsibility, EC 2–20.

reasonable contingent fee is permissible in civil cases because it may be the only means by which a layman can obtain the services of a lawyer of his choice. But a lawyer, because he is in a better position to evaluate a cause of action, should enter into a continent fee arrangement only in those instances where the arrangement will be beneficial to the client.

EC 5–8 A financial interest in the outcome of litigation also results if monetary advances are made by the lawyer to his client.[8] Although this assistance generally is not encouraged, there are instances when it is not improper to make loans to a client. For example, the advancing or guaranteeing of payment of the costs and expenses of litigation by a lawyer may be the only way a client can enforce his cause of action,[9] but the ultimate liability for such costs and expenses must be that of the client.

EC 5–9 Occasionally a lawyer is called upon to decide in a particular case whether he will be a witness or an advocate. If a lawyer is both counsel and witness, he becomes more easily impeachable for interest and thus may be a less effective witness. Conversely, the opposing counsel may be handicapped in challenging the credibility of the lawyer when the lawyer also appears as an advocate in the case. An advocate who becomes a witness is in the unseemly and ineffective position of arguing his own credibility. The roles of an advocate and of a witness are inconsistent; the function of an advocate is to advance or argue the cause of another, while that of a witness is to state facts objectively.

EC 5–10 Problems incident to the lawyer-witness relationship arise at different stages; they relate either to whether a lawyer should accept employment or should withdraw from employment.[10] Regardless of

---

8. See ABA Canon 42.

9. "*Rule 3a.* . . . A member of the State Bar shall not directly or indirectly pay or agree to pay, or represent or sanction the representation that he will pay, medical, hospital or nursing bills or other personal expenses incurred by or for a client, prospective or existing; provided this rule shall not prohibit a member:

"(1) with the consent of the client, from paying or agreeing to pay to third persons such expenses from funds collected or to be collected for the client; or

"(2) after he has been employed, from lending money to his client upon the client's promise in writing to repay such loan; or

"(3) from advancing the costs of prosecuting or defending a claim or action. Such costs within the meaning of this subparagraph (3) include all taxable costs or disbursements, costs or investigation and costs

of obtaining and presenting evidence." Cal. Business and Professions Code § 6076 (West Supp.1967).

10. "When a lawyer knows, prior to trial, that he will be a necessary witness, except as to merely formal matters such as identification or custody of a document or the like, neither he nor his firm or associates should conduct the trial. If, during the trial, he discovers that the ends of justice require his testimony, he should, from that point on, if feasible and not prejudicial to his client's case, leave further conduct of the trial to other counsel. If circumstances do not permit withdrawal from the conduct of the trial, the lawyer should not argue the credibility of his own testimony." *A Code of Trial Conduct: Promulgated by the American College of Trial Lawyers,* 43 A.B.A.J. 223, 224–25 (1957).

when the problem arises, his decision is to be governed by the same basic considerations. It is not objectionable for a lawyer who is a potential witness to be an advocate if it is unlikely that he will be called as a witness because his testimony would be merely cumulative or if his testimony will relate only to an uncontested issue.[11] In the exceptional situation where it will be manifestly unfair to the client for the lawyer to refuse employment or to withdraw when he will likely be a witness on a contested issue, he may serve as advocate even though he may be a witness.[12] In making such decision, he should determine the personal or financial sacrifice of the client that may result from his refusal of employment or withdrawal therefrom, the materiality of his testimony, and the effectiveness of his representation in view of his personal involvement. In weighing these factors, it should be clear that refusal or withdrawal will impose an unreasonable hardship upon the client before the lawyer accepts or continues the employment.[13] Where the question arises, doubts should be resolved in favor of the lawyer testifying and against his becoming or continuing as an advocate.[14]

EC 5–11 A lawyer should not permit his personal interests to influence his advice relative to a suggestion by his client that additional counsel be employed.[15] In like manner, his personal interests should not deter him from suggesting that additional counsel be employed; on the contrary, he should be alert to the desirability of recommending additional counsel when, in his judgment, the proper representation of his client requires it. However, a lawyer should advise his client not to employ additional counsel suggested by the client if the lawyer believes

11. Cf. Canon 19: "When a lawyer is a witness for his client, except as to merely formal matters, such as the attestation or custody of an instrument and the like, he should leave the trial of the case to other counsel."

12. "It is the general rule that a lawyer may not testify in litigation in which he is an advocate unless circumstances arise which could not be anticipated and it is necessary to prevent a miscarriage of justice. In those rare cases where the testimony of an attorney is needed to protect his client's interests, it is not only proper but mandatory that it be forthcoming." Schwartz v. Wenger, 267 Minn. 40, 43–44, 124 N.W.2d 489, 492 (1963).

13. "The great weight of authority in this country holds that the attorney who acts as counsel and witness, in behalf of his client, in the same cause on a material matter, not of a merely formal character, and not in an emergency, but having knowl-

edge that he would be required to be a witness in ample time to have secured other counsel and given up his service in the case, violates a highly important provision of the Code of Ethics and a rule of professional conduct, but does not commit a legal error in so testifying, as a result of which a new trial will be granted." Erwin M. Jennings Co. v. DiGenova, 107 Conn. 491, 499, 141 A. 866, 869 (1928).

14. "[C]ases may arise, and in practice often do arise, in which there would be a failure of justice should the attorney withhold his testimony. In such a case it would be a vicious professional sentiment which would deprive the client of the benefit of his attorney's testimony." Connolly v. Straw, 53 Wis. 645, 649, 11 N.W. 17, 19 (1881).

But see Canon 19. "Except when essential to the ends of justice, a lawyer should avoid testifying in court in behalf of his client."

15. Cf. ABA Canon 7.

that such employment would be a disservice to the client, and he should disclose the reasons for his belief.

EC 5-12 Inability of co-counsel to agree on a matter vital to the representation of their client requires that their disagreement be submitted by them jointly to their client for his resolution, and the decision of the client shall control the action to be taken.[16]

EC 5-13 A lawyer should not maintain membership in or be influenced by any organization of employees that undertakes to prescribe, direct, or suggest when or how he should fulfill his professional obligations to a person or organization that employs him as a lawyer. Although it is not necessarily improper for a lawyer employed by a corporation or similar entity to be a member of an organization of employees, he should be vigilant to safeguard his fidelity as a lawyer to his employer, free from outside influences.

Interests of Multiple Clients

EC 5-14 Maintaining the independence of professional judgment required of a lawyer precludes his acceptance or continuation of employment that will adversely affect his judgment on behalf of or dilute his loyalty to a client.[17] This problem arises whenever a lawyer is asked to represent two or more clients who may have differing interests, whether such interests be conflicting, inconsistent, diverse, or otherwise discordant.[18]

EC 5-15 If a lawyer is requested to undertake or to continue representation of multiple clients having potentially differing interests, he must weigh carefully the possibility that his judgment may be impaired or his loyalty divided if he accepts or continues the employment. He should resolve all doubts against the propriety of the representation. A lawyer should never represent in litigation multiple clients with differing interests;[19] and there are few situations in which he would be justified in

---

16. See ABA Canon 7.

17. See ABA Canon 6; cf. *ABA Opinions* 261 (1944), 242 (1942), 142 (1935), and 30 (1931).

18. The ABA Canons speak of "conflicting interests" rather than "differing interests" but make no attempt to define such other than the statement in Canon 6: "Within the meaning of this canon, a lawyer represents conflicting interests when, in behalf of one client, it is his duty to contend for that which duty to another client requires him to oppose."

19. "Canon 6 of the Canons of Professional Ethics, adopted by the American Bar Association on September 30, 1937, and by the Pennsylvania Bar Association on Janu-

ary 7, 1938, provides in part that 'It is unprofessional to represent conflicting interests, except by express consent of all concerned given after a full disclosure of the facts. Within the meaning of this Canon, a lawyer represents conflicting interests when, in behalf of one client, it is his duty to contend for that which duty to another client requires him to oppose.' The full disclosure required by this canon contemplates that the possibly adverse effect of the conflict be fully explained by the attorney to the client to be affected and by him thoroughly understood....

"The foregoing canon applies to cases where the circumstances are such that possibly conflicting interests may permissibly

representing in litigation multiple clients with potentially differing interests. If a lawyer accepted such employment and the interests did become actually differing, he would have to withdraw from employment with likelihood of resulting hardship on the clients; and for this reason it is preferable that he refuse the employment initially. On the other hand, there are many instances in which a lawyer may properly serve multiple clients having potentially differing interests in matters not involving litigation. If the interests vary only slightly, it is generally likely that the lawyer will not be subjected to an adverse influence and that he can retain his independent judgment on behalf of each client; and if the interests become differing, withdrawal is less likely to have a disruptive effect upon the causes of his clients.

EC 5-16 In those instances in which a lawyer is justified in representing two or more clients having differing interests, it is nevertheless essential that each client be given the opportunity to evaluate his need for representation free of any potential conflict and to obtain other counsel if he so desires.[20] Thus before a lawyer may represent multiple clients, he should explain fully to each client the implications of the common representation and should accept or continue employment only if the clients consent.[21] If there are present other circumstances that might cause any of the multiple clients to question the undivided loyalty of the lawyer, he should also advise all of the clients of those circumstances.[22]

EC 5-17 Typically recurring situations involving potentially differing interests are those in which a lawyer is asked to represent co-defendants in a criminal case, co-plaintiffs in a personal injury case, an insured and his insurer,[23] and beneficiaries of the estate of a decedent. Whether a

be represented by the same attorney. But manifestly, there are instances where the conflicts of interest are so critically adverse as not to admit of one attorney's representing both sides. Such is the situation which this record presents. No one could conscionably contend that the same attorney may represent both the plaintiff and defendant in an adversary action. Yet, that is what is being done in this case." Jedwabny v. Philadelphia Transportation Co., 390 Pa. 231, 235, 135 A.2d 252, 254 (1957), cert. denied, 355 U.S. 966, 2 L.Ed.2d 541, 78 S.Ct. 557 (1958).

20. "Glasser wished the benefit of the undivided assistance of counsel of his own choice. We think that such a desire on the part of an accused should be respected. Irrespective of any conflict of interest, the additional burden of representing another party may conceivably impair counsel's effectiveness.

"To determine the precise degree of prejudice sustained by Glasser as a result of the court's appointment of Stewart as counsel for Kretske is at once difficult and unnecessary. The right to have the assistance of counsel is too fundamental and absolute to allow courts to indulge in nice calculations as to the amount of prejudice arising from its denial." Glasser v. United States, 315 U.S. 60, 75–76, 86 L.Ed. 680, 62 S.Ct. 457, 467 (1942).

21. See ABA Canon 6.

22. Id.

23. Cf. *ABA Opinion* 282 (1950).

"When counsel, although paid by the casualty company, undertakes to represent the policyholder and files his notice of appearance, he owes to his client, the assured, an undeviating and single allegiance. His fealty embraces the requirement to produce

lawyer can fairly and adequately protect the interests of multiple clients in these and similar situations depends upon an analysis of each case. In certain circumstances, there may exist little chance of the judgment of the lawyer being adversely affected by the slight possibility that the interests will become actually differing; in other circumstances, the chance of adverse effect upon his judgment is not unlikely.

EC 5–18 A lawyer employed or retained by a corporation or similar entity owes his allegiance to the entity and not to a stockholder, director, officer, employee, representative, or other person connected with the entity. In advising the entity, a lawyer should keep paramount its interests and his professional judgment should not be influenced by the personal desires of any person or organization. Occasionally a lawyer for an entity is requested by a stockholder, director, officer, employee, representative, or other person connected with the entity to represent him in an individual capacity; in such case the lawyer may serve the individual only if the lawyer is convinced that differing interests are not present.

EC 5–19 A lawyer may represent several clients whose interests are not actually or potentially differing. Nevertheless, he should explain any circumstances that might cause a client to question his undivided loyalty.[24] Regardless of the belief of a lawyer that he may properly represent multiple clients, he must defer to a client who holds the contrary belief and withdraw from representation of that client.

EC 5–20 A lawyer is often asked to serve as an impartial arbitrator or mediator in matters which involve present or former clients. He may serve in either capacity if he first discloses such present or former relationships. After a lawyer has undertaken to act as an impartial arbitrator or mediator, he should not thereafter represent in the dispute any of the parties involved.

in court all witnesses, fact and expert, who are available and necessary for the proper protection of the rights of his client....

"... The Canons of Professional Ethics make it pellucid that there are not two standards, one applying to counsel privately retained by a client, and the other to counsel paid by an insurance carrier." American Employers Ins. Co. v. Goble Aircraft Specialties, 205 Misc. 1066, 1075, 131 N.Y.S.2d 393, 401 (1954), motion to withdraw appeal granted, 1 App.Div.2d 1008, 154 N.Y.S.2d 835 (1956).

"[C]ounsel, selected by State Farm to defend Dorothy Walker's suit for $50,000 damages, was apprised by Walker that his earlier version of the accident was untrue and that actually the accident occurred because he lost control of his car in passing a Cadillac just ahead. At that point, Walker's counsel should have refused to participate further in view of the conflict of interest between Walker and State Farm.... Instead he participated in the ensuing deposition of the Walkers, even took an *ex parte* sworn statement from Mr. Walker in order to advise State Farm what action it should take, and later used the statement against Walker in the District Court. This action appears to contravene an Indiana attorney's duty 'at every peril to himself, to preserve the secrets of his client'...." State Farm Mut. Auto Ins. Co. v. Walker, 382 F.2d 548, 552 (1967), cert. denied, 389 U.S. 1045, 19 L.Ed.2d 837, 88 S.Ct. 789 (1968).

24. See ABA Canon 6.

Desires of Third Persons

EC 5–21 The obligation of a lawyer to exercise professional judgment solely on behalf of his client requires that he disregard the desires of others that might impair his free judgment.[25] The desires of a third person will seldom adversely affect a lawyer unless that person is in a position to exert strong economic, political, or social pressures upon the lawyer. These influences are often subtle, and a lawyer must be alert to their existence. A lawyer subjected to outside pressures should make full disclosure of them to his client;[26] and if he or his client believes that the effectiveness of his representation has been or will be impaired thereby, the lawyer should take proper steps to withdraw from representation of his client.

EC 5–22 Economic, political, or social pressures by third persons are less likely to impinge upon the independent judgment of a lawyer in a matter in which he is compensated directly by his client and his professional work is exclusively with his client. On the other hand, if a lawyer is compensated from a source other than his client, he may feel a sense of responsibility to someone other than his client.

EC 5–23 A person or organization that pays or furnishes lawyers to represent others possesses a potential power to exert strong pressures against the independent judgment of those lawyers. Some employers may be interested in furthering their own economic, political, or social goals without regard to the professional responsibility of the lawyer to his individual client. Others may be far more concerned with establishment or extension of legal principles than in the immediate protection of the rights of the lawyer's individual client. On some occasions, decisions on priority of work may be made by the employer rather than the lawyer with the result that prosecution of work already undertaken for clients is postponed to their detriment. Similarly, an employer may seek, consciously or unconsciously, to further its own economic interests through the action of the lawyers employed by it. Since a lawyer must always be free to exercise his professional judgment without regard to the interests or motives of a third person, the lawyer who is employed by one to

25. See ABA Canon 35.

"Objection to the intervention of a lay intermediary, who may control litigation or otherwise interfere with the rendering of legal services in a confidential relationship, ... derives from the element of pecuniary gain. Fearful of dangers thought to arise from that element, the courts of several States have sustained regulations aimed at these activities. We intimate no view one way or the other as to the merits of those decisions with respect to the particular arrangements against which they are directed. It is enough that the superficial resemblance in form between those arrangements and that at bar cannot obscure the vital fact that here the entire arrangement employs constitutionally privileged means of expression to secure constitutionally guaranteed civil rights." NAACP v. Button, 371 U.S. 415, 441–42, 9 L.Ed.2d 405, 423–24, 83 S.Ct. 328, 342–43 (1963).

26. Cf. ABA Canon 38.

represent another must constantly guard against erosion of his professional freedom.[27]

EC 5–24 To assist a lawyer in preserving his professional independence, a number of courses are available to him. For example, a lawyer should not practice with or in the form of a professional legal corporation, even though the corporate form is permitted by law,[28] if any director, officer, or stockholder of it is a non-lawyer. Although a lawyer may be employed by a business corporation with non-lawyers serving as directors or officers, and they necessarily have the right to make decisions of business policy, a lawyer must decline to accept direction of his professional judgment from any layman. Various types of legal aid offices are administered by boards of directors composed of lawyers and laymen. A lawyer should not accept employment from such an organization unless the board sets only broad policies and there is no interference in the relationship of the lawyer and the individual client he serves. Where a lawyer is employed by an organization, a written agreement that defines the relationship between him and the organization and provides for his independence is desirable since it may serve to prevent misunderstanding as to their respective roles. Although other innovations in the means of supplying legal counsel may develop, the responsibility of the lawyer to maintain his professional independence remains constant, and the legal profession must insure that changing circumstances do not result in loss of the professional independence of the lawyer.

DISCIPLINARY RULES

DR 5–101 Refusing Employment When the Interests of the Lawyer May Impair His Independent Professional Judgment.

(A) Except with the consent of his client after full disclosure, a lawyer shall not accept employment if the exercise of his professional judgment on behalf of his client will be or

27. "Certainly it is true that 'the professional relationship between an attorney and his client is highly personal, involving an intimate appreciation of each individual client's particular problem.' And this Committee does not condone practices which interfere with that relationship. However, the mere fact the lawyer is actually paid by some entity other than the client does not affect that relationship, so long as the lawyer is selected by and is directly responsible to the client. See Informal Opinions 469 and 679. Of course, as the latter decision points out, there must be full disclosure of the arrangement by the attorney to the client. . . ." *ABA Opinion* 320 (1968).

"[A] third party may pay the cost of legal services as long as control remains in the client and the responsibility of the lawyer is solely to the client. Informal Opinions 469 ad [*sic*] 679. See also *Opinion* 237." Id.

28. *ABA Opinion* 303 (1961) recognized that "[s]tatutory provisions now exist in several states which are designed to make [the practice of law in a form that will be classified as a corporation for federal income tax purposes] legally possible, either as a result of lawyers incorporating or forming associations with various corporate characteristics."

reasonably may be affected by his own financial, business, property, or personal interests.[29]

(B) A lawyer shall not accept employment in contemplated or pending litigation if he knows or it is obvious that he or a lawyer in his firm ought to be called as a witness, except that he may undertake the employment and he or a lawyer in his firm may testify:

(1) If the testimony will relate solely to an uncontested matter.

(2) If the testimony will relate solely to a matter of formality and there is no reason to believe that substantial evidence will be offered in opposition to the testimony.

(3) If the testimony will relate solely to the nature and value of legal services rendered in the case by the lawyer or his firm to the client.

(4) As to any matter, if refusal would work a substantial hardship on the client because of the distinctive value of the lawyer or his firm as counsel in the particular case.

DR 5-102   Withdrawal as Counsel When the Lawyer Becomes a Witness.[30]

(A) If, after undertaking employment in contemplated or pending litigation, a lawyer learns or it is obvious that he or a lawyer in his firm ought to be called as a witness on behalf of his client, he shall withdraw from the conduct of the trial and his firm, if any, shall not continue representation in the trial, except that he may continue the representation and he or a lawyer in his firm may testify in the circumstances enumerated in DR 5-101(B)(1) through (4).

(B) If, after undertaking employment in contemplated or pending litigation, a lawyer learns or it is obvious that he or a

29. Cf. ABA Canon 6 and *ABA Opinions* 181 (1938), 104 (1934), 103 (1933), 72 (1932), 50 (1931), 49 (1931), and 33 (1931).

"New York County [Opinion] 203.... [A lawyer] should not advise a client to employ an investment company in which he is interested, without informing him of this." Drinker, *Legal Ethics* 956 (1953).

"In *Opinions* 72 and 49 this Committee held: The relations of partners in a law firm are such that neither the firm nor any member or associate thereof, may accept any professional employment which any member of the firm cannot properly accept.

"In *Opinion* 16 this Committee held that a member of a law firm could not represent a defendant in a criminal case which was being prosecuted by another member of the firm who was public prosecuting attorney. The Opinion stated that it was clearly unethical for one member of the firm to oppose the interest of the state while another member represented those interests.... Since the prosecutor himself could not represent both the public and the defendant, no member of his law firm could either." *ABA Opinion* 296 (1959).

30. Cf. ABA Canon 19 and *ABA Opinions* 220 (1941), 185 (1938), 50 (1931), and 33 (1931); but cf. Erwin M. Jennings Co. v. DiGenova, 107 Conn. 491, 498–99, 141 A. 866, 868 (1928).

lawyer in his firm may be called as a witness other than on behalf of his client, he may continue the representation until it is apparent that his testimony is or may be prejudicial to his client.[31]

DR 5–103   Avoiding Acquisition of Interest in Litigation.

(A) A lawyer shall not acquire a proprietary interest in the cause of action or subject matter of litigation he is conducting for a client,[32] except that he may:

   (1) Acquire a lien granted by law to secure his fee or expenses.

   (2) Contract with a client for a reasonable contingent fee in a civil case.[33]

(B) While representing a client in connection with contemplated or pending litigation, a lawyer shall not advance or guarantee financial assistance to his client,[34] except that a lawyer may advance or guarantee the expenses of litigation, including court costs, expenses of investigation, expenses of medical examination, and costs of obtaining and presenting evidence, provided the client remains ultimately liable for such expenses.

DR 5–104   Limiting Business Relations With a Client

(A) A lawyer shall not enter into a business transaction with a client if they have differing interests therein and if the client expects the lawyer to exercise his professional judgment therein for the protection of the client, unless the client has consented after full disclosure.

(B) Prior to conclusion of all aspects of the matter giving rise to his employment, a lawyer shall not enter into any arrangement or understanding with a client or a prospective client by which he acquires an interest in publication rights with respect to the subject matter of his employment or proposed employment.

---

31. "This *Canon* [19] *of Ethics* needs no elaboration to be applied to the facts here. Apparently, the object of this precept is to avoid putting a lawyer in the obviously embarrassing predicament of testifying and then having to argue the credibility and effect of his own testimony. It was not designed to permit a lawyer to call opposing counsel as a witness and thereby disqualify him as counsel." Galarowicz v. Ward, 119 Utah 611, 620, 230 P.2d 576, 580 (1951).

32. ABA Canon 10 and *ABA Opinions* 279 (1949), 246 (1942) and 176 (1938).

33. See Code of Professional Responsibility, DR 2–106(C).

34. See ABA Canon 42; cf. *ABA Opinion* 288 (1954).

DR 5–105 **Refusing to Accept or Continue Employment if the Interests of Another Client May Impair the Independent Professional Judgment of the Lawyer.**

(A) A lawyer shall decline proffered employment if the exercise of his independent professional judgment in behalf of a client will be or is likely to be adversely affected by the acceptance of the proffered employment,[35] or if it would be likely to involve him in representing differing interests, except to the extent permitted under DR 5–105(C).[36]

(B) A lawyer shall not continue multiple employment if the exercise of his independent professional judgment in behalf of a client will be or is likely to be adversely affected by his representation of another client, or if it would be likely to involve him in representing differing interests, except to the extent permitted under DR 5–105(C).[37]

(C) In the situations covered by DR 5–105(A) and (B), a lawyer may represent multiple clients if it is obvious that he can adequately represent the interest of each and if each consents to the representation after full disclosure of the possible effect of such representation on the exercise of his independent professional judgment on behalf of each.

(D) If a lawyer is required to decline employment or to withdraw from employment under a Disciplinary Rule, no partner or associate, or any other lawyer affiliated with him or his firm may accept or continue such employment.

As amended in 1974.

DR 5–106 **Settling Similar Claims of Clients.[38]**

(A) A lawyer who represents two or more clients shall not make or participate in the making of an aggregate settlement of the claims of or against his clients, unless each client has consented to the settlement after being advised of the existence and nature of all the claims involved in the proposed settlement, of the total amount of the settlement, and of the participation of each person in the settlement.

35. See ABA Canon 6; cf. *ABA Opinions* 167 (1937), 60 (1931), and 40 (1931).

36. *ABA Opinion* 247 (1942) held that an attorney could not investigate a night club shooting on behalf of one of the owner's liability insurers, obtaining the cooperation of the owner, and later represent the injured patron in an action against the owner and a different insurance company unless the attorney obtain the "express consent of all concerned given after a full disclosure of the facts," since to do so would be to represent conflicting interests.

See *ABA Opinions* 247 (1942), 224 (1941), 222 (1941), 218 (1941), 112 (1934), 83 (1932), and 86 (1932).

37. Cf. *ABA Opinions* 231 (1941) and 160 (1936).

38. Cf. *ABA Opinions* 243 (1942) and 235 (1941).

DR 5–107   Avoiding Influence by Others Than the Client.

(A) Except with the consent of his client after full disclosure, a lawyer shall not:

(1) Accept compensation for his legal services from one other than his client.

(2) Accept from one other than his client any thing of value related to his representation of or his employment by his client.[39]

(B) A lawyer shall not permit a person who recommends, employs, or pays him to render legal services for another to direct or regulate his professional judgment in rendering such legal services.[40]

(C) A lawyer shall not practice with or in the form of a professional corporation or association authorized to practice law for a profit, if:

(1) A non-lawyer owns any interest therein,[41] **except that a fiduciary representative of the estate of a lawyer may hold the stock or interest of the lawyer for a reasonable time during administration;**

(2) A non-lawyer is a corporate director or officer thereof;[42] **or**

(3) A non-lawyer has the right to direct or control the professional judgment of a lawyer.[43]

---

39. See ABA Canon 38.

"A lawyer who receives a commission (whether delayed or not) from a title insurance company or guaranty fund for recommending or selling the insurance to his client, or for work done for the client or the company, without either fully disclosing to the client his financial interest in the transaction, or crediting the client's bill with the amount thus received, is guilty of unethical conduct." *ABA Opinion* 304 (1962).

40. See ABA Canon 35; cf. *ABA Opinion* 237 (1941).

"When the lay forwarder, as agent for the creditor, forwards a claim to an attorney, the direct relationship of attorney and client shall then exist between the attorney and the creditor, and the forwarder shall not interpose itself as an intermediary to control the activities of the attorney." *ABA Opinion* 294 (1958).

41. "Permanent beneficial and voting rights in the organization set up to practice law, whatever its form, must be restricted to lawyers while the organization is engaged in the practice of law." *ABA Opinion* 303 (1961).

42. "*Canon 33* ... promulgates underlying principles that must be observed no matter in what form of organization lawyers practice law. Its requirement that no person shall be admitted or held out as a practitioner or member who is not a member of the legal profession duly authorized to practice, and amendable to professional discipline, makes it clear that any centralized management must be in lawyers to avoid a violation of this Canon." *ABA Opinion* 303 (1961).

43. "There is no intervention of any lay agency between lawyer and client when centralized management provided only by lawyers may give guidance or direction to the services being rendered by a lawyer-member of the organization to a client. The language in *Canon 35* that a lawyer should avoid all relations which direct the performance of his duties by or in the interest of an intermediary refers to lay intermediaries and not lawyer intermediaries with

---

CANON 6

A Lawyer Should Represent a Client Competently

ETHICAL CONSIDERATIONS

EC 6–1 Because of his vital role in the legal process, a lawyer should act with competence and proper care in representing clients. He should strive to become and remain proficient in his practice [1] and should accept employment only in matters which he is or intends to become competent to handle.

EC 6–2 A lawyer is aided in attaining and maintaining his competence by keeping abreast of current legal literature and developments, participating in continuing legal education programs,[2] concentrating in particular areas of the law, and by utilizing other available means. He has the additional ethical obligation to assist in improving the legal profession, and he may do so by participating in bar activities intended to advance the quality and standards of members of the profession. Of particular importance is the careful training of his younger associates and the giving of sound guidance to all lawyers who consult him. In short, a

whom he is associated in the practice of law." *ABA Opinion* 303 (1961).

1. "[W]hen a citizen is faced with the need for a lawyer, he wants, and is entitled to, the best informed counsel he can obtain. Changing times produce changes in our laws and legal procedures. The natural complexities of law require continuing intensive study by a lawyer if he is to render his clients a maximum of efficient service. And, in so doing, he maintains the high standards of the legal profession; and he also increases respect and confidence by the general public." Rochelle & Payne, *The Struggle for Public Understanding*, 25 Texas B.J. 109, 160 (1962).

"We have undergone enormous changes in the last fifty years within the lives of most of the adults living today who may be seeking advice. Most of these changes have been accompanied by changes and developments in the law.... Every practicing lawyer encounters these problems and is often perplexed with his own inability to keep up, not only with changes in the law, but also with changes in the lives of his clients and their legal problems.

"To be sure, no client has a right to expect that his lawyer will have all of the answers at the end of his tongue or even in

the back of his head at all times. But the client does have the right to expect that the lawyer will have devoted his time and energies to maintaining and improving his competence to know where to look for the answers, to know how to deal with the problems, and to know how to advise to the best of his legal talents and abilities." Levy & Sprague, *Accounting and Law: Is Dual Practice in the Public Interest?*, 52 A.B.A.J. 1110, 1112 (1966).

2. "The whole purpose of continuing legal education, so enthusiastically supported by the ABA, is to make it possible for lawyers to make themselves better lawyers. But there are no nostrums for proficiency in the law; it must come through the hard work of the lawyer himself. To the extent that that work, whether it be in attending institutes or lecture courses, in studying after hours or in the actual day in and day out practice of his profession, can be concentrated within a limited field, the greater the proficiency and expertness that can be developed." *Report of the Special Committee on Specialization and Specialized Legal Education*, 79 A.B.A.Rep. 582, 588 (1954).

lawyer should strive at all levels to aid the legal profession in advancing the highest possible standards of integrity and competence and to meet those standards himself.

EC 6-3 While the licensing of a lawyer is evidence that he has met the standards then prevailing for admission to the bar, a lawyer generally should not accept employment in any area of the law in which he is not qualified.[3] However, he may accept such employment if in good faith he expects to become qualified through study and investigation, as long as such preparation would not result in unreasonable delay or expense to his client. Proper preparation and representation may require the association by the lawyer of professionals in other disciplines. A lawyer offered employment in a matter in which he is not and does not expect to become so qualified should either decline the employment or, with the consent of his client, accept the employment and associate a lawyer who is competent in the matter.

EC 6-4 Having undertaken representation, a lawyer should use proper care to safeguard the interests of his client. If a lawyer has accepted employment in a matter beyond his competence but in which he expected to become competent, he should diligently undertake the work and study necessary to qualify himself. In addition to being qualified to handle a particular matter, his obligation to his client requires him to prepare adequately for and give appropriate attention to his legal work.

EC 6-5 A lawyer should have pride in his professional endeavors. His obligation to act competently calls for higher motivation than that arising from fear of civil liability or disciplinary penalty.

EC 6-6 A lawyer should not seek, by contract or other means, to limit his individual liability to his client for his malpractice. A lawyer who handles the affairs of his client properly has no need to attempt to limit his liability for his professional activities and one who does not handle the affairs of his client properly should not be permitted to do so. A lawyer who is a stockholder in or is associated with a professional legal corporation may, however, limit his liability for malpractice of his associates in the corporation, but only to the extent permitted by law.[4]

DISCIPLINARY RULES

DR 6-101 Failing to Act Competently.

(A) A lawyer shall not:

3. "If the attorney is not competent to skillfully and properly perform the work, he should not undertake the service." *Degen v. Steinbrink*, 202 App.Div. 477, 481, 195 N.Y.S. 810, 814 (1922), aff'd mem., 236 N.Y. 669, 142 N.E. 328 (1923).

4. See *ABA Opinion* 303 (1961); cf. Code of Professional Responsibility EC 2-11.

(1) Handle a legal matter which he knows or should know that he is not competent to handle, without associating with him a lawyer who is competent to handle it.

(2) Handle a legal matter without preparation adequate in the circumstances.

(3) Neglect a legal matter entrusted to him.[5]

DR 6–102 Limiting Liability to Client.

(A) A lawyer shall not attempt to exonerate himself from or limit his liability to his client for his personal malpractice.

CANON 7

A Lawyer Should Represent a Client Zealously Within the Bounds of the Law

ETHICAL CONSIDERATIONS

EC 7–1 The duty of a lawyer, both to his client[1] and to the legal system, is to represent his client zealously[2] within the bounds of the law,[3] which includes Disciplinary Rules and enforceable professional

5. The annual report for 1967–1968 of the Committee on Grievances of the Association of the Bar of the City of New York showed a receipt of 2,232 complaints; of the 828 offenses against clients, 76 involved conversion, 49 involved "overreaching," and 452, or more than half of all such offenses, involved neglect. *Annual Report of the Committee on Grievances of the Association of the Bar of the City of New York,* N.Y.L.J., Sept. 12, 1968, at 4, col. 5.

1. "The right to be heard would be, in many cases, of little avail if it did not comprehend the right to be heard by counsel. Even the intelligent and educated layman has small and sometimes no skill in the science of law." Powell v. Alabama, 287 U.S. 45, 68–69, 77 L.Ed. 158, 170, 53 S.Ct. 55, 64 (1932).

2. Cf. ABA Canon 4.

"At times ... [the tax lawyer] will be wise to discard some arguments and he should exercise discretion to emphasize the arguments which in his judgment are most likely to be persuasive. But this process involves legal judgment rather than moral attitudes. The tax lawyer should put aside private disagreements with Congressional and Treasury policies. His own notions of policy, and his personal view of what the

law should be, are irrelevant. The job entrusted to him by his client is to use all his learning and ability to protect his client's rights, not to help in the process of promoting a better tax system. The tax lawyer need not accept his client's economic and social opinions, but the client is paying for technical attention and undivided concentration upon his affairs. He is equally entitled to performance unfettered by his attorney's economic and social predilections." Paul, *The Lawyer is a Tax Advisor,* 25 Rocky Mt.L.Rev. 412, 418 (1953).

3. See ABA Canons 15 and 32.

ABA Canon 5, although only speaking of one accused of crime, imposes a similar obligation on the lawyer: "[T]he lawyer is bound, by all fair and honorable means, to present every defense that the law of the land permits, to the end that no person may be deprived of life or liberty, but by due process of law."

"Any persuasion or pressure on the advocate which deters him from planning and carrying out the litigation on the basis of 'what, within the framework of the law, is best for my client's interest?' interferes with the obligation to represent the client fully within the law.

regulations.[4]   The professional responsibility of a lawyer derives from his

"This obligation, in its fullest sense, is the heart of the adversary process. Each attorney, as an advocate, acts for and seeks that which in his judgment is best for his client, within the bounds authoritatively established. The advocate does not *decide* what is just in this case—he would be usurping the function of the judge and jury—he acts for and seeks for his client that which he is entitled to under the law. He can do no less and properly represent the client." Thode, *The Ethical Standard for the Advocate,* 39 Texas L.Rev. 575, 584 (1961).

"The [Texas public opinion] survey indicates that distrust of the lawyer can be traced directly to certain factors. Foremost of these is a basic misunderstanding of the function of the lawyer as an advocate in an adversary system.

"Lawyers are accused of taking advantage of 'loopholes' and 'technicalities' to win. Persons who make this charge are unaware, or do not understand, that the lawyer is hired to win, and if he does not exercise every legitimate effort in his client's behalf, then he is betraying a sacred trust." Rochelle & Payne, *The Struggle for Public Understanding,* 25 Texas B.J. 109, 159 (1962).

"The importance of the attorney's undivided allegiance and faithful service to one accused of crime, irrespective of the attorney's personal opinion as to the guilt of his client, lies in Canon 5 of the American Bar Association Canon of Ethics.

"The difficulty lies, of course, in ascertaining whether the attorney has been guilty of an error of judgment, such as an election with respect to trial tactics, or has otherwise been actuated by his conscience or belief that his client should be convicted in any event. All too frequently courts are called upon to review actions of defense counsel which are, at the most, errors of judgment, not properly reviewable on habeas corpus unless the trial is a farce and a mockery of justice which requires the court to intervene.... But when defense counsel, in a truly adverse proceeding, admits that his conscience would not permit him to adopt certain customary trial procedures, this extends beyond the realm of judgment

and strongly suggests an invasion of constitutional rights." Johns v. Smyth, 176 F.Supp. 949, 952 (E.D.Va.1959), modified, United States ex rel. Wilkins v. Banmiller, 205 F.Supp. 123, 128, n. 5 (E.D. Pa.1962), aff'd 325 F.2d 514 (3d Cir.1963), cert. denied, 379 U.S. 847, 13 L.Ed.2d 51, 85 S.Ct. 87 (1964).

"The adversary system in law administration bears a striking resemblance to the competitive economic system. In each we assume that the individual through partisanship or through self-interest will strive mightily for his side, and that kind of striving we must have. But neither system would be tolerable without restraints and modifications, and at times without outright departures from the system itself. Since the legal profession is entrusted with the system of law administration, a part of its task is to develop in its members appropriate restraints without impairing the values of partisan striving. An accompanying task is to aid in the modification of the adversary system or departure from it in areas to which the system is unsuited." Cheatham, *The Lawyer's Role and Surroundings,* 25 Rocky Mt.L.Rev. 405, 410 (1953).

4. "Rule 4.15 prohibits, in the pursuit of a client's cause, 'any manner of fraud or chicane'; Rule 4.22 requires 'candor and fairness' in the conduct of the lawyer, and forbids the making of knowing misquotations; Rule 4.47 provides that a lawyer 'should always maintain his integrity,' and generally forbids all misconduct injurious to the interests of the public, the courts, or his clients, and acts contrary to 'justice, honesty, modesty or good morals.' Our Commissioner has accurately paraphrased these rules as follows: 'An attorney does not have the duty to do all and whatever he can that may enable him to win his client's cause or to further his client's interest. His duty and efforts in these respects, although they should be prompted by his "entire devotion" to the interest of his client, must be within and not without the bounds of the law.' " In re Wines, 370 S.W.2d 328, 333 (Mo.1963).

See Note, 38 Texas L.Rev. 107, 110 (1959).

membership in a profession which has the duty of assisting members of the public to secure and protect available legal rights and benefits. In our government of laws and not of men, each member of our society is entitled to have his conduct judged and regulated in accordance with the law;[5] to seek any lawful objective[6] through legally permissible means;[7] and to present for adjudication any lawful claim, issue, or defense.

EC 7–2 The bounds of the law in a given case are often difficult to ascertain.[8] The language of legislative enactments and judicial opinions may be uncertain as applied to varying factual situations. The limits and specific meaning of apparently relevant law may be made doubtful by changing or developing constitutional interpretations, inadequately expressed statutes or judicial opinions, and changing public and judicial attitudes. Certainty of law ranges from well-settled rules through areas of conflicting authority to areas without precedent.

EC 7–3 Where the bounds of law are uncertain, the action of a lawyer may depend on whether he is serving as advocate or adviser. A lawyer may serve simultaneously as both advocate and adviser, but the two roles are essentially different.[9] In asserting a position on behalf of his

---

5. "Under our system of government the process of adjudication is surrounded by safeguards evolved from centuries of experience. These safeguards are not designed merely to lend formality and decorum to the trial of causes. They are predicated on the assumption that to secure for any controversy a truly informed and dispassionate decision is a difficult thing, requiring for its achievement a special summoning and organization of human effort and the adoption of measures to exclude the biases and prejudgments that have free play outside the courtroom. All of this goes for naught if the man with an unpopular cause is unable to find a competent lawyer courageous enough to represent him. His chance to have his day in court loses much of its meaning if his case is handicapped from the outset by the very kind of prejudgment our rules of evidence and procedure are intended to prevent." *Professional Responsibility: Report of the Joint Conference,* 44 A.B.A.J. 1159, 1216 (1958).

6. "[I]t is ... [the tax lawyer's] positive duty to show the client how to avail himself to the full of what the law permits. He is not the keeper of the Congressional conscience." Paul, *The Lawyer as a Tax Adviser,* 25 Rocky Mt.L.Rev. 412, 418 (1953).

7. See ABA Canons 15 and 30.

8. "The fact that it desired to evade the law, as it is called, is immaterial, because the very meaning of a line in the law is that you intentionally may go as close to it as you can if you do not pass it.... It is a matter of proximity and degree as to which minds will differ...." Justice Holmes, in Superior Oil Co. v. Mississippi, 280 U.S. 390, 395–96, 74 L.Ed. 504, 508, 50 S.Ct. 169, 170 (1930).

9. "Today's lawyers perform two distinct types of functions, and our ethical standards should, but in the main do not, recognize these two functions. Judge Philbrick McCoy recently reported to the American Bar Association the need for a reappraisal of the Canons in light of the new and distinct function of counselor, as distinguished from advocate, which today predominates in the legal profession....

"... In the first place, any revision of the canons must take into account and speak to this new and now predominant function of the lawyer.... It is beyond the scope of this paper to discuss the ethical standards to be applied to the counselor except to state that in my opinion such standards should require a greater recognition and protection for the interest of the public generally than is presently expressed in the canons. Also, the counselor's obligation

client, an advocate for the most part deals with past conduct and must take the facts as he finds them. By contrast, a lawyer serving as adviser primarily assists his client in determining the course of future conduct and relationships. While serving as advocate, a lawyer should resolve in favor of his client doubts as to the bounds of the law.[10] In serving a client as adviser, a lawyer in appropriate circumstances should give his professional opinion as to what the ultimate decisions of the courts would likely be as to the applicable law.

Duty of the Lawyer to a Client

EC 7–4 The advocate may urge any permissible construction of the law favorable to his client, without regard to his professional opinion as to the likelihood that the construction will ultimately prevail.[11] His conduct is within the bounds of the law, and therefore permissible, if the position taken is supported by the law or is supportable by a good faith argument for an extension, modification, or reversal of the law. However, a lawyer is not justified in asserting a position in litigation that is frivolous.[12]

should extend to requiring him to inform and to impress upon the client a just solution of the problem, considering all interests involved." Thode, *The Ethical Standard for the Advocate,* 39 Texas L.Rev. 575, 578–79 (1961).

"The man who has been called into court to answer for his own actions is entitled to fair hearing. Partisan advocacy plays its essential part in such a hearing, and the lawyer pleading his client's case may properly present it in the most favorable light. A similar resolution of doubts in one direction becomes inappropriate when the lawyer acts as counselor. The reasons that justify and even require partisan advocacy in the trial of a cause do not grant any license to the lawyer to participate as legal advisor in a line of conduct that is immoral, unfair, or of doubtful legality. In saving himself from this unworthy involvement, the lawyer cannot be guided solely by an unreflective inner sense of good faith; he must be at pains to preserve a sufficient detachment from his client's interests so that he remains capable of a sound and objective appraisal of the propriety of what his client proposes to do." *Professional Responsibility: Report of the Joint Conference,* 44 A.B.J. 1159, 1161 (1958).

10. "[A] lawyer who is asked to advise his client . . . may freely urge the statement of positions most favorable to the client just as long as there is reasonable basis for those positions." *ABA Opinion* 314 (1965).

11. "The lawyer . . . is not an umpire, but an advocate. He is under no duty to refrain from making every proper argument in support of any legal point because he is not convinced of its inherent soundness. . . . His personal belief in the soundness of his cause or of the authorities supporting it, is irrelevant." *ABA Opinion* 280 (1949).

"Counsel apparently misconceived his role. It was his duty to honorably present his client's contentions in the light most favorable to his client. Instead he presumed to advise the court as to the validity and sufficiency of prisoner's motion, by letter. We therefore conclude that the prisoner had no effective assistance of counsel and remand this case to the District Court with instructions to set aside the Judgment, appoint new counsel to represent the prisoner if he makes no objection thereto, and proceed anew." McCartney v. United States, 343 F.2d 471, 472 (9th Cir.1965).

12. "Here the court-appointed counsel had the transcript but refused to proceed with the appeal because he found no merit in it. . . . We cannot say that there was a finding of frivolity by either of the California courts or that counsel acted in any greater capacity than merely as *amicus curiae* which was condemned in *Ellis,* supra.

EC 7–5   A lawyer as adviser furthers the interest of his client by giving his professional opinion as to what he believes would likely be the ultimate decision of the courts on the matter at hand and by informing his client of the practical effect of such decision.[13] He may continue in the representation of his client even though his client has elected to pursue a course of conduct contrary to the advice of the lawyer so long as he does not thereby knowingly assist the client to engage in illegal conduct or to take a frivolous legal position. A lawyer should never encourage or aid his client to commit criminal acts or counsel his client on how to violate the law and avoid punishment therefor.[14]

EC 7–6   Whether the proposed action of a lawyer is within the bounds of the law may be a perplexing question when his client is contemplating a course of conduct having legal consequences that vary according to the client's intent, motive, or desires at the time of the action. Often a lawyer is asked to assist his client in developing evidence relevant to the state of mind of the client at a particular time. He may properly assist

Hence California's procedure did not furnish petitioner with counsel acting in the role of an advocate nor did it provide that full consideration and resolution of the matter as is obtained when counsel is acting in that capacity....

"The constitutional requirement of substantial equality and fair process can only be attained where counsel acts in the role of an active advocate in behalf of his client, as opposed to that of *amicus curiae*. The nomerit letter and the procedure it triggers do not reach that dignity. Counsel should, and can with honor and without conflict, be of more assistance to his client and to the court. His role as advocate requires that he support his client's appeal to the best of his ability. Of course, if counsel finds his case to be wholly frivolous, after a conscientious examination of it, he should so advise the court and request permission to withdraw. That request must, however, be accompanied by a brief referring to anything in the record that might arguably support the appeal. A copy of counsel's brief should be furnished the indigent and time allowed him to raise any points that he chooses; the court—not counsel—then proceeds, after a full examination of all the proceedings, to decide whether the case is wholly frivolous. If it so finds it may grant counsel's request to withdraw and dismiss the appeal insofar as federal requirements are concerned, or proceed to a decision on the merits, if state law so requires. On the other hand, if it

finds any of the legal points arguable on their merits (and therefore not frivolous) it must, prior to decision afford the indigent the assistance of counsel to argue the appeal." *Anders v. California,* 386 U.S. 738, 744, 18 L.Ed.2d 493, 498, 87 S.Ct. 1396, 1399–1400 (1967), rehearing denied, 388 U.S. 924, 18 L.Ed.2d 1377, 87 S.Ct. 2094 (1967).

See Paul, *The Lawyer As a Tax Adviser,* 25 Rocky Mt.L.Rev. 412, 432 (1953).

13.   See ABA Canon 32.

14.   "For a lawyer to represent a syndicate notoriously engaged in the violation of the law for the purpose of advising the members how to break the law and at the same time escape it, is manifestly improper. While a lawyer may see to it that anyone accused of crime, no matter how serious and flagrant, has a fair trial, and present all available defenses, he may not co-operate in planning violations of the law. There is a sharp distinction, of course, between advising what can lawfully be done and advising how unlawful acts can be done in a way to avoid conviction. Where a lawyer accepts a retainer from an organization, known to be unlawful, and agrees in advance to defend its members when from time to time they are accused of crime arising out of its unlawful activities, this is equally improper."

"See also *Opinion 155.*" *ABA Opinion* 281 (1952).

his client in the development and preservation of evidence of existing motive, intent, or desire; obviously, he may not do anything furthering the creation or preservation of false evidence. In many cases a lawyer may not be certain as to the state of mind of his client, and in those situations he should resolve reasonable doubts in favor of his client.

EC 7–7 In certain areas of legal representation not affecting the merits of the cause or substantially prejudicing the rights of a client, a lawyer is entitled to make decisions on his own. But otherwise the authority to make decisions is exclusively that of the client and, if made within the framework of the law, such decisions are binding on his lawyer. As typical examples in civil cases, it is for the client to decide whether he will accept a settlement offer or whether he will waive his right to plead an affirmative defense. A defense lawyer in a criminal case has the duty to advise his client fully on whether a particular plea to a charge appears to be desirable and as to the prospects of success on appeal, but it is for the client to decide what plea should be entered and whether an appeal should be taken.[15]

EC 7–8 A lawyer should exert his best efforts to insure that decisions of his client are made only after the client has been informed of relevant considerations. A lawyer ought to initiate this decision-making process if the client does not do so. Advice of a lawyer to his client need not be confined to purely legal considerations.[16] A lawyer should advise his client of the possible effect of each legal alternative.[17] A lawyer should bring to bear upon this decision-making process the fullness of his experience as well as his objective viewpoint.[18] In assisting his client to reach a proper decision, it is often desirable for a lawyer to point out those factors which may lead to a decision that is morally just as well as legally permissible.[19] He may emphasize the possibility of harsh conse-

---

15. See ABA Special Committee on Minimum Standards for the Administration of Criminal Justice, *Standards Relating to Pleas of Guilty,* pp. 69–70 (1968).

16. "First of all, a truly great lawyer is a wise counselor to all manner of men in the varied crises of their lives when they most need disinterested advice. Effective counseling necessarily involves a thoroughgoing knowledge of the principles of the law not merely as they appear in the books but as they actually operate in action." Vanderbilt, *The Five Functions of the Lawyer: Service to Clients and the Public,* 40 A.B.A.J. 31 (1954).

17. "A lawyer should endeavor to obtain full knowledge of his client's cause before advising thereon...." ABA Canon 8.

18. "[I]n devising charters of collaborative effort the lawyer often acts where all of the affected parties are present as participants. But the lawyer also performs a similar function in situations where this is not so, as, for example, in planning estates and drafting wills. Here the instrument defining the terms of collaboration may affect persons not present and often not born. Yet here, too, the good lawyer does not serve merely as a legal conduit for his client's desires, but as a wise counselor, experienced in the art of devising arrangements that will put in workable order the entangled affairs and interests of human beings." *Professional Responsibility: Report of the Joint Conference,* 44 A.B.A.J. 1159, 1162 (1958).

19. See ABA Canon 8.

quences that might result from assertion of legally permissible positions. In the final analysis, however, the lawyer should always remember that the decision whether to forego legally available objectives or methods because of non-legal factors is ultimately for the client and not for himself. In the event that the client in a non-adjudicatory matter insists upon a course of conduct that is contrary to the judgment and advice of the lawyer but not prohibited by Disciplinary Rules, the lawyer may withdraw from the employment.[20]

EC 7-9 In the exercise of his professional judgment on those decisions which are for his determination in the handling of a legal matter,[21] a lawyer should always act in a manner consistent with the best interests of his client.[22] However, when an action in the best interest of his client seems to him to be unjust, he may ask his client for permission to forego such action.[23]

EC 7-10 The duty of a lawyer to represent his client with zeal does not militate against his concurrent obligation to treat with consideration all persons involved in the legal process and to avoid the infliction of needless harm.

EC 7-11 The responsibilities of a lawyer may vary according to the intelligence, experience, mental condition or age of a client, the obligation of a public officer, or the nature of a particular proceeding. Examples include the representation of an illiterate or an incompetent, service as a public prosecutor or other government lawyer, and appearances before administrative and legislative bodies.

EC 7-12 Any mental or physical condition of a client that renders him incapable of making a considered judgment on his own behalf casts

---

"Vital as is the lawyer's role in adjudication, it should not be thought that it is only as an advocate pleading in open court that he contributes to the administration of the law. The most effective realization of the law's aims often takes place in the attorney's office, where litigation is forestalled by anticipating its outcome, where the lawyer's quiet counsel takes the place of public force. Contrary to popular belief, the compliance with the law thus brought about is not generally lip-serving and narrow, for by reminding him of its long-run costs the lawyer often deters his client from a course of conduct technically permissible under existing law, though inconsistent with its underlying spirit and purpose." *Professional Responsibility: Report of the Joint Conference,* 44 A.B.A.J. 1159, 1161 (1958).

20. "My summation of Judge Sharswood's view of the advocate's duty to the client is that he owes to the client the duty to use all legal means in support of the client's case. However, at the same time Judge Sharswood recognized that many advocates would find this obligation unbearable if applicable without exception. Therefore, the individual lawyer is given the choice of representing his client fully within the bounds set by the law *or of telling his client that he cannot do so,* so that the client may obtain another attorney if he wishes." Thode, *The Ethical Standard for the Advocate,* 39 Texas L.Rev. 575, 582 (1961).

Cf. Code of Professional Responsibility, DR 2-110(C).

21. See ABA Canon 24.

22. Thode, *The Ethical Standard for the Advocate,* 39 Texas L.Rev. 575, 592 (1961).

23. Cf. *ABA Opinions* 253 (1946) and 178 (1938).

additional responsibilities upon his lawyer. Where an incompetent is acting through a guardian or other legal representative, a lawyer must look to such representative for those decisions which are normally the prerogative of the client to make. If a client under disability has no legal representative, his lawyer may be compelled in court proceedings to make decisions on behalf of the client. If the client is capable of understanding the matter in question or of contributing to the advancement of his interests, regardless of whether he is legally disqualified from performing certain acts, the lawyer should obtain from him all possible aid. If the disability of a client and the lack of a legal representative compel the lawyer to make decisions for his client, the lawyer should consider all circumstances then prevailing and act with care to safeguard and advance the interests of his client. But obviously a lawyer cannot perform any act or make any decision which the law requires his client to perform or make, either acting for himself if competent, or by a duly constituted representative if legally incompetent.

EC 7–13 The responsibility of a public prosecutor differs from that of the usual advocate; his duty is to seek justice, not merely to convict.[24] This special duty exists because: (1) the prosecutor represents the sovereign and therefore should use restraint in the discretionary exercise of governmental powers, such as in the selection of cases to prosecute; (2) during trial the prosecutor is not only an advocate but he also may make decisions normally made by an individual client, and those affecting the public interest should be fair to all; and (3) in our system of criminal justice the accused is to be given the benefit of all reasonable doubts. With respect to evidence and witnesses, the prosecutor has responsibilities different from those of a lawyer in private practice: the prosecutor should make timely disclosure to the defense of available evidence, known to him, that tends to negate the guilt of the accused, mitigate the degree of the offense, or reduce the punishment. Further, a prosecutor should not intentionally avoid pursuit of evidence merely because he believes it will damage the prosecutor's case or aid the accused.

---

24. See ABA Canon 5 and Berger v. United States, 295 U.S. 78, 79 L.Ed. 1314, 55 S.Ct. 629 (1935).

"The public prosecutor cannot take as a guide for the conduct of his office the standards of an attorney appearing on behalf of an individual client. The freedom elsewhere wisely granted to a partisan advocate must be severely curtailed if the prosecutor's duties are to be properly discharged. The public prosecutor must recall that he occupies a dual role, being obligated, on the one hand, to furnish that adversary element essential to the informed decision of any controversy, but being possessed, on the other, of important governmental powers that are pledged to the accomplishment of one objective only, that of impartial justice. Where the prosecutor is recreant to the trust implicit in his office, he undermines confidence, not only in his profession, but in government and the very ideal of justice itself." *Professional Responsibility: Report of the Joint Conference*, 44 A.B.A.J. 1159, 1218 (1958).

"The prosecuting attorney is the attorney for the state, and it is his primary duty not to convict but to see that justice is done." *ABA Opinion* 150 (1936).

EC 7-14 A government lawyer who has discretionary power relative to litigation should refrain from instituting or continuing litigation that is obviously unfair. A government lawyer not having such discretionary power who believes there is lack of merit in a controversy submitted to him should so advise his superiors and recommend the avoidance of unfair litigation. A government lawyer in a civil action or administrative proceeding has the responsibility to seek justice and to develop a full and fair record, and he should not use his position or the economic power of the government to harass parties or to bring about unjust settlements or results.

EC 7-15 The nature and purpose of proceedings before administrative agencies vary widely. The proceedings may be legislative or quasi-judicial, or a combination of both. They may be *ex parte* in character, in which event they may originate either at the instance of the agency or upon motion of an interested party. The scope of an inquiry may be purely investigative or it may be truly adversary looking toward the adjudication of specific rights of a party or of classes of parties. The foregoing are but examples of some of the types of proceedings conducted by administrative agencies. A lawyer appearing before an administrative agency,[25] regardless of the nature of the proceeding it is conducting, has the continuing duty to advance the cause of his client within the bounds of the law.[26] Where the applicable rules of the agency impose specific obligations upon a lawyer, it is his duty to comply therewith, unless the lawyer has a legitimate basis for challenging the validity thereof. In all appearances before administrative agencies, a lawyer should identify himself, his client if identity of his client is not privileged,[27] and the representative nature of his appearance. It is not improper, however, for a lawyer to seek from an agency information available to the public without identifying his client.

EC 7-16 The primary business of a legislative body is to enact laws rather than to adjudicate controversies, although on occasion the activities of a legislative body may take on the characteristics of an adversary proceeding, particularly in investigative and impeachment matters. The role of a lawyer supporting or opposing proposed legislation normally is quite different from his role in representing a person under investigation or on trial by a legislative body. When a lawyer appears in connection with proposed legislation, he seeks to affect the lawmaking process, but

25. As to appearances before a department of government, Canon 26 provides: "A lawyer openly ... may render professional services ... in advocacy of claims before departments of government, upon the same principles of ethics which justify his appearance before the Courts...."

26. "But as an advocate before a service which itself represents the adversary point of view, where his client's case is fairly arguable, a lawyer is under no duty to disclose its weaknesses, any more than he would be to make such a disclosure to a brother lawyer. The limitations within which he must operate are best expressed in Canon 22...." *ABA Opinion* 314 (1965).

27. See Baird v. Koerner, 279 F.2d 623 (9th Cir.1960).

when he appears on behalf of a client in investigatory or impeachment proceedings, he is concerned with the protection of the rights of his client. In either event, he should identify himself and his client, if identity of his client is not privileged, and should comply with applicable laws and legislative rules.[28]

EC 7–17 The obligation of loyalty to his client applies only to a lawyer in the discharge of his professional duties and implies no obligation to adopt a personal viewpoint favorable to the interests or desires of his client.[29] While a lawyer must act always with circumspection in order that his conduct will not adversely affect the rights of a client in a matter he is then handling, he may take positions on public issues and espouse legal reforms he favors without regard to the individual views of any client.

EC 7–18 The legal system in its broadest sense functions best when persons in need of legal advice or assistance are represented by their own counsel. For this reason a lawyer should not communicate on the subject matter of the representation of his client with a person he knows to be represented in the matter by a lawyer, unless pursuant to law or rule of court or unless he has the consent of the lawyer for that person.[30] If one is not represented by counsel, a lawyer representing another may have to deal directly with the unrepresented person; in such an instance, a lawyer should not undertake to give advice to the person who is attempting to represent himself,[31] except that he may advise him to obtain a lawyer.

Duty of the Lawyer to the Adversary System of Justice

EC 7–19 Our legal system provides for the adjudication of disputes governed by the rules of substantive, evidentiary, and procedural law. An adversary presentation counters the natural human tendency to judge too swiftly in terms of the familiar that which is not yet fully known;[32] the advocate, by his zealous preparation and presentation of

28. See ABA Canon 26.

29. "Law should be so practiced that the lawyer remains free to make up his own mind how he will vote, what causes he will support, what economic and political philosophy he will espouse. It is one of the glories of the profession that it admits of this freedom. Distinguished examples can be cited of lawyers whose views were at variance from those of their clients, lawyers whose skill and wisdom make them valued advisers to those who had little sympathy with their views as citizens." *Professional Responsibility: Report of the Joint Conference,* 44 A.B.A.J. 1159, 1217 (1958).

"No doubt some tax lawyers feel constrained to abstain from activities on behalf of a better tax system because they think that their clients may object. Clients have no right to object if the tax adviser handles their affairs competently and faithfully and independently of his private views as to tax policy. They buy his expert services, not his private opinions or his silence on issues that gravely affect the public interest." Paul, *The Lawyer as a Tax Adviser,* 25 Rocky Mt.L.Rev. 412, 434 (1953).

30. See ABA Canon 9.

31. Id.

32. See *Professional Responsibility: Report of the Joint Conference,* 44 A.B.A.J. 1159, 1160 (1958).

facts and law, enables the tribunal to come to the hearing with an open and neutral mind and to render impartial judgments.[33] The duty of a lawyer to his client and his duty to the legal system are the same: to represent his client zealously within the bounds of the law.[34]

EC 7–20 In order to function properly, our adjudicative process requires an informed, impartial tribunal capable of administering justice promptly and efficiently [35] according to procedures that command public confidence and respect.[36] Not only must there be competent, adverse presentation of evidence and issues, but a tribunal must be aided by rules appropriate to an effective and dignified process. The procedures under which tribunals operate in our adversary system have been prescribed largely by legislative enactments, court rules and decisions, and administrative rules. Through the years certain concepts of proper professional conduct have become rules of law applicable to the adversary adjudicative process. Many of these concepts are the bases for standards of professional conduct set forth in the Disciplinary Rules.

EC 7–21 The civil adjudicative process is primarily designed for the settlement of disputes between parties, while the criminal process is designed for the protection of society as a whole. Threatening to use, or using, the criminal process to coerce adjustment of private civil claims or controversies is a subversion of that process; [37] further, the person against whom the criminal process is so misused may be deterred from asserting his legal rights and thus the usefulness of the civil process in settling private disputes is impaired. As in all cases of abuse of judicial

33. "Without the participation of someone who can act responsibly for each of the parties, this essential narrowing of the issues [by exchange of written pleadings or stipulations of counsel] becomes impossible. But here again the true significance of partisan advocacy lies deeper, touching once more the integrity of the adjudicative process itself. It is only through the advocate's participation that the hearing may remain in fact what it purports to be in theory: a public trial of the facts and issues. Each advocate comes to the hearing prepared to present his proofs and arguments, knowing at the same time that his arguments may fail to persuade and that his proof may be rejected as inadequate. . . . The deciding tribunal, on the other hand, comes to the hearing uncommitted. It has not represented to the public that any fact can be proved, that any argument is sound, or that any particular way of stating a litigant's case is the most effective expression of its merits." *Professional Responsibility: Report of the Joint Conference,* 44 A.B.A.J. 1159, 1160–61 (1958).

34. Cf. ABA Canons 15 and 32.

35. Cf. ABA Canon 21.

36. See *Professional Responsibility: Report of the Joint Conference,* 44 A.B.A.J. 1159, 1216 (1958).

37. "We are of the opinion that the letter in question was improper, and that in writing and sending it respondent was guilty of unprofessional conduct. This court has heretofore expressed its disapproval of using threats of criminal prosecution as a means of forcing settlement of civil claims. . . .

"Respondent has been guilty of a violation of a principle which condemns any confusion of threats of criminal prosecution with the enforcement of civil claims. For this misconduct he should be severely censured." Matter of Gelman, 230 App.Div. 524, 527, 245 N.Y.S. 416, 419 (1930).

process, the improper use of criminal process tends to diminish public confidence in our legal system.

EC 7–22 Respect for judicial rulings is essential to the proper administration of justice; however, a litigant or his lawyer may, in good faith and within the framework of the law, take steps to test the correctness of a ruling of a tribunal.[38]

EC 7–23 The complexity of law often makes it difficult for a tribunal to be fully informed unless the pertinent law is presented by the lawyers in the cause. A tribunal that is fully informed on the applicable law is better able to make a fair and accurate determination of the matter before it. The adversary system contemplates that each lawyer will present and argue the existing law in the light most favorable to his client.[39] Where a lawyer knows of legal authority in the controlling jurisdiction directly adverse to the position of his client, he should inform the tribunal of its existence unless his adversary has done so; but, having made such disclosure, he may challenge its soundness in whole or in part.[40]

EC 7–24 In order to bring about just and informed decisions, evidentiary and procedural rules have been established by tribunals to permit the inclusion of relevant evidence and argument and the exclusion of all other considerations. The expression by a lawyer of his personal opinion as to the justness of a cause, as to the credibility of a witness, as to the culpability of a civil litigant, or as to the guilt or innocence of an accused is not a proper subject for argument to the trier of fact.[41] It is improper as to factual matters because admissible evidence possessed by a lawyer should be presented only as sworn testimony. It is improper as to all other matters because, were the rule otherwise, the silence of a lawyer

---

38. "An attorney has the duty to protect the interests of his client. He has a right to press legitimate argument and to protest an erroneous ruling." Gallagher v. Municipal Court, 31 Cal.2d 784, 796, 192 P.2d 905, 913 (1948).

"There must be protection, however, in the far more frequent case of the attorney who stands on his rights and combats the order in good faith and without disrespect believing with good cause that it is void, for it is here that the independence of the bar becomes valuable." Note, 39 Colum.L.Rev. 433, 438 (1939).

39. "Too many do not understand that accomplishment of the layman's abstract ideas of justice is the function of the judge and jury, and that it is the lawyer's sworn duty to portray his client's case in its most favorable light." Rochelle and Payne, *The*

Struggle for Public Understanding, 25 Texas B.J. 109, 159 (1962).

40. "We are of the opinion that this Canon requires the lawyer to disclose such decisions [that are adverse to his client's contentions] to the court. He may, of course, after doing so, challenge the soundness of the decisions or present reasons which he believes would warrant the court in not following them in the pending case." *ABA Opinion* 146 (1935).

Cf. *ABA Opinion* 280 (1949) and Thode, *The Ethical Standard for the Advocate,* 39 Texas L.Rev. 575, 585–86 (1961).

41. See ABA Canon 15.

"The traditional duty of an advocate is that he honorably uphold the contentions of his client. He should not voluntarily undermine them." Harders v. State of California, 373 F.2d 839, 842 (9th Cir.1967).

on a given occasion could be construed unfavorably to his client. However, a lawyer may argue, on his analysis of the evidence, for any position or conclusion with respect to any of the foregoing matters.

EC 7–25 Rules of evidence and procedure are designed to lead to just decisions and are part of the framework of the law. Thus while a lawyer may take steps in good faith and within the framework of the law to test the validity of rules, he is not justified in consciously violating such rules and he should be diligent in his efforts to guard against his unintentional violation of them.[42] As examples, a lawyer should subscribe to or verify only those pleadings that he believes are in compliance with applicable law and rules; a lawyer should not make any prefatory statement before a tribunal in regard to the purported facts of the case on trial unless he believes that his statement will be supported by admissible evidence; a lawyer should not ask a witness a question solely for the purpose of harassing or embarrassing him; and a lawyer should not by subterfuge put before a jury matters which it cannot properly consider.

EC 7–26 The law and Disciplinary Rules prohibit the use of fraudulent, false, or perjured testimony or evidence.[43] A lawyer who knowingly[44] participates in introduction of such testimony or evidence is subject to discipline. A lawyer should, however, present any admissible evidence his client desires to have presented unless he knows, or from facts within his knowledge should know, that such testimony or evidence is false, fraudulent, or perjured.[45]

EC 7–27 Because it interferes with the proper administration of justice, a lawyer should not suppress evidence that he or his client has a legal obligation to reveal or produce. In like manner, a lawyer should not advise or cause a person to secrete himself or to leave the jurisdiction of a tribunal for the purpose of making him unavailable as a witness therein.[46]

EC 7–28 Witnesses should always testify truthfully[47] and should be free from any financial inducements that might tempt them to do

---

42. See ABA Canon 22.

43. Id. Cf. ABA Canon 41.

44. See generally *ABA Opinion* 287 (1953) as to a lawyer's duty when he unknowingly participates in introducing perjured testimony.

45. "Under any standard of proper ethical conduct an attorney should not sit by silently and permit his client to commit what may have been perjury, and which certainly would mislead the court and the opposing party on a matter vital to the issue under consideration. . . .

. . .

"Respondent next urges that it was his duty to observe the utmost good faith toward his client, and therefore he could not divulge any confidential information. This duty to the client of course does not extend to the point of authorizing collaboration with him in the commission of fraud." In re Carroll, 244 S.W.2d 474, 474–75 (Ky. 1951).

46. See ABA Canon 5; cf. *ABA Opinion* 131 (1935).

47. Cf. ABA Canon 39.

otherwise.[48] A lawyer should not pay or agree to pay a non-expert witness an amount in excess of reimbursement for expenses and financial loss incident to his being a witness; however, a lawyer may pay or agree to pay an expert witness a reasonable fee for his services as an expert. But in no event should a lawyer pay or agree to pay a contingent fee to any witness. A lawyer should exercise reasonable diligence to see that his client and lay associates conform to these standards.[49]

EC 7-29 To safeguard the impartiality that is essential to the judicial process, veniremen and jurors should be protected against extraneous influences.[50] When impartiality is present, public confidence in the judicial system is enhanced. There should be no extrajudicial communication with veniremen prior to trial or with jurors during trial by or on behalf of a lawyer connected with the case. Furthermore, a lawyer who is not connected with the case should not communicate with or cause another to communicate with a venireman or a juror about the case. After the trial, communication by a lawyer with jurors is permitted so long as he refrains from asking questions or making comments that tend to harass or embarrass the juror [51] or to influence actions of the juror in future cases. Were a lawyer to be prohibited from communicating after a trial with a juror, he could not ascertain if the verdict might be subject to legal challenge, in which event the invalidity of a verdict might go undetected.[52] When an extrajudicial communication by a lawyer with a

48. "The prevalence of perjury is a serious menace to the administration of justice, to prevent which no means have as yet been satisfactorily devised. But there certainly can be no greater incentive to perjury than to allow a party to make payments to its opponents witnesses under any guise or on any excuse, and at least attorneys who are officers of the court to aid it in the administration of justice, must keep themselves clear of any connection which in the slightest degree tends to induce witnesses to testify in favor of their clients." In re Robinson, 151 App.Div. 589, 600, 136 N.Y.S. 548, 556–57 (1912), aff'd, 209 N.Y. 354, 103 N.E. 160 (1913).

49. "It will not do for an attorney who seeks to justify himself against charges of this kind to show that he has escaped criminal responsibility under the Penal Law, nor can he blindly shut his eyes to a system which tends to suborn witnesses, to produce perjured testimony, and to suppress the truth. He has an active affirmative duty to protect the administration of justice from perjury and fraud, and that duty is not performed by allowing his subordinates and

assistants to attempt to subvert justice and procure results for his clients based upon false testimony and perjured witnesses." Id., 151 App.Div. at 592, 136 N.Y.S. at 551.

50. See ABA Canon 23.

51. "[I]t is unfair to jurors to permit a disappointed litigant to pick over their private associations in search of something to discredit them and their verdict. And it would be unfair to the public too if jurors should understand that they cannot convict a man of means without risking an inquiry of that kind by paid investigators, with, to boot, the distortions an inquiry of that kind can produce." State v. LaFera, 42 N.J. 97, 107, 199 A.2d 630, 636 (1964).

52. *ABA Opinion* 319 (1968) points out that "[m]any courts today, and the trend is in this direction, allow the testimony of jurors as to all irregularities in and out of the courtroom except those irregularities whose existence can be determined only by exploring the consciousness of a single particular juror, New Jersey v. Kociolek, 20 N.J. 92, 118 A.2d 812 (1955). Model Code

juror is permitted by law, it should be made considerately and with deference to the personal feelings of the juror.

EC 7–30 Vexatious or harassing investigations of veniremen or jurors seriously impair the effectiveness of our jury system. For this reason, a lawyer or anyone on his behalf who conducts an investigation of veniremen or jurors should act with circumspection and restraint.

EC 7–31 Communications with or investigations of members of families of veniremen or jurors by a lawyer or by anyone on his behalf are subject to the restrictions imposed upon the lawyer with respect to his communications with or investigations of veniremen and jurors.

EC 7–32 Because of his duty to aid in preserving the integrity of the jury system, a lawyer who learns of improper conduct by or towards a venireman, a juror, or a member of the family of either should make a prompt report to the court regarding such conduct.

EC 7–33 A goal of our legal system is that each party shall have his case, criminal or civil, adjudicated by an impartial tribunal. The attainment of this goal may be defeated by dissemination of news or comments which tend to influence judge or jury.[53] Such news or comments may

of Evidence Rule 301. Certainly as to states in which the testimony and affidavits of jurors may be received in support of or against a motion for new trial, a lawyer, in his obligation to protect his client, must have the tools for ascertaining whether or not grounds for a new trial exist and it is not unethical for him to talk to and question jurors."

53. Generally see ABA Advisory Committee on Fair Trial and Free Press, Standards Relating to Fair Trial and Free Press (1966).

"[T]he trial court might well have proscribed extrajudicial statements by any lawyer, party, witness, or court official which divulged prejudicial matters.... See State v. Van Dwyne, 43 N.J. 369, 389, 204 A.2d 841, 852 (1964), in which the court interpreted Canon 20 of the American Bar Association's Canons of Professional Ethics to prohibit such statements. Being advised of the great public interest in the case, the mass coverage of the press, and the potential prejudicial impact of publicity, the court could also have requested the appropriate city and county officials to promulgate a regulation with respect to dissemination of information about the case by their employees. In addition, reporters who wrote or broadcast prejudicial stories, could have

been warned as to the impropriety of publishing material not introduced in the proceedings.... In this manner, Sheppard's right to a trial free from outside interference would have been given added protection without corresponding curtailment of the news media. Had the judge, the other officers of the court, and the police placed the interest of justice first, the news media would have soon learned to be content with the task of reporting the case as it unfolded in the courtroom—not pieced together from extrajudicial statements." Sheppard v. Maxwell, 384 U.S. 333, 361–62, 16 L.Ed.2d 600, 619–20, 86 S.Ct. 1507, 1521–22 (1966).

"Court proceedings are held for the solemn purpose of endeavoring to ascertain the truth which is the *sine qua non* of a fair trial. Over the centuries Anglo-American courts have devised careful safeguards by rule and otherwise to protect and facilitate the performance of this high function. As a result, at this time those safeguards do not permit the televising and photographing of a criminal trial, save in two States and there only under restrictions. The federal courts prohibit it by specific rule. This is weighty evidence that our concepts of a fair trial do not tolerate such an indulgence. We have always held that the atmosphere essential to the preservation of a fair trial—

461

prevent prospective jurors from being impartial at the outset of the trial [54] and may also interfere with the obligation of jurors to base their verdict solely upon the evidence admitted in the trial.[55] The release by a lawyer of out-of-court statements regarding an anticipated or pending trial may improperly affect the impartiality of the tribunal.[56] For these

the most fundamental of all freedoms—must be maintained at all costs." Estes v. State of Texas, 381 U.S. 532, 540, 14 L.Ed.2d 543, 549, 85 S.Ct. 1628, 1631–32 (1965), rehearing denied, 382 U.S. 875, 15 L.Ed.2d 118, 86 S.Ct. 18 (1965).

54. "Pretrial can create a major problem for the defendant in a criminal case. Indeed, it may be more harmful than publicity during the trial for it may well set the community opinion as to guilt or innocence.... The trial witnesses present at the hearing, as well as the original jury panel, were undoubtedly made aware of the peculiar public importance of the case by the press and television coverage being provided, and by the fact that they themselves were televised live and their pictures rebroadcast on the evening show." Id., 381 U.S. at 536–37, 14 L.Ed.2d at 546–47, 85 S.Ct. at 1629–30.

55. "The undeviating rule of this Court was expressed by Mr. Justice Holmes over half a century ago in Patterson v. Colorado, 205 U.S. 454, 462 (1907):

"The theory of our system is that the conclusions to be reached in a case will be induced only by evidence and argument in open court, and not by any outside influence, whether of private talk or public print."

Sheppard v. Maxwell, 384 U.S. 333, 351, 16 L.Ed.2d 600, 614, 86 S.Ct. 1507, 1516 (1966).

"The trial judge has a large discretion in ruling on the issue of prejudice resulting from the reading by jurors of news articles concerning the trial.... Generalizations beyond that statement are not profitable, because each case must turn on its special facts. We have here the exposure of jurors to information of a character which the trial judge ruled was so prejudicial it could not be directly offered as evidence. The prejudice to the defendant is almost certain to be as great when that evidence reaches

the jury through news accounts as when it is a part of the prosecution's evidence.... It may indeed be greater for it is then not tempered by protective procedures." Marshall v. United States, 360 U.S. 310, 312–13, 3 L.Ed.2d 1250, 1252, 79 S.Ct. 1171, 1173 (1959).

"The experienced trial lawyer knows that an adverse public opinion is a tremendous disadvantage to the defense of his client. Although grand jurors conduct their deliberations in secret, they are selected from the body of the public. They are likely to know what the general public knows and to reflect the public attitude. Trials are open to the public, and aroused public opinion respecting the merits of a legal controversy creates a court room atmosphere which, without any vocal expression in the presence of the petit jury, makes itself felt and has its effect upon the action of the petit jury. Our fundamental concepts of justice and our American sense of fair play requires that the petit jury shall be composed of persons with fair and impartial minds and without preconceived views as to the merits of the controversy, and that it shall determine the issues presented to it solely upon the evidence adduced at the trial and according to the law given in the instructions of the trial judge.

"While we may doubt that the effect of public opinion would sway or bias the judgment of the trial judge in an equity proceeding, the defendant should not be called upon to run that risk and the trial court should not have his work made more difficult by any dissemination of statements to the public that would be calculated to create a public demand for a particular judgment in a prospective or pending case." ABA Opinion 199 (1940).

Cf. Estes v. State of Texas, 381 U.S. 532, 544–45, 14 L.Ed.2d 543, 551, 85 S.Ct. 1628, 1634 (1965), rehearing denied, 381 U.S. 875, 15 L.Ed.2d 118, 86 S.Ct. 18 (1965).

56. See ABA Canon 20.

reasons, standards for permissible and prohibited conduct of a lawyer with respect to trial publicity have been established.

EC 7–34 The impartiality of a public servant in our legal system may be impaired by the receipt of gifts or loans. A lawyer,[57] therefore, is never justified in making a gift or a loan to a judge, a hearing officer, or an official or employee of a tribunal, except as permitted by Section C(4) of Canon 5 of the Code of Judicial Conduct, but a lawyer may make a contribution to the campaign fund of a candidate for judicial office in conformity with Section B(2) under Canon 7 of the Code of Judicial Conduct.[58]

As amended in 1974.

EC 7–35 All litigants and lawyers should have access to tribunals on an equal basis. Generally, in adversary proceedings a lawyer should not communicate with a judge relative to a matter pending before, or which is to be brought before, a tribunal over which he presides in circumstances which might have the effect or give the appearance of granting undue advantage to one party.[59] For example, a lawyer should not communicate with a tribunal by a writing unless a copy thereof is promptly delivered to opposing counsel or to the adverse party if he is not represented by a lawyer. Ordinarily an oral communication by a lawyer with a judge or hearing officer should be made only upon adequate notice to opposing counsel, or, if there is none, to the opposing party. A lawyer should not condone or lend himself to private importunities by another with a judge or hearing officer on behalf of himself or his client.

EC 7–36 Judicial hearings ought to be conducted through dignified and orderly procedures designed to protect the rights of all parties. Although a lawyer has the duty to represent his client zealously, he should not engage in any conduct that offends the dignity and decorum of proceedings.[60] While maintaining his independence, a lawyer should be respectful, courteous, and above-board in his relations with a judge or hearing officer before whom he appears.[61] He should avoid undue

---

57. Canon 3 observes that a lawyer "deserves rebuke and denunciation for any device or attempt to gain from a Judge special personal consideration or favor."

See ABA Canon 32.

58. "*Judicial Canon 32* provides:

" 'A judge should not accept any presents or favors from litigants, or from lawyers practicing before him or from others whose interests are likely to be submitted to him for judgment.'

"The language of this Canon is perhaps broad enough to prohibit campaign contributions by lawyers, practicing before the court upon which the candidate hopes to sit. However, we do not think it was intended to prohibit such contributions when the candidate is obligated, by force of circumstances over which he has no control, to conduct a campaign, the expense of which exceeds that which he should reasonably be expected to personally bear!" *ABA Opinion* 226 (1941).

59. See ABA Canons 3 and 32.

60. Cf. ABA Canon 18.

61. See ABA Canons 1 and 3.

solicitude for the comfort or convenience of judge or jury and should avoid any other conduct calculated to gain special consideration.

EC 7–37　In adversary proceedings, clients are litigants and though ill feeling may exist between clients, such ill feeling should not influence a lawyer in his conduct, attitude, and demeanor towards opposing lawyers.[62]　A lawyer should not make unfair or derogatory personal reference to opposing counsel.　Haranguing and offensive tactics by lawyers interfere with the orderly administration of justice and have no proper place in our legal system.

EC 7–38　A lawyer should be courteous to opposing counsel and should accede to reasonable requests regarding court proceedings, settings, continuances, waiver of procedural formalities, and similar matters which do not prejudice the rights of his client.[63]　He should follow local customs of courtesy or practice, unless he gives timely notice to opposing counsel of his intention not to do so.[64]　A lawyer should be punctual in fulfilling all professional commitments.[65]

EC 7–39　In the final analysis, proper functioning of the adversary system depends upon cooperation between lawyers and tribunals in utilizing procedures which will preserve the impartiality of tribunals and make their decisional processes prompt and just, without impinging upon the obligation of lawyers to represent their clients zealously within the framework of the law.

DISCIPLINARY RULES

DR 7–101　Representing a Client Zealously.

(A) A lawyer shall not intentionally:[66]
　　(1) Fail to seek the lawful objectives of his client through reasonably available means[67] permitted by law and the Disciplinary Rules, except as provided by DR 7–101(B).　A lawyer does not violate this Disciplinary Rule, however, by acceding to reasonable requests of opposing counsel which do not prejudice the rights of his client, by being punctual in fulfilling all professional commitments, by avoiding offensive tactics, or by treating with courtesy and consideration all persons involved in the legal process.
　　(2) Fail to carry out a contract of employment entered into with a client for professional services, but he may withdraw as permitted under DR 2–110, DR 5–102, and DR 5–105.

62.　See ABA Canon 17.

63.　See ABA Canon 24.

64.　See ABA Canon 25.

65.　See ABA Canon 21.

66.　See ABA Canon 15.

67.　See ABA Canons 5 and 15; cf. ABA Canons 4 and 32.

(3) Prejudice or damage his client during the course of the professional relationship [68] except as required under DR 7–102(B).

(B) In his representation of a client, a lawyer may:

(1) Where permissible, exercise his professional judgment to waive or fail to assert a right or position of his client.

(2) Refuse to aid or participate in conduct that he believes to be unlawful, even though there is some support for an argument that the conduct is legal.

DR 7–102 Representing a Client Within the Bounds of the Law.

(A) In his representation of a client, a lawyer shall not:

(1) File a suit, assert a position, conduct a defense, delay a trial, or take other action on behalf of his client when he knows or when it is obvious that such action would serve merely to harass or maliciously injure another.[69]

(2) Knowingly advance a claim or defense that is unwarranted under existing law, except that he may advance such claim or defense it if can be supported by good faith argument for an extension, modification, or reversal of existing law.

(3) Conceal or knowingly fail to disclose that which he is required by law to reveal.

(4) Knowingly use perjured testimony or false evidence.[70]

(5) Knowingly make a false statement of law or fact.

(6) Participate in the creation or preservation of evidence when he knows or it is obvious that the evidence is false.

(7) Counsel or assist his client in conduct that the lawyer knows to be illegal or fraudulent.

(8) Knowingly engage in other illegal conduct or conduct contrary to a Disciplinary Rule.

(B) A lawyer who receives information clearly establishing that:

(1) His client has, in the course of the representation, perpetrated a fraud upon a person or tribunal shall promptly call upon his client to rectify the same, and if his client refuses or is unable to do so, he shall reveal the fraud to the affected person or tribunal, except when the information is protected as a privileged communication.[71]

68. Cf. ABA Canon 24.

69. See ABA Canon 30.

70. Cf. ABA Canons 22 and 29.

71. See ABA Canon 41; cf. Hinds v. State Bar, 19 Cal.2d 87, 92–93, 119 P.2d 134, 137 (1941); but see *ABA Opinion* 287 (1953) and Texas Canon 38. Also see Code of Professional Responsibility. DR 4–101(C)(2).

(2) **A person other than his client has perpetrated a fraud upon a tribunal shall promptly reveal the fraud to the tribunal.**[72]

As amended in 1974.

DR 7-103 Performing the Duty of Public Prosecutor or Other Government Lawyer.[73]

(A) **A public prosecutor or other government lawyer shall not institute or cause to be instituted criminal charges when he knows or it is obvious that the charges are not supported by probable cause.**

(B) **A public prosecutor or other government lawyer in criminal litigation shall make timely disclosure to counsel for the defendant, or to the defendant if he has no counsel, of the existence of evidence, known to the prosecutor or other government lawyer, that tends to negate the guilt of the accused, mitigate the degree of the offense, or reduce the punishment.**

DR 7-104 Communicating With One of Adverse Interest.[74]

(A) **During the course of his representation of a client a lawyer shall not:**

(1) **Communicate or cause another to communicate on the subject of the representation with a party he knows to be represented by a lawyer in that matter unless he has the prior consent of the lawyer representing such other party[75] or is authorized by law to do so.**

(2) **Give advice to a person who is not represented by a lawyer, other than the advice to secure counsel,[76] if the interests of such person are or have a reasonable possibility of being in conflict with the interests of his client.[77]**

---

72. See Precision Inst. Mfg. Co. v. Automotive M.M. Co., 324 U.S. 806, 89 L.Ed. 1381, 65 S.Ct. 993 (1945).

73. Cf. ABA Canon 5.

74. *"Rule 12. ... A member of the State Bar shall not communicate with a party represented by counsel upon a subject of controversy, in the absence and without the consent of such counsel. This rule shall not apply to communications with a public officer, board, committee or body."* Cal. Business and Professions Code § 6076 (West 1962).

75. See ABA Canon 9; cf. *ABA Opinions* 124 (1934), 108 (1934), 95 (1933), and 75 (1932); also see In re Schwabe, 242 Or. 169, 174–75, 408 P.2d 922, 924 (1965).

"It is clear from the earlier opinions of this committee that *Canon 9* is to be construed literally and does not allow a communication with an opposing party, without the consent of his counsel, though the purpose merely be to investigate the facts. *Opinions 117, 55, 66,*" ABA Opinion 187 (1938).

76. Cf. *ABA Opinion* 102 (1933).

77. Cf. ABA Canon 9 and *ABA Opinion* 58 (1931).

DR 7-105 Threatening Criminal Prosecution.

(A) A lawyer shall not present, participate in presenting, or threaten to present criminal charges solely to obtain an advantage in a civil matter.

DR 7-106 Trial Conduct.

(A) A lawyer shall not disregard or advise his client to disregard a standing rule of a tribunal or a ruling of a tribunal made in the course of a proceeding, but he may take appropriate steps in good faith to test the validity of such rule or ruling.

(B) In presenting a matter to a tribunal, a lawyer shall disclose:[78]

(1) Legal authority in the controlling jurisdiction known to him to be directly adverse to the position of his client and which is not disclosed by opposing counsel.[79]

(2) Unless privileged or irrelevant, the identities of the clients he represents and of the persons who employed him.[80]

(C) In appearing in his professional capacity before a tribunal, a lawyer shall not:

78. Cf. Note, 38 Texas L.Rev. 107, 108–09 (1959).

79. "In the brief summary in the 1947 edition of the Committee's decisions (p. 17), *Opinion 146* was thus summarized: *Opinion 146*—A lawyer should disclose to the court a decision directly adverse to his client's case that is unknown to his adversary.

. . .

"We would not confine the Opinion to 'controlling authorities'—i.e., those decisive of the pending case—but, in accordance with the tests hereafter suggested, would apply it to a decision directly adverse to any proposition of law on which the lawyer expressly relies, which would reasonably be considered important by the judge sitting on the case.

* * *

". . . The test in every case should be: Is the decision which opposing counsel has overlooked one which the court should clearly consider in deciding the case? Would a reasonable judge properly feel that a lawyer who advanced, as the law, a proposition adverse to the undisclosed decision, was lacking in candor and fairness to him? Might the judge consider himself misled by an implied representation that the lawyer knew of no adverse authority?" *ABA Opinion* 280 (1949).

80. "The authorities are substantially uniform against any privilege as applied to the fact of retainer or identity of the client. The privilege is limited to confidential communications, and a retainer is not a confidential communication, although it cannot come into existence without some communication between the attorney and the—at that stage prospective—client." United States v. Pape, 144 F.2d 778, 782 (2d Cir. 1944), cert. denied, 323 U.S. 752 89 L.Ed.2d 602, 65 S.Ct. 86 (1944).

"To be sure, there may be circumstances under which the identification of a client may amount to the prejudicial disclosure of a confidential communication, as where the substance of a disclosure has already been revealed but not its source." Colton v. United States, 306 F.2d 633, 637 (2d Cir. 1962).

(1) State or allude to any matter that he has no reasonable basis to believe is relevant to the case or that will not be supported by admissible evidence.[81]

(2) Ask any question that he has no reasonable basis to believe is relevant to the case and that is intended to degrade a witness or other person.[82]

(3) Assert his personal knowledge of the facts in issue, except when testifying as a witness.

(4) Assert his personal opinion as to the justness of a cause, as to the credibility of a witness, as to the culpability of a civil litigant, or as to the guilt or innocence of an accused;[83] but he may argue, on his analysis of the evidence, for any position or conclusion with respect to the matters stated herein.

(5) Fail to comply with known local customs of courtesy or practice of the bar or a particular tribunal without giving to opposing counsel timely notice of his intent not to comply.[84]

(6) Engage in undignified or discourteous conduct which is degrading to a tribunal.

(7) Intentionally or habitually violate any established rule of procedure or of evidence.

---

81. See ABA Canon 22; cf. ABA Canon 17.

"The rule allowing counsel when addressing the jury the widest latitude in discussing the evidence and presenting the client's theories falls far short of authorizing the statement by counsel of matter not in evidence, or indulging in argument founded on no proof, or demanding verdicts for purposes other than the just settlement of the matters at issue between the litigants, or appealing to prejudice or passion. The rule confining counsel to legitimate argument is not based on etiquette, but on justice. Its violation is not merely an overstepping of the bounds of propriety, but a violation of a party's rights. The jurors must determine the issues upon the evidence. Counsel's address should help them do this, not tend to lead them astray." Cherry Creek Nat. Bank v. Fidelity & Cas. Co., 207 App.Div. 787, 790–91, 202 N.Y.S. 611, 614 (1924).

82. Cf. ABA Canon 18.

§ 6068. ... It is the duty of an attorney:

* * *

"(f) To abstain from all offensive personality, and to advance no fact prejudicial to the honor or reputation of a party or witness, unless required by the justice of the cause with which he is charged." Cal.Business and Professions Code § 6068 (West 1962).

83. "The record in the case at bar was silent concerning the qualities and character of the deceased. It is especially improper, in addressing the jury in a murder case, for the prosecuting attorney to make reference to his knowledge of the good qualities of the deceased where there is no evidence in the record bearing upon his character.... A prosecutor should never inject into his argument evidence not introduced at the trial." People v. Dukes, 12 Ill.2d 334, 341, 146 N.E.2d 14, 17–18 (1957).

84. "A lawyer should not ignore known customs or practice of the Bar or of a particular Court, even when the law permits, without giving timely notice to the opposing counsel." ABA Canon 25.

DR 7-107 Trial Publicity.[85]

(A) A lawyer participating in or associated with the investigation of a criminal matter shall not make or participate in making an extrajudicial statement that a reasonable person would expect to be disseminated by means of public communication and that does more than state without elaboration:

(1) Information contained in a public record.

(2) That the investigation is in progress.

(3) The general scope of the investigation including a description of the offense and, if permitted by law, the identity of the victim.

(4) A request for assistance in apprehending a suspect or assistance in other matters and the information necessary thereto.

(5) A warning to the public of any dangers.

(B) A lawyer or law firm associated with the prosecution or defense of a criminal matter shall not, from the time of the filing of a complaint, information, or indictment, the issuance of an arrest warrant, or arrest until the commencement of the trial or disposition without trial, make or participate in making an extrajudicial statement that a reasonable person would expect to be disseminated by means of public communication and that relates to:

85. The provisions of Sections (A), (B), (C), and (D) of this Disciplinary Rule incorporate the fair trial-free press standards which apply to lawyers as adopted by the ABA House of Delegates, Feb. 19, 1968, upon the recommendation of the Fair Trial and Free Press Advisory Committee of the ABA Special Committee on Minimum Standards for the Administration of Criminal Justice.

Cf. ABA Canon 20; see generally ABA Advisory Committee on Fair Trial and Free Press, Standards Relating to Fair Trial and Free Press (1966).

"From the cases coming here we note that unfair and prejudicial news comment on pending trials has become increasingly prevalent. Due process requires that the accused receive a trial by an impartial jury free from outside influences. Given the pervasiveness of modern communications and the difficulty of effacing prejudicial publicity from the minds of the jurors, the trial courts must take strong measures to ensure that the balance is never weighed against the accused. And appellate tribunals have the duty to make an independent evaluation of the circumstances. Of course, there is nothing that prescribes the press from reporting events that transpire in the courtroom. But where there is a reasonable likelihood that prejudicial news prior to trial will prevent a fair trial, the judge should continue the case until the threat abates, or transfer it to another county not so permeated with publicity.... The courts must take such steps by rule and regulation that will protect their processes from prejudicial outside interferences. Neither prosecutors, counsel for defense, the accused, witnesses, court staff nor enforcement officers coming under the jurisdiction of the court should be permitted to frustrate its function. Collaboration between counsel and the press as to information affecting the fairness of a criminal trial is not only subject to regulation, but is highly censurable and worthy of disciplinary measures." Sheppard v. Maxwell, 384 U.S. 333, 362–63, 16 L.Ed.2d 600, 620, 86 S.Ct. 1507, 1522 (1966).

    (1) The character, reputation, or prior criminal record (including arrests, indictments, or other charges of crime) of the accused.

    (2) The possibility of a plea of guilty to the offense charged or to a lesser offense.

    (3) The existence or contents of any confession, admission, or statement given by the accused or his refusal or failure to make a statement.

    (4) The performance or results of any examinations or tests or the refusal or failure of the accused to submit to examinations or tests.

    (5) The identity, testimony, or credibility of a prospective witness.

    (6) Any opinion as to the guilt or innocence of the accused, the evidence, or the merits of the case.

(C) DR 7-107(B) does not preclude a lawyer during such period from announcing:

    (1) The name, age, residence, occupation, and family status of the accused.

    (2) If the accused has not been apprehended, any information necessary to aid in his apprehension or to warn the public of any dangers he may present.

    (3) A request for assistance in obtaining evidence.

    (4) The identity of the victim of the crime.

    (5) The fact, time, and place of arrest, resistance, pursuit, and use of weapons.

    (6) The identity of investigating and arresting officers or agencies and the length of the investigation.

    (7) At the time of seizure, a description of the physical evidence seized, other than a confession, admission, or statement.

    (8) The nature, substance, or text of the charge.

    (9) Quotations from or references to public records of the court in the case.

    (10) The scheduling or result of any step in the judicial proceedings.

    (11) That the accused denies the charges made against him.

(D) During the selection of a jury or the trial of a criminal matter, a lawyer or law firm associated with the prosecution or defense of a criminal matter shall not make or participate in making an extra-judicial statement that a reasonable person would expect to be disseminated by means of public communication and that relates to the trial, parties, or issues in the trial or other matters that are reasonably likely to interfere with a fair trial, except that he may quote from or refer without comment to public records of the court in the case.

(E) After the completion of a trial or disposition without trial of a criminal matter and prior to the imposition of sentence, a lawyer or law firm associated with the prosecution or defense shall not make or participate in making an extra-judicial statement that a reasonable person would expect to be disseminated by public communication and that is reasonably likely to affect the imposition of sentence.

(F) The foregoing provisions of DR 7-107 also apply to professional disciplinary proceedings and juvenile disciplinary proceedings when pertinent and consistent with other law applicable to such proceedings.

(G) A lawyer or law firm associated with a civil action shall not during its investigation or litigation make or participate in making an extra-judicial statement, other than a quotation from or reference to public records, that a reasonable person would expect to be disseminated by means of public communication and that relates to:

(1) Evidence regarding the occurrence or transaction involved.

(2) The character, credibility, or criminal record of a party, witness, or prospective witness.

(3) The performance or results of any examinations or tests or the refusal or failure of a party to submit to such.

(4) His opinion as to the merits of the claims or defenses of a party, except as required by law or administrative rule.

(5) Any other matter reasonably likely to interfere with a fair trial of the action.

(H) During the pendency of an administrative proceeding, a lawyer or law firm associated therewith shall not make or participate in making a statement, other than a quotation from or reference to public records, that a reasonable person would expect to be disseminated by means of public communication if it is made outside the official course of the proceeding and relates to:

(1) Evidence regarding the occurrence or transaction involved.

(2) The character, credibility, or criminal record of a party, witness, or prospective witness.

(3) Physical evidence or the performance or results of any examinations or tests or the refusal or failure of a party to submit to such.

(4) His opinion as to the merits of the claims, defenses, or positions of an interested person.

(5) Any other matter reasonably likely to interfere with a fair hearing.

(I) The foregoing provisions of DR 7-107 do not preclude a lawyer from replying to charges of misconduct publicly made against him or from participating in the proceedings of legislative, administrative, or other investigative bodies.

471

(J) A lawyer shall exercise reasonable care to prevent his employees and associates from making an extra-judicial statement that he would be prohibited from making under DR 7–107.

DR 7–108   Communication With or Investigation of Jurors.

(A) Before the trial of a case a lawyer connected therewith shall not communicate with or cause another to communicate with anyone he knows to be a member of the venire from which the jury will be selected for the trial of the case.

(B) During the trial of a case:

    (1) A lawyer connected therewith shall not communicate with or cause another to communicate with any member of the jury.[86]

    (2) A lawyer who is not connected therewith shall not communicate with or cause another to communicate with a juror concerning the case.

(C) DR 7–108(A) and (B) do not prohibit a lawyer from communicating with veniremen or jurors in the course of official proceedings.

(D) After discharge of the jury from further consideration of a case with which the lawyer was connected, the lawyer shall not ask questions of or make comments to a member of that jury that are calculated merely to harass or embarrass the juror or to influence his actions in future jury service.[87]

(E) A lawyer shall not conduct or cause, by financial support or otherwise, another to conduct a vexatious or harassing investigation of either a venireman or a juror.

(F) All restrictions imposed by DR 7–108 upon a lawyer also apply to communications with or investigations of members of a family of a venireman or a juror.

(G) A lawyer shall reveal promptly to the court improper conduct by a venireman or a juror, or by another toward a venireman or a juror or a member of his family, of which the lawyer has knowledge.

DR 7–109   Contact With Witnesses.

(A) A lawyer shall not suppress any evidence that he or his client has a legal obligation to reveal or produce.[88]

(B) A lawyer shall not advise or cause a person to secrete himself or to leave the jurisdiction of a tribunal for the purpose of making him unavailable as a witness therein.[89]

---

86. See ABA Canon 23.

87. "[I]t would be unethical for a lawyer to harass, entice, induce or exert influence on a juror to obtain his testimony." *ABA Opinion* 319 (1968).

88. See ABA Canon 5.

89. Cf. ABA Canon 5.

(C) A lawyer shall not pay, offer to pay, or acquiesce in the payment of compensation to a witness contingent upon the content of his testimony or the outcome of the case.[90] But a lawyer may advance, guarantee, or acquiesce in the payment of:

(1) Expenses reasonably incurred by a witness in attending or testifying.

(2) Reasonable compensation to a witness for his loss of time in attending or testifying.

(3) A reasonable fee for the professional services of an expert witness.

DR 7–110 Contact With Officials.[91]

(A) A lawyer shall not give or lend any thing of value to a judge, official, or employee of a tribunal, except as permitted by Section C(4) of Canon 5 of the Code of Judicial Conduct, but a lawyer may make a contribution to the campaign fund of a candidate for judicial office in conformity with Section B(2) under Canon 7 of the Code of Judicial Conduct.

(B) In an adversary proceeding, a lawyer shall not communicate, or cause another to communicate, as to the merits of the cause with a judge or an official before whom the proceeding is pending, except:

(1) In the course of official proceedings in the cause.

(2) In writing if he promptly delivers a copy of the writing to opposing counsel or to the adverse party if he is not represented by a lawyer.

(3) Orally upon adequate notice to opposing counsel or to the adverse party if he is not represented by a lawyer.

(4) As otherwise authorized by law, or by Section A(4) under Canon 3 of the Code of Judicial Conduct.[92]

"*Rule 15.* . . . A member of the State Bar shall not advise a person, whose testimony could establish or tend to establish a material fact, to avoid service of process, or secrete himself, or otherwise to make his testimony unavailable." Cal.Business and Professions Code § 6076 (West 1962).

90. See In re O'Keefe, 49 Mont. 369, 142 P. 638 (1914).

91. Cf. ABA Canon 3.

92. "*Rule 16.* . . . A member of the State Bar shall not, in the absence of opposing counsel, communicate with or argue to a judge or judicial officer except in open court upon the merits of a contested matter pending before such judge or judicial officer; nor shall he, without furnishing opposing counsel with a copy thereof, address a written communication to a judge or judicial officer concerning the merits of a con-

As amended in 1974.

CANON 8

A Lawyer Should Assist in Improving the Legal System

ETHICAL CONSIDERATIONS

EC 8–1 Changes in human affairs and imperfections in human institutions make necessary constant efforts to maintain and improve our legal system.[1] This system should function in a manner that commands public respect and fosters the use of legal remedies to achieve redress of grievances. By reason of education and experience, lawyers are especially qualified to recognize deficiencies in the legal system and to initiate corrective measures therein. Thus they should participate in proposing and supporting legislation and programs to improve the system,[2] without regard to the general interests or desires of clients or former clients.[3]

EC 8–2 Rules of law are deficient if they are not just, understandable, and responsive to the needs of society. If a lawyer believes that the existence or absence of a rule of law, substantive or procedural, causes or contributes to an unjust result, he should endeavor by lawful means to obtain appropriate change in the law. He should encourage the simplifi-

---

tested matter pending before such judge or judicial officer. This rule shall not apply to ex parte matters." Cal.Business and Professions Code § 6076 (West 1962).

1. ". . . [Another] task of the great lawyer is to do his part individually and as a member of the organized bar to improve his profession, the courts, and the law. As President Theodore Roosevelt aptly put it, 'Every man owes some of his time to the upbuilding of the profession to which he belongs.' Indeed, this obligation is one of the great things which distinguishes a profession from a business. The soundness and the necessity of President Roosevelt's admonition insofar as it relates to the legal profession cannot be doubted. The advances in natural science and technology are so startling and the velocity of change in business and in social life is so great that the law along with the other social sciences, and even human life itself, is in grave danger of being extinguished by new gods of its own invention if it does not awake from its lethargy." Vanderbilt, *The Five Functions of the Lawyer: Service to Clients and the Public*, 40 A.B.A.J. 31, 31–32 (1954).

2. See ABA Cannon 29; Cf. Cheatham, *The Lawyer's Role and Surroundings*, 25 Rocky Mt.L.Rev. 405, 406–07 (1953).

"The lawyer tempted by repose should recall the heavy costs paid by his profession when needed legal reform has to be accomplished through the initiative of public-spirited laymen. Where change must be thrust from without upon an unwilling Bar, the public's least flattering picture of the lawyer seems confirmed. The lawyer concerned for the standing of his profession will, therefore, interest himself actively in the improvement of the law. In doing so he will not only help to maintain confidence in the Bar, but will have the satisfaction of meeting a responsibility inhering in the nature of his calling." *Professional Responsibility: Report of the Joint Conference*, 44 A.B.A.J. 1159, 1217 (1958).

3. See Stayton, *Cum Honore Officium*, 19 Tex.B.J. 765, 766 (1956); *Professional Responsibility: Report of the Joint Conference*, 44 A.B.A.J. 1159, 1162 (1958); and Paul, *The Lawyer as a Tax Adviser*, 25 Rocky Mt.L.Rev. 412, 433–34 (1953).

cation of laws and the repeal or amendment of laws that are outmoded.[4] Likewise, legal procedures should be improved whenever experience indicates a change is needed.

EC 8–3 The fair administration of justice requires the availability of competent lawyers. Members of the public should be educated to recognize the existence of legal problems and the resultant need for legal services, and should be provided methods for intelligent selection of counsel. Those persons unable to pay for legal services should be provided needed services. Clients and lawyers should not be penalized by undue geographical restraints upon representation in legal matters, and the bar should address itself to improvements in licensing, reciprocity, and admission procedures consistent with the needs of modern commerce.

EC 8–4 Whenever a lawyer seeks legislative or administrative changes, he should identify the capacity in which he appears, whether on behalf of himself, a client, or the public.[5] A lawyer may advocate such changes on behalf of a client even though he does not agree with them. But when a lawyer purports to act on behalf of the public, he should espouse only those changes which he conscientiously believes to be in the public interest.

EC 8–5 Fraudulent, deceptive, or otherwise illegal conduct by a participant in a proceeding before a tribunal or legislative body is inconsistent with fair administration of justice, and it should never be participated in or condoned by lawyers. Unless constrained by his obligation to preserve the confidences and secrets of his client, a lawyer should reveal to appropriate authorities any knowledge he may have of such improper conduct.

EC 8–6 Judges and administrative officials having adjudicatory powers ought to be persons of integrity, competence, and suitable temperament. Generally, lawyers are qualified, by personal observation or investigation, to evaluate the qualifications of persons seeking or being considered for such public offices, and for this reason they have a special responsibility to aid in the selection of only those who are qualified.[6] It is the

---

4. "There are few great figures in the history of the Bar who have not concerned themselves with the reform and improvement of the law. The special obligation of the profession with respect to legal reform rests on considerations too obvious to require enumeration. Certainly it is the lawyer who has both the best chance to know when the law is working badly and the special competence to put it in order." *Professional Responsibility: Report of the Joint Conference,* 44 A.B.A.J. 1159, 1217 (1958).

5. "*Rule 14.* . . . A member of the State Bar shall not communicate with, or appear before, a public officer, board, committee or body, in his professional capacity, without first disclosing that he is an attorney representing interests that may be affected by action of such officer, board, committee or body." Cal.Business and Professions Code § 6076 (West 1962).

6. See ABA Canon 2.

"Lawyers are better able than laymen to appraise accurately the qualifications of candidates for judicial office. It is proper

duty of lawyers to endeavor to prevent political considerations from outweighing judicial fitness in the selection of judges. Lawyers should protest earnestly against the appointment or election of those who are unsuited for the bench and should strive to have elected [7] or appointed thereto only those who are willing to forego pursuits, whether of a business, political, or other nature, that may interfere with the free and fair consideration of questions presented for adjudication. Adjudicatory officials, not being wholly free to defend themselves, are entitled to receive the support of the bar against unjust criticism.[8] While a lawyer as a citizen has a right to criticize such officials publicly,[9] he should be certain of the merit of his complaint, use appropriate language, and avoid petty criticisms, for unrestrained and intemperate statements tend to lessen public confidence in our legal system.[10] Criticisms motivated by reasons other than a desire to improve the legal system are not justified.

EC 8–7 Since lawyers are a vital part of the legal system, they should be persons of integrity, of professional skill, and of dedication to the improvement of the system. Thus a lawyer should aid in establishing, as

that they should make that appraisal known to the voters in a proper and dignified manner. A lawyer may with propriety endorse a candidate for judicial office and seek like endorsement from other lawyers. But the lawyer who endorses a judicial candidate or seeks that endorsement from other lawyers should be actuated by a sincere belief in the superior qualifications of the candidate for judicial service and not by personal or selfish motives; and a lawyer should not use or attempt to use the power or prestige of the judicial office to secure such endorsement. On the other hand, the lawyer whose endorsement is sought, if he believes the candidate lacks the essential qualifications for the office or believes the opposing candidate is better qualified, should have the courage and moral stamina to refuse the request for endorsement." *ABA Opinion* 189 (1938).

7. "[W]e are of the opinion that, whenever a candidate for judicial office merits the endorsement and support of lawyers, the lawyers may make financial contributions toward the campaign if its cost, when reasonably conducted, exceeds that which the candidate would be expected to bear personally." *ABA Opinion* 226 (1941).

8. See ABA Canon 1.

9. "Citizens have a right under our constitutional system to criticize governmental officials and agencies. Courts are not, and should not be, immune to such criticism." Konigsberg v. State Bar of California, 353 U.S. 252, 269 (1957).

10. "[E]very lawyer, worthy of respect, realizes that public confidence in our courts is the cornerstone of our governmental structure, and will refrain from unjustified attack on the character of the judges, while recognizing the duty to denounce and expose a corrupt or dishonest judge." Kentucky State Bar Ass'n v. Lewis, 282 S.W.2d 321, 326 (Ky.1955).

"We should be the last to deny that Mr. Meeker has the right to uphold the honor of the profession and to expose without fear or favor corrupt or dishonest conduct in the profession, whether the conduct be that of a judge or not.... However, this Canon [29] does not permit one to make charges which are false and untrue and unfounded in fact. When one's fancy leads him to make false charges, attacking the character and integrity of others, he does so at his peril. He should not do so without adequate proof of his charges and he is certainly not authorized to make careless, untruthful and vile charges against his professional brethren." In re Meeker, 76 N.M. 354, 364–65, 414 P.2d 862, 869 (1966), appeal dismissed, 385 U.S. 449, 17 L.Ed.2d 510, 87 S.Ct. 613 (1967).

well as enforcing, standards of conduct adequate to protect the public by insuring that those who practice law are qualified to do so.

EC 8–8 Lawyers often serve as legislators or as holders of other public offices. This is highly desirable, as lawyers are uniquely qualified to make significant contributions to the improvement of the legal system. A lawyer who is a public officer, whether full or part-time, should not engage in activities in which his personal or professional interests are or foreseeably may be in conflict with his official duties.[11]

EC 8–9 The advancement of our legal system is of vital importance in maintaining the rule of law and in facilitating orderly changes; therefore, lawyers should encourage, and should aid in making, needed changes and improvements.

DISCIPLINARY RULES

DR 8–101 Action as a Public Official.

(A) A lawyer who holds public office shall not:

    (1) Use his public position to obtain, or attempt to obtain, a special advantage in legislative matters for himself or for a client under circumstances where he knows or it is obvious that such action is not in the public interest.

    (2) Use his public position to influence, or attempt to influence, a tribunal to act in favor of himself or of a client.

    (3) Accept any thing of value from any person when the lawyer knows or it is obvious that the offer is for the purpose of influencing his action as a public official.

---

11. "*Opinions 16, 30, 34, 77, 118* and *134* relate to *Canon 6,* and pass on questions concerning the propriety of the conduct of an attorney who is a public officer, in representing private interests adverse to those of the public body which he represents. The principle applied in those opinions is that an attorney holding public office should avoid all conduct which might lead the layman to conclude that the attorney is utilizing his public position to further his professional success or personal interests." *ABA Opinion* 192 (1939).

"The next question is whether a lawyer-member of a legislative body may appear as counsel or co-counsel at hearings before a zoning board of appeals, or similar tribunal, created by the legislative group of which he is a member. We are of the opinion that he may practice before fact-finding officers, hearing bodies and commissioners, since under our views he may appear as counsel in the courts where his municipality is a party. Decisions made at such hearings are usually subject to administrative review by the courts upon the record there made. It would be inconsistent to say that a lawyer-member of a legislative body could not participate in a hearing at which the record is made, but could appear thereafter when the cause is heard by the courts on administrative review. This is subject to an important exception. He should not appear as counsel where the matter is subject to review by the legislative body of which he is a member.... We are of the opinion that where a lawyer does so appear there would be conflict of interests between his duty as an advocate for his client on the one hand and the obligation to his governmental unit on the other." In re Becker, 16 Ill.2d 488, 494–95, 158 N.E.2d 753, 756–57 (1959).

Cf. *ABA Opinions* 186 (1938), 136 (1935), 118 (1934), and 77 (1932).

DR 8–102   Statements Concerning Judges and Other Adjudicatory Officers.[12]

(A) A lawyer shall not knowingly make false statements of fact concerning the qualifications of a candidate for election or appointment to a judicial office.

(B) A lawyer shall not knowingly make false accusations against a judge or other adjudicatory officer.

DR 8–103   Lawyer Candidate for Judicial Office.

(A) A lawyer who is a candidate for judicial office shall comply with the applicable provisions of Canon 7 of the Code of Judicial Conduct.

Added in 1974.

CANON 9

A Lawyer Should Avoid Even the Appearance of Professional Impropriety

ETHICAL CONSIDERATIONS

EC 9–1 Continuation of the American concept that we are to be governed by rules of law requires that the people have faith that justice can be obtained through our legal system.[1] A lawyer should promote public confidence in our system and in the legal profession.[2]

EC 9–2 Public confidence in law and lawyers may be eroded by irresponsible or improper conduct of a lawyer. On occasion, ethical conduct of a lawyer may appear to laymen to be unethical. In order to avoid misunderstandings and hence to maintain confidence, a lawyer should fully and promptly inform his client of material developments in the matters being handled for the client. While a lawyer should guard against otherwise proper conduct that has a tendency to diminish public confidence in the legal system or in the legal profession, his duty to clients or to the public should never be subordinate merely because the full discharge of his obligation may be misunderstood or may tend to

---

12. Cf. ABA Canons 1 and 2.

1. "Integrity is the very breath of justice. Confidence in our law, our courts, and in the administration of justice is our supreme interest. No practice must be permitted to prevail which invites towards the administration of justice a doubt or distrust of its integrity." Erwin M. Jennings Co. v. DiGenova, 107 Conn. 491, 499, 141 A. 866, 868 (1928).

2. "A lawyer should never be reluctant or too proud to answer unjustified criticism of his profession, of himself, or of his brother lawyer. He should guard the reputation of his profession and of his brothers as zealously as he guards his own." Rochelle and Payne, *The Struggle for Public Understanding*, 25 Texas B.J. 109, 162 (1962).

subject him or the legal profession to criticism. When explicit ethical guidance does not exist, a lawyer should determine his conduct by acting in a manner that promotes public confidence in the integrity and efficiency of the legal system and the legal profession.[3]

EC 9–3 After a lawyer leaves judicial office or other public employment, he should not accept employment in connection with any matter in which he had substantial responsibility prior to his leaving, since to accept employment would give the appearance of impropriety even if none exists.[4]

EC 9–4 Because the very essence of the legal system is to provide procedures by which matters can be presented in an impartial manner so that they may be decided solely upon the merits, any statement or suggestion by a lawyer that he can or would attempt to circumvent those procedures is detrimental to the legal system and tends to undermine public confidence in it.

EC 9–5 Separation of the funds of a client from those of his lawyer not only serves to protect the client but also avoids even the appearance of impropriety, and therefore commingling of such funds should be avoided.

EC 9–6 Every lawyer owes a solemn duty to uphold the integrity and honor of his profession; to encourage respect for the law and for the courts and the judges thereof; to observe the Code of Professional Responsibility; to act as a member of a learned profession, one dedicated to public service; to cooperate with his brother lawyers in supporting the organized bar through the devoting of his time, efforts, and financial support as his professional standing and ability reasonably permit; to conduct himself so as to reflect credit on the legal profession and to inspire the confidence, respect, and trust of his clients and of the public; and to strive to avoid not only professional impropriety but also the appearance of impropriety.[5]

3. See ABA Canon 29.

4. See ABA Canon 36.

5. "As said in Opinion 49 of the Committee on Professional Ethics and Grievances of the American Bar Association, page 134: 'An attorney should not only avoid impropriety but should avoid the appearance of impropriety.'" State ex rel. Nebraska State Bar Ass'n v. Richards, 165 Neb. 80, 93, 84 N.W.2d 136, 145 (1957).

"It would also be preferable that such contribution [to the campaign of a candidate for judicial office] be made to a campaign committee rather than to the candidate personally. In so doing, possible appearances of impropriety would be re-duced to a minimum." *ABA Opinion* 226 (1941).

"The lawyer assumes high duties, and has imposed upon him grave responsibilities. He may be the means of much good or much mischief. Interests of vast magnitude are entrusted to him; confidence is reposed in him; life, liberty, character and property should be protected by him. He should guard, with jealous watchfulness, his own reputation, as well as that of his profession." People ex rel. Cutler v. Ford, 54 Ill. 520, 522 (1870), and also quoted in State Board of Law Examiners v. Sheldon, 43 Wyo. 522, 526, 7 P.2d 226, 227 (1932).

See *ABA Opinion* 150 (1936).

EC 9–7 A lawyer has an obligation to the public to participate in collective efforts of the bar to reimburse persons who have lost money or property as a result of the misappropriation or defalcation of another lawyer, and contribution to a clients' security fund is an acceptable method of meeting this obligation.

DISCIPLINARY RULES

DR 9–101   Avoiding Even the Appearance of Impropriety.[6]

(A) **A lawyer shall not accept private employment in a matter upon the merits of which he has acted in a judicial capacity.[7]**

(B) **A lawyer shall not accept private employment in a matter in which he had substantial responsibility while he was a public employee.[8]**

(C) **A lawyer shall not state or imply that he is able to influence improperly or upon irrelevant grounds any tribunal, legislative body,[9] or public official.**

6. Cf. Code of Professional Responsibility, EC 5–6.

7. See *ABA* Canon 36.

"It is the duty of the judge to rule on questions of law and evidence in misdemeanor cases and examinations in felony cases. That duty calls for impartial and uninfluenced judgment, regardless of the effect on those immediately involved or others who may, directly or indirectly, be affected. Discharge of that duty might be greatly interfered with if the judge, in another capacity, were permitted to hold himself out to employment by those who are to be, or who may be, brought to trial in felony cases, even though he did not conduct the examination. His private interests as a lawyer in building up his clientele, his duty as such zealously to espouse the cause of his private clients and to defend against charges of crime brought by law-enforcement agencies of which he is a part, might prevent, or even destroy, that unbiased judicial judgment which is so essential in the administration of justice.

"In our opinion, acceptance of a judgeship with the duties of conducting misdemeanor trials, and examinations in felony cases to determine whether those accused should be bound over for trial in a higher court, ethically bars the judge from acting as attorney for the defendants upon such trial, whether they were examined by him or by some other judge. Such a practice would not only diminish public confidence in the administration of justice in both courts, but would produce serious conflict between the private interests of the judge as a lawyer, and of his clients, and his duties as a judge in adjudicating important phases of criminal processes in other cases. The public and private duties would be incompatible. The prestige of the judicial office would be diverted to private benefit, and the judicial office would be demeaned thereby." *ABA Opinion* 242 (1942).

"A lawyer, who has previously occupied a judicial position or acted in a judicial capacity, should refrain from accepting employment in any matter involving the same facts as were involved in any specific question which he acted upon in a judicial capacity and, for the same reasons, should also refrain from accepting any employment which might reasonably appear to involve the same facts." *ABA Opinion* 49 (1931).

See *ABA Opinion* 110 (1934).

8. See *ABA Opinions* 135 (1935) and 134 (1935); cf. ABA Canon 36 and *ABA Opinions* 39 (1931) and 26 (1930). But see *ABA Opinion* 37 (1931).

9. "[A statement by a governmental department or agency with regard to a lawyer resigning from its staff that includes a lau-

DR 9–102 Preserving Identity of Funds and Property of a Client.[10]

(A) All funds of clients paid to a lawyer or law firm, other than advances for costs and expenses, shall be deposited in one or more identifiable bank accounts maintained in the state in which the law office is situated and no funds belonging to the lawyer or law firm shall be deposited therein except as follows:

(1) Funds reasonably sufficient to pay bank charges may be deposited therein.

(2) Funds belonging in part to a client and in part presently or potentially to the lawyer or law firm must be deposited therein, but the portion belonging to the lawyer or law firm may be withdrawn when due unless the right of the lawyer or law firm to receive it is disputed by the client, in which event the disputed portion shall not be withdrawn until the dispute is finally resolved.

(B) A lawyer shall:

(1) Promptly notify a client of the receipt of his funds, securities, or other properties.

(2) Identify and label securities and properties of a client promptly upon receipt and place them in a safe deposit box or other place of safekeeping as soon as practicable.

(3) Maintain complete records of all funds, securities, and other properties of a client coming into the possession of the lawyer and render appropriate accounts to his client regarding them.

---

dation of his legal ability] carries implications, probably not founded in fact, that the lawyer's acquaintance and previous relations with the personnel of the administrative agencies of the government place him in an advantageous position in practicing before such agencies. So to imply would not only represent what probably is untrue, but would be highly reprehensible." *ABA Opinion* 184 (1938).

10. See ABA Canon 11.

"*Rule 9.* ... A member of the State Bar shall not commingle the money or other property of a client with his own; and he shall promptly report to the client the receipt by him of all money and other property belonging to such client. Unless the client otherwise directs in writing, he shall promptly deposit his client's funds in a bank or trust company ... in a bank account separate from his own account and clearly designated as 'Clients' Funds Account' or 'Trust Funds Account' or words of

similar import. Unless the client otherwise directs in writing, securities of a client in bearer form shall be kept by the attorney in a safe deposit box at a bank or trust company, ... which safe deposit box shall be clearly designated as 'Client's Account' or 'Trust Account' or words of similar import, and be separate from the attorney's own safe deposit box." Cal.Business and Professions Code § 6076 (West 1962).

"[C]ommingling is committed when a client's money is intermingled with that of his attorney and its separate identity lost so that it may be used for the attorney's personal expenses or subjected to claims of his creditors.... The rule against commingling was adopted to provide against the probability in some cases, the possibility in many cases, and the danger in all cases that such commingling will result in the loss of clients' money." Black v. State Bar, 57 Cal.2d 219, 225–26, 368 P.2d 118, 122, 18 Cal.Rptr. 518, 522 (1962).

(4) **Promptly pay or deliver to the client as requested by a client the funds, securities, or other properties in the possession of the lawyer which the client is entitled to receive.**

DEFINITIONS *

As used in the Disciplinary Rules of the Code of Professional Responsibility:

(1) "Differing interests" include every interest that will adversely affect either the judgment or the loyalty of a lawyer to a client, whether it be a conflicting, inconsistent, diverse, or other interest.

(2) "Law firm" includes a professional legal corporation.

(3) "Person" includes a corporation, an association, a trust, a partnership, and any other organization or legal entity.

(4) "Professional legal corporation" means a corporation, or an association treated as a corporation, authorized by law to practice law for profit.

(5) "State" includes the District of Columbia, Puerto Rico, and other federal territories and possessions.

(6) "Tribunal" includes all courts and all other adjudicatory bodies.

(7) "A Bar association" includes a bar association of specialists as referred to in DR 2–105(A)(1) or (3).

(8) "Qualified legal assistance organization" means an office or organization of one of the four types listed in DR 2–103(D)(1)–(4), inclusive that meets all the requirements thereof.

As amended in 1974.

* "Confidence" and "secret" are defined in DR 4–101(A).

INDEX TO ABA MODEL CODE

A

Acceptance of Employment. *See* Employment, acceptance of.

Acquiring interest in litigation. *See* Adverse effect on professional judgment, interests of lawyer.

Address change, notification of, DR 2–102 (A) (2)

Administrative agencies and tribunals,
    former employee, rejection of employment by, DR 9–101 (B)
    improper influences on, EC 5–13, EC 5–21, EC 5–24, DR 5–107 (A), (B), EC 8–5, EC 8–6, DR 8–101 (A)
    representation of client, generally, Canon 7, EC 7–15, EC 7–16, EC 8–4, EC 8–8, DR 8–101 (A)

Admiralty practitioners, EC 2–14

Admission to practice,
    duty of lawyers as to applicants, EC 1–3, DR 1–101 (B)
    requirements for, EC 1–2, EC 1–3, EC 1–6, DR 1–101 (A)

Advancing funds to clients, EC 5–8, DR 5–103 (B)
    court costs, EC 5–8, DR 5–103 (B)
    investigation expenses, EC 5–8, DR 5–103 (B)
    litigation expenses, EC 5–7, EC 5–8, DR 5–103 (B)
    medical examination, EC 5–8, DR 5–103 (B)
    personal expenses, EC 5–8, DR 5–103 (B)

Adversary system, duty of lawyer to, Canon 7

Adverse effect on professional judgment of lawyer, Canon 5
    desires of third persons, EC 5–21 – EC 5–24, DR 5–107
    interests of lawyer, EC 5–2 – EC 5–13, DR 5–101, DR 5–104
    interests of other clients, EC 5–14 – EC 5–20, DR 5–105, DR 5–106

Adverse legal authority, duty to reveal, EC 7–23, DR 7–106 (B) (1)

Advertising,
    See also Name, use of. EC 2–6 – EC 2–15, DR 2–101, DR 2–102
    announcement of change of association, DR 2–102 (A) (2)

Advertising—Cont'd
    announcement of change of firm name, DR 2–102 (A) (2)
    announcement of change of office address, DR 2–102 (A) (2)
    announcement of establishment of law office, DR 2–102 (A) (2)
    announcement of office opening, DR 2–102 (A) (2)
    books written by lawyer, DR 2–101 (H) (5)
    building directory, DR 2–102 (A) (3)
    cards, professional announcement, DR 2–102 (A) (1), (2)
    commercial publicity, EC 2–8 – EC 2–10, DR 2–101
    compensation for, EC 2–8, DR 2–101 (B), DR 2–101 (I)
    jurisdictional limitations of members of firm, required, notice of, DR 2–102 (D)
    legal documents, DR 2–101 (H) (4)
    letterheads,
        of clients, DR 2–102 (A) (4)
        of law firm, DR 2–102 (A) (4), DR 2–102 (B)
        of lawyer, DR 2–102 (A) (4), DR 2–102 (B)
    limited practice, EC 2–14, DR 2–101 (B) (2), DR 2–105
    magazine, DR 2–101 (B), DR 2–101 (I)
    name, *See* Name, use of newspaper, DR 2–101 (B), DR 2–101 (I)
    office, identification of, DR 2–101 (B) (1), DR 2–102 (A)
    office address change, DR 2–102 (A) (2)
    office building directory, DR 2–102 (A) (3)
    office establishment, DR 2–102 (A) (2)
    office sign, DR 2–102 (A) (3)
    political, DR 2–101 (H) (1)
    public notices, DR 2–101 (H) (2)
    radio, DR 2–101 (B), DR 2–101 (D), DR 2–101 (I)
    reasons for regulating, EC 2–6 – EC 2–10
    sign, DR 2–102 (A) (3)
    specialization, EC 2–14, DR 2–101 (B) (2), DR 2–105
    television, EC 2–8, DR 2–101 (B), (D)
    textbook, DR 2–101 (H) (5)
    treatises, DR 2–101 (H) (5)

Advice by lawyer to secure legal services, EC 24 – EC 2–5, DR 2–104
   client, former or regular, EC 2–4, DR 2–104 (A) (1)
   close friend, EC 2–4, DR 2–104 (A) (1)
   employment resulting from, EC 2–4, DR 2–104
   motivation, effect of, EC 2–4
   other laymen parties to class action, DR 2–104 (A) (5)
   relative, EC 2–4, DR 2–104 (A) (1)
   volunteered, EC 2–4, DR 2–104
   within permissible legal service programs, DR 2–104 (A) (3)
Advocacy, professional, Canon 7
Aiding unauthorized practice of law, Canon 3
Ambulance chasing. *See* Recommendation of professional employment.
Announcement card. *See* Advertising, cards, professional announcement.
Appearance of impropriety, avoiding, EC 5–6, Canon 9
Appearance of lawyer. *See* Administrative agencies, representation of client before; Courts, representation of client before; Legislature, representation of client before; Witness, lawyer acting as.
Applicant for bar admission. *See* Admission to practice.
Arbitrator, lawyer acting as, EC 5–20
Argument,
   before administrative agency, EC 7–15
   before jury, EC 7–24, EC 7–25, DR 7–106 (C)
   before legislature, EC 7–16
   before tribunal, EC 7–19 – EC 7–25, DR 7–102, DR 7–106
Associates of lawyer, duty to control, EC 1–4, DR 2–103, EC 3–8, EC 3–9, EC 4–2, DR 4–101 (D), DR 7–107
Association of counsel,
   See also Co-counsel; Division of legal fees.
   client's suggestion of, EC 5–10, EC 5–11
   lawyer's suggestion of, EC 5–10, EC 5–11, EC 6–3, DR 6–101 (1)
Assumed name. *See* Name, use of, assumed name.
Attempts to exert personal influence on tribunal, EC 7–24, EC 7–29 – EC 7–33, EC 7–36, DR 7–106 (C), DR 7–108, DR 7–110
Attorney-client privilege. *See also* Confidences of client; Secrets of client. EC 4–4, DR 4–101 (A), DR 7–102 (B) (1)
Attorney's lien. *See* Fee for legal services, collection of. Availability of counsel, EC 2–1, EC 2–7, EC 2–24 – EC 2–33

B

Bank accounts for clients' funds, EC 9–5, DR 9–102
Bank charges on clients' accounts, EC 9–5, DR 9–102
Bar applicant. *See* Admission to practice.
   bar examiners, assisting, EC 1–2
Bar associations,
   disciplinary authority, assisting, EC 1–4, DR 1–103
   educational activities, EC 6–2
   lawyer referral service, DR 2–103 (C) (1), DR 2–103 (D) (3)
   legal aid office, DR 2–103 (D) (1) (d)
Barratry. *See* Advice by lawyer to secure legal services; Recommendation of professional employment.
Bequest by client to lawyer, EC 5–5
Best efforts. *See* Zeal.
Bounds of law,
   difficulty of ascertaining, EC 7–2, EC 7–3, EC 7–4, EC 7–6
   duty to observe, EC 7–1, DR 7–102
   generally, Canon 7
Bribes. *See* Gifts to tribunal officer or employee by lawyer.
Building directory. *See* Advertising, building directory.
Business card. *See* Advertising, cards, professional.

C

Calling card. *See* Advertising, cards, professional.
Candidate. *See* Political activity.
Canons, purpose and function of, Preamble & Preliminary Statement
Cards. *See* Advertising, cards.
Change of association. *See* Advertising, announcement of change of association.
Change of firm name. *See* Advertising, announcement of change of firm name.
Change of office address. *See* Advertising, announcement of change of office address.
Character requirements, EC 1–3
Class action. *See* Advice by lawyer to secure legal services, parties to legal action.
Clients,
   See also Employment; Adverse effect on professional judgment of lawyer; Fee for legal services; Indigent parties, representation of; Unpopular party, representation of.
   appearance as witness for, EC 5–9, EC 5–10, DR 5–101 (B), DR 5–102
   attorney-client privilege, Canon 4

D

INDEX

Discretion of government lawyer, exercise of, EC 7–14

Discussion of pending litigation with news media. *See* Trial publicity.

Diverse interests. *See* Adverse effect on professional judgment of lawyer.

Division of legal fees,
consent of client, when required for, EC 2–22, DR 2–107 (A) (1)
reasonableness of total fee, requirement of, EC 2–22, DR 2–107 (A) (3)
with associated lawyer, EC 2–22, DR 2–107 (A)
with estate of deceased lawyer, EC 3–8, DR 3–102 (A) (2), (3)
with laymen, EC 3–8, DR 3–102 (A)

E

Education,
continuing legal education programs, EC 6–2
of laymen to recognize legal problems, EC 2–1 – EC 2–5, EC 8–1
of laymen to select lawyers, EC 2–6 – EC 2–15, EC 8–1
requirement of bar for applicant, EC 1–2

Elections. *See* Political activity.

Emotional instability. *See* Instability, mental or emotional.

Employees of lawyer,
delegation of tasks, EC 3–6
duty of lawyer to control, EC 4–2, EC 4–3, DR 4–101 (D)

Employment,
See also Advice by lawyer to secure legal services; Recommendation of professional employment.
acceptance of,
generally, EC 2–6 – EC 2–33
indigent client, on behalf of, EC 2–25
instances when improper, EC 2–3, EC 2–4, EC 2–30, DR 2–103, DR 2–104, Canon 5, EC 6–1, EC 6–3, DR 6–101 (A) (1), EC 9–3, DR 9–101 (A), (B)
public retirement from, EC 9–3, DR 9–101 (A), (B)
rejection of, EC 2–26 – EC 2–33, DR 2–103 (E), DR 2–104, DR 2–109, DR 2–110, EC 4–5, Canon 5, EC 6–1, EC 6–3, DR 6–101 (A), EC 9–3, DR 9–101 (A), (B)
unpopular cause, on behalf of, EC 2–27
unpopular client, on behalf of, EC 2–27

Employment—Cont'd
acceptance of—Cont'd
when able to render competent service, EC 2–30, EC 6–1, EC 6–3, DR 6–101 (A) (1)
contract of,
desirability of, EC 2–19
restrictive covenant in, DR 2–108
withdrawal from,
generally, EC 2–32, DR 2–110, Canon 5, EC 7–8
harm to client, avoidance of, EC 2–32, DR 2–110 (A) (2), Canon 5
mandatory withdrawal, EC 2–32, DR 2–110 (B), Canon 5
permissive withdrawal, DR 2–110 (C), Canon 5, EC 7–8
refund of unearned fee paid in advance, requirement of, EC 2–32, DR 2–110 (A) (3)
tribunal, consent to, EC 2–32, DR 2–110
when arbitrator or mediator, EC 5–20

Estate of deceased lawyer. *See* Division of legal fees, with estate of deceased lawyer.

Ethical considerations, purpose and function of, Preliminary Statement

Evidence, conduct regarding, EC 7–24, EC 7–25, DR 7–102 (A), (3) – (6)

Excessive fee. *See* Fee for legal services, amount of, excessive.

Expenses of client, advancing or guaranteeing payment of, EC 5–8, DR 5–103

F

Fee for legal services,
adequate fee, need for, EC 2–17
agreement as to, EC 2–19, DR 2–106 (A)
amount of,
excessive, clearly, DR 2–106
reasonableness, desirability of, EC 2–17, EC 2–18
collection of,
avoiding litigation with client, EC 2–23
client's secrets, use of in collecting or establishing, DR 4–101 (C) (4)
liens, use of, EC 5–7, DR 5–103 (A) (1)
contingent fee, EC 2–20, DR 2–106 (B) (8), DR 2–106 (C), EC 5–7, DR 5–103 (A) (2)
contract as to, desirability of written, EC 2–19
controversy over, avoiding, EC 2–23

487

Fee for legal services—Cont'd
determination of, factors to consider,
ability of lawyer, EC 2–18, DR 2–106
(B) (7)
amount involved, DR 2–106 (B) (4)
customary, DR 2–106 (B) (3)
effort required, DR 2–106 (B) (1)
employment, likelihood of preclusion
of other, DR 2–106 (B) (2)
experience of lawyer, EC 2–18, DR
2–106 (B) (7)
fee customarily charged in locality,
DR 2–106 (B) (3)
interests of client and lawyer, EC
2–17
labor required, DR 2–106 (B) (1)
nature of employment, EC 2–18
question involved, difficulty and novelty of, DR 2–106 (B) (1)
relationship with client, professional,
EC 2–17, DR 2–106 (B) (6)
reputation of lawyer, EC 2–18, DR
2–106 (7)
responsibility assumed by lawyer, EC
2–18
results obtained, EC 2–18, DR 2–106
(B) (4)
skill requisite to services, EC 2–18
time required, EC 2–18, DR 2–106
(B) (1)
type of fee, fixed or contingent, EC
2–18, DR 2–106 (B) (8)
division of, EC 2–22, DR 2–107, DR
3–102
establishment of fee, use of client's confidences and secrets, DR 4–101
(C) (4)
excessive fee, EC 2–17, DR 2–106 (A)
explanation of, EC 2–17, EC 2–18
illegal fee, prohibition against, DR 2–106
(A)
persons able to pay reasonable fee, EC
2–17, EC 2–18
persons only able to pay a partial fee,
EC 2–16
persons without means to pay a fee, EC
2–24, EC 2–25
reasonable fee, rational against overcharging, EC 2–17
refund of unearned portion to client, DR
2–110 (A) (3)
Felony. *See* Discipline of lawyer, grounds
for, illegal conduct.
Firm name. *See* Name, use of, firm name.
Framework of law. *See* Bounds of law.
Frivolous position, avoiding, EC 7–4, DR
7–102 (A) (1)
Funds of client, protection of, EC 9–5, DR
9–102
Future conduct of client, counseling as to.
See Clients, counseling.

G

"General counsel" designation, DR 2–102
(A) (4)
Gift to lawyer by client, EC 5–5
Gifts to tribunal officer or employee by lawyer, DR 7–110 (A)
Government legal assistance agencies,
working with, DR 2–103 (C) (2), DR
2–103 (D) (1) (C)
Grievance committee. *See* Bar associations, disciplinary authority, assisting.
Guaranteeing payment of client's cost and
expenses, EC 5–8, DR 5–103 (B)

H

Harassment, duty to avoid litigation involving, EC 2–30, DR 2–109 (A) (1), DR
7–102 (A) (1)
as limiting practice, EC 2–8, EC 2–14,
DR 2–101 (B) (2), DR 2–105
as partnership, EC 2–13, DR 2–102 (C)
as specialist, EC 2–8, EC 2–14, DR
2–101 (B) (2), DR 2–105

I

Identity of client, duty to reveal, EC 7–16,
EC 8–5
Illegal conduct, as cause for discipline, EC
1–5, DR 1–102 (A) (3), DR 7–102 (A)
(7)
Impartiality of tribunal, aiding in the, Canon 7
Improper influences,
gift or loan to judicial officer, EC 7–34,
DR 7–110 (A)
on judgment of lawyer. *See* Adverse
effect on professional judgment of
lawyer.
Improvement of legal system, EC 8–1, EC
8–2, EC 8–9
Incompetence, mental. *See* Instability,
mental or emotional; Mental competence of client.
Incompetence, professional. *See* Competence, professional.
Independent professional judgment, duty to
preserve, Canon 5
Indigent parties,
provision of legal services to, EC 2–24,
EC 2–25
representation of, EC 2–25
Instability, mental or emotional,
of bar applicant, EC 1–6
of lawyer, EC 1–6, DR 2–110 (B) (3), DR
2–110 (C) (4)
recognition of rehabilitation, EC 1–6

Rebate, propriety of accepting, EC 2–24, EC 2–25

Recognition of legal problems, aiding laymen in, EC 2–1, EC 2–5

Recommendation of bar applicant, duty of lawyer to satisfy himself that applicant is qualified, EC 1–3, DR 1–101 (B)

Recommendation of professional employment, EC 2–8, EC 2–15, DR 2–103

Records of funds, securities, and properties of clients, EC 9–5, DR 9–102 (B)

Referral service. *See* Lawyer referral services.

Refund of unearned fee when withdrawing, duty to give to client, EC 2–32, DR 2–110

Regulation of legal profession, Canons 3 and 8, EC 3–1, EC 3–3, EC 3–9, EC 8–7

Rehabilitation of bar applicant or lawyer, recognition of, EC 1–6

Representation of multiple clients. *See* Adverse effect on professional judgment of lawyer, interest of other clients.

Reputation of lawyer, EC 2–6, EC 2–7

Requests for recommendation for employment, EC 2–8, DR 2–103 (C)

Requirements for bar admission, EC 1–2, EC 1–6, DR 1–101 (B)

Respect for law, EC 1–5

Restrictive covenant, DR 2–108

Retention of employment. *See* Employment.

Retirement,
> *See also* Name, use of, retired partner.
>
> from judicial office, EC 9–3, DR 9–101 (A)
>
> from public employment, EC 9–3, DR 9–101 (B)
>
> plan for laymen employees, EC 3–8, DR 3–102 (3)

Revealing of confidences, EC 4–1, EC 4–2, EC 4–6, DR 4–101 (B) (1), (C), (D)

Revealing of secrets, EC 4–1, EC 4–2, EC 4–6, DR 4–101 (B) (1), (C), (D)

Revealing to tribunal jury misconduct, EC 7–32, DR 7–108 (G)

Runner, prohibition against use of, EC 2–8, DR 2–103 (B)

S

Sanction for violating disciplinary rules, Preliminary Statement

Secrets of client, Canon 4

Selection of judges, duty of lawyers, EC 8–6, DR 8–102 (A)

Selection of lawyer, EC 2–6, EC 2–7, EC 2–8, EC 2–9, EC 2–11, EC 2–14, EC 2–15, DR 2–101

Self-interest of lawyer. *See* Adverse effect on professional judgment of lawyer, interests of lawyer.

Self-representation, privilege of, EC 3–7

Settlement agreement, DR 5–106

Solicitation of business. *See* Advertising: Recommendation of professional employment.

Specialist, holding out as, EC 2–14, DR 2–105

Specialization,
> admiralty, EC 2–14
>
> holding out as having, EC 2–14, DR 2–105
>
> patents, EC 2–14, DR 2–105 (A) (1)
>
> trademark, EC 2–14, DR 2–105 (A) (1)

Speeches to lay groups, EC 2–2, EC 2–5

State of mind of client, effect of in advising him, EC 7–11, EC 7–12

State's attorney. *See* Prosecuting attorney.

"Stirring up litigation." *See* Advertising: Advice by lawyer to secure legal services; Recommendation of professional employment.

Stockholders of corporation, corporate counsel's allegiance to, EC 5–18

Suit to harass another, duty to avoid, EC 2–30, DR 2–109 (A) (1), EC 7–10, EC 7–14, DR 7–102 (A) (1)

Suit to maliciously harm another, duty to avoid, EC 2–30, DR 2–109 (A) (1), EC 7–10, EC 7–14, DR 7–102 (A) (1)

Suggested fee schedule. *See* Fees for legal services, determination of minimum fee schedule.

Suggestion of need for legal services. *See* Advice by lawyer to secure legal services.

Suppression of evidence, EC 7–27, DR 7–102 (A) (2), DR 7–103 (B), DR 7–106 (C) (7)

T

Technical and professional licenses, DR 2–101 (B) (12), DR 2–102 (E)

Termination of employment. *See* Confidences of client; Employment, withdrawal from.

Third persons, desires of. *See* Adverse effect on professional judgment of lawyer, desires of third persons.

Threatening criminal process, EC 7–21, DR 7–105 (A)

Trademark practitioner, EC 2–14, DR 2–105 (A) (1)

Trade name. *See* Name, use of, trade name.

AMERICAN BAR ASSOCIATION CANONS OF PROFESSIONAL ETHICS

As amended until 1969.

[The ABA adopted 32 Canons of Professional Ethics at its thirty-first annual meeting on August 27, 1908. Between 1908 and 1969, the ABA added Canons 33 through 47. Although the Canons were in effect for 61 years, the general aspirational approach of the Canons proved to be outmoded to regulate the conduct of lawyers in the 1950s and 1960s. The Canons were superseded in 1969 by the Model Code of Professional Responsibility. Ed.]

CANONS OF PROFESSIONAL ETHICS

Preamble.

In America, where the stability of Courts and of all departments of government rests upon the approval of the people, it is peculiarly essential that the system for establishing and dispensing Justice be developed to a high point of efficiency and so maintained that the public shall have absolute confidence in the integrity and impartiality of its administration. The future of the Republic, to a great extent, depends upon our maintenance of Justice pure and unsullied. It cannot be so maintained unless the conduct and the motives of the members of our profession are such as to merit the approval of all just men.

No code or set of rules can be framed, which will particularize all the duties of the lawyer in the varying phases of litigation or in all the relations of professional life. The following canons of ethics are adopted by the American Bar Association as a general guide, yet the enumeration of particular duties should not be construed as a denial of the existence of others equally imperative, though not specifically mentioned.

CANON 1

The Duty of the Lawyer to the Courts

It is the duty of the lawyer to maintain towards the Courts a respectful attitude, not for the sake of the temporary incumbent of the judicial office, but for the maintenance of its supreme importance. Judges, not being wholly free to defend themselves, are peculiarly entitled to receive the support of the Bar against unjust criticism and

494

ABA CANONS OF PROF. ETHICS **Canon 4**

clamor. Whenever there is proper ground for serious complaint of a judicial officer, it is the right and duty of the lawyer to submit his grievances to the proper authorities. In such cases, but not otherwise, such charges should be encouraged and the person making them should be protected.

CANON 2

The Selection of Judges

It is the duty of the Bar to endeavor to prevent political considerations from outweighing judicial fitness in the selections of Judges. It should protest earnestly and actively against the appointment or election of those who are unsuitable for the Bench; and it should strive to have elevated thereto only those willing to forego other employments, whether of a business, political or other character, which may embarrass their free and fair consideration of questions before them for decision. The aspiration of lawyers for judicial position should be governed by an impartial estimate of their ability to add honor to the office and not by a desire for the distinction the position may bring to themselves.

CANON 3

Attempts to Exert Personal Influence on the Court

Marked attention and unusual hospitality on the part of a lawyer to a Judge, uncalled for by the personal relations of the parties, subject both the Judge and the lawyer to misconstructions of motive and should be avoided. A lawyer should not communicate or argue privately with the Judge as to the merits of a pending cause, and he deserves rebuke and denunciation for any device or attempt to gain from a Judge special personal consideration or favor. A self-respecting independence in the discharge of professional duty, without denial or diminution of the courtesy and respect due the Judge's station, is the only proper foundation for cordial personal and official relations between Bench and Bar.

CANON 4

When Counsel for an Indigent Prisoner

A lawyer assigned as counsel for an indigent prisoner ought not to ask to be excused for any trivial reason, and should always exert his best efforts on his behalf.

CANON 5

The Defense or Prosecution of Those Accused of Crime

It is the right of the lawyer to undertake the defense of a person accused of crime, regardless of his personal opinion as to the guilt of the accused; otherwise innocent persons, victims only of suspicious circumstances, might be denied proper defense. Having undertaken such defense, the lawyer is bound, by all fair and honorable means, to present every defense that the law of the land permits, to the end that no person may be deprived of life or liberty, but by due process of law.

The primary duty of a lawyer engaged in public prosecution is not to convict, but to see that justice is done. The suppression of facts or the secreting of witnesses capable of establishing the innocence of the accused is highly reprehensible.

CANON 6

Adverse Influences and Conflicting Interests

It is the duty of a lawyer at the time of retainer to disclose to the client all the circumstances of his relations to the parties, and any interest in or connection with the controversy, which might influence the client in the selection of counsel.

It is unprofessional to represent conflicting interests, except by express consent of all concerned given after a full disclosure of the facts. Within the meaning of this canon, a lawyer represents conflicting interests when, in behalf of one client, it is his duty to contend for that which duty to another client requires him to oppose.

The obligation to represent the client with undivided fidelity and not to divulge his secrets or confidences forbids also the subsequent acceptance of retainers or employment from others in matters adversely affecting any interest of the client with respect to which confidence has been reposed.

CANON 7

Professional Colleagues and Conflicts of Opinion

A client's proffer of assistance of additional counsel should not be regarded as evidence of want of confidence, but the matter should be left to the determination of the client. A lawyer should decline association as colleague if it is objectionable to the original counsel, but if the lawyer first retained is relieved, another may come into the case.

When lawyers jointly associated in a cause cannot agree as to any matter vital to the interest of the client, the conflict of opinion should be frankly stated to him for his final determination. His decision should be accepted unless the nature of the difference makes it impracticable for the lawyer whose judgment has been overruled to cooperate effectively. In this event it is his duty to ask the client to relieve him.

Efforts, direct or indirect, in any way to encroach upon the professional employment of another lawyer, are unworthy of those who should be brethren at the Bar; but, nevertheless, it is the right of any lawyer, without fear or favor, to give proper advice to those seeking relief against unfaithful or neglectful counsel, generally after communication with the lawyer of whom the complaint is made.

CANON 8

Advising Upon the Merits of a Client's Cause

A lawyer should endeavor to obtain full knowledge of his client's cause before advising thereon, and he is bound to give a candid opinion of the merits and probable result of pending or contemplated litigation. The miscarriages to which justice is subject, by reason of surprises and disappointments in evidence and witnesses, and through mistakes of juries and errors of Courts, even though only occasional, admonish lawyers to beware of bold and confident assurances to clients, especially where the employment may depend upon such assurance. Whenever the controversy will admit of fair adjustment, the client should be advised to avoid or to end the litigation.

CANON 9

Negotiations With Opposite Party

A lawyer should not in any way communicate upon the subject of controversy with a party represented by counsel; much less should he undertake to negotiate or compromise the matter with him, but should deal only with his counsel. It is incumbent upon the lawyer most particularly to avoid everything that may tend to mislead a party not represented by counsel, and he should not undertake to advise him as to the law.

CANON 10

Acquiring Interest in Litigation

The lawyer should not purchase any interest in the subject matter of the litigation which he is conducting.

CANON 11

Dealing With Trust Property

The lawyer should refrain from any action whereby for his personal benefit or gain he abuses or takes advantage of the confidence reposed in him by his client.

Money of the client or collected for the client or other trust property coming into the possession of the lawyer should be reported and accounted for promptly, and should not under any circumstances be commingled with his own or be used by him.

CANON 12

Fixing the Amount of the Fee

In fixing fees, lawyers should avoid charges which overestimate their advice and services, as well as those which undervalue them. A client's ability to pay cannot justify a charge in excess of the value of the service, though his poverty may require a less charge, or even none at all. The reasonable requests of brother lawyers, and of their widows and orphans without ample means, should receive special and kindly consideration.

In determining the amount of the fee, it is proper to consider: (1) the time and labor required, the novelty and difficulty of the questions involved and the skill requisite properly to conduct the cause; (2) whether the acceptance of employment in the particular case will preclude the lawyer's appearance for others in cases likely to arise out of the transaction, and in which there is a reasonable expectation that otherwise he would be employed, or will involve the loss of other employment while employed in the particular case or antagonisms with other clients; (3) the customary charges of the Bar for similar services; (4) the amount involved in the controversy and the benefits resulting to the client from the services; (5) the contingency or the certainty of the compensation; and (6) the character of the employment, whether casual or for an established and constant client. No one of these considerations in itself is controlling. They are mere guides in ascertaining the real value of the service.

In determining the customary charges of the Bar for similar services, it is proper for a lawyer to consider a schedule of minimum fees adopted by a Bar Association, but no lawyer should permit himself to be controlled thereby or to follow it as his sole guide in determining the amount of his fee.

In fixing fees it should never be forgotten that the profession is a branch of the administration of justice and not a mere money-getting trade.

CANON 13

Contingent Fees

A contract for a contingent fee, where sanctioned by law, should be reasonable under all the circumstances of the case, including the risk and uncertainty of the compensation, but should always be subject to the supervision of a court, as to its reasonableness.

CANON 14

Suing a Client for a Fee

Controversies with clients concerning compensation are to be avoided by the lawyer so far as shall be compatible with his self-respect and with his right to receive reasonable recompense for his services; and lawsuits with clients should be resorted to only to prevent injustice, imposition or fraud.

CANON 15

How Far a Lawyer May Go in Supporting a Client's Cause

Nothing operates more certainly to create or to foster popular prejudice against lawyers as a class, and to deprive the profession of that full measure of public esteem and confidence which belongs to the proper discharge of its duties than does the false claim, often set up by the unscrupulous in defense of questionable transactions, that it is the duty of the lawyer to do whatever may enable him to succeed in winning his client's cause.

It is improper for a lawyer to assert in argument his personal belief in his client's innocence or in the justice of his cause.

The lawyer owes "entire devotion to the interest of the client, warm zeal in the maintenance and defense of his rights and the exertion of his utmost learning and ability," to the end that nothing be taken or be withheld from him, save by the rules of law, legally applied. No fear of judicial disfavor or public unpopularity should restrain him from the full discharge of his duty. In the judicial forum the client is entitled to the benefit of any and every remedy and defense that is authorized by the law of the land, and he may expect his lawyer to assert every such remedy or defense. But it is steadfastly to be borne in mind that the great trust of the lawyer is to be performed within and not without the bounds of the law. The office of attorney does not permit, much less does it demand of him for any client, violation of law or any manner of fraud or chicane. He must obey his own conscience and not that of his client.

CANON 16

Restraining Clients From Improprieties

A lawyer should use his best efforts to restrain and to prevent his clients from doing those things which the lawyer himself ought not to do, particularly with reference to their conduct towards Courts, judicial officers, jurors, witnesses and suitors. If a client persists in such wrongdoing the lawyer should terminate their relation.

CANON 17

Ill–Feeling and Personalities Between Advocates

Clients, not lawyers, are the litigants. Whatever may be the ill-feeling existing between clients, it should not be allowed to influence counsel in their conduct and demeanor toward each other or toward suitors in the case. All personalities between counsel should be scrupulously avoided. In the trial of a cause it is indecent to allude to the personal history or the personal peculiarities and idiosyncrasies of counsel on the other side. Personal colloquies between counsel which cause delay and promote unseemly wrangling should also be carefully avoided.

CANON 18

Treatment of Witnesses and Litigants

A lawyer should always treat adverse witnesses and suitors with fairness and due consideration, and he should never minister to the malevolence or prejudices of a client in the trial or conduct of a cause. The client cannot be made the keeper of the lawyer's conscience in professional matters. He has no right to demand that his counsel shall abuse the opposite party or indulge in offensive personalities. Improper speech is not excusable on the ground that it is what the client would say if speaking in his own behalf.

CANON 19

Appearance of Lawyer as Witness for His Client

When a lawyer is a witness for his client, except as to merely formal matters, such as the attestation or custody of an instrument and the like, he should leave the trial of the case to other counsel. Except when essential to the ends of justice, a lawyer should avoid testifying in court in behalf of his client.

CANON 20

Newspaper Discussion of Pending Litigation

Newspaper publications by a lawyer as to pending or anticipated litigation may interfere with a fair trial in the Courts and otherwise prejudice the due administration of justice. Generally they are to be condemned. If the extreme circumstances of a particular case justify a statement to the public, it is unprofessional to make it anonymously. An *ex parte* reference to the facts should not go beyond quotation from the records and papers on file in the court; but even in extreme cases it is better to avoid any *ex parte* statement.

CANON 21

Punctuality and Expedition

It is the duty of the lawyer not only to his client, but also to the Courts and to the public to be punctual in attendance, and to be concise and direct in the trial and disposition of causes.

CANON 22

Candor and Fairness

The conduct of the lawyer before the Court and with other lawyers should be characterized by candor and fairness.

It is not candid or fair for the lawyer knowingly to misquote the contents of a paper, the testimony of a witness, the language or the argument of opposing counsel, or the language of a decision of a textbook; or with knowledge of its invalidity, to cite as authority a decision that has been overruled, or a statute that has been repealed; or in argument to assert as a fact that which has not been proved, or in those jurisdictions where a side has the opening and closing arguments to mislead his opponent by concealing or withholding positions in his opening argument upon which his side then intends to rely.

It is unprofessional and dishonorable to deal other than candidly with the facts in taking the statements of witnesses, in drawing affidavits and other documents, and in the presentation of causes.

A lawyer should not offer evidence which he knows the Court should reject, in order to get the same before the jury by argument for its admissibility, nor should he address to the Judge arguments upon any point not properly calling for determination by him. Neither should he introduce into an argument, addressed to the court, remarks or statements intended to influence the jury or bystanders.

These and all kindred practices are unprofessional and unworthy of an officer of the law charged, as is the lawyer, with the duty of aiding in the administration of justice.

CANON 23

Attitude Toward Jury

All attempts to curry favor with juries by fawning, flattery or pretended solicitude for their personal comfort are unprofessional. Suggestions of counsel, looking to the comfort or convenience of jurors, and propositions to dispense with argument, should be made to the Court out of the jury's hearing. A lawyer must never converse privately with jurors about the case; and both before and during the trial he should avoid communicating with them, even as to matters foreign to the cause.

CANON 24

Right of Lawyer to Control the Incidents of the Trial

As to incidental matters pending the trial, not affecting the merits of the cause, or working substantial prejudice to the rights of the client, such as forcing the opposite lawyer to trial when he is under affliction or bereavement; forcing the trial on a particular day to the injury of the opposite lawyer when no harm will result from a trial at a different time; agreeing to an extension of time for signing a bill of exceptions, cross interrogatories and the like, the lawyer must be allowed to judge. In such matters no client has a right to demand that his counsel shall be illiberal, or that he do anything therein repugnant to his own sense of honor and propriety.

CANON 25

Taking Technical Advantage of Opposite
Counsel; Agreements With Him

A lawyer should not ignore known customs or practice of the Bar or of a particular Court, even when the law permits, without giving timely notice to the opposing counsel. As far as possible, important agreements, affecting the rights of clients, should be reduced to writing; but it is dishonorable to avoid performance of an agreement fairly made because it is not reduced to writing, as required by rules of Court.

CANON 26

Professional Advocacy Other Than Before Courts

A lawyer openly, and in his true character may render professional services before legislative or other bodies, regarding proposed legislation and in advocacy of claims before departments of government, upon the same principles of ethics which justify his appearance before the Courts; but it is unprofessional for a lawyer so engaged to conceal his attorneyship, or to employ secret personal solicitations, or to use means other than those addressed to the reason and understanding, to influence action.

CANON 27

Advertising, Direct or Indirect

It is unprofessional to solicit professional employment by circulars, advertisements, through toutors or by personal communications or interviews not warranted by personal relations. Indirect advertisements for professional employment such as furnishing or inspiring newspaper comments, or procuring his photograph to be published in connection with causes in which the lawyer has been or is engaged or concerning the manner of their conduct, the magnitude of the interest involved, the importance of the lawyer's position, and all other like self-laudation, offend the traditions and lower the tone of our profession and are reprehensible; but the customary use of simple professional cards is not improper.

Publication in reputable law lists in a manner consistent with the standards of conduct imposed by these canons of brief biographical and informative data is permissible. Such data must not be misleading and may include only a statement of the lawyer's name and the names of his professional associates; addresses, telephone numbers, cable addresses; branches of the profession practiced; date and place of birth and admission to the bar; schools attended; with dates of graduation, degrees and other educational distinctions; public or quasi-public offices; posts of honor; legal authorships; legal teaching positions; memberships and offices in bar associations and committees thereof, in legal and scientific societies and legal fraternities; foreign language ability; the fact of listings in other reputable law lists; the names and addresses of references; and, with their written consent, the names of clients regularly represented. A certificate of compliance with the Rules and Standards issued by the Standing Committee on Law Lists may be treated as evidence that such list is reputable.

It is not improper for a lawyer who is admitted to practice as a proctor in admiralty to use that designation on his letterhead or shingle or for a lawyer who has complied with the statutory requirements of admission to practice before the patent office, to so use the designation "patent attorney" or "patent lawyer" or "trademark attorney" or "trademark lawyer" or any combination of those terms.

CANON 28

Stirring Up Litigation, Directly or Through Agents

It is unprofessional for a lawyer to volunteer advice to bring a lawsuit, except in rare cases where ties of blood, relationship or trust make it his duty to do so. Stirring up strife and litigation is not only unprofessional, but it is indictable at common law. It is disreputable to hunt up defects in titles or other causes of action and inform thereof in order to be employed to bring suit or collect judgment, or to breed litigation by seeking out those with claims for personal injuries or those having any other grounds of action in order to secure them as clients, or to employ agents or runners for like purposes, or to pay or reward, directly or indirectly, those who bring or influence the bringing of such cases to his office, or to remunerate policemen, court or prison officials, physicians, hospital *attachés* or others who may succeed, under the guise of giving disinterested friendly advice, in influencing the criminal, the sick and the injured, the ignorant or others, to seek his professional services. A duty to the public and to the profession devolves upon every member of the Bar having knowledge of such practices upon the part of any practitioner immediately to inform thereof, to the end that the offender may be disbarred.

CANON 29

Upholding the Honor of the Profession

Lawyers should expose without fear or favor before the proper tribunals corrupt or dishonest conduct in the profession, and should accept without hesitation employment against a member of the Bar who has wronged his client. The counsel upon the trial of a cause in which perjury has been committed owe it to the profession and to the public to bring the matter to the knowledge of the prosecuting authorities. The lawyer should aid in guarding the Bar against the admission to the profession of candidates unfit or unqualified because deficient in either moral character or education. He should strive at all times to uphold the honor and to maintain the dignity of the profession and to improve not only the law but the administration of justice.

CANON 30

Justifiable and Unjustifiable Litigations

The lawyer must decline to conduct a civil cause or to make a defense when convinced that it is intended merely to harass or to injure the opposite party or to work oppression or wrong. But otherwise it is his right, and, having accepted retainer, it becomes his duty to insist upon the judgment of the Court as to the legal merits of his client's claim. His appearance in Court should be deemed equivalent to an assertion on his honor that in his opinion his client's case is one proper for judicial determination.

CANON 31

Responsibility for Litigation

No lawyer is obliged to act either as adviser or advocate for every person who may wish to become his client. He has the right to decline employment. Every lawyer upon his own responsibility must decide what employment he will accept as counsel, what causes he will bring into Court for plaintiffs, what cases he will contest in Court for defendants. The responsibility for advising as to questionable transactions, for bringing questionable suits, for urging questionable defenses, is the lawyer's responsibility. He cannot escape it by urging as an excuse that he is only following his client's instructions.

CANON 32

The Lawyer's Duty in Its Last Analysis

No client, corporate or individual, however powerful, nor any cause, civil or political, however important, is entitled to receive nor should any lawyer render any service or advice involving disloyalty to the law whose ministers we are, or disrespect of the judicial office, which we are bound to uphold, or corruption of any person or persons exercising a public office or private trust, or deception or betrayal of the public. When rendering any such improper service or advice, the lawyer invites and merits stern and just condemnation. Correspondingly, he advances the honor of his profession and the best interests of his client when he renders service or gives advice tending to impress upon the client and his undertaking exact compliance with the strictest principles of moral law. He must also observe and advise his client to observe the statute law, though until a statute shall have been construed and interpreted by competent adjudication, he is free and is entitled to advise as to its validity and as to what he conscientiously believes to be its just meaning and extent. But above all a lawyer will find his highest honor in a deserved reputation for fidelity to private trust and to public duty, as an honest man and as a patriotic and loyal citizen.

CANON 33

Partnerships—Names

Partnerships among lawyers for the practice of their profession are very common and are not to be condemned. In the formation of partnerships and the use of partnership names care should be taken not to violate any law, custom, or rule of court locally applicable. Where partnerships are formed between lawyers who are not all admitted to practice in the courts of the state, care should be taken to avoid any misleading name or representation which would create a false impression as to the professional position or privileges of the member not locally admitted. In the formation of partnerships for the practice of law, no person should be admitted or held out as a practitioner or member who is not a member of the legal profession duly authorized to practice, and amenable to professional discipline. In the selection and use of a firm name, no false, misleading, assumed or trade name should be used. The continued use of the name of a deceased or former partner, when permissible by local custom, is not unethical, but care should be taken that no imposition or deception is practiced through this use. When a member of the firm, on becoming a judge, is precluded from practicing law, his name should not be continued in the firm name.

Partnerships between lawyers and members of other professions or non-professional persons should not be formed or permitted where any part of the partnership's employment consists of the practice of law.

CANON 34

Division of Fees

No division of fees for legal services is proper, except with another lawyer, based upon a division of service or responsibility.

CANON 35

Intermediaries

The professional services of a lawyer should not be controlled or exploited by any lay agency, personal or corporate, which intervenes between client and lawyer. A lawyer's responsibilities and qualifications are individual. He should avoid all relations which direct the performance of his duties by or in the interest of such intermediary. A lawyer's relation to his client should be personal, and the responsibility should be direct to the client. Charitable societies rendering aid to the indigents are not deemed such intermediaries.

A lawyer may accept employment from any organization, such as an association, club or trade organization, to render legal services in any matter in which the organization, as an entity, is interested, but this employment should not include the rendering of legal services to the members of such an organization in respect to their individual affairs.

CANON 36

Retirement From Judicial Position or Public Employment

A lawyer should not accept employment as an advocate in any matter upon the merits of which he has previously acted in a judicial capacity.

A lawyer, having once held public office or having been in the public employ, should not after his retirement accept employment in connection with any matter which he has investigated or passed upon while in such office or employ.

CANON 37

Confidences of a Client

It is the duty of a lawyer to preserve his client's confidences. This duty outlasts the lawyer's employment, and extends as well to his employees; and neither of them should accept employment which involves or may involve the disclosure or use of these confidences, either for the private advantage of the lawyer or his employees or to the disadvantage of the client, without his knowledge and consent, and even though there are other available sources of such information. A lawyer should not continue employment when he discovers that this obligation prevents the performance of his full duty to his former or to his new client.

If a lawyer is accused by his client, he is not precluded from disclosing the truth in respect to the accusation. The announced intention of a client to commit a crime is not included within the confidences which he is bound to respect. He may properly make such disclosures as may be necessary to prevent the act or protect those against whom it is threatened.

CANON 38

Compensation, Commissions and Rebates

A lawyer should accept no compensation, commissions, rebates or other advantages from others without the knowledge and consent of his client after full disclosure.

CANON 39

Witnesses

A lawyer may properly interview any witness or prospective witness for the opposing side in any civil or criminal action without the consent of opposing counsel or party. In doing so, however, he should scrupulously avoid any suggestion calculated to induce the witness to suppress or deviate from the truth, or in any degree to affect his free and untrammeled conduct when appearing at the trial or on the witness stand.

CANON 40

Newspapers

A lawyer may with propriety write articles for publications in which he gives information upon the law; but he should not accept employment from such publications to advise inquirers in respect to their individual rights.

CANON 41

Discovery of Imposition and Deception

When a lawyer discovers that some fraud or deception has been practiced, which has unjustly imposed upon the court or a party, he should endeavor to rectify it; at first by advising his client, and if his client refuses to forego the advantage thus unjustly gained, he should promptly inform the injured person or his counsel, so that they may take appropriate steps.

CANON 42

Expenses of Litigation

A lawyer may not properly agree with a client that the lawyer shall pay or bear the expenses of litigation; he may in good faith advance expenses as a matter of convenience, but subject to reimbursement.

CANON 43

Approved Law Lists

It shall be improper for a lawyer to permit his name to be published in a law list the conduct, management or contents of which are calculated or likely to deceive or injure the public or the profession, or to lower the dignity or standing of the profession.

CANON 44

Withdrawal From Employment as Attorney or Counsel

The right of an attorney or counsel to withdraw from employment, once assumed, arises only from good cause. Even the desire or consent of the client is not always sufficient. The lawyer should not throw up the unfinished task to the detriment of his client except for reasons of honor or self-respect. If the client insists upon an unjust or immoral course in the conduct of his case, or if he persists over the attorney's remonstrance in presenting frivolous defenses, or if he deliberately disregards an agreement or obligation as to fees or expenses, the lawyer may be warranted in withdrawing on due notice to the client, allowing him time to employ another lawyer. So also when a lawyer discovers that his client has no case and the client is determined to continue it; or even if the lawyer finds himself incapable of conducting the case effectively. Sundry other instances may arise in which withdrawal is to be justified. Upon withdrawing from a case after a retainer has been paid, the attorney should refund such part of the retainer as has not been clearly earned.

CANON 45

Specialists

The canons of the American Bar Association apply to all branches of the legal profession; specialists in particular branches are not to be considered as exempt from the application of these principles.

CANON 46

Notice to Local Lawyers

A lawyer available to act as an associate of other lawyers in a particular branch of the law or legal service may send to local lawyers only and publish in his local legal journal, a brief and dignified announcement of his availability to serve other lawyers in connection therewith. The announcement should be in a form which does not constitute a statement or representation of special experience or expertise.

CANON 47

Aiding the Unauthorized Practice of Law

No lawyer shall permit his professional services, or his name, to be used in aid of, or to make possible, the unauthorized practice of law by any lay agency, personal or corporate.

PARALLEL TABLES BETWEEN THE ABA CANONS OF PROFESSIONAL ETHICS AND THE ABA MODEL CODE OF PROFESSIONAL RESPONSIBILITY *

CANONS OF PROFESSIONAL ETHICS TO CODE OF PROFESSIONAL RESPONSIBILITY

Preamble
Preamble
DR 1–102(A)(5)
EC 7–20
EC 7–39
EC 8–1
EC 9–1
EC 9–2

Canon 1
DR 1–103(B)
EC 7–36
EC 8–6
DR 7–106(C)(6)
DR 8–102(B)

Canon 2
EC 8–6
DR 8–102(A)

Canon 3
EC 7–34
EC 7–35
EC 7–36
DR 7–110

Canon 4
EC 2–29
EC 7–1
EC 7–19
DR 2–110(C)
DR 7–101(A)(1)

Canon 5
EC 1–5
DR 1–102(A)(4)
EC 2–29
EC 7–1
EC 7–4
EC 7–13
EC 7–19
EC 7–27
DR 7–101(A)(1)
DR 7–102(A)(3)–(7)
DR 7–103
DR 7–109(A)–(B)
EC 8–5

Canon 6
EC 4–1

EC 4–5
DR 4–101(B)
EC 5–1
EC 5–3
EC 5–14
EC 5–15
EC 5–16
EC 5–17
EC 5–19
DR 5–101(A)
DR 5–105
DR 5–106
EC 8–8

Canon 7
EC 2–28
EC 2–29
EC 2–30
EC 2–32
DR 2–108
DR 2–110(C)(3)
EC 4–2
EC 5–11
EC 5–12
DR 7–101(A)(2)

Canon 8
EC 2–9
EC 7–5
EC 7–8

Canon 9
EC 7–18
DR 7–104

Canon 10
EC 5–7
DR 5–103(A)

Canon 11
EC 4–5
DR 4–101(B)(3)
EC 9–5
DR 9–102

Canon 12
EC 2–16
EC 2–17
EC 2–18
EC 2–25

DR 2–106

Canon 13
EC 2–20
DR 2–106
EC 5–7
DR 5–103(A)(2)

Canon 14
EC 2–23
EC 5–7
DR 5–103(A)(1)

Canon 15
EC 1–5
DR 1–102(A)(4)
EC 7–1
EC 7–2
EC 7–3
EC 7–4
EC 7–5
EC 7–6
EC 7–19
EC 7–24
EC 7–26
DR 7–101(A)(1)
DR 7–101(B)(2)
DR 7–102(A)(2)
DR 7–102(A)(3)–(7)
DR 7–106(C)(4)
EC 9–2

Canon 16
EC 2–32
DR 2–110(C)(1)(b)
EC 7–28
DR 7–101(A)(2)
EC 8–5

Canon 17
EC 1–5
EC 7–10
EC 7–37
EC 7–38
DR 7–101(A)(1)

Canon 18
EC 1–5
EC 7–10
EC 7–25

EC 7–36
DR 7–101(A)(1)
DR 7–106(C)(2)

Canon 19
EC 5–9
EC 5–10
DR 5–101(B)
DR 5–102

Canon 20
EC 7–33
DR 7–107

Canon 21
EC 6–4
DR 6–101(A)(3)
EC 7–20
EC 7–38
DR 7–101(A)(1)

Canon 22
EC 1–5
DR 1–102(A)(4)
EC 7–6
EC 7–25
EC 7–26
EC 7–27
DR 7–102(A)(3)–(7)
DR 7–106(C)(1)
EC 8–5

Canon 23
EC 7–29
EC 7–31
EC 7–36
DR 7–108

Canon 24
EC 7–7
EC 7–9
EC 7–10
EC 7–38
DR 7–101(A)(1)
DR 7–101(B)(1)

Canon 25

* Compiled by Olavi Maru, Reference Librarian, William Nelson Cromwell Library, American Bar Foundation.

EC 7–38
DR 7–101(A)(1)
DR 7–106(C)(5)

Canon 26
EC 7–15
EC 7–16
EC 7–36
DR 7–106(B)(2)
DR 7–107(F)
DR 7–107(H)
DR 7–107(I)
DR 7–110(B)
EC 8–4

Canon 27
EC 2–21
EC 2–3
EC 2–4
EC 2–8
EC 2–9
EC 2–10
EC 2–14
DR 2–101
DR 2–102(A)
DR 2–102(E)
DR 2–103(A)
DR 2–105(A)

Canon 28
EC 1–4
EC 1–5
EC 2–1
EC 2–2
EC 2–3
EC 2–4
EC 2–8
DR 1–103(A)–(B)
DR 2–103(A)
DR 2–104(A)

Canon 29
EC 1–2
EC 1–3
EC 1–4
DR 1–101(B)
DR 1–103(A)
DR 1–103(B)
EC 2–28

DR 7–102(A)(3)–(7)
DR 7–102(B)(2)
EC 8–1
EC 8–2
EC 8–5
EC 8–7
EC 8–9
EC 9–2
EC 9–6

Canon 30
EC 1–5
DR 1–102(A)(4)
EC 2–3
EC 2–30
DR 2–109(A)(1)
EC 7–1
EC 7–4
EC 7–19
DR 7–101(A)(1)
DR 7–102(A)(1)

Canon 31
EC 2–26
EC 2–27
EC 2–28
EC 2–29
DR 2–109(A)(2)
EC 7–1
EC 7–4
EC 7–5
EC 7–14
EC 7–19
DR 7–101(B)(2)
DR 7–102(A)(2)

Canon 32
EC 1–5
DR 1–102(A)(5)
EC 7–1
EC 7–5
EC 7–19
DR 7–102(A)(3)–(7)
EC 8–5

Canon 33
EC 2–11
EC 2–12
EC 2–13

DR 2–102(B)
DR 2–102(C)
DR 2–102(D)
EC 3–8
DR 3–103
DR 5–107(C)

Canon 34
EC 2–22
DR 2–103(B)
DR 2–107(A)
EC 3–8
DR 3–102

Canon 35
DR 2–103(D)
DR 2–104(A)(2)
DR 2–104(A)(3)
EC 5–1
EC 5–13
EC 5–21
EC 5–22
EC 5–23
EC 5–24
DR 5–107(B)
DR 5–107(C)(3)

Canon 36
EC 9–3
DR 9–101

Canon 37
Canon 4 generally
EC 2–32
DR 2–110
DR 4–101(B)
DR 4–101(B)(2)–(3)
DR 4–101(C)
DR 4–101(D)
DR 7–101(A)(2)

Canon 38
EC 2–21
EC 5–21
DR 5–107(A)(2)

Canon 39
EC 1–5
DR 1–102(A)(4)

EC 7–28
DR 7–102(A)(3)–(7)
DR 7–109(C)

Canon 40
EC 2–2
EC 2–5
DR 2–104(A)(4)

Canon 41
DR 7–102(B)(1)
EC 8–5

Canon 42
EC 5–8
DR 5–103(B)

Canon 43
DR 2–102(A)(6)

Canon 44
EC 1–5
DR 1–102(A)(5)
EC 2–31
EC 2–32
DR 2–110
EC 5–15
EC 5–19
EC 5–21
DR 5–102
DR 5–105(B)
DR 5–105(D)
EC 7–8
DR 7–101(A)(2)

Canon 45
Preliminary statement

Canon 46
EC 2–14
DR 2–105(A)(3)

Canon 47
EC 1–5
DR 1–102(A)(5)
EC 3–1 through
  EC 3–9
DR 3–101

PARALLEL TABLES BETWEEN THE ABA MODEL CODE OF PROFESSIONAL RESPONSIBILITY AND THE ABA CANONS OF PROFESSIONAL ETHICS

Code	Canons	Code	Canons
Preamble	Preamble	EC 2–14	27
Preliminary			46
Statement	45	EC 2–16	12
		EC 2–17	12
Canon 1		EC 2–18	12
EC 1–2	29	EC 2–20	13
EC 1–3	29	EC 2–21	38
EC 1–4	28	EC 2–22	34
	29	EC 2–23	14
EC 1–5	5	EC 2–25	12
	15	EC 2–26	31
	17	EC 2–27	31
	18	EC 2–28	7
	22		29
	28		31
	30	EC 2–29	4
	32		5
	39		7
	44		31
	47	EC 2–30	7
DR 1–101			30
(B)	29	EC 2–31	44
DR 1–102		EC 2–32	7
(A)(4)	5		16
	15		37
	22		44
	30	DR 2–101	27
	39	DR 2–102	
(A)(5)	Preamble	(A)	27
	32	(A)(6)	43
	44	(B)	33
	47	(C)	33
DR 1–103		(D)	33
(A)	28	(E)	27
	29	DR 2–103	
(B)	1	(A)	27
	28		28
	29	(B)	34
		(D)	35
Canon 2		DR 2–104	
EC 2–1	28	(A)	28
EC 2–2	27	(A)(2)	35
	28	(A)(3)	35
	40	DR 2–104	
EC 2–3	27	(A)(4)	40
	28	DR 2–105	
	30	(A)	27
EC 2–4	27	(A)(3)	46
	28	DR 2–106	12
EC 2–5	40		13
EC 2–8	27	DR 2–107	
	28	(A)	34
EC 2–9	8	DR 2–108	7
	27	DR 2–109	
EC 2–10	27	(A)(1)	30
EC 2–11	33	(A)(2)	31
EC 2–12	33	DR 2–110	37
EC 2–13	33		

512

ABA CANONS OF PROF. ETHICS

Code	Canons	Code	Canons
	44	(A)(2)	13
(C)	4	(B)	42
(C)(1)(b)	16	DR 5–105	6
(C)(3)	7	(B)	44
		(D)	44
Canon 3		DR 5–106	6
EC 3–1 through EC 3–9	47	DR 5–107	
EC 3–8	33	(A)(2)	38
	34	(B)	35
DR 3–101	47	(C)	33
DR 3–102	34	(C)(3)	35
DR 3–103	33		
	37	**Canon 6**	
		EC 6–4	21
Canon 4		DR 6–101	
EC 4–1	6	(A)(3)	21
EC 4–2	7		
EC 4–5	6	**Canon 7**	
	11	EC 7–1	4
DR 4–101			5
(B)	6		15
	37		30
(B)(2)	37		31
(B)(3)	11		32
	37	EC 7–2	15
(C)	37	EC 7–3	15
(D)	37	EC 7–4	5
			15
Canon 5			30
EC 5–1	6		31
	35	EC 7–5	8
EC 5–3	6		15
EC 5–7	10		31
	13		32
	14	EC 7–6	15
EC 5–8	42		22
EC 5–9	19	EC 7–7	24
EC 5–11	7	EC 7–8	8
EC 5–12	7		44
EC 5–13	35	EC 7–9	24
EC 5–14	6	EC 7–10	17
EC 5–15	6		18
	44		24
EC 5–16	6	EC 7–13	5
EC 5–17	6	EC 7–14	31
EC 5–19	6	EC 7–15	26
	44	EC 7–16	26
EC 5–21	35	EC 7–18	9
	38	EC 7–19	4
	44		5
EC 5–22	35		15
EC 5–23	35		30
EC 5–24	35		31
DR 5–101			32
(A)	6	EC 7–20	Preamble
(B)	19		21
DR 5–102	19	EC 7–24	15
	44	EC 7–25	18
DR 5–103			22
(A)	10	EC 7–26	15
(A)(1)	14		22
		EC 7–27	2

ABA CANONS OF PROF. ETHICS

Code	Canons	Code	Canons
	22	DR 7–104	9
EC 7–28	16	DR 7–106	
	39	(B)(2)	26
EC 7–29	23	(C)(1)	22
EC 7–31	23	(C)(2)	18
EC 7–33	20	(C)(4)	15
EC 7–34	3	(C)(5)	25
EC 7–35	3	(C)(6)	1
EC 7–36	1	DR 7–107	20
	3	(F)	26
	18	(H)	26
	23	(I)	26
	26	DR 7–108	23
EC 7–37	17	DR 7–109	
EC 7–38	17	(A)–(B)	5
	21	(C)	39
	24	DR 7–110	3
	25	(B)	26
EC 7–39	Preamble		
DR 7–101		**Canon 8**	
(A)(1)	4	EC 8–1	Preamble
	5		29
	15	EC 8–2	29
	17	EC 8–4	26
	18	EC 8–5	5
	21		16
	24		22
	25		29
	30		32
(A)(2)	7		41
	16	EC 8–6	1
	37		2
	44	EC 8–7	29
(B)(1)	24	EC 8–8	6
(B)(2)	15	EC 8–9	29
	31	DR 8–102	
DR 7–102		(A)	2
(A)(1)	30	(B)	1
(A)(2)	15		
	31	**Canon 9**	
(A)(3)–(7)	5	EC 9–1	Preamble
	15	EC 9–2	Preamble
	22		15
	29		29
	32	EC 9–3	36
	39	EC 9–5	11
(B)(1)	41	EC 9–6	29
(B)(2)	29	DR 9–101	36
DR 7–103	5	DR 9–102	11

514

RESTATEMENT OF LAW GOVERNING LAWYERS

In 1986, the American Law Institute began the process of writing the Restatement of Law Governing Lawyers. This long and difficult task has culminated in the anticipated completion of the Restatement in late 1999. However, the proposed final drafts have been approved by the ALI. From the first tentative drafts of the Restatement language, courts, commentators, and bar personnel began to take account of the language and research brought together in this project. The impact and influence of this Restatement cannot be underestimated. The ABA's Ethics 2000 project has explicitly decided to examine and take account of the substance of the Restatement of Law Governing Lawyers. Therefore, this supplement reprints the text of the sections of the Restatement. Due to space considerations, we do not reprint the comments or reporters notes. Of course, those who seek to research areas of professional responsibility should examine the full Restatement document.

Note: Readers must be aware that as this supplement was being prepared the Reporters were finalizing the language and structure of the Restatement of Law Governing Lawyers. At this time, it is anticipated that the final document will be published in late fall of 1999. Therefore, before one relies or cites to the sections reprinted below, one should ascertain whether a more current final draft is available. We of course, will include the final draft in our next supplement. The draft contained below is the most current publicly available draft as of April 1999,

Table of Contents

CHAPTER 3: CLIENT AND LAWYER: THE FINANCIAL AND PROPERTY RELATIONSHIP

CHAPTER 4: LAWYER CIVIL LIABILITY

CHAPTER 5: CONFIDENTIAL CLIENT INFORMATION

CHAPTER 6: REPRESENTING CLIENTS: IN GENERAL

CHAPTER 1: REGULATION OF THE LEGAL PROFESSION

§ 1. Regulation of Lawyers in General

Upon admission to the bar of any jurisdiction, a person becomes a lawyer and as such is subject to applicable law governing such matters as professional discipline, procedure and evidence, civil remedies, and criminal sanctions.

§ 2. Admission to Practice Law

In order to become a lawyer and qualify to practice law in a jurisdiction of admission, a prospective lawyer must comply with requirements of the jurisdiction relating to such matters as education, other demonstration of competence such as success in a bar examination, and character.

§ 3. Jurisdictional Scope of Practice of Law by Lawyer

A lawyer currently admitted to practice in a jurisdiction may provide legal services to clients in a matter:

(1) at any place within the admitting jurisdiction;

(2) before a tribunal or administrative agency of another jurisdiction or the federal government in compliance with requirements for temporary or regular admission to practice before that tribunal or agency; and

(3) at a place within a jurisdiction in which the lawyer is not admitted to the extent the lawyer's activities in the matter arise out of or are otherwise reasonably related to the lawyer's practice in (1) or (2).

§ 4. Unauthorized Practice by Non–Lawyer

A person not admitted to practice as a lawyer (see § 2) may not engage in the unauthorized practice of law, and a lawyer may not assist a person to do so.

§ 5. Professional Discipline

(1) A lawyer is subject to professional discipline for violation of any provision of an applicable lawyer code.

(2) A lawyer is subject to professional discipline under Subsection (1) for committing or attempting to commit a violation, knowingly assisting or inducing another to do so, or knowingly doing so through the acts of another.

§ 6. Judicial Remedies Available to Client and Nonclient for Lawyer Wrongs

For a lawyer's breach of duty owed to the lawyer's client or to a nonclient, judicial remedies may be available through judgment or other order entered in accordance with the standards applicable tot he remedy awarded, including standards concerning limitations of remedies. Judicial remedies include the following:

(1) awarding a sum of money as damages;

(2) providing injunctive relief, including requiring specific performance of a contract or enjoining its non-performance;

(3) requiring restoration of a specific thing or awarding a sum of money to prevent unjust enrichment;

(4) ordering cancellation or reformation of a contract, deed, or similar instrument;

(5) declaring the rights of the parties, such as by directing that an obligation claimed by the lawyer to be owed to the lawyer is not enforceable;

(6) punishing the lawyer for contempt;

(7) enforcing and arbitration award;

(8) disqualifying a lawyer from representation;

(9) forfeiting a lawyer's fee (see § 49);

(10) denying admissibility of evidence wrongfully obtained;

(11) dismissing the claim or defense of a litigant represented by the lawyer;

(12) granting a new trial; and

(13) entering a procedural or other sanction.

§ 7. Judicial Remedies Available to Lawyer for Client Wrongs

When a lawyer seeks from a present or former client a remedy based on the client's breach of a duty to the lawyer, a tribunal will provide relief in favor of the lawyer if the tribunal is persuade that the remedy sought by the lawyer is:

(1) appropriate under otherwise applicable principles governing the remedy; and

(2) does not put the lawyer in a position otherwise prohibited by an applicable lawyer code.

§ 8. Lawyer Criminal Offense

The traditional and appropriate activities of lawyers in representing clients consistent with the requirements of the applicable lawyer code are relevant factors for the tribunal in assessing propriety of a lawyer's conduct under the law of crimes. In other respects, a lawyer is guilty of an offense for acts committed in the course of representing a client to the same extent and on the same basis as would a non-lawyer similarly acting.

§ 10. Law Practice Organization in General

(1) A lawyer may practice as a solo practitioner, as a employee of another lawyer or firm of lawyers, as a member of a law firm constituted as a partnership, professional corporation, or similar organization, or as an employee of an organization.

(2) A lawyer in an organization described in Subsection (1) is subject to otherwise-applicable law governing the particular legal form in which the association practices with respect to questions concerning its creation, operation, management, and dissolution.

(3) Absent agreement with the firm providing a more permissive role, a lawyer leaving a law firm may solicit firm clients on whose matters the lawyer has actively and substantially worked either after the lawyer has left the firm or after the lawyer has adequately and timely

informed the firm of the lawyer's intent to contact firm clients for that purpose.

§ 11. Limitations on Non–Lawyer Involvement in Law Firm

(1) In a law firm, a non-lawyer may not own any interest in the firm, and a non-lawyer may not be empowered to or actually exercise the right to direct or control the professional activities of a lawyer in the firm.

(2) A lawyer may not form a partnership or other business enterprise with a non-lawyer if any of the activities of the enterprise consist of the practice of law.

(3) A lawyer of law firm may not share legal fees with a person not admitted to practice as a lawyer, except that:

    (a) an agreement by a lawyer with the lawyer's firm or another lawyer in the firm may provide for payment, over a reasonable period of time after the lawyer's death, to the lawyer's estate or to one or more specified persons;

    (b) a lawyer who undertakes to complete unfinished legal business of a deceased lawyer may pay to the estate of the deceased lawyer a portion of the total compensation that fairly represents services rendered by the deceased lawyer; and

    (c) a lawyer or law firm may include non-lawyer employees in a compensation or retirement plan, even though the plan is based in whole or in part on a profit-sharing arrangement.

§ 12. Duty of Supervision by Lawyer

(1) A lawyer who is a partner in a law partnership or principal in a law firm corporation or similar organization is subject to professional discipline if the lawyer fails to make reasonable efforts to endure that the firm has in effect measures giving reasonable assurance that all lawyers in the firm conform to the applicable lawyer code.

(2) A lawyer who has direct supervisory authority over another lawyer is subject to professional discipline if the supervisory lawyer fails to make reasonable efforts to ensure that the other lawyer conforms to applicable rules of a lawyer code.

(3) A lawyer is subject to responsibility for professional discipline for another lawyer's violation of the rules of professional conduct if:

    (a) the lawyer orders, or with knowledge of the specific conduct, ratifies the conduct involved; or

    (b) the lawyer is a partner in the law firm in which the other lawyer practices, or has direct supervisory authority over the other lawyer, and knows of the conduct at a time when its consequences can be avoided or mitigated but fails to take reasonable remedial measures.

(4) With respect to a non-lawyer associated with a lawyer or the lawyer's firm, the lawyer is subject to professional discipline if either:

    (a) the lawyer fails to make reasonable efforts to ensure

       (i) that the firm in which that lawyer practices has in effect measures giving reasonable assurance that the non-lawyer's conduct is compatible with the professional obligations of the lawyer; and

       (ii) that the conduct of a non-lawyer over whom the lawyer has direct supervisory authority conforms to the professional obligations of the lawyer; or

    (b) the non-lawyer's conduct would be a violation of the applicable lawyer code if engage in by a lawyer, and

       (i) the lawyer orders or, with knowledge of the specific conduct, ratifies that conduct; or

       (ii) the lawyer is a partner in the law firm in which the non-lawyer is employed, or has direct supervisory authority over the non-lawyer, and knows of the conduct at a time when the consequences can be avoided or mitigated but fails to take reasonable remedial measures.

§ 13. Duty of a Lawyer Subject to Suervision

(1) For purposes of professional discipline, a lawyer must conform to provisions of an applicable lawyer code notwithstanding that the lawyer acted at the direction of another lawyer or other person.

(2) For purposes of professional discipline, a lawyer under the direct supervisory authority of another lawyer does not violate an applicable lawyer code if that lawyer acts in accordance with the supervisory lawyer's direction based on a reasonable resolution of an arguable question of professional duty.

§ 14. Restrictions on the Right to Practice Law

(1) A lawyer may not offer or enter into a law firm agreement that restricts the right of the lawyer to practice law after termination of the relationship, except for a restriction incident to the lawyer's retirement from the practice of law.

(2) A lawyer may not offer or enter into an agreement in settling a client claim restricting the right of the lawyer to practice law, including the right to represent or take particular action on behalf of other clients.

CHAPTER 2: THE CLIENT–LAWYER RELATIONSHIP

§ 26. Formation of Client–Lawyer Relationship

A relationship of client and lawyer arises when:

(1) a person manifests to a lawyer the person's intent that the lawyer provide legal services for the person; and either

(a) the lawyer manifests to the person consent to do so; or

(b) the lawyer fails to manifest lack of consent to do so, and the lawyer knows or reasonably should know that the person reasonably relies on the lawyer to provide the services; or

(2) a tribunal with power to do so appoints the lawyer to provide the services.

§ 27. Lawyer's Duties to Prospective Client

When a person discusses with a lawyer the possibility of their forming a client-lawyer relationship for a matter or matters, and no such relationship ensues, the lawyer must:

(1) protect the person's confidential information by:

(a) not subsequently using or disclosing confidential information learned in the consultation, except to the extent permitted with respect to confidential information of a client; and

(b) not representing a client whose interests are materially adverse to those of the prospective client in the same or a substantially related matter, but only when the lawyer (or another lawyer whose disqualification is imputed to the lawyer under the standards of §§ 203 & 204) has received from the prospective client confidential information that could be significantly harmful to the prospective client in the matter, unless:

(i) any personally-prohibited lawyer is screened as stated in § 204(2)(b) & (c); or

(ii) both the affected client and the prospective client have given informed consent to the representation under the limitations and conditions provided in § 202;

(2) protect the person's property in the lawyer's custody as stated in §§ 56–58; and

(3) use reasonable care to the extent the lawyer gives the person legal advice or provides other legal services for the person.

§ 28. Lawyer's Duties to Client in General

To the extent consistent with the lawyer's other legal duties and subject to the other provisions of this Restatement, a lawyer must, in matters within the scope of the representation:

(1) proceed in a manner reasonably calculated to advance a client's lawful objectives, as defined by the client after consultation;

(2) act with reasonable competence and diligence;

(3) comply with obligations concerning the client's confidences and property, avoid impermissible conflicting interests, deal honestly with the client, and not employ advantages arising from the client-lawyer relationship in a manner adverse to the client; and

(4) fulfill valid contractual obligations to the client.

§ 29. Client's Duties to Lawyer

Subject to the other provisions of this Restatement, in matters covered by the representation a client must:

(1) compensate a lawyer for services and expenses as stated in Chapter 3;

(2) indemnify the lawyer for liability to which the client has exposed the lawyer without the lawyer's fault; and

(3) fulfill any valid contractual obligations to the lawyer.

§ 29A. Client–Lawyer Agreements

(1) An agreement between a lawyer and client concerning the client-lawyer relationship, including an agreement modifying an existing agreement, may be enforced by either party if the agreement meets other applicable requirements, except that:

(a) if the agreement or modification is made after a reasonable time after the lawyer has begun to represent the client in the matter (see § 50(1)), the client may avoid it unless the lawyer shows that the agreement and the circumstances of its formation were fair and reasonable to the client; and

(b) if the agreement is made after the lawyer has finished providing services, the client may avoid it if the client was not informed of facts needed to evaluate the appropriateness of the lawyer's compensation or other benefits conferred on the lawyer by the agreement.

(2) A tribunal should construe an agreement between client and lawyer as a reasonable person in the circumstances of the client would have construed it.

§ 30. Limitation of Client or Lawyer Duties

(1) Subject to other requirements stated in this Restatement, a client and lawyer may agree to limit a duty that a lawyer would otherwise owe to the client if:

(a) the client is adequately informed and consents; and

(b) the terms of the limitation are reasonable in the circumstances.

(2) A lawyer may agree to waive a client's duty to pay or other duty owed to the lawyer.

§ 31. Lawyer's Duty to Inform and Consult With Client

(1) A lawyer must keep a client reasonably informed about the matter and must consult with a client to a reasonable extent concerning decisions to be made by the lawyer under §§ 32–34.

(2) A lawyer must promptly comply with a client's reasonable requests for information.

(3) A lawyer must notify a client of decisions to be made by the client under §§ 32–34 and must explain a matter to the extent reasonably necessary to permit the client to make informed decisions regarding the representation.

§ 32. Allocating Authority to Decide Between Client and Lawyer

As between client and lawyer:

(1) A client and lawyer may agree which of them will make specified decisions, subject to the requirements stated in §§ 29A, 30, 33, 34, and other provisions of this Restatement. The agreement may be superseded by another valid agreement.

(2) A client may instruct a lawyer during the representation, subject to the requirements stated in §§ 33, 34, and other provisions of this Restatement.

(3) Subject to Subsections (1) and (2) a lawyer may take any lawful measure within the scope of representation that is reasonably calculated to advance a client's objectives as defined by the client, consulting with the client as required by § 31.

(4) A client may ratify an act of a lawyer that was not previously authorized.

§ 33. Authority Reserved to Client

(1) As between client and lawyer, subject to Subsection (2) and § 34, the following and comparable decisions are reserved to the client except when the client has validly authorized the lawyer to make the particular decision: whether and on what terms to settle a claim; how a criminal defendant should plead; whether a criminal defendant should waive jury trial; whether a criminal defendant should testify; and whether to appeal in a civil proceeding or criminal prosecution.

(2) A client may not validly authorize a lawyer to make the decisions described in Subsection (1) when other law (such as criminal procedure rules governing pleas, jury trial waiver, and defendant testimony) requires the client's personal participation or approval.

(3) Regardless of any contrary agreement with a lawyer, a client may revoke a lawyer's authority to make the decisions described in Subsection (1).

§ 34. Authority Reserved to Lawyer

As between client and lawyer, a lawyer retains authority that may not be overridden by an agreement with or an instruction from the client:

(1) to refuse to perform, counsel, or assist future or ongoing acts in the representation that the lawyer reasonably believes to be unlawful;

(2) to make decisions or take actions in the representation that the lawyer reasonably believes to be required by law or an order of a tribunal.

§ 35. Client Under Disability

(1) When a client's ability to make adequately considered decisions in connection with the representation is impaired, whether because of minority, physical illness, mental disability, or other cause, the lawyer must, as far as reasonably possible, maintain a normal client-lawyer relationship with the client and act in the best interests of the client as stated in Subsection (2).

(2) A lawyer representing a client impaired as described in Subsection (1) and for whom no guardian or other representative is available to act, must, with respect to a matter within the scope of the representation, pursue the lawyer's reasonable view of the client's objectives or interests as the client would define them if able to make adequately considered decisions on the matter, even if the client expresses no wishes or gives contrary instructions.

(3) If a client impaired as described in Subsection (1) has a guardian or other person legally entitled to act for the client, the client's lawyer must treat that person as entitled to act with respect to the client's interests in the matter, unless:

(a) the lawyer represents the client in a matter against the interests of that person; or

(b) that person instructs the lawyer to act in a manner that the lawyer knows will violate the person's legal duties toward the client.

(4) A lawyer representing a client impaired as described in Subsection (1) may seek the appointment of a guardian or take other protective action within the scope of the representation when doing so is practical and will advance the client's objectives or interests, determined as stated in Subsection (2).

§ 37. Appearance Before Tribunal

A lawyer who enters an appearance before a tribunal on behalf of a person is presumed to represent that person as a client. The presumption may be rebutted.

§ 38. Lawyer's Actual Authority

A lawyer's act is considered to be that of a client in proceedings before a tribunal or in dealings with third persons when:

    (1) the client has expressly or impliedly authorized the act;

    (2) authority concerning the act is reserved to the lawyer as stated in § 34; or

    (3) the client ratifies the act.

§ 39. Lawyer's Apparent Authority

A lawyer's act is considered to be that of the client in proceedings before a tribunal or in dealings with a third person if the tribunal or third person reasonably assumes that the lawyer is authorized to do the act on the basis of the client's (and not the lawyer's) manifestations of such authorization.

§ 40. Lawyer's Knowledge; Notification to Lawyer; and Statements of Lawyer

(1) Information imparted to a lawyer during and relating to the representation of a client is attributed to the client for the purpose of determining the client's rights and liabilities in matters in which the lawyer represents the client, unless those rights or liabilities require proof of the client's personal knowledge or intentions, or the lawyer's legal duties preclude disclosure of the information to the client.

(2) Unless applicable law otherwise provides, a third person may give notification to a client, in a matter in which the client is represented by a lawyer, by giving notification to the client's lawyer, unless the third person knows of circumstances reasonably indicating that the client has abrogated the lawyer's authority to receive notification.

(3) A lawyer's unprivileged statement is admissible in evidence against a client as if it were the client's statement if either:

    (a) the client authorized the lawyer to make a statement concerning the subject; or

    (b) the statement concerns a matter within the scope of the representation and was made by the lawyer during it.

§ 41. Lawyer's Act or Advice as Mitigating or Avoiding Client's Responsibility

(1) When a client's intent or mental state is in issue, a tribunal may consider otherwise admissible evidence of a lawyer's advice to the client.

(2) In deciding whether to impose a sanction on a person or to relieve a person from a criminal or civil ruling, default, or judgment, a tribunal may consider otherwise admissible evidence to prove or disprove that the lawyer who represented the person did so inadequately or contrary to the client's instructions.

§ 42. Lawyer's Liability to Third Person for Conduct on Behalf of Client

(1) For improper conduct while representing a client, a lawyer is subject to professional discipline as stated in [Chapter 1], to civil liability as stated in [Chapter 4], and to prosecution as provided in the criminal law.

(2) A lawyer is subject to liability to third persons on contracts the lawyer entered into on behalf of a client, unless the lawyer or third person disclaimed such liability, if:

    (a) the client's existence or identity was not disclosed to the third person; or

    (b) the contract is between the lawyer and a third person who provides goods or services used by lawyers and who, as the lawyer knows or reasonably should know, relies on the lawyer's credit.

(3) A lawyer is subject to liability to a third person for damages for loss proximately caused by the lawyer's acting without authority from a client under § 38 if:

    (a) the lawyer tortiously misrepresents to the third person that the lawyer has authority to make a contract, conveyance, or affirmation on behalf of the client and the third person reasonably relies on the misrepresentation; or

    (b) the lawyer purports to make a contract, conveyance, or affirmation on behalf of the client, unless the lawyer manifests that the lawyer does not warrant that the lawyer is authorized to act or the other party knows that the lawyer is not authorized to act.

§ 43. Termination of Lawyer's Authority

(1) A lawyer must comply with applicable law requiring notice to or permission of a tribunal when terminating a representation and with an order of a tribunal requiring the representation to continue.

(2) Subject to Subsection (1) and § 45, a lawyer's actual authority to represent a client ends when:

    (a) the client discharges the lawyer;

    (b) the client dies or, in the case of a corporation or similar organization, loses its capacity to function as such;

    (c) the lawyer withdraws;

    (d) the lawyer dies or becomes physically or mentally incapable of providing representation, is disbarred or suspended from practicing law, or is ordered by a tribunal to cease representing a client; or

    (e) the representation ends as provided by agreement or because the lawyer has completed the contemplated services.

(3) A lawyer's apparent authority to act for a client with respect to another person ends when the other person knows or should know of

facts from which it can be reasonably inferred that the lawyer lacks actual authority, including knowledge of any event described in Subsection (2).

§ 44. Discharge by Client and Withdrawal by Lawyer

(1) Subject to Subsection (4), a client may discharge a lawyer at any time.

(2) Subject to Subsection (4), a lawyer may not represent a client or, where representation has commenced, must withdraw from the representation of a client if:

(a) the representation will result in the lawyer's violating rules of professional conduct or other law;

(b) the lawyer's physical or mental condition materially impairs the lawyer's ability to represent the client; or

(c) the client discharges the lawyer.

(3) Subject to Subsection (4), a lawyer may withdraw from representing a client if:

(a) withdrawal can be accomplished without material adverse effect on the interests of the client;

(b) the lawyer reasonably believes withdrawal is required in circumstances stated in Subsection (2);

(c) the client gives informed consent;

(d) the client persists in a course of action involving the lawyer's services that the lawyer reasonably believes is criminal, fraudulent, or in breach of the client's fiduciary duty;

(e) the lawyer reasonably believes the client has used or threatens to use the lawyer's services to perpetrate a crime or fraud;

(f) the client insists on taking action that the lawyer considers repugnant or imprudent;

(g) the client fails to fulfill a substantial financial or other obligation to the lawyer regarding the lawyer's services and the lawyer has given the client reasonable warning that the lawyer will withdraw unless the client fulfills the obligation;

(h) the representation has been rendered unreasonably difficult by the client or by the irreparable breakdown of the client-lawyer relationship; or

(i) other good cause for withdrawal exists.

(4) Notwithstanding Subsections (1), (2), and (3), a lawyer must comply with applicable law requiring notice to or permission of a tribunal when terminating a representation and with a valid order of a tribunal requiring the representation to continue.

§ 45. Lawyer's Duties When Representation Terminates

(1) In terminating a representation, a lawyer must take steps to the extent reasonably practicable to protect the client's interests, such as giving notice to the client of the termination, allowing time for employment of other counsel, surrendering papers and property to which the client is entitled, and refunding any advance payment of fee the lawyer has not earned.

(2) Following termination of a representation, a lawyer must:

(a) observe obligations to a former client such as those dealing with client confidences (see Chapter 5), conflicts of interest (see Chapter 8), client property and documents (see §§ 56–58), and fee collection (see § 53);

(b) take no action on behalf of a former client without new authorization and give reasonable notice, to those who might otherwise be misled, that the lawyer lacks authority to act for the client;

(c) take reasonable steps to convey to the former client any material communication the lawyer receives relating to the matter involved in the representation; and

(d) take no unfair advantage of a former client by abusing knowledge or trust acquired by means of the representation.

CHAPTER 3: CLIENT AND LAWYER: THE FINANCIAL AND PROPERTY RELATIONSHIP

§ 46. Reasonable and Lawful Fees

A lawyer may not charge a fee larger than is reasonable in the circumstances or that is prohibited by law.

§ 47. Contingent–Fee Arrangements

(1) A lawyer may agree with a client for a fee the size or payment of which is contingent on the outcome of a matter, unless the agreement violates § 46 or another provision of this Restatement or the size or payment of the fee is:

(a) contingent on success in prosecuting or defending a criminal proceeding; or

(b) contingent on a specified result in a divorce proceeding or a proceeding concerning custody of a child.

(2) Unless the agreement construed in the circumstances indicates otherwise, when a lawyer has contracted for a contingent fee, the lawyer is entitled to receive the specified fee only when and to the extent the client receives payment.

§ 48. Forbidden Client–Lawyer Financial Arrangements

(1) A lawyer may not acquire a proprietary interest in the cause of action or subject matter of litigation that the lawyer is conducting for a client, except that the lawyer may:

(a) acquire a lien as provided by § 55 to secure the lawyer's fee or expenses; and

(b) contract with a client for a contingent fee in a civil case except when prohibited as stated in § 47.

(2) A lawyer may not make or guarantee a loan to a client in connection with pending or contemplated litigation that the lawyer is conducting for the client, except that the lawyer may[:

(a) make or guarantee a loan covering court costs and expenses of litigation, the repayment of which to the lawyer may be contingent on the outcome of the matter.[; and

[(b) make or guarantee a loan on fair terms, the repayment of which to the lawyer may be contingent on the outcome of the matter, if: (i) the loan is needed to enable the client to withstand delay in litigation that otherwise might unjustly induce the client to settle or dismiss a case because of financial hardship rather than on the merits; and (ii) if the lawyer does not promise or offer the loan before being retained.]

(3) A lawyer may not, before the lawyer ceases to represent a client, make an agreement giving the lawyer literary or media rights to a portrayal or account based in substantial part on information relating to the representation.

§ 49. Partial or Complete Forfeiture of Lawyer's Compensation

A lawyer engaging in clear and serious violation of duty to a client may be required to forfeit some or all of the lawyer's compensation for the matter. In determining whether and to what extent forfeiture is appropriate, relevant considerations include the gravity and timing of the violation, its willfulness, its effect on the value of the lawyer's work for the client, any other threatened or actual harm to the client, and the adequacy of other remedies.

§ 50. Client–Lawyer Fee Agreements

(1) Before or within a reasonable time after beginning to represent a client in a matter, a lawyer must communicate to the client, in writing when applicable rules so provide, the basis or rate of the fee, unless the communication is unnecessary for the client because the lawyer has previously represented that client on the same basis or at the same rate.

(2) The validity and construction of an agreement between a client and a lawyer concerning the lawyer's fees are governed by § 29A.

(3) Unless an agreement construed in the circumstances indicates otherwise:

(a) a lawyer may not charge separately for the lawyer's general office and overhead expenses;

(b) payments that the law requires an opposing party or that party's lawyer to pay as attorney-fee awards or sanctions are credited to the client, not the client's lawyer, absent a contrary statute or court order; and

(c) when a lawyer requests and receives a fee payment that is not for services already rendered, that payment is to be credited against whatever fee the lawyer is entitled to collect.

§ 51. Lawyer's Fee in Absence of Agreement

If a client and lawyer have not made a valid agreement providing for another measure of compensation, a client owes a lawyer who has performed legal services for the client the fair value of the lawyer's services.

§ 52. Fees on Termination

If a client-lawyer relationship ends before the lawyer has completed the services due for a matter and the lawyer's fee has not been forfeited under § 49:

(1) a lawyer who has been discharged or withdraws may recover the lesser of the fair value of the lawyer's services as determined under § 51 and the ratable proportion of the compensation provided by any otherwise enforceable agreement between lawyer and client for the services performed; except that

(2) the tribunal may allow such a lawyer to recover the ratable proportion of the compensation provided by such an agreement if:

(a) the discharge or withdrawal is not attributable to misconduct of the lawyer;

(b) the lawyer has performed severable services; and

(c) allowing contractual compensation would not burden the client's choice of counsel or the client's ability to replace counsel.

§ 53. Fee Collection Methods

In seeking compensation claimed from a client or former client, a lawyer may not employ collection methods forbidden by law, use confidential information (as defined in Chapter 5) when not permitted under § 117, or harass the client.

§ 54. Remedies and Burden of Persuasion

(1) A fee dispute between a lawyer and a client may be adjudicated in any appropriate proceeding, including a suit by the lawyer to recover an unpaid fee, a suit for a refund by a client, an arbitration to which both parties consent unless applicable law renders the lawyer's consent

unnecessary, or in the court's discretion a proceeding ancillary to a pending suit in which the lawyer performed the services in question.

(2) In any such proceeding the lawyer has the burden of persuading the trier of fact, when relevant, of the existence and terms of any fee agreement, the making of any disclosures to the client required to render an agreement enforceable, and the extent and value of the lawyer's services.

§ 55. Lawyer Liens

(1) Except as provided in Subsection (2) or by statute or rule, a lawyer does not acquire a lien entitling the lawyer to retain the client's property in the lawyer's possession in order to secure payment of the lawyer's fees and disbursements. A lawyer may decline to deliver to a client or former client an original or copy of any document prepared by the lawyer or at the lawyer's expense if the client or former client has not paid all fees and disbursements due for the lawyer's work in preparing the document and nondelivery would not unreasonably harm the client or former client.

(2) Unless otherwise provided by statute or rule, client and lawyer may agree that the lawyer shall have a security interest in property of the client recovered for the client through the lawyer's efforts, as follows:

    (a) the lawyer may contract in writing with the client for a lien on the proceeds of the representation to secure payment for the lawyer's services and disbursements in that matter;

    (b) the lien becomes binding on a third party when the party has notice of the lien;

    (c) the lien applies only to the amount of fees and disbursements claimed reasonably and in good faith for the lawyer's services performed in the representation; and

    (d) the lawyer may not unreasonably impede the speedy and inexpensive resolution of any dispute concerning those fees and disbursements or the lien.

(3) A tribunal where an action is pending may in its discretion adjudicate any fee or other dispute concerning a lien asserted by a lawyer on property of a party to the action, provide for custody of the property, release all or part of the property to the client or lawyer, and grant such other relief as justice may require.

(4) With respect to property neither in the lawyer's possession nor recovered by the client through the lawyer's efforts, the lawyer may obtain a security interest on property of a client only as provided by other law and consistent with §§ 29A and 207. Acquisition of such a security interest is a business or financial transaction with a client within the meaning of § 207.

§ 56. Safeguarding and Segregating Property

(1) A lawyer holding funds or other property of a client in connection with a representation, or such funds or other property in which a client claims an interest, must take reasonable steps to safeguard the funds or property. A similar obligation may be imposed by law on funds or other property so held and owned or claimed by a third person. In particular, the lawyer must hold such property separate from the lawyer's property, keep records of it, deposit funds in an account separate from the lawyer's own funds, identify tangible objects, and comply with related requirements imposed by regulatory authorities.

(2) Upon receiving funds or other property in a professional capacity and in which a client or a third person owns or claims an interest, a lawyer shall promptly notify the client or third person. The lawyer shall promptly render a full accounting regarding such property upon request by the client or third person.

§ 57. Surrendering Possession of Property

(1) Except as provided in Subsection (2), a lawyer must promptly deliver, to the client or third person so entitled, funds or other property in the lawyer's possession belonging to a client or third person.

(2) A lawyer may retain possession of funds or other property of a client or third person if:

    (a) the client or third person consents;

    (b) the lawyer's client is entitled to the property, the lawyer appropriately possesses the property for purposes of the representation, and the client has not asked for delivery of the property;

    (c) the lawyer has a valid lien on the property (see § 55);

    (d) there are substantial grounds for dispute as to the person entitled to the property; or

    (e) delivering the property to the client or third person would violate a court order or other legal obligation of the lawyer.

§ 58. Documents Relating to Representation

(1) A lawyer must take reasonable steps to safeguard documents in the lawyer's possession relating to the representation of a client or former client.

(2) On request, a lawyer must allow a client or former client to inspect and copy any document possessed by the lawyer relating to the representation, unless substantial grounds exist to refuse.

(3) Unless a client or former client consents to nondelivery or substantial grounds exist for refusing to make delivery, a lawyer must deliver to the client or former client, at an appropriate time and in any event promptly after the representation ends, such originals and copies

of other documents possessed by the lawyer relating to the representation as the client or former client reasonably needs.

(4) Notwithstanding Subsections (2) and (3), a lawyer may decline to deliver to a client or former client an original or copy of any document under circumstances permitted by § 55(1).

§ 59. Fee–Splitting With Lawyer Not in Same Firm

A division of fees between lawyers who are not in the same firm may be made only if:

(1)(a) the division is in proportion to the services performed by each lawyer or (b) by agreement with the client, each lawyer assumes joint responsibility for the representation;

(2) the client is informed of and does not object to the fact of division and the participation of the lawyers involved; and

(3) the total fee in reasonable (see § 46).

CHAPTER 4: LAWYER CIVIL LIABILITY

§ 71. Elements and Defenses Generally

In addition to the other possible bases of civil liability described in §§ 76A and 77, a lawyer is civilly liable to a person to whom the lawyer owes a duty of care within the meaning of § 72 or § 73, if the lawyer fails to exercise care within the meaning of § 74 and if that failure is a legal cause of injury within the meaning of § 75, unless the lawyer has a defense within the meaning of § 76.

§ 72. Duty of Care to Client

For purposes of liability under § 71, a lawyer owes a client the duty to exercise care within the meaning of § 74 in pursuing the client's lawful objectives in matters covered by the representation and in fulfilling the fiduciary duties to the client set forth in § 28(3).

§ 73. Duty of Care to Certain Non–Clients

For purposes of liability under § 71, a lawyer owes a duty to use care within the meaning of § 74:

(1) to a prospective client, as stated in § 27;

(2) to a non-client when and to the extent that:

(a) the lawyer or (with the lawyer's acquiescence) the lawyer's client invites the non-client to rely on the lawyer's opinion or provision of other legal services, and the non-client so relies, and

(b) the non-client is not, under applicable tort law, too remote from the lawyer to be entitled to protection;

(3) to a non-client when and to the extent that:

(a) the lawyer knows that a client intends as one of the primary objectives of the representation that the lawyer's services benefit the non-client; and

(b) such a duty would not significantly impair the lawyer's performance of obligations to the client, and the absence of such a duty would make enforcement of those obligations unlikely;

(4) to a non-client when and to the extent that:

(a) the lawyer's client is a trustee, guardian, executor, or fiduciary acting primarily to perform similar functions for the non-client;

(b) circumstances known to the lawyer make it clear that appropriate action by the lawyer is necessary with respect to a matter within the scope of the representation to prevent or rectify the breach of a fiduciary duty owed by the client to the non-client, where (i) the breach is a crime or fraud or (ii) the lawyer has assisted or is assisting the breach;

(c) the non-client is not reasonably able to protect its rights; and

(d) such a duty would not significantly impair the performance of the lawyer's obligations to the client.

§ 74. Standard of Care

(1) For purposes of liability under § 71, a lawyer who owes a duty of care must exercise the competence and diligence normally exercised by lawyers in similar circumstances, unless the lawyer represents that the lawyer will exercise greater competence or diligence.

(2) Proof of a violation of a rule or statute regulating the conduct of lawyers:

(a) does not give rise to an implied cause of action for lack of care;

(b) does not preclude other proof concerning the duty of care in Subsection (1); and

(c) may be considered by a trier of fact as an aid in understanding and applying the standard of Subsection (1) to the extent that

(i) the rule or statute was designed for the protection of persons in the position of the claimant and

(ii) proof of the content and construction of such a rule or statute is relevant to the claimant's claim.

§ 75. Causation and Damages

A lawyer is liable under § 71 only for injury of which the lawyer's breach of a duty of care was a legal cause, as determined under generally applicable principles of causation and damages.

§ 76. Defenses; Prospective Liability Waiver; Settlement

(1) An agreement prospectively limiting a lawyer's liability to a client for malpractice is unenforceable.

(2) The client or former client may void an agreement settling a claim by the client or former client against the person's lawyer if:

(a) the client or former client was subjected to improper pressure by the lawyer in reaching the settlement; or

(b)(i) the client or former client was not independently represented in negotiating the settlement, and (ii) the settlement was not fair and reasonable to the client or former client.

(3) For purposes of professional discipline, a lawyer may not:

(a) make an agreement prospectively limiting the lawyer's liability to a client for malpractice; or

(b) settle a claim for such liability with an unrepresented client or former client without first advising that person in writing that independent representation is appropriate in connection therewith.

(4) Except as otherwise provided in this Section, liability under § 71 is subject to the defenses available under generally applicable principles of law governing professional negligence actions. A lawyer is not liable under § 71 for any action or inaction the lawyer reasonably believed to be required by law, including a professional rule.

§ 76A. Civil Liability to Client Other Than for Malpractice

(1) A lawyer is subject to liability to a client for injury caused by breach of contract in the circumstances and to the extent provided by contract law.

(2) A lawyer is subject to liability to a client for injury caused by intentional breach of the fiduciary duties set forth in § 28(3) in the circumstances and to the extent provided by law governing intentional breach of fiduciary duties.

(3) A client is entitled to restitutionary, injunctive, or declaratory remedies against a lawyer in the circumstances and to the extent provided by generally applicable law governing such remedies.

§ 77. Liability to Client or Non–Client Under General Law

Except as provided in § 78, and in addition to liability under §§ 71–76A, a lawyer is subject to liability to a client or non-client when a nonlawyer would be in similar circumstances.

§ 78. Non–Client Claims—Certain Defenses and Exceptions to Liability

(1) In addition to other absolute or conditional privileges provided by the law of defamation, a lawyer is absolutely privileged under the law of defamation to publish defamatory matter concerning a non-client in

communications preliminary to a reasonably anticipated proceeding before a tribunal, or in the institution or during the course and as a part of such a proceeding, in which the lawyer participates as counsel, if the matter is published to a person who will be involved in the proceeding and has some relation to the proceeding.

(2) A lawyer representing a client in a civil proceeding, or procuring the institution of criminal proceedings by a client, is not liable to a non-client for wrongful use of civil proceedings or for malicious prosecution if the lawyer has probable cause for acting, or if the lawyer acts primarily to help the client obtain a proper adjudication of the client's claim.

(3) A lawyer who advises or assists a client to make or break a contract, to enter or dissolve a legal relationship, or to enter or not enter a contractual relation, is not liable to a non-client for interference with contract or with prospective contractual relations or with a legal relationship, if the lawyer acts to advance the client's objectives without using wrongful means.

§ 79. Vicarious Liability

(1) A law firm is subject to civil liability for injury legally caused to a person by any wrongful act or omission of any principal or employee of the firm who was acting in the ordinary course of the firm's business or with actual authority.

(2) Each of the principals of a law firm organized as a general partnership is liable jointly and severally with the firm.

(3) A principal of a law firm organized other than as a general partnership as authorized by law is vicariously liable for the acts of another principal or employee of the firm to the extent provided by law.

CHAPTER 5: CONFIDENTIAL CLIENT INFORMATION

§ 111. Definition of "Confidential Client Information"

Confidential client information consists of information relating to that client, acquired by a lawyer or agent of the lawyer in the course of or as the result of representing the client, other than information that is generally known.

§ 112. Lawyer's Duty to Safeguard Confidential Client Information

(1) Except as provided in §§ 113–117A, during and after representation of a client:

(a) the lawyer may not use or disclose confidential client information as defined in § 111 if there is a reasonable prospect that doing so will adversely affect a material interest of the client or if the client has instructed the lawyer not to use or disclose such information;

(b) the lawyer must take steps reasonable in the circumstances to protect confidential client information against impermissible use or disclosure by the lawyer's associates or agents that may adversely affect a material interest of the client or otherwise than as instructed by the client.

(2) Except as stated in § 114, a lawyer who uses confidential information of a client for the lawyer's pecuniary gain other than in the practice of law must account to the client for any profits made.

§ 113. Using or Disclosing Information to Advance Client Interests

A lawyer may use or disclose confidential client information when the lawyer reasonably believes that doing so will advance the interests of the client in the representation.

§ 114. Using or Disclosing Information With Client Consent

A lawyer may use or disclose confidential client information when the client consents after being adequately informed concerning the use or disclosure.

§ 115. Using or Disclosing Information When Required by Law

A lawyer may use or disclose confidential client information when required by law, after the lawyer takes reasonably appropriate steps to assert that the information is privileged or otherwise protected against disclosure.

§ 116. Using or Disclosing Information in Lawyer's Self–Sefense

A lawyer may use or disclose confidential client information when and to the extent that the lawyer reasonably believes it necessary in order to defend the lawyer or the lawyer's associate or agent against a charge or threatened charge by any person that the lawyer or such associate or agent acted wrongfully in the course of representing that client.

§ 117. Using or Disclosing Information in Compensation Dispute

A lawyer may use or disclose confidential client information when and to the extent that the lawyer reasonably believes necessary in order to permit the lawyer to resolve a dispute with the client concerning compensation or reimbursements that the lawyer reasonably claims to be due.

§ 117A. Using or Disclosing Information to Prevent Death or Serious Bodily Harm

(1) A lawyer may use or disclose confidential client information when and to the extent that the lawyer reasonably believes such use or disclosure is necessary to prevent certain death o serious bodily harm to a person.

(2) Before using or disclosing information pursuant to the Section, the lawyer must, if feasible, make a good faith effort to persuade the client either not to act or, if the client or another person has already acted, to warn the victim or take other action to prevent the harm and, if relevant, to advise the client of the lawyer's ability to use or disclose pursuant to the Section and the consequences thereof.

(3) A lawyer who, in a situation described in this Section, takes action or decides not to take action permitted under this Section is not, solely by reason of such action or inaction, subject to professional discipline, liable for damages to the lawyer's client or any third person, or barred from recovery against a client or third person by an affirmative defense based solely thereon.

§ 117B. Using or Disclosing Information to Prevent, Rectify, or Mitigate Substantial Financial Loss

(1) A lawyer may use or disclose confidential client information when and to the extent that the lawyer reasonably believes such use or disclosure is necessary to prevent a crime or fraud, and:

(a) the crime or fraud threatens substantial loss to a person;

(b) the loss has not yet occurred;

(c) the lawyer's client intends to commit the crime or fraud either directly or through a third person; and

(d) the client has employed or is employing the lawyer's services in committing the crime or fraud.

(2) In addition of a loss otherwise described in Subsection (1) but that has already occurred, a lawyer may use or disclose confidential client information when and to the extent that the lawyer reasonably believes such use or disclosure is necessary to rectify or mitigate the loss.

(3) Before using or disclosing information pursuant to this Section, the lawyer must, if feasible, make a good faith effort to persuade the client either not to act or, if the client has already acted, to warn the victim or take other action to prevent, rectify, or mitigate the loss and, if relevant, to advise the client of the lawyer's ability to use or disclose pursuant to this Section and the consequences thereof.

(4) A lawyer who, in a situation described in this Section, takes action or decides not to take action permitted under this Section is not, solely by reason of such action or inaction, subject to professional discipline, liable for damages to the lawyer's client or any third person,

or barred from recovery against a client or third person by an affirmative defense based solely thereon.

§ 118. Attorney–Client Privilege

Except as otherwise provided in this Restatement, the attorney-client privilege may be invoked as provided in § 135 with respect to:

(1) a communication

(2) made between privileged persons

(3) in confidence

(4) for the purpose of obtaining or providing legal assistance for the client.

§ 119. Attorney–Client Privilege—"Communication"

A communication within the meaning of § 118 is any expression through which a privileged person, as defined in § 120, undertakes to convey information to another privileged person and any document or other record revealing such an expression.

§ 120. Attorney–Client Privilege—"Privileged Persons"

Privileged persons within the meaning of § 118 are the client (including a prospective client), the client's lawyer, agents of either who facilitate communications between them, and agents of the lawyer who facilitate the representation.

§ 121. Attorney–Client Privilege—"In Confidence"

A communication is in confidence within the meaning of § 118 if, at the time and in the circumstances of the communication, the communicating person reasonably believes that no one will learn the contents of the communication except a privileged person as defined in § 120 or another person with whom communications are protected under a similar evidentiary privilege.

§ 122. Attorney–Client Privilege—Legal Assistance as Object of Privileged Communication

A communication is made for the purpose of obtaining or providing legal assistance within the meaning of § 118 if it is made to or to assist a person:

(1) who is a lawyer or who the client or prospective client reasonably believes to be a lawyer; and

(2) whom the client or prospective client consults for the purpose of obtaining legal assistance.

§ 123. Privilege for Organizational Client

When a client is a corporation, unincorporated association, partnership, trust, estate, sole proprietorship, or other for-profit or not-for-profit organization, the attorney-client privilege extends to a communication that:

(1) otherwise qualifies as privileged under §§ 118–122;

(2) is between an agent of the organization and a privileged person as defined in § 120;

(3) concerns a legal matter of interest to the organization; and

(4) is disclosed only to:

(a) privileged persons as defined in § 120; and

(b) other agents of the organization who reasonably need to know of the communication in order to act for the organization.

§ 124. Privilege for Governmental Client

Unless applicable law otherwise provides, the attorney-client privilege extends to a communication of a governmental organization as stated in § 123 and of an individual officer, employee, or other agent of a governmental organization n as a client with respect to his or her personal interest as stated in §§ 118–122.

§ 125. Privilege of Co–Clients

(1) If two or more persons are jointly represented by the same lawyer in a matter, a communication of either co-client that otherwise qualifies as privileged under §§ 118–122 and relates to matters of common interest is privileged as against third persons, and any co-client may invoke the privilege, unless it has been waived by the client who made the communication.

(2) Unless the co-clients have agreed otherwise, a communication described in Subsection (1) is not privileged as between the co-clients in a subsequent adverse proceeding between them.

§ 126. Common–Interest Arrangement

(1) If two or more clients with a common interest in a litigated or non-litigated matter are represented by separate lawyers and they agree to exchange information concerning the matter, a communication of any such client that otherwise qualifies as privileged under §§ 118–122 that relates to the matter is privileged as against third persons. Any such client may invoke the privilege, unless it has been waived by the client who made the communication.

(2) Unless the clients have agreed otherwise, a communication described in Subsection (1) is not privileged as between clients described in Subsection (1) in a subsequent adverse proceeding between them.

§ 127. Duration of Privilege

Unless waived (see §§ 128–130) or subject to exception (see §§ 131–134B), the attorney-client privilege may be invoked as provided in § 135 at any time during or after termination of the relationship between client or prospective client and lawyer.

§ 128. Waiver by Agreement, Disclaimer, or Failure to Object

The attorney-client privilege is waived if the client, the client's lawyer, or another authorized agent of the client:

(1) agrees to waive the privilege;

(2) disclaims protection of the privilege and

(a) another person reasonably relies on the disclaimer to that person's detriment; or

(b) reasons of judicial administration require that the client not be permitted to revoke the disclaimer; or

(3) in a proceeding before a tribunal, fails to object properly to an attempt by another person to give or exact testimony or other evidence of a privileged communication.

§ 129. Subsequent Disclosure

The attorney-client privilege is lost if the client, the client's lawyer, or another authorized agent of the client voluntarily discloses the communication in a non-privileged communication.

§ 130. Waiver by Putting Assistance or Communication in Issue

(1) The attorney-client privilege is waived for any relevant communication if the client asserts as to a material issue in a proceeding that:

(a) the client acted upon the advice of a lawyer or that the advice was otherwise relevant to the legal significance of the client's conduct; or

(b) a lawyer's assistance was ineffective, negligent, or otherwise wrongful.

(2) The attorney-client privilege is waived for a recorded communication if a witness:

(a) employs the communication to aid the witness while testifying; or

(b) employed the communication in preparing to testify, and the tribunal finds that disclosure is required in the interests of justice.

§ 131. Exception for Dispute Concerning Decedent's Disposition of Property

The attorney-client privilege does not apply to a communication from or to a decedent relevant to an issue between parties who claim an interest through the same deceased client, either by testate or intestate succession or by an inter vivos transaction.

§ 132. Exception for Client Crime or Fraud

The attorney-client privilege does not apply to a communication occurring when a client:

(a) consults a lawyer for the purpose, later accomplished, of obtaining assistance to engage in a crime or fraud or aiding a third person to do so, or

(b) regardless of the client's purpose at the time of consultation, uses the lawyer's advice or other services to engage in or assist a crime or fraud.

§ 133. Exceptions for Lawyer Self–Protection

The attorney-client privilege does not apply to a communication that is relevant and reasonably necessary for a lawyer to employ in a proceeding:

(1) to resolve a dispute with a client concerning compensation or reimbursement that the lawyer reasonably claims the client owes the lawyer; or

(2) to defend the lawyer against an allegation by any person that the lawyer, an agent of the lawyer, or another person for whose conduct the lawyer is responsible acted wrongfully during the course of representing a client.

§ 134A. Exception for Fiduciary–Lawyer Communication

In a proceeding in which a trustee of an express trust or similar fiduciary is charged with breach of fiduciary duties by a beneficiary, a communication otherwise within § 118 is nonetheless not privileged if the communication:

(a) is relevant to the claimed breach; and

(b) was between the trustee and a lawyer (or other privileged person within the meaning of § 120) who was retained to advise the trustee concerning the administration of the trust.

§ 134B. Exception for Organizational Fiduciary

In a proceeding involving a dispute between an organizational client and shareholders, members, or other constituents of the organization toward whom the directors, officers, or similar persons managing the organization bear fiduciary responsibilities, the attorney-client privilege of the organization may be withheld from a communication otherwise within § 118 if the tribunal finds that:

(a) those managing the organization are charged with breach of their obligations toward the shareholders, members, or other constituents or toward the organization itself;

(b) the communication occurred prior to the assertion of the charges and relates directly to those charges; and

(c) the need of the requesting party to discover or introduce the communication is sufficiently compelling and the threat to confidentiality sufficiently confined to justify setting the privilege aside.

§ 135. Invoking the Privilege and Its Exceptions

(1) When an attempt is made to introduce in evidence or obtain discovery of a communication privileged under § 118:

(a) A client, a personal representative of an incompetent or deceased client, or a person succeeding to the interest of a client may invoke or waive the privilege, either personally or through counsel or another authorized agent.

(b) A lawyer, an agent of the lawyer, or an agent of a client from whom a privileged communication is sought must invoke the privilege when doing so appears reasonably appropriate, unless the client:

(i) has waived the privilege; or

(ii) has authorized the lawyer or agent to waive it.

(c) Notwithstanding failure to invoke the privilege as specified in Subsections (1)(a) and (1)(b), the tribunal has discretion to invoke the privilege.

(2) A person invoking the privilege must ordinarily object contemporaneously to an attempt to disclose the communication and, if the objection is contested, demonstrate each element of the privilege under § 118.

(3) A person invoking a waiver of or exception to the privilege (§§ 128–134B) must assert it and, if the assertion is contested, demonstrate each element of the waiver or exception.

§ 136. Work–Product Immunity

(1) Work product consists of tangible material or its intangible equivalent in unwritten or oral form, other than underlying facts, prepared by a lawyer for litigation then in progress or in reasonable anticipation of future litigation.

(2) Opinion work product consists of the opinions or mental impressions of a lawyer; all other work product is ordinary work product.

(3) Except for material which by applicable law is not so protected, work product is immune from discovery or other compelled disclosure to the extent stated in §§ 137 (ordinary work product) and 138 (opinion work product) when the immunity is invoked as described in § 139.

§ 137. Ordinary Work Product

When work product protection is invoked as described in § 139, ordinary work product (§ 136(2)) is immune from discovery or other compelled disclosure unless either an exception recognized in §§ 140–142 applies or the inquiring party:

> (1) has a substantial need for the material in order to prepare for trial; and

> (2) is unable without undue hardship to obtain the substantial equivalent of the material by other means.

§ 138. Opinion Work Product

When work product protection is invoked as described in § 139, opinion work product (§ 136(2)) is immune from discovery or other compelled disclosure unless either the immunity is waived or an exception applies (§§ 140–142) or extraordinary circumstances justify disclosure.

§ 139. Invoking Work–Product Immunity and Its Exceptions

(1) Work-product immunity may be invoked by or for a person on whose behalf the work product was prepared.

(2) The person invoking work-product immunity must object and, if the objection is contested, demonstrate each element of the immunity.

(3) Once a claim of work product has been adequately supported, a person entitled to invoke a waiver or exception must assert it and, if the assertion is contested, demonstrate each element of the waiver or exception.

§ 140. Waiver of Work–Product Immunity by Voluntary Act

Work-product immunity is waived if the client, the client's lawyer, or another authorized agent of the client:

> (1) agrees to waive the immunity;

> (2) disclaims protection of the immunity and:

>> (a) another person reasonably relies on the disclaimer to that person's detriment; or

>> (b) reasons of judicial administration require that the client not be permitted to revoke the disclaimer; or

> (3) in a proceeding before a tribunal, fails to object properly to an attempt by another person to give or exact testimony or other evidence of work product; or

> (4) discloses the material to third persons in circumstances in which there is a significant likelihood that an adversary or potential adversary in anticipated litigation will obtain it.

§ 141. Waiver of Work–Product Immunity by Use in Litigation

(1) Work-product immunity is waived for any relevant material if the client asserts as to a material issue in a proceeding that:

(a) the client acted upon the advice of a lawyer or that the advice was otherwise relevant to the legal significance of the client's conduct; or

(b) a lawyer's assistance was ineffective, negligent, or otherwise wrongful.

(2) The work-product immunity is waived for recorded material if a witness

(a) employs the material to aid the witness while testifying, or

(b) employed the material in preparing to testify, and the tribunal finds that disclosure is required in the interests of justice.

§ 142. Exception for Crime or Fraud

Work-product immunity does not apply to materials prepared when a client consults a lawyer for the purpose of obtaining assistance to engage in a crime or fraud or to aid a third person to do so or uses the materials for such a purpose.

CHAPTER 6: REPRESENTING CLIENTS: IN GENERAL

§ 151. Advising and Assisting Client—In General

(1) A lawyer who counsels or assists a client to engage in conduct that violates the rights of a third person is subject to liability:

(a) to the third person to the extent stated in §§ 73 and 77–78; and

(b) to the client to the extent stated in § 72, 76A, and 77.

(2) For purposes of professional discipline, a lawyer may not counsel or assist a client to take or fail to take an action that the lawyer knows to be criminal or fraudulent or in violation of a court order with the intent of facilitating or encouraging the action, but the lawyer may counsel or assist a client to take or fail to take action for which the lawyer reasonably believes the client can assert a non-frivolous argument that the client's action will not constitute a crime or fraud or violate a court order, such as when the action constitutes a good faith effort to determine the validity, scope, meaning, or application of a law or court order.

(3) In counseling a client, a lawyer may address non-legal aspects of a proposed course of conduct, including moral, reputational, economic, social, political, and business aspects.

§ 152. Evaluation Undertaken for Third Person

(1) In furtherance of the objectives of a client in a representation, a lawyer may provide to a non-client the results of the lawyer's investigation and analysis of facts or the lawyer's professional evaluation or opinion on the matter.

(2) When providing the information, evaluation, or opinion under Subsection (1) is reasonably likely to affect the client's interests materially and adversely, the lawyer shall first obtain the client's consent after the client is adequately informed concerning important possible effects on the client's interests.

(3) In providing the information, evaluation, or opinion under Subsection (1), the lawyer shall exercise care with respect to the non-client to the extent stated in § 73(2) and not make false statements prohibited under § 157.

§ 155. Representing Organization as Client

(1) When a lawyer is employed or retained to represent an organization:

(a) the lawyer represents the interests of the organization as defined by its responsible agents acting pursuant to the organization's decision-making procedures; and

(b) subject to Subsection (2), the lawyer must follow instructions in the representation, as stated in § 32(2), given by persons authorized so to act on behalf of the organization.

(2) If a lawyer representing an organization knows of circumstances indicating that a constituent of the organization has engaged in action or intends to act in a way that violates a legal obligation to the organization that will likely cause substantial injury to it, or that reasonably can be foreseen to be imputable to the organization and thus likely to result in substantial injury to it, the lawyer must proceed in what the lawyer reasonably believes to be the best interests of the organization.

(3) In the circumstances described in Subsection (2), the lawyer may, in circumstances warranting such steps, ask the constituent to reconsider the matter, recommend that a second legal opinion be sought, and seek review by appropriate supervisory authority within the organization, including referring the matter to the highest authority that can act in behalf of the organization.

§ 156. Representing Governmental Client

A lawyer representing a governmental client must proceed in the representation as stated in § 155, except that the lawyer:

(1) possesses such rights and responsibilities as may be defined by law to make decisions on behalf of the governmental client that are within the authority of a client under §§ 33 and 32(2);

(2) except as otherwise provided by law, must proceed as stated in §§ 155(2) and 155(3) with respect to an act of a constituent of the governmental client that violates a legal obligation that will likely cause substantial public or private injury or that reasonably can be foreseen to be imputable to and thus likely result in substantial injury to the client;

(3) if a prosecutor or similar lawyer determine whether to file criminal proceedings, or take other steps in such proceedings, must do so only when based on probable cause and the lawyer's belief, formed after due investigation, that there are good factual and legal grounds to support the step taken; and

(4) must observe other applicable restrictions imposed by law on those similarly functioning for the governmental client.

§ 157. Statements to Non–Clients

A lawyer communicating on behalf of client with a non-client may not:

(1) knowingly make a false statement of material fact or law to a non-client,

(2) make other statements prohibited by law; or

(3) fail to make a disclosure required by law.

§ 158. Represented Non–Client—General Anti–Contact Rule

(1) A lawyer representing a client in a matter may not communicate about the subject of the representation with a non-client whom the lawyer knows to be represented in the matter by another lawyer, or with a representative of an organizational non-client so represented as defined in § 159, unless:

(a) the communication is with a public officer or agency to the extent stated in § 161;

(b) the lawyer is a party and represents no other client in the matter;

(c) the communication is authorized by law;

(d) the communication reasonably responds to an emergency; or

(e) the other lawyer consents.

(2) Subsection (1) does not prohibit the lawyer from assisting the client in otherwise proper communication by the lawyer's client with a represented non-client, unless the lawyer thereby seeks to deceive or overreach the non-client.

§ 159. Definition of Represented Non–Client

Within the meaning of § 158, a represented non-client includes:

(1) a natural person represented by a lawyer; and

(2) a representative of an organization represented by a lawyer:

(a) who supervises, directs or regularly consults with the lawyer concerning the matter or who has power to compromise or settle the matter;

(b) whose acts or omissions may be imputed to the organization for purposes of civil or criminal liability in the matter; or

(c) whose statements, under applicable rules of evidence, would have the effect of binding the organization with respect to proof of the matter.

§ 161. Represented Governmental Agency or Officer

Unless otherwise provided by law and except when a represented governmental agency or officer is engaged in litigation of a specific claim that does not involve broad public policy issues, the rule stated in § 158 does not apply to communications with the agency or the officer in the officer's official capacity. In specific-claim litigation, contact is permissible so long as it does not create an opportunity for substantially unfair advantage against the governmental party.

§ 162. Information of Non–Client Known to Be Legally Protected

A lawyer representing a client in a matter and communicating with a non-client in a situation permitted under § 158 may not seek to obtain information that the lawyer reasonably should know the non-client may not reveal without violating a duty of confidentiality to another imposed by law.

§ 163. Dealings With Unrepresented Non–client

In the course of representing a client and dealing with a non-client who is not represented by a lawyer:

(1) the lawyer may not mislead the non-client, to the prejudice of the non-client, concerning the identity and interests of the person the lawyer represents; and

(2) when the lawyer knows or reasonably should know that the unrepresented non-client misunderstands the lawyer's role in the matter, the lawyer must make reasonable efforts to correct the misunderstanding when failure to do so would materially prejudice the non-client.

§ 164. Representing Client in Legislative and Administrative Matters

A lawyer representing a client before a legislature or administrative agency:

(1) must disclose that the appearance is in a representative capacity and not misrepresent the capacity in which the lawyer appears;

(2) must comply with applicable law and regulations governing such representations; and

(3) except as applicable law otherwise provides:

(a) in an adjudicative proceeding before a government agency or involving such an agency as a participant, has the legal rights and responsibilities of an advocate in a proceeding before a judicial tribunal; and

(b) in other types of proceedings and matters, has the legal rights and responsibilities applicable in the lawyer's dealings with a private person.

CHAPTER 7: REPRESENTING CLIENTS IN LITIGATION

§ 165. Complying With Law and Tribunal Rulings

In representing a client in a matter before a tribunal, a lawyer must comply with applicable law, including rules of procedure and evidence and specific tribunal rulings.

§ 166. Dealing With Other Participants in Proceedings

In representing a client in a matter before a tribunal, a lawyer may not use means that have no substantial purpose other than to embarrass, delay, or burden a third person, or use methods of obtaining evidence that are prohibited by law.

§ 167. Prohibited Forensic Tactics

In representing a client in a matter before a tribunal, a lawyer may not, in the presence of the trier of fact:

(1) state a personal opinion about the justness of a cause, the creditability of a witness, the culpability of a civil litigant, or the guilt or innocence of an accused, but the lawyer may argue any position or conclusion adequately supported by the lawyer's analysis of the evidence; or

(2) allude to any factual matter that the lawyer does not reasonably believe is relevant or supportable by admissible evidence.

§ 168. Advocate as Witness

(1) Except as provided in Subsection (2), a lawyer may not represent a client in a contested hearing or trial of a matter in which:

(a) the lawyer is expected to testify for the lawyer's client; or

(b) the lawyer does not intend to testify but (i) the lawyer's testimony would be material to establishing a claim or defense of the client, and (ii) the client has not consented as stated in § 202 to the lawyer's failure to testify.

(2) A lawyer may represent a client when the lawyer will testify as stated in Subsection (1)(a) if:

(a) the lawyer's testimony relates to an issue that the lawyer reasonably believes will not be contested or to the nature and value of legal services rendered in the proceeding;

(b) deprivation of the lawyer's services as advocate would work a substantial hardship on the client; or

(c) consent has been given by (i) opposing parties who would be adversely affected by the lawyer's testimony, and (ii) if relevant, the lawyer's client, as stated in § 202 with respect to any conflict of interest between lawyer and client (see § 206) that the lawyer's testimony would create.

(3) A lawyer may not represent a client in a litigated matter pending before a tribunal when the lawyer or a lawyer in the lawyer's firm will give testimony materially adverse to the position of the lawyer's client or materially adverse to a former client of any such lawyer with respect to a matter substantially related to the earlier representation, unless the affected client has consented as stated in § 202 with respect to any conflict of interest between lawyer and client (see § 206) that the testimony would create.

(4) A tribunal should not permit a lawyer to call opposing trial counsel as a witness unless the testifying lawyer would give testimony that is not merely cumulative of evidence readily available by less intrusive means.

§ 169. Advocate's Public Comment on Pending Litigation

(1) In representing a client in a matter before a tribunal, a lawyer may not make a statement outside the proceeding that a reasonable person would expect to be disseminated by means of public communications when the lawyer knows or reasonably should know that the statement will have a substantial likelihood of materially prejudicing a juror or influencing or intimidating a prospective witness in the proceeding. However, a lawyer may in any event make a statement that is reasonably necessary to mitigate the impact on the lawyer's client of substantial, undue, and prejudicial publicity recently initiated by one other than the lawyer or the lawyer's client.

(2) A prosecutor must, except for statements necessary to inform the public of the nature and extent of the prosecutor's actions and that serve a legitimate law enforcement purpose, refrain from making extrajudicial comments that have a substantial likelihood of heightening public condemnation of the accused.

§ 170. Frivolous Advocacy

(1) A lawyer may not bring or defend a proceeding, or assert or controvert an issue therein, unless there is a basis for doing so that is not frivolous, which includes a good-faith argument for an extension, modification, or reversal of existing law.

(2) Notwithstanding Subsection (1), a lawyer for the defendant in a criminal proceeding, or respondent in a proceeding that could result in incarceration, may so defend the proceeding as to require that the prosecutor establish every necessary element.

(3) A lawyer may not make a frivolous discovery request or fail to make a reasonably diligent effort to comply with a proper discovery request of another party.

§ 171. Disclosure of Legal Authority

In representing a client in a matter before a tribunal, a lawyer may not knowingly:

(1) make a false statement of a material proposition of law to the tribunal; or

(2) fail to disclose to the tribunal legal authority in the controlling jurisdiction known to the lawyer to be directly adverse to the position asserted by the client and not disclosed by opposing counsel.

§ 172. Advocacy in Ex Parte and Other Proceedings

In representing a client in a matter before a tribunal, a lawyer applying for ex parte relief must comply with the requirements of § 170 and §§ 178–180 and further:

(1) must not present evidence the lawyer reasonably believes is false;

(2) must disclose all material and relevant facts known to the lawyer that will enable the tribunal to reach an informed decision; and

(3) must comply with any other applicable special requirements of candor imposed by law.

§ 173. Improperly Influencing Judicial Officer

(1) A lawyer representing a client may not knowingly communicate ex parte with a judge or an official before whom a proceeding is pending concerning the matter, except as authorized by law.

(2) A lawyer may not make a gift or loan prohibited by law to a judicial officer, attempt to influence the officer otherwise than by legally proper procedures, or state or imply an ability so to influence a judicial officer.

§ 174. Lawyer Statement Concerning Judicial or Legal Officer

A lawyer may not knowingly or recklessly make publicly a false derogatory statement of fact concerning the qualifications or integrity of an incumbent of a judicial or other public legal office or a candidate for election to such an office.

§ 175. Lawyer Contact With Jurors

A lawyer may not:

(1) except as allowed by law, communicate with or seek to influence a person known by the lawyer to be a member of a jury pool from which the jury will be drawn;

(2) except as allowed by law, communicate with or seek to influence a member of the jury;

communicate with a juror who has been excused from further service:

(a) when that would harass the juror or constitute an attempt to influence the juror's actions as a juror in future cases; pr

(b) in any other way prohibited by law.

§ 176. Interviewing and Preparing Prospective Witness

(1) A lawyer may interview a witness for the purpose of preparing the witness to testify.

(2) A lawyer may not unlawfully obstruct another party's access to a witness.

(3) A lawyer may not unlawfully induce or assist a prospective witness to evade or ignore process obliging the witness to appear to testify.

(4) A lawyer may not request a person to refrain from voluntarily giving relevant testimony or information to another party, unless:

(a) the person is the lawyer's client in the matter; or

(b)(i) the person is not the lawyer's client but is a relative or employee or other agent of the lawyer's client, and (ii) the lawyer reasonably believes compliance will not materially and adversely affect the person's interests.

§ 177. Compensating Witness

A lawyer may not offer or pay to a witness any consideration:

(1) in excess of the reasonable expenses of the witness incurred in providing evidence, except that an expert witness may be offered and paid a non-contingent fee;

(2) contingent on the content of the witness's testimony or the outcome of the litigation; or

(3) otherwise prohibited by law.

§ 178. Falsifying or Destroying Evidence

(1) A lawyer may not falsify documentary or other evidence.

(2) A lawyer may not destroy or obstruct another party's access to documentary or other evidence when doing so would violate a court order or a criminal statute dealing with obstruction of justice or a similar offense, or counsel or assist a client to do so.

§ 179. Physical Evidence of Client Crime

With respect to physical evidence to a client crime, a lawyer:

(1) may, when reasonably necessary for purposes of the representation, take possession of the evidence and retain it for the time reasonably necessary to examine it and subject it to tests that do not alter or destroy material characteristics of the evidence; but

(2) following possession under Subsection (1), the lawyer must:

(a) return the evidence to the site from which it was taken, when that can be accomplished without destroying or altering material characteristics of the evidence; or

(b) notify prosecuting authorities of the lawyer's possession of the evidence or turn the evidence over to them.

§ 180. False Testimony or Evidence

(1) A lawyer may not:

(a) knowingly counsel or assist a witness to testify falsely or otherwise to offer false evidence;

(b) knowingly make a false statement of fact to the tribunal;

(c) offer testimony or other evidence known by the lawyer to be false.

(2) If a lawyer has offered testimony or other evidence as to a material issue of fact and comes to know of its falsity, the lawyer must take reasonable remedial measures and may disclose confidential client information when necessary to take such a measure.

(3) A lawyer may refuse to offer testimony or other evidence that the lawyer reasonably believes is false, even if the lawyer does not know it to be false.

CHAPTER 8: CONFLICT OF INTEREST

§ 201. Basic Prohibition of Conflict of Interest

Unless all affected clients and other necessary persons consent to the representation under the limitations and conditions provided in § 202, a lawyer may not represent a client if the representation would involve a conflict of interest. A conflict of interest is involved if there is a substantial risk that the lawyer's representation of the client would be materially and adversely affected by the lawyer's own interests or by the lawyer's duties to another current client, a former client, or a third person.

§ 202.   Client Consent to a Conflict of Interest

(1) A lawyer may represent a client notwithstanding a conflict of interest prohibited by § 201 if each affected client or former client gives informed consent to the lawyer's representation. Informed consent requires that the client or former client have reasonably adequate information about the material risks of such representation to that client or former client.

(2) Notwithstanding the informed consent of each affected client or former client, a lawyer may not represent a client if:

(a) the representation is prohibited by law;

(b) one client will assert a claim against the other in the same litigation; or

(c) in the circumstances, it is not reasonably likely that the lawyer will be able to provide adequate representation to one or more of the clients.

§ 203.   Imputation of Conflict of Interest to Affiliated Lawyers

Unless all affected clients consent to the representation under the limitations and conditions provided in § 202 or unless imputation hereunder is removed as provided in § 204, the restrictions upon a lawyer imposed by §§ 206–216 also restrict other affiliated lawyers who:

(1) are associated with that lawyer in rendering legal services to others through a law partnership, professional corporation, sole proprietorship, or similar association;

(2) are employed with that lawyer by an organization to render legal services either to that organization or to others to advance the interests or objectives of the organization; or

(3) share office facilities without reasonable adequate measures to protect confidential client information so that it will not be available to other lawyers in the shared office.

§ 204.   Removing Imputation

(1) Imputation specified in § 203 does not restrict an affiliated lawyer when the affiliation between the affiliated lawyer and the personally-prohibited lawyer that required the imputation has been terminated, and no material confidential information of the client, relevant to the matter, has been communicated by the personally-prohibited lawyer to the affiliated lawyer or that lawyer's firm.

(2) Imputation specified in § 203 does not restrict an affiliated lawyer with respect to a former-client conflict under § 213, when there is no reasonably apparent risk that confidential information of the

former client will be used with material adverse effect on the former client because:

(a) any confidential client information communicated to the personally-prohibited lawyer is unlikely to be significant in the subsequent matter;

(b) the personally-prohibited lawyer is subject to screening measures adequate to eliminate involvement by that lawyer in the representation; and

(c) timely and adequate notice of the screening has been provided to all affected clients.

(3) Imputation specified in § 203 does not restrict a lawyer affiliated with a former government lawyer with respect to a conflict under § 214 if:

(a) the personally-prohibited lawyer is subject to screening measures adequate to eliminate involvement by that lawyer in the representation; and

(b) timely and adequate notice of the screening has been provided to the appropriate government agency and to affected clients.

§ 206. Lawyer's Personal Interest Affecting Representation of Client

Unless the affected client consents to the representation under the limitations and conditions provided in § 202, a lawyer may not represent a client if there is a substantial risk that the lawyer's representation of the client would be materially and adversely affected by the lawyer's financial or other personal interests.

§ 207. Business Transaction Between Lawyer and Client

A lawyer may not participate in a business or financial transaction with a client, except a standard commercial transaction in which the lawyer does not render legal services, unless:

(1) the client has adequate information about the terms of the transaction and the risks presented by the lawyer's involvement in it;

(2) the terms and circumstances of the transaction are fair and reasonable to the client; and

(3) the client consents to the lawyer's role in the transaction under the limitations and conditions provided in § 202 after being encouraged, and given a reasonable opportunity, to seek independent legal advice concerning the transaction.

§ 208. Client Gift to Lawyer

(1) A lawyer may not prepare any instrument effecting any gift from a client to the lawyer, including a testamentary gift, unless the lawyer is

a relative or other natural object of the client's generosity and the gift is not significantly disproportionate to those given other donees similarly related to the donor.

(2) A lawyer may not accept a gift from a client, including a testamentary gift, unless:

(a) the lawyer is a relative or other natural object of the client's generosity;

(b) the value conferred by the client and the benefit to the lawyer are insubstantial in amount; or

(c) the client, before making the gift, has received independent advice or has been encouraged, and given a reasonable opportunity, to seek such advice.

§ 209. Representing Parties With Conflicting Interests in Civil Litigation

Unless all affected clients consent to the representation under the limitations and conditions provided in § 202, a lawyer in civil litigation may not:

(1) represent two or more clients in a matter if there is substantial risk that the lawyer's representation of one of the clients would be materially and adversely affected by the lawyer's duties to another client in the matter; or

(2) represent one client in asserting or defending a claim against another client currently represented by the lawyer, even if the matters are not related.

§ 210. Conflicts of Interest in Criminal Litigation

Unless all affected clients consent to the representation under the limitations and conditions provided in § 202, a lawyer in a criminal matter may not represent:

(1) two or more defendants or potential defendants in the same matter; or

(2) a single defendant, if the representation would involve a conflict of interest as defined in § 201.

§ 211. Multiple Representation in Non–Litigated Matter

Unless all affected clients consent to the representation under the limitations and conditions provided in § 202, a lawyer may not represent two or more clients in a matter not involving litigation if there is a substantial risk that the lawyer's representation of one or more of the clients would be materially and adversely affected by the lawyer's duties to one or more of the other clients.

§ 212. Conflicts of Interest in Representing Organization

Unless all affected clients consent to the representation under the limitations and conditions provided in § 202, a lawyer may not represent both an organization and a director, officer, employee, shareholder, owner, partner, member, or other individual or organization associated with the organization if there is a substantial risk that the lawyer's representation of either would be materially and adversely affected by the lawyer's duties to the other.

§ 213. Representation Adverse to Interest of Former Client

Unless both the affected present and former clients consent to the representation under the limitations and conditions provided in § 202, a lawyer who has represented a client in a matter may not thereafter represent another client in the same or a substantially related matter in which the interests of the former client are materially adverse. The current matter is substantially related to the earlier matter if:

> (1) the current matter involves the work the lawyer performed for the former client; or

> (2) there is a substantial risk that representation of the present client will involve the use of information acquired in the course of representing the former client, unless that information has become generally known.

§ 214. Former Government Lawyer or Officer

(1) A lawyer may not act on behalf of a client with respect to a matter in which the lawyer participated personally and substantially while acting as a government lawyer or officer unless both the government and the client consent to the representation under the limitations and conditions provided in § 202.

(2) A lawyer who acquires confidential information while acting as a government lawyer or officer may not:

> (a) if the information concerns a person, represent a client whose interests are materially adverse to that person in a matter in which the information could be used to the material disadvantage of that person; or

> (b) if the information concerns the governmental client or employer, represent another public or private client in circumstances described in § 213(2).

§ 215. Compensation or Direction by Third Person

(1) A lawyer may not represent a client under circumstances in which someone other than the client will wholly or partly compensate the lawyer for the representation, unless the client consents under the limitations and conditions provided in § 202, with knowledge of the circumstances and conditions of the payment.

(2) A lawyer's professional conduct on behalf of a client may be directed by someone other than the client when:

(a) the direction is reasonable in scope and character, such as by reflecting obligations borne by the person directing the lawyer; and

(b) the client consents to the direction under the limitations and conditions provided in § 202.

§ 216. Lawyer With Fiduciary or Other Legal Obligation to Third Person

Unless the affected client consents to the representation under the limitations and conditions provided in § 202, a lawyer may not represent a client in any matter with respect to which the lawyer has a fiduciary or other legal obligation to another if there is a substantial risk that the lawyer's representation of the client would be materially and adversely affected by the lawyer's obligation.

SELECTED STANDARDS ON PROFESSIONALISM AND COURTESY

Table of Contents

AMERICAN BAR ASSOCIATION REPORT OF COMMISSION ON PROFESSIONALISM (1986)

(Selected sections)

[The report has been approved for distribution by the House of Delegates of the American Bar Association. However, the views expressed are those of the Commission on Professionalism. They have not been approved by the House of Delegates or the Board of Governors and, accordingly, should not be construed as representing the policy of the Association. Ed.]

* * *

III. THE MEANING OF PROFESSIONALISM

"Professionalism" is an elastic concept the meaning and application of which are hard to pin down. That is perhaps as it should be. The term has a rich, long-standing heritage, and any single definition runs the risk of being too confining.

Yet the term is so important to lawyers that at least a working definition seems essential. Lawyers are proud of being part of one of the "historic" or "learned" professions, along with medicine and the clergy, which have been seen as professions through many centuries.

When he was asked to define a profession, Dean Roscoe Pound of Harvard Law School said:

> The term refers to a group ... pursuing a learned art as a common calling in the spirit of public service—no less a public service

561

because it may incidentally be a means of livelihood. Pursuit of the learned art in the spirit of a public service is the primary purpose.

The rhetoric may be dated, but the Commission believes the spirit of Dean Pound's definition stands the test of time. The practice of law "in the spirit of a public service" can and ought to be the hallmark of the legal profession.

More recently, others have identified some common elements which distinguish a profession from other occupations. Commission member Professor Eliot Freidson of New York University defines our profession as:

An occupation whose members have special privileges, such as exclusive licensing, that are justified by the following assumptions:

1. That its practice requires substantial intellectual training and the use of complex judgments.

2. That since clients cannot adequately evaluate the quality of the service, they must trust those they consult.

3. That the client's trust presupposes that the practitioner's self-interest is overbalanced by devotion to serving both the client's interest and the public good, and

4. That the occupation is self-regulating—that is, organized in such a way as to assure the public and the courts that its members are competent, do not violate their client's trust, and transcend their own self-interest.

Again, the Commission suggests that this list of elements is useful in thinking through the issues which follow.

Some may argue on the basis of the cases previously discussed that the legal profession is no longer "special." They might say that lawyers should treat their ideals as archaic, construe the rules of professional conduct as narrowly as possible, and try only to maximize their incomes. The Commission disagrees. Moreover, the testimony we have heard and the surveys we have examined indicate that the public wants the legal profession to maintain its long-held professional ideals. Indeed, the public should expect no less.

We have earlier described the diversity of the Bar, both in terms of demographics and areas of practice. One can properly ask whether any common ideas of professionalism can suffice for such a varied institution. We believe they can. While one must always be conscious of the variety within the legal profession, more unites than separates us.

* * *

The suggestions and conclusions which follow are grouped by the role to be played by each segment of the Bar. In discussing the practicing Bar, we want it to be clear that we are including in that category all lawyers—whether litigators or non-litigators, whether sole practitioners, members or employees of firms, government lawyers or lawyers employed by corporations, educational institutions or other entities.

It is our hope that the recommendations which follow will not be unobserved aspirations, but will represent concrete ways in which lawyers can inspire a rebirth of respect and confidence in themselves, in the services they provide and in the legal system itself. We believe that much can be done. Taken individually, the proposals may not appear substantial, but in the aggregate we believe they can have a significant impact. However, to be effective, they must have the support not only of every part of the legal community, but also of the citizens of this country—the public whose interests lawyers are to serve.

We first present a summary of our recommendations, and then a discussion of each.

IV. SUMMARY OF RECOMMENDATIONS

A. LAW SCHOOLS

1. Law schools should give continuing attention to the form and content of their courses in ethics and professionalism. They should weave ethical and professional issues into courses in both substantive and procedural fields. They should give serious consideration to supplementing courses in ethics and professionalism with a required summer reading list for entering students and with a film or videotape on ethics, along the lines discussed later in this report.

2. Law schools should expose students to promising new methods of dealing with legal problems. Thus, for example, consideration should be given to instruction in such matters as alternative methods of dispute resolution and processes of negotiation.

3. Deans and faculties of law schools should keep in mind that the law school experience provides a student's first exposure to the profession, and that professors inevitably serve as important role models for students. Therefore, the highest standards of ethics and professionalism should be adhered to within law schools.

4. Law schools should adopt codes of student conduct, possibly based on the Model Rules of Professional Conduct. They should report convictions of serious infractions of law school rules to the Character and Fitness Committees, or their equivalent, of states in which the student applies for admission to the Bar.

5. Law schools should retain high admission standards in the face of declining applications and should not lower their standards for graduation.

B. PRACTICING BAR AND BAR ASSOCIATIONS

1. Law firms should help their newly-admitted associates to face the practical and ethical issues which inevitably arise in practice. This

can be done in a variety of ways, and small firms or sole practitioners should work together to sponsor programs to facilitate such training. Local bar associations and law schools should assist in such efforts.

2. In order to assure greater competence of practicing lawyers, continuing legal education courses should be strengthened and made mandatory. Where practical, some form of examination in courses taken should be required.

3. The Commission recommends that the American Bar Association prepare a series of six to eight films or videotapes dealing with ethical and professional issues. The tapes should effectively present a wide range of such issues and should use the Socratic approach so effectively used in the Columbia University Media & Society Seminar programs. If feasible, at least one such tape should be designed especially for use in law schools. The tapes also should be made available to state and local bar associations for use in mandatory continuing legal education programs.

4. False, fraudulent or misleading advertising is not constitutionally protected and should be referred to disciplinary authorities for action against offending lawyers. Appropriate measures short of disciplinary action should be considered. Such measures could include requiring an advertisement to contain warnings or disclaimers.

5. The Bar should place increasing emphasis on the role of lawyers as officers of the court, or more broadly, as officers of the system of justice. Lawyers should exercise independent judgment as to how to pursue legal matters. They have a duty to make the system of justice work properly. Ideally, clients should recognize this duty and appreciate the importance to society of maintaining the system of justice.

6. The Bar should study the issue of the participation of law firms and individual lawyers in business activities, certainly where either actual or potential conflicts of interest may be involved.

7. When not representing clients before legislative bodies, lawyers should put aside self-interest and should support legislation that is in the public interest. In addition, the Bar should urge legislative bodies to consider the consequences of proposed legislation on the courts. All too frequently, such legislation, when enacted, inundates the courts with cases never contemplated by the drafters.

8. Fees are a source of misunderstanding between many lawyers and their clients. Further, the amount of fees charged by lawyers in some instances results in bitter criticism of the Bar. The Commission suggests:

a. Fee arrangements between lawyers and their clients should be in writing, where feasible.

b. If, at the end of a lawyer's services in any matter, the client believes that the fee charged was inappropriate, the client should be able to have the matter reviewed by an impartial fee review committee, possibly appointed by the state Supreme

Court. All such committees or entities should include lay members.

9. Lawyers and judges should report to the appropriate disciplinary committee or prosecuting attorney any serious misconduct on the part of other lawyers and judges which they believe would support a complaint for discipline or criminal charges.

10. Bar associations should be constantly alert to seek improvements in the system of justice. This should embrace such activities as supporting an expanded use of alternative methods of dispute resolution.

C. JUDGES

1. Trial judges should take a more active role in the conduct of litigation. They should see that cases advance promptly, fairly and without abuse. Granting increased authority to judges runs the risk of arbitrary behavior on their part, but reviewing courts should provide whatever counterbalance is needed.

2. Judges should impose sanctions for abuse of the litigation process. Currently, the Federal Rules of Civil Procedure permit the imposition of sanctions for such abuses, and increasing use is being made of the sanctions to penalize the lawyer or the client, or both. In many state systems, the Supreme Courts have not promulgated such rules. State Supreme Courts should adopt rules similar to Rule 11 of the Federal Rules, so that authority to act is clearly given to trial judges.

3. Merit selection should be the means by which judges are chosen. The Commission believes that a bench of the quality that merit selection can provide is essential to improve our system of justice.

4. State disciplinary agencies under the control of state supreme courts are, in general, insufficiently funded and staffed. They now cannot do much more than deal with charges of theft, neglect or the commission of a felony. Adequate funding should be made available to the disciplinary agencies, enabling them to do a thorough and competent job in pursuing the full range of offenses which occur.

5. State supreme courts control admission to the Bar. They often charge character and fitness committees or their equivalent with the responsibility of reviewing the qualifications of applicants. Adequate funding and authority should be provided to such committees so that they can do a thorough job of investigation.

D. IN GENERAL

All segments of the Bar should:

1. Preserve and develop within the profession integrity, competence, fairness, independence, courage and a devotion to the public interest.

2. Resolve to abide by higher standards of conduct than the minimum required by the Code of Professional Responsibility and the Model Rules of Professional Conduct.

3. Increase the participation of lawyers in *pro bono* activities and help lawyers recognize their obligation to participate.

4. Resist the temptation to make the acquisition of wealth a primary goal of law practice.

5. Encourage innovative methods which simplify and make less expensive the rendering of legal services.

6. Educate the public about legal processes and the legal system.

7. Resolve to employ all the organizational resources necessary in order to assure that the legal profession is effectively self-regulating.

* * *

AMERICAN BAR ASSOCIATION
A LAWYER'S CREED OF PROFESSIONALISM

On August 9th, 1988, the American Bar Association House of Delegates adopted the following resolutions regarding so-called "Codes of Courtesy."

BE IT RESOLVED that the American Bar Association recommends to state and local bar associations that they encourage their members to accept as a guide for their individual conduct, and to comply with, a lawyer's creed of professionalism.

BE IT FURTHER RESOLVED that nothing contained in such a creed shall be deemed to supersede or in any way amend the Model Rules of Professional Conduct or other disciplinary codes, alter existing standards of conduct against which lawyer negligence might be judged or become a basis for the imposition of civil penalty of any kind.

Following is a proposed example of "A Lawyer's Creed of Professionalism."

Preamble

As a lawyer I must strive to make our system of justice work fairly and efficiently. In order to carry out that responsibility, not only will I comply with the letter and spirit of the disciplinary standards applicable to all lawyers, but I will also conduct myself in accordance with the following Creed of Professionalism when dealing with my client, opposing parties, their counsel, the courts and the general public.

A. With respect to my client:

PROFESSIONALISM AND COURTESY

1. I will be loyal and committed to my client's cause, but I will not permit that loyalty and commitment to interfere with my ability to provide my client with objective and independent advice;

2. I will endeavor to achieve my client's lawful objectives in business transactions and in litigation as expeditiously and economically as possible;

3. In appropriate cases, I will counsel my client with respect to mediation, arbitration and other alternative methods of resolving disputes;

4. I will advise my client against pursuing litigation (or any other course of action) that is without merit and against insisting on tactics which are intended to delay resolution of the matter or to harass or drain the financial resources of the opposing party;

5. I will advise my client that civility and courtesy are not to be equated with weakness;

6. While I must abide by my client's decision concerning the objectives of the representation, I nevertheless will counsel my client that a willingness to initiate or engage in settlement discussions is consistent with zealous and effective representation.

B. With respect to opposing parties and their counsel:

1. I will endeavor to be courteous and civil, both in oral and in written communications;

2. I will not knowingly make statements of fact or of law that are untrue;

3. In litigation proceedings I will agree to reasonable requests for extensions of time or for waiver of procedural formalities when the legitimate interests of my client will not be adversely affected;

4. I will endeavor to consult with opposing counsel before scheduling depositions and meetings and before re-scheduling hearings, and I will cooperate with opposing counsel when scheduling changes are requested;

5. I will refrain from utilizing litigation or any other course of conduct to harass the opposing party;

6. I will refrain from engaging in excessive and abusive discovery, and I will comply with all reasonable discovery requests;

7. I will refrain from utilizing delaying tactics;

8. In depositions and other proceedings, and in negotiations, I will conduct myself with dignity, avoid making groundless objections and refrain from engaging in acts of rudeness or disrespect;

9. I will not serve motions and pleadings on the other party, or his counsel, at such a time or in such a manner as will unfairly limit the other party's opportunity to respond;

10. In business transactions I will not quarrel over matters of form or style, but will concentrate on matters of substance and content;

11. I will clearly identify, for other counsel or parties, all changes that I have made in documents submitted to me for review.

C. With respect to the courts and other tribunals:

1. I will be a vigorous and zealous advocate on behalf of my client, while recognizing, as an officer of the court, that excessive zeal may be detrimental to my client's interests as well as to the proper functioning of our system of justice;

2. Where consistent with my client's interests, I will communicate with opposing counsel in an effort to avoid litigation and to resolve litigation that has actually commenced;

3. I will voluntarily withdraw claims or defenses when it becomes apparent that they do not have merit or are superfluous;

4. I will refrain from filing frivolous motions;

5. I will make every effort to agree with other counsel, as early as possible, on a voluntary exchange of information and on a plan for discovery;

6. I will attempt to resolve, by agreement, my objections to matters contained in my opponent's pleadings and discovery requests;

7. When scheduled hearings or depositions have to be cancelled, I will notify opposing counsel, and, if appropriate, the court (or other tribunal) as early as possible;

8. Before dates for hearings or trials are set—or, if that is not feasible, immediately after such dates have been set—I will attempt to verify the availability of key participants and witnesses so that I can promptly notify the court (or other tribunal) and opposing counsel of any likely problem in that regard;

9. In civil matters, I will stipulate to facts as to which there is no genuine dispute;

10. I will endeavor to be punctual in attending court hearings, conferences and depositions;

11. I will at all times be candid with the court.

D. With respect to the public and to our system of justice:

1. I will remember that, in addition to commitment to my client's cause, my responsibilities as a lawyer include a devotion to the public good;

2. I will endeavor to keep myself current in the areas in which I practice and, when necessary, will associate with, or refer my client to, counsel knowledgeable in another field of practice;

3. I will be mindful of the fact that, as a member of a self-regulating profession, it is incumbent on me to report violations by fellow lawyers of any disciplinary rule;

4. I will be mindful of the need to protect the image of the legal profession in the eyes of the public and will be so guided when considering methods and contents of advertising;

5. I will be mindful that the law is a learned profession and that among its desirable goals are devotion to public service, improvement of administration of justice, and the contribution of uncompensated time and civic influence on behalf of those persons who cannot afford adequate legal assistance.

AMERICAN BAR ASSOCIATION LAWYER'S PLEDGE OF PROFESSIONALISM

I will remember that the practice of law is first and foremost a profession, and I will subordinate business concerns to professionalism concerns.

I will encourage respect for the law and our legal system through my words and actions.

I will remember my responsibilities to serve as an officer of the court and protector of individual rights.

I will contribute time and resources to public service, public education, charitable, and *pro bono* activities in my community.

I will work with the other participants in the legal system, including judges, opposing counsel and those whose practices are different from mine, to make our legal system more accessible and responsive.

I will resolve matters expeditiously and without unnecessary expense.

I will resolve disputes through negotiation whenever possible.

I will keep my clients well-informed and involved in making the decisions that affect them.

I will continue to expand my knowledge of the law.

I will achieve and maintain proficiency in my practice.

I will be courteous to those with whom I come into contact during the course of my work.

I will honor the spirit and intent, as well as the requirements, of the applicable rules or code of professional conduct for my jurisdiction, and will encourage others to do the same.

AMERICAN BAR ASSOCIATION ASPIRATIONAL GOALS ON LAWYER ADVERTISING

Preamble

During the past decade, the courts have sought to define the nature and extent of permissible advertising by lawyers. In a series of decisions, the U.S. Supreme Court has held that lawyer advertising which is not false or misleading is commercial speech entitled to protection under the First Amendment of the U.S. Constitution.

Pending further clarification by the courts, some advertising practices exist which may be detrimental. Some forms of advertising may adversely affect public perceptions about the justice system itself. For example, empirical evidence suggests that undignified advertising can detract from the public's confidence in the legal profession and respect for the justice system.

Under present case law, the matter of dignity is widely believed to be so subjective as to be beyond the scope of constitutionally permitted regulation. Nevertheless, it seems entirely proper for the organized bar to suggest non-binding aspirational goals urging lawyers who wish to advertise to do so in a dignified manner. Although only aspirational, such goals must be scrupulously sensitive to fundamental constitutional rights of lawyers and the needs of the public.

It is the role and responsibility of lawyers to provide legal services to the public. It has been demonstrated by responsible studies that people sometimes do not receive needed legal services, either because they are unaware of available services, don't understand how they can benefit from those services or don't understand how to obtain them. Therefore, it is also the legal profession's responsibility to inform the public about the availability of legal services and how to obtain and use them.

Advertising is one of many methods by which lawyers can inform the public about legal services. Although most people find a lawyer through word-of-mouth networks of family, friends and work associates, when properly done, advertising can help people to better understand the legal services available to them and how to obtain those services.

When properly done, advertising can also be a productive way for lawyers to build and maintain their client bases. Advertising and other forms of marketing can enable lawyers to attain efficiencies of scale which may help make legal services more affordable. As the Supreme Court pointed out in *Bates v. State Bar of Arizona,* 433 U.S. 350, 377 (1977), it is "entirely possible that advertising will serve to reduce, not advance, the cost of legal services to the consumer."

Lawyers are at all times officers of the court, and as such, they have a special obligation to assure that their conduct conforms to the highest ideals of the legal profession. Thus, lawyers who advertise should be mindful not only of the effect their advertising may have on their own professional image but also of the effect it may have on the public's overall perception of the judicial system.

If lawyer advertising avoids false, misleading or deceptive representations, or coercive or misleading solicitation, it advances the goal of bringing needed legal services to more people than are now being served.

However, when advertising though not false, misleading or deceptive degenerates into undignified and unprofessional presentations, the public is not served, the lawyer who advertised does not benefit and the image of the judicial system may be harmed.

Accordingly, lawyer advertising should exemplify the inherent dignity and professionalism of the legal community. Dignified lawyer advertising tends to inspire public confidence in the professional competence and ability of lawyers and portrays the commitment of lawyers to serve clients' legal needs in accordance with the ethics and public service tradition of a learned profession.

Lawyer advertising is a key facet of the marketing and delivery of legal services to the public. The professional conduct rules for lawyers adopted by the states regulate some aspects of lawyer advertising, but they also leave lawyers much latitude to decide how to advertise. The following Aspirational Goals are presented in an effort to suggest how lawyers can achieve the beneficial goals of advertising while minimizing or eliminating altogether its negative implications.

These aspirational goals are not intended to establish mandatory requirements which might form the basis for disciplinary enforcement. Rules of Professional Conduct and Disciplinary Rules of Codes of Professional Responsibility in effect in all jurisdictions establish the standards which all lawyers who advertise must meet. Rather, these aspirational goals are intended to provide suggested objectives which all lawyers who engage in advertising their services should be encouraged to achieve in order that lawyer advertising may be more effective and reflect the professionalism of the legal community.

Aspirational Goals

1. Lawyer advertising should encourage and support the public's confidence in the individual lawyer's competence and integrity as well as the commitment of the legal profession to serve the public's legal needs in the tradition of the law as a learned profession.

2. Since advertising may be the only contact many people have with lawyers, advertising by lawyers should help the public understand its legal rights and the judicial process and should uphold the dignity of the legal profession.

3. While "dignity" and "good taste" are terms open to subjective interpretation, lawyers should consider that advertising which reflects the ideals stated in these Aspirational Goals is likely to be dignified and suitable to the profession.

4. Since advertising must be truthful and accurate, and not false or misleading, lawyers should realize that ambiguous or confusing advertising can be misleading.

5. Particular care should be taken in describing fees and costs in advertisements. If an advertisement states a specific fee for a particular service, it should make clear whether or not all problems of that type can be handled for that specific fee. Similar care should be taken in describing the lawyer's areas of practice.

6. Lawyers should consider that the use of inappropriately dramatic music, unseemly slogans, hawkish spokespersons, premium offers, slapstick routines or outlandish settings in advertising does not instill confidence in the lawyer or the legal profession and undermines the serious purpose of legal services and the judicial system.

7. Advertising developed with a clear identification of its potential audience is more likely to be understandable, respectful and appropriate to that audience, and, therefore, more effective. Lawyers should consider using advertising and marketing professionals to assist in identifying and reaching an appropriate audience.

8. How advertising conveys its message is as important as the message itself. Again, lawyers should consider using professional consultants to help them develop and present a clear message to the audience in an effective and appropriate way.

9. Lawyers should design their advertising to attract legal matters which they are competent to handle.

10. Lawyers should be concerned with making legal services more affordable to the public. Lawyer advertising may be designed to build up client bases so that efficiencies of scale may be achieved that will translate into more affordable legal services.

THE TEXAS LAWYER'S CREED— A MANDATE FOR PROFESSIONALISM

Promulgated by the Supreme Court of Texas and the Texas Court of Criminal Appeals (1989)

I am a lawyer; I am entrusted by the People of Texas to preserve and improve our legal system. I am licensed by the Supreme Court of Texas. I must therefore abide by the Texas Disciplinary Rules of Professional Conduct, but I know that Professionalism requires more than merely avoiding the violation of laws and rules. I am committed to this Creed for no other reason than it is right.

I. OUR LEGAL SYSTEM

A lawyer owes to the administration of justice personal dignity, integrity, and independence. A lawyer should always adhere to the highest principles of professionalism.

1. I am passionately proud of my profession. Therefore, "My word is my bond."

2. I am responsible to assure that all persons have access to competent representation regardless of wealth or position in life.

3. I commit myself to an adequate and effective pro bono program.

4. I am obligated to educate my clients, the public, and other lawyers regarding the spirit and letter of this Creed.

5. I will always be conscious of my duty to the judicial system.

II. LAWYER TO CLIENT

A lawyer owes to a client allegiance, learning, skill, and industry. A lawyer shall employ all appropriate means to protect and advance the client's legitimate rights, claims, and objectives. A lawyer shall not be deterred by any real or imagined fear of judicial disfavor or public unpopularity, nor be influenced by mere self-interest.

1. I will advise my client of the contents of this Creed when undertaking representation.

2. I will endeavor to achieve my client's lawful objectives in legal transactions and in litigation as quickly and economically as possible.

3. I will be loyal and committed to my client's lawful objectives, but I will not permit that loyalty and commitment to interfere with my duty to provide objective and independent advice.

4. I will advise my client that civility and courtesy are expected and are not a sign of weakness.

5. I will advise my client of proper and expected behavior.

6. I will treat adverse parties and witnesses with fairness and due consideration. A client has no right to demand that I abuse anyone or indulge in any offensive conduct.

7. I will advise my client that we will not pursue conduct which is intended primarily to harass or drain the financial resources of the opposing party.

8. I will advise my client that we will not pursue tactics which are intended primarily for delay.

9. I will advise my client that we will not pursue any course of action which is without merit.

10. I will advise my client that I reserve the right to determine whether to grant accommodations to opposing counsel in all matters that do not adversely affect my client's lawful objectives. A client has no right to instruct me to refuse reasonable requests made by other counsel.

11. I will advise my client regarding the availability of mediation, arbitration, and other alternative methods of resolving and settling disputes.

III. LAWYER TO LAWYER

A lawyer owes to opposing counsel, in the conduct of legal transactions and the pursuit of litigation, courtesy, candor, cooperation, and scrupulous observance of all agreements and mutual understandings. Ill feelings between clients shall not influence a lawyer's conduct, attitude, or demeanor toward opposing counsel. A lawyer shall not engage in unprofessional conduct in retaliation against other unprofessional conduct.

1. I will be courteous, civil, and prompt in oral and written communications.

2. I will not quarrel over matters of form or style, but I will concentrate on matters of substance.

3. I will identify for other counsel or parties all changes I have made in documents submitted for review.

4. I will attempt to prepare documents which correctly reflect the agreement of the parties. I will not include provisions which have not been agreed upon or omit provisions which are necessary to reflect the agreement of the parties.

5. I will notify opposing counsel, and, if appropriate, the Court or other persons, as soon as practicable, when hearings, depositions, meetings, conferences or closings are cancelled.

6. I will agree to reasonable requests for extensions of time and for waiver of procedural formalities, provided legitimate objectives of my client will not be adversely affected.

7. I will not serve motions or pleadings in any manner that unfairly limits another party's opportunity to respond.

8. I will attempt to resolve by agreement my objections to matters contained in pleadings and discovery requests and responses.

9. I can disagree without being disagreeable. I recognize that effective representation does not require antagonistic or obnoxious behavior. I will neither encourage nor knowingly permit my client

or anyone under my control to do anything which would be unethical or improper if done by me.

10. I will not, without good cause, attribute bad motives or unethical conduct to opposing counsel nor bring the profession into disrepute by unfounded accusations of impropriety. I will avoid disparaging personal remarks or acrimony towards opposing counsel, parties and witnesses. I will not be influenced by any ill feeling between clients. I will abstain from any allusion to personal peculiarities or idiosyncrasies of opposing counsel.

11. I will not take advantage, by causing any default or dismissal to be rendered, when I know the identity of an opposing counsel, without first inquiring about that counsel's intention to proceed.

12. I will promptly submit orders to the Court. I will deliver copies to opposing counsel before or contemporaneously with submission to the Court. I will promptly approve the form of orders which accurately reflect the substance of the rulings of the Court.

13. I will not attempt to gain an unfair advantage by sending the Court or its staff correspondence or copies of correspondence.

14. I will not arbitrarily schedule a deposition, Court appearance, or hearing until a good faith effort has been made to schedule it by agreement.

15. I will readily stipulate to undisputed facts in order to avoid needless costs or inconvenience for any party.

16. I will refrain from excessive and abusive discovery.

17. I will comply with all reasonable discovery requests. I will not resist discovery requests which are not objectionable. I will not make objections nor give instructions to a witness for the purpose of delaying or obstructing the discovery process. I will encourage witnesses to respond to all deposition questions which are reasonably understandable. I will neither encourage nor permit my witness to quibble about words where their meaning is reasonably clear.

18. I will not seek Court intervention to obtain discovery which is clearly improper and not discoverable.

19. I will not seek sanctions or disqualification unless it is necessary for protection of my client's lawful objectives or is fully justified by the circumstances.

IV. LAWYER AND JUDGE

Lawyers and judges owe each other respect, diligence, candor, punctuality, and protection against unjust and improper criticism and attack. Lawyers and judges are equally responsible to protect the dignity and independence of the Court and the profession.

SELECTED STANDARDS

1. I will always recognize that the position of judge is the symbol of both the judicial system and administration of justice. I will refrain from conduct that degrades this symbol.

2. I will conduct myself in Court in a professional manner and demonstrate my respect for the Court and the law.

3. I will treat counsel, opposing parties, the Court, and members of the Court staff with courtesy and civility.

4. I will be punctual.

5. I will not engage in any conduct which offends the dignity and decorum of proceedings.

6. I will not knowingly misrepresent, mischaracterize, misquote or miscite facts or authorities to gain an advantage.

7. I will respect the rulings of the Court.

8. I will give the issues in controversy deliberate, impartial and studied analysis and consideration.

9. I will be considerate of the time constraints and pressures imposed upon the Court, Court staff and counsel in efforts to administer justice and resolve disputes.

PART TWO

CODES OF JUDICIAL CONDUCT

Table of Contents

Introduction

As in the case of regulating lawyers' conduct, the ABA has sought to provide standards for regulating judicial conduct. In 1924, the ABA adopted the Canons of Judicial Ethics. During the 1960s, the federal Judicial Conference of the United States developed standards for federal judges. Soon after the ABA adopted the Model Code of Professional Responsibility, the ABA appointed a commission to produce a revised code of conduct for judges. The resulting document is the 1972 Code of Judicial Conduct. In 1990, the ABA replaced the 1972 Code with a new Code of Judicial Conduct. Both the 1990 and the 1972 codes are reproduced in this part.

By 1999, twenty state supreme courts had adopted new standards of judicial conduct based in whole or in part on the 1990 Model Code of Judicial Conduct.

ABA MODEL CODE OF JUDICIAL CONDUCT (1990) [†]

Table of Contents

PREAMBLE

Our legal system is based on the principle that an independent, fair and competent judiciary will interpret and apply the laws that govern us. The role of the judiciary is central to American concepts of justice and the rule of law. Intrinsic to all sections of this Code are the precepts that judges, individually and collectively, must respect and honor the judicial office as a public trust and strive to enhance and maintain confidence in our legal system. The judge is an arbiter of facts and law for the resolution of disputes and a highly visible symbol of government under the rule of law.

The Code of Judicial Conduct is intended to establish standards for ethical conduct of judges. It consists of broad statements called Canons, specific rules set forth in Sections under each Canon, a Terminology Section, an Application Section and Commentary. The text of the Canons and the Sections, including the Terminology and Application Sections, is authoritative. The Commentary, by explanation and example, provides guidance with respect to the purpose and meaning of the Canons and Sections. The Commentary is not intended as a statement of additional rules. When the text uses "shall" or "shall not," it is intended to impose binding obligations the violation of which can result

† Model Code of Judicial Conduct (August 1990) was adopted by the House of Delegates of the American Bar Association on August 7, 1990.

in disciplinary action. When "should" or "should not" is used, the text is intended as hortatory and as a statement of what is or is not appropriate conduct but not as a binding rule under which a judge may be disciplined. When "may" is used, it denotes permissible discretion or, depending on the context, it refers to action that is not covered by specific proscriptions.

The Canons and Sections are rules of reason. They should be applied consistent with constitutional requirements, statutes, other court rules and decisional law and in the context of all relevant circumstances. The Code is to be construed so as not to impinge on the essential independence of judges in making judicial decisions.

The Code is designed to provide guidance to judges and candidates for judicial office and to provide a structure for regulating conduct through disciplinary agencies. It is not designed or intended as a basis for civil liability or criminal prosecution. Furthermore, the purpose of the Code would be subverted if the Code were invoked by lawyers for mere tactical advantage in a proceeding.

The text of the Canons and Sections is intended to govern conduct of judges and to be binding upon them. It is not intended, however, that every transgression will result in disciplinary action. Whether disciplinary action is appropriate, and the degree of discipline to be imposed, should be determined through a reasonable and reasoned application of the text and should depend on such factors as the seriousness of the transgression, whether there is a pattern of improper activity and the effect of the improper activity on others or on the judicial system. See ABA Standards Relating to Judicial Discipline and Disability Retirement.[†]

The Code of Judicial Conduct is not intended as an exhaustive guide for the conduct of judges. They should also be governed in their judicial and personal conduct by general ethical standards. The Code is intended, however, to state basic standards which should govern the conduct of all judges and to provide guidance to assist judges in establishing and maintaining high standards of judicial and personal conduct.

TERMINOLOGY

Terms explained below are noted with an asterisk (*) in the Sections where they appear. In addition, the Sections where terms appear are referred to after the explanation of each term below.

"Appropriate authority" denotes the authority with responsibility for initiation of disciplinary process with respect to the violation to be reported. See Sections 3D(1) and 3D(2).

[†] Judicial disciplinary procedures adopted in the jurisdictions should comport with the requirements of due process. The ABA Standards Relating to Judicial Discipline and Disability Retirement are cited as an example of how these due process requirements may be satisfied.

"Candidate." A candidate is a person seeking selection for or retention in judicial office by election or appointment. A person becomes a candidate for judicial office as soon as he or she makes a public announcement of candidacy, declares or files as a candidate with the election or appointment authority, or authorizes solicitation or acceptance of contributions or support. The term "candidate" has the same meaning when applied to a judge seeking election or appointment to non-judicial office. See Preamble and Sections 5A, 5B, 5C and 5E.

"Continuing part-time judge." A continuing part-time judge is a judge who serves repeatedly on a part-time basis by election or under a continuing appointment, including a retired judge subject to recall who is permitted to practice law. See Application Section C.

"Court personnel" does not include the lawyers in a proceeding before a judge. See Sections 3B(7)(c) and 3B(9).

"De minimis" denotes an insignificant interest that could not raise reasonable question as to a judge's impartiality. See Sections 3E(1)(c) and 3E(1)(d).

"Economic interest" denotes ownership of a more than de minimis legal or equitable interest, or a relationship as officer, director, advisor or other active participant in the affairs of a party, except that:

(i) ownership of an interest in a mutual or common investment fund that holds securities is not an economic interest in such securities unless the judge participates in the management of the fund or a proceeding pending or impending before the judge could substantially affect the value of the interest;

(ii) service by a judge as an officer, director, advisor or other active participant in an educational, religious, charitable, fraternal or civic organization, or service by a judge's spouse, parent or child as an officer, director, advisor or other active participant in any organization does not create an economic interest in securities held by that organization;

(iii) a deposit in a financial institution, the proprietary interest of a policy holder in a mutual insurance company, of a depositor in a mutual savings association or of a member in a credit union, or a similar proprietary interest, is not an economic interest in the organization unless a proceeding pending or impending before the judge could substantially affect the value of the interest;

(iv) ownership of government securities is not an economic interest in the issuer unless a proceeding pending or impending before the judge could substantially affect the value of the securities.

580

See Sections 3E(1)(c) and 3E(2).

"Fiduciary" includes such relationships as executor, administrator, trustee, and guardian. See Sections 3E(2) and 4E.

"Knowingly," "knowledge," "known" or "knows" denotes actual knowledge of the fact in question. A person's knowledge may be inferred from circumstances. See Sections 3D, 3E(1), and 5A(3).

"Law" denotes court rules as well as statutes, constitutional provisions and decisional law. See Sections 2A, 3A, 3B(2), 3B(6), 4B, 4C, 4D(5), 4F, 4I, 5A(2), 5A(3), 5B(2), 5C(1), 5C(3) and 5D.

"Member of the candidate's family" denotes a spouse, child, grandchild, parent, grandparent or other relative or person with whom the candidate maintains a close familial relationship. See Section 5A(3)(a).

"Member of the judge's family" denotes a spouse, child, grandchild, parent, grandparent, or other relative or person with whom the judge maintains a close familial relationship. See Sections 4D(3), 4E and 4G.

"Member of the judge's family residing in the judge's household" denotes any relative of a judge by blood or marriage, or a person treated by a judge as a member of the judge's family, who resides in the judge's household. See Sections 3E(1) and 4D(5).

"Nonpublic information" denotes information that, by law, is not available to the public. Nonpublic information may include but is not limited to: information that is sealed by statute or court order, impounded or communicated in camera; and information offered in grand jury proceedings, presentencing reports, dependency cases or psychiatric reports. See Section 3B(11).

"Periodic part-time judge." A periodic part-time judge is a judge who serves or expects to serve repeatedly on a part-time basis but under a separate appointment for each limited period of service or for each matter. See Application Section D.

"Political organization" denotes a political party or other group, the principal purpose of which is to further the election or appointment of candidates to political office. See Sections 5A(1), 5B(2) and 5C(1).

"Pro tempore part-time judge." A pro tempore part-time judge is a judge who serves or expects to serve once or only sporadically on a part-time basis under a separate appointment for each period of service or for each case heard. See Application Section E.

"Public election." This term includes primary and general elections; it includes partisan elections, nonpartisan elections and retention elections. See Section 5C.

"Require." The rules prescribing that a judge "require" certain conduct of others are, like all of the rules in this Code,

581

rules of reason. The use of the term "require" in that context means a judge is to exercise reasonable direction and control over the conduct of those persons subject to the judge's direction and control. See Sections 3B(3), 3B(4), 3B(6), 3B(9) and 3C(2).

"Third degree of relationship." The following persons are relatives within the third degree of relationship: great-grandparent, grandparent, parent, uncle, aunt, brother, sister, child, grandchild, great-grandchild, nephew or niece. See Section 3E(1)(d).

CANON 1

A Judge Shall Uphold the Integrity and Independence of the Judiciary

A. An independent and honorable judiciary is indispensable to justice in our society. A judge should participate in establishing, maintaining and enforcing high standards of conduct, and shall personally observe those standards so that the integrity and independence of the judiciary will be preserved. The provisions of this Code are to be construed and applied to further that objective.

Commentary

Deference to the judgments and rulings of courts depends upon public confidence in the integrity and independence of judges. The integrity and independence of judges depends in turn upon their acting without fear or favor. Although judges should be independent, they must comply with the law, including the provisions of this Code. Public confidence in the impartiality of the judiciary is maintained by the adherence of each judge to this responsibility. Conversely, violation of this Code diminishes public confidence in the judiciary and thereby does injury to the system of government under law.

CANON 2

A Judge Shall Avoid Impropriety and the Appearance of Impropriety in All of the Judge's Activities

A. A judge shall respect and comply with the law * and shall act at all times in a manner that promotes public confidence in the integrity and impartiality of the judiciary.

Commentary

Public confidence in the judiciary is eroded by irresponsible or improper conduct by judges. A judge must avoid all impropriety and

* See Terminology, "law."

appearance of impropriety. A judge must expect to be the subject of constant public scrutiny. A judge must therefore accept restrictions on the judge's conduct that might be viewed as burdensome by the ordinary citizen and should do so freely and willingly.

The prohibition against behaving with impropriety or the appearance of impropriety applies to both the professional and personal conduct of a judge. Because it is not practicable to list all prohibited acts, the proscription is necessarily cast in general terms that extend to conduct by judges that is harmful although not specifically mentioned in the Code. Actual improprieties under this standard include violations of law, court rules or other specific provisions of this Code. The test for appearance of impropriety is whether the conduct would create in reasonable minds a perception that the judge's ability to carry out judicial responsibilities with integrity, impartiality and competence is impaired.

See also Commentary under Section 2C.

B.   A judge shall not allow family, social, political or other relationships to influence the judge's judicial conduct or judgment.   A judge shall not lend the prestige of judicial office to advance the private interests of the judge or others;   nor shall a judge convey or permit others to convey the impression that they are in a special position to influence the judge.   A judge shall not testify voluntarily as a character witness.

Commentary

Maintaining the prestige of judicial office is essential to a system of government in which the judiciary functions independently of the executive and legislative branches. Respect for the judicial office facilitates the orderly conduct of legitimate judicial functions. Judges should distinguish between proper and improper use of the prestige of office in all of their activities. For example, it would be improper for a judge to allude to his or her judgeship to gain a personal advantage such as deferential treatment when stopped by a police officer for a traffic offense. Similarly, judicial letterhead must not be used for conducting a judge's personal business.

A judge must avoid lending the prestige of judicial office for the advancement of the private interests of others. For example, a judge must not use the judge's judicial position to gain advantage in a civil suit involving a member of the judge's family. In contracts for publication of a judge's writings, a judge should retain control over the advertising to avoid exploitation of the judge's office. As to the acceptance of awards, see Section 4D(5)(a) and Commentary.

Although a judge should be sensitive to possible abuse of the prestige of office, a judge may, based on the judge's personal knowledge, serve as a reference or provide a letter of recommendation. However, a judge must not initiate the communication of information to a sentencing judge or a probation or corrections officer but may provide to such persons information for the record in response to a formal request.

Judges may participate in the process of judicial selection by cooperating with appointing authorities and screening committees seeking names for consideration, and by responding to official inquiries concerning a person being considered for a judgeship. See also Canon 5 regarding use of a judge's name in political activities.

A judge must not testify voluntarily as a character witness because to do so may lend the prestige of the judicial office in support of the party for whom the judge testifies. Moreover, when a judge testifies as a witness, a lawyer who regularly appears before the judge may be placed in the awkward position of cross-examining the judge. A judge may, however, testify when properly summoned. Except in unusual circumstances where the demands of justice require, a judge should discourage a party from requiring the judge to testify as a character witness.

C. A judge shall not hold membership in any organization that practices invidious discrimination on the basis of race, sex, religion or national origin.

Commentary

Membership of a judge in an organization that practices invidious discrimination gives rise to perceptions that the judge's impartiality is impaired. Section 2C refers to the current practices of the organization. Whether an organization practices invidious discrimination is often a complex question to which judges should be sensitive. The answer cannot be determined from a mere examination of an organization's current membership rolls but rather depends on how the organization selects members and other relevant factors, such as that the organization is dedicated to the preservation of religious, ethnic or cultural values of legitimate common interest to its members, or that it is in fact and effect an intimate, purely private organization whose membership limitations could not be constitutionally prohibited. Absent such factors, an organization is generally said to discriminate invidiously if it arbitrarily excludes from membership on the basis of race, religion, sex or national origin persons who would otherwise be admitted to membership. *See New York State Club Ass'n. Inc. v. City of New York,* 108 S.Ct. 2225, 101 L.Ed.2d 1 (1988); *Board of Directors of Rotary International v. Rotary Club of Duarte,* 481 U.S. 537, 107 S.Ct. 1940, 95 L.Ed.2d 474 (1987); *Roberts v. United States Jaycees,* 468 U.S. 609, 104 S.Ct. 3244, 82 L.Ed.2d 462 (1984).

Although Section 2C relates only to membership in organizations that invidiously discriminate on the basis of race, sex, religion or national origin, a judge's membership in an organization that engages in any discriminatory membership practices prohibited by the law of the jurisdiction also violates Canon 2 and Section 2A and gives the appearance of impropriety. In addition, it would be a violation of Canon 2 and

Section 2A for a judge to arrange a meeting at a club that the judge knows practices invidious discrimination on the basis of race, sex, religion or national origin in its membership or other policies, or for the judge to regularly use such a club. Moreover, public manifestation by a judge of the judge's knowing approval of invidious discrimination on any basis gives the appearance of impropriety under Canon 2 and diminishes public confidence in the integrity and impartiality of the judiciary, in violation of Section 2A.

When a person who is a judge on the date this Code becomes effective [in the jurisdiction in which the person is a judge] [1] learns that an organization to which the judge belongs engages in invidious discrimination that would preclude membership under Section 2C or under Canon 2 and Section 2A, the judge is permitted, in lieu of resigning, to make immediate efforts to have the organization discontinue its invidiously discriminatory practices, but is required to suspend participation in any other activities of the organization. If the organization fails to discontinue its invidiously discriminatory practices as promptly as possible (and in all events within a year of the judge's first learning of the practices), the judge is required to resign immediately from the organization.

CANON 3

A Judge Shall Perform the Duties of Judicial Office Impartially and Diligently

A. Judicial Duties in General. The judicial duties of a judge take precedence over all the judge's other activities. The judge's judicial duties include all the duties of the judge's office prescribed by law.* In the performance of these duties, the following standards apply.

B. Adjudicative Responsibilities.

(1) A judge shall hear and decide matters assigned to the judge except those in which disqualification is required.

(2) A judge shall be faithful to the law * and maintain professional competence in it. A judge shall not be swayed by partisan interests, public clamor or fear of criticism.

(3) A judge shall require * order and decorum in proceedings before the judge.

(4) A judge shall be patient, dignified and courteous to litigants, jurors, witnesses, lawyers and others with whom the judge deals in an official capacity, and shall require * similar

---

1. The language within the brackets should be deleted when the jurisdiction adopts this provision.

* See Terminology.

conduct of lawyers, and of staff, court officials and others subject to the judge's direction and control.

Commentary

The duty to hear all proceedings fairly and with patience is not inconsistent with the duty to dispose promptly of the business of the court. Judges can be efficient and businesslike while being patient and deliberate.

(5) A judge shall perform judicial duties without bias or prejudice. A judge shall not, in the performance of judicial duties, by words or conduct manifest bias or prejudice, including but not limited to bias or prejudice based upon race, sex, religion, national origin, disability, age, sexual orientation or socioeconomic status, and shall not permit staff, court officials and others subject to the judge's direction and control to do so.

Commentary

A judge must refrain from speech, gestures or other conduct that could reasonably be perceived as sexual harassment and must require the same standard of conduct of others subject to the judge's direction and control.

A judge must perform judicial duties impartially and fairly. A judge who manifests bias on any basis in a proceeding impairs the fairness of the proceeding and brings the judiciary into disrepute. Facial expression and body language, in addition to oral communication, can give to parties or lawyers in the proceeding, jurors, the media and others an appearance of judicial bias. A judge must be alert to avoid behavior that may be perceived as prejudicial.

(6) A judge shall require * lawyers in proceedings before the judge to refrain from manifesting, by words or conduct, bias or prejudice based upon race, sex, religion, national origin, disability, age, sexual orientation or socioeconomic status, against parties, witnesses, counsel or others. This Section 3B(6) does not preclude legitimate advocacy when race, sex, religion, national origin, disability, age, sexual orientation or socioeconomic status, or other similar factors, are issues in the proceeding.

(7) A judge shall accord to every person who has a legal interest in a proceeding, or that person's lawyer, the right to be heard according to law.* A judge shall not initiate, permit, or consider ex parte communications, or consider other communications made to the judge outside the presence of the parties concerning a pending or impending proceeding except that:

* See Terminology.

(a) **Where circumstances require, ex parte communications for scheduling, administrative purposes or emergencies that do not deal with substantive matters or issues on the merits are authorized; provided:**

(i) **the judge reasonably believes that no party will gain a procedural or tactical advantage as a result of the ex parte communication, and**

(ii) **the judge makes provision promptly to notify all other parties of the substance of the ex parte communication and allows an opportunity to respond.**

(b) **A judge may obtain the advice of a disinterested expert on the law * applicable to a proceeding before the judge if the judge gives notice to the parties of the person consulted and the substance of the advice, and affords the parties reasonable opportunity to respond.**

(c) **A judge may consult with court personnel * whose function is to aid the judge in carrying out the judge's adjudicative responsibilities or with other judges.**

(d) **A judge may, with the consent of the parties, confer separately with the parties and their lawyers in an effort to mediate or settle matters pending before the judge.**

(e) **A judge may initiate or consider any ex parte communications when expressly authorized by law * to do so.**

Commentary

The proscription against communications concerning a proceeding includes communications from lawyers, law teachers, and other persons who are not participants in the proceeding, except to the limited extent permitted.

To the extent reasonably possible, all parties or their lawyers shall be included in communications with a judge.

Whenever presence of a party or notice to a party is required by Section 3B(7), it is the party's lawyer, or if the party is unrepresented the party, who is to be present or to whom notice is to be given.

An appropriate and often desirable procedure for a court to obtain the advice of a disinterested expert on legal issues is to invite the expert to file a brief amicus curiae.

Certain ex parte communication is approved by Section 3B(7) to facilitate scheduling and other administrative purposes and to accommodate emergencies. In general, however, a judge must discourage ex parte communication and allow it only if all the criteria stated in Section 3B(7) are clearly met. A judge must disclose to all parties all ex parte

---

* See Terminology.

communications described in Sections 3B(7)(a) and 3B(7)(b) regarding a proceeding pending or impending before the judge.

A judge must not independently investigate facts in a case and must consider only the evidence presented.

A judge may request a party to submit proposed findings of fact and conclusions of law, so long as the other parties are apprised of the request and are given an opportunity to respond to the proposed findings and conclusions.

A judge must make reasonable efforts, including the provision of appropriate supervision, to ensure that Section 3B(7) is not violated through law clerks or other personnel on the judge's staff.

If communication between the trial judge and the appellate court with respect to a proceeding is permitted, a copy of any written communication or the substance of any oral communication should be provided to all parties.

(8) A judge shall dispose of all judicial matters promptly, efficiently and fairly.

Commentary

In disposing of matters promptly, efficiently and fairly, a judge must demonstrate due regard for the rights of the parties to be heard and to have issues resolved without unnecessary cost or delay. Containing costs while preserving fundamental rights of parties also protects the interests of witnesses and the general public. A judge should monitor and supervise cases so as to reduce or eliminate dilatory practices, avoidable delays and unnecessary costs. A judge should encourage and seek to facilitate settlement, but parties should not feel coerced into surrendering the right to have their controversy resolved by the courts.

Prompt disposition of the court's business requires a judge to devote adequate time to judicial duties, to be punctual in attending court and expeditious in determining matters under submission, and to insist that court officials, litigants and their lawyers cooperate with the judge to that end.

(9) A judge shall not, while a proceeding is pending or impending in any court, make any public comment that might reasonably be expected to affect its outcome or impair its fairness or make any nonpublic comment that might substantially interfere with a fair trial or hearing. The judge shall require * similar abstention on the part of court personnel * subject to the judge's direction and control. This Section does not prohibit judges from making public statements in the course of their official duties or from explaining for public information the

* See Terminology.

588

procedures of the court. **This Section does not apply to proceedings in which the judge is a litigant in a personal capacity.**

Commentary

The requirement that judges abstain from public comment regarding a pending or impending proceeding continues during any appellate process and until final disposition. This Section does not prohibit a judge from commenting on proceedings in which the judge is a litigant in a personal capacity, but in cases such as a writ of mandamus where the judge is a litigant in an official capacity, the judge must not comment publicly. The conduct of lawyers relating to trial publicity is governed by [Rule 3.6 of the ABA Model Rules of Professional Conduct]. (Each jurisdiction should substitute an appropriate reference to its rule.)

(10) A judge shall not commend or criticize jurors for their verdict other than in a court order or opinion in a proceeding, but may express appreciation to jurors for their service to the judicial system and the community.

Commentary

Commending or criticizing jurors for their verdict may imply a judicial expectation in future cases and may impair a juror's ability to be fair and impartial in a subsequent case.

(11) A judge shall not disclose or use, for any purpose unrelated to judicial duties, nonpublic information * acquired in a judicial capacity.

C. Administrative Responsibilities.

(1) A judge shall diligently discharge the judge's administrative responsibilities without bias or prejudice and maintain professional competence in judicial administration, and should cooperate with other judges and court officials in the administration of court business.

(2) A judge shall require staff, court officials and others subject to the judge's direction and control to observe the standards of fidelity and diligence that apply to the judge and to refrain from manifesting bias or prejudice in the performance of their official duties.

(3) A judge with supervisory authority for the judicial performance of other judges shall take reasonable measures to assure the prompt disposition of matters before them and the proper performance of their other judicial responsibilities.

(4) A judge shall not make unnecessary appointments. A judge shall exercise the power of appointment impartially and on the basis of merit. A judge shall avoid nepotism and favorit-

* See Terminology.

ism. A judge shall not approve compensation of appointees beyond the fair value of services rendered.

Commentary

Appointees of a judge include assigned counsel, officials such as referees, commissioners, special masters, receivers and guardians and personnel such as clerks, secretaries and bailiffs. Consent by the parties to an appointment or an award of compensation does not relieve the judge of the obligation prescribed by Section 3C(4).

D. Disciplinary Responsibilities.

(1) A judge who receives information indicating a substantial likelihood that another judge has committed a violation of this Code should take appropriate action. A judge having knowledge* that another judge has committed a violation of this Code that raises a substantial question as to the other judge's fitness for office shall inform the appropriate authority.*

(2) A judge who receives information indicating a substantial likelihood that a lawyer has committed a violation of the Rules of Professional Conduct [substitute correct title if the applicable rules of lawyer conduct have a different title] should take appropriate action. A judge having knowledge* that a lawyer has committed a violation of the Rules of Professional Conduct [substitute correct title if the applicable rules of lawyer conduct have a different title] that raises a substantial question as to the lawyer's honesty, trustworthiness or fitness as a lawyer in other respects shall inform the appropriate authority.*

(3) Acts of a judge, in the discharge of disciplinary responsibilities, required or permitted by Sections 3D(1) and 3D(2) are part of a judge's judicial duties and shall be absolutely privileged, and no civil action predicated thereon may be instituted against the judge.

Commentary

Appropriate action may include direct communication with the judge or lawyer who has committed the violation, other direct action if available, and reporting the violation to the appropriate authority or other agency or body.

E. Disqualification.

(1) A judge shall disqualify himself or herself in a proceeding in which the judge's impartiality might reasonably be questioned, including but not limited to instances where:

* See Terminology.

Commentary

Under this rule, a judge is disqualified whenever the judge's impartiality might reasonably be questioned, regardless whether any of the specific rules in Section 3E(1) apply. For example, if a judge were in the process of negotiating for employment with a law firm, the judge would be disqualified from any matters in which that law firm appeared, unless the disqualification was waived by the parties after disclosure by the judge.

A judge should disclose on the record information that the judge believes the parties or their lawyers might consider relevant to the question of disqualification, even if the judge believes there is no real basis for disqualification.

By decisional law, the rule of necessity may override the rule of disqualification. For example, a judge might be required to participate in judicial review of a judicial salary statute, or might be the only judge available in a matter requiring immediate judicial action, such as a hearing on probable cause or a temporary restraining order. In the latter case, the judge must disclose on the record the basis for possible disqualification and use reasonable efforts to transfer the matter to another judge as soon as practicable.

(a) the judge has a personal bias or prejudice concerning a party or a party's lawyer, or personal knowledge * of disputed evidentiary facts concerning the proceeding;

(b) the judge served as a lawyer in the matter in controversy, or a lawyer with whom the judge previously practiced law served during such association as a lawyer concerning the matter, or the judge has been a material witness concerning it;

Commentary

A lawyer in a government agency does not ordinarily have an association with other lawyers employed by that agency within the meaning of Section 3E(1)(b); a judge formerly employed by a government agency, however, should disqualify himself or herself in a proceeding if the judge's impartiality might reasonably be questioned because of such association.

(c) the judge knows * that he or she, individually or as a fiduciary, or the judge's spouse, parent or child wherever residing, or any other member of the judge's family residing in the judge's household,* has an economic interest * in the subject matter in controversy or in a party to the proceeding

* See Terminology.

or has any other more than de minimis * interest that could be substantially affected by the proceeding;

(d) the judge or the judge's spouse, or a person within the third degree of relationship * to either of them, or the spouse of such a person:

(i) is a party to the proceeding, or an officer, director or trustee of a party;

(ii) is acting as a lawyer in the proceeding;

(iii) is known * by the judge to have a more than de minimis * interest that could be substantially affected by the proceeding;

(iv) is to the judge's knowledge * likely to be a material witness in the proceeding.

Commentary

The fact that a lawyer in a proceeding is affiliated with a law firm with which a relative of the judge is affiliated does not of itself disqualify the judge. Under appropriate circumstances, the fact that "the judge's impartiality might reasonably be questioned" under Section 3E(1), or that the relative is known by the judge to have an interest in the law firm that could be "substantially affected by the outcome of the proceeding" under Section 3E(1)(d)(iii) may require the judge's disqualification.

(2) A judge shall keep informed about the judge's personal and fiduciary * economic interests,* and make a reasonable effort to keep informed about the personal economic interests of the judge's spouse and minor children residing in the judge's household.

F. **Remittal of Disqualification.** A judge disqualified by the terms of Section 3E may disclose on the record the basis of the judge's disqualification and may ask the parties and their lawyers to consider, out of the presence of the judge, whether to waive disqualification. If following disclosure of any basis for disqualification other than personal bias or prejudice concerning a party, the parties and lawyers, without participation by the judge, all agree that the judge should not be disqualified, and the judge is then willing to participate, the judge may participate in the proceeding. The agreement shall be incorporated in the record of the proceeding.

Commentary

A remittal procedure provides the parties an opportunity to proceed without delay if they wish to waive the disqualification. To assure that

* See Terminology.

consideration of the question of remittal is made independently of the judge, a judge must not solicit, seek or hear comment on possible remittal or waiver of the disqualification unless the lawyers jointly propose remittal after consultation as provided in the rule. A party may act through counsel if counsel represents on the record that the party has been consulted and consents. As a practical matter, a judge may wish to have all parties and their lawyers sign the remittal agreement.

CANON 4

A Judge Shall So Conduct the Judge's Extra–Judicial Activities as to Minimize the Risk of Conflict With Judicial Obligations

A. Extra-judicial Activities in General. A judge shall conduct all of the judge's extra-judicial activities so that they do not:

(1) cast reasonable doubt on the judge's capacity to act impartially as a judge;

(2) demean the judicial office; or

(3) interfere with the proper performance of judicial duties.

Commentary

Complete separation of a judge from extra-judicial activities is neither possible nor wise; a judge should not become isolated from the community in which the judge lives.

Expressions of bias or prejudice by a judge, even outside the judge's judicial activities, may cast reasonable doubt on the judge's capacity to act impartially as a judge. Expressions which may do so include jokes or other remarks demeaning individuals on the basis of their race, sex, religion, national origin, disability, age, sexual orientation or socioeconomic status. See Section 2C and accompanying Commentary.

B. Avocational Activities. A judge may speak, write, lecture, teach and participate in other extra-judicial activities concerning the law,* the legal system, the administration of justice and non-legal subjects, subject to the requirements of this Code.

Commentary

As a judicial officer and person specially learned in the law, a judge is in a unique position to contribute to the improvement of the law, the legal system, and the administration of justice, including revision of substantive and procedural law and improvement of criminal and juvenile justice. To the extent that time permits, a judge is encouraged to do so, either independently or through a bar association, judicial conference

* See Terminology.

593

or other organization dedicated to the improvement of the law. Judges may participate in efforts to promote the fair administration of justice, the independence of the judiciary and the integrity of the legal profession and may express opposition to the persecution of lawyers and judges in other countries because of their professional activities.

In this and other Sections of Canon 4, the phrase "subject to the requirements of this Code" is used, notably in connection with a judge's governmental, civic or charitable activities. This phrase is included to remind judges that the use of permissive language in various Sections of the Code does not relieve a judge from the other requirements of the Code that apply to the specific conduct.

C. Governmental, Civic or Charitable Activities.

(1) A judge shall not appear at a public hearing before, or otherwise consult with, an executive or legislative body or official except on matters concerning the law,* the legal system or the administration of justice or except when acting pro se in a matter involving the judge or the judge's interests.

Commentary

See Section 2B regarding the obligation to avoid improper influence.

(2) A judge shall not accept appointment to a governmental committee or commission or other governmental position that is concerned with issues of fact or policy on matters other than the improvement of the law,* the legal system or the administration of justice. A judge may, however, represent a country, state or locality on ceremonial occasions or in connection with historical, educational or cultural activities.

Commentary

Section 4C(2) prohibits a judge from accepting any governmental position except one relating to the law, legal system or administration of justice as authorized by Section 4C(3). The appropriateness of accepting extra-judicial assignments must be assessed in light of the demands on judicial resources created by crowded dockets and the need to protect the courts from involvement in extra-judicial matters that may prove to be controversial. Judges should not accept governmental appointments that are likely to interfere with the effectiveness and independence of the judiciary.

Section 4C(2) does not govern a judge's service in a nongovernmental position. See Section 4C(3) permitting service by a judge with organizations devoted to the improvement of the law, the legal system or the administration of justice and with educational, religious, charitable, fraternal or civic organizations not conducted for profit. For example, service on the board of a public educational institution, unless it were a law school, would be prohibited under Section 4C(2), but service on the board of a public law school or any private educational institution would generally be permitted under Section 4C(3).

(3) A judge may serve as an officer, director, trustee or non-legal advisor of an organization or governmental agency devoted to the improvement of the law,* the legal system or the administration of justice or of an educational, religious, charitable, fraternal or civic organization not conducted for profit, subject to the following limitations and the other requirements of this Code.

Commentary

Section 4C(3) does not apply to a judge's service in a governmental position unconnected with the improvement of the law, the legal system or the administration of justice; see Section 4C(2).

See Commentary to Section 4B regarding use of the phrase "subject to the following limitations and the other requirements of this Code." As an example of the meaning of the phrase, a judge permitted by Section 4C(3) to serve on the board of a fraternal institution may be prohibited from such service by Sections 2C or 4A if the institution practices invidious discrimination or if service on the board otherwise casts reasonable doubt on the judge's capacity to act impartially as a judge.

Service by a judge on behalf of a civic or charitable organization may be governed by other provisions of Canon 4 in addition to Section 4C. For example, a judge is prohibited by Section 4G from serving as a legal advisor to a civic or charitable organization.

(a) A judge shall not serve as an officer, director, trustee or non-legal advisor if it is likely that the organization

(i) will be engaged in proceedings that would ordinarily come before the judge, or

(ii) will be engaged frequently in adversary proceedings in the court of which the judge is a member or in any court subject to the appellate jurisdiction of the court of which the judge is a member.

Commentary

The changing nature of some organizations and of their relationship to the law makes it necessary for a judge regularly to reexamine the activities of each organization with which the judge is affiliated to determine if it is proper for the judge to continue the affiliation. For example, in many jurisdictions charitable hospitals are now more fre-

* See Terminology.

595

quently in court than in the past. Similarly, the boards of some legal aid organizations now make policy decisions that may have political significance or imply commitment to causes that may come before the courts for adjudication.

(b) A judge as an officer, director, trustee or non-legal advisor, or as a member or otherwise:

(i) may assist such an organization in planning fund-raising and may participate in the management and investment of the organization's funds, but shall not personally participate in the solicitation of funds or other fund-raising activities, except that a judge may solicit funds from other judges over whom the judge does not exercise supervisory or appellate authority;

(ii) may make recommendations to public and private fund-granting organizations on projects and programs concerning the law,* the legal system or the administration of justice;

(iii) shall not personally participate in membership solicitation if the solicitation might reasonably be perceived as coercive or, except as permitted in Section 4C(3)(b)(i), if the membership solicitation is essentially a fund-raising mechanism;

(iv) shall not use or permit the use of the prestige of judicial office for fund-raising or membership solicitation.

Commentary

A judge may solicit membership or endorse or encourage membership efforts for an organization devoted to the improvement of the law, the legal system or the administration of justice or a nonprofit educational, religious, charitable, fraternal or civic organization as long as the solicitation cannot reasonably be perceived as coercive and is not essentially a fund-raising mechanism. Solicitation of funds for an organization and solicitation of memberships similarly involve the danger that the person solicited will feel obligated to respond favorably to the solicitor if the solicitor is in a position of influence or control. A judge must not engage in direct, individual solicitation of funds or memberships in person, in writing or by telephone except in the following cases: 1) a judge may solicit for funds or memberships other judges over whom the judge does not exercise supervisory or appellate authority, 2) a judge may solicit other persons for membership in the organizations described above if neither those persons nor persons with whom they are affiliated are likely ever to appear before the court on which the judge serves and

* See Terminology.

3) a judge who is an officer of such an organization may send a general membership solicitation mailing over the judge's signature.

Use of an organization letterhead for fund-raising or membership solicitation does not violate Section 4C(3)(b) provided the letterhead lists only the judge's name and office or other position in the organization, and, if comparable designations are listed for other persons, the judge's judicial designation. In addition, a judge must also make reasonable efforts to ensure that the judge's staff, court officials and others subject to the judge's direction and control do not solicit funds on the judge's behalf for any purpose, charitable or otherwise.

A judge must not be a speaker or guest of honor at an organization's fund-raising event, but mere attendance at such an event is permissible if otherwise consistent with this Code.

D. Financial Activities.

(1) A judge shall not engage in financial and business dealings that:

(a) may reasonably be perceived to exploit the judge's judicial position, or

(b) involve the judge in frequent transactions or continuing business relationships with those lawyers or other persons likely to come before the court on which the judge serves.

Commentary

The Time for Compliance provision of this Code (Application, Section F) postpones the time for compliance with certain provisions of this Section in some cases.

When a judge acquires in a judicial capacity information, such as material contained in filings with the court, that is not yet generally known, the judge must not use the information for private gain. See Section 2B; see also Section 3B(11).

A judge must avoid financial and business dealings that involve the judge in frequent transactions or continuing business relationships with persons likely to come either before the judge personally or before other judges on the judge's court. In addition, a judge should discourage members of the judge's family from engaging in dealings that would reasonably appear to exploit the judge's judicial position. This rule is necessary to avoid creating an appearance of exploitation of office or favoritism and to minimize the potential for disqualification. With respect to affiliation of relatives of judge with law firms appearing before the judge, see Commentary to Section 3E(1) relating to disqualification.

Participation by a judge in financial and business dealings is subject to the general prohibitions in Section 4A against activities that tend to reflect adversely on impartiality, demean the judicial office, or interfere with the proper performance of judicial duties. Such participation is also subject to the general prohibition in Canon 2 against activities involving impropriety or the appearance of impropriety and the prohibition in Section 2B against the misuse of the prestige of judicial office. In addition, a judge must maintain high standards of conduct in all of the judge's activities, as set forth in Canon 1. See Commentary for Section 4B regarding use of the phrase "subject to the requirements of this Code."

(2) A judge may, subject to the requirements of this Code, hold and manage investments of the judge and members of the judge's family,* including real estate, and engage in other remunerative activity.

Commentary

This Section provides that, subject to the requirements of this Code, a judge may hold and manage investments owned solely by the judge, investments owned solely by a member or members of the judge's family, and investments owned jointly by the judge and members of the judge's family.

(3) A judge shall not serve as an officer, director, manager, general partner, advisor or employee of any business entity except that a judge may, subject to the requirements of this Code, manage and participate in:

  (a) a business closely held by the judge or members of the judge's family,* or

  (b) a business entity primarily engaged in investment of the financial resources of the judge or members of the judge's family.

Commentary

Subject to the requirements of this Code, a judge may participate in a business that is closely held either by the judge alone, by members of the judge's family, or by the judge and members of the judge's family.

Although participation by a judge in a closely-held family business might otherwise be permitted by Section 4D(3), a judge may be prohibited from participation by other provisions of this Code when, for example, the business entity frequently appears before the judge's court or the participation requires significant time away from judicial duties. Similarly, a judge must avoid participating in a closely-held family business if the judge's participation would involve misuse of the prestige of judicial office.

---

* See Terminology.

(4) A judge shall manage the judge's investments and other financial interests to minimize the number of cases in which the judge is disqualified. As soon as the judge can do so without serious financial detriment, the judge shall divest himself or herself of investments and other financial interests that might require frequent disqualification.

(5) A judge shall not accept, and shall urge members of the judge's family residing in the judge's household,* not to accept, a gift, bequest, favor or loan from anyone except for:

Commentary

Section 4D(5) does not apply to contributions to a judge's campaign for judicial office, a matter governed by Canon 5.

Because a gift, bequest, favor or loan to a member of the judge's family residing in the judge's household might be viewed as intended to influence the judge, a judge must inform those family members of the relevant ethical constraints upon the judge in this regard and discourage those family members from violating them. A judge cannot, however, reasonably be expected to know or control all of the financial or business activities of all family members residing in the judge's household.

(a) a gift incident to a public testimonial, books, tapes and other resource materials supplied by publishers on a complimentary basis for official use, or an invitation to the judge and the judge's spouse or guest to attend a bar-related function or an activity devoted to the improvement of the law,* the legal system or the administration of justice;

Commentary

Acceptance of an invitation to a law-related function is governed by Section 4D(5)(a); acceptance of an invitation paid for by an individual lawyer or group of lawyers is governed by Section 4D(5)(h).

A judge may accept a public testimonial or a gift incident thereto only if the donor organization is not an organization whose members comprise or frequently represent the same side in litigation, and the testimonial and gift are otherwise in compliance with other provisions of this Code. See Sections 4A(1) and 2B.

(b) a gift, award or benefit incident to the business, profession or other separate activity of a spouse or other family member of a judge residing in the judge's household, including gifts, awards and benefits for the use of both the spouse or other family member and the judge (as spouse or family member), provided the gift, award or benefit could

---

* See Terminology.

not reasonably be perceived as intended to influence the judge in the performance of judicial duties;

(c) ordinary social hospitality;

(d) a gift from a relative or friend, for a special occasion, such as a wedding, anniversary or birthday, if the gift is fairly commensurate with the occasion and the relationship;

Commentary

A gift to a judge, or to a member of the judge's family living in the judge's household, that is excessive in value raises questions about the judge's impartiality and the integrity of the judicial office and might require disqualification of the judge where disqualification would not otherwise be required. See, however, Section 4D(5)(e).

(e) a gift, bequest, favor or loan from a relative or close personal friend whose appearance or interest in a case would in any event require disqualification under Section 3E;

(f) a loan from a lending institution in its regular course of business on the same terms generally available to persons who are not judges;

(g) a scholarship or fellowship awarded on the same terms and based on the same criteria applied to other applicants; or

(h) any other gift, bequest, favor or loan, only if: the donor is not a party or other person who has come or is likely to come or whose interests have come or are likely to come before the judge; and, if its value exceeds $150.00, the judge reports it in the same manner as the judge reports compensation in Section 4H.

Commentary

Section 4D(5)(h) prohibits judges from accepting gifts, favors, bequests or loans from lawyers or their firms if they have come or are likely to come before the judge; it also prohibits gifts, favors, bequests or loans from clients of lawyers or their firms when the clients' interests have come or are likely to come before the judge.

E. Fiduciary Activities.

(1) A judge shall not serve as executor, administrator or other personal representative, trustee, guardian, attorney in fact or other fiduciary,* except for the estate, trust or person of

* See Terminology.

a member of the judge's family,* and then only if such service will not interfere with the proper performance of judicial duties.

(2) A judge shall not serve as a fiduciary * if it is likely that the judge as a fiduciary will be engaged in proceedings that would ordinarily come before the judge, or if the estate, trust or ward becomes involved in adversary proceedings in the court on which the judge serves or one under its appellate jurisdiction.

(3) The same restrictions on financial activities that apply to a judge personally also apply to the judge while acting in a fiduciary * capacity.

Commentary

The Time for Compliance provision of this Code (Application, Section F) postpones the time for compliance with certain provisions of this Section in some cases.

The restrictions imposed by this Canon may conflict with the judge's obligation as a fiduciary. For example, a judge should resign as trustee if detriment to the trust would result from divestiture of holdings the retention of which would place the judge in violation of Section 4D(4).

F. Service as Arbitrator or Mediator. A judge shall not act as an arbitrator or mediator or otherwise perform judicial functions in a private capacity unless expressly authorized by law.*

Commentary

Section 4F does not prohibit a judge from participating in arbitration, mediation or settlement conferences performed as part of judicial duties.

G. Practice of Law. A judge shall not practice law. Notwithstanding this prohibition, a judge may act pro se and may, without compensation, give legal advice to and draft or review documents for a member of the judge's family.*

Commentary

This prohibition refers to the practice of law in a representative capacity and not in a pro se capacity. A judge may act for himself or herself in all legal matters, including matters involving litigation and matters involving appearances before or other dealings with legislative and other governmental bodies. However, in so doing, a judge must not abuse the prestige of office to advance the interests of the judge or the judge's family. See Section 2(B).

The Code allows a judge to give legal advice to and draft legal documents for members of the judge's family, so long as the judge receives no compensation. A judge must not, however, act as an

* See Terminology.

advocate or negotiator for a member of the judge's family in a legal matter.

* * *

Canon 6, new in the 1972 Code, reflected concerns about conflicts of interest and appearances of impropriety arising from compensation for off-the-bench activities. Since 1972, however, reporting requirements that are much more comprehensive with respect to what must be reported and with whom reports must be filed have been adopted by many jurisdictions. The Committee believes that although reports of compensation for extra-judicial activities should be required, reporting requirements preferably should be developed to suit the respective jurisdictions, not simply adopted as set forth in a national model code of judicial conduct. Because of the Committee's concern that deletion of this Canon might lead to the misconception that reporting compensation for extra-judicial activities is no longer important, the substance of Canon 6 is carried forward as Section 4H in this Code for adoption in those jurisdictions that do not have other reporting requirements. In jurisdictions that have separately established reporting requirements, Section 4H(2) (Public Reporting) may be deleted and the caption for Section 4H modified appropriately.

* * *

H. Compensation, Reimbursement and Reporting.

(1) Compensation and Reimbursement. A judge may receive compensation and reimbursement of expenses for the extra-judicial activities permitted by this Code, if the source of such payments does not give the appearance of influencing the judge's performance of judicial duties or otherwise give the appearance of impropriety.

> **(a) Compensation shall not exceed a reasonable amount nor shall it exceed what a person who is not a judge would receive for the same activity.**

> **(b) Expense reimbursement shall be limited to the actual cost of travel, food and lodging reasonably incurred by the judge and, where appropriate to the occasion, by the judge's spouse or guest. Any payment in excess of such an amount is compensation.**

(2) Public Reports. A judge shall report the date, place and nature of any activity for which the judge received compensation, and the name of the payor and the amount of compensation so received. Compensation or income of a spouse attributed to the judge by operation of a community property law is not extra-judicial compensation to the judge. The judge's report shall be made at least annually and shall be filed as a public

document in the office of the clerk of the court on which the judge serves or other office designated by law.*

Commentary

See Section 4D(5) regarding reporting of gifts, bequests and loans.

The Code does not prohibit a judge from accepting honoraria or speaking fees provided that the compensation is reasonable and commensurate with the task performed. A judge should ensure, however, that no conflicts are created by the arrangement. A judge must not appear to trade on the judicial position for personal advantage. Nor should a judge spend significant time away from court duties to meet speaking or writing commitments for compensation. In addition, the source of the payment must not raise any question of undue influence or the judge's ability or willingness to be impartial.

I. Disclosure of a judge's income, debts, investments or other assets is required only to the extent provided in this Canon and in Sections 3E and 3F, or as otherwise required by law.*

Commentary

Section 3E requires a judge to disqualify himself or herself in any proceeding in which the judge has an economic interest. See "economic interest" as explained in the Terminology Section. Section 4D requires a judge to refrain from engaging in business and from financial activities that might interfere with the impartial performance of judicial duties; Section 4H requires a judge to report all compensation the judge received for activities outside judicial office. A judge has the rights of any other citizen, including the right to privacy of the judge's financial affairs, except to the extent that limitations established by law are required to safeguard the proper performance of the judge's duties.

CANON 5 [2]

A Judge or Judicial Candidate Shall Refrain From Inappropriate Political Activity

A. All Judges and Candidates.

---

* See Terminology.

2. Introductory Note to Canon 5: There is wide variation in the methods of judicial selection used, both among jurisdictions and within the jurisdictions themselves. In a given state, judges may be selected by one method initially, retained by a different method, and selected by still another method to fill interim vacancies.

According to figures compiled in 1987 by the National Center for State Courts, 32 states and the District of Columbia use a merit selection method (in which an executive such as a governor appoints a judge from a group of nominees selected by a judicial nominating commission) to select judges in the state either initially or to fill an interim vacancy. Of those 33 jurisdic-

(1) Except as authorized in Sections 5B(2), 5C(1) and 5C(3), a judge or a candidate* for election or appointment to judicial office shall not:

(a) act as a leader or hold an office in a political organization *;

(b) publicly endorse or publicly oppose another candidate for public office;

(c) make speeches on behalf of a political organization;

(d) attend political gatherings; or

(e) solicit funds for, pay an assessment to or make a contribution to a political organization or candidate, or purchase tickets for political party dinners or other functions.

Commentary

A judge or candidate for judicial office retains the right to participate in the political process as a voter.

Where false information concerning a judicial candidate is made public, a judge or another judicial candidate having knowledge of the facts is not prohibited by Section 5A(1) from making the facts public.

Section 5A(1)(a) does not prohibit a candidate for elective judicial office from retaining during candidacy a public office such as county prosecutor, which is not "an office in a political organization."

Section 5A(1)(b) does not prohibit a judge or judicial candidate from privately expressing his or her views on judicial candidates or other candidates for public office.

A candidate does not publicly endorse another candidate for public office by having that candidate's name on the same ticket.

(2) A judge shall resign from judicial office upon becoming a candidate * for a non-judicial office either in a primary or in a general election, except that the judge may continue to hold judicial office while being a candidate for election to or serving

tions, a merit selection method is used in 18 jurisdictions to choose judges of courts of last resort, in 13 jurisdictions to choose judges of intermediate appellate courts, in 12 jurisdictions to choose judges of general jurisdiction courts and in 5 jurisdictions to choose judges of limited jurisdiction courts.

Methods of judicial selection other than merit selection include nonpartisan election (10 states use it for initial selection at all court levels, another 10 states use it for initial selection for at least one court level) and partisan election (8 states use it for initial selection at all court levels, another 7 states use it for initial selection for at least one level). In a small minority of the states, judicial selection methods include executive or legislative appointment (without nomination of a group of potential appointees by a judicial nominating commission) and court selection. In addition, the federal judicial system utilizes an executive appointment method. See State Court Organization 1987 (National Center for State Courts, 1988).

as a delegate in a state constitutional convention if the judge is otherwise permitted by law * to do so.

(3) A candidate * for a judicial office:

(a) shall maintain the dignity appropriate to judicial office and act in a manner consistent with the integrity and independence of the judiciary, and shall encourage members of the candidate's family * to adhere to the same standards of political conduct in support of the candidate as apply to the candidate;

Commentary

Although a judicial candidate must encourage members of his or her family to adhere to the same standards of political conduct in support of the candidate that apply to the candidate, family members are free to participate in other political activity.

(b) shall prohibit employees and officials who serve at the pleasure of the candidate,* and shall discourage other employees and officials subject to the candidate's direction and control from doing on the candidate's behalf what the candidate is prohibited from doing under the Sections of this Canon;

(c) except to the extent permitted by Section 5C(2), shall not authorize or knowingly * permit any other person to do for the candidate * what the candidate is prohibited from doing under the Sections of this Canon;

(d) shall not:

(i) make pledges or promises of conduct in office other than the faithful and impartial performance of the duties of the office;

(ii) make statements that commit or appear to commit the candidate with respect to cases, controversies or issues that are likely to come before the court; or

(iii) knowingly * misrepresent the identity, qualifications, present position or other fact concerning the candidate or an opponent;

Commentary

Section 5A(3)(d) prohibits a candidate for judicial office from making statements that appear to commit the candidate regarding cases, controversies or issues likely to come before the court. As a corollary, a candidate should emphasize in any public statement the candidate's duty to uphold the law regardless of his or her personal views. See also

* See Terminology.   * See Terminology.

Section 3B(9), the general rule on public comment by judges. Section 5A(3)(d) does not prohibit a candidate from making pledges or promises respecting improvements in court administration. Nor does this Section prohibit an incumbent judge from making private statements to other judges or court personnel in the performance of judicial duties. This Section applies to any statement made in the process of securing judicial office, such as statements to commissions charged with judicial selection and tenure and legislative bodies confirming appointment. See also Rule 8.2 of the ABA Model Rules of Professional Conduct.

(e) may respond to personal attacks or attacks on the candidate's record as long as the response does not violate Section 5A(3)(d).

B. Candidates Seeking Appointment to Judicial or Other Governmental Office.

(1) A candidate * for appointment to judicial office or a judge seeking other governmental office shall not solicit or accept funds, personally or through a committee or otherwise, to support his or her candidacy.

(2) A candidate * for appointment to judicial office or a judge seeking other governmental office shall not engage in any political activity to secure the appointment except that:

(a) such persons may:

(i) communicate with the appointing authority, including any selection or nominating commission or other agency designated to screen candidates;

(ii) seek support or endorsement for the appointment from organizations that regularly make recommendations for reappointment or appointment to the office, and from individuals to the extent requested or required by those specified in Section 5B(2)(a); and

(iii) provide to those specified in Sections 5B(2)(a)(i) and 5B(2)(a)(ii) information as to his or her qualifications for the office;

(b) a non-judge candidate * for appointment to judicial office may, in addition, unless otherwise prohibited by law *;

(i) retain an office in a political organization,*

(ii) attend political gatherings, and

(iii) continue to pay ordinary assessments and ordinary contributions to a political organization or candidate and purchase tickets for political party dinners or other functions.

Commentary

Section 5B(2) provides a limited exception to the restrictions imposed by Sections 5A(1) and 5D. Under Section 5B(2), candidates seeking reappointment to the same judicial office or appointment to another judicial office or other governmental office may apply for the appointment and seek appropriate support.

Although under Section 5B(2) non-judge candidates seeking appointment to judicial office are permitted during candidacy to retain office in a political organization, attend political gatherings and pay ordinary dues and assessments, they remain subject to other provisions of this Code during candidacy. See Sections 5B(1), 5B(2)(a), 5E and Application Section.

C. Judges and Candidates Subject to Public Election.

(1) **A judge or a candidate * subject to public election * may, except as prohibited by law:***

(a) **at any time**

(i) **purchase tickets for and attend political gatherings;**

(ii) **identify himself or herself as a member of a political party; and**

(iii) **contribute to a political organization *;**

(b) **when a candidate for election**

(i) **speak to gatherings on his or her own behalf;**

(ii) **appear in newspaper, television and other media advertisements supporting his or her candidacy;**

(iii) **distribute pamphlets and other promotional campaign literature supporting his or her candidacy; and**

(iv) **publicly endorse or publicly oppose other candidates for the same judicial office in a public election in which the judge or judicial candidate is running.**

Commentary

Section 5C(1) permits judges subject to election at any time to be involved in limited political activity. Section 5D, applicable solely to incumbent judges, would otherwise bar this activity.

(2) **A candidate * shall not personally solicit or accept campaign contributions or personally solicit publicly stated support. A candidate may, however, establish committees of responsible persons to conduct campaigns for the candidate through media**

* See Terminology.   * See Terminology.

advertisements, brochures, mailings, candidate forums and other means not prohibited by law. Such committees may solicit and accept reasonable campaign contributions, manage the expenditure of funds for the candidate's campaign and obtain public statements of support for his or her candidacy. Such committees are not prohibited from soliciting and accepting reasonable campaign contributions and public support from lawyers. A candidate's committees may solicit contributions and public support for the candidate's campaign no earlier than [one year] before an election and no later than [90] days after the last election in which the candidate participates during the election year. A candidate shall not use or permit the use of campaign contributions for the private benefit of the candidate or others.

Commentary*

There is legitimate concern about a judge's impartiality when parties whose interests may come before a judge, or the lawyers who represent such parties, are known to have made contributions to the election campaigns of judicial candidates. This is among the reasons that merit selection of judges is a preferable manner in which to select the judiciary. Notwithstanding that preference, Section 5C(2) recognizes that in many jurisdictions judicial candidates must raise funds to support their candidates for election to judicial office. It therefore permits a candidate, other than a candidate for appointment, to establish campaign committees to solicit and accept public support and reasonable financial contributions. In order to guard against the possibility that conflicts of interest will arise, the candidate must instruct his or her campaign committees at the start of the campaign to solicit or accept only contributions that are reasonable and appropriate under the circumstances. Though not prohibited, campaign contributions of which a judge has knowledge, made by lawyers or others who appear before the judge may, by virtue of their size or source, raise questions about a judge's impartiality and be cause for ~~relevant to~~ disqualification as provided under Section 3(E).

Campaign committees established under Section 5C(2) should manage campaign finances responsibly, avoiding deficits that might necessitate post-election fund-raising, to the extent possible. Such committees must at all times comply with applicable statutory provisions governing their conduct.

Section 5C(2) does not prohibit a candidate from initiating an evaluation by a judicial selection commission or bar association, or, subject to the requirements of this Code, from responding to a request for information from any organization.

* In 1997, the ABA amended the Commentary to Canon 5C(2).

(3) Except as prohibited by law,* a candidate * for judicial office in a public election * may permit the candidate's name: (a) to be listed on election materials along with the names of other candidates for elective public office, and (b) to appear in promotions of the ticket.

Commentary

Section 5C(3) provides a limited exception to the restrictions imposed by Section 5A(1).

D. Incumbent Judges. A judge shall not engage in any political activity except (i) as authorized under any other Section of this Code, (ii) on behalf of measures to improve the law,* the legal system or the administration of justice, or (iii) as expressly authorized by law.

Commentary

Neither Section 5D nor any other section of the Code prohibits a judge in the exercise of administrative functions from engaging in planning and other official activities with members of the executive and legislative branches of government. With respect to a judge's activity on behalf of measures to improve the law, the legal system and the administration of justice, see Commentary to Section 4B and Section 4C(1) and its Commentary.

E. Applicability. Canon 5 generally applies to all incumbent judges and judicial candidates.* A successful candidate, whether or not an incumbent, is subject to judicial discipline for his or her campaign conduct; an unsuccessful candidate who is a lawyer is subject to lawyer discipline for his or her campaign conduct. A lawyer who is a candidate for judicial office is subject to [Rule 8.2(b) of the ABA Model Rules of Professional Conduct]. (An adopting jurisdiction should substitute a reference to its applicable rule.)

APPLICATION OF THE CODE OF JUDICIAL CONDUCT

A. Anyone, whether or not a lawyer, who is an officer of a judicial system[3] and who performs judicial functions, including an officer such as a magistrate, court commissioner, special

---

* See Terminology.

3. Applicability of this Code to administrative law judges should be determined by each adopting jurisdiction. Administrative law judges generally are affiliated with the executive branch of government rather than the judicial branch and each adopting jurisdiction should consider the unique characteristics of particular administrative law judge positions in adopting and adapting the Code for administrative law judges. See, e.g., Model Code of Judicial Conduct for Federal Administrative Law Judges, endorsed by the National Conference of Administrative Law Judges in February 1989.

master or referee, is a judge within the meaning of this Code. All judges shall comply with this Code except as provided below.

Commentary

The four categories of judicial service in other than a full-time capacity are necessarily defined in general terms because of the widely varying forms of judicial service. For the purposes of this Section, as long as a retired judge is subject to recall the judge is considered to "perform judicial functions." The determination of which category and, accordingly, which specific Code provisions apply to an individual judicial officer, depend upon the facts of the particular judicial service.

B. Retired Judge Subject to Recall. A retired judge subject to recall who by law is not permitted to practice law is not required to comply:
    (1) except while serving as a judge, with Section 4F; and
    (2) at any time with Section 4E.
    C. Continuing Part-time Judge. A continuing part-time judge *:
    (1) is not required to comply:
        (a) except while serving as a judge, with Section 3B(9); and

        (b) at any time with Sections 4C(2), 4D(3), 4E(1), 4F, 4G, 4H, 5A(1), 5B(2) and 5D.

(2) shall not practice law in the court on which the judge serves or in any court subject to the appellate jurisdiction of the court on which the judge serves, and shall not act as a lawyer in a proceeding in which the judge has served as a judge or in any other proceeding related thereto.

Commentary

When a person who has been a continuing part-time judge is no longer a continuing part-time judge, including a retired judge no longer subject to recall, that person may act as a lawyer in a proceeding in which he or she has served as a judge or in any other proceeding related thereto only with the express consent of all parties pursuant to [Rule 1.12(a) of the ABA Model Rules of Professional Conduct]. (An adopting jurisdiction should substitute a reference to its applicable rule).

D. Periodic Part-time Judge. A periodic part-time judge *:
(1) is not required to comply
    (a) except while serving as a judge, with Section 3B(9);
    (b) at any time, with Sections 4C(2), 4C(3)(a), 4D(1)(b), 4D(3), 4D(4), 4D(5), 4E, 4F, 4G, 4H, 5A(1), 5B(2) and 5D.

* See Terminology.

(2) shall not practice law in the court on which the judge serves or in any court subject to the appellate jurisdiction of the court on which the judge serves, and shall not act as a lawyer in a proceeding in which the judge has served as a judge or in any other proceeding related thereto.

Commentary

When a person who has been a periodic part-time judge is no longer a periodic part-time judge (no longer accepts appointments), that person may act as a lawyer in a proceeding in which he or she has served as a judge or in any other proceeding related thereto only with the express consent of all parties pursuant to [Rule 1.12(a) of the ABA Model Rules of Professional Conduct]. (An adopting jurisdiction should substitute a reference to its applicable rule).

E. Pro Tempore Part–Time Judge. A pro tempore part-time judge *:

(1) is not required to comply:

(a) except while serving as a judge, with Sections 2A, 2B, 3B(9) and 4C(1);

(b) at any time with Sections 2C, 4C(2), 4C(3)(a), 4C(3)(b), 4D(1)(b), 4D(3), 4D(4), 4D(5), 4E, 4F, 4G, 4H, 5A(1), 5A(2), 5B(2) and 5D.

(2) A person who has been a pro tempore part-time judge * shall not act as a lawyer in a proceeding in which the judge has served as a judge or in any other proceeding related thereto except as otherwise permitted by [Rule 1.12(a) of the ABA Model Rules of Professional Conduct]. (An adopting jurisdiction should substitute a reference to its applicable rule.)

F. Time for Compliance. A person to whom this Code becomes applicable shall comply immediately with all provisions of this Code except Sections 4D(2), 4D(3) and 4E and shall comply with these Sections as soon as reasonably possible and shall do so in any event within the period of one year.

Commentary

If serving as a fiduciary when selected as judge, a new judge may, notwithstanding the prohibitions in Section 4E, continue to serve as fiduciary but only for that period of time necessary to avoid serious adverse consequences to the beneficiary of the fiduciary relationship and in no event longer than one year. Similarly, if engaged at the time of judicial selection in a business activity, a new judge may, notwithstanding the prohibitions in Section 4D(3), continue in that activity for a reasonable period but in no event longer than one year.

* See Terminology.

AMERICAN BAR ASSOCIATION CODE OF JUDICIAL CONDUCT (1972)

As amended until 1989.

[In 1969, the ABA created a commission chaired by California Supreme Court Justice Traynor to draft a code of conduct for judges. The new code of conduct was to replace the Canons of Judicial Ethics, which had been adopted by the ABA in 1924. This committee produced the Code of Judicial Conduct and this document was adopted by the ABA in 1972. Most state courts have adopted codes based largely upon the 1972 Code of Judicial Conduct. Note, however, that the ABA replaced the 1972 Code with a 1990 Code of Judicial Conduct. Ed.]

Contents

INTRODUCTION

Almost fifty years ago the American Bar Association formulated the original *Canons of Judicial Ethics*. Those Canons, occasionally amended, have been adopted in most states. In 1969 the Association determined that current needs and problems required revision of the Canons.

In the revision process, the Association has sought and considered the views of the Bench and Bar and other interested persons. In the judgment of the Association this Code, consisting of statements of norms denominated canons, the accompanying text setting forth specific rules, and the commentary, states the standards that judges should observe. The canons and text establish mandatory standards unless otherwise indicated. It is hoped that all jurisdictions will adopt this Code and establish effective disciplinary procedures for its enforcement.

CANON 1

A Judge Should Uphold the Integrity and Independence of the Judiciary

An independent and honorable judiciary is indispensable to justice in our society. A judge should participate in establishing, maintaining, and enforcing, and should himself observe, high standards of conduct so that the integrity and independence of the judiciary may be preserved. The provisions of this Code should be construed and applied to further that objective.

CANON 2

A Judge Should Avoid Impropriety and the Appearance of Impropriety in All His Activities

A. A judge should respect and comply with the law and should conduct himself at all times in a manner that promotes public confidence in the integrity and impartiality of the judiciary.

B. A judge should not allow his family, social, or other relationships to influence his judicial conduct or judgment. He should not lend the prestige of his office to advance the private interests of others; nor should he convey or permit others to convey the impression that they are in a special position to influence him. He should not testify voluntarily as a character witness.

Commentary

Public confidence in the judiciary is eroded by irresponsible or improper conduct by judges. A judge must avoid all impropriety and appearance of impropriety. He must expect to be the subject of constant public scrutiny. He must therefore accept restrictions on his conduct that might be viewed as burdensome by the ordinary citizen and should do so freely and willingly.

The testimony of a judge as a character witness injects the prestige of his office into the proceeding in which he testifies and may be misunderstood to be an official testimonial. This Canon, however, does not afford him a privilege against testifying in response to an official summons.

It is inappropriate for a judge to hold membership in any organization that practices invidious discrimination on the basis of race, sex, religion, or national origin. Membership of a judge in an organization that practices invidious discrimination may give rise to perceptions by minorities, women, and others, that the judge's impartiality is impaired. Whether an organization practices invidious discrimination is often a complex question to which judges should be sensitive. The answer cannot be determined by a mere examination of an organization's current membership rolls but rather depends upon the history of the organization's selection of members and other relevant factors. Ultimately, each judge must determine in the judge's own conscience whether an organization of which the judge is a member practices invidious discrimination.[1]

CANON 3

A Judge Should Perform the Duties of His Office Impartially and Diligently

The judicial duties of a judge take precedence over all his other activities. His judicial duties include all the duties of his office prescribed by law. In the performance of these duties, the following standards apply:
A. Adjudicative Responsibilities.

    (1) A judge should be faithful to the law and maintain professional competence in it. He should be unswayed by partisan interests, public clamor, or fear of criticism.

    (2) A judge should maintain order and decorum in proceedings before him.

    (3) A judge should be patient, dignified, and courteous to litigants, jurors, witnesses, lawyers, and others with whom he deals in his official capacity, and should require similar conduct of lawyers, and of his staff, court officials, and others subject to his direction and control.

Commentary

The duty to hear all proceedings fairly and with patience is not inconsistent with the duty to dispose promptly of the business of the court. Courts can be efficient and business-like while being patient and deliberate.

---

1. This paragraph was added on August 7, 1984, by the American Bar Association House of Delegates meeting in Chicago.

(4) A judge should accord to every person who is legally interested in a proceeding, or his lawyer, full right to be heard according to law, and, except as authorized by law, neither initiate nor consider *ex parte* or other communications concerning a pending or impending proceeding. A judge, however, may obtain the advice of a disinterested expert on the law applicable to a proceeding before him if he gives notice to the parties of the person consulted and the substance of the advice, and affords the parties reasonable opportunity to respond.

Commentary

The proscription against communications concerning a proceeding includes communications from lawyers, law teachers, and other persons who are not participants in the proceeding, except to the limited extent permitted. It does not preclude a judge from consulting with other judges, or with court personnel whose function is to aid the judge in carrying out his adjudicative responsibilities.

An appropriate and often desirable procedure for a court to obtain the advice of a disinterested expert on legal issues is to invite him to file a brief *amicus curiae*.

(5) A judge should dispose promptly of the business of the court.

Commentary

Prompt disposition of the court's business requires a judge to devote adequate time to his duties, to be punctual in attending court and expeditious in determining matters under submission, and to insist that court officials, litigants and their lawyers cooperate with him to that end.

(6) A judge should abstain from public comment about a pending or impending proceeding in any court, and should require similar abstention on the part of court personnel subject to his direction and control. This subsection does not prohibit judges from making public statements in the course of their official duties or from explaining for public information the procedures of the court.

Commentary

"Court personnel" does not include the lawyers in a proceeding before a judge. The conduct of lawyers is governed by DR7–107 of the *Code of Professional Responsibility*.

(7) A judge should prohibit broadcasting, televising, recording or photographing in courtrooms and areas immediately adjacent thereto during sessions of court, or recesses between sessions, except that under rules prescribed by a supervising appellate court or other appropriate authority, a judge may authorize broadcasting, televising, recording and photographing of judicial proceedings in courtrooms and areas immediately adjacent thereto consistent with the right of the parties to a fair trial and subject to express conditions, limitations, and guidelines which allow such coverage in a manner that will be unobtrusive, will not distract the trial participants, and will not otherwise interfere with the administration of justice.[2]

B. Administrative Responsibilities.

(1) A judge should diligently discharge his administrative responsibilities, maintain professional competence in judicial administration, and facilitate the performance of the administrative responsibilities of other judges and court officials.

(2) A judge should require his staff and court officials subject to his direction and control to observe the standards of fidelity and diligence that apply to him.

(3) A judge should take or initiate appropriate disciplinary measures against a judge or lawyer for unprofessional conduct of which the judge may become aware.

Commentary

Disciplinary measures may include reporting a lawyer's misconduct to an appropriate disciplinary body.

(4) A judge should not make unnecessary appointments. He should exercise his power of appointment only on the basis of merit, avoiding nepotism and favoritism. He should not approve compensation of appointees beyond the fair value of services rendered.

Commentary

Appointees of the judge include officials such as referees, commissioners, special masters, receivers, guardians and personnel such as clerks, secretaries, and bailiffs. Consent by the parties to an appointment or an award of compensation does not relieve the judge of the obligation prescribed by this subsection.

2. As amended August 11, 1982, American Bar Association House of Delegates, San Francisco, per Report 107.

C. Disqualification.

(1) A judge should disqualify himself in a proceeding in which his impartiality might reasonably be questioned, including but not limited to instances where:

(a) he has a personal bias or prejudice concerning a party, or personal knowledge of disputed evidentiary facts concerning the proceeding;

(b) he served as lawyer in the matter in controversy, or a lawyer with whom he previously practiced law served during such association as a lawyer concerning the matter, or the judge or such lawyer has been a material witness concerning it;

Commentary

A lawyer in a governmental agency does not necessarily have an association with other lawyers employed by that agency within the meaning of this subsection; a judge formerly employed by a governmental agency, however, should disqualify himself in a proceeding if his impartiality might reasonably be questioned because of such association.

(c) he knows that he, individually or as a fiduciary, or his spouse or minor child residing in his household, has a financial interest in the subject matter in controversy or in a party to the proceeding, or any other interest that could be substantially affected by the outcome of the proceeding;

(d) he or his spouse, or a person within the third degree of relationship to either of them, or the spouse of such a person:

(i) is a party to the proceeding, or an officer, director, or trustee of a party;

(ii) is acting as a lawyer in the proceeding;

Commentary

The fact that a lawyer in a proceeding is affiliated with a law firm with which a lawyer-relative of the judge is affiliated does not of itself disqualify the judge. Under appropriate circumstances, the fact that "his impartiality might reasonably be questioned" under Canon 3C(1), or that the lawyer-relative is known by the judge to have an interest in the law firm that could be "substantially affected by the outcome of the proceeding" under Canon 3C(1)(d)(iii) may require his disqualification.

(iii) is known by the judge to have an interest that could be substantially affected by the outcome of the proceeding;

(iv) is to the judge's knowledge likely to be a material witness in the proceeding;

(2) A judge should inform himself about his personal and fiduciary financial interests, and make a reasonable effort to inform himself about the personal financial interests of his spouse and minor children residing in his household.

(3) For the purposes of this section:

(a) the degree of relationship is calculated according to the civil law system;

Commentary

According to the civil law system, the third degree of relationship test would, for example, disqualify the judge if his or his spouse's father, grandfather, uncle, brother, or niece's husband were a party or lawyer in the proceeding, but would not disqualify him if a cousin were a party or lawyer in the proceeding.

(b) "fiduciary" includes such relationships an executor, administrator, trustee, and guardian;

(c) "financial interest" means ownership of a legal or equitable interest, however small, or a relationship as director, advisor, or other active participant in the affairs of a party, except that:

(i) ownership in a mutual or common investment fund that holds securities is not a "financial interest" in such securities unless the judge participates in the management of the fund;

(ii) an office in an educational, religious, charitable, fraternal, or civic organization is not a "financial interest" in securities held by the organization;

(iii) the proprietary interest of a policy holder in a mutual insurance company, of a depositor in a mutual savings association, or a similar proprietary interest, is a "financial interest" in the organization only if the outcome of the proceeding could substantially affect the value of the interest;

(iv) ownership of government securities is a "financial interest" in the issuer only if the outcome of the proceeding could substantially affect the value of the securities.

D. **Remittal of Disqualification.** A judge disqualified by the terms of Canon 3C(1)(c) or Canon 3C(1)(d) may, instead of withdrawing from the proceeding, disclose on the record the basis of his disqualification. If, based on such disclosure, the parties and lawyers, independently of the judge's participation, all agree in writing that the judge's relationship is immaterial or that his financial interest is insubstantial, the judge is no longer disqualified, and may participate in the proceeding. The agreement, signed by all parties and lawyers, shall be incorporated in the record of the proceeding.

Commentary

This procedure is designed to minimize the chance that a party or lawyer will feel coerced into an agreement. When a party is not immediately available, the judge without violating this section may proceed on the written assurance of the lawyer that his party's consent will be subsequently filed.

CANON 4

A Judge May Engage in Activities to Improve the Law, the Legal System, and the Administration of Justice

A judge, subject to the proper performance of his judicial duties, may engage in the following quasi-judicial activities, if in doing so he does not cast doubt on his capacity to decide impartially any issue that may come before him:

A. He may speak, write, lecture, teach, and participate in other activities concerning the law, the legal system, and the administration of justice.

B. He may appear at a public hearing before an executive or legislative body or official on matters concerning the law, the legal system, and the administration of justice, and he may otherwise consult with an executive or legislative body or official, but only on matters concerning the administration of justice.

C. He may serve as a member, officer, or director of an organization or governmental agency devoted to the improvement of the law, the legal system, or the administration of justice. He may assist such an organization in raising funds and may participate in their management and investment, but should not personally participate in public fund raising activities. He may make recommendations to public and private fund-granting agencies on projects and programs concerning the law, the legal system, and the administration of justice.

Commentary

As a judicial officer and person specially learned in the law, a judge is in a unique position to contribute to the improvement of the law, the legal system, and the administration of justice, including revision of substantive and procedural law and improvement of criminal and juvenile justice. To the extent that his time permits, he is encouraged to do so, either independently or through a bar association, judicial conference, or other organization dedicated to the improvement of the law.

619

Extra-judicial activities are governed by Canon 5.

CANON 5

A Judge Should Regulate His Extra-Judicial Activities to Minimize the Risk of Conflict with His Judicial Duties

A. Avocational Activities. A judge may write, lecture, teach, and speak on non-legal subjects, and engage in the arts, sports, and other social and recreational activities, if such avocational activities do not detract from the dignity of his office or interfere with the performance of his judicial duties.

Commentary

Complete separation of a judge from extra judicial activities is neither possible nor wise; he should not become isolated from the society in which he lives.

B. Civic and Charitable Activities. A judge may participate in civic and charitable activities that do not reflect adversely upon his impartiality or interfere with the performance of his judicial duties. A judge may serve as an officer, director, trustee, or non-legal advisor of an educational, religious, charitable, fraternal, or civic organization not conducted for the economic or political advantage of its members, subject to the following limitations:

(1) A judge should not serve if it is likely that the organization will be engaged in proceedings that would ordinarily come before him or will be regularly engaged in adversary proceedings in any court.

Commentary

The changing nature of some organizations and of their relationship to the law makes it necessary for a judge regularly to reexamine the activities of each organization with which he is affiliated to determine if it is proper for him to continue his relationship with it. For example, in many jurisdictions charitable hospitals are now more frequently in court than in the past. Similarly, the boards of some legal aid organizations now make policy decisions that may have political significance or imply commitment to causes that may come before the courts for adjudication.

(2) A judge should not solicit funds for any educational, religious, charitable, fraternal, or civic organization, or use or permit the use of the prestige of his office for that purpose, but he may be listed as an officer, director, or

trustee of such an organization. He should not be a speaker or the guest of honor at an organization's fund raising events, but he may attend such events.

(3) **A judge should not give investment advice to such an organization, but he may serve on its board of directors or trustees even though it has the responsibility for approving investment decisions.**

Commentary

A judge's participation in an organization devoted to quasi-judicial activities is governed by Canon 4.

C. Financial Activities.

(1) **A judge should refrain from financial and business dealings that tend to reflect adversely on his impartiality, interfere with the proper performance of his judicial duties, exploit his judicial position, or involve him in frequent transactions with lawyers or persons likely to come before the court on which he serves.**

(2) **Subject to the requirements of subsection (1), a judge may hold and manage investments, including real estate, and engage in other remunerative activity, but should not serve as an officer, director, manager, advisor, or employee of any business.**

Commentary

The Effective Date of Compliance provision of this Code qualifies this subsection with regard to a judge engaged in a family business at the time this Code becomes effective.

Canon 5 may cause temporary hardship in jurisdictions where judicial salaries are inadequate and judges are presently supplementing their income through commercial activities. The remedy, however, is to secure adequate judicial salaries.

[**Canon 5C(2) sets the minimum standard to which a full-time judge should adhere. Jurisdictions that do not provide adequate judicial salaries but are willing to allow full-time judges to supplement their incomes through commercial activities may adopt the following substitute until such time as adequate salaries are provided:**

* **(2) Subject to the requirement of subsection (1), a judge may hold and manage investments, including real estate, and engage in other remunerative activity including the operation of a business.**

Jurisdictions adopting the foregoing substitute may also wish to prohibit a judge from engaging in certain types of

businesses such as that of banks, public utilities, insurance companies, and other businesses affected with a public interest.]

(3) A judge should manage his investments and other financial interests to minimize the number of cases in which he is disqualified. As soon as he can do so without serious financial detriment, he should divest himself of investments and other financial interests that might require frequent disqualification.

(4) Neither a judge nor a member of his family residing in his household should accept a gift, bequest, favor, or loan from anyone except as follows:

(a) a judge may accept a gift incident to public testimonial to him; books supplied by publishers on a complimentary basis for official use; or an invitation to the judge and his spouse to attend a bar-related function or activity devoted to the improvement of the law, the legal system, or the administration of justice;

(b) a judge or a member of his family residing in his household may accept ordinary social hospitality; a gift, bequest, favor, or loan from a relative; a wedding or engagement gift; a loan from a lending institution in its regular course of business on the same terms generally available to persons who are not judges; or a scholarship or fellowship awarded on the same terms applied to other applicants;

(c) a judge or a member of his family residing in his household may accept any other gift, bequest, favor, or loan only if the donor is not a party or other person whose interests have come or are likely to come before him, and, if its value exceeds $100, the judge reports it in the same manner as he reports compensation in Canon 6C.

Commentary

This subsection does not apply to contributions to a judge's campaign for judicial office, a matter governed by Canon 7.

(5) For the purposes of this section "member of his family residing in his household" means any relative of a judge by blood or marriage, or a person treated by a judge as a member of his family, who resides in his household.

(6) A judge is not required by this Code to disclose his income, debts, or investments, except as provided in this Canon and Canons 3 and 6.

Commentary

Canon 3 requires a judge to disqualify himself in any proceeding in which he has a financial interest, however small; Canon 5 requires a judge to refrain from engaging in business and from financial activities that might interfere with the impartial performance of his judicial duties; Canon 6 requires him to report all compensation he receives for activities outside his judicial office. A judge has the rights of an ordinary citizen, including the right to privacy of his financial affairs, except to the extent that limitations thereon are required to safeguard the proper performance of his duties. Owning and receiving income from investments do not as such affect the performance of a judge's duties.

(7) Information acquired by a judge in his judicial capacity should not be used or disclosed by him in financial dealings or for any other purpose not related to his judicial duties.

D. Fiduciary Activities. A judge should not serve as the executor, administrator, trustee, guardian, or other fiduciary, except for the estate, trust, or person of a member of his family, and then only if such service will not interfere with the proper performance of his judicial duties. "Member of his family" includes a spouse, child, grandchild, parent, grandparent, or other relative or person with whom the judge maintains a close familial relationship. As a family fiduciary a judge is subject to the following restrictions:

(1) He should not serve if it is likely that as a fiduciary he will be engaged in proceedings that would ordinarily come before him, or if the estate, trust, or ward becomes involved in adversary proceedings in the court on which he serves or one under its appellate jurisdiction.

Commentary

The Effective Date of Compliance provision of this Code qualifies this subsection with regard to a judge who is an executor, administrator, trustee, or other fiduciary at the time this Code becomes effective.

(2) While acting as a fiduciary a judge is subject to the same restrictions on financial activities that apply to him in his personal capacity.

Commentary

A judge's obligation under this Canon and his obligation as a fiduciary may come into conflict. For example, a judge should resign as trustee if it would result in detriment to the trust to divest it of holdings whose retention would place the judge in violation of Canon 5C(3).

E. Arbitration. A judge should not act as an arbitrator or mediator.

F. Practice of Law. A judge should not practice law.

G. Extra-judicial Appointments. A judge should not accept appointment to a governmental committee, commission, or

other position that is concerned with issues of fact or policy on matters other than the improvement of the law, the legal system, or the administration of justice. A judge, however, may represent his country, state, or locality on ceremonial occasions or in connection with historical, educational, and cultural activities.

Commentary

Valuable services have been rendered in the past to the states and the nation by judges appointed by the executive to undertake important extra-judicial assignments. The appropriateness of conferring these assignments on judges must be reassessed, however, in light of the demands on judicial manpower created by today's crowded dockets and the need to protect the courts from involvement in extra-judicial matters that may prove to be controversial. Judges should not be expected or permitted to accept governmental appointments that could interfere with the effectiveness and independence of the judiciary.

CANON 6

A Judge Should Regularly File Reports of Compensation Received for Quasi-Judicial and Extra-Judicial Activities

A judge may receive compensation and reimbursement of expenses for the quasi-judicial and extra-judicial activities permitted by this Code, if the source of such payments does not give the appearance of influencing the judge in his judicial duties or otherwise give the appearance of impropriety, subject to the following restrictions:

A. Compensation. Compensation should not exceed a reasonable amount nor should it exceed what a person who is not a judge would receive for the same activity.

B. Expense Reimbursement. Expense reimbursement should be limited to the actual cost of travel, food, and lodging reasonably incurred by the judge and, where appropriate to the occasion by his spouse. Any payment in excess of such an amount is compensation.

C. Public Reports. A judge should report the date, place, and nature of any activity for which he received compensation, and the name of the payor and the amount of compensation so received. Compensation or income of a spouse attributed to the judge by operation of a community property law is not extra-judicial compensation to the judge. His report should be made at least annually and should be filed as a public document in the office of the clerk of the court on which he serves or other office designated by rule of court.

CANON 7

A Judge Should Refrain From Political Activity
Inappropriate to His Judicial Office

A. **Political Conduct in General.**
   (1) A judge or a candidate for election to judicial office should not:
      (a) act as a leader or hold any office in a political organization;
      (b) make speeches for a political organization or candidate or publicly endorse a candidate for public office;

Commentary

A candidate does not publicly endorse another candidate for public office by having his name on the same ticket.

      (c) solicit funds for or pay an assessment or make a contribution to a political organization or candidate, attend political gatherings, or purchase tickets for political party dinners, or other functions, except as authorized in subsection A(2);
   (2) A judge holding an office filled by public election between competing candidates, or a candidate for such office, may, only insofar as permitted by law, attend political gatherings, speak to such gatherings on his own behalf when he is a candidate for election or re-election, identify himself as a member of a political party, and contribute to a political party or organization.
   (3) A judge should resign his office when he becomes a candidate either in a party primary or in a general election for a nonjudicial office, except that he may continue to hold his judicial office while being a candidate for election to or serving as a delegate in a state constitutional convention, if he is otherwise permitted by law to do so.
   (4) A judge should not engage in any other political activity except on behalf of measures to improve the law, the legal system, or the administration of justice.
B. **Campaign Conduct.**
   (1) A candidate, including an incumbent judge, for a judicial office that is filled either by public election between competing candidates or on the basis of a merit system election:
      (a) should maintain the dignity appropriate to judicial office, and should encourage members of his family to

adhere to the same standards of political conduct that apply to him;

(b) **should prohibit public officials or employees subject to his direction or control from doing for him what he is prohibited from doing under this Canon; and except to the extent authorized under subsection B(2) or B(3), he should not allow any other person to do for him what he is prohibited from doing under this Canon;**

(c) **should not make pledges or promises of conduct in office other than the faithful and impartial performance of the duties of the office; announce his views on disputed legal or political issues; or misrepresent his identity, qualifications, present position, or other fact.**

(2) **A candidate, including an incumbent judge, for a judicial office that is filled by public election between competing candidates should not himself solicit or accept campaign funds, or solicit publicly stated support, but he may establish committees of responsible persons to secure and manage the expenditure of funds for his campaign and to obtain public statements of support for his candidacy. Such committees are not prohibited from soliciting campaign contributions and public support from lawyers. A candidate's committees may solicit funds for his campaign no earlier than [90] days before a primary election and no later than [90] days after the last election in which he participates during the election year. A candidate should not use or permit the use of campaign contributions for the private benefit of himself or members of his family.**

Commentary

Unless the candidate is required by law to file a list of his campaign contributors, their names should not be revealed to the candidate.

[Each jurisdiction adopting this Code should prescribe a time limit on soliciting campaign funds that is appropriate to the elective process therein.]

(3) **An incumbent judge who is a candidate for retention in or re-election to office without a competing candidate, and whose candidacy has drawn active opposition, may campaign in response thereto and may obtain publicly stated support and campaign funds in the manner provided in subsection B(2).**

Compliance With the Code of Judicial Conduct

Anyone, whether or not a lawyer, who is an officer of a judicial system performing judicial functions, including an officer such as a referee in bankruptcy, special master, court commissioner, or magistrate, is a judge for the purpose of this Code. All judges should comply with this Code except as provided below.

A. **Part-time Judge. A part-time judge is a judge who serves on a continuing or periodic basis, but is permitted by law to devote time to some other profession or occupation and whose compensation for that reason is less than that of a full-time judge. A part-time judge:**

   (1) **is not required to comply with Canon 5C(2), D, E, F, and G, and Canon 6C;**

   (2) **should not practice law in the court on which he serves or in any court subject to the appellate jurisdiction of the court on which he serves, or act as a lawyer in a proceeding in which he has served as a judge in any other proceeding related thereto.**

B. **Judge Pro Tempore. A judge pro tempore is a person who is appointed to act temporarily as a judge.**

   (1) **While acting as such, a judge pro tempore is not required to comply with Canon 5C(2), (3), D, E, F, and G, and Canon 6C.**

   (2) **A person who has been a judge pro tempore should not act as a lawyer in a proceeding in which he has served as a judge or in any other proceeding related thereto.**

C. **Retired Judge. A retired judge who receives the same compensation as a full-time judge on the court from which he retired and is eligible for recall to judicial service should comply with all the provisions of this Code except Canon 5G, but he should refrain from judicial service during the period of an extra-judicial appointment not sanctioned by Canon 5G. All other retired judges eligible for recall to judicial service should comply with the provisions of this Code governing part-time judges.**

Effective Date of Compliance

A person to whom this Code becomes applicable should arrange his affairs as soon as reasonably possible to comply with it. If, however, the demands on his time and the possibility of conflicts of interest are not substantial, a person who holds judicial office on the date this Code becomes effective may:

   (a) **continue to act as an officer, director, or non-legal advisor of a family business;**

   (b) **continue to act as an executor, administrator, trustee, or other fiduciary for the estate or person of one who is not a member of his family.**

CORRELATION TABLES

The Correlation Tables identify 1990 Code rules that relate to the same subject matter as the corresponding rules of the 1972 Code. The substance of the rules cited is not necessarily identical, and in many instances varies considerably. Although the Commentary is not cross-referenced, the subject matter of certain rules of the 1990 Code may have been addressed by the Commentary in the 1972 Code.

CORRELATION TABLE A

1990 CODE	1972 CODE
Preamble	None
Terminology	Canons 3C(3)(a), (b), (c); 5C(5); 5D
Canon 1	Canon 1
Section 1A	Paragraph to Canon 1
Canon 2	Canon 2
Section 2A	Canon 2A
Section 2B	Canon 2B
Section 2C	None
Canon 3	Canon 3
Section 3A	Paragraph to Canon 3
Section 3B(1)	None
Section 3B(2)	Canon 3A(1)
Section 3B(3)	Canon 3A(2)
Section 3B(4)	Canon 3A(3)
Section 3B(5)	None
Section 3B(6)	None
Section 3B(7)	Canon 3A(4)
Section 3B(7)(a)	None
Section 3B(7)(a)(i)	None
Section 3B(7)(a)(ii)	None
Section 3B(7)(b)	Canon 3A(4)
Section 3B(7)(c)	None
Section 3B(7)(d)	None
Section 3B(7)(e)	None
Section 3B(8)	Canon 3A(5)
Section 3B(9)	Canon 3A(6)
Section 3B(10)	None
Section 3B(11)	Canon 5C(7)
Section 3C(1)	Canon 3B(1)
Section 3C(2)	Canon 3B(2)
Section 3C(3)	None
Section 3C(4)	Canon 3B(4)
Section 3D(1)	Canon 3B(3)
Section 3D(2)	Canon 3B(3)
Section 3D(3)	None
Section 3E(1)	Canon 3C(1)
Section 3E(1)(a)	Canon 3C(1)(a)
Section 3E(1)(b)	Canon 3C(1)(b)

CORRELATION TABLES

CORRELATION TABLES

1990 CODE	1972 CODE
Section 5A(1)(a)	Canon 7A(1)(a)
Section 5A(1)(b)	Canon 7A(1)(b)
Section 5A(1)(c)	Canon 7A(1)(b)
Section 5A(1)(d)	Canon 7A(1)(c)
Section 5A(1)(e)	Canon 7A(1)(c)
Section 5A(2)	Canon 7A(3)
Section 5A(3)	Canon 7B(1)
Section 5A(3)(a)	Canon 7B(1)(a)
Section 5A(3)(b)	Canon 7B(1)(b)
Section 5A(3)(c)	Canon 7B(1)(b)
Section 5A(3)(d)	Canon 7B(1)(c)
Section 5A(3)(d)(i)	Canon 7B(1)(c)
Section 5A(3)(d)(ii)	Canon 7B(1)(c)
Section 5A(3)(d)(iii)	Canon 7B(1)(c)
Section 5A(3)(e)	None
Section 5B(1)	None
Section 5B(2)	None
Section 5B(2)(a)	None
Section 5B(2)(a)(i)	None
Section 5B(2)(a)(ii)	None
Section 5B(2)(a)(iii)	None
Section 5B(2)(b)	None
Section 5B(2)(b)(i)	None
Section 5B(2)(b)(ii)	None
Section 5B(2)(b)(iii)	None
Section 5C(1)	Canon 7A(2)
Section 5C(1)(a)	Canon 7A(2)
Section 5C(1)(a)(i)	Canon 7A(2)
Section 5C(1)(a)(ii)	Canon 7A(2)
Section 5C(1)(a)(iii)	Canon 7A(2)
Section 5C(1)(b)	Canon 7A(2)
Section 5C(1)(b)(i)	Canon 7A(2)
Section 5C(1)(b)(ii)	None
Section 5C(1)(b)(iii)	None
Section 5C(1)(b)(iv)	None
Section 5C(2)	Canon 7B(2)
Section 5C(3)	None
Section 5D	Canon 7A(4)
Section 5E	None
Application	Compliance
Section A	Paragraph to Compliance
Section B	Compliance C
Section B(1)	Compliance C
Section B(2)	Compliance C
Section C	Compliance A
Section C(1)	Compliance A(1)
Section C(1)(a)	Compliance A(1)
Section C(1)(b)	Compliance A(1)
Section C(2)	Compliance A(2)
Section D	Compliance A
Section D(1)	Compliance A(1)
Section D(1)(a)	Compliance A(1)
Section D(1)(b)	Compliance A(1)
Section D(2)	Compliance A(2)
Section E	Compliance B
Section E(1)	Compliance B(1)

1990 CODE	1972 CODE
Section E(1)(a)	Compliance B(1)
Section E(1)(b)	Compliance B(1)
Section E(2)	Compliance B(2)
Section F	Effective Date of Compliance

CORRELATION TABLE B

1972 CODE	1990 CODE
Canon 1	Canon 1
Paragraph to Canon 1	Section 1A
Canon 2	Canon 2
Canon 2A	Sections 2A, 2C
Canon 2B	Section 2B
Canon 3	Canon 3
Paragraph to Canon 3	Section 3A
Canon 3A(1)	Section 3B(2)
Canon 3A(2)	Section 3B(3)
Canon 3A(3)	Section 3B(4)
Canon 3A(4)	Sections 3B(7)(b)
Canon 3A(5)	Section 3B(8)
Canon 3A(6)	Section 3B(9)
Canon 3A(7)	None
Canon 3B(1)	Section 3C(1)
Canon 3B(2)	Section 3C(2)
Canon 3B(3)	Sections 3D(1), (2)
Canon 3B(4)	Section 3C(4)
Canon 3C(1)	Section 3E(1)
Canon 3C(1)(a)	Section 3E(1)(a)
Canon 3C(1)(b)	Section 3E(1)(b)
Canon 3C(1)(c)	Section 3E(1)(c)
Canon 3C(1)(d)	Section 3E(1)(d)
Canon 3C(1)(d)(i)	Section 3E(1)(d)(i)
Canon 3C(1)(d)(ii)	Section 3E(1)(d)(ii)
Canon 3C(1)(d)(iii)	Section 3E(1)(d)(iii)
Canon 3C(1)(d)(iv)	Section 3E(1)(d)(iv)
Canon 3C(2)	Section 3E(2)
Canon 3C(3)	Terminology
Canon 3C(3)(a)	Terminology
Canon 3C(3)(b)	Terminology
Canon 3C(3)(c)	Terminology
Canon 3C(3)(c)(i)	Terminology
Canon 3C(3)(c)(ii)	Terminology
Canon 3C(3)(c)(iii)	Terminology
Canon 3C(3)(c)(iv)	Terminology
Canon 3D	Section 3F
Canon 4	Canon 4
Paragraph to Canon 4	Section 4A
Canon 4A	Section 4B
Canon 4B	Section 4C(1)
Canon 4C	Sections 4C(3)(b), (i), (ii)
Canon 5	Canon 4
Paragraph to Canon 5	Section
Canon 5A	Section 4B
Canon 5B	Section 4C(3)
Canon 5B(1)	Sections 4C(3)(a), (i), (ii)
Canon 5B(2)	Section 4C(3)(b)

CORRELATION TABLES

PART THREE

RULES OF EVIDENCE AND PROCEDURE THAT AFFECT THE LEGAL PROFESSION

Table of Contents

Introduction

Until recently, most courses and casebooks in professional responsibility focused solely on the ABA's model codes of conduct. However, the law which governs and regulates the conduct of lawyers must go far beyond the ABA's pronouncements. One other source of law which affects lawyers' conduct must include rules of evidence, procedure, and court. This part includes rules of evidence and procedure which affect the practice of law.

SELECTED RULES OF EVIDENCE AND PROCEDURE

Federal Rules of Evidence for United States Courts and Magistrates

Appendix of Deleted Rules of Evidence

Federal Rules of Civil Procedure

Federal Rules of Criminal Procedure

Federal Rules of Appellate Procedure

Rules of The Supreme Court of The United States

Draft Federal Rules of Attorney Conduct

FEDERAL RULES OF EVIDENCE FOR UNITED STATES COURTS AND MAGISTRATES

Rule 501. General Rule

Except as otherwise required by the Constitution of the United States or provided by Act of Congress or in rules prescribed by the Supreme Court pursuant to statutory authority, the privilege of a witness, person, government, State, or political subdivision thereof shall be governed by the principles of common law as they may be interpreted by the courts of the United States in the light of reason and experience. However, in civil actions and proceedings, with respect to an element of a claim or defense as to which State law supplies the rule of decision, the privilege of a witness, person, government, State, or political subdivision thereof shall be determined in accordance with State law.

Rule 605. Competency of Judge as Witness

The judge presiding at the trial may not testify in that trial as a witness. No objection need be made in order to preserve the point.

APPENDIX OF DELETED RULES OF EVIDENCE

Rule 503. Lawyer-Client Privilege [Not enacted.]

(a) Definitions. As used in this rule:

(1) A "client" is a person, public officer, or corporation, association, or other organization or entity, either public or private, who is rendered professional legal services by a lawyer, or who consults a lawyer with a view to obtaining professional legal services from him.

(2) A "lawyer" is a person authorized, or reasonably believed by the client to be authorized, to practice law in any state or nation.

(3) A "representative of the lawyer" is one employed to assist the lawyer in the rendition of professional services.

(4) A communication is "confidential" if not intended to be disclosed to third persons other than those to whom disclosure is in furtherance of the rendition of professional legal services to the client or those reasonably necessary for the transmission of the communication.

(b) General rule of privilege. A client has a privilege to refuse to disclose and to prevent any other person from disclosing confidential communications made for the purpose of facilitating the rendition of professional legal services to the client, (1) between himself or his representative and his lawyer or his lawyer's representative, or (2) between his lawyer and the lawyer's representative, or (3) by him or his lawyer to a lawyer representing another in a matter of common interest,

635

or (4) between representatives of the client or between the client and a representative of the client, or (5) between lawyers representing the client.

(c) Who may claim the privilege. The privilege may be claimed by the client, his guardian or conservator, the personal representative of a deceased client, or the successor, trustee, or similar representative of a corporation, association, or other organization, whether or not in existence. The person who was the lawyer at the time of the communication may claim the privilege but only on behalf of the client. His authority to do so is presumed in the absence of evidence to the contrary.

(d) Exceptions. There is no privilege under this rule:

(1) Furtherance of crime or fraud. If the services of the lawyer were sought or obtained to enable or aid anyone to commit or plan to commit what the client knew or reasonably should have known to be a crime or fraud; or

(2) Claimants through same deceased client. As to a communication relevant to an issue between parties who claim through the same deceased client, regardless of whether the claims are by testate or intestate succession or by *inter vivos* transaction; or

(3) Breach of duty by lawyer or client. As to a communication relevant to an issue of breach of duty by the lawyer to his client or by the client to his lawyer; or

(4) Document attested by lawyer. As to a communication relevant to an issue concerning an attested document to which the lawyer is an attesting witness; or

(5) Joint clients. As to a communication relevant to a matter of common interest between two or more clients if the communication was made by any of them to a lawyer retained or consulted in common, when offered in an action between any of the clients.

FEDERAL RULES OF CIVIL PROCEDURE
(as amended to Jan. 1, 1999)

Rule 11. Signing of Pleadings, Motions, and Other Papers; Representations to Court; Sanctions *

(a) Signature. Every pleading, written motion, and other paper shall be signed by at least one attorney of record in the attorney's

---

* [Ed.] This footnote contains the text of Rule 11 after its 1983 Amendment.

Every pleading, motion, and other paper of a party represented by an attorney shall be signed by at least one attorney of record in the attorney's individual name, whose address shall be stated. A party who is not represented by an attorney shall sign the party's pleading, motion, or other paper and state the party's address. Except when otherwise specifically provided by rule or statute, pleadings need not be verified or accompanied by affidavit. The rule in equity that the averments of an answer under oath must be overcome by the testimony of two wit-

individual name, or, if the party is not represented by an attorney, shall be signed by the party. Each paper shall state the signer's address and telephone number, if any. Except when otherwise specifically provided by rule or statute, pleadings need not be verified or accompanied by affidavit. An unsigned paper shall be stricken unless omission of the signature is corrected promptly after being called to the attention of the attorney or party.

(b) Representations to Court. By presenting to the court (whether by signing, filing, submitting, or later advocating) a pleading, written motion, or other paper, an attorney or unrepresented party is certifying that to the best of the person's knowledge, information, and belief, formed after an inquiry reasonable under the circumstances,—

(1) it is not being presented for any improper purpose, such as to harass or to cause unnecessary delay or needless increase in the cost of litigation;

(2) the claims, defenses, and other legal contentions therein are warranted by existing law or by a nonfrivolous argument for the extension, modification, or reversal of existing law or the establishment of new law;

(3) the allegations and other factual contentions have evidentiary support or, if specifically so identified, are likely to have evidentiary support after a reasonable opportunity for further investigation or discovery; and

(4) the denials of factual contentions are warranted on the evidence or, if specifically so identified, are reasonably based on a lack of information or belief.

(c) Sanctions. If, after notice and a reasonable opportunity to respond, the court determines that subdivision (b) has been violated, the court may, subject to the conditions stated below, impose an appropriate sanction upon the attorneys, law firms, or parties that have violated subdivision (b) or are responsible for the violation.

nesses or of one witness sustained by corroborating circumstances is abolished. The signature of an attorney or party constitutes a certificate by the signer that the signer has read the pleading, motion, or other paper; that to the best of the signer's knowledge, information, and belief formed after reasonable inquiry it is well grounded in fact and is warranted by existing law or a good faith argument for the extension, modification, or reversal of existing law, and that it is not interposed for any improper purpose, such as to harass or to cause unnecessary delay or needless increase in the cost of litigation.

If a pleading, motion, or other paper is not signed, it shall be stricken unless it is signed promptly after the omission is called to the attention of the pleader or movant. If a pleading, motion, or other paper is signed in violation of this rule, the court, upon motion or upon its own initiative, shall impose upon the person who signed it, a represented party, or both, an appropriate sanction, which may include an order to pay to the other party or parties the amount of the reasonable expenses incurred because of the filing of the pleading, motion, or other paper, including a reasonable attorney's fee.

(1) How Initiated.

(A) By Motion. A motion for sanctions under this rule shall be made separately from other motions or requests and shall describe the specific conduct alleged to violate subdivision (b). It shall be served as provided in Rule 5, but shall not be filed with or presented to the court unless, within 21 days after service of the motion (or such other period as the court may prescribe), the challenged paper, claim, defense, contention, allegation, or denial is not withdrawn or appropriately corrected. If warranted, the court may award to the party prevailing on the motion the reasonable expenses and attorney's fees incurred in presenting or opposing the motion. Absent exceptional circumstances, a law firm shall be held jointly responsible for violations committed by its partners, associates, and employees.

(B) On Court's Initiative. On its own initiative, the court may enter an order describing the specific conduct that appears to violate subdivision (b) and directing an attorney, law firm, or party to show cause why it has not violated subdivision (b) with respect thereto.

(2) Nature of Sanction; Limitations. A sanction imposed for violation of this rule shall be limited to what is sufficient to deter repetition of such conduct or comparable conduct by others similarly situated. Subject to the limitations in subparagraphs (A) and (B), the sanction may consist of, or include, directives of a nonmonetary nature, an order to pay a penalty into court, or, if imposed on motion and warranted for effective deterrence, an order directing payment to the movant of some or all of the reasonable attorneys' fees and other expenses incurred as a direct result of the violation.

(A) Monetary sanctions may not be awarded against a represented party for a violation of subdivision (b)(2).

(B) Monetary sanctions may not be awarded on the court's initiative unless the court issues its order to show cause before a voluntary dismissal or settlement of the claims made by or against the party which is, or whose attorneys are, to be sanctioned.

(3) Order. When imposing sanctions, the court shall describe the conduct determined to constitute a violation of this rule and explain the basis for the sanction imposed.

(d) Inapplicability to Discovery. Subdivisions (a) through (c) of this rule do not apply to disclosures and discovery requests, responses, objections, and motions that are subject to the provisions of Rules 26 through 37.

(As amended Apr. 22, 1993, eff. Dec. 1, 1993.)

ADVISORY COMMITTEE NOTES
1993 Amendments

Purpose of revision. This revision is intended to remedy problems that have arisen in the interpretation and application of the 1983 revision of the rule. * * *

The rule retains the principle that attorneys and pro se litigants have an obligation to the court to refrain from conduct that frustrates the aims of Rule 1. The revision broadens the scope of this obligation, but places greater constraints on the imposition of sanctions and should reduce the number of motions for sanctions presented to the court. New subdivision (d) removes from the ambit of this rule all discovery requests, responses, objections, and motions subject to the provisions of Rule 26 through 37.

Subdivision (a). Retained in this subdivision are the provisions requiring signatures on pleadings, written motions, and other papers. Unsigned papers are to be received by the Clerk, but then are to be stricken if the omission of the signature is not corrected promptly after being called to the attention of the attorney or pro se litigant. Correction can be made by signing the paper on file or by submitting a duplicate that contains the signature. A court may require by local rule that papers contain additional identifying information regarding the parties or attorneys, such as telephone numbers to facilitate facsimile transmissions, though, as for omission of a signature, the paper should not be rejected for failure to provide such information.

The sentence in the former rule relating to the effect of answers under oath is no longer needed and has been eliminated. The provision in the former rule that signing a paper constitutes a certificate that it has been read by the signer also has been eliminated as unnecessary. The obligations imposed under subdivision (b) obviously require that a pleading, written motion, or other paper be read before it is filed or submitted to the court.

Subdivisions (b) and (c). These subdivisions restate the provisions requiring attorneys and pro se litigants to conduct a reasonable inquiry into the law and facts before signing pleadings, written motions, and other documents, and prescribing sanctions for violation of these obligations. The revision in part expands the responsibilities of litigants to the court, while providing greater constraints and flexibility in dealing with infractions of the rule. The rule continues to require litigants to "stop-and-think" before initially making legal or factual contentions. It also, however, emphasizes the duty of candor by subjecting litigants to potential sanctions for insisting upon a position after it is no longer tenable and by generally providing protection against sanctions if they withdraw or correct contentions after a potential violation is called to their attention.

The rule applies only to assertions contained in papers filed with or submitted to the court. It does not cover matters arising for the first time during oral presentations to the court, when counsel may make statements that would not have been made if there had been more time for study and reflection. However, a litigant's obligations with respect to the contents of these papers are not measured solely as of the time they are filed with or submitted to the court, but include reaffirming to the court and advocating positions contained in those pleadings and motions after learning that they cease to have any merit. For example, an attorney who during a pretrial conference insists on a claim or defense should be viewed as "presenting to the court" that contention and would be subject to the obligations of subdivision (b) measured as of that time. Similarly, if after a notice of removal is filed, a party urges in federal court the allegations of a pleading filed in state court (whether as claims, defenses, or in disputes regarding removal or remand), it would be viewed as "presenting"—and hence certifying to the district court under Rule 11—those allegations.

The certification with respect to allegations and other factual contentions is revised in recognition that sometimes a litigant may have good reason to believe that a fact is true or false but may need discovery, formal or informal, from opposing parties or third persons to gather and confirm the evidentiary basis for the allegation. Tolerance of factual contentions in initial pleadings by plaintiffs or defendants when specifically identified as made on information and belief does not relieve litigants from the obligation to conduct an appropriate investigation into the facts that is reasonable under the circumstances; it is not a license to join parties, make claims, or present defenses without any factual basis or justification. Moreover, if evidentiary support is not obtained after a reasonable opportunity for further investigation or discovery, the party has a duty under the rule not to persist with that contention. Subdivision (b) does not require a formal amendment to pleadings for which evidentiary support is not obtained, but rather calls upon a litigant not thereafter to advocate such claims or defenses.

The certification is that there is (or likely will be) "evidentiary support" for the allegation, not that the party will prevail with respect to its contention regarding the fact. That summary judgment is rendered against a party does not necessarily mean, for purposes of this certification, that it had no evidentiary support for its position. On the other hand, if a party has evidence with respect to a contention that would suffice to defeat a motion for summary judgment based thereon, it would have sufficient "evidentiary support" for purposes of Rule 11.

Denials of factual contentions involve somewhat different considerations. Often, of course, a denial is premised upon the existence of evidence contradicting the alleged fact. At other times a denial is permissible because, after an appropriate investigation, a party has no information concerning the matter or, indeed, has a reasonable basis for doubting the credibility of the only evidence relevant to the matter. A party should not deny an allegation it knows to be true; but it is not required, simply because it lacks contradictory evidence, to admit an allegation that it believes is not true.

The changes in subdivisions (b)(3) and (b)(4) will serve to equalize the burden of the rule upon plaintiffs and defendants, who under Rule 8(b) are in effect allowed to deny allegations by stating that from their initial investigation they lack sufficient information to form a belief as to the truth of the allegation. If, after further investigation or discovery, a denial is no longer warranted, the defendant should not continue to insist on that denial. While sometimes helpful, formal amendment of the pleadings to withdraw an allegation or denial is not required by subdivision (b).

Arguments for extensions, modifications, or reversals of existing law or for creation of new law do not violate subdivision (b)(2) provided they are "nonfrivolous." This establishes an objective standard, intended to eliminate any "empty-head pure-heart" justification for patently frivolous arguments. However, the extent to which a litigant has researched the issues and found some support for its theories even in minority opinions, in law review articles, or through consultation with other attorneys should certainly be taken into account in determining whether paragraph (2) has been violated. Although arguments for a change of law are not required to be specifically so identified, a contention that is so identified should be viewed with greater tolerance under the rule.

The court has available a variety of possible sanctions to impose for violations, such as striking the offending paper; issuing an admonition, reprimand, or censure; requiring participation in seminars or other educational programs; ordering a fine payable to the court; referring the matter to disciplinary authorities (or, in the case of government attorneys, to the Attorney General, Inspector General, or agency head), etc. See Manual for Complex Litigation, Second, § 42.3. The rule does not attempt to enumerate the factors a court should consider in deciding whether to impose a sanction or what sanctions would be appropriate in the circumstances; but, for emphasis, it does specifically note that a sanction may be nonmonetary as well as monetary. Whether the improper conduct was willful, or negligent; whether it was part of a pattern of activity, or an isolated event; whether it infected the entire pleading, or only one particular count or defense; whether the person has engaged in similar conduct in other litigation; whether it was intended to injure; what effect it had on the litigation process in time or expense; whether the responsible person is trained in the law; what amount, given the financial resources of the responsible person, is needed to deter that person from repetition in the same case; what amount is needed to deter similar activity by other litigants: all of these may in a particular case be proper considerations. The court has significant discretion in determining what sanctions, if any, should be imposed for a violation, subject to the principle that the sanctions should not be more severe than reasonably necessary to deter repetition of the conduct by the offending person or comparable conduct by similarly situated persons.

Since the purpose of Rule 11 sanctions is to deter rather than to compensate, the rule provides that, if a monetary sanction is imposed, it should ordinarily be paid into court as a penalty. However, under unusual circumstances, particularly for (b)(1) violations, deterrence may be ineffective unless the sanction not only requires the person violating the rule to make a monetary payment, but also directs that some or all of this payment be made to those injured by the violation. Accordingly, the rule authorizes the court, if requested in a motion and if so warranted, to award attorney's fees to another party. Any such award to another party, however, should not exceed the expenses and attorneys' fees for the services directly and unavoidably caused by the violation of the certification requirement. If, for example, a wholly unsupportable count were included in a multi-count complaint or counterclaim for the purpose of needlessly increasing the cost of litigation to an impecunious adversary, any award of expenses should be limited to those directly caused by inclusion of the improper count, and not those resulting from the filing of the complaint or answer itself. The award should not provide compensation for services that could have been avoided by an earlier disclosure of evidence or an earlier challenge to the groundless claims or defenses. Moreover, partial reimbursement of fees may constitute a sufficient deterrent with respect to violations by persons having modest financial resources. In cases brought under statutes providing for fees to be awarded to prevailing parties, the court should not employ cost-shifting under this rule in a manner that would be inconsistent with the standards that govern the statutory award of fees, such as stated in Christiansburg Garment Co. v. EEOC, 434 U.S. 412 (1978).

The sanction should be imposed on the persons—whether attorneys, law firms, or parties—who have violated the rule or who may be determined to be responsible for the violation. The person signing, filing, submitting, or advocating a document has a nondelegable responsibility to the court, and in most situations is the person to be sanctioned for a violation. Absent exceptional circumstances, a law firm is to be held also responsible when, as a result of a motion under subdivision (c)(1)(A), one of its partners, associates, or employees is determined to have violated the rule. Since such a motion may be filed only if the offending paper is not withdrawn or corrected within 21 days after service of the motion, it is appropriate that the law firm ordinarily be viewed as jointly responsible under established principles of agency. This provision is designed to remove the restrictions of the former rule. Cf. Pavelic & LeFlore v. Marvel Entertainment Group, 493 U.S. 120 (1989) (1983 version of Rule 11 does not permit sanctions against law firm of attorney signing groundless complaint).

The revision permits the court to consider whether other attorneys in the firm, co-counsel, other law firms, or the party itself should be held accountable for their part in causing a violation. When appropriate, the court can make an additional inquiry in order to determine whether the sanction should be imposed on such persons, firms, or parties either in addition to or, in unusual circumstances, instead of the person actually making the presentation to the court. For example, such an inquiry may be appropriate in cases involving governmental agencies or other institutional parties that frequently impose substantial restrictions on the discretion of individual attorneys employed by it.

Sanctions that involve monetary awards (such as a fine or an award of attorney's fees) may not be imposed on a represented party for causing a violation of subdivision (b)(2), involving frivolous contentions of law. Monetary responsibility for such violations is more properly placed solely on the party's attorneys. With this limitation, the rule should not be subject to attack under the Rules Enabling Act. See Willy v. Coastal Corp., ___ U.S. ___ (1992); Business Guides, Inc. v. Chromatic Communications Enter. Inc., ___ U.S. ___ (1991). This restriction does not limit the court's power to impose sanctions or remedial orders that may have collateral financial consequences upon a party, such as dismissal of a claim, preclusion of a defense, or preparation of amended pleadings.

Explicit provision is made for litigants to be provided notice of the alleged violation and an opportunity to respond before sanctions are imposed. Whether the matter should be decided solely on the basis of written submissions or should be scheduled for oral argument (or, indeed, for evidentiary presentation) will depend on the circumstances. If the court imposes a sanction, it must, unless waived, indicate its reasons in a written order or on the record; the court should not ordinarily have to explain its denial of a motion for sanctions. Whether a violation has occurred and what sanctions, if any, to impose for a violation are matters committed to the discretion of the trial court; accordingly, as under current law, the standard for appellate review of these decisions will be for abuse of discretion. See Cooter & Gell v. Hartmarx Corp., 496 U.S. 384 (1990) (noting, however, that an abuse would be established if the court based its ruling on an erroneous view of the law or on a clearly erroneous assessment of the evidence).

The revision leaves for resolution on a case-by-case basis, considering the particular circumstances involved, the question as to when a motion for violation of Rule 11 should be served and when, if filed, it should be decided. Ordinarily the motion should be served promptly after the inappropriate paper is filed, and, if delayed too long, may be viewed as untimely. In other circumstances, it should not be served until the other party has had a reasonable opportunity for discovery. Given the "safe harbor" provisions discussed below, a party cannot delay serving its Rule 11 motion until conclusion of the case (or judicial rejection of the offending contention).

Rule 11 motions should not be made or threatened for minor, inconsequential violations of the standards prescribed by subdivision (b). They should not be employed as a discovery device or to test the legal sufficiency or efficacy of allegations in the pleadings; other motions are available for those purposes. Nor should Rule 11 motions be prepared to emphasize the merits of a party's position, to exact an unjust settlement, to intimidate an adversary into withdrawing contentions that are fairly debatable, to increase the costs of litigation, to create a conflict of interest between attorney and client, or to seek disclosure of matters otherwise protected by the attorney-client privilege or the work-product doctrine. As under the prior rule, the court may defer its ruling (or its decision as to the identity of the persons to be sanctioned) until final resolution of the case in order to avoid immediate conflicts of interest and to reduce the disruption created if a disclosure of attorney-client communications is needed to determine whether a violation occurred or to identify the person responsible for the violation.

The rule provides that requests for sanctions must be made as a separate motion, i.e., not simply included as an additional prayer for relief contained in another motion. The motion for sanctions is not, however, to be filed until at least 21 days (or such other period as the court may set) after being served. If, during this period, the alleged violation is corrected, as by withdrawing (whether formally or informally) some allegation or contention, the motion should not be filed with the court. These provisions are intended to provide a type of "safe harbor" against motions under Rule 11 in that a party will not be subject to sanctions on the basis of another party's motion unless, after receiving the motion, it refuses to withdraw that position or to acknowledge candidly that it does not currently have evidence to support a specified allegation. Under the former rule, parties were sometimes reluctant to abandon a questionable contention lest that be viewed as evidence of a violation of Rule 11; under the revision, the timely withdrawal of a contention will protect a party against a motion for sanctions.

To stress the seriousness of a motion for sanctions and to define precisely the conduct claimed to violate the rule, the revision provides that the "safe harbor" period begins to run only upon service of the motion. In most cases, however, counsel should be expected to give informal notice to the other party, whether in person or by a telephone call or letter, of a potential violation before proceeding to prepare and serve a Rule 11 motion.

As under former Rule 11, the filing of a motion for sanctions is itself subject to the requirements of the rule and can lead to sanctions. However, service of a cross motion under Rule 11 should rarely be needed since under the revision the court may award to the person who prevails on a motion under Rule 11—whether the movant or the target of the motion—reasonable expenses, including attorney's fees, incurred in presenting or opposing the motion.

The power of the court to act on its own initiative is retained, but with the condition that this be done through a show cause order. This procedure provides the person with notice and an opportunity to respond. The revision provides that a monetary sanction imposed after a court-initiated show cause order be limited to a penalty payable to the court and that it be imposed only if the show cause order is issued before any voluntary dismissal or an agreement of the parties to settle the claims made by or against the litigant. Parties settling a case should not be subsequently faced with an unexpected order from the court leading to monetary sanctions that might have affected their willingness to settle or voluntarily dismiss a case. Since show cause orders will ordinarily be issued only in situations that are akin to a contempt of court, the rule does not provide a "safe harbor" to a litigant for withdrawing a claim, defense, etc., after a show cause order has been issued on the court's own initiative. Such corrective action, however, should be taken into account in deciding what—if any—sanction to impose if, after consideration of the litigant's response, the court concludes that a violation has occurred.

Subdivision (d). Rules 26(g) and 37 establish certification standards and sanctions that apply to discovery disclosures, requests, responses, objections, and motions. It is appropriate that Rules 26 through 37, which are specially designed for the discovery process, govern such documents and conduct rather than the more general provisions of Rule 11. Subdivision (d) has been added to accomplish this result.

Rule 11 is not the exclusive source for control of improper presentations of claims, defenses, or contentions. It does not supplant statutes permitting awards of attorney's fees to prevailing parties or alter the principles governing such awards. It does not inhibit the court in punishing for contempt, in exercising its inherent powers, or in imposing sanctions, awarding expenses, or directing remedial action authorized under other rules or under 28 U.S.C. § 1927. See Chambers v. NASCO, __ U.S. __ (1991). Chambers cautions, however, against reliance upon inherent powers if appropriate sanctions can be imposed under provisions such as Rule 11, and the procedures specified in Rule 11—notice, opportunity to respond, and findings—should ordinarily be employed when imposing a sanction under the court's inherent powers. Finally, it should be noted that Rule 11 does not preclude a party from initiating an independent action for malicious prosecution or abuse of process.

Rule 16. Pretrial Conferences; Scheduling; Management

(a) Pretrial Conferences; Objectives. In any action, the court may in its discretion direct the attorneys for the parties and any unrepresented parties to appear before it for a conference or conferences before trial for such purposes as

(1) expediting the disposition of the action;

(2) establishing early and continuing control so that the case will not be protracted because of lack of management;

(3) discouraging wasteful pretrial activities;

(4) improving the quality of the trial through more thorough preparation, and;

(5) facilitating the settlement of the case.

(b) Scheduling and Planning. Except in categories of actions exempted by district court rule as inappropriate, the district judge, or a magistrate judge when authorized by district court rule, shall, after receiving the report from the parties under Rule 26(f) or after consulting with the attorneys for the parties and any unrepresented parties by a scheduling conference, telephone, mail, or other suitable means, enter a scheduling order that limits the time

(1) to join other parties and to amend the pleadings;

(2) to file motions; and

(3) to complete discovery.

The scheduling order may also include

(4) modifications of the times for disclosures under Rules 26(a) and 26(e)(1) and of the extent of discovery to be permitted;

(5) the date or dates for conferences before trial, a final pretrial conference, and trial; and

(6) any other matters appropriate in the circumstances of the case.

The order shall issue as soon as practicable but in any event within 90 days after the appearance of a defendant and within 120 days after the complaint has been served on a defendant. A schedule shall not be modified except upon a showing of good cause and by leave of the district judge or, when authorized by local rule, by a magistrate judge.

(c) Subjects for Consideration at Pretrial Conferences. At any conference under this rule consideration may be given, and the court may take appropriate action, with respect to

(1) the formulation and simplification of the issues, including the elimination of frivolous claims or defenses;

(2) the necessity or desirability of amendments to the pleadings;

(3) the possibility of obtaining admissions of fact and of documents which will avoid unnecessary proof, stipulations regarding the authenticity of documents, and advance rulings from the court on the admissibility of evidence;

(4) the avoidance of unnecessary proof and of cumulative evidence, and limitations or restrictions on the use of testimony under Rule 702 of the Federal Rules of Evidence;

(5) the appropriateness and timing of summary adjudication under Rule 56;

(6) the control and scheduling of discovery, including orders affecting disclosures and discovery pursuant to Rule 26 and Rules 29 through 37;

(7) the identification of witnesses and documents, the need and schedule for filing and exchanging pretrial briefs, and the date or dates for further conferences and for trial;

(8) the advisability of referring matters to a magistrate judge or master;

(9) settlement and the use of special procedures to assist in resolving the dispute when authorized by statute or local rule;

(10) the form and substance of the pretrial order;

(11) the disposition of pending motions;

(12) the need for adopting special procedures for managing potentially difficult or protracted actions that may involve complex issues, multiple parties, difficult legal questions, or unusual proof problems;

(13) an order for a separate trial pursuant to Rule 42(b) with respect to a claim, counterclaim, cross-claim, or third-party claim, or with respect to any particular issue in the case;

(14) an order directing a party or parties to present evidence early in the trial with respect to a manageable issue that could, on the evidence, be the basis for a judgment as a matter of law under Rule 50(a) or a judgment on partial findings under Rule 52(c);

(15) an order establishing a reasonable limit on the time allowed for presenting evidence; and

(16) such other matters as may facilitate the just, speedy, and inexpensive disposition of the action.

At least one of the attorneys for each party participating in any conference before trial shall have authority to enter into stipulations and to make admissions regarding all matters that the participants may reasonably anticipate may be discussed. If appropriate, the court may require that a party or its representative be present or reasonably available by telephone in order to consider possible settlement of the dispute.

(d) Final Pretrial Conference. Any final pretrial conference shall be held as close to the time of trial as reasonable under the circumstances. The participants at any such conference shall formulate a plan for trial, including a program for facilitating the admission of evidence. The conference shall be attended by at least one of the attorneys who will conduct the trial for each of the parties and by any unrepresented parties.

(e) Pretrial Orders. After any conference held pursuant to this rule, an order shall be entered reciting the action taken. This order shall control the subsequent course of the action unless modified by a subsequent order. The order following a final pretrial conference shall be modified only to prevent manifest injustice.

(f) Sanctions. If a party or party's attorney fails to obey a scheduling or pretrial order, or if no appearance is made on behalf of a party at a scheduling or pretrial conference, or if a party or party's attorney is substantially unprepared to participate in the conference, or if a party or party's attorney fails to participate in good faith, the judge, upon motion or the judge's own initiative, may make such orders with regard hereto as are just, and among others any of the orders provided in Rule 37(b)(2)(B), (C), (D). In lieu of or in addition to any other sanction, the judge shall require the party or the attorney representing the party or both to pay the reasonable expenses incurred because of any noncompliance with this rule, including attorney's fees, unless the judge finds that the noncompliance was substantially justified or that other circumstances make an award of expenses unjust.

(As amended Apr. 22, 1993, eff. Dec. 1, 1993).

1993 Amendments

Subdivision (b). One purpose of this amendment is to provide a more appropriate deadline for the initial scheduling order required by the rule. The former rule directed that the order be entered within 120 days from the filing of the complaint. This requirement has created problems because Rule 4(m) allows 120 days for service and ordinarily at least one defendant should be available to participate in the process of formulating the scheduling order. The revision provides that the order is to be entered within 90 days after the date a defendant first appears (whether by answer or by a motion under Rule 12) or, if earlier (as may occur in some actions against the United States or if service is waived under Rule 4), within 120 days after service of the complaint on a defendant. The longer time provided by the revision is not intended to encourage unnecessary delays in entering the scheduling order. Indeed, in most cases the order can and should be entered at a much earlier date. Rather, the additional time is intended to alleviate problems in multi-defendant cases and should ordinarily be adequate to enable participation by all defendants initially named in the action.

In many cases the scheduling order can and should be entered before this deadline. However, when setting a scheduling conference, the court should take into account the effect this setting will have in establishing deadlines for the parties to meet under revised Rule 26(f) and to exchange information under revised Rule 26(a)(1). While the parties are expected to stipulate to additional time for making their disclosures when warranted by the circumstances, a scheduling conference held before defendants have had time to learn much about the case may result in diminishing the value of the Rule 26(f) meeting, the parties' proposed discovery plan, and indeed the conference itself.

New paragraph (4) has been added to highlight that it will frequently be desirable for the scheduling order to include provisions relating to the timing of disclosures under Rule 26(a). While the initial disclosures required by Rule 26(a)(1) will ordinarily have been made before entry of the scheduling order, the timing and sequence for disclosure of expert testimony and of the witnesses and exhibits to be used at trial should be tailored to the circumstances of the case and is a matter that should be considered at the initial scheduling conference. Similarly, the scheduling order might contain provisions modifying the extent of discovery (e.g., number and length of depositions) otherwise permitted under these rules or by a local rule.

The report from the attorneys concerning their meeting and proposed discovery plan, as required by revised Rule 26(f), should be submitted to the court before the scheduling order is entered. Their proposals, particularly regarding matters on which they agree, should be of substantial value to the court in setting the timing and limitations on discovery and should reduce the time of the court needed to conduct a meaningful conference under Rule 16(b). As under the prior rule, while a scheduling order is mandated, a scheduling conference is not. However, in view of the benefits to be derived from the litigants and a judicial officer meeting in person, a Rule 16(b) conference should, to the extent practicable, be held in all cases that will involve discovery.

This subdivision, as well as subdivision (c)(8), also is revised to reflect the new title of United States Magistrate Judges pursuant to the Judicial Improvements Act of 1990.

Subdivision (c). The primary purposes of the changes in subdivision (c) are to call attention to the opportunities for structuring of trial under Rules 42, 50, and 52 and to eliminate questions that have occasionally been raised regarding the authority of the court to make appropriate orders designed either to facilitate settlement or to provide for an efficient and economical trial. The prefatory language of this subdivision is revised to clarify the court's power to enter appropriate orders at a conference notwithstanding the objection of a party. Of course settlement is dependent upon agreement by the parties and, indeed, a conference is most effective and productive when the parties participate in a spirit of cooperation and mindful of their responsibilities under Rule 1.

Paragraph (4) is revised to clarify that in advance of trial the court may address the need for, and possible limitations on, the use of expert testimony under Rule 702 of the Federal Rules of Evidence. Even when proposed expert testimony might be admissible under the standards of Rules 403 and 702 of the evidence rules, the court may preclude or limit such testimony if the cost to the litigants—which may include the cost to adversaries of securing testimony on the same subjects by other experts—would be unduly expensive given the needs of the case and the other evidence available at trial.

Paragraph (5) is added (and the remaining paragraphs renumbered) in recognition that use of Rule 56 to avoid or reduce the scope of trial is a topic that can, and often should, be considered at a pretrial conference. Renumbered paragraph (11) enables the court to rule on pending motions for summary adjudication that are ripe for decision at the time of the conference. Often, however, the potential use of Rule 56 is a matter that arises from discussions during a conference. The court may then call for motions to be filed.

Paragraph (6) is added to emphasize that a major objective of pretrial conferences should be to consider appropriate controls on the extent and timing of discovery. In many cases the court should also specify the times and sequence for disclosure of written reports from experts under revised Rule 26(a)(2)(B) and perhaps direct changes in the types of experts from whom written reports are required. Consideration should also be given to possible changes in the timing or form of the disclosure of trial witnesses and documents under Rule 26(a)(3).

Paragraph (9) is revised to describe more accurately the various procedures that, in addition to traditional settlement conferences, may be helpful in settling litigation. Even if a case cannot immediately be settled, the judge and attorneys can explore possible use of alternative procedures such as mini-trials, summary jury trials, mediation, neutral evaluation, and nonbinding arbitration that can lead to consensual resolution of the dispute without a full trial on the merits. The rule acknowledges the presence of statutes and local rules or plans that may authorize use of some of these procedures even when not agreed to by the parties. See 28 U.S.C. §§ 473(a)(6), 473(b)(4), 651–58; Section 104(b)(2), Pub.L. 101–650. The rule does not attempt to resolve questions as to the extent a court would be authorized to require such proceedings as an exercise of its inherent powers.

The amendment of paragraph (9) should be read in conjunction with the sentence added to the end of subdivision (c), authorizing the court to direct that, in appropriate cases, a responsible representative of the parties be present or available by telephone during a conference in order to discuss possible settlement of the case. The sentence refers to participation by a party or its representative. Whether this would be the individual party, an officer of a corporate party, a representative from an insurance carrier, or someone else would depend on the circumstances. Particularly in litigation in which governmental agencies or large amounts of money are involved, there may be no one with on-the-spot settlement authority, and the most that should be expected is access to a person who would have a major role in submitting a recommendation to the body or board with ultimate decision-making responsibility. The selection of the appropriate representative should ordinarily be left to the party and its counsel. Finally, it should be noted that the unwillingness of a party to be available, even by telephone, for a settlement conference may be a clear signal that the time and expense involved in pursuing settlement is likely to be unproductive and that personal participation by the parties should not be required.

The explicit authorization in the rule to require personal participation in the manner stated is not intended to limit the reasonable exercise of the court's inherent powers, e.g., G. Heileman Brewing Co. v. Joseph Oat Corp., 871 F.2d 648 (7th Cir.1989), or its power to require party participation under the Civil Justice Reform Act of 1990. See 28 U.S.C. § 473(b)(5) (civil justice expense and delay reduction plans adopted by district courts may include requirement that representatives "with authority to bind [parties] in settlement discussions" be available during settlement conferences).

New paragraphs (13) and (14) are added to call attention to the opportunities for structuring of trial under Rule 42 and under revised Rules 50 and 52.

Paragraph (15) is also new. It supplements the power of the court to limit the extent of evidence under Rules 403 and 611(a) of the Federal Rules of Evidence, which typically would be invoked as a result of developments during trial. Limits on the length of trial established at a conference in advance of trial can provide the parties with a better opportunity to determine priorities and exercise selectivity in presenting evidence than when limits are imposed during trial. Any such limits must be reasonable under the circumstances, and ordinarily the court should impose them only after receiving appropriate submissions from the parties outlining the nature of the testimony expected to be presented through various witnesses, and the expected duration of direct and cross-examination.

1983 Amendment

. . .

Subdivision (f); Sanctions. Original Rule 16 did not mention the sanctions that might be imposed for failing to comply with the rule. However, courts have not hesitated to enforce it by appropriate measures. See, *e.g., Link v. Wabash R. Co.*, 370 U.S. 626 (1962) (district court's dismissal under Rule 41(b) after plaintiff's attorney failed to appear at a pretrial conference upheld); *Admiral Theatre Corp. v. Douglas Theatre*, 585 F.2d 877 (8th Cir.1978) (district court has discretion to exclude exhibits or refuse to permit the testimony of a witness not listed prior to trial in contravention of its pretrial order).

To reflect that existing practice, and to obviate dependence upon Rule 41(b) or the court's inherent power to regulate litigation, *cf. Societe Internationale Pour Participations Industrielles et Commerciales, S.A. v. Rogers*, 357 U.S. 197 (1958), Rule 16(f) expressly provides for imposing sanctions on disobedient or recalcitrant parties, their attorneys, or both in four types of situations. Rodes, Ripple & Mooney, *Sanctions Imposable for Violations of the Federal Rules of Civil Procedure* 65–67, 80–84, Federal Judicial Center (1981). Furthermore, explicit reference to sanctions reenforces the rule's intention to encourage forceful judicial management.

Rule 16(f) incorporates portions of Rule 37(b)(2), which prescribes sanctions for failing to make discovery. This should facilitate application of Rule 16(f), since courts and lawyers already are familiar with the Rule 37 standards. Among the sanctions authorized by the new subdivision are: preclusion order, striking a pleading, staying the proceeding, default judgment, contempt, and charging a party, his attorney, or both with the expenses, including attorney's fees, caused by noncompliance. The contempt sanction, however, is only available for a violation of a court order. The references in Rule 16(f) are not exhaustive.

As is true under Rule 37(b)(2), the imposition of sanctions may be sought by either the court or a party. In addition, the court has discretion to impose whichever sanction it feels is appropriate under the circumstances. Its action is reviewable under the abuse-of-discretion standard. See *National Hockey League v. Metropolitan Hockey Club, Inc.,* 427 U.S. 639 (1976).

Rule 26. General Provisions Governing Discovery; Duty of Disclosure

(a) Required Disclosures; Methods to Discover Additional Matter.

(1) Initial Disclosures. Except to the extent otherwise stipulated or directed by order or local rule, a party shall, without awaiting a discovery request, provide to other parties:

(A) the name and, if known, the address and telephone number of each individual likely to have discoverable information relevant to disputed facts alleged with particularity in the pleadings, identifying the subjects of the information;

(B) a copy of, or a description by category and location of, all documents, data compilations, and tangible things in the possession, custody, or control of the party that are relevant to disputed facts alleged with particularity in the pleadings;

(C) a computation of any category of damages claimed by the disclosing party, making available for inspection and copying as under Rule 34 the documents or other evidentiary material, not privileged or protected from disclosure, on which such computation is based, including materials bearing on the nature and extent of injuries suffered; and

(D) for inspection and copying as under Rule 34 any insurance agreement under which any person carrying on an insurance business may be liable to satisfy part or all of a judgment which may be entered in the action or to indemnify or reimburse for payments made to satisfy the judgment.

Unless otherwise stipulated or directed by the court, these disclosures shall be made at or within 10 days after the meeting of the parties under subdivision (f). A party shall make its initial disclosures based on the information then reasonably available to it and is not excused from making its disclosures because it has not fully completed its investigation of the case or because it challenges the sufficiency of another party's disclosures or because another party has not made its disclosures.

(2) **Disclosure of Expert Testimony.**

(A) In addition to the disclosures required by paragraph (1), a party shall disclose to other parties the identity of any person who may be used at trial to present evidence under Rule 702, 703, or 705 of the Federal Rules of Evidence.

(B) Except as otherwise stipulated or directed by the court, this disclosure shall, with respect to a witness who is retained or specially employed to provide expert testimony in the case or whose duties as an employee of the party regularly involve giving expert testimony, be accompanied by a written report prepared and signed by the witness. The report shall contain a complete statement of all opinions to be expressed and the basis and reasons therefor; the data or other information considered by the witness in forming the opinions; any exhibits to be used as a summary of or support for the opinions; the qualifications of the witness, including a list of all publications authored by the witness within the preceding ten years; the compensation to be paid for the study and testimony; and a listing of any other cases in which the witness has testified as an expert at trial or by deposition within the preceding four years.

(C) These disclosures shall be made at the times and in the sequence directed by the court. In the absence of other directions from the court or stipulation by the parties, the disclosures shall be made at least 90 days before the trial date or the date the case is to be ready for trial or, if the evidence is intended solely to contradict or rebut evidence on the same subject matter identified by another party under paragraph (2)(B), within 30 days after the disclosure made by the other party. The parties shall supplement these disclosures when required under subdivision (e)(1).

(3) Pretrial Disclosures. In addition to the disclosures required in the preceding paragraphs, a party shall provide to other parties the following information regarding the evidence that it may present at trial other than solely for impeachment purposes:

(A) the name and, if not previously provided, the address and telephone number of each witness, separately identifying those whom the party expects to present and those whom the party may call if the need arises;

(B) the designation of those witnesses whose testimony is expected to be presented by means of a deposition and, if not taken stenographically, a transcript of the pertinent portions of the deposition testimony; and

(C) an appropriate identification of each document or other exhibit, including summaries of other evidence, separately identifying those which the party expects to offer and those which the party may offer if the need arises.

Unless otherwise directed by the court, these disclosures shall be made at least 30 days before trial. Within 14 days thereafter, unless a different time is specified by the court, a party may serve and file a list disclosing (i) any objections to the use under Rule 32(a) of a deposition designated by another party under subparagraph (B) and (ii) any objection, together with the grounds therefor, that may be made to the admissibility of materials identified under subparagraph (C). Objections not so disclosed, other than objections under Rules 402 and 403 of the Federal Rules of Evidence, shall be deemed waived unless excused by the court for good cause shown.

(4) Form of Disclosures; Filing. Unless otherwise directed by order or local rule, all disclosures under paragraphs (1) through (3) shall be made in writing, signed, served, and promptly filed with the court.

(5) Methods to Discover Additional Matter. Parties may obtain discovery by one or more of the following methods: depositions upon oral examination or written questions; written interrogatories; production of documents or things or permission to enter upon land or other property under Rule 34 or 45(a)(1)(C), for inspection and other purposes; physical and mental examinations; and requests for admission.

(b) Discovery Scope and Limits. Unless otherwise limited by order of the court in accordance with these rules, the scope of discovery is as follows:

(1) In General. Parties may obtain discovery regarding any matter, not privileged, which is relevant to the subject matter involved in the pending action, whether it relates to the claim or defense of the party seeking discovery or to the claim or defense of any other party, including the existence, description, nature, custody, condition, and location of any books, documents, or other tangible things and the identity and location of persons having knowledge of any discoverable matter. The information sought need not be admissible at the trial if the information sought appears reasonably calculated to lead to the discovery of admissible evidence.

(2) Limitations. By order or by local rule, the court may alter the limits in these rules on the number of depositions and interrogatories and may also limit the length of depositions under Rule 30 and the number of requests under Rule 36. The frequency or extent of use of the discovery methods otherwise permitted under these rules and by any local rule shall be limited by the court if it determines that: (i) the discovery sought is unreasonably cumulative or duplicative, or is obtainable from some other source that is more convenient, less burdensome, or less expensive; (ii) the party seeking discovery has had ample opportunity by discovery in the action to obtain the information sought; or (iii) the burden or expense of the proposed discovery outweighs its likely benefit, taking into account the needs of the case, the amount in controversy, the parties' resources, the importance of the issues at stake in the litigation, and the importance of the proposed discovery in resolving the issues. The court may act upon its own initiative after reasonable notice or pursuant to a motion under subdivision (c).

(3) Trial Preparation: Materials. Subject to the provisions of subdivision (b)(4) of this rule, a party may obtain discovery of documents and tangible things otherwise discoverable under subdivision (b)(1) of this rule and prepared in anticipation of litigation or for trial by or for another party or by or for that other party's representative (including the other party's attorney, consultant, surety, indemnitor, insurer, or agent) only upon a showing that the party seeking discovery has substantial need of the materials in the preparation of the party's case and that the party is unable without undue hardship to obtain the substantial equivalent of the materials by other means. In ordering discovery of such materials when the required showing has been made, the court shall protect against disclosure of the mental impressions, conclusions, opinions, or legal theories of an attorney or other representative of a party concerning the litigation.

A party may obtain without the required showing a statement concerning the action or its subject matter previously made by that party. Upon request, a person not a party may obtain without the required showing a statement concerning the action or its subject matter previously made by that person. If the request is refused, the person may move for a court order. The provisions of Rule 37(a)(4) apply to the award of expenses incurred in relation to the motion. For purposes of this paragraph, a statement previously made is (A) a written statement signed or otherwise adopted or approved by the person making it, or (B) a stenographic, mechanical, electrical, or other recording, or a transcription thereof, which is a substantially verbatim recital of an oral statement by the person making it and contemporaneously recorded.

(4) Trial Preparation: Experts.

(A) A party may depose any person who has been identified as an expert whose opinions may be presented at trial. If a report from the expert is required under subdivision (a)(2)(B), the deposition shall not be conducted until after the report is provided.

(B) A party may, through interrogatories or by deposition, discover facts known or opinions held by an expert who has been retained or specially employed by another party in anticipation of litigation or preparation for trial and who is not expected to be called as a witness at trial, only as provided in Rule 35(b) or upon a showing of exceptional circumstances under which it is impracticable for the party seeking discovery to obtain facts or opinions on the same subject by other means.

(C) Unless manifest injustice would result, (i) the court shall require that the party seeking discovery pay the expert a reasonable fee for time spent in responding to discovery under this subdivision; and (ii) with respect to discovery obtained under subdivision (b)(4)(B) of this rule the court shall require the party seeking discovery to pay the other party a fair portion of the fees and expenses reasonably incurred by the latter party in obtaining facts and opinions from the expert.

(5) Claims of Privilege or Protection of Trial Preparation Materials. When a party withholds information otherwise discoverable under these rules by claiming that it is privileged or subject to protection as trial preparation material, the party shall make the claim expressly and shall describe the nature of the documents, communications, or things not produced or disclosed in a manner that, without revealing information itself privileged or protected, will enable other parties to assess the applicability of the privilege or protection.

(c) Protective Orders. Upon motion by a party or by the person from whom discovery is sought, accompanied by a certification that the movant has in good faith conferred or attempted to confer with other affected parties in an effort to resolve the dispute without court action, and for good cause shown, the court in which the action is pending or alternatively, on matters relating to a deposition, the court in the district where the deposition is to be taken may make any order which justice requires to protect a party or person from annoyance, embarrassment, oppression, or undue burden or expense, including one or more of the following:

(1) that the disclosure or discovery not be had;

(2) that the disclosure or discovery may be had only on specified terms and conditions, including a designation of the time or place;

(3) that the discovery may be had only by a method of discovery other than that selected by the party seeking discovery;

(4) that certain matters not be inquired into, or that the scope of the disclosure or discovery be limited to certain matters;

(5) that discovery be conducted with no one present except persons designated by the court;

(6) that a deposition, after being sealed, be opened only by order of the court;

(7) that a trade secret or other confidential research, development, or commercial information not be revealed or be revealed only in a designated way; and

(8) that the parties simultaneously file specified documents or information enclosed in sealed envelopes to be opened as directed by the court.

If the motion for a protective order is denied in whole or in part, the court may, on such terms and conditions as are just, order that any party or other person provide or permit discovery. The provisions of Rule 37(a)(4) apply to the award of expenses incurred in relation to the motion.

(d) Timing and Sequence of Discovery. Except when authorized under these rules or by local rule, order, or agreement of the parties, a party may not seek discovery from any source before the parties have met and conferred as required by subdivision (f). Unless the court upon motion, for the convenience of parties and witnesses and in the interests of justice, orders otherwise, methods of discovery may be used in any sequence, and the fact that a party is conducting discovery, whether by deposition or otherwise, shall not operate to delay any other party's discovery.

(e) Supplementation of Disclosures and Responses. A party who has made a disclosure under subdivision (a) or responded to a request for discovery with a disclosure or response is under a duty to supplement or correct the disclosure or response to include information thereafter acquired if ordered by the court or in the following circumstances:

(1) A party is under a duty to supplement at appropriate intervals its disclosures under subdivision (a) if the party learns that in some material respect the information disclosed is incomplete or incorrect and if the additional or corrective information has not otherwise been made known to the other parties during the discovery process or in writing. With respect to testimony of an expert from whom a report is required under subdivision (a)(2)(B) the duty extends both to information contained in the report and to information provided through a deposition of the expert, and any additions or other changes to this information shall be disclosed by the time the party's disclosures under Rule 26(a)(3) are due.

(2) A party is under a duty seasonably to amend a prior response to an interrogatory, request for production, or request for admission if the party learns that the response is in some material respect incomplete or incorrect and if the additional or corrective information has not otherwise been made known to the other parties during the discovery process or in writing.

(f) Meeting of Parties; Planning for Discovery. Except in actions exempted by local rule or when otherwise ordered, the parties shall, as soon as practicable and in any event at least 14 days before a scheduling conference is held or a scheduling order is due under Rule 16(b), meet to discuss the nature and basis of their claims and defenses and the possibilities for a prompt settlement or resolution of the case, to make or arrange for the disclosures required by subdivision (a)(1), and to develop a proposed discovery plan. The plan shall indicate the parties' views and proposals concerning:

    (1) what changes should be made in the timing, form, or requirement for disclosures under subdivision (a) or local rule, including a statement as to when disclosures under subdivision (a)(1) were made or will be made;

    (2) the subjects on which discovery may be needed, when discovery should be completed, and whether discovery should be conducted in phases or be limited to or focused upon particular issues;

    (3) what changes should be made in the limitations on discovery imposed under these rules or by local rule, and what other limitations should be imposed; and

    (4) any other orders that should be entered by the court under subdivision (c) or under Rule 16(b) and (c).

The attorneys of record and all unrepresented parties that have appeared in the case are jointly responsible for arranging and being present or represented at the meeting, for attempting in good faith to agree on the proposed discovery plan, and for submitting to the court within 10 days after the meeting a written report outlining the plan.

(g) Signing of Disclosures, Discovery Requests, Responses, and Objections.

    (1) Every disclosure made pursuant to subdivision (a)(1) or subdivision (a)(3) shall be signed by at least one attorney of record in the attorney's individual name, whose address shall be stated. An unrepresented party shall sign the disclosure and state the party's address. The signature of the attorney or party constitutes a certification that to the best of the signer's knowledge, information, and belief, formed after a reasonable inquiry, the disclosure is complete and correct as of the time it is made.

    (2) Every discovery request, response, or objection made by a party represented by an attorney shall be signed by at least one attorney of record in the attorney's individual name, whose address shall be stated. An unrepresented party shall sign the request, response, or objection and state the party's address. The signature of the attorney or party constitutes a certification that to the best of the signer's knowledge, information, and belief, formed after a reasonable inquiry, the request, response, or objection is:

(A) consistent with these rules and warranted by existing law or a good faith argument for the extension, modification, or reversal of existing law;

(B) not interposed for any improper purpose, such as to harass or to cause unnecessary delay or needless increase in the cost of litigation; and

(C) not unreasonable or unduly burdensome or expensive, given the needs of the case, the discovery already had in the case, the amount in controversy, and the importance of the issues at stake in the litigation.

If a request, response, or objection is not signed, it shall be stricken unless it is signed promptly after the omission is called to the attention of the party making the request, response, or objection, and a party shall not be obligated to take any action with respect to it until it is signed.

(3) If without substantial justification a certification is made in violation of the rule, the court, upon motion or upon its own initiative, shall impose upon the person who made the certification, the party on whose behalf the disclosure, request, response, or objection is made, or both, an appropriate sanction, which may include an order to pay the amount of the reasonable expenses incurred because of the violation, including a reasonable attorney's fee.

(As amended Apr. 22, 1993, eff. Dec. 1, 1993.)

ADVISORY COMMITTEE NOTES
1993 Amendments

Subdivision (a). Through the addition of paragraphs (1)–(4), this subdivision imposes on parties a duty to disclose, without awaiting formal discovery requests, certain basic information that is needed in most cases to prepare for trial or make an informed decision about settlement. The rule requires all parties (1) early in the case to exchange information regarding potential witnesses, documentary evidence, damages, and insurance, (2) at an appropriate time during the discovery period to identify expert witnesses and provide a detailed written statement of the testimony that may be offered at trial through specially retained experts, and (3) as the trial date approaches to identify the particular evidence that may be offered at trial. The enumeration in Rule 26(a) of items to be disclosed does not prevent a court from requiring by order or local rule that the parties disclose additional information without a discovery request. Nor are parties precluded from using traditional discovery methods to obtain further information regarding these matters, as for example asking an expert during a deposition about testimony given in other litigation beyond the four-year period specified in Rule 26(a)(2)(B).

A major purpose of the revision is to accelerate the exchange of basic information about the case and to eliminate the paper work involved in requesting such information, and the rule should be applied in a manner to achieve those objectives. The concepts of imposing a duty of disclosure were set forth in Brazil, The Adversary Character of Civil Discovery: A Critique and Proposals for Change, 31 Vand.L.Rev. 1348 (1978), and Schwarzer, The Federal Rules, the Adversary Process, and Discovery Reform, 50 U.Pitt.L.Rev. 703, 721–23 (1989).

The rule is based upon the experience of district courts that have required disclosure of some of this information through local rules, court-approved standard interrogatories, and standing orders. Most have required pretrial disclosure of the kind of information described in Rule 26(a)(3). Many have required written reports from experts containing information like that specified in Rule 26(a)(2)(B). While far more limited, the experience of the few state and federal courts that have required pre-discovery exchange of core information such as is contemplated in Rule 26(a)(1) indicates that savings in time and expense can be achieved, particularly if the litigants meet and discuss the issues in the case as a predicate for this exchange and if a judge supports the process, as by using the results to guide further proceedings in the case. Courts in Canada and the United Kingdom have for many years required disclosure of certain information without awaiting a request from an adversary.

Paragraph (1). As the functional equivalent of court-ordered interrogatories, this paragraph requires early disclosure, without need for any request, of four types of information that have been customarily secured early in litigation through formal discovery. The introductory clause permits the court, by local rule, to exempt all or particular types of cases from these disclosure requirement or to modify the nature of the information to be disclosed. It is expected that courts would, for example, exempt cases like Social Security reviews and government collection cases in which discovery would not be appropriate or would be unlikely. By order the court may eliminate or modify the disclosure requirements in a particular case, and similarly the parties, unless precluded by order or local rule, can stipulate to elimination or modification of the requirements for that case. The disclosure obligations specified in paragraph (1) will not be appropriate for all cases, and it is expected that changes in these obligations will be made by the court or parties when the circumstances warrant.

Authorization of these local variations is, in large measure, included in order to accommodate the Civil Justice Reform Act of 1990, which implicitly directs districts to experiment during the study period with differing procedures to reduce the time and expense of civil litigation. The civil justice delay and expense reduction plans adopted by the courts under the Act differ as to the type, form, and timing of disclosures required. Section 105(c)(1) of the Act calls for a report by the Judicial Conference to Congress by December 31, 1995, comparing experience in twenty of these courts; and section 105(c)(2)(B) contemplates that some changes in the Rules may then be needed. While these studies may indicate the desirability of further changes in Rule 26(a)(1), these changes probably could not become effective before December 1998 at the earliest. In the meantime, the present revision puts in place a series of disclosure obligations that, unless a court acts affirmatively to impose other requirements or indeed to reject all such requirements for the present, are designed to eliminate certain discovery, help focus the discovery that is needed, and facilitate preparation for trial or settlement.

Subparagraph (A) requires identification of all persons who, based on the investigation conducted thus far, are likely to have discoverable information relevant to the factual disputes between the parties. All persons with such information should be disclosed, whether or not their testimony will be supportive of the position of the disclosing party. As officers of the court, counsel are expected to disclose the identity of those persons who may be used by them as witnesses or who, if their potential testimony were known, might reasonably be expected to be deposed or called as a witness by any of the other parties. Indicating briefly the general topics on which such persons have information should not be burdensome, and will assist other parties in deciding which depositions will actually be needed.

Subparagraph (B) is included as a substitute for the inquiries routinely made about the existence and location of documents and other tangible things in the possession, custody, or control of the disclosing party. Although, unlike subdivision (a)(3)(C), an itemized listing of each exhibit is not required, the disclosure should describe and categorize, to the extent identified during the initial investigation, the nature and location of potentially relevant documents and records, including computerized data and other electronically-recorded information, sufficiently to enable opposing parties (1) to make an informed decision concerning which documents might need to be examined, at least initially, and (2) to frame their document requests in a manner likely to avoid squabbles resulting from the wording of the requests. As with potential witnesses, the requirement for disclosure of documents applies to all potentially relevant items then known to the party, whether or not supportive of its contentions in the case.

Unlike subparagraphs (C) and (D), subparagraph (B) does not require production of any documents. Of course, in cases involving few documents a disclosing party may prefer to provide copies of the documents rather than describe them, and the rule is written to afford this option to the disclosing party. If, as will be more typical, only the description is provided, the other parties are expected to obtain the documents desired by proceeding under Rule 34 or through informal requests. The disclosing party does not, by describing documents under subparagraph (B), waive its right to object to production on the basis of privilege or work product protection, or to assert that the documents are not sufficiently relevant to justify the burden or expense of production.

The initial disclosure requirements of subparagraphs (A) and (B) are limited to identification of potential evidence "relevant to disputed facts alleged with particularity in the pleadings." There is no need for a party to identify potential evidence with respect to allegations that are admitted. Broad, vague, and conclusory allegations sometimes tolerated in notice pleading—for example, the assertion that a product with many component parts is defective in some unspecified manner—should not impose upon responding parties the obligation at that point to search for and identify all persons possibly involved in, or all documents affecting, the design, manufacture, and assembly of the product. The greater the specificity and clarity of the allegations in the pleadings, the more complete should be the listing of potential witnesses and types of documentary evidence. Although paragraphs (1)(A) and (1)(B) by their terms refer to the factual disputes defined in the pleadings, the rule contemplates that these issues would be informally refined and clarified during the meeting of the parties under subdivision (f) and that the disclosure obligations would be adjusted in the light of these discussions. The disclosure requirements should, in short, be applied with common sense in light of the principles of Rule 1, keeping in mind the salutary purposes that the rule is intended to accomplish. The litigants should not indulge in gamesmanship with respect to the disclosure obligations.

Subparagraph (C) imposes a burden of disclosure that includes the functional equivalent of a standing Request for Production under Rule 34. A party claiming damages or other monetary relief must, in addition to disclosing the calculation of such damages, make available the supporting documents for inspection and copying as if a request for such materials had been made under Rule 34. This obligation applies only with respect to documents then reasonably available to it and not privileged or protected as work product. Likewise, a party would not be expected to provide a calculation of damages which, as in many patent infringement actions, depends on information in the possession of another party or person.

Subparagraph (D) replaces subdivision (b)(2) of Rule 26, and provides that liability insurance policies be made available for inspection and copying. The last two sentences of that subdivision have been omitted as unnecessary, not to signify any change of law. The disclosure of insurance information does not thereby render such information admissible in evidence. See Rule 411, Federal Rules of Evidence. Nor does subparagraph (D) require disclosure of applications for insurance, though in particular cases such information may be discoverable in accordance with revised subdivision (a)(5).

Unless the court directs a different time, the disclosures required by subdivision (a)(1) are to be made at or within 10 days after the meeting of the parties under subdivision (f). One of the purposes of this meeting is to refine the factual disputes with respect to which disclosures should be made under paragraphs (1)(A) and (1)(B), particularly if an answer has not been filed by a defendant, or, indeed, to afford the parties an opportunity to modify by stipulation the timing or scope of these obligations. The time of this meeting is generally left to the parties provided it is held at least 14 days before a scheduling conference is held or before a scheduling order is due under Rule 16(b). In cases in which no scheduling conference is held, this will mean that the meeting must ordinarily be held within 75 days after a defendant has first appeared in the case and hence that the initial disclosures would be due no later than 85 days after the first appearance of a defendant.

Before making its disclosures, a party has the obligation under subdivision (g)(1) to make a reasonable inquiry into the facts of the case. The rule does not demand an exhaustive investigation at this stage of the case, but one that is reasonable under the circumstances, focusing on the facts that are alleged with particularity in the pleadings. The type of investigation that can be expected at this point will vary based upon such factors as the number and complexity of the issues; the location, nature, number, and availability of potentially relevant witnesses and documents; the extent of past working relationships between the attorney and the client, particularly in handling related or similar litigation; and of course how long the party has to conduct an investigation, either before or after filing of the case. As provided in the last sentence of subdivision (a)(1), a party is not excused from the duty of disclosure merely because its investigation is incomplete. The party should make its initial disclosures based on the pleadings and the information then reasonably available to it. As its investigation continues and as the issues in the pleadings are clarified, it should supplement its disclosures as required by subdivision (e)(1). A party is not relieved from its obligation of disclosure merely because another party has not made its disclosures or has made an inadequate disclosure.

It will often be desirable, particularly if the claims made in the complaint are broadly stated, for the parties to have their Rule 26(f) meeting early in the case, perhaps before a defendant has answered the complaint or had time to conduct other than a cursory investigation. In such circumstances, in order to facilitate more meaningful and useful initial disclosures, they can and should stipulate to a period of more than 10 days after the meeting in which to make these disclosures, at least for defendants who had no advance notice of the potential litigation. A stipulation at an early meeting affording such a defendant at least 60 days after receiving the complaint in which to make its disclosures under subdivision (a)(1)—a period that is two weeks longer than the time formerly specified for responding to interrogatories served with a complaint—should be adequate and appropriate in most cases.

Paragraph (2). This paragraph imposes an additional duty to disclose information regarding expert testimony sufficiently in advance of trial that opposing parties have a reasonable opportunity to prepare for effective cross examination and perhaps arrange for expert testimony from other witnesses. Normally the court should prescribe a time for these disclosures in a scheduling order under Rule 16(b), and in most cases the party with the burden of proof on an issue should disclose its expert testimony on that issue before other parties are required to make their disclosures with respect to that issue. In the absence of such a direction, the disclosures are to be made by all parties at least 90 days before the trial date or the date by which the case is to be ready for trial, except that an additional 30 days is allowed (unless the court specifies another time) for disclosure of expert testimony to be used solely to contradict or rebut the testimony that may be presented by another party's expert. For a discussion of procedures that have been used to enhance the reliability of expert testimony, see M. Graham, Expert Witness Testimony and the Federal Rules of Evidence: Insuring Adequate Assurance of Trustworthiness, 1986 U.Ill.L.Rev. 90.

Paragraph (2)(B) requires that persons retained or specially employed to provide expert testimony, or whose duties as an employee of the party regularly involve the giving of expert testimony, must prepare a detailed and complete written report, stating the testimony the witness is expected to present during direct examination, together with the reasons therefor. The information disclosed under the former rule in answering interrogatories about the "substance" of expert testimony was frequently so sketchy and vague that it rarely dispensed with the need to depose the expert and often was even of little help in preparing for a deposition of the witness. Revised Rule 37(c)(1) provides an incentive for full disclosure; namely, that a party will not ordinarily be permitted to use on direct examination any expert testimony not so disclosed. Rule 26(a)(2)(B) does not preclude counsel from providing assistance to experts in preparing the reports, and indeed, with experts such as automobile mechanics, this assistance may be needed. Nevertheless, the report, which is intended to set forth the substance of the direct examination, should be written in a manner that reflects the testimony to be given by the witness and it must be signed by the witness.

The report is to disclose the data and other information considered by the expert and any exhibits or charts that summarize or support the expert's opinions. Given this obligation of disclosure, litigants should no longer be able to argue that materials furnished to their experts to be used in forming their opinions—whether or not ultimately relied upon by the expert—are privileged or otherwise protected from disclosure when such persons are testifying or being deposed.

Revised subdivision (b)(4)(A) authorizes the deposition of expert witnesses. Since depositions of experts required to prepare a written report may be taken only after the report has been served, the length of the deposition of such experts should be reduced, and in many cases the report may eliminate the need for a deposition. Revised subdivision (e)(1) requires disclosure of any material changes made in the opinions of an expert from whom a report is required, whether the changes are in the written report or in testimony given at a deposition.

For convenience, this rule and revised Rule 30 continue to use the term "expert" to refer to those persons who will testify under Rule 702 of the Federal Rules of Evidence with respect to scientific, technical, and other specialized matters. The requirement of a written report in paragraph (2)(B), however, applies only to those experts who are retained or specially employed to provide such testimony in the case or whose duties as an employee of a party regularly involve the giving of such testimony. A treating physician, for example, can be deposed or called to testify at trial without any requirement for a written report. By local rule, order, or written stipulation, the requirement of a written report may be waived for particular experts or imposed upon additional persons who will provide opinions under Rule 702.

Paragraph (3). This paragraph imposes an additional duty to disclose, without any request, information customarily needed in final preparation for trial. These disclosures are to be made in accordance with schedules adopted by the court under Rule 16(b) or by special order. If no such schedule is directed by the court, the disclosures are to be made at least 30 days before commencement of the trial. By its terms, rule 26(a)(3) does not require disclosure of evidence to be used solely for impeachment purposes; however, disclosure of such evidence—as well as other items relating to conduct of trial—may be required by local rule or a pretrial order.

Subparagraph (A) requires the parties to designate the persons whose testimony they may present as substantive evidence at trial, whether in person or by deposition. Those who will probably be called as witnesses should be listed separately from those who are not likely to be called but who are being listed in order to preserve the right to do so if needed because of developments during trial. Revised Rule 37(c)(1) provides that only persons so listed may be used at trial to present substantive evidence. This restriction does not apply unless the omission was "without substantial justification" and hence would not bar an unlisted witness if the need for such testimony is based upon developments during trial that could not reasonably have been anticipated—e.g., a change of testimony.

Listing a witness does not obligate the party to secure the attendance of the person at trial, but should preclude the party from objecting if the person is called to testify by another party who did not list the person as a witness.

Subparagraph (B) requires the party to indicate which of these potential witnesses will be presented by deposition at trial. A party expecting to use at trial a deposition not recorded by stenographic means is required by revised Rule 32 to provide the court with a transcript of the pertinent portions of such depositions. This rule requires that copies of the transcript of a nonstenographic deposition be provided to other parties in advance of trial for verification, an obvious concern since counsel often utilize their own personnel to prepare transcripts from audio or video tapes. By order or local rule, the court may require that parties designate the particular portions of stenographic depositions to be used at trial.

Subparagraph (C) requires disclosure of exhibits, including summaries (whether to be offered in lieu of other documentary evidence or to be used as an aid in understanding such evidence), that may be offered as substantive evidence. The rule requires a separate listing of each such exhibit, though it should permit voluminous items of a similar or standardized character to be described by meaningful categories. For example, unless the court has otherwise directed, a series of vouchers might be shown collectively as a single exhibit with their starting and ending dates. As with witnesses, the exhibits that will probably be offered are to be listed separately from those which are unlikely to be offered but which are listed in order to preserve the right to do so if needed because of developments during trial. Under revised Rule 37(c)(1) the court can permit use of unlisted documents the need for which could not reasonably have been anticipated in advance of trial.

Upon receipt of these final pretrial disclosures, other parties have 14 days (unless a different time is specified by the court) to disclose any objections they wish to preserve to the usability of the deposition testimony or to the admissibility of the documentary evidence (other than under Rules 402 and 403 of the Federal Rules of Evidence). Similar provisions have become commonplace either in pretrial orders or by local rules, and significantly expedite the presentation of evidence at trial, as well as eliminate the need to have available witnesses to provide "foundation" testimony for most items of documentary evidence. The listing of a potential objection does not constitute the making of that objection or require the court to rule on the objection; rather, it preserves the right of the party to make the objection when and as appropriate during trial. The court may, however, elect to treat the listing as a motion "in limine" and rule upon the objections in advance of trial to the extent appropriate.

The time specified in the rule for the final pretrial disclosures is relatively close to the trial date. The objective is to eliminate the time and expense in making these disclosures of evidence and objections in those cases that settle shortly before trial, while affording a reasonable time for final preparation for trial in those cases that do not settle. In many cases, it will be desirable for the court in a scheduling or pretrial order to set an earlier time for disclosures of evidence and provide more time for disclosing potential objections.

Paragraph (4). This paragraph prescribes the form of disclosures. A signed written statement is required, reminding the parties and counsel of the solemnity of the obligations imposed; and the signature on the initial or pretrial disclosure is a certification under subdivision (g)(1) that it is complete and correct as of the time when made. Consistent with Rule 5(d), these disclosures are to be filed with the court unless otherwise directed. It is anticipated that many courts will direct that expert reports required under paragraph (2)(B) not be filed until needed in connection with a motion or for trial.

Paragraph (5). This paragraph is revised to take note of the availability of revised Rule 45 for inspection from non-parties of documents and premises without the need for a deposition.

Subdivision (b). This subdivision is revised in several respects. First, former paragraph (1) is subdivided into two paragraphs for ease of reference and to avoid renumbering of paragraphs (3) and (4). Textual changes are then made in new paragraph (2) to enable the court to keep tighter rein on the extent of discovery. The information explosion of recent decades has greatly increased both the potential cost of wide-ranging discovery and the potential for discovery to be used as an instrument for delay or oppression. Amendments to Rules 30, 31, and 33 place presumptive limits on the number of depositions and interrogatories, subject to leave of court to pursue additional discovery. The revisions in Rule 26(b)(2) are intended to provide the court with broader discretion to impose additional restrictions on the scope and extent of discovery and to authorize courts that develop case tracking systems based on the complexity of cases to increase or decrease by local rule the presumptive number of depositions and interrogatories allowed in particular types or classifications of cases. The revision also dispels any doubt as to the power of the court to impose limitations on the length of depositions under Rule 30 or on the number of requests for admission under Rule 36.

Second, former paragraph (2), relating to insurance, has been relocated as part of the required initial disclosures under subdivision (a)(1)(D), and revised to provide for disclosure of the policy itself.

Third, paragraph (4)(A) is revised to provide that experts who are expected to be witnesses will be subject to deposition prior to trial, conforming the norm stated in the rule to the actual practice followed in most courts, in which depositions of experts have become standard. Concerns regarding the expense of such depositions should be mitigated by the fact that the expert's fees for the deposition will ordinarily be borne by the party taking the deposition. The requirement under subdivision (a)(2)(B) of a complete and detailed report of the expected testimony of certain forensic experts may, moreover, eliminate the need for some such depositions or at least reduce the length of the depositions. Accordingly, the deposition of an expert required by subdivision (a)(2)(B) to provide a written report may be taken only after the report has been served.

Paragraph (4)(C), bearing on compensation of experts, is revised to take account of the changes in paragraph (4)(A).

Paragraph (5) is a new provision. A party must notify other parties if it is withholding materials otherwise subject to disclosure under the rule or pursuant to a discovery request because it is asserting a claim of privilege or work product protection. To withhold materials without such notice is contrary to the rule, subjects the party to sanctions under Rule 37(b)(2), and may be viewed as a waiver of the privilege or protection.

The party must also provide sufficient information to enable other parties to evaluate the applicability of the claimed privilege or protection. Although the person from whom the discovery is sought decides whether to claim a privilege or protection, the court ultimately decides whether, if this claim is challenged, the privilege or protection applies. Providing information pertinent to the applicability of the privilege or protection should reduce the need for in camera examination of the documents.

The rule does not attempt to define for each case what information must be provided when a party asserts a claim of privilege or work product protection. Details concerning time, persons, general subject matter, etc., may be appropriate if only a few items are withheld, but may be unduly burdensome when voluminous documents are claimed to be privileged or protected, particularly if the items can be described by categories. A party can seek relief through a protective order under subdivision (c) if compliance with the requirement for providing this information would be an unreasonable burden. In rare circumstances some of the pertinent information affecting applicability of the claim, such as the identity of the client, may itself be privileged; the rule provides that such information need not be disclosed.

The obligation to provide pertinent information concerning withheld privileged materials applies only to items "otherwise discoverable." If a broad discovery request is made—for example, for all documents of a particular type during a twenty year period—and the responding party believes in good faith that production of documents for more than the past believes in good faith that production of documents for more than the past three years would be unduly burdensome, it should make its objection to the breadth of the request and, with respect to the documents generated in that three year period, produce the unprivileged documents and describe those withheld under the claim of privilege. If the court later rules that documents for a seven year period are properly discoverable, the documents for the additional four years should then be either produced (if not privileged) or described (if claimed to be privileged).

Subdivision (c). The revision requires that before filing a motion for a protective order the movant must confer—either in person or by telephone—with the other affected parties in a good faith effort to resolve the discovery dispute without the need for court intervention. If the movant is unable to get opposing parties even to discuss the matter, the efforts in attempting to arrange such a conference should be indicated in the certificate.

Subdivision (d). This subdivision is revised to provide that formal discovery—as distinguished from interviews of potential witnesses and other informal discovery—not commence until the parties have met and conferred as required by subdivision (f). Discovery can begin earlier if authorized under Rule 30(a)(2)(C) (deposition of person about to leave the country) or by local rule, order, or stipulation. This will be appropriate in some cases, such as those involving requests for a preliminary injunction or motions challenging personal jurisdiction. If a local rule exempts any types of cases in which discovery may be needed from the requirement of a meeting under Rule 26(f), it should specify when discovery may commence in those cases.

The meeting of counsel is to take place as soon as practicable and in any event at least 14 days before the date of the scheduling conference under Rule 16(b) or the date a scheduling order is due under Rule 16(b). The court can assure that discovery is not unduly delayed either by entering a special order or by setting the case for a scheduling conference.

Subdivision (e). This subdivision is revised to provide that the requirement for supplementation applies to all disclosures required by subdivisions (a)(1)–(3). Like the former rule, the duty, while imposed on a "party," applies whether the corrective information is learned by the client or by the attorney. Supplementations need not be made as each new item of information is learned but should be made at appropriate intervals during the discovery period, and with special promptness as the trial date approaches. It may be useful for the scheduling order to specify the time or times when supplementations should be made.

The revision also clarifies that the obligation to supplement responses to formal discovery requests applies to interrogatories, requests for production, and requests for admissions, but not ordinarily to deposition testimony. However, with respect to experts from whom a written report is required under subdivision (a)(2)(B), changes in the opinions expressed by the expert whether in the report or at a subsequent deposition are subject to a duty of supplemental disclosure under subdivision (e)(1).

The obligation to supplement disclosures and discovery responses applies whenever a party learns that its prior disclosures or responses are in some material respect incomplete or incorrect. There is, however, no obligation to provide supplemental or corrective information that has been otherwise made known to the parties in writing or during the discovery process, as when a witness not previously disclosed is identified during the taking of a deposition or when an expert during a deposition corrects information contained in an earlier report.

Subdivision (f). This subdivision was added in 1980 to provide a party threatened with abusive discovery with a special means for obtaining judicial intervention other than through discrete motions under Rules 26(c) and 37(a). The amendment envisioned a two-step process: first, the parties would attempt to frame a mutually agreeable plan; second, the court would hold a "discovery conference" and then enter an order establishing a schedule and limitations for the conduct of discovery. It was contemplated that the procedure, an elective one triggered on request of a party, would be used in special cases rather than as a routine matter. As expected, the device has been used only sparingly in most courts, and judicial controls over the discovery process have ordinarily been imposed through scheduling orders under Rule 16(b) or through rulings on discovery motions.

The provisions relating to a conference with the court are removed from subdivision (f). This change does not signal any lessening of the importance of judicial supervision. Indeed, there is a greater need for early judicial involvement to consider the scope and timing of the disclosure requirements of Rule 26(a) and the presumptive limits on discovery imposed under these rules or by local rules. Rather, the change is made because the provisions addressing the use of conferences with the court to control discovery are more properly included in Rule 16, which is being revised to highlight the court's powers regarding the discovery process.

The desirability of some judicial control of discovery can hardly be doubted. Rule 16, as revised, requires that the court set a time for completion of discovery and authorizes various other orders affecting the scope, timing, and extent of discovery and disclosures. Before entering such orders, the court should consider the views of the parties, preferably by means of a conference, but at the least through written submissions. Moreover, it is desirable that the parties' proposals regarding discovery be developed through a process where they meet in person, informally explore the nature and basis of the issues, and discuss how discovery can be conducted most efficiently and economically.

As noted above, former subdivision (f) envisioned the development of proposed discovery plans as an optional procedure to be used in relatively few cases. The revised rule directs that in all cases not exempted by local rule or special order the litigants must meet in person and plan for discovery. Following this meeting, the parties submit to the court their proposals for a discovery plan and can begin formal discovery. Their report will assist the court in seeing that the timing and scope of disclosures under revised Rule 26(a) and the limitations on the extent of discovery under these rules and local rules are tailored to the circumstances of the particular case.

To assure that the court has the litigants' proposals before deciding on a scheduling order and that the commencement of discovery is not delayed unduly, the rule provides that the meeting of the parties take place as soon as practicable and in any event at least 14 days before a scheduling conference is held or before a scheduling order is due under Rule 16(b). (Rule 16(b) requires that a scheduling order be entered within 90 days after the first appearance of a defendant or, if earlier, within 120 days after the complaint has been served on any defendant.) The obligation to participate in the planning process is imposed on all parties that have appeared in the case, including defendants who, because of a pending Rule 12 motion, may not have yet filed an answer in the case. Each such party should attend the meeting, either through one of its attorneys or in person if unrepresented. If more parties are joined or appear after the initial meeting, an additional meeting may be desirable.

Subdivision (f) describes certain matters that should be accomplished at the meeting and included in the proposed discovery plan. This listing does not exclude consideration of other subjects, such as the time when any dispositive motions should be filed and when the case should be ready for trial.

The parties are directed under subdivision (a)(1) to make the disclosures required by that subdivision at or within 10 days after this meeting. In many cases the parties should use the meeting to exchange, discuss, and clarify their respective disclosures. In other cases, it may be more useful if the disclosures are delayed until after the parties have discussed at the meeting the claims and defenses in order to define the issues with respect to which the initial disclosures should be made. As discussed in the Notes to subdivision (a)(1), the parties may also need to consider whether a stipulation extending this 10–day period would be appropriate, as when a defendant would otherwise have less than 60 days after being served in which to make its initial disclosure. The parties should also discuss at the meeting what additional information, although not subject to the disclosure requirements, can be made available informally without the necessity for formal discovery requests.

The report is to be submitted to the court within 10 days after the meeting and should not be difficult to prepare. In most cases counsel should be able to agree that one of them will be responsible for its preparation and submission to the court. Form 35 has been added in the Appendix to the Rules, both to illustrate the type of report that is contemplated and to serve as a checklist for the meeting.

The litigants are expected to attempt in good faith to agree on the contents of the proposed discovery plan. If they cannot agree on all aspects of the plan, their report to the court should indicate the competing proposals of the parties on those items, as well as the matters on which they agree. Unfortunately, there may be cases in which, because of disagreements about time or place or for other reasons, the meeting is not attended by all parties or, indeed, no meeting takes place. In such situations, the report—or reports— should describe the circumstances and the court may need to consider sanctions under Rule 37(g).

By local rule or special order, the court can exempt particular cases or types of cases from the meet-and-confer requirement of subdivision (f). In general this should include any types of cases which are exempted by local rule from the requirement for a scheduling order under Rule 16(b), such as cases in which there will be no discovery (e.g., bankruptcy appeals and reviews of social security determinations). In addition, the court may want to exempt cases in which discovery is rarely needed (e.g., government collection cases and proceedings to enforce administrative summonses) or in which a meeting of the parties might be impracticable (e.g., actions by unrepresented prisoners). Note that if a court exempts from the requirements for a meeting any types of cases in which discovery may be needed, it should indicate when discovery may commence in those cases.

Subdivision (g). Paragraph (1) is added to require signatures on disclosures, a requirement that parallels the provisions of paragraph (2) with respect to discovery requests, responses, and objections. The provisions of paragraph (3) have been modified to be consistent with Rules 37(a)(4) and 37(c)(1); in combination, these rules establish sanctions for violation of the rules regarding disclosures and discovery matters. Amended Rule 11 no longer applies to such violations.

Rule 37. Failure to Make or Cooperate in Discovery: Sanctions

(a) Motion For Order Compelling Disclosure or Discovery. A party, upon reasonable notice to other parties and all persons affected thereby, may apply for an order compelling disclosure or discovery as follows:

(1) Appropriate Court. An application for an order to a party shall be made to the court in which the action is pending. An application for an order to a person who is not a party shall be made to the court in the district where the discovery is being, or is to be, taken.

(2) Motion.

(A) If a party fails to make a disclosure required by Rule 26(a), any other party may move to compel disclosure and for appropriate sanctions. The motion must include a certification that the movant has in good faith conferred or attempted to confer with the party not making the disclosure in an effort to secure the disclosure without court action.

663

(B) If a deponent fails to answer a question propounded or submitted under Rules 30 or 31, or a corporation or other entity fails to make a designation under Rule 30(b)(6) or 31(a), or a party fails to answer an interrogatory submitted under Rule 33, or if a party, in response to a request for inspection submitted under Rule 34, fails to respond that inspection will be permitted as requested or fails to permit inspection as requested, the discovering party may move for an order compelling an answer, or a designation, or an order compelling inspection in accordance with the request. The motion must include a certification that the movant has in good faith conferred or attempted to confer with the person or party failing to make the discovery in an effort to secure the information or material without court action. When taking a deposition on oral examination, the proponent of the question may complete or adjourn the examination before applying for an order.

(3) Evasive or Incomplete Disclosure, Answer, or Response. For purposes of this subdivision an evasive or incomplete disclosure, answer, or response is to be treated as a failure to disclose, answer, or respond.

(4) Expenses and Sanctions.

(A) If the motion is granted or if the disclosure or requested discovery is provided after the motion was filed, the court shall, after affording an opportunity to be heard, require the party or deponent whose conduct necessitated the motion or the party or attorney advising such conduct or both of them to pay to the moving party the reasonable expenses incurred in making the motion, including attorney's fees, unless the court finds that the motion was filed without the movant's first making a good faith effort to obtain the disclosure or discovery without court action, or that the opposing party's nondisclosure, response, or objection was substantially justified, or that other circumstances make an award of expenses unjust.

(B) If the motion is denied, the court may enter any protective order authorized under Rule 26(c) and shall, after affording an opportunity to be heard, require the moving party or the attorney filing the motion or both of them to pay to the party or deponent who opposed the motion the reasonable expenses incurred in opposing the motion, including attorney's fees, unless the court finds that the making of the motion was substantially justified or that other circumstances make an award of expenses unjust.

(C) If the motion is granted in part and denied in part, the court may enter any protective order authorized under Rule 26(c) and may, after affording an opportunity to be heard, apportion the reasonable expenses incurred in relation to the motion among the parties and persons in a just manner.

(b) Failure to Comply with Order.

(1) Sanctions by Court in District Where Deposition is Taken. If a deponent fails to be sworn or to answer a question after being directed to do so by the court in the district in which the deposition is being taken, the failure may be considered a contempt of that court.

(2) Sanctions by Court in Which Action Is Pending. If a party or an officer, director, or managing agent of a party or a person designated under Rule 30(b)(6) or 31(a) to testify on behalf of a party fails to obey an order to provide or permit discovery, including an order made under subdivision (a) of this rule or Rule 35, or if a party fails to obey an order entered under Rule 26(f), the court in which the action is pending may make such orders in regard to the failure as are just, and among others the following:

(A) An order that the matters regarding which the order was made or any other designated facts shall be taken to be established for the purposes of the action in accordance with the claim of the party obtaining the order;

(B) An order refusing to allow the disobedient party to support or oppose designated claims or defenses, or prohibiting that party from introducing designated matters in evidence;

(C) An order striking out pleadings or parts thereof, or staying further proceedings until the order is obeyed, or dismissing the action or proceeding or any part thereof, or rendering a judgment by default against the disobedient party;

(D) In lieu of any of the foregoing orders or in addition thereto, an order treating as a contempt of court the failure to obey any orders except an order to submit to a physical or mental examination;

(E) Where a party has failed to comply with an order under Rule 35(a) requiring that party to produce another for examination, such orders as are listed in paragraphs (A), (B), and (C) of this subdivision, unless the party failing to comply shows that that party is unable to produce such person for examination.

In lieu of any of the foregoing orders or in addition thereto, the court shall require the party failing to obey the order or the attorney advising that party or both to pay the reasonable expenses, including attorney's fees, caused by the failure, unless the court finds that the failure was substantially justified or that other circumstances make an award of expenses unjust.

(c) Failure to Disclose; False or Misleading Disclosure; Refusal to Admit.

(1) A party that without substantial justification fails to disclose information required by Rule 26(a) or 26(e)(1) shall not, unless such failure is harmless, be permitted to use as evidence at a trial, at a hearing, or on a motion any witness or information not so disclosed. In addition to or in lieu of this sanction, the court, on motion and after affording an opportunity to be heard, may impose other appropriate sanctions. In addition to requiring payment of reasonable expenses, including attorney's fees, caused by the failure, these sanctions may include any of the actions authorized under subparagraphs (A), (B), and (C) of subdivision (b)(2) of this rule and may include informing the jury of the failure to make the disclosure.

(2) If a party fails to admit the genuineness of any document or the truth of any matter as requested under Rule 36, and if the party requesting the admissions thereafter proves the genuineness of the document or the truth of the matter, the requesting party may apply to the court for an order requiring the other party to pay the reasonable expenses incurred in making that proof, including reasonable attorney's fees. The court shall make the order unless it finds that (A) the request was held objectionable pursuant to Rule 36(a), or (B) the admission sought was of no substantial importance, or (C) the party failing to admit had reasonable ground to believe that the party might prevail on the matter, or (D) there was other good reason for the failure to admit.

(d) Failure of Party to Attend at Own Deposition or Serve Answers to Interrogatories or Respond to Request for Inspection. If a party or an officer, director, or managing agent of a party or a person designated under Rule 30(b)(6) or 31(a) to testify on behalf of a party fails (1) to appear before the officer who is to take the deposition, after being served with a proper notice, or (2) to serve answers or objections to interrogatories submitted under Rule 33, after proper service of the interrogatories, or (3) to serve a written response to a request for inspection submitted under Rule 34, after proper service of the request, the court in which the action is pending on motion may make such orders in regard to the failure as are just, and among others it may take any action authorized under subparagraphs (A), (B), and (C) of subdivision (b)(2) of this rule. Any motion specifying a failure under clause (2) or (3) of this subdivision shall include a certification that the movant has in good faith conferred or attempted to confer with the party failing to answer or respond in an effort to obtain such answer or response without court action. In lieu of any order or in addition thereto, the court shall require the party failing to act or the attorney advising that party or both to pay the reasonable expenses, including attorney's fees, caused by the failure unless the court finds that the failure was substantially justified or that other circumstances make an award of expenses unjust.

The failure to act described in this subdivision may not be excused on the ground that the discovery sought is objectionable unless the party failing to act has a pending motion for a protective order as provided by Rule 26(c).

(e) [Abrogated].

(f) [Repealed. Pub.L. 96–481, Title II, § 205(a), Oct. 21, 1980, 94 Stat. 2330.]

(g) Failure to Participate in the Framing of a Discovery Plan. If a party or a party's attorney fails to participate in good faith in the development and submission of a proposed discovery plan as required by Rule 26(f), the court may, after opportunity for hearing, require such party or attorney to pay to any other party the reasonable expenses, including attorney's fees, caused by the failure.
(As amended Apr. 22, 1993, eff. Dec. 1, 1993.)

ADVISORY COMMITTEE NOTES
1993 Amendments

Subdivision (a). This subdivision is revised to reflect the revision of Rule 26(a), requiring disclosure of matters without a discovery request.

Pursuant to new subdivision (a)(2)(A), a party dissatisfied with the disclosure made by an opposing party may under this rule move for an order to compel disclosure. In providing for such a motion, the revised rule parallels the provisions of the former rule dealing with failures to answer particular interrogatories. Such a motion may be needed when the information to be disclosed might be helpful to the party seeking the disclosure but not to the party required to make the disclosure. If the party required to make the disclosure would need the material to support its own contentions, the more effective enforcement of the disclosure requirement will be to exclude the evidence not disclosed, as provided in subdivision (c)(1) of this revised rule.

Language is included in the new paragraph and added to the subparagraph (B) that requires litigants to seek to resolve discovery disputes by informal means before filing a motion with the court. This requirement is based on successful experience with similar local rules of court promulgated pursuant to Rule 83.

The last sentence of paragraph (2) is moved into paragraph (4).

Under revised paragraph (3), evasive or incomplete disclosures and responses to interrogatories and production requests are treated as failures to disclose or respond. Interrogatories and requests for production should not be read or interpreted in an artificially restrictive or hypertechnical manner to avoid disclosure of information fairly covered by the discovery request, and to do so is subject to appropriate sanctions under subdivision (a).

Revised paragraph (4) is divided into three subparagraphs for ease of reference, and in each the phrase "after opportunity for hearing" is changed to "after affording an opportunity to be heard" to make clear that the court can consider such questions on written submission as well as on oral hearings.

Subparagraph (A) is revised to cover the situation where information that should have been produced without a motion to compel is produced after the motion is filed but before it is brought on for hearing. The rule also is revised to provide that a party should not be awarded its expenses for filing a motion that could have been avoided by conferring with opposing counsel.

Subparagraph (C) is revised to include the provision that formerly was contained in subdivision (a)(2) and to include the same requirement of an opportunity to be heard that is specified in subparagraphs (A) and (B).

Subdivision (c). The revision provides a self-executing sanction for failure to make a disclosure required by Rule 26(a), without need for a motion under subdivision (a)(2)(A).

Paragraph (1) prevents a party from using as evidence any witnesses or information that, without substantial justification, has not been disclosed as required by Rules 26(a) and 26(e)(1). This automatic sanction provides a strong inducement for disclosure of material that the disclosing party would expect to use as evidence, whether at a trial, at a hearing, or on a motion, such as one under Rule 56. As disclosure of evidence offered solely for impeachment purposes is not required under those rules, this preclusion sanction likewise does not apply to that evidence.

Limiting the automatic sanction to violations "without substantial justification," coupled with the exception for violations that are "harmless," is needed to avoid unduly harsh penalties in a variety of situations: e.g., the inadvertent omission from a Rule 26(a)(1)(A) disclosure of the name of a potential witness known to all parties; the failure to list as a trial witness a person so listed by another party; or the lack of knowledge of a pro se litigant of the requirement to make disclosures. In the latter situation, however, exclusion would be proper if the requirement for disclosure had been called to the litigant's attention by either the court or another party.

Preclusion of evidence is not an effective incentive to compel disclosure of information that, being supportive of the position of the opposing party, might advantageously be concealed by the disclosing party. However, the rule provides the court with a wide range of other sanctions—such as declaring specified facts to be established, preventing contradictory evidence, or, like spoliation of evidence, allowing the jury to be informed of the fact of nondisclosure—that, though not self-executing, can be imposed when found to be warranted after a hearing. The failure to identify a witness or document in a disclosure statement would be admissible under the Federal Rules of Evidence under the same principles that allow a party's interrogatory answers to be offered against it.

Subdivision (d). This subdivision is revised to require that, where a party fails to file any response to interrogatories or a Rule 34 request, the discovering party should informally seek to obtain such responses before filing a motion for sanctions.

The last sentence of this subdivision is revised to clarify that it is the pendency of a motion for protective order that may be urged as an excuse for a violation of subdivision (d). If a party's motion has been denied, the party cannot argue that its subsequent failure to comply would be justified. In this connection, it should be noted that the filing of a motion under Rule 26(c) is not self-executing—the relief authorized under that rule depends on obtaining the court's order to that effect.

Subdivision (g). This subdivision is modified to conform to the revision of Rule 26(f).

Notes of Advisory Committee on Rules

The provisions of this rule authorizing orders establishing facts or excluding evidence or striking pleadings, or authorizing judgments of dismissal or default, for refusal to answer questions or permit inspection or otherwise make discovery, are in accord with *Hammond Packing Co. v. Arkansas,* 1909, 29 S.Ct. 370, 212 U.S. 322, 53 L.Ed. 530, 15 Ann.Cas. 645, which distinguishes between the justifiable use of such measures as a means of compelling the production of evidence, and their unjustifiable use, as in *Hovey v. Elliott,* 1897, 17 S.Ct. 841, 167 U.S. 409, 42 L.Ed. 215, for the mere purpose of punishing for contempt.

1970 Amendment

Rule 37 provides generally for sanctions against parties or persons unjustifiably resisting discovery. Experience has brought to light a number of defects in the language of the rule as well as instances in which it is not serving the purposes for which it was designed. See Rosenberg, *Sanctions to Effectuate Pretrial Discovery,* 58 Col.L.Rev. 480 (1958). In addition, changes being made in other discovery rules require conforming amendments to Rule 37.

Rule 37 sometimes refers to a "failure" to afford discovery and at other times to a "refusal" to do so. Taking note of this dual terminology, courts have imported into "refusal" a requirement of "willfulness." See *Roth v. Paramount Pictures Corp.,* 8 F.R.D. 31 (W.D.Pa.1948); *Campbell v. Johnson,* 101 F.Supp. 705, 707 (S.D.N.Y.1951). In *Societe Internationale v. Rogers,* 357 U.S. 197 (1958), the Supreme Court concluded that the rather random use of these two terms in Rule 37 showed no design to use them with consistently distinctive meanings, that "refused" in Rule 37(b)(2) meant simply a failure to comply, and that willfulness was relevant only to the selection of sanctions, if any, to be imposed. Nevertheless, after the decision in *Societe*, the court in *Hinson v. Michigan Mutual Liability Co.*, 275 F.2d 537 (5th Cir.1960) once again ruled that "refusal" required willfulness. Substitution of "failure" for "refusal" throughout Rule 37 should eliminate this confusion and bring the rule into harmony with the *Societe Internationale* decision. See Rosenberg, supra, 58 Col.L.Rev. 480, 489–490 (1958).

* * *

Subdivision (b). This subdivision deals with sanctions for failure to comply with a court order. The present captions for subsections (1) and (2) entitled, "Contempt" and "Other Consequences," respectively, are confusing. One of the consequences listed in (2) is the arrest of the party, representing the exercise of the contempt power. The contents of the subsections show that the first authorizes the sanction of contempt (and no other) by the court in which the deposition is taken, whereas the second subsection authorizes a variety of sanctions, including contempt, which may be imposed by the court in which the action is pending. The captions of the subsections are changed to reflect their contents.

The scope of Rule 37(b)(2) is broadened by extending it to include any order "to provide or permit discovery," including orders issued under Rules 37(a) and 35. Various rules authorize orders for discovery—e.g., Rule 35(b)(1), Rule 26(c) as revised, Rule 37(d). See Rosenberg, supra, 58 Col.L.Rev. 480, 484–486. Rule 37(b)(2) should provide comprehensively for enforcement of all these orders. Cf. *Societe Internationale v. Rogers*, 357 U.S. 197, 207 (1958). On the other hand, the reference to Rule 34 is deleted to conform to the changed procedure in that rule.

A new subsection (E) provides that sanctions which have been available against a party for failure to comply with an order under Rule 35(a) to submit to examination will now be available against him for his failure to comply with a Rule 35(a) order to produce a third person for examination, unless he shows that he is unable to produce the person. In this context, "unable" means in effect "unable in good faith." See *Societe Internationale v. Rogers*, 357 U.S. 197 (1958).

Subdivision (b)(2) is amplified to provide for payment of reasonable expenses caused by the failure to obey the order. Although Rules 37(b)(2) and 37(d) have been silent as to award of expenses, courts have nevertheless ordered them on occasion. E.g., *United Sheeplined Clothing Co. v. Arctic Fur Cap Corp.*, 165 F.Supp. 193 (S.D.N.Y.1958); *Austin Theatre, Inc. v. Warner Bros. Pictures, Inc.*, 22 F.R.D. 302 (S.D.N.Y.1958). The provision places the burden on the disobedient party to avoid expenses by showing that his failure is justified or that special circumstances make an award of expenses unjust. Allocating the burden in this way conforms to the changed provisions as to expenses in Rule 37(a), and is particularly appropriate when a court order is disobeyed.

An added reference to directors of a party is similar to a change made in subdivision (d) and is explained in the note to that subdivision. The added reference to persons designated by a party under Rules 30(b)(6) or 31(a) to testify on behalf of the party carries out the new procedure in those rules for taking a deposition of a corporation or other organization.

* * *

Additional provisions in Rule 37(c) protect a party from having to pay expenses if the request for admission was held objectionable under Rule 36(a) or if the party failing to admit had reasonable ground to believe that he might prevail on the matter. The latter provision emphasizes that the true test under Rule 37(c) is not whether a party prevailed at trial but whether he acted reasonably in believing that he might prevail.

* * *

Rule 60. Relief From Judgment or Order

(a) **Clerical Mistakes.** Clerical mistakes in judgments, orders or other parts of the record and errors therein arising from oversight or omission may be corrected by the court at any time of its own initiative or on the motion of any party and after such notice, if any, as the court orders. During the pendency of an appeal, such mistakes may be so corrected before the appeal is docketed in the appellate court, and thereafter while the appeal is pending may be so corrected with leave of the appellate court.

(b) Mistakes; Inadvertence; Excusable Neglect; Newly Discovered Evidence; Fraud, etc. On motion and upon such terms as are just, the court may relieve a party or a party's legal representative from a final judgment, order, or proceeding for the following reasons: (1) mistake, inadvertence, surprise, or excusable neglect; (2) newly discovered evidence which by due diligence could not have been discovered in time to move for a new trial under Rule 59(b); (3) fraud (whether heretofore denominated intrinsic or extrinsic), misrepresentation, or other misconduct of an adverse party; (4) the judgment is void; (5) the judgment has been satisfied, released, or discharged, or a prior judgment upon which it is based has been reversed or otherwise vacated, or it is no longer equitable that the judgment should have prospective application; or (6) any other reason justifying relief from the operation of the judgment. The motion shall be made within a reasonable time, and for reasons (1), (2), and (3) not more than one year after the judgment, order, or proceeding was entered or taken. A motion under this subdivision (b) does not affect the finality of a judgment or suspend its operation. This rule does not limit the power of a court to entertain an independent action to relieve a party from a judgment, order, or proceeding, or to grant relief to a defendant not actually personally notified as provided in Title 28, U.S.C. § 1655, or to set aside a judgment for fraud upon the court. Writs of coram nobis, coram vobis, audita querela, and bills of review and bills in the nature of a bill of review, are abolished, and the procedure for obtaining any relief from a judgment shall be by motion as prescribed in these rules or by an independent action.

(As amended Dec. 27, 1946, eff. Mar. 19, 1948; Dec. 29, 1948, eff. Oct. 20, 1949; Mar. 2, 1987, eff. Aug. 1, 1987.)

Rule 63. Disability of a Judge

If a trial or hearing has been commenced and the judge is unable to proceed, any other judge may proceed with it upon certifying familiarity with the record and determining that the proceedings in the case may be completed without prejudice to the parties. In a hearing or trial without a jury, the successor judge shall at the request of a party recall any witness whose testimony is material and disputed and who is available to testify again without undue burden. The successor judge may also recall any other witness.

(As amended Mar. 2, 1987, eff. Aug. 1, 1987; Apr. 30, 1991, eff. Dec. 1, 1991.)

Rule 68. Offer of Judgment

At any time more than 10 days before the trial begins, a party defending against a claim may serve upon the adverse party an offer to allow judgment to be taken against the defending party for the money or property or to the effect specified in the offer, with costs then accrued. If within 10 days after the service of the offer the adverse party serves written notice that the offer is accepted, either party may then file the offer and notice of acceptance together with proof of service thereof and thereupon the clerk shall enter judgment. An offer not accepted shall be deemed withdrawn and evidence thereof is not admissible except in a proceeding to determine costs. If the judgment finally obtained by the offeree is not more favorable than the offer, the offeree must pay the costs incurred after the making of the offer. The fact that an offer is made but not accepted does not preclude a subsequent offer. When the liability of one party to another has been determined by verdict or order or judgment, but the amount or extent of the liability remains to be determined by further proceedings, the party adjudged liable may make an offer of judgment, which shall have the same effect as an offer made before trial if it is served within a reasonable time not less than 10 days prior to the commencement of hearings to determine the amount or extent of liability.

(As amended Dec. 27, 1946, eff. Mar. 19, 1948; Feb. 28, 1966, eff. July 1, 1966; Mar. 2, 1987, eff. Aug. 1, 1987.)

FEDERAL RULES OF CRIMINAL PROCEDURE

Rule 44. Right to and Assignment of Counsel

(a) Right to Assigned Counsel. Every defendant who is unable to obtain counsel shall be entitled to have counsel assigned to represent that defendant at every stage of the proceedings from initial appearance before the federal magistrate judge or the court through appeal, unless that defendant waives such appointment.

(b) Assignment Procedure. The procedures for implementing the right set out in subdivision (a) shall be those provided by law and by local rules of court established pursuant thereto.

(c) Joint Representation. Whenever two or more defendants have been jointly charged pursuant to Rule 8(b) or have been joined for trial pursuant to Rule 13, and are represented by the same retained or assigned counsel or by retained or assigned counsel who are associated in the practice of law, the court shall promptly inquire with respect to such joint representation and shall personally advise each defendant of the right to the effective assistance of counsel, including separate representation. Unless it appears that there is good cause to believe no conflict of interest is likely to arise, the court shall take such measures as may be appropriate to protect each defendant's right to counsel.

(As amended Apr. 30, 1979, eff. Dec. 1, 1980; Mar. 9, 1987, eff. Aug. 1, 1987; Apr. 22, 1993, eff. Dec. 1, 1993.)

1979 Amendment

Rule 44(c) establishes a procedure for avoiding the occurrence of events which might otherwise give rise to a plausible post-conviction claim that because of joint representation the defendants in a criminal case were deprived of their Sixth Amendment right to the effective assistance of counsel. Although "courts have differed with respect to the scope and nature of the affirmative duty of the trial judge to assure that criminal defendants are not deprived of their right to the effective assistance of counsel by joint representation of conflicting interests." *Holloway v. Arkansas*, 98 S.Ct. 1173 (1978) (where the Court found it unnecessary to reach this issue), this amendment is generally consistent with the current state of the law in several circuits. As held in *United States v. Carrigan*, 543 F.2d 1053 (2d Cir.1976):

> When a potential conflict of interest arises, either where a court has assigned the same counsel to represent several defendants or where the same counsel has been retained by co-defendants in a criminal case, the proper course of action for the trial judge is to conduct a hearing to determine whether a conflict exists to the degree that a defendant may be prevented from receiving advice and assistance sufficient to afford him the quality of representation guaranteed by the Sixth Amendment. The defendant should be fully advised by the trial court of the facts underlying the potential conflict and be given the opportunity to express his views.

See also *United States v. Lawriw*, 568 F.2d 98 (8th Cir.1977) (duty on trial judge to make inquiry where joint representation by appointed or retained counsel, and "without such an inquiry a finding of knowing and intelligent waiver will seldom, if ever, be sustained by this Court"); *Abraham v. United States*, 549 F.2d 236 (2d Cir.1977); *United States v. Mari*, 526 F.2d 117 (2d Cir.1975); *United States v. Truglio*, 493 F.2d 574 (4th Cir.1974) (joint representation should cause trial judge "to inquire whether the defenses to be presented in any way conflict"); *United States v. DeBerry*, 487 F.2d 488 (2d Cir.1973); *United States ex rel. Hart v. Davenport*, 478 F.2d 203 (3d Cir.1973) (noting there "is much to be said for the rule ... which assumes prejudice and nonwaiver if there has been no on-the-record inquiry by the court as to the hazards to defendants from joint representation"); *United States v. Alberti*, 470 F.2d 878 (2d Cir.1973); *United States v. Foster*, 469 F.2d 1 (1st Cir.1972) (lack of sufficient inquiry shifts the burden of proof on the question of prejudice to the government); *Campbell v. United States*, 352 F.2d 359 (D.C.Cir.1965) (where joint representation, court "has a duty to ascertain whether each defendant has an awareness of the potential risks of that course and nevertheless has knowingly chosen it"). Some states have taken a like position; see, e.g., *State v. Olsen*, Minn.1977, 258 N.W.2d 898.

This procedure is also consistent with that recommended in the ABA Standards Relating to the Function of the Trial Judge (Approved Draft, 1972), which provide in § 3.4(b):

> Whenever two or more defendants who have been jointly charged, or whose cases have been consolidated, are represented by the same attorney, the trial judge should inquire into potential conflicts with may jeopardize the right of each defendant to the fidelity of his counsel.

Avoiding a conflict-of-interest situation is in the first instance a responsibility of the attorney. If a lawyer represents "multiple clients having potentially differing interests, he must weigh carefully the possibility that his judgment may be impaired or his loyalty divided if he accepts or continues the employment," and he is to "resolve all doubts against the propriety of the representation." Code of Professional Responsibility, Ethical Consideration 5–15. See also ABA Standards Relating to the Defense Function § 3.5(b) (Approved Draft, 1971) concluding that the "potential for conflict of interest in representing multiple defendants is so grave that ordinarily a lawyer should decline to act for more than one of several co-defendants except in unusual situations when, after careful investigation, it is clear that no conflict is likely to develop and when the several defendants give an informed consent to such multiple representation."

It by no means follows that the inquiry provided for by rule 44(c) is unnecessary. For one thing, even the most diligent attorney may be unaware of facts giving rise to a potential conflict. Often "counsel must operate somewhat in the dark and feel their way uncertainly to an understanding of what their clients may be called upon to meet upon a trial" and consequently "are frequently unable to foresee developments which may require changes in strategy." *United States v. Carrigan,* supra (concurring opinion). "Because the conflicts are often subtle it is not enough to rely upon counsel, who may not be totally disinterested, to make sure that each of his joint clients has made an effective waiver." *United States v. Lawriw,* supra.

Moreover, it is important that the trial judge ascertain whether the effective and fair administration of justice would be adversely affected by continued joint representation, even when an actual conflict is not then apparent. As noted in *United States v. Mari,* supra (concurring opinion):

> Trial court insistence that, except in extraordinary circumstances, codefendants retain separate counsel will in the long run ... prove salutary not only to the administration of justice and the appearance of justice but the cost of justice; habeas corpus petitions, petitions for new trials, appeals and occasionally retrials ... can be avoided. Issues as to whether there is an actual conflict of interest, whether the conflict has resulted in prejudice, whether there has been a waiver, whether the waiver is intelligent and knowledgeable, for example, can all be avoided. Where a conflict that first did not appear subsequently arises in or before trial, ... continuances or mistrials can be saved. Essentially by the time a case ... gets to the appellate level the harm to the appearance of justice has already been done, whether or not reversal occurs; at the trial level it is a matter which is so easy to avoid.

A rule 44(c) inquiry is required whether counsel is assigned or retained. It "makes no difference whether counsel is appointed by the court or selected by the defendants; even where selected by the defendants the same dangers of potential conflict exist, and it is also possible that the rights of the public to the proper administration of justice may be affected adversely." *United States v. Mari,* supra (concurring opinion). See also *United States v. Lawriw,* supra. When there has been "no discussion as to possible conflict initiated by the court," it cannot be assumed that the choice of counsel by the defendants "was intelligently made with knowledge of any possible conflict." *United States v. Carrigan,* supra. As for assigned counsel, it is provided by statute that "the court shall appoint separate counsel for defendants having interests that cannot properly be represented by the same counsel, or when other good cause is shown." 18 U.S.C. § 3006(A)(b). Rule 44(c) is not intended to prohibit the automatic appointment of separate counsel in the first instance, see *Ford v. United States,* 379 F.2d 123 (D.C.Cir.1967); *Lollar v. United States,* 376 F.2d 243 (D.C.Cir.1967), which would obviate the necessity for an inquiry.

Under rule 44(c), an inquiry is called for when the joined defendants are represented by the same attorney and also when they are represented by attorneys "associated in the practice of law." This is consistent with Code of Professional Responsibility, Disciplinary Rule 5–105(D) (providing that if "a lawyer is required to decline employment or to withdraw from employment" because of a potential conflict, "no partner or associate of his or his firm may accept or continue such employment"); and ABA Standards Relating to the Defense Function § 3.5(b) (Approved Draft, 1971) (applicable to "a lawyer or lawyers who are associated in practice"). Attorneys representing joined defendants should so advise the court if they are associated in the practice of law.

The rule 44(c) procedure is not limited to cases expected to go to trial. Although the more dramatic conflict situations, such as when the question arises as to whether the several defendants should take the stand, *Morgan v. United States,* 396 F.2d 110 (2d Cir.1968), tend to occur in a trial context, serious conflicts may also arise when one or more of the jointly represented defendants pleads guilty.

> The problem is that even where as here both codefendants pleaded guilty there are frequently potential conflicts of interest.... [T]he prosecutor may be inclined to accept a guilty plea from one codefendant which may harm the interests of the other. The contrast in the dispositions of the cases may have a harmful impact on the codefendant who does not initially plead guilty; he may be pressured into pleading guilty himself rather than face his codefendant's bargained-for testimony at a trial. And it will be his own counsel's recommendation to the initially pleading codefendant which will have contributed to this harmful impact upon him.... [I]n a given instance it would be at least conceivable that the prosecutor would be willing to accept pleas to lesser offenses from two defendants in preference to a plea of guilty by one defendant to a greater offense.

United States v. Mari, supra (concurring opinion). To the same effect is ABA Standards Relating to the Defense Function at 213–14.

It is contemplated that under rule 44(c) the court will make appropriate inquiry of the defendants and of counsel regarding the possibility of a conflict of interest developing. Whenever it is necessary to make a more particularized inquiry into the nature of the contemplated defense, the court should "pursue the inquiry with defendants and their counsel on the record but in chambers" so as "to avoid the possibility of prejudicial disclosures to the prosecution." *United States v. Foster,* supra. It is important that each defendant be "fully advised of the facts underlying the potential conflict and is given an opportunity to express his or her views." *United States v. Alberti,* supra. The rule specifically requires that the court personally advise each defendant of his right to effective assistance of counsel, including separate representation. See *United States v. Foster,* supra, requiring that the court make a determination that jointly represented defendants "understand that they may retain separate counsel, or if qualified, may have such counsel appointed by the court and paid for by the government."

Under rule 44(c), the court is to take appropriate measures to protect each defendant's right to counsel unless it appears "there is good cause to believe no conflict of interest is likely to arise" as a consequence of the continuation of such joint representation. A less demanding standard would not adequately protect the Sixth Amendment right to effective assistance of counsel or the effective administration of criminal justice. Although joint representation "is not per se violative of constitutional guarantees of effective assistance of counsel," *Holloway v. Arkansas,* supra, it would not suffice to require the court to act only when a conflict of interest is then apparent, for it is not possible to "anticipate with complete accuracy the course that a criminal trial may take." *Fryar v. United States,* 404 F.2d 1071 (10th Cir.1968). This is particularly so in light of the fact that if a conflict later arises and a defendant thereafter raises a Sixth Amendment objection, a court must grant relief without indulging "in nice calculations as to the amount of prejudice arising from its denial." *Glasser v. United States,* 315 U.S. 60 (1942). This is because, as the Supreme Court more recently noted in *Holloway v. Arkansas,* supra, "in a case of joint representation of conflicting interests the evil ... is in what the advocate finds himself compelled to refrain from doing," and this makes it "virtually impossible" to assess the impact of the conflict.

Rule 44(c) does not specify what particular measures must be taken. It is appropriate to leave this within the court's discretion, for the measures which will best protect each defendant's right to counsel may well vary from case to case. One possible course of action is for the court to obtain a knowing, intelligent and voluntary waiver of the right to separate representation, for, as noted in *Holloway v. Arkansas,* supra, "a defendant may waive his right to the assistance of an attorney unhindered by a conflict of interests." See *United States v. DeBerry,* supra, holding that defendants should be jointly represented only if "the court has ascertained that ... each understands clearly the possibilities of a conflict of interest and waives any rights in connection with it." It must be emphasized that a "waiver of the right to separate representation should not be accepted by the court unless the defendants have each been informed of the probable hazards; and the voluntary character of their waiver is apparent." ABA Standards Relating to the Function of the Trial Judge at 45. *United States v. Garcia,* supra, spells out in significant detail what should be done to assure an adequate waiver:

> As in Rule 11 procedures, the district court should address each defendant personally and forthrightly advise him of the potential dangers of representation by counsel with a conflict of interest. The defendant must be at liberty to question the district court as to the nature and consequences of his legal representation. Most significantly, the court should seek to elicit a narrative response from each defendant that he has been advised of his right to effective representation, that he understands the details of his attorney's possible conflict of interest and the potential perils of such a conflict, that he has discussed the matter with his attorney or if he wishes with outside counsel, and that he voluntarily waives his Sixth Amendment protections. It is, of course, vital that the waiver be established by "clear, unequivocal, and unambiguous language." ... Mere assent in response to a series of questions from the bench may in some circumstances constitute an adequate waiver, but the court should nonetheless endeavor to have each defendant personally articulate in detail his intent to forego this significant constitutional protection. Recordation of the waiver colloque between defendant and judge, will also serve the government's interest by assisting in

shielding any potential conviction from collateral attack, either on Sixth Amendment grounds or on a Fifth or Fourteenth Amendment "fundamental fairness" basis.

See also Hyman, Joint Representation of Multiple Defendants in a Criminal Trial: The Court's Headache, 5 Hofstra L.Rev. 315, 334 (1977).

Another possibility is that the court will order that the defendants be separately represented in subsequent proceedings in the case.

> Though the court must remain alert to and take account of the fact that "certain advantages might accrue from joint representation," *Holloway v. Arkansas, supra,* it need not permit the joint representation to continue merely because the defendants express a willingness to so proceed. That is, there will be cases where the court should require separate counsel to represent certain defendants despite the expressed wishes of such defendants. Indeed, failure of the trial court to require separate representation may ... require a new trial, even though the defendants have expressed a desire to continue with the same counsel. The right to effective representation by counsel whose loyalty is undivided is so paramount in the proper administration of criminal justice that it must in some cases take precedence over all other considerations, including the expressed preference of the defendants concerned and their attorney.

United States v. Carrigan, supra (concurring opinion). See also *United States v. Lawriw,* supra; *Abraham v. United States,* supra; ABA Standards Relating to the Defense Function at 213, concluding that in some circumstances "even full disclosure and consent of the client may not be an adequate protection." As noted in *United States v. Dolan,* 570 F.2d 1177 (3d Cir.1978), such an order may be necessary where the trial judge is

> not satisfied that the waiver is proper. For example, a defendant may be competent enough to stand trial, but not competent enough to understand the complex, subtle, and sometimes unforeseeable dangers inherent in multiple representation. More importantly, the judge may find that the waiver cannot be intelligently made simply because he is not in a position to inform the defendant of the foreseeable prejudices multiple representation might entail for him.

As concluded in *Dolan,* "exercise of the court's supervisory powers by disqualifying an attorney representing multiple criminal defendants in spite of the defendants' express desire to retain that attorney does not necessarily abrogate defendant's sixth amendment rights". It does not follow from the absolute right of self-representation recognized in *Faretta v. California,* 422 U.S. 806 (1975), that there is an *absolute* right to counsel of one's own choice. Thus,

> when a trial court finds an actual conflict of interest which impairs the ability of a criminal defendant's chosen counsel to conform with the ABA Code of Professional Responsibility, the court should not be required to tolerate an inadequate representation of a defendant. Such representation not only constitutes a breach of professional ethics and invites disrespect for the integrity of the court, but it is also detrimental to the independent interest of the trial judge to be free from future attacks over the adequacy of the waiver or the fairness of the proceedings in his own court and the subtle problems implicating the defendant's comprehension of the waiver. Under such circumstances, the court can elect to exercise its supervisory authority over members of the bar to enforce the ethical standard requiring an attorney to decline multiple representation.

United States v. Dolan, supra. See also Geer, Conflict of Interest and Multiple Defendants in a Criminal Case: Professional Responsibilities of the Defense Attorney, 62 Minn.L.Rev. 119 (1978); Note, Conflict of Interests in Multiple Representation of Criminal Co-Defendants, 68 J.Crim.L. & C. 226 (1977).

The failure in a particular case to conduct a rule 44(c) inquiry would not, standing alone, necessitate the reversal of a conviction of a jointly represented defendant. However, as is currently the case, a reviewing court is more likely to assume a conflict resulted from the joint representation when no inquiry or an inadequate inquiry was conducted. *United States v. Carrigan,* supra; *United States v. DeBerry,* supra. On the other hand, the mere fact that a rule 44(c) inquiry was conducted in the early stages of the case does not relieve the court of all responsibility in this regard thereafter. The obligation placed upon the court by rule 44(c) is a continuing one, and thus in a particular case further inquiry may be necessary on a later occasion because of new developments suggesting a potential conflict of interest.

FEDERAL RULES OF APPELLATE PROCEDURE

Rule 38. Damages and Costs for Frivolous Appeals

If a court of appeals determines that an appeal is frivolous, it may, after a separately filed motion or notice from the court and reasonable opportunity to respond, award just damages and single or double costs to the appellee.

(As amended Apr. 29, 1994, eff. Dec. 1, 1994; April 24, 1998, effective December 1, 1998.)

ADVISORY COMMITTEE NOTES
1994 Amendments

The amendment requires that before a court of appeals may impose sanctions, the person to be sanctioned must have notice and an opportunity to respond. The amendment reflects the basic principle enunciated in the Supreme Court's opinion in Roadway Express, Inc. v. Piper, 447 U.S. 752, 767 (1980), that notice and opportunity to respond must precede the imposition of sanctions. A separately filed motion requesting sanctions constitutes notice. A statement inserted in a party's brief that the party moves for sanctions is not sufficient notice. Requests in briefs for sanctions have become so commonplace that it is unrealistic to expect careful responses to such requests without any indication that the court is actually contemplating such measures. Only a motion, the purpose of which is to request sanctions, is sufficient. If there is no such motion filed, notice must come from the court. The form of notice from the court and of the opportunity for comment purposely are left to the court's discretion.

Rule 46. Attorneys

(a) Admission to the Bar.

(1) *Eligibility.* An attorney is eligible for admission to the bar of a court of appeals if that attorney is of good moral and professional character and is admitted to practice before the Supreme Court of the United States, the highest court of a state, another United States court of appeals, or a United States district court (including the district courts for Guam, the Northern Mariana Islands, and the Virgin Islands).

(2) *Application.* An applicant must file an application for admission, on a form approved by the court that contains the applicant's personal statement showing eligibility for membership. The applicant must subscribe to the following oath or affirmation:

"I, _____, do solemnly swear (or affirm) that I will conduct myself as an attorney and counselor of this court, uprightly and according to law; and that I will support the Constitution of the United States.

(3) *Admission Procedures.* On written or oral motion of a member of the court's bar, the court will act on the application. An applicant may be admitted by oral motion in open court. But, unless the court orders otherwise, an applicant need not appear before the court to be admitted. Upon admission, an applicant must pay the clerk the fee prescribed by local rule or court order.

(b) Suspension or Disbarment.

(1) *Standard.* A member of the court's bar is subject to suspension or disbarment by the court if the member:

(A) has been suspended or disbarred from practice in any other court; or

(B) is guilty of conduct unbecoming a member of the court's bar.

(2) *Procedure.* The member must be given an opportunity to show good cause, within the time prescribed by the court, why the member should not be suspended or disbarred.

(3) *Order.* The court must enter an appropriate order after the member responds and a hearing is held, if requested, or after the time prescribed for a response expires, if no response is made.

(c) Discipline. A court of appeals may discipline an attorney who practices before it for conduct unbecoming a member of the bar or for failure to comply with any court rule. First, however, the court must afford the attorney reasonable notice, an opportunity to show cause to the contrary, and, if requested, a hearing.

(Amended March 10, 1986, effective July 1, 1986; April 24, 1998, effective December 1, 1998.)

RULES OF THE SUPREME COURT OF THE UNITED STATES

PART II. ATTORNEYS AND COUNSELORS

Rule 5. Admission to the Bar

1. It shall be requisite for admission to the Bar of this Court that the applicant shall have been admitted to practice in the highest court of a State, Commonwealth, Territory or Possession, or of the District of Columbia for the three years immediately preceding the date of application and shall have been free from any adverse disciplinary action whatsoever during that 3–year period, and that the applicant appears to the Court to be of good moral and professional character.

2. Each applicant shall file with the Clerk (1) a certificate from the presiding judge, clerk, or other authorized official of that court evidencing the applicant's admission to practice there and the applicant's current good standing, and (2) a completely executed copy of the form approved by the Court and furnished by the Clerk containing (i) the applicant's personal statement and (ii) the statement of two sponsors (who must be members of the Bar of this Court and who must personally know, but not be related to, the applicant) endorsing the correctness of the applicant's statement, stating that the applicant possesses all the qualifications required for admission, and affirming that the applicant is of good moral and professional character.

3. If the documents submitted demonstrate that the applicant possesses the necessary qualifications, has signed the oath or affirmation, and has paid the required fee, the Clerk will notify the applicant of acceptance by the Court as a member of the Bar and issue a certificate of admission. An applicant who so desires may be admitted in open court on oral motion by a member of the Bar of this Court, provided that all other requirements for admission have been satisfied.

4. Each applicant shall take or subscribe to the following oath or affirmation:

I, _____, do solemnly swear (or affirm) that as an attorney and as a counselor of this Court, I will conduct myself uprightly and according to law, and that I will support the Constitution of the United States.

* * *

Rule 6. Argument Pro Hac Vice

1. An attorney not admitted to practice in the highest court of a State, Commonwealth, Territory or Possession, or of the District of Columbia for the requisite three years, but who is otherwise eligible for admission to practice in this Court under Rule 5.1, may be permitted to argue *pro hac vice*.

2. An attorney, barrister, or advocate who is qualified to practice in the courts of a foreign state may be permitted to argue *pro hac vice*.

3. Oral argument *pro hac vice* will be allowed only on motion of the attorney of record for the party on whose behalf leave is requested. The motion must briefly and distinctly state the appropriate qualifications of the attorney who is to argue *pro hac vice*. It must be filed with the Clerk, in the form prescribed by Rule 21, no later than the date on which the respondent's or appellee's brief on the merits is due to be filed and must be accompanied by proof of service pursuant to Rule 29.

Rule 7. Prohibition Against Practice

No employee of this Court shall practice as an attorney or counselor in any court or before any agency of government while employed by the Court; nor shall any person after leaving such employment participate in any professional capacity in any case pending before this Court or in any case being considered for filing in this Court, until two years have elapsed after separation; nor shall a former employee ever participate in any professional capacity in any case that was pending in this Court during the employee's tenure.

Rule 8. Disbarment and Disciplinary Action

1. Whenever it is shown to the Court that a member of the Bar of this Court has been disbarred or suspended from practice in any court of record, or has engaged in conduct unbecoming a member of the Bar of this Court, that member will be suspended from practice before this

Court forthwith and will be afforded the opportunity to show cause, within 40 days, why a disbarment order should not be entered. Upon response, or upon the expiration of the 40 days if no response is made, the Court will enter an appropriate order.

2. The Court may, after reasonable notice and an opportunity to show cause why disciplinary action should not be taken, and after a hearing if material facts are in dispute, take any appropriate disciplinary action against any attorney who practices before it for conduct unbecoming a member of the Bar or for failure to comply with these Rules or any Rule of the Court.

DRAFT FEDERAL RULES OF ATTORNEY CONDUCT

The federal courts are considering a proposal to standardize certain rules of ethics that would apply in all federal courts and then to leave the remainder of the ethics issues to state ethics law. On February 11, 1998, the federal judiciary rules committee referred the following proposed ten ethics rules to its advisory committees. On June 18, 1998, the rules committee established a special ad hoc committee to study the proposed rules. It is anticipated that these rules, if adopted, would replace nearly 100 local rules current in place in the federal system.

Table of Contents

Rule 1. General Rule

(a) Standards for Attorney Conduct. Except as provided by subdivision (c) of this rule, or a rule adopted in accordance with 28 U.S.C. Section Section 2072, or a rule of the Federal rules of Attorney Conduct, the standards for attorney conduct for United States district courts and courts of appeals are as follows:

(1) Conduct in Proceedings Before District Court. For conduct in connection with a case or proceeding pending in a district court before which a lawyer has been admitted to practice (either generally or for purposes of that proceeding), the standards to be applied must be the standards of attorney conduct currently adopted by the state authority responsible for adopting rules of attorney conduct of the state in which the district court sits; and

679

(2) All Other Conduct. For any other act or omission by an attorney admitted to practice before a district court or court of appeals, the standards for attorney conduct are:

(A) if the attorney is licensed to practice only in one state, the rules of that state as currently adopted by its highest court, or

(B) if the attorney is licensed to practice in more than one state, the rules of the state in which the attorney principally practices as currently adopted by its highest court; but if particular conduct has its predominant effect in another state in which the attorney is licensed to practice, then the rules of that state as currently adopted by its highest court.

(3) Violation as Misconduct. If an attorney violates the rules— whether individually or in concert with others, and whether or not the violation occurred in the course of the attorney-client relationship—the violation constitutes misconduct and is grounds for discipline.

(b) Sanctions. For misconduct defined in the Federal Rules of Attorney Conduct, for good cause shown, and after notice and opportunity to be heard, an attorney admitted to practice before a district court or court of appeals may be disbarred, suspended, reprimanded, or subjected to any other disciplinary action that the court deems appropriate. The same misconduct may also subject an attorney to the disciplinary authority of the state or state where the attorney is admitted to practice.

(c) Applicability. Rules 2–10 of the Federal Rules of Attorney Conduct apply only in a case or proceeding pending in a United States district court or court of appeals. Rule 1(a) and (b) and Rules 2–10 of the Federal Rules of Attorney Conduct do not apply in a case or proceeding pending in the district court within the jurisdiction conferred by 28 U.S.C. Section Section 1334 or 158, or in a case or proceeding referred to a bankruptcy judge under 28 U.S.C. Section 157 (a), unless otherwise provided by the Federal Rules of Bankruptcy Procedure or by local bankruptcy rules promulgated in accordance with F.R. Bankr. P. 9029.

Note

This rule is based on Model Local Rule IV of the Federal Rules of Disciplinary Enforcement as recommended by the Committee on Court Administration and Case Management in 1978 and ABA Model Rule of Professional Conduct 8.5 governing choice of law for disciplinary authority. See D.R. Coquillette, Report on Local Rules Regulating Attorney Conduct in the Federal Courts, Appendix V (July 5, 1995) (original version of Rule IV of the Federal Rules of Disciplinary Enforcement), republished in D.R. Coquillette, M. Leary, Working Papers of the Committee on Rules of Practice and Procedure: Special Studies of Federal Rules Governing Attorney Conduct (1997), 1–95. (Hereafter, "Working Papers.")

The words "case or proceeding pending before" a court mean any matter which is actually before such a court, or is certain to be before such a court.

The Federal Rules of Attorney Conduct were not designed to govern bankruptcy cases and proceedings. The Committee on Rules of Practice and Procedure recognizes that there may be situations in which standards for attorney conduct in bankruptcy cases and proceedings should or must differ in some respects from standards applicable in other federal cases. First, there are statutory provisions that govern aspects of attorney conduct in bankruptcy cases, but have no application in other federal litigation. The Bankruptcy Code contains several provisions that govern attorney conduct, such as the requirement that an attorney for a trustee or committee be "disinterested," limitations on compensation, and a prohibition against sharing compensation. See 11 U.S.C. Section Section 327–331, 504. Second, the Federal Rules of Bankruptcy Procedure contain several rules governing aspects of attorney conduct, such as Rule 2014 on disclosures of relationships with parties in interest.

Rule 1(c) renders the Federal Rules of Attorney Conduct generally inapplicable in bankruptcy cases and proceedings. It is anticipated that the Advisory Committee on Bankruptcy Rules will consider formulating additional standards for attorney conduct applicable in bankruptcy cases and proceedings if, by local bankruptcy rule, the attorney conduct standards of the district court are made applicable.

Rule 2. Confidentiality of Information

(a) A lawyer must not reveal information relating to representation of a client unless the client consents after consultation, except for disclosures that are impliedly authorized in order to carry out the representation, for disclosures required by law or court order, and except as stated in paragraph (b).

(b) A lawyer may reveal, and to the extent required by Federal Rules of Attorney Conduct 7 and 9(b) must reveal, such information to the extent the lawyer reasonably believes necessary:

(1) to prevent the client from committing a criminal or fraudulent act that the lawyer believes is likely to result in death or substantial bodily harm, or in substantial injury to another's financial interests or property; or

(2) to establish a claim or defense on behalf of the lawyer in a controversy between the lawyer and the client, to establish a defense to a criminal charge or civil claim against the lawyer based upon conduct in which the client was involved, or to respond to allegations in any proceeding concerning the lawyer's representation of the client.

Note

This rule adopts ABA Model Rule of Professional Conduct 1.6 almost in its entirety. There is one significant exception. The rule modifies Rule 1.6 to permit disclosures of confidential information in order to prevent a fraudulent act which would result in substantial injury to the financial interests or property of another. (ABA Model Rule 1.6 only permits such disclosure in the cases of criminal acts "likely to result in imminent death or substantial bodily harm.") The rule was modified to reflect prevailing state views which permit this type of disclosure. Thirty-six states permit disclosure under these circumstances, and five states mandate disclosure in these circumstances. By permitting disclosure, the federal rule comports with or avoids conflict with forty-one jurisdictions, and follows the trend in the most recent state adoption of the Model Rules, such as in Massachusetts, effective Jan. 1, 1998. See Roger C. Cramton, Memorandum to Participants of the Special Study Conference, 2 (Jan. 8, 1996). In addition, an exception for disclosures "required by law or court order" has been added. See ABA Code of Professional Responsibility DR 4–101(C)(2). Finally, the rule provides a reference to Federal Rules of Attorney Conduct 7 and 9 which are based on the ABA Model Rules of Professional Conduct 3.3 and 4.1 respectively. This reference emphasizes that Federal Rule of Attorney Conduct 2(b) is not the only provision of these rules which deals with disclosure of information and that in some circumstances disclosure of such information may be required and not merely permitted.

Small stylistic changes have been made in all of the ABA Model Rules, even those adopted without substantive changes. For example, in Rule 2 the ABA Model Rule 1.6 (a) uses "shall," and the Federal Rule 2(a) uses "must." This is to comport with uniform federal drafting guidelines. See Bryan A. Garner, Guidelines for Drafting and Editing Court Rules (1997), 29.

While the "Comments" published with the ABA Model Rules have not been formally adopted, even for those federal rules that closely follow the ABA models, they are useful as "guides to interpretation." See ABA Model Rules, "Preamble," Sec. 21, in Model Rules of Professional Conduct (1998 ed.), 8.

Rule 3.   Conflict of Interest: General Rule

(a) A lawyer must not represent a client if that representation will be directly adverse to another client, unless:

(1) the lawyer reasonably believes the representation will not adversely affect the relationship with the other client; and

(2) each client consents after consultation.

(b) A lawyer must not represent a client if that representation may be materially limited by the lawyer's responsibilities to another client or to a third person, or by the lawyer's own interests, unless:

(1) the lawyer reasonably believes the representation will not be adversely affected; and

(2) the client consents after consultation; when representation of multiple clients in a single matter is undertaken, the consultation must include explanation of the implications of the common representation and the advantages and risks involved.

Note

This rule adopts ABA Model Rule of Professional Conduct 1.7 in its entirety, with small stylistic changes. Over the last five years, the largest number of federal disputes involving attorney conduct concerned conflict of interest rules. See Daniel R. Coquillette, Study of Recent Federal Cases (1990–95) Involving Rules of Attorney Conduct, 3 (Dec. 1, 1995) (forty-six percent of reported federal disputes involved conflict of interest rules). See Working Papers, supra, 100–102, 107–116, 189–210.

This rule, and Rules 5, 6 and 8, do not prevent a trial judge from disqualifying an attorney when necessary to protect the integrity of a judicial proceeding, despite client consent to the representation. See Wheat v. United States, 486 U.S. 153 (1988).

Rule 4.   Conflict of Interest: Prohibited Transactions

(a) A lawyer must not enter into a business transaction with a client or knowingly acquire an ownership, possessory, security, or other pecuniary interest adverse to a client unless:

(1) the transaction and terms on which the lawyer acquires the interest are fair and reasonable to the client and are fully disclosed and transmitted in writing to the client in a manner that can be reasonably understood by the client;

(2) the client is given reasonable opportunity to seek the advice of independent counsel in the transaction; and

(3) the client consents in writing.

(b) A lawyer must not use information relating to representation of a client to the client's disadvantage unless the client consents after consultation, except as permitted or required by Federal Rules of Attorney Conduct 2 or 7.

(c) A lawyer must not prepare an instrument giving the lawyer or a person related to the lawyer as parent, child, sibling, or spouse any substantial gift from a client, including a testamentary gift, except where the client is related to the donee.

(d) Until the representation of a client ends, a lawyer must not make or negotiate an agreement giving the lawyer literary or media rights to a portrayal or account based in substantial part on information relating to the representation.

(e) A lawyer must not provide financial assistance to a client in connection with pending or contemplated litigation, except that:

(1) a lawyer may advance court costs and expenses of litigation, the repayment of which may be contingent on the outcome of the matter; and

(2) a lawyer representing an indigent client may pay court costs and expenses of litigation on the client's behalf.

(f) A lawyer must not accept compensation for representing a client from one other than the client unless:

(1) the client consents after consultation;

(2) there is no interference with the lawyer's independence of professional judgment or with the attorney-client relationship; and

(3) information relating to the representation of a client is protected as required by Federal Rules of Attorney Conduct 2, 7, and 9.

(g) A lawyer who represents two or more clients must not participate in making aggregate settlement of claims of or against the clients, or in a criminal case an aggregated agreement on guilty or nolo contendere pleas, unless each client consents after consultation, including disclosure of the existence and nature of all the claims or pleas involved and of the participation of each person in the settlement.

(h) A lawyer must not make an agreement prospectively limiting the lawyer's liability to a client for malpractice unless permitted by law and the client is independently represented in making the agreement. Nor may a lawyer settle a claim for such liability with an unrepresented person or former client without first advising that person in writing to seek independent representation.

(i) A lawyer related to another lawyer as parent, child, sibling, or spouse must not represent a client whose interests in that matter are directly adverse to a person whom the lawyer knows is represented by the other lawyer unless the client consents after a consultation about the relationship.

(j) A lawyer must not acquire a proprietary interest in a claim or in the subject matter of litigation that the lawyer is conducting for a client, except that the lawyer may:

(1) acquire a lien granted by law to secure the lawyer's fee or expenses; and

(2) contract with a client for a reasonable contingent fee in a civil case.

Note

This rule adopts ABA Model Rule of Professional Conduct 1.8 in its entirety except for small stylistic changes and cross references to these rules. Again, over the last five years, the largest category of federal disputes involving attorney conduct centered on conflict of interest rules. See Daniel R. Coquillette, Study of Recent Federal Cases (1990–95) Involving Rules of Attorney Conduct, 3 (Dec. 1, 1995) (forty-six percent of reported federal disputes involved conflict of interest rules). See Working Papers, supra, 100–102, 107–116. DR 4–101(B)(2) and (3), DR 5–103, DR 5–104, DR 5–106, DR 5–107(A) and (B), DR 5–108 and DR 6–102 are the corresponding provisions of the ABA Code of Professional Responsibility. See Working Papers, supra, 115–116, 199–200, 205–210.

Rule 5.   Conflict of Interest: Former Client

(a) A lawyer who has formerly represented a client in a matter must not later represent another person in the same or a substantially related matter in which that person's interests are materially adverse to the former client's interests unless the former client consents after consultation.

(b)(1) Except as noted in (b)(2), a lawyer must not knowingly represent a person in the same or a substantially related matter in which a firm with which the lawyer was formerly associated had previously represented a client:

(A) whose interests are materially adverse to that person; and

(B) about whom the lawyer had acquired information protected by Federal Rules of Attorney Conduct 2 and 5(c), that is material to the matter.

(2) The former client may, after consultation, consent to the type of representation described in (b)(1).

(c) A lawyer who has formerly represented a client in a matter or whose present or former firm has formerly represented a client in a matter must not later:

(1) use information relating to the representation to the disadvantage of the former client except as Federal Rule of Attorney Conduct 2 and 7 would permit or require with respect to a client, or when the information has become generally known; or

(2) reveal information relating to the representation except as Federal Rule of Attorney Conduct 2 or 7 would permit or require with respect to a client.

Note

This rule adopts the substance of ABA Model Rule of Professional Conduct 1.9 in its entirety except for the cross references to these rules. DR 4–101(B) and (C) and DR 5–105(C) are the corresponding provisions of the ABA Code of Professional Responsibility. See Working Papers, supra, 100–102, 107–116, 189–210.

Rule 6.   Imputed Disqualification: General Rule

(a) While lawyers are associated in a firm, they must not knowingly represent a client when any one of them practicing alone would be prohibited from doing so by Federal Rules of Attorney Conduct 4, 5(c), or 6.

(b) When a lawyer has terminated an association with a firm, the firm is not prohibited from later representing a person with interests materially adverse to those of a client represented by the formerly associated lawyer, and not currently represented by the firm, unless:

(1) the matter is the same or substantially related to that in which the formerly associated lawyer represented the client; and

(2) any lawyer remaining in the firm has information that is both protected by Federal Rules of Attorney Conduct 2 and 5(c), and material to the matter.

(c) A disqualification prescribed by this rule may be waived by the affected client under the conditions stated in Federal Rule of Attorney Conduct 3.

Note

This rule adopts ABA Model Rule of Professional Conduct 1.10 almost in its entirety except for small stylistic changes and cross references to these rules. The rule does not include a federal rule similar to ABA Model Rule 2.2, dealing with the lawyer as an intermediary. No recent federal cases have involved ABA Model Rule 2.2, and the matter should be left to state rules. See Daniel R. Coquillette, Study of Recent Federal Cases (1990–95) Involving Rules of Attorney Conduct, 3 (Dec. 1, 1995) (no reported federal disputes involve Model Rule 2.2). See Working Papers, supra, 189–210. DR 5–105(D) is the corresponding provision of the ABA Code of Professional Responsibility. See Working Papers, supra, 115–116, 199–200, 209–210.

Rule 7.   Candor Toward the Tribunal

(a) A lawyer must not knowingly:

(1) make a false statement of material fact or law to a tribunal;

(2) fail to disclose a material fact to a tribunal when disclosure is necessary to avoid assisting a criminal or fraudulent act by the client;

(3) fail to disclose to the tribunal legal authority in the controlling jurisdiction known to the lawyer to be directly adverse to the client's position and not disclosed by opposing counsel; or

(4) offer evidence that the lawyer knows to be false. If a lawyer has offered material evidence and comes to know of its falsity, the lawyer must take reasonable remedial measures.

(b) The duties stated in paragraph (a) continue to the conclusion of the proceeding, and apply even if compliance requires disclosure of information otherwise protected by Federal Rule of Attorney Conduct 2.

(c) A lawyer may refuse to offer evidence that the lawyer reasonably believes is false.

(d) In an ex parte proceeding, a lawyer must inform the tribunal of all known material facts that will enable the tribunal to make an informed decision, even if the facts are adverse.

Note

This rule adopts ABA Model Rule of Professional Conduct 3.3 in its entirety except for small stylistic changes and a cross reference to these rules. To preserve the integrity of the court proceedings, candor toward the tribunal is a matter of significant federal interest, and as such, requires a single uniform standard applicable in all federal courts. See Roger C. Cramton, Memorandum to Participants of the Special Study Conference, 2–3 (Jan. 8, 1996). The rule is also needed in continuing Federal Rules of Attorney Conduct Rule 2 and 4, where it is cross-cited. DR 7–102 and DR 7–106(B) are the corresponding provisions of the ABA Code of Professional Responsibility. See Working Papers, supra, 100–102, 107–116, 189–210.

Rule 8.   Lawyer as Witness

(a) A lawyer must not act as an advocate at a trial in which the lawyer is likely to be a necessary witness except where:

(1) the testimony relates to an uncontested issue;

(2) the testimony relates to the nature and value of legal services rendered in the case; or

(3) the lawyer's disqualification would work a substantial hardship on the client.

(b) A lawyer may act as advocate in a trial in which another lawyer in the lawyer's firm is likely to be called as a witness unless precluded from so doing by Federal Rules of Attorney Conduct 3 or 5.

Note

This rule adopts ABA Model Rule of Professional Conduct 3.7 in its entirety, except for small stylistic changes and a cross reference to these rules. Between 1990–1995, ten percent of reported federal disputes involve lawyer as witness rules. See Daniel R. Coquillette, Study of Recent Federal Cases (1990–95) Involving Rules of Attorney Conduct, 3 (Dec. 1, 1995). See Working Papers, supra, 100–102, 107–116, 189–210. This trend dropped to five percent between July 1, 1995 and March 23, 1996, id., 196, but the 1990–1996 culminated totals are still high at 49 cases, or more than nine percent. Id., 203. Thus, a federal lawyer as witness rule is needed to create uniform standards of conduct for attorneys practicing in the federal courts. The corresponding provisions of the ABA Code of Professional Responsibility are DR 5–101(B) and DR 5–102. See Working Papers, supra, 115–116, 199–200, 209–210.

Rule 9.   Truthfulness in Statements to Others

In the course of representing a client a lawyer must not knowingly:

(a) make a false statement of material fact or law to a third person; or

(b) fail to disclose a material fact to a third person when disclosure is necessary to avoid assisting in a criminal or fraudulent act by a client, unless disclosure is prohibited by Federal Rule of Attorney Conduct 2.

Note

This rule adopts ABA Model Rule of Professional Conduct 4.1 in its entirety except for a small stylistic change and a cross reference to these rules. This rule is rarely invoked in federal court proceedings, but it is a central rule of conduct. See Working Papers, supra, 203. See Roger C. Cramton, Memorandum to Participants of the Special Study Conference (Jan. 8, 1996). It is also needed in applying Rule 2, supra, where it is cross-cited. The corresponding provision of the ABA Model Code of Professional Responsibility is DR 7–102. See Working Papers, supra, pp. 116, 210.

Rules 10.   Communications with Persons Represented by Counsel.

(a) General Rule. A lawyer who is representing a client in a matter must not communicate about the subject of the representation with a person the lawyer knows to be represented by another lawyer in the matter, unless the lawyer has the consent of the other lawyer or is authorized to do so by:

(1) constitutional law, statute, or an agency regulation having the force of law;

(2) a decision or rule of a court of competent jurisdiction;

(3) a prior written authorization by a court of competent jurisdiction obtained by the lawyer in good faith; or

(4) paragraph (b) of this rule.

(b) Rules Relating to Government Lawyers Engaged in Civil or Criminal Law Enforcement. A government lawyer engaged in a criminal or civil law enforcement matter, or a person acting under the lawyer's direction, may communicate with a person known by the government lawyer to be represented by a lawyer in the matter if:

(1) the communication occurs prior to the person's having been arrested, charged in a criminal case, or named as a defendant in a civil law enforcement proceeding brought by the governmental agency that seeks to engage in the communication, and the communication relates to the investigation of criminal activity or other unlawful conduct; or

(2) the communication occurs after the represented person has been arrested, charged in a criminal case, or named as a defendant in a civil law enforcement proceeding brought by the governmental agency that seeks to engage in the communication, and the communication is:

(A) made in the course of any investigation of additional, different, or ongoing criminal activity or other unlawful conduct; or

(B) made to protect against a risk of death or bodily harm that the governmental lawyer reasonably believes may occur; or

(C) made at the time of the arrest of the represented person and after he or she is advised of his or her rights to remain silent and to counsel and voluntarily and knowingly waives those rights; or

(D) initiated by the represented person, either directly or through an intermediary, if prior to the communication the represented person has given a written or recorded voluntary and informed waiver of counsel for that communication.

(c) Organizations as Represented Persons.

(1) When the represented "person" is an organization, an individual is "represented" by counsel for the organization if the individual is not separately represented with respect to the subject matter of the communication, and

(A) with respect to a communication by a government lawyer in a civil or criminal law enforcement matter, is known by the government lawyer to be a current member of the control group of the represented organization; or

(B) with respect to a communication by a lawyer in any other matter, is known by the lawyer to be

(i) a current member of the control group of the represented organization; or

(ii) a representative of the organization whose acts or omissions in the matter may be imputed to the organization under applicable law; or

(iii) a representative of the organization whose statements under applicable rules of evidence would have the effect of binding the organization with respect to proof of the matter.

(2) The term "control group" means the following persons (A) the chief executive officer, chief operating officer, chief financial officer, and chief legal officer of the organization; and (B) to the extent not encompassed by the foregoing, the chair of the organization's governing body, president, treasurer, and secretary, and a vice-president or vice-chair who is in charge of a principal business unit, division, or function (such as salaries, administration, or finance) or performs a major policy making function for the organization; and (C) any other current employee or official who is known to be participating as a principal decision maker in the determination of the organization's legal position in the matter.

(d) Limitations on Communications. When communicating with a represented person pursuant to this Rule, a lawyer must not:

(1) inquire about information regarding litigation strategy or legal arguments for counsel, or seek to induce the person to forego representation or disregard the advice of the person's counsel; or

(2) engage in negotiations of a plea agreement, settlement, statutory or non-statutory immunity agreement, or other disposition of actual or potential criminal charges or civil enforcement claims, or sentences or penalties with respect to the matter in which the person is represented by counsel unless such negotiations are permitted by paragraph (a) or (b)(2)(D).

Note

This rule is based on the tentative outcome of negotiations between the Department of Justice and the Conference of Chief Justices, "Discussion Draft, December 19, 1997," with the addition of some technical stylistic changes. As such, if differs from the comparable ABA rule, ABA Model Rule 4.2, in many respects. See ABA Formal Opinion 97–408 (1997); ABA Formal Opinion 95–396 (1995) and ABA Informal Opinion 1377 (1977). This rule, as negotiated, has an extensive "Comment." See "Discussion Draft, December 19, 1997." "Comment," pp. 1–6.

The Conference of Chief Justices considered this "Discussion Draft" at its regular Midwinter Meeting on January 25–29, 1998. At the request of officials of the American Bar Association and others, the Conference postponed the matter to its next meeting, scheduled for August 2–6, 1998. See Memorandum of February 6, 1998 from Chief Justice Thomas R. Phillips, President, Conference of Chief Justices. Obviously, if the Conference of Chief Justices, the Department of Justice, and the American Bar Association can agree on a draft rule, it will be the presumptive candidate for the final version of Rule 10.

From 1990–1995, twelve percent of reported federal cases involve rules governing communications with represented persons. See Daniel R. Coquillette, Study of Recent Federal Cases (1990–95) Involving Rules of Attorney Conduct, 3 (Dec. 1, 1995). See Working Papers, supra, 99–211. This trend increased between July 1, 1995 and March 23, 1996, to sixteen percent. Id., 196. Thus, a federal rule is needed to create uniform standards of conduct for attorneys practicing in the federal courts. The corresponding provision of the ABA Code of Professional Responsibility is DR 7–104. See id., 115–116, 199–200, 209–210.